This registration code provides access to

documents and other sources available at the

Western Civilizations, 17th Edition StudySpace site:

wwnorton.com/studyspace

LDES-RUIP

Western Civilizations

Their History &
Their Culture

Judith Coffin

Robert Stacey

Joshua Cole

Carol Symes

Western Civilizations

Their History & Their Culture

SEVENTEENTH EDITION

VOLUME B

W. W. NORTON & COMPANY · NEW YORK · LONDON

W. W. Norton & Company has been independent since its founding in 1923, when William Warder Norton and Mary D. Herter Norton first published lectures delivered at the People's Institute, the adult education division of New York City's Cooper Union. The firm soon expanded its program beyond the Institute, publishing books by celebrated academics from America and abroad. By midcentury, the two major pillars of Norton's publishing program—trade books and college texts—were firmly established. In the 1950s, the Norton family transferred control of the company to its employees, and today—with a staff of four hundred and a comparable number of trade, college, and professional titles published each year—W. W. Norton & Company stands as the largest and oldest publishing house owned wholly by its employees.

Editor: Jon Durbin
Project editor: Kathleen Feighery
Managing editor, College: Marian Johnson
Copyeditors: Candace Levy and Michael Fleming
E-media editor: Steve Hoge
Ancillary editor: Lorraine Klimowich
Editorial assistant: Jason Spears
Photo editor: Junenoire Mitchell
Photo research: Donna Ranieri
Senior production manager, College: Benjamin Reynolds
Design director: Rubina Yeh
Book designer: Judith Abbate / Abbate Design
Composition: TexTech, Inc.—Brattleboro, VT
Cartographers: Mapping Specialists—Madison, WI
Manufacturing: R. R. Donnelley & Sons—Jefferson City, MO

The Library of Congress has Cataloged the one-volume edition as follows:

Coffin, Judith G., 1952–
    Western civilizations : their history & their culture / Judith G. Coffin ... [et al.]. — Seventeenth ed.
        p. cm.
    Includes bibliographical references and index.
    ISBN 978-0-393-93481-6 (hardcover)
    1. Civilization, Western—Textbooks.   2. Europe—Civilization—Textbooks.   I. Title.
    CB245.C65 2011
    909'.09821—dc22

                                                          2010038141

This edition:
ISBN: **978-0-393-93485-4 (pbk.)**

W. W. Norton & Company, Inc., 500 Fifth Avenue, New York, N. Y. 10110
wwnorton.com

W. W. Norton & Company Ltd., Castle House, 75/76 Wells Street, London W1T 3QT

1 2 3 4 5 6 7 8 9 0

To our families:

Willy, Zoe, and Aaron Forbath
Robin, Will, and Anna Stacey
Kate Tremel, Lucas and Ruby Cole
Tom, Erin, and Connor Wilson

with love and gratitude for their support.
And to all our students, who have also been
our teachers.

JUDITH COFFIN (Ph.D. Yale University) is an associate professor at the University of Texas, Austin, where she won University of Texas President's Associates' Award for Teaching Excellence. Previously, she taught at Harvard University and the University of California, Riverside. Her research interests are the social and cultural history of gender, mass culture, slavery, race relations, and colonialism. She is the author of *The Politics of Women's Work: The Paris Garment Trades, 1750–1915*.

ROBERT STACEY (Ph.D. Yale University) is professor of history, Dean of the Humanities, and a member of the Jewish Studies faculty at the University of Washington, Seattle. A long-time teacher of Western civilization and medieval European history, he has received Distinguished Teaching Awards from both the University of Washington and Yale University, where he taught from 1984 to 1988. He has authored and coauthored four books, including a textbook, *The Making of England to 1399*. He holds an M.A. from Oxford University and a Ph.D. from Yale.

JOSHUA COLE (Ph.D. University of California, Berkeley) is Associate Professor of History at the University of Michigan at Ann Arbor. His publications include work on gender and the history of the population sciences, colonial violence, and the politics of memory in 19th and 20th century France, Germany, and Algeria. His first book was *The Power of Large Numbers: Population, Politics and Gender in Nineteenth-Century France* (Ithaca, NY: Cornell University Press, 2000).

CAROL SYMES (Ph.D. Harvard University) is Associate Professor of history and Director of Undergraduate Studies in the history department at the University of Illinois, Urbana-Champaign, where she has won the top teaching award in the College of Liberal Arts and Sciences. Her main areas of study include medieval Europe, the history of information media and communication technologies, and the history of theatre. Her first book was *A Common Stage: Theater and Public Life in Medieval Arras* (Ithaca: Cornell University Press, 2007).

Brief Contents

Contents

Maps

The motivating principle for this edition of *Western Civilizations* is a relatively simple idea: that history students will be inspired to engage more effectively with the past if they are given a flexible set of tools to use as they approach their readings. *Western Civilizations* has always been known for its clear and vigorous account of Europe's past, and previous editions have been noteworthy for their selection of primary sources and visual images. As the authors of this new edition, we have made a special effort to bring greater unity to the pedagogical elements that accompany each chapter, so that students will be able to work more productively with the textbook in mastering this rich history. This pedagogical structure is designed to empower the students to analyze and interpret the historical evidence on their own, and thus to become participants in the work of history.

Undergraduates today have more choices in introductory history courses than they did only twenty or thirty years ago. As public awareness of the importance of global connections grew in the late twentieth century, many colleges and universities enriched their programs by adding courses in world history as well as introductory surveys in Latin American, African, and Asian history alongside the traditional offerings in the history of the United States and Europe. These developments can only be seen as enormously positive, but they do not in any way diminish the need for a broad-based history of European society and culture such as that represented in *Western Civilizations*. The wide chronological scope of this work offers an unusual opportunity to trace the development of central human themes—population movements, economic development, politics and state-building, changing religious beliefs, and the role of the arts and technology—in a dynamic and complex part of the world whose cultural diversity has been constantly invigorated and renewed by its interactions with peoples living in other places. As in previous editions, we have attempted to balance the coverage of political, social, economic, and cultural phenomena, and the chapters also include extensive coverage of material culture, daily life, gender, sexuality, art, and technology. And following the path laid out by the book's previous authors, Judith Coffin and Robert Stacey, we have insisted that the history of European peoples can be best understood through their interactions with people in other parts of the world. The portrait of European society that emerges from this text is thus both rich and dynamic, attentive to the latest developments in historical scholarship and fully aware of the ways that the teaching of European history has changed in the past decades.

Given the general consensus about the importance of seeing human history in its broadest—and if possible, global—context, Europeanists who teach the histories of ancient, medieval, and modern societies have been mindful of the need to rethink the ways that this history should be taught. For good reasons, few historians at the dawn of the twenty-first century uphold a monolithic vision of a single and enduring "Western civilization" whose inevitable march through history can be traced chapter by chapter through time. This idea, strongly associated with the curriculum of early twentieth-century American colleges and universities, no longer conforms to what we know about the human past. Neither the "West" nor "Europe" can be seen as distinct, unified entities in space or time; the meanings attributed to these geographical expressions have changed in significant ways. Most historians now agree that a linear notion of "civilization" persisting over the centuries was made coherent only by leaving out the intense conflicts, extraordinary ruptures, and dynamic processes of change at the heart of the societies that are the subject of this book. Smoothing out the rough edges of the past does students no favors—even an introductory text such as this one should present the past as it appears to the historians who study it—that is, as an ever-changing panorama of human effort and creation, filled with possibility, but also fraught with discord, uncertainty, accident, and tragedy.

New Pedagogical Features

Our goals as the new authors of this dynamic text are to provide a book that students will read, that reinforces your course objectives, that helps your students master core content, and that provides tools for your students to use in thinking critically about our human past. In order to achieve these primary goals, the traditional strengths of the book have been augmented by several exciting new features. The most revolutionary is the new pedagogical framework that supports each chapter. Many students in introductory survey courses find the sheer quantity of information to be a challenge, and so we have created these new pedagogical features to help them approach their reading in a more systematic way. At the outset of every chapter, a *Before You Read This Chapter* box offers three preliminary windows onto the material to be covered: *Story Lines, Chronology*, and *Core Objectives*. The *Story Lines* allow the student to become familiar with the primary narrative threads that tie the chapter's elements together, and the *Chronology* grounds these *Story Lines* in the period under study. The *Core Objectives* provide a checklist to ensure that the student is aware of the primary teaching points in the chapter. The student is then reminded of these teaching points on completing the chapter, in the *After You Read This Chapter* section, which prompts the student to revisit the chapter in three ways. The first, *Reviewing the Core Objectives*, asks the reader to reconsider core objectives by answering a pointed question about each one. The second, *People, Ideas, and Events in Context*, summarizes some of the particulars that students should retain from their reading, through questions that allow them to relate individual terms to the major objectives and story lines. Finally, questions about long-term *Consequences* allow for more open-ended reflection on the significance of the chapter's material, drawing students' attention to issues that connect the chapter to previous chapters and giving them insight into what comes next. As a package, the pedagogical features at the beginning and end of each chapter work together to empower the student, by breaking down the process of reading and learning into manageable tasks.

A second package of pedagogical features is designed to help students think about history and its underlying issues more critically. For us as teachers, good pedagogy and critical thinking begin with good narrative writing. Each chapter starts with an opening vignette that showcases a particular person or event representative of the era as a whole. Within each chapter, an expanded program of illustrations and maps has been enhanced by the addition of **Guiding Questions** that challenge the reader to explore the historical contexts and significance of the maps and illustrations in a more critical way. The historical value of images, artifacts, and material culture is further emphasized in a new feature, *Interpreting Visual Evidence*. We anticipate that this section will provide discussion leaders with a provocative departure point for conversations about the key issues raised by visual sources, which students often find more approachable than texts. Once this conversation has begun, students will further be able to develop the tools they need to read the primary texts. In this new edition, the selection of primary source texts, *Analyzing Primary Sources*, has been carefully revised and many new questions have been added to frame the readings. The dynamism and diversity of Western civilizations is also illuminated through a look at **Competing Viewpoints** in each chapter, in which specific debates are presented through paired primary source texts. Finally, the bibliographical *For Further Reading* section has been edited and brought up-to-date and is now located at the end of the book.

REVISED CHAPTER TOURS

There are significant changes to each chapter of the book, as well. In Chapter 1, the challenges of locating and interpreting historical evidence drawn from nontextual sources (archaeological, environmental, anthropological, mythic) is a special focus. Chapter 2 further underscores the degree to which recent archeological discoveries and new historical techniques have revolutionized our understanding of ancient history, and have also corroborated ancient peoples' own understandings of their past. Chapter 3 offers expanded coverage of the diverse polities that emerged in ancient Greece, and of Athens' closely related political, documentary, artistic, and intellectual achievements. Chapter 4's exploration of the Hellenistic world is more wide-ranging than before, and it includes an entirely new discussion of the scientific revolution powered by this first cosmopolitan civilization.

With Chapter 5, the unique values and institutions of the Roman Republic are the focus of a new segment, while the account of the Republic's expansion and transformation under the Principate has been sharpened and clarified. Chapter 6's treatment of early Christianity has been deepened and expanded, and more attention has been paid to the fundamental ways in which this fledgling religion itself changed as a result of its changing status within the Roman Empire. This chapter also draws on cutting-edge scholarship that has significantly revised our understanding of the so-called "Crisis of the Third Century" and the question of Rome's fragmentation and "fall."

Beginning with this chapter, the chronological structure of Volume 1 has been adjusted in order to make the periodization of the Middle Ages more conceptually manageable and the material easier to teach. Chapter 6 therefore ends with the reign of Theodoric in the West and the consolidation of Christian and pagan cultures in the fifth century. Chapter 7 now begins with the reign of Justinian; and while it still examines Rome's three distinctive successor civilizations, it no longer attempts to encapsulate all of Byzantine and Islamic history down to the fifteenth century. Instead, these interlocking histories and that of northwestern Europe are carried forward to about 950 C.E. in this chapter, and continue to intersect with one another in subsequent chapters. And whereas Chapters 8 and 9 used to cover the period 1000–1300 from two different angles (political, social, and economic *versus* religious and intellectual), the new structure interweaves these forces, with Chapter 8 covering the period 950–1100 and Chapter 9 extending from 1100 to 1300.

Chapters 10–12 all assess the transition from medieval to nearly modern. Chapter 10 looks at Europe in the years 1300 to 1500, the centuries of "Crisis, Unrest, and Opportunity." Chapter 11 explores the simultaneous expansion of Europe through "Commerce, Conquest, and Colonization" between 1300 and 1600. And Chapter 12 examines the "Renaissance Ideals and Realities" that stemmed from, and contributed to, these same events. All three chapters have been revised and expanded for this edition. Thereafter, Chapter 13 characterizes the sixteenth century as "The Age of Dissent and Division," while Chapter 14 surveys the religious, political, and military struggles that arose in the era of confessional difference, contested sovereignty, and military escalation between 1540 and 1660.

Chapters 15–17 cover the history of early modern Europe between the sixteenth and eighteenth centuries, a time that saw powerful absolutist regimes emerge on the continent; the establishment of wealthy European trading empires in Asia, Africa, and the Americas; and successive periods of intense intellectual and philosophical discussion during the Scientific Revolution and the Enlightenment. Chapter 15 has been reorganized to better relate the emergence of absolutist regimes on the continent with the alternatives to absolutism that developed in England, and to clarify the differences between the colonial empires of France, Britain, and Spain. Chapter 16 emphasizes the many facets of scientific inquiry during the Scientific Revolution and introduces a new section on women scientists. Meanwhile, Chapter 17 adds new emphasis to the ways that Enlightenment figures dealt with cultures and peoples in the parts of the world that Europeans confronted in building their empires.

Chapters 18–19 cover the political and economic revolutions of the late eighteenth and early nineteenth centuries. Chapter 18 covers the French Revolution and the Napoleonic empires in depth, while also drawing attention to the way that these central episodes were rooted in a larger pattern of revolutionary political change that engulfed the Atlantic world. Chapter 19 emphasizes both the economic growth and the technological innovations that were a part of the Industrial Revolution, while also exploring the social and cultural consequences of industrialization for men and women in Europe's new industrial societies. The *Interpreting Visual Evidence* box in Chapter 19 allows students to explore the ways that industrialization created new perceptions of the global economy in Europe, changing the way people thought of their place in the world.

Chapters 20–21 explore the successive struggles between conservative reaction and revolutionaries in Europe, as the revolutionary forces of nationalism unleashed by the French Revolution redrew the map of Europe and threatened the dynastic regimes that had ruled for centuries. In all of these chapters, new visual images have been added to focus students' attention on the many ways that "the people" were represented by liberals, conservatives, and revolutionaries, and the consequences of these contesting representations.

Chapter 22 takes on the history of nineteenth-century colonialism, exploring both its political and economic origins and its consequences for the peoples of Africa and Asia. The chapter gives new emphasis to the significance of colonial conquest for European culture, as colonial power became increasingly associated with national greatness, both in conservative monarchies and in more democratic regimes. Meanwhile, Chapter 23 brings the narrative back to the heart of Europe, covering the long-term consequences of industrialization and the consolidation of a conservative form of nationalism in many European nations even as the electorate was being expanded. The chapter emphasizes the varied nature of the new forms of political dissent, from the feminists who claimed the right to vote to the newly organized socialist movements that proved so enduring in many European countries.

Chapters 24 and 25 bring new vividness to the history of the First World War and the intense conflicts of the interwar period, while Chapter 26 uses the history of the Second World War as a hinge for understanding European and global developments in the second half of the twentieth century. The *Interpreting Visual Evidence* box in Chapter 24 allows for a special focus on the role of propaganda among the belligerent nations in 1914–1918, and the chapter's section on the diplomatic crisis that preceded the First World War has been streamlined to allow students to more easily comprehend the essential issues at the heart of the conflict. In Chapter 25 the *Interpreting Visual Evidence* box continues to explore the theme touched on in earlier chapters, political representations of "the people," this time in the context of fascist spectacles in Germany and Italy in the 1930s. These visual sources help students to understand the vulnerability of Europe's democratic regimes during these years as they faced the dual assault from fascists on the right and Bolsheviks on the left.

Chapters 27–29 bring the volumes to a close in a thorough exploration of the Cold War, decolonization, the collapse of the Soviet Union and the Eastern Bloc in 1989–1991, and the roots of the multifaceted global conflicts that beset the world in the first decade of the twenty-first century. Chapter 27 juxtaposes the Cold War with decolonization, showing how this combination sharply diminished the ability of European nations to control events in the international arena, even as they succeeded in rebuilding their economies at home. Chapter 28 explores the vibrancy of European culture in the crucial period of the 1960s to the early 1990s, bringing new attention to the significance of 1989 as a turning point in European history. Finally, a completely new set of primary documents and questions accompanies Chapter 29, which covers the benefits and tensions of a a newly globalized world. The chapter's conclusion now covers the financial crisis of 2008 and the subsequent election of Barack Obama, as well as recent debates within Islam about Muslims living as minorities in non-Muslim nations.

A Few Words of Thanks

Our first year as members of *Western Civilizations'* authorial team has been a challenging and rewarding one. We are honored to be the partners of two historians whose work we have long admired, and who have been formative influences on us in our careers as students, scholars, and teachers of history. We would also like to thank a number of our colleagues around the country who provided in-depth critiques of large sections of the book: Paul Freedman (Yale University), Sheryl Kroen (University of Florida), Michael Kulikowski (Pennsylvania State University), Harry Liebersohn (University of Illinois, Urbana-Champaign), and Helmut Smith (Vanderbilt University). We are very grateful for the expert assistance and support of the Norton team, especially that of our editor, Jon Durbin. Kate Feighery, our fabulous project editor, has driven the book beautifully through the manuscript process. Jason Spears has skillfully dealt with a myriad of issues pertaining to

the preparation of the text. Junenoire Mitchell and Donna Ranieri did an excellent job finding many of the exact images we specified. Lorraine Klimowich did an expert job developing the print ancillaries. Ben Reynolds has efficiently marched us through the production process. Steve Hoge has done a great job developing the book's fantastic emedia, particularly the new Author Insight Podcasts and Euro History Tours powered by Google Maps. Michael Fleming, Candace Levy, Robin Cook, and John Gould were terrific in skillfully guiding the manuscript through the copyediting and proofreading stages. Finally, we want to thank Tamara McNeill for spearheading the marketing campaign for the new edition. We are also indebted to the numerous expert readers who commented on various chapters and who thereby strengthened the book as a whole. We are thankful to our families, for their patience and advice, and to our students, whose questions and comments over the years have been essential to the framing of this book. And we extend a special thanks to, and hope to hear from, all the teachers and students we may never meet—their engagement with this book will frame new understandings of our shared past and its bearing on our future.

NEW EDITION REVIEWERS

Donna Allen, Glendale Community College
Ken Bartlett, University of Toronto
Volker Benkert, Arizona State University
Dean Bennett, Schenectady City Community College
Patrick Brennan, Gulf Coast Community College
Neil Brooks, Community College of Baltimore County, Essex
James Brophy, University of Delaware
Kevin Caldwell, Blue Ridge Community College
Keith Chu, Bergen Community College
Alex D'erizans, Borough of Manhattan Community College, CUNY
Hilary Earl, Nipissing University
Kirk Ford, Mississippi College
Michael Gattis, Gulf Coast Community College
David M. Gallo, College of Mount Saint Vincent
Jamie Gruring, Arizona State University
Tim Hack, Salem Community College
Bernard Hagerty, University of Pittsburg
Paul T. Hietter, Mesa Community College
Paul Hughes, Sussex County Community College
Kyle Irvin, Jefferson State Community College
Llana Krug, York College of Pennsylvania
Guy Lalande, St. Francis Xavier University
Chris Laney, Berkshire Community College

Charles Levine, Mesa Community College
Michael Mckeown, Daytona State University
Dan Puckett, Troy State University
Dan Robinson, Troy State University
Craig Saucier, Southeastern Louisiana University
Aletia Seaborn, Southern Union State College
Victoria Thompson, Arizona State University
Donna Trembinski, St. Francis Xavier University
Pamela West, Jefferson State Community College
Julianna Wilson, Pima Community College

PREVIOUS EDITION REVIEWERS

Eric Ash, Wayne State University
Sacha Auerbach, Virginia Commonwealth University
Ken Bartlett, University of Toronto
Benita Blessing, Ohio University
Chuck Boening, Shelton State Community College
John Bohstedt, University of Tennessee, Knoxville
Dan Brown, Moorpark College
Kevin Caldwell, Blue Ridge Community College
Jodi Campbell, Texas Christian University
Annette Chamberlain, Virginia Western Community
  College
Jason Coy, College of Charleston
Benjamin Ehlers, University of Georgia
Maryann Farkas, Dawson College
Gloria Fitzgibbon, Wake Forest University
Tina Gaddis, Onondaga Community College
Alex Garman, Eastern New Mexico State University
Norman Goda, Ohio University
Andrew Goldman, Gonzaga University
Robert Grasso, Monmouth University

Sylvia Gray, Portland Community College
Susan Grayzel, University of Mississippi
Timothy Hack, University of Delaware
Hazel Hahn, Seattle University
Derek Hastings, Oakland University
Dawn Hayes, Montclair State University
John Houston, Fordham University
Michael Hughes, Wake Forest University
Bruce Hunt, University of Texas, Austin
Ahmed Ibrahim, Southwest Missouri State
  University
Kevin James, University of Guelph
Lars Jones, Florida Institute of Technology
John Kearney, Cy Fair Community College
Roman Laba, Hudson Valley Community College
Elizabeth Lehfeldt, Cleveland State University
Thomas Maulucci, State University of New York,
  Fredonia
Amy McCandless, College of Charleston
John McGrath, Boston University
Nicholas Murray, Adirondack College
Charles Odahl, Boise State University
Bill Olejniczak, College of Charleston
Jeffrey Plaks, University of Central Oklahoma
Peter Pozesky, College of Wooster
Rebecca Schloss, Texas A&M University
James Shedel, Georgetown University
Rebecca Spang, Indiana University, Bloomington
Patrick Speelman, College of Charleston
Robert Taylor, Florida Institute of Technology
Paul Teverow, Missouri Southern State University
James Vanstone, John Abbott College
Kirk Willis, University of Georgia
Ian Worthington, University of Missouri, Columbia

Before You Read This Chapter

Crisis, Unrest, and Opportunity, 1300–1500

CORE OBJECTIVES

- **EXPLAIN** the economic and social effects of the Black Death.

- **DEFINE** the concept of national monarchy and summarize its implications.

- **IDENTIFY** the factors leading to the rise of Muscovy.

- **UNDERSTAND** the significance of the conciliar movement and its defeat by the papacy.

- **DESCRIBE** the spiritual, cultural, and technological innovations of the later Middle Ages.

In June of 1381, thousands of laborers from the English countryside rose up in rebellion. Most were peasants or village craftsmen, yet the revolt was carefully coordinated. Plans were spread in coded messages circulated by word of mouth and by the followers of a renegade Oxford professor, John Wyclif, who had called for the redistribution of Church property and taught that common people should be able to read the Bible in their own language. The rebellion's immediate cause had been a series of exorbitant taxes levied by Parliament for the support of an ongoing war with France, but its more fundamental cause was an epidemic that had occurred thirty years earlier. The Black Death had reduced the entire population of Europe by 30 to 50 percent, and had drastically altered the world of the survivors. In this new world, workers were valuable and could rebel against those who paid them poorly or treated them like slaves. In that fateful summer of 1381, the workers of England even vowed to kill all the representatives of both the Church and the government—to kill (as they put it) all the lawyers—and to destroy all the documents that had been used to keep them down. It was a revolution, and it partly succeeded. Although the leaders were eventually captured and executed, the rebellion had made the strength of the common people known to all.

The fourteenth and fifteenth centuries are often seen as a time of crisis. And certainly, this was an age of adversity in Europe. Famine and plague cut fearful swaths through the population; war was a brutally recurrent fact of life; and the papacy spent seventy years in continuous exile from Italy, only to see its prestige decline further after its return to Rome. But this period was also a time of opportunity. The exhausted land of Europe recovered from centuries of overfarming while workers gained the economic edge and, eventually, social and political power. Meanwhile, the people of Europe's various monarchies came to identify themselves as members of a new political entity, the nation-state; popular and intellectual movements sought to reform the Church; and a host of artistic and scientific innovations contributed to all of these phenomena. It was a period of intense creativity that would redefine European civilization.

THE BLACK DEATH AND ITS CONSEQUENCES

By 1300, the European economy was reaching its limits. Between 1000 and 1300, the population had tripled and the continent had become a sea of grain fields that stretched, almost unbroken, from Ireland to Ukraine. Forests were cleared, marshes drained, and pastureland reduced—but still, Europe was barely able to feed itself. At the same time, the warming trend that had begun in the late eighth century (Chapter 8) reversed itself. For even a reduction of one or two degrees centrigrade is enough to cause substantial changes in rainfall patterns, shorten growing seasons, and lessen agricultural productivity.

The new vulnerability of the European economy and ecosystem was dramatically revealed in the great famine that lasted from 1315 to 1322. In these years, adverse weather conditions were nearly continuous, and the result was starvation on a very large scale. Weakened by malnutrition, people and domestic animals also fell victim to epidemic diseases. Approximately 10 to 15 percent of the population north of the Alps perished. In the decades following, cold winters and floods threatened southern Europe, too, and in 1343 a tsunami destroyed ports in southern Italy. Earthquakes and comets seemed like further terrifying portents of disaster.

THE PLAGUE CLAIMS A VICTIM. A priest gives last rites to a bedridden plague victim, as a smiling devil pierces him with a spear and Christ looks mercifully down from Heaven. ■ *What are the possible meanings of this image?* ■ *What does it reveal about contemporary attitudes toward death?*

Tracking the Black Death

The Black Death is the name given to a deadly plague that spread from Mongolia to China, northern India, and the Middle East during the 1330s and 1340s. By 1346, the disease had reached the Black Sea. From there, in 1347, Genoese ships inadvertently brought it to Sicily and northern Italy. From Italy it spread westward along trade routes, first striking seaports, then moving inland. It moved with astonishing rapidity, advancing about two miles per day during both summer and winter. By 1350 it had reached Scandinavia and northern Russia, then spread southward until it linked up with the earlier waves of infection that had brought it from Central Asia to the Black Sea. It continued to erupt in local epidemics for the next 300 years; some localities could expect a renewed outbreak every decade. The last Europe-wide instance occurred between 1661 and

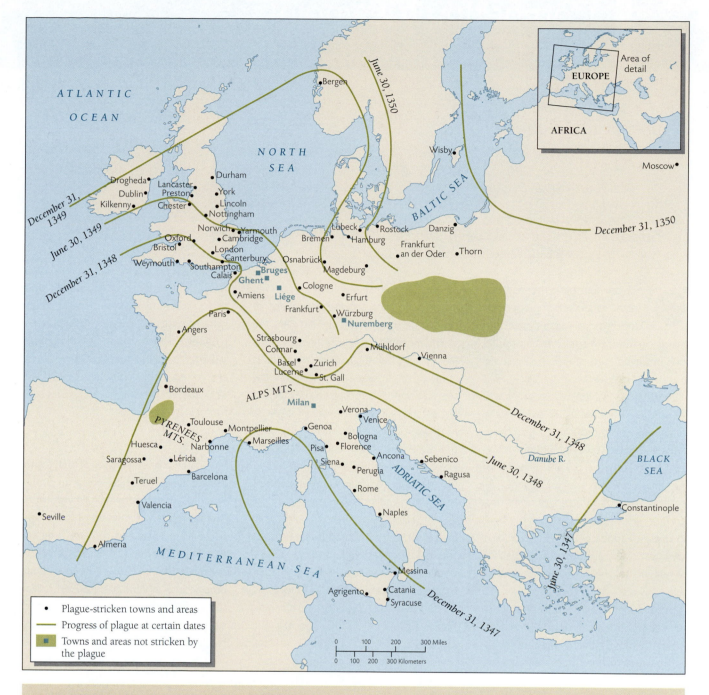

THE PROGRESS OF THE BLACK DEATH, FOURTEENTH CENTURY. ▪ *What trajectories did the Black Death follow once it was introduced into Europe?* ▪ *How might the growth of towns, trade, and travel have contributed to the spread of the Black Death?* ▪ *Would such a rapid advance have been likely during the early Middle Ages or even in the ancient world?*

1669, although there were sporadic outbreaks in Poland and Russia until the end of the eighteenth century.

The scale of mortality caused by the Black Death is almost unimaginable. At least a third, and probably half, of Europe's people died between 1347 and 1350. By the following century, the combined effects of plague, famine, and warfare had reduced the total population by at least 50 percent, perhaps by as much as two thirds. This massive mortality also had dramatic effects on the landscape. In Germany, more than 40,000 villages disappeared. And even when villages survived, the shortage of workers forced changes in agricultural practice. Around Paris, more than half the farmland cultivated in 1348 had become pasture by 1450. Elsewhere, abandoned fields reverted to woodland,

Competing Viewpoints

Responses to the Black Death

Many chroniclers, intellectuals, and private individuals have left accounts of the plague and its effects, and many attempted to understand why it had occurred, how it spread, and how communities should respond to it.

The Spread of the Plague According to Gabriele D'Mussis (d. 1356), a Lawyer in Piacenza (Northern Italy)

Oh God! See how the heathen Tartar races, pouring together from all sides, suddenly invested the city of Caffa [near Constantinople] and besieged the trapped Christians there for almost three years. . . . But behold, [in 1346] the whole army was affected by a disease which overran the Tartars and killed thousands upon thousands every day. It was as though arrows were raining down from heaven to strike and crush the Tartars' arrogance. All medical advice and attention was useless; the Tartars died as soon as the signs of disease appeared on their bodies: swellings in the armpit or groin caused by coagulating humours, followed by a putrid fever.

The dying Tartars, stunned and stupefied by the immensity of the disaster brought about by the disease, and realising that they had no hope of escape, lost interest in the siege. But they ordered corpses to be placed in catapults and lobbed into the city in the hope that the intolerable stench would kill everyone inside. What seemed like mountains of dead were thrown into the city, and the Christians could not hide or flee or escape from them, although they dumped as many of the bodies as they could in the sea. And soon the rotting corpses tainted the air and poisoned the water supply. . . . Moreover one infected man could carry the poison to others, and infect people and places with the disease by look alone. No one knew, or could discover, a means of defence.

Thus almost everyone who had been in the East . . . fell victim . . . through the bitter events of 1346 to 1348—the Chinese, Indians, Persians, Medes, Kurds, Armenians, Cilicians, Georgians, Mesopotamians, Nubians, Ethiopians, Turks, Egyptians, Arabs, Saracens and Greeks. . . .

* * *

As it happened, among those who escaped from Caffa by boat were a few sailors who had been infected with the poisonous disease. Some boats were bound for Genoa, others went to Venice and to other Christian areas. When the sailors reached these places and mixed with the people there, it was as if they had brought evil spirits with them. . . .

* * *

Scarcely one in seven of the Genoese survived. In Venice, where an inquiry was held into the mortality, it was found that more than 70 percent of the people had died. . . . The rest of Italy, Sicily and Apulia and the neighbouring regions maintain that they have been virtually emptied of inhabitants. . . . The Roman Curia at Avignon, the provinces on both sides of the Rhône, Spain, France, and the Empire cry up their griefs. . . .

* * *

Everyone has a responsibility to keep some record of the disease and the increasing the forested areas in parts of Europe by as much as one third.

Immediate reactions to the Black Death ran the gamut from panic to resignation. Observers quickly realized that the plague was contagious, but precisely how it spread remained enigmatic. Some believed that it was caused by breathing "bad air" and so urged people to flee from stricken areas, which caused the disease to spread even faster. Others looked for scapegoats, and revived old conspiracy theories that implicated Jews in the poisoning of wells. Scores of Jewish communities were attacked and thousands of their inhabitants massacred in the Rhineland,

deaths, and because I am myself from Piacenza I have been urged to write more about what happened there in 1348. . . .

I don't know where to begin. Cries and laments arise on all sides. Day after day one sees the Cross and the Host being carried about the city, and countless dead being buried. . . . The living made preparations for their [own] burial, and because there was not enough room for individual graves, pits had to be dug in colonnades and piazzas, where nobody had ever been buried before. It often happened that man and wife, father and son, mother and daughter, and soon the whole household and many neighbours, were buried together in one place. . . .

A Letter From the Town Council of Cologne to the Town Council of Strasbourg (Germany), 12 January 1349

Very dear friends, all sorts of rumours are now flying about against Judaism and the Jews prompted by this unexpected and unparalleled mortality of Christians. . . . Throughout our city, as in yours, many-winged Fame clamours that this mortality was initially caused, and is still being spread, by the poisoning of springs and wells, and that the Jews must have dropped poisonous substances into them. When it came to our knowledge that serious charges had been made against the Jews in several small towns and villages on the basis of this mortality, we sent numerous letters to you and to other cities and towns to uncover the truth behind these rumours, and set a thorough investigation in train. . . .

If a massacre of the Jews were to be allowed in the major cities (something which we are determined to prevent in our city, if we can, as long as the Jews are found to be innocent of these or similar actions) it could lead to the sort of outrages and disturbances which would whip up a popular revolt among the common people—and such revolts have in the past brought cities to misery and desolation. In any case we are still of the opinion that this mortality and its attendant circumstances are caused by divine vengeance and nothing else. Accordingly we intend to forbid any harassment of the Jews in our city because of these flying rumours, but to defend them faithfully and keep them safe, as our predecessors did—and we are convinced that you ought to do the same. . . .

Source: From Rosemary Horrox, ed. and trans. *The Black Death* (Manchester: 1994), pp. 16–21, 219–20.

Questions for Analysis

1. How does Gabriele d'Mussis initially explain the causes of the plague? How and why does his understanding of it change as he traces its movements from East to West?

2. Why does the Council of Cologne wish to quell violence against the Jews? How does this reasoning complement or challenge what we have learned so far about the treatment of Jews in medieval Europe?

3. In your view, do these two perspectives display a rational approach to the horrors of the Black Death? Why or why not?

southern France, and Christian Spain. (No such attacks on Jews are known to have occurred in Muslim areas of Spain or elsewhere in the Muslim world.) The papacy and some local authorities tried to halt these attacks, but these admonitions came too late. Another response to the plague was the Flagellant movement, so called because of the whips (*flagella* in Latin) with which traveling bands of penitents lashed themselves in order to appease the wrath of God. But the unruly and sometimes hysterical mobs that gathered around the flagellants aroused the concern of both ecclesiastical and secular authorities, and the movement was suppressed by papal order.

What caused the Black Death? Most evidence points to the deadly microbe *Yersinia pestis*, which causes bubonic plague and its even deadlier cousins, pneumonic and septicemic plague. In its bubonic form, this microbe is carried by fleas that travel on the backs of rats; humans catch it only if they are bitten by an infected flea or rat. Bubonic plague attacks the lymphatic system, producing enormous swellings (buboes) of the lymph nodes in the groin, neck, and armpits. Pneumonic plague results when *Y. pestis* infects the lungs, allowing the contagion to spread in the same ways as the common cold. Septicemic plague occurs when an infected flea introduces the microbe directly into the human bloodstream, causing death within hours, often before any symptoms of the disease can manifest themselves. One of the things that made the Black Death so frightening, therefore, is that it manifested itself in different ways. Those afflicted by the hideous bubonic plague might actually recover, while others—seemingly untouched—might die suddenly and mysteriously.

The Impact on the Countryside

The economic and social consequences of the plague were profound. Crops rotted in the fields, manufacturing ceased, and trade was disrupted. Basic commodities became scarcer and prices rose, prompting ineffectual efforts to control prices and to force surviving laborers to work. But these were short-term effects. In the decades following, the new demographic reality permanently altered established social and economic patterns.

First and foremost, the drastic decrease in population meant a relative abundance of food. The price of grain eventually fell, which made it more affordable. At the same time, the scarcity of workers made peasant labor valuable: wages rose and work became easily obtainable. With wages high and food prices low, ordinary people could now afford more bread, and could also spend their surplus cash on dairy products, meat, fish, fruits, and wine. As a result, the people of Europe in the later Middle Ages were better nourished than they had ever been—better than many are today. A recent study of fifteenth-century rubbish dumps has concluded that the people of Glasgow (Scotland) ate a healthier diet in 1405 than they did in 2005.

A healthier ecological balance was also reestablished in the wake of the plague. With the lessened demand for fuel, forests that had almost disappeared by 1300 began to recover and expand. Meanwhile, the declining demand for grain allowed many farmers to expand their livestock herds. By turning arable land into pasture land, farmers reduced the need to hire workers and thus increased their

profits while improving the fertility of the soil through manuring. Some farmers were even able to enlarge their holdings because so much land had been abandoned.

Most of these innovations were made by small farmers, because great lords—individuals, as well as monasteries—were slower to adjust to the changing circumstances. Some landholders responded to the shortage of workers and the rising costs of wages by forcing their tenants to perform additional unpaid labor. In eastern Europe, many free peasants became serfs for the first time. In Castile, Poland, and Germany, too, lords succeeded in imposing new forms of servitude. In other parts of Iberia and in Italy, actual slavery—which had nearly been eradicated during the economic boom of the twelfth and thirteenth centuries—became common for the first time in centuries.

In France, by contrast, peasants remained relatively free, although many were forced to pay a variety of fees and taxes to their lords and to the king. In England, where peasant bondage had been more common than in France, serfdom ultimately disappeared altogether. In the new world of geographical mobility and economic opportunity, English serfs were able to vote with their feet, either by moving to town or to the lands of a lord who offered more favorable terms: lower rents, more animals, fewer work requirements, and greater personal freedoms.

The Urban Impact

Towns were especially sensitive to the changing economic and social climate. Some had already shrunk in size as a result of the Great Famine. Others, overcrowded and unsanitary, were particularly vulnerable to plague. Thereafter, they were vulnerable to the effects of violence. In Florence, the population rebounded quickly after the Black Death only to be depleted again by civil unrest: by 1427, it had dropped from around 300,000 to about 100,000. In Toulouse (southern France), the population remained fairly stable until 1430, when it was reduced by over 75 percent by the Hundred Years' War (see below). In London and Paris, however, large-scale immigration from the countryside reversed the short-term declines of the plague. Many of these new workers were women, whose economic opportunities were greatly enhanced by urban labor shortages.

Although the overall population declined, a far larger percentage of all people were living in towns by 1500: approximately 20 precent, as opposed to 10 or 15 percent prior to the Black Death. Fueling this urban growth was the increasing specialization of the late-medieval economy. With farmers under less pressure to produce grain in bulk, land could be devoted to livestock, dairy farming, and the production of a more diverse array of fruits and vegetables; and these could now be exchanged efficiently on the open market. Towns with links to extant trading networks benefited accordingly. In northern Germany, a group of cities even formed a coalition to build a new network, the Hanseatic League, whose members controlled commerce from Britain and Scandinavia to the Baltic. In northern Italy, the increased demand for luxury goods—which even some peasants and urban laborers could now afford—brought new wealth to the spice- and silk-trading city of Venice and also to the fine-cloth manufacturers of Milan and the jewelers of Florence. Milan's armaments industry also prospered, supplying its warring neighbors and the armies of Europe.

Not all the urban areas of Europe fared well. The Franco-Flemish cities that had played such a large role in the economic and cultural life of the High Middle Ages suffered a serious economic depression and the ravages of various wars. But on the whole, Europe profited from the plague, and was poised to extend its commercial networks into Africa, Asia, and ultimately, in the fifteenth century, the Americas (see Chapter 11).

The economic boom also stimulated the development of business practices and accounting techniques. New forms of partnership and the development of insurance contracts helped to minimize the risks associated with long-distance trading. Double-entry bookkeeping, widely used in Italy by the mid-fourteenth century, gave merchants a much clearer picture of their profits and losses than had been possible before. The Medici family of Florence established branches of their bank in each of the major cities of Europe and were careful that the failure of one would no longer bankrupt the entire firm, as previous branch-banking arrangements had done. Banks also experimented with advanced credit techniques borrowed from Muslim and Jewish financiers, allowing their clients to transfer funds between branches without any real money changing hands. Such transfers were carried out by written orders, the ancestors of the modern check.

SOCIAL MOBILITY AND SOCIAL INEQUALITY

The consequences of the Black Death were ultimately beneficial for many of those who survived it. But European society did not adjust easily to the new world created by the plague. It seemed to many like a world turned upside down, so rapidly had changes occurred.

Revolts and Rebellions

Between 1350 and 1425, hundreds of popular rebellions challenged the status quo in many regions of Europe. In 1358, for example, peasants in northeastern France rose up violently against their lords, destroying property, burning buildings and crops, and even murdering or raping targeted individuals. This incident is known as the Jacquerie Rebellion because all French peasants were caricatured by the aristocracy as "Jacques" ("Jack"). In England, as we have already noted, a very different uprising occurred in June of 1381, much more organized and involving a much wider segment of society. Thousands of people marched on London, targeting the bureaucracies of the royal government and the Church, capturing and killing the archbishop of Canterbury, and meeting personally with the fourteen-year-old king, Richard II, to demand an end to serfdom and taxation, and the redistribution of property. It ended with the arrest and execution of the ringleaders. In Florence, workers in the cloth industry—known as the Ciompi (*chee-OM-pee*)—protested high unemployment and mistreatment by the manufacturers who also ran the Florentine government.

THE BANKER AND HIS WIFE BY QUENTIN MASSYS (1466–1530). This painting exemplifies the realistic art of the later Middle Ages: the wealthy banker and his wife display all the fashionable trappings and gadgets of the era, including an illuminated prayer book and a mirror. *What does this image convey about the values and lifestyle of the merchant class?*

They seized control of the city, demanding relief from taxes, full employment, and political representation. They maintained power for a remarkable six weeks before their reforms were revoked.

The local circumstances that lay behind each of these revolts are unique, but these and hundreds of other rebellions exhibit certain common features. First of all, these uprisings were not bread riots spurred by destitution. Those who took part in them had actually been empowered by the new economic conditions and wanted to leverage their position in order to enact even larger changes. Some rebellions, like the English Peasants' Revolt, were touched off by resistance to new and higher taxes. Others, like the Jacquerie and the revolt of the Ciompi, took place at moments when unpopular governments were weakened by factionalism and military defeat. The English revolt was also fueled by the widespread perception of corruption within the Church and the royal administration.

Behind this social and political unrest, therefore, lies not poverty and hunger but the growing prosperity and self-confidence that village communities and urban workers felt in the changed economic circumstances that arose from the plague. For the most part, the rebels' hopes that they could fundamentally alter the conditions of their lives were frustrated. Kings, aristocrats, and urban oligarchs sometimes lost their nerve in the middle of an uprising, but they were almost always successful, after a time, in reasserting dominance. Yet this tradition of popular rebellion, established during the the later Middle Ages, would remain an important feature of Western civilizations and would culminate in the French Revolution (Chapter 18). It continues to this day.

Aristocratic Life in the Later Middle Ages

The urban elites and rural aristocracies of Europe did not adapt easily to the new world created by the plague. Yet the later Middle Ages was a hardly a period of crisis for those in power. Quite the contrary: the great noble families of Europe were far wealthier than their ancestors had been. Nor did the plague undermine the dominant position they had established in European society. It did, however, make

A HUNTING PARTY. This fifteenth-century illustration shows an elaborately dressed group of noble men and women setting out with falcons, accompanied by their servants and their dogs. Hunting was an activity restricted to the aristocracy, and an occasion for conspicuous consumption and display.

their world substantially more complex and uncertain, at a time when the costs of maintaining a fashionable lifestyle were escalating rapidly.

Across Europe, most noble families continued to derive much of their revenue from vast landholdings. But many lords also tried to increase their sources of income through investment in trading ventures. In Catalonia, Italy, Germany, and England, this became common practice. In France and Castile, however, direct involvement in commerce was regarded as socially demeaning and was, therefore, avoided by established families. Commerce could still be a route to ennoblement in these kingdoms, but once aristocratic rank was achieved one was expected to abandon these employments and adopt an appropriate way of life: living in a rural castle or urban palace surrounded by a lavish household, embracing the values and conventions of chivalry (including hunting and a family coat of arms), and serving the prince at court and in war.

Nobility became, as a result, even more difficult to define than it had been during the twelfth and thirteenth centuries. In countries where nobility entailed clearly defined legal privileges—such as the right to be tried only in special courts—proven descent from noble ancestors might be sufficient to qualify a family as noble in the eyes of the law. Legal nobility of this sort was, however, a somewhat less exclusive distinction than one might expect. In fifteenth-century Castile and Navarre, 10 to 15 percent of the total population had claims to be recognized as noble on these terms. In Poland, Hungary, and Scotland, the legally privileged nobility was closer to 5 percent; whereas in England and France, fewer than 2 percent could plausibly claim the legal privileges of noble status.

Fundamentally, however, nobility was a marker of social rank, expressed and epitomized by an individual's lifestyle. Hereditary land ownership, political influence, deference from social inferiors, courtly manners, and the ostentatious display of wealth: these combined to constitute a family's honor and hence to mark it as noble. But in practice, the lines of social distinction between noble and non-noble families remained fuzzy. Even on the battlefield, the supremacy of the mounted noble knight was being threatened by the growing importance of professional soldiers, archers, and artillery experts. There were even hints of a more radical critique of claims to innate superiority. As the English rebels put it in 1381: "When Adam dug and Eve spun, Who then was a gentleman?" In other words, they recognized that all human beings are equal and that social distinctions are entirely artificial.

Precisely because nobility was contested during the later Middle Ages, those who claimed the status took elaborate measures to assert its exclusivity. This accounts, in part, for the extraordinary number, variety, and richness of the artifacts and artworks that survive from this period. Aristocrats vied with one another in hosting lavish banquets. They dressed in rich and extravagant clothing: close-fitting doublets and hose with long pointed shoes for men, multilayered silk dresses with ornately festooned headdresses for women. They maintained enormous households: in France around 1400, the duke of Berry had 400 matched pairs of hunting dogs and 1,000 servants. They took part in elaborately ritualized tournaments and pageants, in which the participants pretended to be the heroes of chivalric romances. Aristocrats also emphasized their tastes and refinement by supporting authors and artists, and sometimes by becoming accomplished poets themselves. Nobility existed only if it was recognized; and to be recognized, noble status had to be constantly reasserted and displayed.

Rulers contributed to this process of noble self-assertion; indeed, they were among its principal supporters and patrons. Kings and princes across Europe competed in founding chivalric orders such as the Knights of the Garter in England and the Order of the Star in France. These orders honored men who had demonstrated the idealized virtues of knighthood, virtues celebrated as characteristic of the nobility as a whole. By exalting the nobility as a class, then, chivalric orders helped cement the links that bound the nobility to their kings and princes. So too did the gifts, pensions, offices, and marriage prospects that kings and princes could bestow on their noble followers. Given the decline in the agricultural revenues of noble estates, such rewards of princely service were critically important to maintaining noble fortunes. Indeed, the alliance that was forged in the fifteenth century between kings and their noble supporters would become one of the most characteristic features of "old regime" (in

A NOBLE BANQUET. Uncle of the mad king Charles VI, the duke of Berry left politics to his brothers, the dukes of Burgundy and Anjou. In return, he received enormous subsidies from the royal government, which he spent on sumptuous buildings, festivals, and artworks, including the famous Book of Hours (prayer book) that includes this image. Here, the duke (seated at right, in blue) gives a New Year's Day banquet for his household, who exchange gifts while his hunting dogs dine on scraps from the table. In the background, knights confront one another in a battle—or a tournament.

French, *ancien régime*) Europe. In France, this alliance lasted until the French Revolution of 1789. In Germany, Austria, and Russia it would last until the outbreak of World War I. In England, it persisted in some respects until World War II.

WARFARE AND NATION-BUILDING

The partnership between royalty and nobility was partly a response to the new social and economic world created by the plague. But it was also a product of the unprecedented prevalence and scale of warfare. Beginning in the fourteenth century and continuing into the twentieth, Europeans were almost constantly at war. To fight these wars, governments claimed new powers to tax their subjects and to control their subjects' lives. Armies became larger, military technology deadlier. Wars became more destructive, society more militarized. As a result of these developments, the most successful European states—the monarchies of Portugal, Spain, and France—were aggressively expansionist. By 1600, their impact would be global (see Chapter 11).

England, France, and the Hundred Years' War

The Hundred Years' War was the largest, longest, and most wide-ranging military conflict since Rome's wars with Carthage in the third and second centuries B.C.E. (Chapter 5). England and France were its principal antagonists, but almost all of the major European powers became involved in it at some stage. Active hostilities lasted from 1337 until 1453, interrrupted by truces of varying lengths. The roots of the conflict, however, reached back into the 1290s, when King Edward I of England attempted to conquer the neighboring kingdom of Scotland, thereby provoking the Scots to ally with France. And the threat of war continued until 1558, when Calais, the last English toehold on the Continent, passed into French hands.

The war had several causes. The most fundamental source of conflict, and the most difficult to resolve, was the fact that the kings of England held the duchy of Gascony as vassals of the French king; this was part of Eleanor of Aquitaine's domains, added to the Anglo-Norman Empire in 1154 (Chapter 9). In the twelfth and thirteenth centuries, when the French kings had not yet absorbed this region, this fact had seemed less of an anomaly. But as Europe's territorial monarchies began to claim sovereignty based on the free

exercise of power within the "natural" boundaries of their domains, the English presence in "French" Gascony became more and more problematic. That England also had close commercial links, through the wool trade, with Flanders—which consistently resisted French imperialism—added fuel to the fire. So did the French alliance with the Scots, who had been resolutely resisting English imperialism.

Complicating this volatile situation was the disputed succession of the French crown. In 1328, the last of King Philip IV's three sons died without leaving a son to succeed him: the Capetian dynasty, founded by the Frankish warlord Hugh Capet in 987 (Chapter 8), had finally exhausted itself. A new dynasty, the Valois, came to the throne—but only by insisting that women could neither inherit royal power nor pass it on. For otherwise, the heir to France was Edward III of England, whose mother, Isabella, was Philip IV's only daughter. When his claim was initially passed over, Edward was only fifteen and in no position to protest. In 1337, however, when the disputes over Gascony and Scotland erupted into war, Edward raised the stakes by claiming to be the rightful king of France, a claim that subsequent English kings would maintain until the eighteenth century.

The hostilities that make up the Hundred Years' War can be divided into three main phases (see the maps on page 321). In the first phase, from 1337 until 1360, the English won a series of startling military victories, most famously at Crécy (1346), Calais (1347), and Poitiers (1356). Although France was richer and more populous than England by a factor of at least three to one, the English government was more effective in mobilizing the entire population, for reasons that were discussed in Chapter 9. King Edward was therefore able to levy and maintain a professional army of seasoned and well-disciplined soldiers, cavalry, and longbowmen. The huge but poorly led armies assembled by the French proved no match for the tactical superiority of these smaller English forces. English armies pillaged the French countryside at will, while civil wars broke out between individual French lords. Meanwhile, mercenary bands of soldiers roamed the countryside, attacking and looting peasant villages and holding towns to ransom just at the time when they were struggling to recover from the Black Death. In 1358, popular frustration boiled over in the savage rebellion of the Jacquerie (discussed above).

In 1360, Edward III agreed to renounce his claim to the French throne in return for full sovereignty over a greatly enlarged duchy of Gascony and the promise of a huge ransom for the king of France, whom he held captive. But the terms of the treaty were never honored. The French king continued to treat the English king as his vassal, and the king of England never ceased to claim the throne of France. Nor did the treaty resolve the underlying issues that had

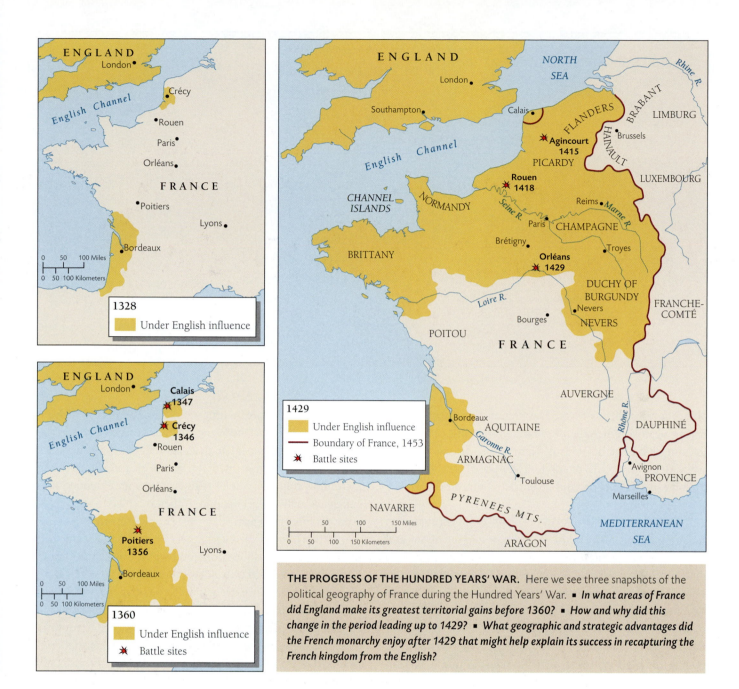

THE PROGRESS OF THE HUNDRED YEARS' WAR. Here we see three snapshots of the political geography of France during the Hundred Years' War. ▪ *In what areas of France did England make its greatest territorial gains before 1360?* ▪ *How and why did this change in the period leading up to 1429?* ▪ *What geographic and strategic advantages did the French monarchy enjoy after 1429 that might help explain its success in recapturing the French kingdom from the English?*

led to the war itself. Instead, a proxy war developed during the 1360s and 1370s, in which English and French troops organized into "Free Companies" hired themselves out in the service of warring factions in Castile and competing city-states in northern Italy. By 1376, when hostilties resumed between England and France, the Hundred Years' War had become a Europe-wide phenomenon.

In this second phase of the war, the tide quickly shifted in favor of France. In England, the aging Edward III was succeeded by his nine-year-old grandson, Richard II (r. 1377–99). Meanwhile, the new king of France, Charles V (r. 1364–80), imposed a series of new national taxes on the common people, restored order by disbanding the Free

Companies, and hired the leader of one of these bands as the commander of his army. He thereby created a professional military that could match the English in discipline and tactics. By 1380, English territories in France had been reduced to a core area around the southwestern city of Bordeaux and the port of Calais in the extreme northeast.

Unlike his grandfather Edward III, Richard II had no interest in the French war. And although the war had been extremely popular in England, it ceased to be so during Richard's minority, when its conduct was mismanaged by his advisors. Indeed, this was one of the issues that had triggered the Peasants' Revolt in 1381. However, the nobility stood to gain from the war's continuation, and Richard's

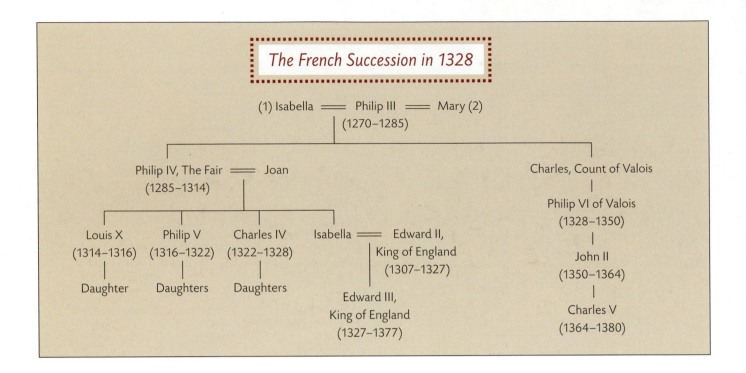

The French Succession in 1328

(1) Isabella ══ Philip III ══ Mary (2)
(1270–1285)

Philip IV, The Fair ══ Joan
(1285–1314)

Charles, Count of Valois
|
Philip VI of Valois
(1328–1350)

Louis X
(1314–1316)
|
Daughter

Philip V
(1316–1322)
|
Daughters

Charles IV
(1322–1328)
|
Daughters

Isabella ══ Edward II,
King of England
(1307–1327)

Edward III,
King of England
(1327–1377)

John II
(1350–1364)
|
Charles V
(1364–1380)

---

failure to press his claims to the French throne turned the barons against him. When Richard attempted to confiscate the inheritance of his cousin, Henry of Lancaster, Henry's supporters used this as pretext for rebellion. In 1399, Richard was deposed and eventually murdered. Henry seized the throne.

As a usurper, Henry IV (r. 1399–1413) struggled to maintain his authority in the face of repeated rebellions and challenges. Frequently ill, he was in no position to pursue the French war. When his son Henry V succeeded him in 1413, however, the new king immediately began to prepare for renewed war with France. A brilliant diplomat, Henry sealed alliances with both the emperor in Germany and the powerful duke of Burgundy, who was in control of the French royal government, then foundering due to the insanity of the French king, Charles VI (r. 1380–1422). When Henry V invaded France in 1415, he therefore faced only a partial army representing the anti-Burgundian faction within the royal court; the duke of Burgundy and his forces stayed home. Then, at Agincourt, Henry managed to win a crushing victory over a vastly larger, but badly disciplined French force. By 1420, he had conquered most of northern France and had forced the aged and infirm King Charles VI to give him his daughter Catherine's hand in marriage and to recognize him as heir to the throne of France—thus dispossessing the heir apparent, known as the Dauphin ("the dolphin"), the future King Charles VII.

Unlike his great-grandfather Edward III, who used his claim to the French throne largely as a bargaining chip to secure sovereignty over Gascony, Henry V honestly believed

himself to be the rightful king of France. And his astonishing success in capturing the French kingdom seemed to put the stamp of divine approval on that claim. But Henry's successes in France also transformed the nature of the war, turning it from a profitable war of conquest into an extended and expensive military occupation. It thereby sowed the seeds of eventual English defeat.

Henry himself died early in 1422, still actively engaged in extending English control southward, toward the Loire. King Charles VI died only a few months later. The new king of England and France, Henry VI (r. 1422–61), was an infant, but the English armies under the command of his advisors continued to press southward. Meanwhile, the Dauphin's confidence in his right to the throne had been shattered by his own mother's declaration that he was illegitimate. Although it seemed unlikely that English forces would ever succeed in dislodging him from territories south of the Loire, it might have happened that England would once again rule an empire comprising much of northern France, as it had for a century and a half after the Norman Conquest.

But this scenario fails to reckon with Joan of Arc. In 1429, a peasant girl from Lorraine (a territory only nominally part of France) made her way to the Dauphin's court and announced that an angel had told her that he, Charles, was the rightful king, and that she, Joan, should drive the English out of France. The fact that she even got a hearing underscores the hopelessness of the Dauphin's position, as does the extraordinary fact that he gave her a contingent of troops. With this force, Joan liberated the strategic city of Orléans, then under siege, after which a series of victories

Analyzing Primary Sources

The Condemnation of Joan of Arc by the University of Paris, 1431

After Joan's capture by the Burgundians, she was handed over to the English and tried for heresy at an ecclesiastical court set up in Rouen. It was on this occasion that the theology faculty of Paris pronounced the following verdict on her actions.

ou, Joan, have said that, since the age of thirteen, you have experienced revelations and the appearance of angels, of St. Catherine and St. Margaret, and that you have very often seen them with your bodily eyes, and that they have spoken to you. As for the first point, the clerks of the University of Paris have considered the manner of the said revelations and appearances . . . Having considered all . . . they have declared that all the things mentioned above are lies, falsenesses, misleading and pernicious things and that such revelations are superstitions, proceeding from wicked and diabolical spirits.

Item: You have said that your king had a sign by which he knew that you were sent by God, for St. Michael, accompanied by several angels, some of which having wings, the others crowns, with St. Catherine and St. Margaret, came to you at the chateau of Chinon. All the company ascended through the floors of the castle until they came to the room of your king, before whom the angel bearing the crown bowed. . . .

As for this matter, the clerks say that it is not in the least probable, but it is rather a presumptuous lie, misleading and pernicious, a false statement, derogatory of the dignity of the Church and of the angels. . . .

Item: you have said that, at God's command, you have continually worn men's clothes, and that you have put on a short robe, doublet, shoes attached by points, also that you have had short hair, cut around above the ears, without retaining anything on your person which shows that you are a woman, and that several times you have received the body of Our Lord dressed in this fashion, despite having been admonished to give it up several times, the which you would not do. You have said that you would rather die than abandon the said clothing, if it were not at God's command, and that if you were wearing those clothes and were with the king, and those of your party, it would be one of the greatest benefits for the kingdom of France. You have also said that not for anything would you swear an oath not to wear the said clothing and carry arms any longer. And all these things you say you

have done for the good and at the command of God. As for these things, the clerics say that you blaspheme God and hold him in contempt in his sacraments; you transgress Divine Law, Holy Scripture, and canon law. You err in the faith. You boast in vanity. You are suspected of idolatry and you have condemned yourself in not wishing to wear clothing suitable to your sex, but you follow the custom of Gentiles and Saracens.

Source: Carolyne Larrington, ed. and trans., *Women and Writing in Medieval Europe* (New York: 1995), pp. 183–84.

Questions for Analysis

1. Paris was in the hands of the English when this condemnation was issued. Is there any evidence that its authors were coerced into making this pronouncement?

2. On what grounds was Joan condemned for heresy?

3. In what ways does Joan's behavior highlight larger trends in late medieval spirituality and popular piety?

culminated in Charles's coronation in the cathedral of Reims, the traditional site for the crowning of French kings. But despite her victories, Joan was an embarrassment whose very charisma made her dangerous: a peasant leading aristocrats, a woman leading men, and a commoner who claimed to have been commissioned by God. When, a few months later, the Burgundians captured her in battle

and handed her over to the English, King Charles VII did nothing to save her. Accused of witchcraft, condemned by the theologians of Paris, and tried for heresy by an English ecclesiastical court, Joan was burned to death in the market square at Rouen in 1431. She was nineteen years old.

The French forces whom Joan had inspired, however, continued on the offensive. In 1435, the Duke of Burgundy

JOAN OF ARC. A contemporary sketch of Joan was drawn in the margin of this register documenting official proceedings at the Parlement of Paris in 1429.

were successful, the king rode a wave of popularity that fueled an emerging sense of English identity. When the war turned against the English, however, defeats abroad undermined support for the monarch at home. Of the nine English kings who ruled England between 1307 and 1485, five were deposed and murdered by factions. This was a consequence of England's peculiar form of kingship, whose strength depended on the king's ability to mobilize popular support through Parliament while maintaining the support of his nobility through successful wars. Failure to maintain this balance was even more destablizing in England than it would have been elsewhere, precisely because royal power was so centralized. In France, the nobility could endure the insanity of Charles VI because his government was not powerful enough to threaten them. In England, neither the nobility nor the nation could afford the incompetent kingship of Henry VI. The result was an aristocratic rebellion against the king that led to a full-blown civil war: the Wars of the Roses, so called—by the novelist Sir Walter Scott (1771–1832)—because of the emblems of the two competing noble families descended from Edward III, Lancaster and York. It ended only when a Lancastrian claimant, Henry Tudor (r. 1485–1509), resolved the dynastic feud by marrying Elizabeth of York, ruling as Henry VII and establishing a new Tudor dynasty whose symbol was a rose with both white and red petals. His son was Henry VIII (see Chapter 13).

Despite England's ultimate defeat, the Hundred Years' War strengthened a characteristically English equation between national identity and the power of the state. Mounting anti-French sentiment also contributed to the triumph of the English vernacular over French for the first time since the Norman Conquest. And having lost its continental possessions, England became, for the first time, a self-contained island nation that looked to the sea for defense and opportunity. This would later prove to be an advantage in many ways.

withdrew from his alliance with England; and when the young English king, Henry VI, proved first incompetent and then insane, a series of French military victories brought hostilities to an end with the capture of Bordeaux in 1453. English kings would threaten to renew the war for another century, and Anglo-French hostility would last until the defeat of Napoleon in 1815. But after 1453, English control over French territory would be limited to the port of Calais, which fell in 1558.

The Effects of the Hundred Years' War

The Hundred Years' War challenged the very existence of France. The disintegration of that kingdom, first during the 1350s and 1360s, and again between 1415 and 1435, glaringly revealed the fragility of the bonds that tied the king to the nobility, and Paris to the outlying regions. Nonetheless, the king's power was actually increased by the war's end, laying the foundations on which the power of early modern France would be built.

The Hundred Years' War also had dramatic effects on the English monarchy. When English armies in France

Conflict in the Holy Roman Empire and Italy

The endemic warfare that begins to characterize the history of Europe in the later Middle Ages was usually even more destructive than it proved to be in the struggle between England and France. In the lands of the Holy Roman Empire, armed conflict among territorial princes, and between these princes and the German emperors, weakened all the principal combatants significantly. Periodically, a powerful emperor would emerge to play a major role, but the dominant trend was toward the continuing dissolution of power, with German princes dividing their territories among their heirs while free cities and local lords strove to shake off the princes' rule. Between 1350 and 1450, near anarchy prevailed in many regions. In the eastern empire, however, the rulers of Bavaria, Austria, and Brandenburg-Prussia were able to strengthen their authority by supporting the efforts of the nobility to subject their peasants to serfdom and by conquering and colonizing new territories on their eastern frontiers.

In northern and central Italy, the last half of the fourteenth century was also marked by incessant conflict. With the papacy based in Avignon from 1309 until 1377, the Papal States collapsed and Rome itself was riven by factional violence. Warfare among northern city-states added to the violence caused by urban rebellions in the wake of the plague. By around 1400, however, Venice, Milan, and Florence had succeeded in stabilizing their differing forms of government. Venice was now ruled by an oligarchy of merchants; Milan by a family of despots; and Florence was ruled as a republic but dominated by the influence of a few wealthy clans, especially the Medici banking family. Having settled their internal problems, these three cities then began to expand their territories by subordinating other cities to their rule. By 1454, almost all the towns of northern Italy were allied with one of these powers. An exception was the port of Genoa, which remained prosperous and independent as a shipping and trading hub. The papacy, meanwhile, reasserted its control over central Italy when it was restored to Rome in 1377, while the southern kingdom of Naples persisted as a separate entity, but plagued by constant local warfare and poor government.

For about forty years, a treaty negotiated in 1454 brought peace among this cluster of Italian powers, while frequently shifting alliances checked the ambitions of any one state for further expansion. In 1494, however, a large-scale invasion of Italy by the French destroyed the diplomatic and military balance. Moreover, it revealed that none of these small-scale Italian states could oppose the powerful national monarchies that had developed north of the Alps—or the new kingdom of Spain.

The Emergence of Spain

The kingdoms of the Iberian peninsula were also in constant conflict during the fourteenth and fifteenth centuries. In Castile, civil war and incompetent governance allowed the Castilian nobility to gain greater control over the peasantry and greater independence from the crown. In Aragon, the crown preserved its authority and benefitted

from the extended commercial influence of Catalonia. But after 1458, Aragon was enmeshed in a civil war over a disputed succession, a war in which both France and Castile became involved.

The solution would ultimately lie in the blending of powerful families. In 1469, Prince Ferdinand of Aragon was recognized as the undisputed heir to that throne and, in the same year, secured this position by marrying Isabella, the heiress to Castile. Isabella became a queen in 1474, Ferdinand a king in 1479, and although Castile and Aragon continued to be ruled as separate kingdoms until 1714 (even now, tensions between the two former kingdoms continue), the marriage of Ferdinand and Isabella enabled the pursuit of several ambitious policies. Their union allowed them to spend their extraordinary resources on the creation of Europe's most powerful army, which was initially employed to conquer Granada, the last remaining Muslim principality in Spain. Granada fell in 1492, and a decade later Spanish armies intervened in Italy, eventually turning all of Italy into a Spanish protectorate.

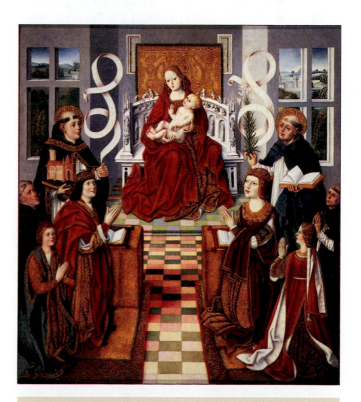

FERDINAND AND ISABELLA HONORING THE VIRGIN. In this contemporary Spanish painting, the royal couple are shown with two of their children and two household chaplains, and in the company of the Blessed Virgin, the Christ Child, and saints from the Dominican order (the Dominicans were instrumental in conducting the affairs of the Spanish Inquisition). ■ *How clear is the distinction between these holy figures and the royal family?* ■ *What message is conveyed by their proximity?*

The conquest of Granada was a turning point for the emerging Spanish monarchy. Both Castile and Aragon had been shaped for centuries by their involvement in the "reconquest" of Iberia, and the victory of 1492 earned Ferdinand and Isabella the title of Europe's "Most Catholic" monarchs. It also associated Castile, in particular, with the crusading ethos, which now sought outlets elsewhere. Only a few months after the conquest of Granada, Queen Isabella granted three ships to a Genoese adventurer who promised to reach India by sailing westward across the Atlantic Ocean. He failed, of course; but by landing in two new continents, which he claimed for Spain, Columbus extended the Castilian crusading tradition to the New World, with enduring consequences (see Chapter 11).

The year 1492 also saw the expulsion of the entire Jewish community from Spain, the culmination of a process of Jewish exclusion from Christian Europe that had accelerated in the late thirteenth century (Chapter 9). The Spanish expulsion stands out, however, for the total number of Jews involved (at least 100,000 and possibly as many as 200,000) and because of the rich cultural legacy fostered by the Jews of this region over a period of a thousand years. The Catholic monarchs' motives for ordering this expulsion are still debated. Tens of thousands of Spanish Jews had converted to Christianity between 1391 and 1420, many as a result of coercion but some from sincere religious conviction. And for a generation or so it seemed possible that these converts, known as *conversos*, might successfully assimilate into Christian society. But the internal and external conflicts that led to the union of Ferdinand and Isabella made the *conversos* targets of discriminatory legislation and may also have fueled popular suspicions that they remained Jews in secret. To make "proper" Christians out of the *conversos*, the "Most Catholic" monarchs may have concluded that they needed to remove the "bad influence" posed by the continuing presence of a Jewish community in Spain.

The expulsion of Jews thus enabled the creation of a new and explicitly Christian identity for the hybrid Spanish nation, transcending the many rival regional identities there. Like other contemporary monarchs, Ferdinand and Isabella may have sought to strengthen their emerging nation-state by constructing an exclusively Christian identity for its people, and by attaching that new identity to the crown.

The Growth of National Monarchies

In France, England, and Spain, as well as in smaller kingdoms like Scotland and Portugal, the later Middle Ages thus saw the emergence of European states more powerful and cohesive than any that had existed before. The basic political patterns established in the formative twelfth and thirteenth centuries had made this possible, yet the active construction of a sense of national identity in these territories, and the fusion of that identity with kingship, were new phenomena. Forged by war and fueled by the growing cultural importance of vernacular languages, this fusion produced a new type of political organization: the national monarchy.

The advantages of these national monarchies when compared to older forms of political organization—such as the empire and the city-state—is most clearly visible in Italy. Until the end of the fifteenth century, the Italian city-states had appeared to be well governed and powerful, and Venice even had a maritime empire of its own. But when the armies of France and Spain invaded the Italian peninsula, neither the militias of the city-states nor the far-flung resources of Venice were a match for them. Germany and the Low Countries would suffer the same fate only a few generations later, and would remain battlegrounds for competing armies until the early nineteenth century. But the new national monarchies brought significant disadvantages, too. They guaranteed the continued prevalence of warfare in Europe, and they eventually transported their rivalry to every corner of the globe in the late nineteenth and early twentieth centuries.

THE RISE OF MUSCOVY, "THE THIRD ROME"

The fourteenth and fifteenth centuries also witnessed the consolidation of a state that would become the dominant power in eastern Europe and, in the twentieth century, one of the great powers of the world. Yet Russia developed very differently from the national monarchies of western Europe. It was, instead, the largest multiethnic empire in the pre-modern world. And by 1500, it claimed to be the rightful successor to the Rome of the Caesars, as well as to that of Constantine.

Kievan Rus' and the Mongol Khanate

As we saw in Chapter 8, the Viking people known as Rus' had played a key role in establishing a principality at Kiev (now in Ukraine), which maintained diplomatic and trading relations with both western Europe and Byzantium throughout the tenth and eleventh centuries. That dynamic changed with the arrival of the Mongols (whose movements will be discussed more fully in Chapter 11). Commanded by a grandson of the great Chingiz (Genghis) Khan, the Mongols overran Kiev in 1240. Two years later, they created their own state on the lower Volga River, known as the Khanate of the Golden Horde, and from this base they wielded power for 150 years.

Initially, the Mongols ruled their Russian territories directly, installing their own administrative officials and requiring Russian princes to subject themselves to the Great Khan himself, by traveling to Mongolia. Around 1300, however, the Mongols began to tolerate the existence of several semi-independent principalities from which they demanded regular tribute. Kiev never recovered its dominant position, but one of the newer principalities would enable the construction of a Russian state: Muscovy, the duchy centered on Moscow.

The Rise of Muscovy

In the early fourteenth century, Moscow was the tribute-collecting center for the Mongol Khanate. This did not always protect it from attack, but Mongol support did help Moscow's dukes to absorb neighboring territories. And because Moscow was far from the Mongol base on the lower Volga, its dukes could further consolidate their strength without attracting too much attention from the khans. This location was also advantageous for forging commercial contacts with the Baltic and Black Sea regions.

Yet Moscow's ties with western Europe remained undeveloped—not because it was under the thumb of the Mongols, but because it was loyal to the Orthodox Church of Byzantium. Relations between eastern and western Christians had deteriorated steadily during the Crusades and were openly hostile after Constantinople was captured and sacked by crusaders in 1204, a calamity from which it never recovered. Then, during the fourteenth and fifteenth centuries, Moscow's sensitivity to threats from European Christianity was escalated by the growing strength of a Catholic kingdom on its borders.

The Expansion of Poland

In the thirteenth century, the small kingdom of Poland had struggled to defend itself from neighboring German princes and from absorption into the Holy Roman Empire. But when the empire's strength waned after the death of Frederick the Great (Chapter 9), Poland's situation grew more secure. In 1386, its reigning queen, Jadwiga, enabled its dramatic expansion when she married Jagiello, the duke of neighboring

Lithuania, thus doubling the size of her kingdom. Lithuania had begun to carve out an extensive territory stretching from the Baltic to modern-day Belarus and Ukraine, and this expansionist momentum increased after its union with Poland. In 1410, at the Battle of Tannenberg, combined Polish and Lithuanian forces defeated the Teutonic Knights, a military order that controlled a crucial region lying between the allied kingdoms. Thereafter, Poland-Lithuania began to push eastward toward Muscovy.

Although many of Lithuania's aristocratic families were Orthodox Christians, the established church in Lithuania was loyal to Rome, as it was in Poland. Thus when the inhabitants of the region around Moscow began to feel threatened by Poland-Lithuania, one way of constructing a shared Muscovite identity was to direct shared hostility toward Latin Christendom.

The Russian Church and the Third Rome

Muscovy's alienation from western Europe increased as Byzantium grew weaker and the responsibility for defending Orthodox Christianity devolved onto the Russian Church. Muscovites prided themselves on their descent from the Rus' who had been converted by Byzantine missionaries in the tenth century (Chapter 8), and they saw themselves as the natural champions of Constantinople, which was now surrounded by the Muslim empire of the Ottoman Turks (to be discussed further in Chapter 11). But when the patriarch of Constantinople agreed to submit to the authority of Rome in 1438, in the desperate hope that the papacy would rally military support for the besieged city, Russian clergy refused to follow suit. After Constantinople fell to the Turks in 1453—predictably, without any help from Latin Christendom—the Russian Church therefore emerged as the only surviving proponent of Orthodox Christianity, while the Muscovite state declared itself the divinely appointed successor to Rome. To drive the point home, Muscovite dukes began to take the title of *tsar*, "caesar." In their eyes, Moscow had become the last and greatest heir of the Roman Empire. "Two Romes have fallen," said a Muscovite chonicler, "the third is still standing, and a fourth there shall not be."

The Reign of Ivan the Great (1462–1505)

Along with the imperial title, the Muscovite rulers borrowed the Byzantine ideology of the ruler's divine election,

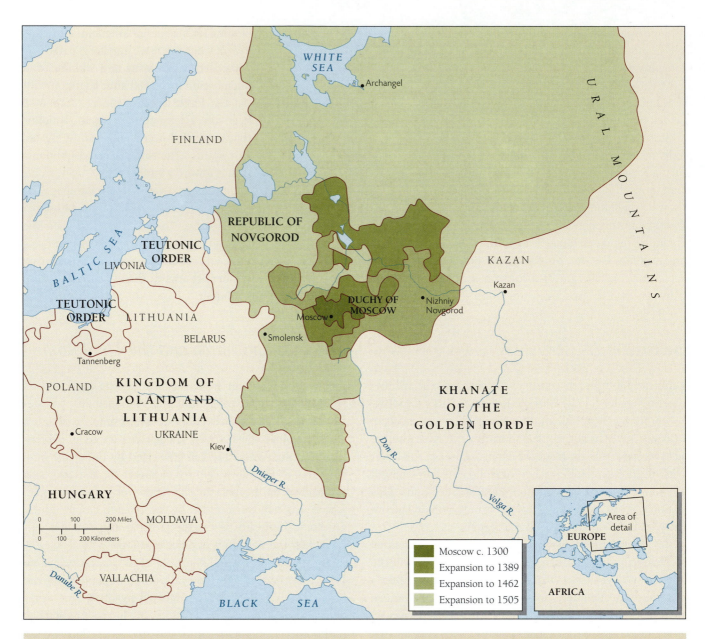

THE EXPANSION OF MUSCOVITE RUSSIA TO 1505. The grand duchy of Moscow was the heart of what would soon become the Russian Empire. ■ *With what other empires and polities did the Muscovites have to compete during this period of expansion?* ■ *How did the relative isolation of Moscow, compared with early Kiev, allow for the growth of Muscovite power on the one hand and Moscow's distinctively non-Western culture on the other?* ■ *How might the natural direction of the expansion of Muscovite power until 1505 help to encourage attitudes often at odds with those of western European civilization?*

and this undergirded the sacred position later ascribed to the tsars. But ideology alone could not have built the Russian Empire. Behind its growth lay the steadily growing power of Moscow's rulers, who achieved effective independence from the Mongols when a rebellious Mongol warlord named Timur the Lame (Tamburlane) destroyed the Khanate of the Golden Horde at the end of the fourteenth century. This allowed the Muscovite grand duke,

Ivan III, known as Ivan the Great, to fill the power vacuum and carry forward his own imperial agenda.

Ivan launched a series of conquests that annexed all the independent Russian principalities lying between Moscow and the border of Poland-Lithuania. After invading Lithuania in 1492 and 1501, Ivan even succeeded in bringing parts of that domain (portions of modern Belarus and Ukraine) under his control. Meanwhile, he married the

IVAN THE GREAT. This modern tribute to Ivan III prominently displays the two-headed eagle of imperial Rome. *What is the significance of this symbolic choice?*

niece of the last Byzantine emperor, giving substance to the claim that Muscovy was a new New Rome. He also rebuilt his fortified Moscow residence, known as the Kremlin, in magnificent Italianate style. He would later adopt, as his imperial insignia, the double-headed eagle of Rome and its legions. By the time of his death in 1505, Muscovy was firmly established as a dominant power and the power of the tsar was revealed as more absolute than that of any European monarch.

THE TRIALS OF THE ROMAN CHURCH

The later Middle Ages changed the Roman Church in ways that would prove definitive. Like other large land-owners, monasteries suffered from the economic changes brought about by the Black Death, as did bishops, who confronted the same dilemmas as the secular nobility. But no ecclesiastical institution suffered more severe trials than the papacy, which endured almost seventy years of exile from Rome followed by a debilitating forty-year schism. It then faced a protracted battle with reformers who sought to reduce the pope's role in Church governance. Even though the papacy won this battle in the short term, the renewed abuse of papal power would, in the long run, bring about the permanent schism caused by the Reformation of the sixteenth century (Chapter 13).

The "Babylonian Captivity" of the Papacy

As we saw in Chapter 9, Boniface VIII's humiliation at the hands of the French king Philip IV was followed by the wholesale subjugation of papal authority to the French crown. This period is often called the "Babylonian Captivity" of the papacy, recalling the Jews' exile in Babylon during the sixth century B.C.E. (see Chapter 2). From 1309 until 1378, the papal court resided at Avignon, a small city in southern France. It had not intended to remain there and, after Philip's death in 1314, it probably could have left. But Avignon soon proved to have a number of advantages over Rome. It was closer to the major centers of power, it was far removed from the tumultuous politics of Rome and the Papal States, and it was safe from the aggressive attentions of the German emperors. And as the papal bureaucracy grew in size, it became more difficult to move. In time, Avignon began to feel like home; in fact it *was* home for all of the popes elected there, who were natives of the region, as were nearly all the cardinals whom they appointed. This helped to cement their loyalty to the French king.

The papacy never abandoned its claims to the overlordship of Rome and the Papal States, but making good on these claims took decades of planning and a great deal of money. The Avignon popes accordingly imposed new taxes and obligations on the dioceses of France, England, Germany, and Spain. Judicial cases from ecclesiastical courts also brought large revenues into the papal coffers. Most controversially, the Avignon popes claimed the right to appoint bishops and priests to vacant offices, bypassing the electoral rights of individual dioceses and collecting huge fees from successful appointees.

By these and other measures, the Avignon popes strengthened their administrative control over the Church but weakened their moral authority. Stories of the court's unseemly luxury circulated widely, especially during the

THE PAPAL PALACE AT AVIGNON. This great palace was begun in 1339, and symbolizes the apparent permanence of the papal residence in Avignon.

reign of the notoriously corrupt Clement VI (r. 1342–52), whose rule coincided with the Black Death. Clement openly sold spiritual benefits for money, boasted that he would appoint a jackass to a bishopric if he thought it would turn a profit, and defended his sexual transgressions by insisting that they were therapeutic. After his death, in the decades that were transforming European society in so many other ways, calls for the papacy's return to Rome grew more insistent. The most successful of these was the letter-writing campaign of the nun and mystic Catherine of Siena (1347–1380), whose teasing but pious missives to Gregory XI (r. 1370–78) ultimately persuaded him to make the move.

The Great Schism and the Conciliar Movement

The papacy's restoration was short-lived. A year after Gregory's return to Rome, he died. His cardinals—many of them Frenchmen—struggled to interpret the wishes of the volatile Romans, whose habit of expressing themselves through violence was unsettling to outsiders. Later, the cardinals would claim to have capitulated to the Roman mob when they elected an Italian candidate, Urban VI. When Urban fell out with them soon afterward, the cardinals fled the city and, from a safe distance, declared his selection invalid because it had been made under duress. They then elected a new pope, a Frenchman who took the name Clement VII. Urban retaliated by naming a new, entirely Italian, College of Cardinals and by refusing Clement access to the city. The French pope and his cardinals withdrew ignominiously to Avignon, while the Italian pope remained in Rome. The resulting rift is known as the Great Western Schism. For between 1378 and 1417, the Latin Church was divided between two (and, ultimately, three) competing papacies, each claiming to be legitimate and each denouncing the heresy of the others.

Not surprisingly, Europe's religious allegiances fractured along the political lines drawn by the ongoing Hundred Years' War: France and her allies Scotland, Castile, Aragon, and Naples recognized the pope in Avignon; while England, Germany, northern Italy, Scandinavia, Bohemia, Poland, and Hungary recognized the Roman pope. Nor was there any obvious way to end this embarrassing state of affairs. The two rival Colleges of Cardinals continued to elect successors every time a pope died, perpetuating the problem. Finally, in 1409, some cardinals from both camps met at Pisa, where they ceremoniously declared the deposition of both popes and named a new one from among their number. But neither of the popes reigning in Rome and Avignon accepted that decision, so there were now three rival popes excommunicating each other, instead of only two.

This debacle was ultimately addressed between 1417 and 1420 at the Council of Constance, the largest and longest ecclesiastical gathering since the Council of Nicea, over a thousand years before (Chapter 6). Its chief mission was to remove all rival claimants for papal office before agreeing on the election of a new pope: an Italian who took the name Martin V. But many of the council's delegates had even more far-reaching plans for the reform of the Church, ambitions that stemmed from the legal doctrine that gave the council power to depose and elect popes in the first place. This doctrine, known as conciliarism, holds that supreme authority within the Church rests not with the pope, but with a representative general council—and not just the council convened at Constance, but any future council. The delegates at Constance thus decreed that general councils should meet

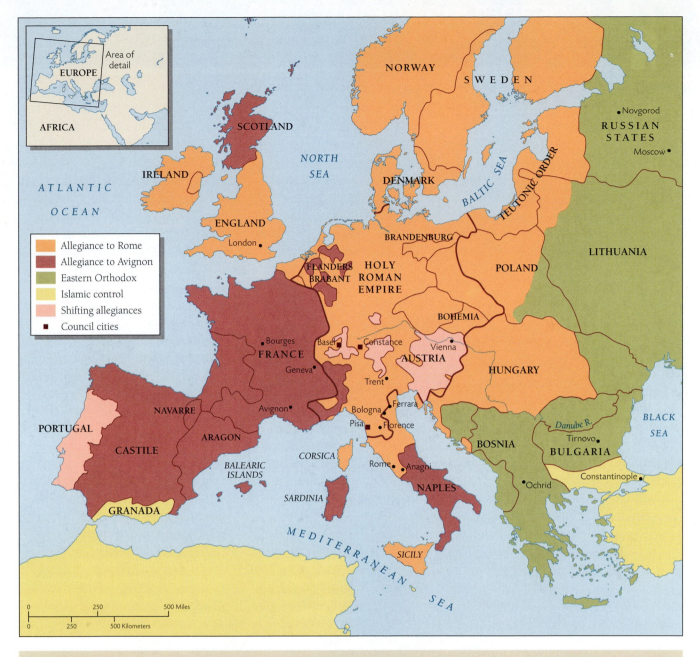

THE GREAT SCHISM, 1378–1417. During the Great Schism, the various territories of Europe were divided in their allegiances. ■ *According to the map key, who were they choosing between?* ■ *What common interests would have united the supporters of the Avignon pope, or the Roman pope?* ■ *Why would areas like Portugal and Austria waver in their support?*

regularly to oversee the governance of the Church and to act as a check on the unbridled use of papal power.

Had conciliarism triumphed, the Reformation of the following century might not have occurred. But, predictably, Martin V and his successors did everything they could to undermine this doctrine, precisely because it limited their power. So when the next general council met at Siena in 1423, Pope Martin duly sent representatives—who then turned around and went back to Rome. (The Council of Constance had specified that councils must meet frequently, but had not specified how long those meetings should last.) The following year, the delegates to a general council at Basel took steps to ensure that the pope could not dismiss it, after which a lengthy struggle for power ensued between the advocates of papal monarchy and the conciliarists. Twenty-five years later, in 1449, the Council of Basel dissolved itself, bringing to an end a radical experiment in conciliar government—and dashing the hopes of those who thought

Competing Viewpoints

Council or Pope?

The Great Schism spurred a fundamental and far-reaching debate about the nature of authority within the Church. Arguments for papal supremacy rested on traditional claims that the popes were the successors of Saint Peter, to whom Jesus Christ had delegated his own authority. Arguments for the supremacy of a general council had been advanced by many intellectuals throughout the fourteenth century, but it was only in the circumstances of the schism that these arguments found a wide audience. The following documents trace the history of the controversy, from the declaration of conciliar supremacy at the Council of Constance (Haec Sancta), to the council's efforts to guarantee regular meetings of general councils thereafter (Frequens), to the papal condemnation of appeals to the authority of general councils issued in 1460 (Execrabilis).

Haec Sancta Synodus (1415)

This holy synod of Constance . . . declares that being lawfully assembled in the Holy Spirit, constituting a general council and representing the Catholic Church Militant, it has its power directly from Christ, and that all persons of whatever rank or dignity, even a Pope, are bound to obey it in matters relating to faith and the end of the Schism and the general reformation of the church of God in head and members.

Further, it declares that any person of whatever position, rank, or dignity, even a Pope, who contumaciously refuses to obey the mandates, statutes, ordinances, or regulations enacted or to be enacted by this holy synod, or by any other general council lawfully assembled, relating to the matters aforesaid or to other matters involved with them, shall, unless he repents, be . . . duly punished. . . .

Source: R. L. Loomis, ed. and trans., *The Council of Constance* (New York: 1961), p. 229

Frequens (1417)

The frequent holding of general councils is the best method of cultivating the field of the Lord, for they root out the briars, thorns, and thistles of heresies, errors, and schisms, correct abuses, make crooked things straight, and prepare the Lord's vineyard for fruitfulness and rich fertility. Neglect of general councils sows the seeds of these evils and encourages their growth. This truth is borne in upon us as we recall times past and survey the present.

Therefore by perpetual edict we . . . ordain that henceforth general councils shall be held as follows: the first within the five years immediately following the end of the present council, the second within seven years from the end of the council next after this, and subsequently every ten years forever. . . . Thus there will always be a certain continuity. Either

---

it would lead to an internal reformation thorough enough to keep the Roman Church intact.

The Growth of National Churches

The papacy's victory over the conciliarists was a costly one in the short term, as well as in the long term. To win the support of Europe's kings and princes, various popes negotiated a series of treaties, known as "concordats," which granted these rulers extensive authority over churches within their domains. The popes thus secured their own theoretical supremacy by surrendering their real power. For under the terms of these concordats, kings now received many of the revenues that had previously gone to the papacy. They also acquired new powers to appoint candidates to church offices. It was a reversal of the hard-won reforms of the eleventh and twelfth centuries.

With both papal authority and spiritual prestige in decline, kings and princes became the primary figures to whom both clergy and laity looked for religious and moral guidance. Many secular rulers responded to such expec-

a council will be in session or one will be expected at the end of a fixed period. . . .

Source: R. L. Loomis, ed. and trans., *The Council of Constance* (New York: 1961), pp. 246–47

Execrabilis (1460)

An execrable abuse, unheard of in earlier times, has sprung up in our period. Some men, imbued with a spirit of rebellion and moved not by a desire for sound decisions but rather by a desire to escape the punishment for sin, suppose that they can appeal from the Pope, Vicar of Jesus Christ—from the Pope, to whom in the person of blessed Peter it was said, "Feed my sheep" and "whatever you bind on earth will be bound in heaven"—from this Pope to a future council. How harmful this is to the Christian republic, as well as how contrary to canon law, anyone who is not ignorant of the law can understand. For . . . who would not consider it ridiculous to appeal to something which does not now exist anywhere nor does anyone know when it will exist? The poor are heavily oppressed by the powerful, offenses remain unpunished, rebellion against the Holy See is encouraged, license for sin is granted, and all ecclesiastical discipline and hierarchical ranking of the Church are turned upside down.

Wishing therefore to expel this deadly poison from the Church of Christ, and concerned with the salvation of the sheep committed to us . . . with the counsel and assent of our venerable brothers, the Cardinals of the Holy Roman Church, together with the counsel and assent of all those prelates who have been trained in canon and civil law who follow our Court, and with our own certain knowledge, we condemn appeals of this kind, reject them as erroneous and abominable, and declare them to be completely null and void. And we lay down that from now on, no one should dare . . . to make such an appeal from our decisions, be they legal or theological, or from any commands at all from us or our successors. . . .

Source: Reprinted by permission of the publisher from *Defensorum Obedientiae Apostolicae Et Alia Documenta* by Gabriel Biel, edited and translated by Heiko A. Oberman, Daniel E. Zerfoss, and William J. Courtenay, pp. 224–27, Cambridge, Mass.: The Belknap Press of Harvard University Press, Copyright © 1968 by the President and Fellows of Harvard College.

Questions for Analysis

1. On what grounds does *Haec Sancta* establish the authority of a council? Why would this be considered a threat to papal power?

2. Why was it considered necessary for councils to meet regularly (*Frequens*)? What might have been the logical consequences of such regular meetings?

3. On what grounds does *Execrabilis* condemn the appeals to future councils that have no specified meeting date? Why would it not have condemned the conciliar movement altogether?

---

tations aggressively, closing scandal-ridden monasteries, suppressing alleged heretics, regulating prostitution, and prohibiting the lower classes from dressing as if they were nobles. By these and other such measures, rulers could present themselves as champions of moral reform while also strengthening their political power. The result was an increasingly close link between national monarchies and national churches, a link that would become even stronger after the Reformation (see Chapter 13).

Having given away so many sources of revenue, the popes of the late fifteenth century became even more dependent on their own territories in central Italy. But to tighten their hold on the Papal States they had to rule like other Italian princes: leading armies, jockeying for alliances, and undermining their opponents by every possible means—including covert operations, murder, and assassination. Judged by the secular standards of the day, these efforts paid off: the Papal States became one of the better-governed and wealthier principalities in Italy. But such methods did nothing to increase the popes' reputation for piety, and disillusionment with the papacy as a force for the advancement of spirituality became even more widespread.

THE PURSUIT OF HOLINESS

Despite the travails of the institutional Church, religious devotion among the laity was more widespread and intense during the later Middle Ages than it had ever been. The fundamental theme of preachers in this era, that salvation lay open to any Christian who strove for it, bore fruit in the multiplying variety of paths that could lead to God. Some of these paths led believers in directions the Church declared heretical. But for the vast majority of Christians, extreme forms of dissent held no appeal. The local parish church, and especially the sacraments performed by the parish priest, became the center of religious life. To understand late medieval Christianity, we therefore need to start in the parish.

Sacrament and Ritual

Innocent III's insistence that all Christians should have direct access to sound religious instruction (Chapter 9) ensured that nearly all of Europe was covered by a network of local parish churches by the time of the Black Death. In these churches, parish priests administered the sacraments ("holy rites") that conveyed the grace of God to individual Christians and that marked significant moments in the lifecycle of every person. Late medieval piety revolved around these sacraments, of which there were seven: baptism, confirmation, confession (or penance), marriage, extreme unction, ordination, and communion. Baptism, a ceremony of initiation administered in the early centuries of Christianity to adults (Chapter 6), became in the course of the Middle Ages a sacrament administered to infants as soon as possible after birth. Confirmation of adolescents therefore "confirmed" the promises made on a child's behalf at baptism by parents and godparents. Periodic confession of sins to a priest guaranteed forgiveness by God, for if a sinner did not perform appropriate acts of penance to atone for sins, penance would have to be completed in Purgatory, the netherworld between Heaven and Hell. Marriage was a relatively new sacrament, increasingly emphasized in the later Middle Ages but very seldom practiced; for in order to be valid, marriage in this period required only that solemn promises be exchanged by a man and a woman, and in many cases the fact of cohabitation was taken to be proof of marriage. Extreme unction (or last rites) was administered to a dying person. It ensured the final absolution of all sins and so was essential to the assurance of salvation.

Like baptism, extreme unction could, in an emergency, be administered by any Christian believer. The other sacraments, however, could be administered only by a properly ordained priest—or, in the case of confirmation and ordination, by a bishop. Ordination was therefore the only sacrament reserved for the small percentage of Christians who became priests, and it conveyed to the priest his special authority to share God's grace through the sacraments: a power that could never be lost, even by a priest who led an immoral life.

This sacramental system was the foundation on which the practices of late medieval popular piety rested. Pilgrimages, for example, were a form of penance, and could lessen one's time in Purgatory. Crusading was a kind of extreme pilgrimage that promised the complete fulfillment of all

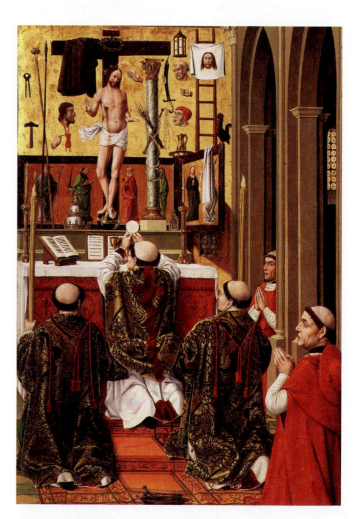

THE REAL PRESENCE OF CHRIST. This painting, executed in the mid-fifteenth century, refers to a popular legend underscoring the truth of transubstantiation. According to this legend, Pope Gregory the Great (c. 540–604) was celebrating Mass in his private chapel when he had a vision of the crucified Christ, whose body and blood were rendered visible when he consecrated the bread and wine on the altar. Here, Christ displays his wounds to the astonished onlookers. The instruments of Christ's passion—the people and implements that tortured and killed him—are also displayed.

penances the crusader might owe for all the sins of his (or her) life. Many other pious acts—saying the prayers of the rosary, for example, or giving alms to the poor—could also serve as penance for one's sins while constituting good works that would help the believer in his or her journey toward salvation.

But the sacrament that was most central to the religious lives of medieval Christians was the communion ceremony of the Mass (or the Eucharist). As we noted in Chapter 9, the ritual power of the Mass was greatly enhanced in the twelfth century, when the Church began promoting the doctrine of transubstantiation. Christians attending Mass understood that when the priest spoke the ritual words "This is my body" and "This is my blood," the substances of bread and wine held in the priest's hands were miraculously transformed into the body and blood of Jesus Christ. To consume one or both of these substances was to ingest holiness; and so powerful was this idea that many Christians only received the sacramental bread once a year, at Easter.

But to share in the miracle of the Eucharist one did not have to consume it: one had only to witness the elevation of the Host. So daily attendance at Mass merely to view the Host became a common form of devotion, as did the practice of displaying a consecrated wafer in a special reliquary called a monstrance ("show case"), which could be set up on a special altar or carried through the streets on feast days. Believers sometimes attributed astonishing properties to the eucharistic Host, feeding it to sick animals or rushing from church to church to see the consecrated bread as many times as possible in a day. Some of these practices were criticized by reformers as superstitious or even heretical. But by and large, these expressions of devotion were encouraged, and efforts to stop them were also met with staunch opposition from faithful laymen and laywomen.

Spirituality and the Social Order

The spiritual and social lives of medieval Christians were inextricably intertwined; indeed, any distinction between the two would have made little sense to the people of this era. The parish church stood literally at the center of their lives. Churchyards were communal meeting places, sometimes even the sites of markets, and church buildings were a refuge from attack and a gathering place for parish business. The church's holidays marked the passage of the year, and the church's bells marked the hours of the day. The church was holy, but it was also essential to daily life.

Yet some medieval Christians—many regarded today as saints—were not satisfied with these conventional practices and developed forms of piety that were distinctly controversial during their lifetimes. Indeed, the distinction between the superhuman powers of a saint and those of a witch could be difficult to discern. As Joan of Arc's predicament reveals, medieval women found it particularly challenging to find outlets for their piety that would not earn them the condemnation of the Church. Many women therefore internalized those practices or confined them to the domestic sphere—sometimes to the inconvenience of their families and communities. For example, the young Catherine of Siena refused to help with the housework or to support her working-class family, and instead took over one of the house's two rooms for her own private prayers, confining her parents and a dozen siblings to the remaining room. Julianna of Norwich (1342–1416) withdrew from the world into a small cell built next to her local church, where she spent the rest of her life in prayer and contemplation. Her younger contemporary, the housewife Margery Kempe (c. 1372–c. 1439), resented the fact that she had a husband, several children, and a household to support, and thus could not take such a step. In later life, she renounced her wifely duties and devoted her life to performing acts of histrionic piety which alienated most of those who came into contact with her. For example, she was so moved by the contemplation of Jesus' sufferings on the cross that she would cry hysterically for hours, disrupting the Mass. When on pilgrimage in Rome, she cried at the sight of babies that reminded her of the infant Jesus, or young men whom she thought resembled him.

The extraordinary piety of such individuals could be inspiring, but it could also threaten the Church's control over religious life and the links that bound individuals to their communities. It could, therefore, be dangerous. Some believers who sought to achieve a mystical union with God through rigorous prayer, penance, and personal sacrifice were ultimately condemned for heresy because they did not subordinate their mystical quests to the authority of the Church, and indeed declared that it was not necessary to obey God's Church on earth. Even less radical figures might find themselves treading on dangerous ground, especially if they published their experiences and ideas in the vernacular. The preacher Master Eckhart (c. 1260–1327), a German Dominican, taught that there was a "spark" deep within every human soul, and it was in this spark that God lived. Through prayer and self-renunciation, any person could therefore retreat into the inner recesses of her being and access divinity. This conveyed the message that a layperson might attain salvation through her own efforts, without the intervention of a priest. As a result, many of Eckhart's teachings were condemned as heretical. More safely orthodox was the practical mysticism preached by Thomas à Kempis, whose *Imitation of Christ* (c. 1427) taught readers how to appreciate aspects of the divine in their everyday lives. Originally written in Latin, the *Imitation* was quickly translated into many vernacular languages and is now more widely read than any other Christian book except the Bible.

Lollards and Hussites

For the most part, the threat of heretical movements was less dangerous to the Church than the corruption of the papacy. But in England and Bohemia, some popular movements did pose serious challenges. The key figure in both cases was John Wyclif (c. 1330–1384), an Oxford theologian and powerful critic of the Church. A survivor of the Black Death, Wyclif lived at a time when the authority and integrity of the papacy were at a particularly low ebb. Indeed, he concluded that the empty sacraments of a corrupt Church could not save anyone. He therefore urged the English king to confiscate ecclesiastical wealth and to replace corrupt priests and bishops with men who would live according to apostolic standards of poverty and piety. Some of Wyclif's followers, known to their detractors as Lollards (from a word meaning "mumblers" or "beggars"), went even further, dismissing the sacraments as fraudulent attempts to extort money from the faithful. Lollard preachers also advocated for direct access to the Scriptures, and promoted an English translation of the Bible attributed to Wyclif himself.

Wylclif's teachings played an important role in the Peasants' Revolt of 1381, and Lollardy gained numerous adherents in the decades after his death. The movement was even supported by a number of aristocratic families; certainly the idea of the dissolving the Church's wealth would have been attractive to many of those who stood to gain from it. But after a failed Lollard uprising in 1414, both the movement and its supporters went underground in England.

In Bohemia and eastern Europe, however, Wyclif's ideas lived on and struck even deeper roots. They were adopted by Jan Hus (c. 1373–1415), a charismatic teacher at the royal university in Prague. In contrast to the Lollards, who had scornfully dismissed the Mass and thereby lost much popular support, Hus emphasized the centrality of the Eucharist to Christian piety. Indeed, he demanded that the laity be allowed to receive not only the consecrated bread but also the consecrated wine, which was usually reserved solely for priests. This demand became a rallying cry for the Hussite movement. Influential nobles also supported Hus, partly in the hope that the reforms he demanded might restore revenues they had lost to the Church over the previous century. Accordingly, most of Bohemia was behind him when Hus traveled to the Council of Constance to publish his views and to urge the assembled delegates to undertake sweeping reforms.

But rather than giving him a hearing, the other delegates to the council convicted Hus of heresy and had him burned at the stake. Back home, Hus's supporters raised the banner of open revolt, and the aristocracy took advantage of the situation to seize Church property. Between 1420 and 1424, armed bands of fervent Hussites resoundingly

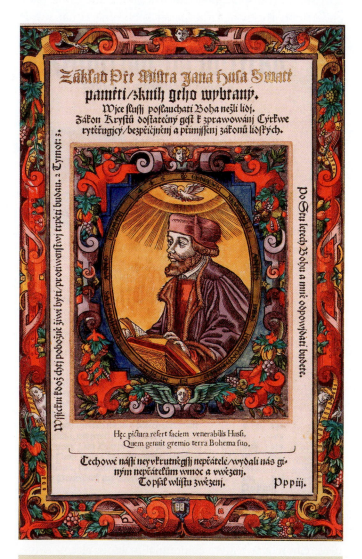

THE TEACHINGS OF JAN HUS. An eloquent religious reformer, Jan Hus was burned at the stake in 1415 after having been found guilty of heresy at the Council of Constance. This lavishly illustrated booklet of his teachings was published over a century later in his native Bohemia, and includes texts in the Czech vernacular and in Latin. ▪ *What does its later publication suggest about the uses to which Hus's image and theology were put during the Protestant Reformation?*

defeated several armies, as priests, artisans, and peasants rallied to pursue Hus's goals of religious reform and social justice. These victories increased popular fervor, but they also made these radical reformers increasingly volatile. In 1434, accordingly, a more conservative arm of the Hussite movement was able to negotiate a settlement with the Bohemian church. By the terms of this settlement, Bohemians could receive both the bread and wine of the Mass, which thus placed them beyond the pale of Latin orthodoxy and effectively separated the Bohemian national church from the Church of Rome.

Lollardy and Hussitism exhibit a number of striking similarities. Both began in the university and then spread to the countryside. Both called for the clergy to live in simplicity and poverty, and both attracted noble support, especially in their early days. Both movements were also strongly nationalistic, employing their own vernacular languages (English and Czech) and identifying themselves with the English or Czech people in opposition to a "foreign" Church. They also relied on vernacular preaching and social activism. In all these respects, they established patterns that would emerge again in the vastly larger currents of the Protestant Reformation (Chapter 13).

MEDIEVAL CREATIVITY AND INNOVATION

Many of the extraordinary achievements of the later Middle Ages have often been ascribed to the Renaissance, the name given to an intellectual and artistic movement that began concurrently in Italy, in the fourteenth and fifteenth centuries. We will discuss the causes and outcomes of this movement more fully in Chapter 12. For now, we focus on parallel developments closely tied to the trends discussed above.

Knowledge of the World and of God

In the thirteenth century, Thomas Aquinas had constructed a theological view of the world as rational, organized, and comprehensible to the inquiring human mind (Chapter 9). Confidence in this picture began to wane in the fourteenth century, even before the Black Death posed a new challenge to it. Philosophers such as the English Franciscan William of Ockham (d. 1349) denied that human reason could prove fundamental theological truths such as the existence of God. Instead, he argued that human knowledge

of God, and hence salvation, depends entirely on what God himself has chosen to reveal through scripture. Humans can investigate the natural world, but there is no necessary connection between the observable regularities of nature and the unknowable essence of divinity.

This philosophical position, known as nominalism, has its roots in the philosophy of Plato (Chapter 4) and has had an enormous impact on modern thought. The nominalists' distinction between the rational comprehensibility of the natural world and the incomprehensibility of God encourages investigation of the natural world without reference to supernatural explanations: one of the most important foundations of the modern scientific method (see Chapter 16). Nominalism also encourages empirical observation by positing that knowledge of the world should rest on sensory experience rather than abstraction. Late medieval philosophy is thus fundamental to modern science.

Capturing Reality in Writing

The entertainments of the later Middle Ages also exhibit an intense interest in the the world as it is. Such naturalism was not new, but later medieval authors were able to reach a far larger and more diverse audience than their predecessors. For increasingly, the most innovative and ambitious ideas were expressed in the vernacular languages of Europe. Behind this phenomenon lay three interrelated developments: the growing identification between vernacular language and nationalism, the increasing accessibility of lay education, and the emergence of a substantial reading public for vernacular literature. We can see these influences at work in three of the major authors of this period: Giovanni Boccaccio, Geoffrey Chaucer, and Christine de Pisan.

Boccaccio (*bohk-KAHT-chee-oh*, 1313–1375) is best known for the *Decameron*, a collection of prose tales about sex, adventure, and trickery which he represents as being told over a period of ten days by a sophisticated party of ten young women and men temporarily residing in a country villa outside Florence to escape the Black Death. Boccaccio borrowed the outlines of many of these tales from earlier sources, especially the fabliaux discussed in Chapter 9, but he couched them in a freely colloquial style, in an attempt to capture the relationships and foibles of real human beings. His men and women are flesh-and-blood creatures with minds and bodies, who interact comfortably and naturally. Indeed, Boccaccio's treatment of sexual relations is often graphic.

Similar in many ways to Boccaccio, whose influence on him was profound, is the English poet Geoffrey Chaucer (c. 1340–1400). Chaucer was among the first generation of

English authors whose compositions can be understood by modern readers with relatively little effort. For by the fourteenth century, the Anglo-Saxon language of England's pre-Conquest inhabitants had mixed with the French spoken by their Norman conquerors, to create the language which is the ancestor of our own. Chaucer's masterpiece is the *Canterbury Tales*. Like the *Decameron*, this is a collection of stories held together by a framing narrative: in this case, the stories are told by an array of people traveling together on a pilgrimage from London to the shrine of Saint Thomas Becket at Canterbury. But there are also significant differences between the *Decameron* and the *Canterbury Tales*. Chaucer's stories are in verse, for the most part, and they are recounted by people of all different classes—from a high-minded knight to a poor university student to a lusty widow. Each character tells a story that is particularly illustrative of his or her own occupation and outlook on the world, forming a kaleidoscopic human comedy.

The later Middle Ages also saw the emergence of professional authors who made their living with their pens. Significantly, one of the first was a woman, Christine de Pisan (c. 1365–c. 1434). Although born in northern Italy, Christine spent her adult life in France, where her husband was a member of the king's household. When he died, the widowed Christine wrote to support herself and her children. She mastered a wide variety of literary genres, including treatises on chivalry and warfare that she dedicated to her patron, Charles VI of France. She also wrote for a larger and more popular audience. Her imaginative *Book of the City of Ladies* is an extended defense of the character, capacities, and history of women, designed to refute their male detractors. Christine also took part in a vigorous pamphlet campaign that refuted misogynistic claims made by male authors like Boccaccio. This debate was ongoing for several hundred years, and became so famous that it was given a name: the *querelle des femmes*, "the debate over women." Remarkably, Christine also wrote a song in praise of Joan of Arc. Sadly, she probably lived long enough to learn that this other extraordinary woman had been put to death for behaving in a way that was considered unwomanly.

Visualizing Reality

Just as naturalism was a dominant trait of late medieval literature, so it was of later medieval art. Whereas earlier medieval art had emphasized abstract design, the sculptors of the thirteenth century were already paying close attention to the way plants, animals, and human beings really looked. Carvings of leaves and flowers were now being made from direct observation and are clearly recognizable to modern botanists as distinct species. Statues of humans also became more realistic in their portrayals of facial expressions and bodily proportions. According to a story in circulation around 1290, a sculptor working on a likeness of the German emperor allegedly made a hurried return trip to study his subject's face a second time, because he'd heard that a new wrinkle had appeared on the emperor's brow.

In the fourteenth and fifteenth centuries, the trend toward naturalism in sculpture was extended to manuscript illumination and painting. The latter was, to a large extent, a new art. As we saw in Chapter 1, walls paintings are one of the oldest forms of artistic expression in human history, and throughout antiquity and the Middle Ages artists had decorated the walls of public and private buildings with frescoes (paintings executed on "fresh"—wet—plaster). But in addition to frescoes, Italian artists in the thirteenth century began to

CHRISTINE DE PISAN. One of the most prolific authors of the fifteenth century, Christine used her influence to uphold the dignity of women and to celebrate their history and achievements. Here she is seen describing the prowess of an Amazon warrior who could defeat men effortlessly in armed combat.

Analyzing Primary Sources

Why a Woman Can Write about Warfare

Christine de Pisan (c. 1365–c. 1434) was one of the West's first professional writers, best known today for her Book of the City of Ladies *and* The Treasure of the City of Ladies, *works which aimed to provide women with an honorable and rich history, and to combat generations of institutionalized misogyny. But in her own time, she was probably best known for the work excerpted here,* The Book of the Deeds of Arms and of Chivalry, *a manual of military strategy and conduct written at the height of the Hundred Years' War, in 1410.*

s boldness is essential for great undertakings, and without it nothing should be risked, I think it is proper in this present work to set forth my unworthiness to treat such exalted matter. I should not have dared even to think about it, but although boldness is blameworthy when it is foolhardy, I should state that I have not been inspired by arrogance or foolish presumption, but rather by true affection and a genuine desire for the welfare of noble men engaging in the profession of arms. I am encouraged, in the light of my other writings, to undertake to speak in this book of the most honorable office of arms and chivalry. . . . So to this end I have gathered together facts and subject matter from various books to produce this present volume. But inasmuch as it is fitting for this matter to be discussed factually, diligently, and sensibly . . . and also in consideration of the fact that military and lay experts in the aforesaid art of chivalry are not usually clerks or writers who are expert in language, I intend to treat the matter in the plainest possible language. . . .

As this is unusual for women, who generally are occupied in weaving, spinning, and household duties, I humbly invoke . . . the wise lady Minerva [Athena], born in the land of Greece, whom the ancients esteemed highly for her great wisdom. Likewise the poet Boccaccio praises her in his *Book of Famous Women*, as do other writers praise her art and manner of making trappings of iron and steel, so let it not be held against me if I, as a woman, take it upon myself to treat of military matters. . . .

O Minerva! goddess of arms and of chivalry, who, by understanding beyond that of other women, did find and initiate among the other noble arts and sciences the custom of forging iron and steel armaments and harness both proper and suitable for covering and protecting men's bodies against arrows slung in battle—helmets, shields, and protective covering having come first from you—you instituted and gave directions for drawing up a battle order, how to begin an assault and to engage in proper combat. . . . In the aforementioned country of Greece, you provided the usage of this office, and insofar as it may please you to be favorably disposed, and I in no way appear to be against the nation from which you came, the country beyond the Alps that is now called Apulia and Calabria in Italy, where you were born, let me say that like you I am an Italian woman.

Source: From *The Book of the Deeds of Arms and of Chivalry*, trans. Sumner Willard and ed. Charity Cannon Willard (University Park, PA: 1999), pp. 11–13.

Questions for Analysis

1. Christine very cleverly deflects potential criticism for her "boldness" in writing about warfare. What tactics does she use?

2. The Greco-Roman goddess Athena (Minerva) was the goddess of wisdom, weaving, and warfare. Why does Christine invoke her aid? What parallels does she draw between her own attributes and those of Minerva?

---

adapt the techniques used by icon painters in Byzantium, painting free-standing pictures on pieces of wood or canvas using tempera (pigments mixed with water and natural gums). Around 1400, painting in oils was introduced in the Low Countries, and these techniques soon spread southward to Italy and beyond.

This diversification of artistic media created new aesthetic and commercial opportunities. Artists were now able to paint and sell portable altarpieces, devotional images, and portraits. And so long as they could afford the necessary materials, they did not have to wait for a specific commission from a patron. This meant that they had more freedom to choose their subject matter and to put an individual stamp on their work—one of the reasons why we know the names of so many late-medieval artists. One of these, Giotto di Bondone of Florence (c. 1267–1337), painted both walls and portable wooden panels. Giotto (*gee-AHT-toh*) was preeminently an imitator of nature. Not only do his human beings and animals look lifelike, they seem to do natural things. When Christ enters Jerusalem on Palm Sunday, boys climb trees to get a better view; when Saint Francis is laid out in death, someone checks to see whether he has really received the marks of Christ's wounds, the *stigmata*; and when the Virgin's parents, Joachim and Anna, meet after a long separation, they embrace and kiss one another tenderly. Although many of the artists who came after Giotto moved away from naturalism, this style became the norm by 1400. It is for this reason that he is often regarded as the first painter of the Renaissance, a movement that is really an outgrowth of the later Middle Ages (see Chapter 12).

In northern Europe, manuscript illumination remained the dominant artistic medium, and during this period many breathtaking books were created for wealthy

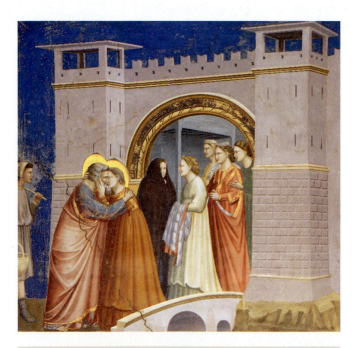

THE MEETING OF JOACHIM AND ANNA BY GIOTTO. According to legend, Anna and Joachim were an aged and infertile couple who were able to conceive their only child, Mary, through divine intervention. Since Mary was supposed to have been conceived without the taint of sin, theologians taught that she had been miraculously engendered without sexual contact. Hence, this painting may portray the moment of her conception—but it also portrays the affection of husband and wife. ▪ *What values does it convey to the viewer?*

patrons like the duke of Berry (noted above). But oil painting also caught on, especially in Flanders, where artists found a market for their works among the nobility and wealthy merchants. Practitioners like Rogier van der Weyden (c. 1400–1464) excelled at communicating both deep piety and the minute details of everyday experience (see **Interpreting Visual Evidence**). Just as contemporary spirituality saw divinity in material objects, so a Flemish painter could portray the Virgin and Child against a background vista of contemporary life, with people going about their business or a man urinating against a wall. This was not blasphemous; quite the contrary. It conveyed the message that the events of the Bible are constantly present, here and now: Christ is contemporary, not some distant figure whose life and experiences are irrelevant to us.

The same immediacy is also evident in medieval drama. Plays were often devotional exercises that involved the efforts of an entire community. In the English city of York, for example, an annual series of pageants reenacted the entire history of human salvation from the Creation to the Last Judgment in a single summer day, beginning at dawn and ending late at night. Each pageant was produced by a particular craft guild and showcased that guild's special talents: "The Last Supper" was performed by the bakers, whose bread was a key element in their reenactment of the first Eucharist, while "The Crucifixion" was performed by the nail-makers, whose wares were thereby put on prominent display. In Italy, confraternities competed with one another to honor the saints with songs and processions. In Spain and Catalonia, there were elaborate dramas celebrating the life and miracles of the Virgin, one of which is still performed every year in the Basque town of Elche: it is the oldest European play in continuous production. Elsewhere on the Continent there were civic spectacles performed over a period of several days. But not all plays were pious. Some honored visiting kings and princes. Others celebrated the flouting of social conventions, featuring cross-dressing and the reversal of hierarchies.

Technological Advances

In the later Middle Ages, as in other places and times, warfare was the engine driving the development of many new technologies. Although explosive powder had been invented in China, it was first put to devastating use in the guns of the Hundred Years' War. The earliest cannons were as dangerous to those who fired them as to those who were targeted, but by the middle of the fifteenth century they were reliable enough to revolutionize the nature of warfare. In 1453, heavy artillery played a leading role in

Interpreting Visual Evidence

Realizing Devotion

These two paintings by the Flemish artist Rogier van der Weyden (*FAN-der-VIE-den*, c. 1400–1464) capture some of the most compelling characteristics of late medieval art, particularly the trend toward realistic representations of holy figures and sacred stories. On the left (image A), the artist depicts himself as the evangelist Luke, regarded in Christian tradition as a painter of portraits; he sketches the Virgin nursing the infant Jesus in a town house overlooking a Flemish city. On the right (image B), van der Weyden imagines the entombment of the dead Christ by his followers, including the Virgin (left), Mary Magdalene (kneeling), and the disciple John (right). Here, he makes use of a motif that became increasingly prominent in the later Middle Ages: Christ as the Man of Sorrows, displaying his wounds and inviting the viewer to share in his suffering. In both paintings, van der Weyden emphasizes the humanity of his subjects rather than their iconic status (see Chapter 7), and he places them in the urban and rural landscapes of his own world.

Questions for Analysis

1. How are these paintings different from the sacred images of the earlier Middle Ages (see, for example, pages 213 and 290)? What messages does the artist convey by setting these events in his own immediate present?

2. In what ways do these paintings reflect broad changes in popular piety and medieval devotional practices? Why, for example, would the artist display the dead and wounded body of Christ—rather than depicting him as resurrected and triumphant, or as an all-seeing creator and judge?

3. In general, how would you use these images as evidence of the worldview of the fifteenth century? What do they tell us about people's attitudes, emotions, and values?

A. Saint Luke drawing the portrait of the Virgin.

B. The Deposition.

the outcomes of two crucial conflicts: the Ottoman Turks breached the defenses of Constantinople (see Chapter 11) and the French captured the city of Bordeaux, thereby ending the Hundred Years' War. Thereafter, cannons made it more difficult for rebellious aristocrats to hole up in their stone castles, and so consequently aided in the consolidation of national monarchies. Cannons placed aboard ships made Europe's developing navies more effective. A handheld firearm, the pistol, was also invented in the fourteenth century, and around 1500 the musket ended forever the military dominance of heavily armored cavalry, giving the advantage to foot soldiers.

Other late medieval technologies were more life enhancing. Eyeglasses, first invented in the 1280s, were perfected in the fourteenth century, extending the careers of those who made a living by reading and writing. The use of the magnetic compass helped ships sail farther away from land. Subsequently, numerous improvements in shipbuilding, mapmaking, and navigational devices enabled Europeans to venture out into the Atlantic. We will discuss the implications of these developments in Chapter 11.

Among the many implements of modern daily life invented in this era, the most familiar are clocks and printed books. Mechanical clocks came into use shortly before 1300 and proliferated immediately thereafter. They were too large and expensive for private purchase, but towns vied with one another to install them in prominent public buildings, thus advertising municipal wealth and good governance. Mechanical timekeeping had two profound effects. One was the further stimulation of interest in complex machinery of all sorts, an interest already awakened by the widespread use of mills in the eleventh and twelfth centuries (Chapter 8). More significant was the way that clocks regulated daily life. Until the advent of clocks, time was flexible. Days had been theoretically divided into hours and hours into minutes and minutes into seconds since the time of the Sumerians (Chapter 1), but there had never been a way of mapping these temporal measurements onto an actual day. Clocks relentlessly divided time into exact units and thus gave rise to new expectations about labor and productivity. People were expected to start and end work "on time," and many came to believe that "time is money." This emphasis on timekeeping brought new efficiencies but also created new tensions and obsessions.

The development of printing was even more momentous. A major stimulus for this was the more widespread availability of paper. Parchment, Europe's chief writing material since the seventh century, was extremely expensive

A FIFTEENTH-CENTURY SIEGE WITH CANNON. Cannons were an essential element in siege warfare during the Hundred Years' War and thereafter.

Area of detail

EUROPE

AFRICA

NORWAY

SWEDEN

Stockholm
1483

BALTIC SEA

SCOTLAND

NORTH SEA

Edinburgh
1507

Copenhagen
1490

DENMARK

Odense
1482

POLAND

Dublin
1551

ENGLAND

Utrecht
1470

London
1492

Westminster
1476

Brussels
1475

Leipzig
1481

ATLANTIC OCEAN

Cologne
1465

HOLY ROMAN EMPIRE

Paris
1470

Eltville
1467

Mainz
1450

Bamberg
1460

Pilsen
1468

Nuremberg
1470

Strasbourg
1458

Augsburg
1468

Danube R.

Vienna
1482

Basel
1468

Beromünster
1470

AUSTRIA

HUNGARY

FRANCE

SWITZERLAND

Lyons
1473

Milan
1471

Venice
1469

VENETIAN EMPIRE

ADRIATIC SEA

Florence
1482

PAPAL STATES

PORTUGAL

CORSICA

Rome
1467

Naples
1471

Lisbon
1489

SPAIN

Valencia
1474

SARDINIA

KINGDOM OF TWO SICILIES

Seville
1478

BALEARIC ISLANDS

MEDITERRANEAN SEA

0   100   200   300 Miles

0   100   200   300 Kilometers

THE SPREAD OF PRINTING

■ Up until 1470   ■ 1471–1500

THE SPREAD OF PRINTING. This map shows how quickly the technology of printing spread throughout Europe between 1470 and 1500.
■ *In what regions were printing presses most heavily concentrated?* ■ *What factors would have led to their proliferation in the Low Countries, northern Italy, and Germany—as compared to France, Spain, and England?* ■ *Why would so many have been located along waterways?*

DEVIL WITH EYEGLASSES. Spectacles were most commonly worn by those who made a living by reading and writing, notably bureaucrats and lawyers. In this conceptualization of Hell, the devil charged with keeping track of human sin wears eyeglasses.
■ *What might this image reveal about popular attitudes toward record-keeping and the growing legal and administrative bureaucracies of the later Middle Ages?*

to manufacture and even required special training on the part of scribes—one reason why writing remained a specialized skill for much of the Middle Ages, while the ability to read was common. Paper, made from rags turned into pulp by mills, was both cheaper and far easier to use. Accordingly, reading and writing also became cheaper and easier. Increased literacy led to a growing demand for books, which in turn led to experimentation with different methods of book production. A breakthrough came around 1450, when it was discovered that movable type (cast-iron letter forms and punctuation marks) could be slotted into frames to form lines of words, and whole pages could thus be reproduced by coating those frames with ink and pressing them onto paper or parchment, after which the type could be reused. The most famous early result of this technique is the Bible completed in the workshop of Johann Gutenberg in Mainz, around 1454.

By saving labor and time, the printing press made the cost of printed books about one fifth as expensive as hand-copied books and made book culture a more basic part of daily life. Printing thereby facilitated the more rapid exchange of information and ideas, and also made it more difficult for those in power to suppress these ideas effectively. Martin Luther could create an immediate and far-flung network of support by employing this new communication technology (Chapter 13); had printing not been available, he might have died ignominiously, as Hus had done a century before. The spread of books also standardized national languages. Regional dialects were often so diverse that

After You Read This Chapter

Ⓢ Visit StudySpace for quizzes, additional review materials, and multi-media documents. **wwnorton.com/studyspace**

REVIEWING THE OBJECTIVES

■ The Black Death had short-term and long-term effects on the economy and societies of Europe. What were some of the most important changes?

■ The melding of strong kingship with the promotion of national identity was a new development in the later Middle Ages. What circumstances made this possible? Why is this development significant?

■ Several key factors enabled the growth of a Russian state centered on Muscovy. What were they?

■ The conciliar movement sought to limit the power of the papacy. How? Why was this movement unsuccessful?

■ In what ways do the spiritual, cultural, and technological innovations of the later Middle Ages reflect the political, social, and economic changes brought about by the Black Death?

people living within the same state could not understand each other. Now, each European country began to develop its own linguistic standards, which could be disseminated more uniformly through the imposition of these standards. For example, the "king's English," the dialect of London, could be promulgated throughout the realm, allowing the government to operate more efficiently.

CONCLUSION

The later Middle Ages constitute a period of tremendous creativity and revolutionary change. The effects of the Black Death were catastrophic, but the resulting labor shortages encouraged experimentation and opened up new opportunities. Europe's economy diversified and expanded. Increasing wealth and access to education produced new inventions, ideas, and forms of art. Between 1300 and 1500, hundreds and perhaps thousands of new schools were established, and scores of new universities emerged. Medieval intellectuals came to see the natural world as operating according to its own laws, which were empirically verifiable and which did not necessarily reflect the mind of God: an essential step toward the emergence of a scientific worldview. Women were still excluded from formal schooling, but nevertheless became active—and perhaps dominant—participants in literate culture and in the religious life of their communities. Average men and women also became more active in cultivating their own individual spiritualities, at a time when the institutional Church provided little inspiring leadership. Meanwhile, incessant warfare enabled more powerful governments to harvest a larger percentage of their subjects' wealth through taxation, which they proceeded to invest in ships, guns, and the standing armies made possible by new technologies and more effective administration.

In short, the generations who survived the calamaties of famine, plague, and warfare seized the opportunities their new world presented to them. By 1500, most Europeans lived more secure lives than their ancestors had, and they stood on the verge of an extraordinary period of expansion and conquest that enabled them to dominate the globe.

PEOPLE, IDEAS, AND EVENTS IN CONTEXT

- Compare and contrast the **BLACK DEATH'S** effects on rural and urban areas.
- In what ways do the rebellions of the later fourteenth and fifteenth centuries reflect the changes brought about by the plague? How did the nobility of Europe respond to this changing world?
- What were the main causes and consequences of the **HUNDRED YEARS' WAR?** How did **FERDINAND AND ISABELLA** begin to construct a national monarchy in Spain?
- On what grounds did **MUSCOVY** claim to be "the third Rome"? What is the significance of **IVAN THE GREAT'S** use of the title *TSAR?*
- How did the **COUNCIL OF CONSTANCE** respond to the crisis of the **GREAT SCHISM?**
- How did the teachings of **JOHN WYCLIF** and **JAN HUS** critique religious trends?
- What were the major artistic and technological innovations of the later Middle Ages?

CONSEQUENCES

- In 2000, a group of historians was asked to identify the most significant historical figure of the past millennium; but rather than choosing a person (e.g., Martin Luther, Napoleon, Adolf Hitler) they chose the microbe *Yersinia pestis*. Do you agree with this assessment? Why or why not?
- In your view, which was more crucial to the formation of the modern state: the political and legal developments we surveyed in Chapter 9 or the emergence of national identities in the later Middle Ages? Why?
- Was the conciliar movement doomed to failure, given what we have learned about the history of the Roman Church? How far back does one need to go, in order to trace the development of disputes over ecclesiastical governance?

Before You Read This Chapter

Commerce, Conquest, and Colonization, 1300–1600

CORE OBJECTIVES

- **DESCRIBE** the effects of the Mongol conquests.

- **EXPLAIN** the consequences of the Ottoman Empire's dependence on slave labor.

- **IDENTIFY** the factors that drove exploration and colonialism in the fourteenth and fifteenth centuries.

- **DEFINE** the essential difference between modern slavery and that of all previous civilizations.

- **UNDERSTAND** the far-reaching impact of the New World conquests.

When Christopher Columbus set sail from Genoa in 1492, he carried with him two influential travel narratives. One was largely factual and one was fantastic, but it is doubtful that Columbus could tell the difference between them. The first was the *Book of Marvels*, attributed to Jehan de Mandeville, an English adventurer (writing in French) who claimed to have traveled beyond the boundaries of the known world. The second was Marco Polo's account of his journeys in the Far East and of his sojourn at the court of the Great Khan in China. Both of these books shaped the Genoese mariner's expectations of what he would find when he embarked on his travels, and they also shaped his descriptions of the places and peoples he encountered. As a result, it is difficult to separate fiction from fact when we read his accounts—or those of many other European explorers. What we can now for certain is that the civilizations of the New World and those of the Old had a profound impact on one another.

In 1352, when Mandeville's *Book of Marvels* began to circulate, Europe had become a politically consolidated and culturally unified region. It had also reached its geographical limits;

347

there was, it seemed, no more room for expansion. With the completed conquest of Muslim territory in 1492, Ferdinand and Isabella eradicated an Islamic presence in western Europe that dated to the seventh century. Yet there was no longer any viable prospect of Latin Christendom's dominion in the Holy Land, North Africa, or any of the other Muslim territories that had been targeted by crusaders. The growing power of the Ottoman Turks was forging a new empire that would soon come to encompass all these regions, as well as the lands of the eastern Roman Empire in Byzantium. Meanwhile, German princes' drive to conquer territories in eastern Europe was slowed by the rise of Poland-Lithuania and the emergence of Muscovy as a contender for power on Europe's northeastern frontier; and their efforts would be halted altogether by the arrival of the Mongols and the eventual absorption of eastern Europe into the Ottoman Empire. Europe was also reaching its ecological limits. Indeed, the pressure on its natural resources was eased only by the dramatic population losses that had resulted from the combined effects of famine, plague, and war in the fourteenth and fifteenth centuries.

But despite these checks—or because of them—Europeans did not turn inward. As land-based conquests became less viable, new maritime empires coalesced around chains of colonies that extended from the Black Sea to Canary Islands. Trade routes were opened through the Strait of Gibraltar, resulting in greater economic integration between the Mediterranean and Atlantic economies and increasing Europe's demand for Asian spices and African gold. By the late fifteenth century, Mediterranean mariners and colonists were reaching farther into the Atlantic and pushing down the west coast of Africa. In 1498, one such expedition would make its way to India.

This fifteenth-century expansion of the Mediterranean world into the Atlantic was the essential preliminary to Columbus's voyages, and to the eventual conquests of the Americas. Because these events seem so familiar, we can easily underestimate both their improbability and their significance for the Western civilizations we have been studying, and for the "new world" they encountered. For the indigenous peoples and empires of the Americas, the results were cataclysmic. Within a hundred years of Europeans' arrival, between 50 and 90 percent of the native population had perished from disease, massacre, and enslavement. Moreover, Europeans' capacity to further their imperial ambitions wherever ships could sail and guns could penetrate profoundly destabilized Europe and its neighbors, sharpening the divisions among competing kingdoms and empires. The effects of this process, which reached its apogee in the nineteenth century, are still being felt today.

MONGOLS, EUROPEANS, AND THE FAR EAST

Trade between the Mediterranean world and the Far East dates back to antiquity, but it was not until the late thirteenth century that Europeans began to establish direct trading connections with India, China, and the so-called Spice Islands of the Indonesian archipelago. For Europeans, these connections would prove profoundly important, as much for their impact on the European imagination as for their economic significance. For the peoples of Asia, however, the appearance of European traders on the fabled Silk Road between Central Asia and China was merely a curiosity. The really consequential event was the rise of the Mongol Empire that made such connections possible.

THE HEAD OF TIMUR THE LAME. This bust of the Mongol leader known in the West as Tamerlane is based on a forensic reconstruction of his exhumed skull.

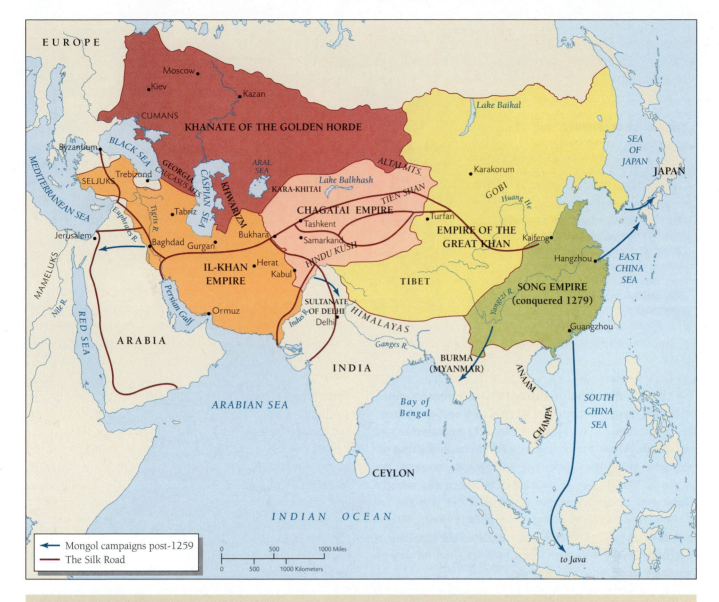

THE MONGOL SUCCESSOR STATES. Like Alexander's, Chingiz Khan's empire was swiftly assembled and encompassed vast portions of Europe and Asia. ▪ *How many separate Mongol empires were there after 1259, and how far did they stretch geographically?* ▪ *How might the Mongol occupation of the Muslim world have aided the expansion of European trade?* ▪ *At the same time, why would it have complicated the efforts of Crusader armies in the Holy Land?*

The Expansion of the Mongol Empire

The Mongols were one of many nomadic peoples inhabiting the steppes of Central Asia. Although closely connected with the Turkish populations with whom they frequently intermarried, the Mongols spoke their own distinctive language and had their own homeland, to the north of the Gobi Desert in present-day Mongolia. Sheep provided them with shelter (sheepskin tents), woolen clothing, milk, and meat. Like many nomadic peoples, the Mongols were highly accomplished horsemen and raiders. Indeed, it was in part to control their raiding ventures that the Chinese

had built the fortified Great Wall, many centuries before. Primarily, though, China defended itself by attempting to ensure that the Mongols remained internally divided, with their energies turned against each other.

In the late twelfth century, however, a Mongol chief named Temüjin began to unite the various tribes under his rule. He did so by incorporating the warriors of each defeated tribe into his own army, thus building up a large military force. In 1206 his supremacy was formally acknowledged by all the Mongols, and he took the title Chingiz (Genghis) Khan, or "universal ruler." He now directed his enormous army against his neighbors, taking advantage of the fact

THE BATTLE OF LEIGNITZ, 1241. This image from a fourteenth-century chronicle shows heavily armored knights from Poland and Germany confronting the swift-moving mounted archers of the Mongol cavalry. Mongol warriors often had the advantage over Europeans because their smaller, faster horses carried lighter loads, and because the warriors themselves could shoot down their opponents at long range. ▪ *Which army appears to be gaining the upper hand here?*

that China was at this time divided into three hostile states. In 1209, Chingiz Khan launched an attack on one of these, the Chin Empire of the north, and in 1211 managed to raid its interior. These initial attacks were probably looting expeditions rather than deliberate attempts at conquest, but by the 1230s a full-scale invasion of northern and western China was under way, culminating in 1234 wih the fall of these regions to the Mongols. In 1279, Chingiz Khan's grandson Qubilai (Kublai) Khan completed the conquest of southern China, thus reuniting China for the first time in centuries, and under Mongol rule.

At the same time, Chingiz Khan was also turning his forces westward, conquering much of Central Asia and incorporating the important commercial cities of Tashkent, Samarkand, and Bukhara into his empire. When he died in 1227, his son and successor, Ögedei (*EHRG-uh-day*), not only completed the conquest of the China, he laid plans for a massive invasion of the West. Between 1237 and 1240, the Mongol horde (so called from the Turkish word *ordu*, meaning "tent" or "encampment") conquered southern Russia and then launched a two-pronged assault that pushed them farther west. The smaller of the two Mongol armies swept through Poland toward eastern Germany; the larger army went southwest toward Hungary. In April of 1241, the smaller Mongol force met a hastily assembled army of Germans and Poles at the battle of Liegnitz, where the two sides fought to a bloody standstill. Two days later, the larger Mongol army annihilated the Hungarian army at the River Sajo.

It is possible that the Mongol armies could have moved even farther west after this important victory, but when the Great Khan Ögedei died in December of that same year, 1241, the leaderless Mongol forces withdrew from eastern Europe. It took five years for a new great khan to establish himself, only to die a few years later, leaving the Mongols without a leader for another three years. Although Mongol conquests continued in Persia, the Middle East, and China, attacks on Europe never resumed. By 1300, the period of Mongol expansion had come to an end. Yet the descendants of Chingiz Khan continued to rule this enormous empire—the largest land empire in the history of the world—for another half-century. Later, under the leadership of Timur the Lame (known as Tamerlane to Europeans) it looked briefly as if the Mongol Empire might be reunited. But Timur died in 1405 on his way to invade China; thereafter the various parts of the Mongol Empire fell into the hands of local rulers, including (in Asia Minor) the Ottoman Turks. Mongol influence continued, however, in the Mughal Empire of India, whose rulers were descended from the followers of Chingiz Khan.

The Mongols owed their success to the size, speed, and training of their mounted armies; to the intimidating savagery with which they treated those who resisted them; and to their ability to adapt the administrative traditions of their subjects to their own purposes. They were also highly tolerant of the religious beliefs of others—a distinct advantage in controlling an empire that comprised an array of Buddhist, Christian, and Muslim sects. And for the most part, Mongol governance was directed at securing the steady payment of tribute from the empire's subjects, which meant that local rulers could retain much of their power. Except in China, where the Mongol Yuan Dynasty maintained a complex administrative bureaucracy, Mongol rule was highly decentralized.

A Bridge to the East

The Mongols had a keen eye for the commercial advantages of their empire. They began to control the caravan routes that led from China through Central Asia to the Black Sea. They also encouraged commercial contacts with European traders, especially through the Persian city of Tabriz, from which both land and sea routes led on to China. Until the Mongol conquests, the Silk Road to China had been closed to most Western merchants and travelers. But almost as soon as the Mongol Empire was established, we find Europeans venturing on these routes. The first such travelers were Franciscan missionaries like William of Rubruck,

sent by King Louis IX of France in 1253 as his ambassador to the Mongol court. But Western merchants quickly followed. The most famous of these were three Venetians: the brothers Niccolò and Matteo Polo, and Niccolò's son, Marco. Marco Polo's account of his travels, which began when he was seventeen, includes details of his twenty-year sojourn in the service of Qubilai Khan and of his journey home through the Spice Islands, India, and Persia. The book had an enormous effect on the imagination of his contemporaries: for the next two centuries, most of what Europeans knew about the Far East they learned from Marco Polo's *Travels*. Christopher Columbus's copy of this book still survives.

European connections with the western ends of the Silk Road would continue until the mid-fourteenth century. The Genoese were especially active in this trade, not least because their rivals, the Venetians, already dominated the Mediterranean trade with Alexandria and Beirut, through

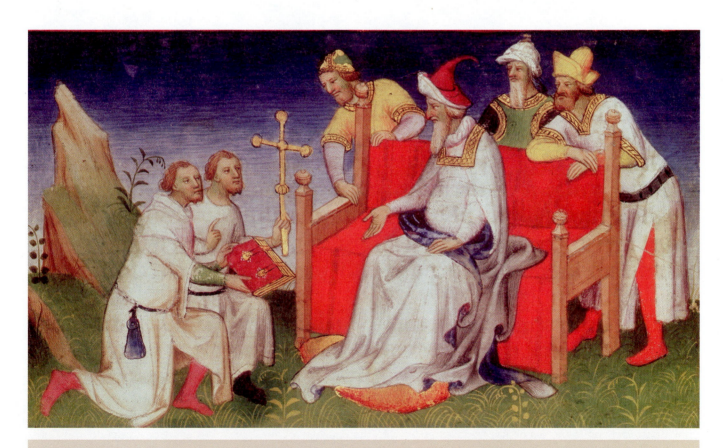

VENETIAN AMBASSADORS TO THE GREAT KHAN. Around 1270, the Venetian merchants Niccolò and Matteo Polo returned to Europe after their first prolonged journey through the empire of the Great Khan, bearing with them an official letter to the Roman pope. This image shows them at the moment of their arrival at the Great Khan's court, to which they have allegedly carried a Christian cross and a Bible. It comes from a manuscript copy of Jehan de Mandeville's *Book of Marvels*, which offered readers an alternative vision of the lands and peoples also described by Niccolò's famous son, Marco, who accompanied his father and uncle when they made their second journey to the Great Khan's court several years later. ■ *Why might many such visual references to the Polo family's adventures have been included in Mandeville's more fanciful travel narrative?*

Competing Viewpoints

Two Travel Accounts

Two of the books that influenced Columbus and his contemporaries were travel narratives describing the exotic worlds that lay beyond Europe: worlds that may or may not have existed as they are described. The first excerpt below is taken from the account published by Marco Polo of Venice in the early fourteenth century. The young Marco traveled overland from Constantinople to the court of Qubilai Khan in the early 1270s, together with his father and uncle. He became a gifted linguist, and remained at the Mongol court until the early 1290s, when he returned to Europe after a journey through Southeast Asia, Indonesia, and the Indian Ocean. The second excerpt is from the Book of Marvels *attributed to Jehan de Mandeville, an almost entirely fictional account of wonders that also became a source for European ideas about South and East Asia. This particular passage concerns a legendary Christian figure called Prester ("Priest") John, who is alleged to have traveled to the East and become a great ruler.*

Marco Polo's Description of Java

Departing from Ziamba, and steering between south and south-east, fifteen hundred miles, you reach an island of very great size, named Java. According to the reports of some well-informed navigators, it is the greatest in the world, and has a compass above three thousand miles. It is under the dominion of one king only, nor do the inhabitants pay tribute to any other power. They are worshipers of idols.

The country abounds with rich commodities. Pepper, nutmegs, spikenard, galangal, cubebs, cloves and all the other valuable spices and drugs, are the produce of the island; which occasion it to be visited by many ships laden with merchandise, that yields to the owners considerable profit.

The quantity of gold collected there exceeds all calculation and belief. From thence it is that . . . merchants . . . have imported, and to this day import, that metal to a great amount, and from thence also is obtained the greatest part of the spices that are distributed throughout the world. That the Great Khan [Qubilai] has not brought the island under subjection to him, must be attributed to the length of the voyage and the dangers of the navigation.

Source: *The Travels of Marco Polo,* rev and ed. Manuel Komroff (New York: 1926), pp. 267–68.

Mandeville's Description of Prester John

This emperor Prester John has great lands and has many noble cities and good towns in his realm and many great, large islands. For all the country of India is separated into islands by the great floods that come from Paradise, that divide the land into many parts. And also in the sea he has many islands. . . .

This Prester John has under him many kings and many islands and many varied people of various conditions. And this land is full good and rich, but not so rich as is the land of the Great Khan. For the merchants do not come there so

commonly to buy merchandise as they do in the land of the Great Khan, for it is too far to travel to. . . .

[Mandeville then goes on to describe the difficulties of reaching Prester John's lands by sea.]

This emperor Prester John always takes as his wife the daughter of the Great Khan, and the Great Khan in the same way takes to wife the daughter of Prester John. For these two are the greatest lords under the heavens.

In the land of Prester John there are many diverse things, and many precious stones so great and so large that men

make them into vessels such as platters, dishes, and cups. And there are many other marvels there that it would be too cumbrous and too long to put into the writing of books. But of the principal islands and of his estate and of his law I shall tell you some part.

This emperor Prester John is Christian and a great part of his country is Christian also, although they do not hold to all the articles of our faith as we do. . . .

And he has under him 72 provinces, and in every province there is a king. And these kings have kings under them, and all are tributaries to Prester John.

And he has in his lordships many great marvels. For in his country is the sea that men call the Gravelly Sea, that is all gravel and sand without any drop of water. And it ebbs and flows in great waves as other seas do, and it is never still. . . . And a three-day journey from that sea there are great mountains out of which flows a great flood that comes out of Paradise. And it is full of precious stones without any drop of water. . . .

He dwells usually in the city of Susa [in Persia]. And there is his principal palace, which is so rich and so noble that no one will believe the report unless he has seen it. And above the chief tower of the palace there are two round pommels of gold and in each of them are two great, large rubies that shine full brightly upon the night. And the principal gates of his palace are of a precious stone that men call sardonyxes [a type of onyx], and the frames and the bars are made of ivory. And the windows of the halls and chambers are of crystal. And the tables upon which men eat, some are made of emeralds, some of amethyst, and some of gold full of precious stones. And the legs that hold up the tables are made of the same precious stones. . . .

Source: *Mandeville's Travels,* ed. M. C. Seymour (Oxford: 1967), pp. 195–99 (language modernized from Middle English by R. C. Stacey).

Questions for Analysis

1. What does Marco Polo want his readers to know about Java, and why? What does this suggest about the interests of these intended readers?

2. What does Mandeville want his readers to know about Prester John and his domains? Why are these details so important?

3. Which of these accounts seems more trustworthy, and why? Even if we cannot accept one or both at face value, what insight do they give us into the expectations of Columbus and the other Europeans adventurers who relied on these accounts?

which the bulk of Europe's Far Eastern luxury goods continued to pass. But the Mongols of Persia became progressively more hostile to Westerners, and the Genoese finally abandoned Tabriz after attacks had made their position there untenable. Then, in 1346, the Mongols of the Golden Horde besieged the Genoese colony at Caffa on the Black Sea, a siege memorable chiefly because it became a conduit for the Black Death, which was passed from the Mongol army to the Genoese defenders, who returned with it to western Europe (see Chapter 10).

The window of opportunity that made Marco Polo's travels possible was thus relatively small. By the middle of the fourteenth century, hostilities between the various parts of the Mongol Empire were already making travel along the Silk Road perilous. After 1368, when the last Mongol dynasty was overthrown, most Westerners were excluded from China and Mongols were restricted to cavalry service in the imperial armies of the new Ming Dynasty. The overland trade routes from China to the Black Sea continued to operate, but Europeans had no direct access to them. Yet the new, more integrated world that Mongol rule had created continued to exercise a lasting effect on Europe, despite the relatively short time during which Europeans themselves were able to participate directly in it. European memories of the Far East would be preserved, and the dream of reestablishing close connections between Europe and China would survive to influence a new round of European commercial and imperial expansion from the late fifteenth century onward.

THE RISE OF THE OTTOMAN EMPIRE

Like the Mongols, the Turks were initially a nomadic people whose economy depended on raiding. They were already established in northwestern Anatolia when the Mongols arrived there, and were being converted to Islam. But unlike the established Muslim powers in the region, whom the Mongols weakened and ultimately destroyed, the Turks were the principal beneficiaries of the Mongol conquest. For when the Mongols toppled the Seljuk sultanate and the Abbasid caliphate of Baghdad, they eliminated the two traditional authorities that had previously kept Turkish border chieftains like the Ottomans in check. Now they were free to raid, unhindered, along the soft frontiers of Byzantium. At the same time, they remained far enough from the centers of Mongol authority to avoid being destroyed themselves.

The Conquest of Constantinople

By the end of the thirteenth century, members of the Ottoman dynasty had established themselves as leaders among the Turks of the Anatolian frontier. By the mid-fourteenth century, they had solidified their preeminence by capturing a number of important cities. These successes brought the Ottomans to the attention of the Byzantine emperor, who hired a contingent of them as mercenaries in 1345. They were extraordinarily successful—so much so that the eastern Roman Empire could not control their movements. By 1370, they had extended their control all the way to the Danube. In 1389, Ottoman forces defeated a powerful coalition of Serbian forces at the battle of Kosovo, enabling them to extend control over Greece, Bulgaria, and the Balkans.

In 1396, the Ottoman army attacked Constantinople, but withdrew to repel a Western crusading force that had been sent against them. In 1402 they attacked Constantinople again, but were once more were forced to withdraw, this time to confront a Mongolian invasion of Anatolia. Led by Timur the Lame, the Mongol army captured the Ottoman sultan and destroyed his army; for the next decade it appeared that Ottoman hegemony over Anatolia might have ended. By 1413, however, Timur was dead, a new sultan had emerged, and the Ottomans were able to resume their conquests.

Ottoman pressure on Constantinople continued during the 1420s and 1430s, producing a steady stream of Byzantine refugees who brought with them to Italy the surviving masterworks of classical Greek literature (see Chapter 12). But it was not until 1451 that a new sultan, Mehmet II, turned his full attention to the conquest of the imperial city. In 1453, after a brilliantly executed siege, Mehmet succeeded in breaching the city walls. The Byzantine emperor was killed in the assault, the city itself was thoroughly plundered, and its remaining population was sold into slavery. The Ottomans then settled down to rule their new capital in a style reminiscent of their Byzantine predecessors.

The Ottoman conquest of Constantinople administered an enormous psychological shock to many European

rulers and intellectuals, but its economic impact was minor. Ottoman control over the former Byzantine Empire reduced European access to the Black Sea, but the bulk of the Far Eastern luxury trade with Europe had never passed through the Black Sea ports in the first place. Europeans got most of their spices and silks through Venice, which imported them from Alexandria and Beirut, and these two cities did not fall to the Ottomans until the 1520s. So the Ottoman Empire was not necessarily the force that propelled Portuguese efforts to locate a sea route to India and the Spice Islands. If anything, it was Portuguese access to India, and European attempts to exclude Muslims from

SULTAN MEHMET II, "THE CONQUEROR" (r. 1451–81). This portrait, executed by the Ottoman artist Siblizade Ahmed, exhibits features characteristic of both Central Asia and Europe. The sultan's pose—his aesthetic appreciation of the rose, his elegant handkerchief—are indicative of the former, as is the fact that he wears the white turban of a scholar and the thumb ring of an archer. But the subdued coloring and three-quarter profile may reflect the influence of Italian portraits. ▪ *What did the artist achieve through this blending of styles and symbols?* ▪ *What messages does this portrait convey?*

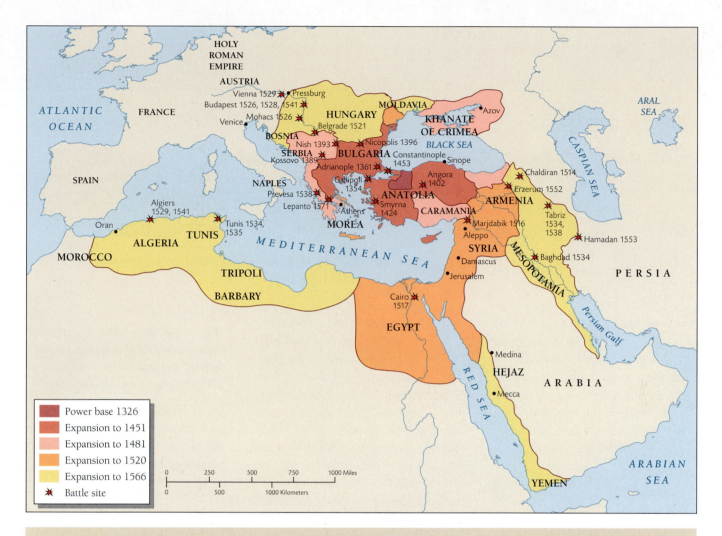

THE GROWTH OF THE OTTOMAN EMPIRE. Consider the patterns of Ottoman expansion revealed in this map. ▪ *Where is Constantinople, and how might the capture of Constantinople in 1453 have facilitated further conquests?* ▪ *Compare the extent of the Ottoman Empire in 1566 with that of the Byzantine Empire under Justinian (see the map on page 208). How would you account for their similarities?* ▪ *How might you explain the fact that the Ottoman Empire did not continue its rapid expansion after 1566?*

the Indian spice trade, that helped spur the Ottoman conquests of Syria, Egypt, and Hungary during the 1520s and 1530s. To be sure, these conquests had other motives, too, including control of Egyptian grain exports. And by eliminating the merchants who had traditionally dominated the overland spice trade through Beirut and Alexandria, the Ottomans also hoped to redirect this trade through Constantinople, and so up the Danube into western Europe.

But if the practical effects of the Ottoman conquest were modest where western Europe was concerned, the effects on the Turks themselves were transformative. Vast new wealth poured into Anatolia, which the Ottomans increased by carefully tending to the industrial and commercial interests of their new capital city Constantinople, which they also called Istanbul—the Turkish pronunciation of the Greek phrase "in the city." Trade routes were redirected to

feed the capital, and the Ottomans became a naval power in the eastern Mediterranean and the Black Sea. As a result, Constantinople's population grew from fewer than 100,000 in 1453 to more than 500,000 in 1600, making it the largest city in the world outside of China.

War, Slavery, and Social Advancement

Despite the Ottomans' careful attention to commerce, their empire continued to rest on the spoils of conquest until the end of the sixteenth century. In order to manage this continual expansion, the size of the Ottoman army and administration grew exponentially, drawing more and more manpower from the empire. And because the Ottoman army and administration were largely composed of slaves,

Analyzing Primary Sources

Ottoman Janissaries

The following account is from a memoir written by Konstantin Mihailovic, a Serbian Christian who was captured as a youth by the army of Sultan Mehmet II. For eight years, he served in the Ottoman janissary ("gate-keeper") corps. In 1463, the fortress he was defending for the Sultan was captured by the Hungarians, after which he recorded his experiences for a Christian audience.

henever the Turks invade foreign lands and capture their people, an imperial scribe follows immediately behind them, and whatever boys there are, he takes them all into the janissaries and gives five gold pieces for each one and sends them across the sea [to Anatolia]. There are about two thousand of these boys. If, however, the number of them from enemy peoples does not suffice, then he takes from the Christians in every village in his land who have boys, having established what is the most every village can give so that the quota will always be full. And the boys whom he takes in his own land are called *cilik*. Each one of them can leave his property to whomever he wants after his death. And those whom he takes among the enemies are called *pendik*. These latter after their deaths can leave nothing; rather, it goes to the emperor, except that if someone comports himself well and is so deserving that he be freed, he may leave it to whomever he wants. And on the boys who are across the sea the emperor spends nothing; rather, those to whom they are entrusted must maintain them and send them where he orders. Then they take those who are suited for it on ships and there they study and train to skirmish in battle. There the emperor already provides for them and gives them a wage. From there he chooses for his own court those who are trained and then raises their wages.

Source: Konstantin Mihailovic, *Memoirs of a Janissary* (Michigan Slavic Translations 3), trans. Benjamin Stolz (Ann Arbor, MI: 1975), pp. 157–59.

Questions for Analysis

1. Why might the Ottoman emperor have established this system for "recruiting" and training janissaries? What are its strengths and weaknesses?

2. Based on your knowledge of Western civilizations, how unusual would you deem this method of raising troops? How does it compare to the strategies of other rulers we have studied?

---

the demand for more soldiers and administrators could best be met through further conquests that would capture yet more slaves. Further conquests, however, required a still larger army and an even more extensive bureaucracy; and so the cycle continued. It mirrors, in many respects, the dilemma of the Roman Empire (Chapter 5). Indeed, another way in which the Ottoman Empire resembled that of Rome was in this insatiable demand for slaves.

Not only were slaves were the backbone of the Ottoman army administration, they were also critical to the lives of the Turkish upper class. One of the important measures of status in Ottoman society was the number of slaves in one's household. After 1453, new wealth permitted some elites to maintain households in the thousands. In the sixteenth century, the sultan alone possessed more than 20,000 slave attendants, not including his bodyguard and elite infantry units, both of which were also composed of slaves.

Where did all of these slaves come from? Many were captured in war. Many others were taken on raiding forays into Poland and Ukraine and sold to Crimean slave merchants, who shipped their captives to the slave markets of Constantinople. But slaves were also recruited (some willingly, some by coercion) from rural areas of the Ottoman Empire itself. Because the vast majority of slaves were household servants and administrators rather than laborers, some people willingly accepted enslavement, believing that they would be better off as slaves in Constantinople than as impoverished peasants in the countryside. In the Balkans especially, many people were enslaved as children, handed over by their families to pay the "child tax" the Ottomans imposed on rural areas too poor to pay a monetary tribute. Although unquestionably a wrenching experience for families, this practice did open up opportunities for social advancement. Special academies were created at

Constantinople to train the most able of the enslaved male children to act as administrators and soldiers, and some rose to become powerful figures in the Ottoman Empire. Slavery, indeed, carried relatively little social stigma. Even the sultan himself was most often the son of an enslaved woman.

Because Muslims were not permitted to enslave other Muslims, the vast majority of Ottoman slaves were Christian—although many eventually converted to Islam. And because so many of the elite positions within Ottoman government were held by these slaves, the paradoxical result was that Muslims, including the Turks themselves, were effectively excluded from the main avenues of social and political influence in the Ottoman Empire. Nor was Ottoman society dominated by a powerful hereditary nobility like those of contemporary European society. Avenues to power were therefore remarkably open to men of ability and talent, most of them non-Muslim slaves. Nor was this power limited to the government and the army. Commerce and business also remained largely in the hands of non-Muslims, most frequently Greeks, Syrians, and Jews. Jews in particular found in the Ottoman Empire a welcome refuge from the persecutions and expulsions that had characterized Jewish life in late-medieval Europe. After their expulsion from Spain in 1492, more than 100,000 Spanish (Sephardic) Jews ultimately immigrated to the territories of the Ottoman Empire.

Religious Conflicts

The Ottoman sultans were Sunni Muslims who lent staunch support to the religious and legal pronouncements of the Islamic schools in their realm. When Ottomans captured the cities of Medina and Mecca in 1516, they also became the defenders of the two principal holy sites of Islam. Soon after, they captured Jerusalem and Cairo too, putting an end to the Mamluk sultanate of Egypt and becoming the keepers of the Holy Land. In 1538, accordingly, the Ottoman ruler formally adopted the title of caliph, thereby declaring himself to be the legitimate successor of the Prophet Muhammad.

In keeping with Sunni traditions, the Ottomans were tolerant of non-Muslims, especially during the fifteenth and sixteenth centuries. They organized the major religious groups of their empire into legally recognized units and permitted them considerable rights of self-government. After 1453, however, when they gained control of Constantinople, the Ottomans were especially careful to protect and promote the authority of the Greek Orthodox patriarch of Constantinople over the Orthodox Christians of their empire. As a result, the Ottomans enjoyed staunch support from their Orthodox Christian subjects during their wars

with the Christians of western Europe. The Ottomans' principal religious conflicts were therefore not with their own subjects, but with the Shi'ite Muslim dynasty that ruled neighboring Persia. Time and again during the sixteenth century, Ottoman expeditions into western Europe had to be abandoned when hostilities erupted with the Persians.

OTTOMAN ORTHODOXY. This genealogical chart is designed to show the descent of Sultan Mehmet III (1595–1603) from his own illustrious ancestors—both warriors and scholars—as well as from Muhammad, whose central image is piously veiled. ▪ *Why was it desirable for the Ottoman sultans to proclaim themselves caliphs, too, and therefore heirs to Muhammad?* ▪ *How might this have increased the hostility between the Sunni Turks and the Shi'ite Muslims of neighboring Persia?*

The Ottomans and Europe

For a variety of reasons, the contest between the Ottoman Empire and the rulers of western Europe never lived up to the rhetoric of holy war that both sides employed in their propaganda. In Europe, especially, there were internal divisions that frustrated any attempts to mount a unified campaign. By the sixteenth century, as we shall see (Chapters 13 and 14), Catholic and Protestant sects were turning that same crusading rhetoric against one another. But even before that, Christian military initiatives were ineffectual. In 1396, a Western crusader army was annihilated by the Ottomans at the battle of Nicopolis, and Ottoman armies besieged Vienna several times during the following two centuries.

But apart from these few dramatic events, conflicts between the Ottomans and the rulers of western Europe were fought out mainly through pirate raids and naval battles in the Mediterranean. The result was a steady escalation in the scale and cost of navies. In 1571, when a combined Habsburg and Venetian force defeated the Ottoman fleet at Lepanto, more than 400 ships took part, with both sides deploying naval forces ten times larger than they had possessed half a century before. Although undeniably a victory for the Habsburgs and their Venetian allies, the battle of Lepanto was far less decisive than is often suggested. The Ottoman navy was speedily rebuilt; and by no means did Lepanto put an end to Ottoman influence over the eastern Mediterranean Sea.

In any case, both Ottoman and Habsburg interests soon shifted away from their conflict with each other. The Ottomans embarked on a long and costly war with Persia, while the Spanish Habsburgs turned their attention toward their new empire in the Atlantic. By the mid-seventeenth century, when a new round of Ottoman-European conflicts began, the strength of the Ottoman Empire had been sapped by a series of indolent sultans and by the tensions that arose within the empire itself as it ceased to expand. Although the empire would last until 1918 (see Chapter 24), it was in no position to rival the global hegemony that European powers were beginning to achieve.

MEDITERRANEAN COLONIALISM

During the fifteenth century, Europeans focused their commercial ambitions more and more on the western Mediterranean and Atlantic. As we noted above, however, this reorientation can only partially be attributed to the rising power of the Ottoman Empire. It was more significantly the product of two related developments: the growing importance of the African gold trade and the growth of European colonial empires in the western Mediterranean.

The Search for African Gold

The European trade in African gold was not new. It had been going on for centuries, facilitated by Muslim middlemen whose caravans brought it from the Niger River to the North African ports of Algiers and Tunis. In the thirteenth century, Catalan and Genoese merchants established trading colonies in Tunis to expedite this process, exchanging woolen cloth from northern Europe for North African grain and sub-Saharan gold.

But the medieval demand for gold was greatly accelerated during the fourteenth century, when a silver shortage began to affect the entire European economy. Silver production—which enabled the circulation of coinage in

THE BATTLE OF LEPANTO, 1571. This oil painting by the Venetian artist Paolo Veronese (1528–1588) celebrates the victory of a Christian navy over the forces of the Ottoman Empire. Over 400 ships took part in the massive engagement. In the lower register of his canvas, Veronese strives to capture the tumult and confusion. In the upper register, warlike saints and angels gather to support the efforts of the Spanish and Venetian mariners.

Europe—fell markedly during the 1340s and remained at a low level thereafter, as Europeans reached the limits of their technological capacity to extract silver ore from deep mines. This shortfall was compounded during the fifteenth century by a serious cash-flow problem: more European silver was moving east in the spice trade than could be now be replenished from extant sources. Gold therefore represented an obvious alternative currency for large transactions, and in the thirteenth century some European rulers began minting gold coins. But Europe itself had few natural gold reserves. To maintain and expand these gold coinages, new and larger supplies of gold were needed. The most obvious source was Africa.

Mediterranean Empires: Catalonia, Venice, and Genoa

European interest in the African gold trade coincided with the creation of entrepreneurial empires in the Mediterranean. During the thirteenth century, the Catalans conquered and colonized a series of western Mediterranean islands, including Majorca, Ibiza, Minorca, Sicily, and Sardinia. Except in Sicily, the pattern of Catalan exploitation was largely the same on all these islands: expulsion or extermination of the existing population, usually Muslim; the extension of economic concessions to attract new settlers; and a heavy reliance on slave labor to produce foodstuffs and raw materials for export.

These new colonial efforts were mainly carried out by private individuals operating under royal charters. They therefore contrast strongly with older patterns of Venetian colonization, which had long been directed by the city's rulers and which were focused mainly on the eastern Mediterranean, where the Venetians dominated the trade in spices and silks. The Genoese, to take yet another case, also had extensive interests in the western Mediterranean, where they traded bulk goods such as cloth, hides, grain, timber, and sugar. But Genoese colonies tended to be more informal than either Venetian or Catalan colonies, constituting family networks rather than an extension of state sovereignty. The Genoese were also more closely integrated with the societies of North Africa, Spain, and the Black Sea than were their Venetian or Catalan counterparts.

Genoese colonists pioneered the production of sugar and sweet wines in the western Mediterranean and later in the Atlantic islands off the west coast of Africa, particularly Madeira. They also moved away from reliance on the oared galleys favored by the Venetians toward larger, fuller-bodied sailing ships that could carry greater volumes of cargo. With further modifications to accommodate the rougher sailing conditions of the Atlantic Ocean, these were the ships that would carry sixteenth-century Europeans around the globe.

SPANISH GALLEON. The larger, full-bottomed ships that came into use during the fifteenth century would become engines of imperial conquest and the vessels that brought the riches of those conquests back to Europe. This wooden model was made for the Museo Storico Navale di Venezia (Naval History Museum) in Venice.

From the Mediterranean to the Atlantic

For centuries, European maritime commerce had been divided between a Mediterranean and a northeastern Atlantic world. Starting around 1270, however, Italian merchants began to sail through the Strait of Gibraltar and on up to the wool-producing regions of England and the Netherlands. This was a step toward the extension of Mediterranean patterns of commerce and colonization into the Atlantic Ocean. Another step was the discovery (or possibly the rediscovery) of the Atlantic island chains known as the Canaries and the Azores, which Genoese sailors reached in the fourteenth century. Efforts to colonize the Canary Islands, and to convert and enslave their inhabitants, began almost immediately. But an effective conquest of the Canary Islands did not really begin until the fifteenth century, when it was undertaken by Portugal and completed by

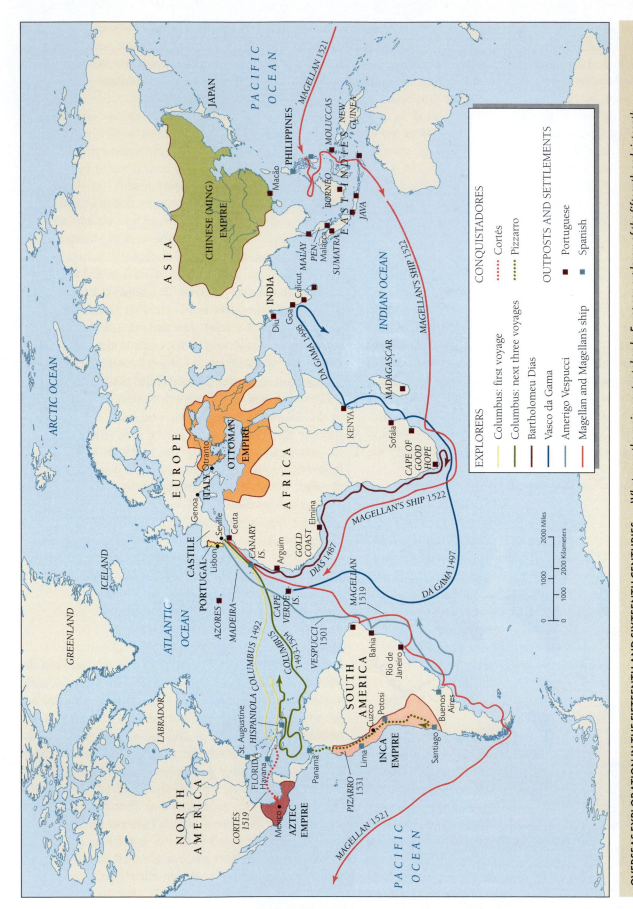

OVERSEAS EXPLORATION IN THE FIFTEENTH AND SIXTEENTH CENTURIES. ▪ *What were the major routes taken by European explorers of the fifteenth and sixteenth centuries?* ▪ *What was the explorers' main goal?* ▪ *How might the establishment of outposts in Africa, America, and the East Indies have radically altered the balance of power in the Old World, and why?*

Castile. The Canaries, in turn, became the base from which further Portuguese voyages down the west coast of Africa proceeded. They were also the jumping-off point from which Christopher Columbus would sail westward across the Atlantic Ocean in the hope of reaching Asia.

Naval Technology and Navigation

The new European empires of the fifteenth and sixteenth centuries rested on a mastery of the oceans. The Portuguese caravel—the workhorse ship of the fifteenth-century voyages to Africa—was based on ship and sail designs that had been in use among Portuguese fishermen since the thirteenth century. Starting in the 1440s, however, Portuguese shipwrights began building larger caravels of about 50 tons displacement with two masts, each carrying a triangular (lateen) sail. Columbus's *Niña* was of this design, having been refitted with two square sails in the Canary Islands to enable it to sail more efficiently before the wind during the Atlantic crossing. Such ships required much smaller crews than did the multi-oared galleys that were still commonly used in the Mediterranean. By the end of the fifteenth century, even larger caravels of around 200 tons were being constructed, with a third mast and a combination of square and lateen sails.

Europeans were also making significant advances in navigation during the fifteenth and sixteenth centuries. Quadrants, which could calculate latitude in the Northern Hemisphere by the height of the North Star above the horizon, were in widespread use by the 1450s. As sailors approached the equator, however, the quadrant became less and less useful, and navigators instead made use of astrolabes, which reckoned latitude by the height of the sun. Like quadrants, astrolabes had been known in western Europe for centuries. But it was not until the 1480s that the astrolabe became a really useful instrument for seaborne navigation, with the preparation of standard tables sponsored by the Portuguese crown. Compasses, too, were coming into more widespread use during the fifteenth century. Longitude, however, remained impossible to calculate accurately until the eighteenth century, when the invention

PORTOLAN CHART. Maritime maps like this one were crucial navigational aids, and came to be widely used outside the Mediterranean in the fifteenth century. This chart, made by Vesconte Maggiolo in 1541, shows the Mediterranean and Atlantic coastlines of Europe and North Africa.

of the marine chronometer finally made it possible to keep accurate time at sea. In the sixteenth century, Europeans sailing east or west across the oceans generally had to rely on their skill at dead reckoning to determine where they were on the globe.

European sailors also benefited from a new interest in maps and navigational charts. Especially important to Atlantic sailors were books known as *rutters* or *routiers*. These contained detailed sailing instructions and descriptions of the coastal landmarks a pilot could expect to encounter en route to a variety of destinations. Mediterranean sailors had used similar books since at least the fourteenth century. Known as *portolani*, or portolan charts, they mapped the ports along the coastlines, tracked prevailing winds and tides, and warned of reefs and shallow harbors. In the fifteenth century, these map-making techniques were extended to the Atlantic Ocean; by the end of the sixteenth century, the accumulated knowledge contained in rutters spanned the globe.

Portugal, Africa, and the Sea Route to India

It was among the Portuguese that two critical interests— the African gold trade and Atlantic colonization—first came together. In 1415, a Portuguese expedition captured the North African port of Ceuta. During the 1420s, the Portuguese colonized both the island of Madeira and the Canary Islands. During the 1430s, they extended these colonization efforts to the Azores. By the 1440s, they had reached the Cape Verde Islands. In 1444, Portuguese explorers first landed on the African mainland in the area between the Senegal and the Gambia river mouths, where they began to collect cargoes of gold and slaves for export back to Portugal. By the 1470s, Portuguese sailors had rounded the West African "bulge" and were exploring the Gulf of Guinea.

In 1483, they reached the mouth of the Congo River. In 1488, the Portuguese captain Bartholomeu Dias was accidentally blown around the southern tip of Africa by a gale, after which he named the point "Cape of Storms." But the king of Portugal, João II (r. 1481–95), took a more optimistic view of Dias's achievement: he renamed it the Cape of Good Hope and began planning a naval expedition to India. In 1497–98, accordingly, Vasco da Gama rounded the cape, and then, with the help of a Muslim naviga-

tor named Ibn Majid, crossed the Indian Ocean to Calicut, on the southwestern coast of India, opening up for the first time a sea route between Europe and the Far Eastern spice trade. Although da Gama lost half his fleet and one-third of his men on his two-year voyage, his cargo of spices was so valuable that his losses were deemed insignificant. His heroism became legendary, and his story became the basis for the Portuguese national epic, the *Lusiads*.

Now masters of the quickest route to riches in the world, the Portuguese swiftly capitalized on da Gama's accomplishment. After 1500, Portuguese trading fleets sailed regularly to India. In 1509, the Portuguese defeated an Ottoman fleet and then blockaded the mouth of the Red Sea, attempting to cut off one of the traditional routes by which spices had traveled to Alexandria and Beirut. By 1510, Portuguese military forces had established a series of forts along the western Indian coastline, including their headquarters at Goa. In 1511 Portuguese ships seized Malacca, a center of the spice trade on the Malay peninsula. By 1515, they had reached the Spice Islands and the coast of China. So completely did the Portuguese now dominate the spice trade that by the 1520s even the Venetians were forced to buy their pepper in the Portuguese capital of Lisbon.

Artillery and Empire

Larger, more maneuverable ships and improved navigational aids made it possible for the Portuguese and other European mariners to reach Africa, Asia, and the Americas by sea. But fundamentally, these sixteenth-century European commercial empires were a military achievement. As such, they reflected what Europeans had learned in their wars against each other during the fourteenth and fifteenth centuries. Perhaps the most critical military advance was the increasing sophistication of artillery, a development made possible not only by gunpowder, but also by improved metallurgical

A TURKISH BRASS CANNON OF THE FIFTEENTH CENTURY. This eighteen-ton gun fired iron projectiles twenty-five inches in diameter.

techniques for casting cannon barrels. By the middle of the fifteenth century, as we observed in Chapter 10, the use of artillery pieces had rendered the stone walls of medieval castles and towns obsolete, a fact brought home in 1453 by the successful French siege of Bordeaux (which ended the Hundred Years' War), and by the Ottoman siege of Constantinople (which ended the Byzantine Empire).

Indeed, the new ship designs (first caravels, and later the larger galleons) were important in part because their larger size made it possible to mount more effective artillery pieces on them. European vessels were now conceived as floating artillery platforms, with scores of guns mounted in fixed positions along their sides and swivel guns mounted fore and aft. These guns were vastly expensive, as were the ships that carried them; but for those rulers who could afford them, such ships made it possible to project military power around the world. Even though Vasco da Gama had been able to sail into the Indian Ocean in 1498, the Portuguese did not gain control of that ocean until 1509, when they defeated a combined Ottoman and Indian naval force at the battle of Div. Portuguese trading outposts in Africa and Asia were also fortifications, built not so much to guard against the attacks of native peoples as to ward off assaults from other Europeans. Without this essential military component, the European maritime empires of the sixteenth century could not have existed.

Prince Henry the Navigator

Because we know that Portuguese expeditions down the African coast ultimately opened up a sea route to India and the Far East, it is tempting to presume that this was their goal from the beginning. The traditional narrative of these events presents exploration as their mission, India as their goal, and Prince Henry the Navigator (1394–1460) as the guiding genius behind them. But it was only a generation after Henry's death, in the 1480s, that India became the target toward which these voyages were directed. Before this time, Portuguese involvement in Africa was driven instead by much more traditional goals: crusading ambitions against the Muslims of North Africa; the desire to establish direct links with the sources of African gold production south of the Sahara Desert; the desire to colonize the Atlantic islands; the burgeoning market for slaves in Europe and in the Ottoman Empire; and the hope that somewhere in Africa they might find the kingdom of the legendary Prester John, the mythical Christian king whom Europeans believed would be their ally against the Muslims if only they could locate him (see page 352). In the twelfth and thirteenth centuries, they had sought him in Asia. But from the 1340s on, he was believed to

PRINCE HENRY THE NAVIGATOR. This image shows a detail from a larger group portrait of the Portuguese royal family.

reside in Ethiopia, an expansive term that to most Europeans seems to have meant "somewhere in Africa."

Still, Prince Henry (whose nickname, "the Navigator," was assigned to him in the seventeenth century) remains a central figure in the history of Portuguese exploration, even though the stories about his school for navigators and cartographers, as well as his role in designing improved ships and navigational instruments, are probably exaggerated. He personally directed eight of the thirty-five Portuguese voyages to Africa that occurred during his lifetime, and he played an important part in organizing the Portuguese colonization of Madeira, the Canary Islands, and the Azores. He also pioneered the Portuguese slave trade, first on the Canaries (whose population was almost entirely eradicated) and then along the Senegambian coast of western Africa. His main motivation was to outflank the cross-Saharan African gold trade by intercepting this trade at its source. To this end, he built a series of forts along the African coastline, most famously at Arguim, to which he hoped to divert the trans-Saharan gold caravans. This was also his reason for colonizing the Canary Islands, which he saw as a staging ground for expeditions into the African interior. He was therefore a man of his time, rather than a visionary: a crusader against Islam, a prince in search of an empire, a lord seeking resources to support his followers, and an aspiring merchant who hoped to make a killing in the gold trade but instead found his main profits in slaving.

Atlantic Colonization and Slave Networks

Although slavery had effectively disappeared in much of northwestern Europe by the early twelfth century, slavery continued in Iberia, Italy, and elsewhere in the Mediterranean world. It existed, however, on a small scale; there were no slave-powered factories or large-scale agricultural systems in this period. The major slave markets and slave economies, as we have noted, were in the Ottoman Empire. And, as had been the case since antiquity, no aspect of this slave trade was racially based. Most slaves of this era were European Christians, predominantly Poles, Ukrainians, Greeks, and Bulgarians; in previous eras, they had been Germanic and Celtic peoples.

What was new about slavery in the fifteenth century, then, was its racialization—an aspect of modern slavery that has made an indelible impact on our own society. To Europeans, African slaves were visible in ways that other slaves were not, and it became convenient for those who dealt in them to justify the mass deportation of entire populations by claiming their racial inferiority and their "natural" fitness for a life of bondage. This nefarious practice, too, has had long-lasting and tragic consequences that still afflict the civilizations of our own world.

From as early as the mid-fifteenth century, Lisbon began to emerge as a significant market for enslaved Africans. Something on the order of 15,000 to 20,000 Africans were sold there within a twenty-year period during Prince Henry's lifetime. In the following half century, the numbers amounted to perhaps 150,000 by 1505. For the most part, the purchasers of these slaves regarded them as status symbols; it became fashionable to have African footmen, page boys, and ladies' maids. Still, in the Atlantic colonies—Madeira, the Canaries, and the Azores—land was worked mainly by European settlers and sharecroppers. Slave labor, if it was employed at all, was generally used only in sugar mills. On Madeira and the Canaries, where sugar became the predominant cash crop during the last quarter of the fifteenth century, some slaves were therefore introduced. But even sugar production did not lead to the widespread introduction of slavery on these islands.

However, a new kind of slave-based sugar plantation began to emerge in Portugal's Atlantic colonies in the 1460s, starting on the Cape Verde Islands and then extending southward into the Gulf of Guinea. These islands were not populated when the Portuguese began to settle them, and their climate generally discouraged most Europeans from living there. They were ideally located, however, along the routes of slave traders venturing outward from the nearby West African coast. It was this plantation model that would be exported to Brazil by the Portuguese and to the Caribbean islands of the Americas by their Spanish conquerors, with incalculable consequences for the peoples of Africa, the Americas, and Europe.

NEW WORLD ENCOUNTERS

When King Ferdinand and Queen Isabella of Spain decided to underwrite a voyage of exploration, they were hoping to steal some thunder from the successful Portuguese ventures of the past half century. For it was clear that tiny Portugal would soon dominate the sea-lanes if rival entrepreneurs

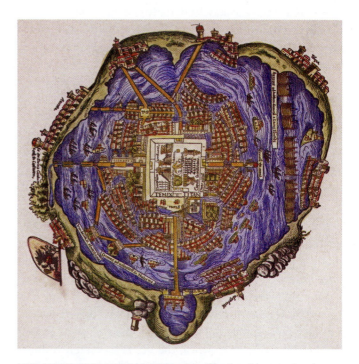

THE AZTEC CITY OF TENOCHTITLAN. The Spanish conquistador Bernal Díaz del Castillo (1492–1585) took part in the conquest of the Aztec Empire and later wrote a historical account of his adventures. His admiring description of the Aztec capital at Tenochtitlan records that the Spaniards were amazed to see such a huge city built in the midst of vast lake, with gigantic buildings arranged in a meticulous urban plan around a central square, and broad causeways linking the city to the mainland. This hand-colored woodcut was included in an early edition of Hernando Cortés's letters to Emperor Charles V, printed at Nuremberg (Germany) in 1524.

Interpreting Visual Evidence

America as an Object of Desire

Under the influence of Mandeville's *Book of Marvels* and a host of other popular narratives, Columbus and his fellow voyagers were prepared to find the New World full of cannibals. They also assumed that the indigenous peoples' custom of wearing little or no clothing—not to mention their "savagery"—would render their women sexually available. In the letters he sent back to Europe, Columbus recounts one notable encounter with a "cannibal girl" whom he had taken captive in his tent. Her naked body aroused his desire, but she resisted his advances so fiercely that he had to tie her up—which of course made it easier for him to "subdue" her. In the end, he cheerfully reports, the girl's sexual performance was so satisfying that she might have been trained, as he put it, in a "school for whores."

The Flemish artist Jan van der Straet (1523–1605) would have heard many such reports of the encounters between (mostly male) Europeans and the peoples of the New World. This engraving, based on one of his drawings, is among the thousands of mass-produced images that circulated widely in Europe, thanks to the invention of printing. It imagines the first encounter between a male "Americus" (like Columbus, or Amerigo Vespucci himself) and the New World, "America," depicted as a voluptuous, available woman. The Latin caption reads: "America rises to meet Americus; and whenever he calls her, she will always be aroused."

Americen Americus retexit, & Semel vocauit inde semper excitam.

AMERICA.

Questions for Analysis

1. Study the details of this image carefully. What does each symbolize, and how do they work together as an allegory of conquest and colonization?

2. On what stereotypes of indigenous peoples does this image draw? Notice, for example, the cannibalistic campfire of the group in the background, or the posture of "America."

3. The New World itself—America—is imagined as female in this image. Why is this? What messages might this—and the suggestive caption—have conveyed to a European viewer?

did not attempt to find alternate routes. Hence the bold—and ill-informed—decision to reach Asia by sailing west. Like his contemporaries, Christoffa Corombo (1451–1506) of Genoa understood that the world was a sphere, but like them he also thought it was much smaller than it actually is. (As we saw in Chapter 4, the accurate calculation of the globe's circumference made in ancient Alexandria had been suppressed centuries later by the Roman geographer Ptolemy.) Furthermore, it had been accepted since antiquity that there were only three continents: Europe, Asia, and Africa.

What made the scheme seem plausible to Ferdinand and Isabella was, first, the discovery and colonization of the Canary Islands and the Azores, which had reinforced the

A Spanish Critique of New World Conquest

Not all Europeans approved of European imperialism or its "civilizing" effects on the peoples of the New World. One of the most influential contemporary critics was Bartolomé de las Casas (1474–1566), who left his home city of Seville at the age of eighteen, joined the Dominican order, and eventually became bishop of Chiapas (Mexico). Although he was a product of his times—he owned many slaves—he was also prescient in discerning the devastating effects of European settlement in the West Indies and Central America, and he particularly deplored the exploitation and extermination of indigenous populations. The following excerpt is from one of the many eloquent manifestos he published in an attempt to gain the sympathies of the Spanish crown and to reach a wide readership. It was printed in 1542.

 od made all the peoples of this area, many and varied as they are, as open and as innocent as can be imagined. The simplest people in the world—unassuming, long-suffering, unassertive, and submissive—they are without malice or guile, and are utterly faithful and obedient both to their own native lords and to the Spaniards in whose service they now find themselves.... They are innocent and pure in mind and have a lively intelligence, all of which makes them particularly receptive to learning and understanding the truths of our Catholic faith and to being instructed in virtue; indeed, God has invested them with fewer impediments in this regard than any other people on earth....

It was upon these gentle lambs... that from the very first day they clapped eyes on them the Spanish fell like ravening wolves upon the fold, or like tigers and savage lions who have not eaten meat for days. The pattern established at the outset has remained unchanged to this day, and the Spaniards still do nothing save tear the natives to shreds, murder them and inflict upon them untold misery, suffering and distress, tormenting, harrying and persecuting them mercilessly....

When the Spanish first journeyed there, the indigenous population of the island of Hispaniola stood at some three million; today only two hundred survive. The island of Cuba, which extends for a distance almost as great as that separating Valladolid from Rome, is now to all intents and purposes uninhabited; and two other large, beautiful and fertile islands, Puerto Rico and Jamaica, have been similarly devastated. Not a living soul remains today on any of the islands

hypothesis that the Atlantic was dotted with islands all the way to Japan; and second, the Genoese mariner's egregious miscalculation of the earth's size, which convinced him that he could reach Japan and China in about a month's clear sailing after leaving the Canary Islands. The man we know as Christopher Columbus never realized his mistake. When he reached the Bahamas and the island of Hispaniola in 1492 after only a month's sailing, he returned to Spain to report that he had reached the outer islands of Asia.

Discoveries

Of course, Columbus was not the first European to set foot on the American continents. As we noted in Chapter 8, Viking sailors briefly settled present-day Newfoundland,

Labrador, and perhaps even portions of New England around the year 1000. But knowledge of these Viking landings had been forgotten or ignored outside of Iceland for hundreds of years. Moreover, the tiny Scandinavian colonies on Greenland had been abandoned by the fifteenth century, when the cooling of the climate (Chapter 10) destroyed the fragile ecosystems that had barely sustained the lives of Norse settlers there.

Although Columbus brought back no Asian spices to prove that he had found an alternate route on his voyages, he did return with some small samples of gold and a few indigenous people—whose existence gave promise of entire tribes that might be "saved" (by conversion to Christianity) and enslaved by Europeans. This provided sufficient incentive for the Spanish monarchs to finance three more expeditions by Columbus, and many more by others. Soon the of the Bahamas . . . even though every single one of the sixty or so islands in the group . . . is more fertile and more beautiful than the Royal Gardens in Seville and the climate is as healthy as anywhere on earth. The native population, which once numbered some five hundred thousand, was wiped out by forcible expatriation to the island of Hispaniola, a policy adopted by the Spaniards in an endeavour to make up losses among the indigenous population of that island. . . .

At a conservative estimate, the despotic and diabolical behaviour of the Christians has, over the last forty years, led to the unjust and totally unwarranted deaths of more than twelve million souls, women and children among them. . . .

The reason the Christians have murdered on such a vast scale and killed anyone and everyone in their way is purely and simply greed. . . . The Spaniards have shown not the slightest consideration for these people, treating them (and I speak from first-hand experience, having been there from the outset) not as brute animals—indeed, I would to God they had done and had shown them the consideration they afford their animals—so much as piles of dung in the middle of the road. They have had as little concern for their souls as for their bodies, all the millions that have perished having gone to their deaths with no knowledge of God and without the benefit of the Sacraments. One fact in all this is widely known and beyond dispute, for even the tyrannical murderers themselves acknowledge the truth of it: the indigenous peoples never did the Europeans any harm whatever. . . .

Source: Bartolomé de la Casas, *A Short Account of the Destruction of the Indies*, trans. Nigel Griffin (Harmondsworth: 1992), pp. 9–12.

Questions for Analysis

1. Given his perspective on the behavior of his countrymen, how might Bartolomé de las Casas have justified his own presence in New Spain (Mexico)? What do you think he may have hoped to achieve by publishing this account?

2. What comparisons does the author make between New Spain (Mexico) and the Old, and between indigenous peoples and Europeans? What is he trying to convey?

3. Compare this account with the contemporary engraving on page 365. What new light does this excerpt throw on that visual allegory? How might a reader-viewer of the time have reconciled these two very different pictures of European imperialism?

---

mainlands of two hitherto unknown continents were identified, as were clusters of new islands. Gradually, Europeans reached the conclusion that what they had encounterd was an entirely "New World," and one that had—shockingly—never been foretold either by the teachings of Christianity or the wisdom of the ancients. Awareness of this fact was most widely publicized by the Italian explorer and geographer Amerigo Vespucci (1454–1512), whose name was soon adapted as a descriptor for the new continents (see **Interpreting Visual Evidence** on page 365).

At first, the realization that this world was not, in fact, an outpost of Asia came as a disappointment to the Spanish: two major land masses and two vast oceans disrupted their plans to beat the Portuguese to the Spice Islands. But this sense of frustration began to lift in 1513, when Vasco Núñez de Balboa first viewed the Pacific Ocean from the Isthmus of Panama. Thereafter, Ferdinand and Isabella's grandson, the Holy Roman Emperor Charles V, renewed their dream when he accepted Ferdinand Magellan's proposal to see whether a route to Asia could be found by sailing around South America. But Magellan's voyage of 1519 demonstrated beyond question that the globe was simply too large for any such plan to be feasible. Of the five ships that left Spain under his command, only one returned, three years later, having been forced to circumnavigate the globe. Out of a crew of 265 sailors, only eighteen survived. Most had died of scurvy or starvation; Magellan himself had been killed in a skirmish with native peoples in the Philippines.

This fiasco ended all hope of discovering an easy southwest passage to Asia—although the deadly dream of a northwest passage survived, and motivated many European explorers of North America into the twentieth century. It has been revived today: in our age of global warming, the retreat of Arctic pack ice has led to the opening of new shipping lanes, and in 2008 the first commercial voyage successfully traversed the Arctic Ocean.

The Spanish Conquest of America

Although the discovery of two continents was initially construed as a setback, it quickly became clear that this New World had great wealth of its own. From the start, Columbus's gold samples, in themselves rather paltry, had nurtured hopes that gold might lie piled in ingots somewhere in these vast new lands, ready to enrich any European adventurer who discovered them. Rumor fed rumor, until a few freelance Spanish soldiers really did strike it rich beyond their most avaricious imaginings. Between 1519 and 1521, the *conquistador* (Spanish for "conqueror") Hernánd Cortés, with a force of only 600 men, overthrew the Aztec Empire of Mexico and plundered its rulers' fabulous wealth. Then in 1533, another conquistador, Francisco Pizarro, toppled the highly centralized South American empire of the Incas and seized its great stores of gold and silver. His force numbered only 180. Despite the vast populations, sophistica-

tion, and enormous resources of these two extraordinary empires—the Aztec capital of Tenochtitlan (*ten-och-tit-LAN*, now Mexico City) rivaled any European city in size and amazed its conquerors by the height and grandeur of its buildings—Cortés and Pizarro had the advantage. They had cannons, firearms, steel swords, armor, and horses, all unknown to the native peoples of the Americas. They were also aided by the indigenous peoples' extreme susceptibility to infectious European diseases, which had already weakened these populations as a result of their earlier contacts with explorers and settlers following in the wake of Columbus. Those who survived were promised liberation from the oppressive regimes of the Aztecs and Incas—little knowing how much worse their new oppressors would be.

The Profits of Empire

Cortés and Pizarro captured hoards of gold and silver that had been accumulated for centuries by the native civilizations of Mexico and Peru. Almost immediately, however, a search for the sources of these precious metals was launched by conquistadors. The first gold deposits were

SPANISH CONQUISTADORS IN MEXICO. This sixteenth-century drawing of conquistadors slaughtering the Aztec aristocracy emphasizes the advantages that plate armor and steel swords gave to the Spanish soldiers.

Analyzing Primary Sources

Enslaved Native Laborers at Potosí

Since the Spanish crown received one-fifth of all revenues from the mines of New Spain, as well as maintaining a monopoly over the mercury used to refine the silver ore into silver, it had an important stake in ensuring the mines' productivity. To this end, the crown granted colonial mine owners the right to conscript native peoples and gave them considerable freedom when it came to the treatment of the workers. This account, dated to about 1620, describes the conditions endured by these native laborers.

According to His Majesty's warrant, the mine owners on this massive range [at Potosí] have a right to the conscripted labor of 13,300 Indians in the working and exploitation of the mines, both those [mines] which have been discovered, those now discovered, and those which shall be discovered. It is the duty of the *Corregidor* [municipal governor] of Potosí to have them rounded up and to see that they come in from all the provinces between Cuzco . . . and as far as the frontiers of Tarija and Tomina. . . .

The conscripted Indians go up every Monday morning to the . . . foot of the range; the *Corregidor* arrives with all the provincial captains or chiefs who have charge of the Indians assigned him for his miner or smelter; that keeps him busy till 1 P.M., by which time the Indians are already turned over to these mine and smelter owners.

After each has eaten his ration, they climb up the hill, each to his mine, and go in, staying there from that hour until Saturday evening without coming out of the mine; their wives bring them food, but they stay constantly underground, excavating and carrying out the ore from which they get the silver. They all have tallow candles, lighted day and night; that is the light they work with, for as they are underground, they have need for it all the time. . . .

These Indians have different functions in the handling of the silver ore; some break it up with bar or pick, and dig down in, following the vein in the mine; others bring it up; others up above keep separating the good and the poor in piles; others are occupied in taking it down from the range to the mills on herds of llamas; every day they bring up more than 8,000 of these native beasts of burden for this task. These teamsters who carry the metal are not conscripted, but are hired.

Source: Antonio Vázquez de Espinosa, *Compendium and Description of the West Indies*, trans. Charles Upson Clark (Washington, DC: 1968), p. 62.

Questions for Analysis

1. From the tone of this account, what do you think was the narrator's purpose in writing? Who is his intended audience?

2. Reconstruct the conditions in which these laborers worked. What would you estimate to be the human costs of this week's labor? Why, for example, would a fresh workforce be needed every Monday?

---

discovered in Hispaniola, where surface mines were speedily established using native laborers, who died in appalling numbers from disease, brutality, and overwork. Of the approximately 1 million native people who had welcomed Columbus in 1492, only 100,000 survived by 1510; 90 percent of the population had died within a generation. By 1538, there were fewer than 500.

With the loss of so many workers, the mines of Hispaniola became uneconomical to operate, and the European colonists turned instead to cattle raising and sugar production. Modeling their sugarcane plantations on those of the Cape Verde Islands and St. Thomas (São Tomé) in the Gulf of Guinea, colonists began to import thousands of African slaves to labor in the new industry. Sugar production was, by its nature, a capital-intensive undertaking. The need to import slave labor added further to its costs, guaranteeing that control over the new industry would fall into the hands of a few extremely wealthy planters and financiers.

Despite the importance of sugar production in the Caribbean and of cattle ranching on the Mexican mainland—which had a devastating effect on the fragile ecosystem of Central America—it was mining that shaped the Spanish colonies of Central and South America most fundamentally. Gold was the lure that had initially drawn the Spanish to the New World, but silver became their most lucrative export. Between 1543 and 1548, vast silver deposits were discovered north of Mexico City and at Potosí in Bolivia. But even before these discoveries, the Spanish crown had taken steps to assume direct control over its new colonies. It was therefore to the Spanish crown that the profits from these astonishingly productive mines accrued. Potosí quickly became the most important mining town in the world. By 1570, it numbered 120,000 inhabitants, despite being located at an altitude of 15,000 feet, where the temperature never climbs above 59° F. As in Hispaniola, enslaved native laborers died by the tens of thousands in these mines and in the disease-infested boom towns that surrounded them (see page 369).

New mining techniques made it possible to produce even greater quantities of silver, though at the cost of even greater mortality among the native laborers. Between 1571 and 1586, silver production at Potosí quadrupled, reaching a peak in the 1590s, when 10 million ounces of silver per year were arriving in Spain from the Americas. In the 1540s, by contrast, the corresponding figure was only 1.5 million ounces. In the peak years of domestic European silver production, by contrast, only about 3 million ounces of silver per year were produced between 1525 and 1535, and this figure dropped steadily from about 1550 on. Europe's silver shortage therefore came to an end during the sixteenth century, but the silver that now circulated there came almost entirely from the New World.

This massive infusion of silver into the European economy accelerated an inflation that had already begun in the late fifteenth century. Initially, it was driven by the renewed growth of the European population, an expanding economy, and a relatively fixed supply of food. From the 1540s on, however, inflation was largely the product of the greatly increased supply of coinage that was now entering the European economy. The result was a rapid rise in prices. Although the effects of this were felt throughout Europe, Spain was particularly hard hit. Prices doubled between 1500 and 1560, and they doubled again between 1560 and 1600. These price spikes in turn undermined the competitiveness of Spanish industries. Then, when the flow of New World silver slowed dramatically during the 1620s and 1630s, the Spanish economy collapsed.

After 1600, when smaller quantities of New World silver were entering the European economy, prices rose more

After You Read This Chapter

 Visit StudySpace for quizzes, additional review materials, and multi-media documents. **wwnorton.com/studyspace**

REVIEWING THE OBJECTIVES

- The conquests of the Mongols had a significant impact on Europe. What were some key effects?
- The Ottomans' dependence on slavery had a number of notable consequences. What were they?
- Colonialism and overseas exploration were driven by an array of factors. Identify some of the main economic and technological changes that occurred during the fourteenth and fifteenth centuries.
- In what ways did the practice of slavery and its justification change in the fifteenth century?
- The "discovery" of the New World had profound effects on the Old World, as well as on the indigenous peoples of the Americas. Describe some of these effects.

slowly. But the price of grain still ballooned to five or six times the level of the previous century by 1650, producing social dislocation and widespread misery for many of Europe's poorest inhabitants (see Chapter 14). In England, for example, the period between about 1590 and 1610 was the most desperate the country had experienced since the Great Famine, nearly three hundred years before. As the population rose and wages fell, living standards declined dramatically. Indeed, if we compute living standards by dividing the price of an average basket of food by the average daily wage of a common laborer, then standards of living were lower in England at the beginning of the modern era than they had been at any time during the Middle Ages. It is no wonder, then, that so many Europeans found emigration to the Americas a tempting prospect.

CONCLUSION

By 1600, commerce, colonization and overseas conquest had profoundly changed both Europe and the wider world. Even though Europeans had little direct contact with China after the fall of the Mongol Empire, the economy of Europe became more closely tied to that of Asia through the trade routes maintained by the Ottoman Empire. At the same time, the emergence of Portugal and Spain as Europe's leading long-distance traders was moving the center of economic gravity away from the Mediterranean toward the Atlantic. Displaced by Ottoman Constantinople from its role as the principal conduit for the spice trade, Venice gradually declined, while the Genoese moved increasingly into the world of finance, backing the commercial ventures of other powers, particularly Spain, whose Atlantic ports bustled with vessels and shone with wealth. By the mid-seventeenth century, however, both Spain and Portugal had become the victims of their own success. They would retain their American colonies until the nineteenth century, but it would be the Dutch, the French, and especially the English who would establish the most successful European empires in North America, Asia, Africa, and Australia. Meanwhile, these and other developments were moving Italy to the center of European affairs for the first time since the fragmentation of the Roman Empire. How this happened is the subject of Chapter 12.

PEOPLE, IDEAS, AND EVENTS IN CONTEXT

- What circumstances enabled **MARCO POLO**'s travels in the East? Why was the period of commercial contact between the **MONGOL EMPIRE** and Europe so brief?
- What forces drove the **OTTOMAN EMPIRE** to expand its reach? Why was the Ottoman caliph more tolerant of Jews and Christians than of dissent within Islam?
- What set the **GENOESE** entrepreneurs apart from other colonial powers in the Mediterranean?
- How does **PRINCE HENRY THE NAVIGATOR** exemplify the motives for pursuing overseas expansion, as well as the mythology that has grown up around these early efforts?
- What were the expectations that launched **COLUMBUS**'s voyage? Why were **FERDINAND AND ISABELLA** of Spain motivated to finance it?
- What advantages did the Spanish **CONQUISTADORS** have over the native peoples of the **AMERICAS**? What were the immediate effects of European conquest on the Americas?

CONSEQUENCES

- How do the patterns of conquest and colonization discussed in this chapter compare to those of earlier periods, particularly those of antiquity? How many of these developments were new?
- In what ways did the slave trade of the Atlantic world differ from the slave economies of antiquity? How might Europeans have used Greek and Roman justifications of slavery in defense of these new ventures? (See Chapters 4 and 5.)
- How important a role does technology play in the developments we have surveyed in this chapter? In your view, which technological innovation was of the greatest historical significance?

Before You Read This Chapter

Renaissance Ideals and Realities, c. 1350–1550

Rummaging through the books in a remote monastic library, an Italian bureaucrat attached to the papal curia at Avignon was surprised to find a manuscript of Cicero's letters—letters that no living person had known to exist. They had probably been copied in the time of Charlemagne, and had then been forgotten for hundreds of years. How many other works of this great Roman orator had met the same fate? he wondered. And how many more books might still remain to be discovered? Clearly, thought Francesco Petrarca (1304–1374), he was living in an age of ignorance. A great gulf seemed to open up between his own time and that of the ancients: a middle age that separated him from those well-loved models.

For centuries, Christian intellectuals had regarded "the dark ages" as the time between Adam's expulsion from Eden and the birth of Christ. But now, Petrarca redefined that concept and applied it to his own era. According to him, the Middle Ages was not the pagan past but the time that separated him from direct communion with the classics. Yet this did not stop him from trying to bridge the gap. "I would have written to you long ago," he said in a Latin letter to the Greek poet Homer (dead for over two thousand years), "had it not been for the fact that we lack a common language."

Petrarca (known to English-speakers as Petrarch) would later become famous in his own day as an Italian poet, a Latin stylist, and a tireless advocate for the resuscitation of the classical past. And the values that he and his contemporaries began to espouse would give rise to a new intellectual and artistic movement in Italy, a movement strongly critical of the present and admiring of a past that had disappeared with the fragmentation of Rome's empire and the end of Italy's greatness. We know this movement as the Renaissance, the French word for "rebirth" that was applied to it in the eighteenth century. It has since become shorthand for the epoch following the Middle Ages, but it is really a parallel phenomenon—as the overlapping chronologies of this chapter and the two previous chapters show. Talking about the Renaissance is therefore a way of talking about some significant changes in education and outlook that transformed the culture of Italy from the late fourteenth to the early sixteenth centuries, and which eventually influenced the rest of Europe in important ways.

These changes were fueled by the intensified warfare, political competition, and commercial expansion of this era. They began in Italy because the intellectuals of its warring city-states desperately sought for new models of governance in the older civilizations of Greece and Rome, and because they were the first to receive the intellectuals of Constantinople after the conquests of the Ottoman Turks spurred a diaspora of Greek-speaking refugees. They resulted in new—or renewed—approaches to education, scholarship, civic engagement, history, literature, and art. And they soon spread beyond Italy, influencing the intellectual and artistic endeavors of other Europeans.

MEDIEVAL OR RENAISSANCE?

The term *renaissance* has usually been taken literally, as though the cultural accomplishments of antiquity had ceased to be appreciated and imitated, and therefore needed to be "reborn." Yet we have been tracing the enduring influence of classical civilization throughout the Middle Ages for many chapters, and we have constantly noted the reverence accorded to Aristotle, Virgil, Cicero, and a host of other figures, as well as the persistence of Roman law and Roman institutions. It is also misleading to characterize the Renaissance as rejecting the fervent Christianity of the Middle Ages, and as a return to the pagan past: however

much the scholars and artists of this age loved the classics, none saw classicism as superseding Christianity. Indeed, all discussions of "the Renaissance" must be qualified by the fact that there was no single set of Renaissance ideals, and that these ideals were constantly reshaped and determined by political, social, and economic realities.

Renaissance Classicism

Renaissance thinkers and artists were enormously diverse in their attitudes, achievements, and approaches. That said, one can certainly find distinguishing traits that make the concept of a "Renaissance" meaningful. With respect to knowledge of the classics, for example, there was a significant quantitative difference between the learning of the Middle Ages and that of the Renaissance. Medieval scholars knew many Roman authors—especially Virgil, Ovid, and Cicero—but the discovery of "new" works by Livy, Tacitus, and Lucretius expanded the classical canon considerably. Equally if not more important was the recovery of Greek literature, whose study had hitherto thrived only in Byzantium. In the twelfth and thirteenth centuries, as we have seen (Chapters 8 and 9), Greek scientific and philosophical works became available to western Europeans thanks to increased contact with Islam; but no Greek poems or plays were available in Latin translations, and neither were the major dialogues of Plato. Nor could more than a handful of western Europeans read the language of classical Greece. But as the Ottomon Turks put increasing pressure on the shrinking borders of the Byzantine Empire (Chapter 11), more and more Greek-speaking intellectuals fled to Italy, bringing their books and their knowledge with them.

Renaissance thinkers not only knew many more classical texts, they used them in new ways. Medieval intellectuals had long regarded ancient sources as complementing and confirming their own assumptions. By contrast, the new reading methods of the Renaissance fostered an increased awareness of the conceptual gap that separated the contemporary world from that of antiquity. At the same time, the structural similarities between ancient Greek poleis and the city-states of Italy encouraged political theorists to use these ancient forms of government as models. This firm determination to learn from antiquity was even more pronounced in the realms of architecture and art, areas in which classical models contributed most strikingly to the creation of a distinctive Renaissance style.

Finally, although Renaissance culture was by no means pagan, it was more overtly materialistic and more commer-

Some Renaissance Attitudes toward Women

Italian society in the fourteenth and fifteenth centuries was characterized by marriage patterns in which men in their late twenties or thirties customarily married women in their mid- to late teens. This demographic fact probably contributed to the widely shared belief that wives were essentially children, who could not be trusted with important matters and who were best trained by being beaten. Renaissance humanism did little to change such attitudes. In some cases, it even reinforced them.

fter my wife had been settled in my house a few days, and after her first pangs of longing for her mother and family had begun to fade, I took her by the hand and showed her around the whole house. I explained that the loft was the place for grain and that the stores of wine and wood were kept in the cellar. I showed her where things needed for the table were kept, and so on, through the whole house. At the end there were no household goods of which my wife had not learned both the place and the purpose. . . .

Only my books and records and those of my ancestors did I determine to keep well sealed. . . . These my wife not only could not read, she could not even lay hands on them. I kept my records at all times . . . locked up and arranged in order in my study, almost like sacred and religious objects. I never gave my wife permission to enter that place, with me or alone. . . .

[Husbands] who take counsel with their wives . . . are madmen if they think true prudence or good counsel lies in the female brain. . . . For this very reason I have always tried carefully not to let any secret of mine be known to a woman. I did not doubt that my wife was most loving, and more discreet and modest in her ways than any, but I still considered it safer to have her unable, and not merely unwilling, to harm me. . . . Furthermore, I made it a rule never to speak with her of anything but household matters or questions of conduct, or of the children.

Source: Leon Battista Alberti, "On the Family," in *The Family in Renaissance Florence*, trans. and ed. Renée N. Watkins. (Columbia, S.C.: 1969), pp. 208–13, as abridged in Julie O'Faolain and Lauro Martines, eds., *Not in God's Image: Women in History from the Greeks to the Victorians* (New York: 1973), pp. 187–88.

Questions for Analysis

1. For what reasons did Alberti argue that a wife should have no access to books or records?

2. Would you have expected humanism to make attitudes to women more liberal and "modern"? How do views like Alberti's challenge such assumptions?

---

cialized. For one thing, the competition among and within Italian city-states fostered a culture of display and conspicuous consumption. The relative weakness of the Church in Italy also contributed to the growth of secular power and a more worldly outlook. Italian bishoprics were small and relatively powerless compared to those north of the Alps, and Italian universities were much more independent of ecclesiastical supervision than those elsewhere. Even the papacy—restored to Rome only after Petrarca's death—was severely limited, not the least because the papacy's role as a political rival in central Italy compromised its moral authority. All these factors fostered the emergence of new aesthetics, ideals, and aspirations.

Renaissance Humanism

The most basic of Renaissance intellectual ideals is summarized in the term *humanism*. This was a program of study that aimed to replace the scholastic emphasis on logic and metaphysics with the study of language, literature, rhetoric, history, and ethics. The humanists always preferred ancient literature to the writings of more recent authors. Although some wrote in both Latin and the vernacular, most humanists regarded vernacular literature as a lesser diversion for the uneducated; serious scholarship and praiseworthy poetry could be written only in Latin or Greek. Latin,

The Humanists' Educational Program

These three selections illustrate the confidence placed by humanists in their elite educational program, and their conviction that it would be of supreme value to the state as well as to the individual students who pursued it. Not everyone agreed with the humanists' claims, however, and a good deal of self-promotion lies behind them.

Vergerius on Liberal Studies

We call those studies *liberal* which are worthy of a free man; those studies by which we attain and practice virtue and wisdom; that education which calls forth, trains, and develops those highest gifts of body and of mind which ennoble men, and which are rightly judged to rank next in dignity to virtue only.... It is, then, of the highest importance that even from infancy this aim, this effort, should constantly be kept alive in growing minds. For ... we shall not have attained wisdom in our later years unless in our earliest we have sincerely entered on its search. [P. P. Vergerius (1370–1444), *"Concerning Excellent Traits."*]

Alberti on the Importance of Literature

Letters are indeed so important that without them one would be considered nothing but a rustic, no matter how much a gentlemen [he may be by birth]. I'd much rather see a young nobleman with a book than with a falcon in his hand....

Be diligent, then, you young people, in your studies. Do all you can to learn about the events of the past that are worthy of memory. Try to understand all the useful things that have been passed on to you. Feed your minds on good maxims. Learn the delights of embellishing your souls with good morals. Strive to be kind and considerate [of others] when conducting civil business. Get to know those things human and divine that have been put at your disposal in books for good reason. Nowhere [else] will you find ... the elegance of a verse of Homer, or Virgil, or of some other excellent poet. You will find no field so delightful or flowering as in one of the orations of Demosthenes, Cicero, Livy, Xenophon, and other such pleasant and perfect orators. No effort is more fully compensated ... as the constant reading and rereading of good things. From such reading you will rise rich in good maxims and good arguments, strong in your ability to persuade others and get them to listen to you; among the citizens you will willingly be heard, admired, praised, and loved. [Leon Battista Alberti (1404–1472), *"On the Family."*]

moreover, had to be the classical Latin of Cicero and Virgil, not the evolving, changing Latin of the universities and the Church.

Renaissance humanists therefore condemned the living Latin of their scholastic contemporaries as a barbarous departure from ancient (and therefore "correct") standards of Latin style. Despite their belief that they were thereby reviving the study of the classics, the humanists actually contributed to Latin's demise. By insisting on ancient standards of grammar, syntax, and diction, they turned Latin into a fossilized language that ceased to have any direct relevance to daily life. They also contributed, ironically and unwittingly, to the ultimate triumph of the various European vernaculars as languages of intellectual and cultural life, and to the death of Latin as a common European language.

Bruni on the Humanist Curriculum

The foundations of all true learning must be laid in the sound and thorough knowledge of Latin: which implies study marked by a broad spirit, accurate scholarship, and careful attention to details. Unless this solid basis be secured it is useless to attempt to rear an enduring edifice. Without it the great monuments of literature are unintelligible, and the art of composition impossible. To attain this essential knowledge we must never relax our careful attention to the grammar of the language, but perpetually confirm and extend our acquaintance with it until it is thoroughly our own. . . .

But the wider question now confronts us, that of the subject matter of our studies, that which I have already called the realities of fact and principle, as distinct from literary form. . . . First among such studies I place History: a subject which must not on any account be neglected by one who aspires to true cultivation. . . . For the careful study of the past enlarges our foresight in contemporary affairs and affords to citizens and to monarchs lessons . . . in the or-dering of public policy. From History, also, we draw our store of examples of moral precepts. . . .

The great Orators of antiquity must by all means be included. Nowhere do we find the virtues more warmly ex-tolled, the vices so fiercely decried. From them we may learn, also, how to express consolation, encouragement, dissuasion or advice. . . .

Familiarity with the great poets of antiquity is essential to any claim to true education. For in their writings we find deep speculations upon Nature, and upon the Causes and Origins of things, which must carry weight with us both from their antiquity and from their authorship. . . .

Proficiency in literary form, not ac-companied by broad acquaintance with facts and truths, is a barren attainment; whilst information, however vast, which lacks all grace of expression would seem to be put under a bushel or partly thrown away. . . . Where, however, this double capacity exists—breadth of learn-ing and grace of style—we allow the highest title to distinction and to abiding fame. . . . [Leonardo Bruni (1369–1444), *"Concerning the Study of Literature."*]

Sources: Vergerius and Bruni: William Harrison Woodward, ed., *Vittorino da Feltre and Other Humanist Educators* (London: 1897), pp. 96–110, 124–29, 132–33. Alberti: Eric Cochrane and Julius Kirshner, eds., *University of Chicago Readings in Western Civilization.* Vol. 5: *The Renaissance* (Chicago: 1986), pp. 81–82.

Questions for Analysis

1. What is the purpose of education, according to these authorities? What elements do their programs share? What are their potential areas of contention?

2. Why did humanists such as Leonardo Bruni consider the study of history essential to education?

Humanists were also convinced that their own educational program—which placed the study of Latin language and literature at the core of the curriculum and then encouraged the study of Greek—was the best way to produce virtuous citizens and able public officials. And because women were excluded from Italian political life, the education of women was therefore of little concern to most humanists, although some aristocratic women did acquire humanist training. Here again there are paradoxes: for as more and more Italian city-states fell into the hands of autocratic rulers, the humanist educational curriculum lost its immediate connection to the republican ideals of Italian political life. Nevertheless, humanists never lost their conviction that the study of the "humanities" (as the humanist curriculum came to be known) was the best way to produce political leaders.

THE RENAISSANCE OF ITALY

Although the Renassiance eventually became a Europe-wide intellectual and artistic movement, it developed first and most distinctively in Italy. Understanding why this happened is important not only to explaining the origins of this movement, but also to understanding its essential characteristics.

The most fundamental reason was that, after the Black Death, northern Italy became the most urbanized region of Europe. Moreover, Italian aristocrats customarily lived in urban centers rather than in rural castles, and consequently became more fully involved in urban public affairs than their counterparts north of the Alps. Elsewhere in Europe, most aristocrats lived on the income from their landed estates, while rich town dwellers gained their living from trade; but in Italy, many town-dwelling aristocrats engaged in banking or mercantile enterprises while many rich mercantile families imitated the manners of the aristocracy. The noted Florentine family the Medici, for example, were originally physicians and apothecaries (as their name suggests). But they eventually made a fortune in banking and commerce, and were able to assimiliate into the aristocracy.

The results of these developments are tied to the history of the new humanist education mentioned above. Not only was there great demand for the skills of reading and accounting necessary to become a successful merchant, but the richest and most prominent families sought above all to find teachers who would impart to their sons the knowledge and skills necessary to cutting a figure in society and speaking with authority in public affairs. Consequently, Italy produced a large number of lay educators, many of whom not only taught students but also demonstrated their learning by producing political and ethical treatises and works of literature. Italian schools and tutors accordingly turned out the best-educated urban elites in all of Europe, men who became wealthy, knowledgeable patrons ready to invest in the cultivation of new ideas and new forms of literary and artistic expression.

A second reason why late-medieval Italy was the birthplace of an intellectual and artistic renaissance has to do with its vexed political situation. Unlike France, England, Spain, and the kingdoms of Scandinavia and eastern Europe, Italy had no unifying political institutions. Italians therefore looked to the classical past for their time of glory, dreaming of a day when Rome would be, again, the center of the world. They boasted that ancient Roman monuments were omnipresent in their landscape, and that classical Latin literature referred to cities and sites they recognized as their own.

Italians were particularly intent on reappropriating their classical heritage because they were seeking to establish an independent cultural identity that could help them oppose the intellectual and political supremacy of France. The removal of the papacy to Avignon for most of the fourteenth century and the subsequent Great Schism (Chapter 10) had heightened antagonism between the city-states of Italy and the burgeoning nation-states and empires of the Continent. This coincided with a rejection of the scholasticism taught in northern Europe's universities, and the embrace of the intellectual alternatives offered by new readings of classical sources. As Roman literature and learning took hold in the imaginations of Italy's intellectuals, so too did Roman art and architecture, for Roman models could help Italians create an artistic alternative to French Gothic, just as Roman learning offered an intellectual alternative to the scholasticism of Paris.

Finally, the Italian Renaissance could not have occurred without the underpinning of Italian wealth gained through the increasing commercial ventures described in Chapter 11. This meant that talented men seeking employment and patronage were more likely to stay at home than

POPE JULIUS II (r. 1503–15). This portrait of one of the most powerful popes of the Renaissance—it was he who commissioned Michelangelo's paintings in the Sistine Chapel—was executed by Raffaello Sanzio da Urbino, known as Raphael (1483–1520). The acorns atop the posts of the throne are visual puns on the pope's family name, della Rovere ("of the oak"). ■ *What impression of the pope's personality does this portrait convey?*

to seek opportunities abroad. Intensive investment in culture also arose from an intensification of urban pride and the concentration of individual and family wealth in urban areas. Cities themselves became the primary patrons of art and learning in the fourteenth century. During the fifteenth century, however, when most city-states succumbed to the hereditary rule of powerful dynasties, patronage was monopolized by the princely aristocracy. Among these great princes were the popes in Rome, who controlled the Papal States, employed the greatest artists of the day, and for a few decades made Rome the artistic capital of Europe.

LITERARY AND INTELLECTUAL ACTIVITY

We have already encountered the man who strove to leave behind "the middle age" of his own time, and who is therefore considered the founder of the Renaissance movement: Francesco Petrarca (1304–1374). Petrarch was an ordained priest, but he believed that the scholastic theology taught in universities was entirely misguided, because it concentrated on abstract speculation rather than the achievement of virtue and ethical conduct. Instead, he felt that the truly Christian writer must cultivate literary eloquence, and so inspire others to do good through the pursuit of beauty and truth. For him, the best models of eloquence were to be found in the classical texts of Latin literature, which were doubly valuable because they were also filled with ethical wisdom. Petrarch dedicated himself, therefore, to rediscovering such texts and to writing his own poems and moral treatises in a Latin style modeled on classical authors. But Petrarch was also a prolific vernacular poet. His Italian sonnets—which spawned a new literary genre—were written in praise of his semi-fictional beloved, Laura, in the chivalrous style of the troubadours. They were widely admired and imitated, inspiring poets in other European vernaculars. William Shakespeare (1564–1616) would later adopt the form.

Petrarch's ultimate ideal for human conduct was a solitary life of contemplation and asceticism. But subsequent Italian thinkers and scholars, located mainly in Florence, developed a different vision of life's true purpose. For them, the goal of classical education was civic. Humanists such as Leonardo Bruni (c. 1370–1444) and Leon Battista Alberti (1404–1472) agreed with Petrarch on the importance of eloquence and the value of classical literature, but they also taught that man's nature equipped him for action, for usefulness to his family and society, and for serving the state—

ideally a city-state after the Florentine model. In their view, ambition and the quest for glory were noble impulses that ought to be encouraged and channeled toward these ends. They also refused to condemn the accumulation of material possessions, arguing that the history of human progress is inseparable from the human dominion of the earth and its resources.

Many of the humanists' civic ideals are expressed Alberti's treatise *On the Family* (1443), in which he argued that the nuclear family was the fundamental unit of the city-state and should be governed in such a way as to further the city-state's political, social, and economic goals. Alberti accordingly argued that the family should mirror the city-state's own organization, and he thus consigned women—who, in reality, governed the household—to child-bearing, child-rearing, and subservience to men (see **Analyzing Primary Sources** on page 375). He asserted, furthermore, that women should play no role whatsoever in the public sphere. Although such dismissals of women's abilities were fiercely resisted by actual women, the humanism of the Renaissance was characterized by a pervasive denigration of them—a denigration often mirrored in the works of classical literature that these humanists so much admired.

The Emergence of Textual Scholarship

The humanists of Florence also went far beyond Petrarch in their knowledge of classical (especially Greek) literature and philosophy. In this they were aided by a number of Byzantine scholars who had migrated to Italy in the first half of the fifteenth century and who gave instruction in the language. There were also attempts on the part of Italians to acquire Greek masterpieces for themselves, which often involved journeys back to Constantinople. In 1423, for example, one adventurous scholar managed to bring back 238 manuscript books, among them rare works of Sophocles, Euripides, and Thucydides, all of which were quickly paraphrased in Latin and thus made accessible to western Europeans for the first time. By 1500, most of the Greek classics, including the writings of Plato, the dramatists, and the historians, had been translated and were more widely available than they had ever been, even in their own day.

This influx of new texts spurred a new interest in textual criticism. A pioneer in this activity was Lorenzo Valla (1407–1457). Born in Rome and active primarily as a secretary to the king of Naples and Sicily, Valla had no allegiance to the republican ideals of the Florentine humanists. Instead, he turned his skills to the painstaking analysis of Greek and Latin texts in order to show how the thorough study of language could discredit old assumptions about these texts' meanings and even unmask some texts as forgeries. For example, propagandists argued that the papacy's claim to secular power in Europe derived from rights granted to the bishop of Rome by the emperor Constantine in the fourth century, enshrined in the so-called Donation of Constantine. By analyzing the language of this spurious document, Valla proved that it could not have been written in the time of Constantine because it contained more recent Latin usages and vocabulary. He concluded that it had in fact been the work of a papal supporter active many centuries after Constantine's death. This demonstration not only discredited the more traditional methods of scholasticism, it introduced the concept of anachronism into all subsequent textual study and historical thought. Indeed, Valla even applied his expert knowledge of Greek to elucidating the meaning of Saint Paul's letters, which he believed had been obscured by Jerome's Latin translation (Chapter 6). This work was to prove an important link between Italian Renaissance scholarship and the subsequent Christian humanism of the north, which in turn fed into the Reformation (see Chapter 13).

PICO DELLA MIRANDOLA. When this young nobleman arrived in Florence at the age of nineteen, he was said to have been "of beauteous feature and shape." This contemporary portrait has often been attributed to Botticelli.

Renaissance Neoplatonism

In the wake of these discoveries, Italian thought became dominated by a new interest in the philosophy of Plato (Chapter 4) and in the Neoplatonism of Plotinus (Chapter 6). So many intellectuals were engaged in the study of Plato that scholars used to believe that there was even a "Platonic Academy" in Florence; but in reality, the work of intellectuals like Marsilio Ficino (1433–1499) and Giovanni Pico della Mirandola (1463–1494) was informally fostered by the patronage of the wealthy Cosimo de' Medici. From the standpoint of posterity, Ficino's greatest achievement was his translation of Plato's works into Latin, which made them widely available to Europeans for the first time. Ficino himself regarded his *Hermetic Corpus*, a collection of passages drawn from ancient mystical writings, to be his greatest contribution to learning. It contained, among other texts, portions of the Hebrew Kabbalah.

Ficino's Platonic philosophy moved away from the ethics of civic humanism. He taught that the individual should look primarily to the salvation of the immortal soul from its "always miserable" mortal body: a very Platonic idea. His disciple Pico likewise rejected the mundanity of public affairs and shared his teacher's penchant for extracting and combining snippets taken out of context from ancient mystical tracts. But he also argued that man has the capacity to achieve union with God through the exercise of his unique talents, a glory that can be attained in life as well as in death.

The Influence of Machiavelli

The greatness of these humanist scholars lay not in their originality but in their efforts to popularize aspects of ancient thought. But none of them was so influential as the era's greatest philosphical pragmatist, the Florentine Niccolò Machiavelli (1469–1527). Machiavelli's political writings both reflect the unstable condition of Italy and strive to address it. Since the end of the fifteenth century, Italy had become the arena of bloody international struggles. Both France and Spain had invaded the peninsula and were competing for the allegiance of the Italian city-states, which in turn were torn by internal dissension.

In 1498, Machiavelli became a prominent official in the government of the Florentine Republic, set up four years earlier when the French invasion had led to the expulsion of the Medici. His duties largely involved diplomatic missions to other Italian city-states. While in Rome, he became fascinated with the attempt of Cesare Borgia, son of Pope Alexander VI, to create his own principality in central Italy.

Analyzing Primary Sources

Machiavelli's Patriotism

These passages are from the concluding chapter to Machiavelli's treatise The Prince. *Like the book itself, they are addressed to Lorenzo de' Medici, head of Florence's most powerful family. In it, Machiavelli laments Italy's "barbarian occupation" by foreign powers, by which he means the invading armies of France, Spain, and the Holy Roman Empire. He may also be alluding to the many companies of foreign mercenaries that fought for Italy's various city-states.*

eflecting on the matters set forth above and considering within myself whether the times were propitious in Italy at present to honor a new prince and whether there is at hand the matter suitable for a prudent and virtuous leader to mold in a new form, giving honor to himself and benefit to the citizens of the country, I have arrived at the opinion that all circumstances now favor such a prince, and I cannot think of a time more propitious for him than the present. If, as I said, it was necessary in order to make apparent the virtue of Moses, that the people of Israel should be enslaved in Egypt, and that the Persians should be oppressed by the Medes to provide an opportunity to illustrate the greatness and the spirit of Cyrus, and that the Athenians should be scattered in order to show the excellence of Theseus, thus at the present time, in order to reveal the valor of an Italian spirit, it was essential that Italy should fall to her present low estate, more enslaved than the Hebrews, more servile than the Persians, more disunited than the Athenians, leaderless and lawless, beaten, despoiled, lacerated, overrun and crushed under every kind of misfortune. . . . So Italy now, left almost lifeless, awaits the coming of one who will heal her wounds, putting an end to the sacking and looting in Lombardy and the spoliation and extortions in the Realm of Naples and Tuscany, and cleanse her sores that have been so long festering. Behold how she prays God to send her some one to redeem her from the cruelty and insolence of the barbarians. See how she is ready and willing to follow any banner so long as there be someone to take it up. Nor has she at present any hope of finding her redeemer save only in your illustrious house [the Medici] which has been so highly exalted both by its own merits and by fortune and which has been favored by God and the church, of which it is now ruler. . . .

This opportunity, therefore, should not be allowed to pass, and Italy, after such a long wait, must be allowed to behold her redeemer. I cannot describe the joy with which he will be received in all these provinces which have suffered so much from the foreign deluge, nor with what thirst for vengeance, nor with what firm devotion, what solemn delight, what tears! What gates could be closed to him, what people could deny him obedience, what envy could withstand him, what Italian could withhold allegiance from him? THIS BARBARIAN OCCUPATION STINKS IN THE NOSTRILS OF ALL OF US. Let your illustrious house then take up this cause with the spirit and the hope with which one undertakes a truly just enterprise. . . .

Source: Niccolò Machiavelli, *The Prince,* trans. and ed. Thomas G. Bergin (Arlington Heights, IL: 1947), pp. 75–76, 78.

Questions for Analysis

1. Why does Machiavelli argue that Italy needed the type of ruler he described in *The Prince*?

2. According to Machiavelli, what was wrong with the Italy of his own day? What does "patriotism" mean for him?

3. How does Machiavelli use historical precedents and parallels to make his argument?

He noted with approval Cesare's ruthlessness and his complete subordination of personal ethics to political ends. In 1512, when the Medici returned to overthrow the republic of Florence, Machiavelli was deprived of his position. Disappointed and embittered, he retired to the country and devoted his energies to the articulation of a new political philosophy that he hoped would earn him a powerful job.

Machiavelli remains a controversial figure. Some modern scholars, like many of his own contemporary readers, see him as disdainful of conventional morality, interested solely in the acquisition and exercise of power as an end in itself. Others see him as an Italian patriot, who viewed princely tyranny as the only way to liberate Italy from its foreign conquerors. Still others see him as influenced by

THE STATES OF ITALY, c. 1494. This map shows the divisions of Italy on the eve of the French invasion in 1494. Contemporary observers often described Italy as being divided among five great powers: Milan, Venice, Florence, the Papal States, and the Kingdom of the Two Sicilies (based in Naples). ▪ *Which of these powers would have been most capable of expanding their territories?* ▪ *Which neighboring states would have been most threatened by such attempts at expansion?* ▪ *Why would Florence and the Papal States so often find themselves in conflict with each other?*

on Livy, which drew on the works of that Roman historian, he praised the ancient Roman Republic as a model for his own contemporaries, lauding constitutional government, equality among citizens, and the subordination of religion to the service of the state. There is little doubt, in fact, that Machiavelli was a committed believer in the free city-state as the ideal form of human government. But Machiavelli also wrote *The Prince*, "a handbook for tyrants" in the eyes of his critics, and he dedicated this work to Lorenzo, son of Piero de' Medici, whose family had overthrown the Florentine republic that Machiavelli himself had served.

Because *The Prince* has been so much more widely read than the *Discourses*, interpretations of Machiavelli's political thought have often mistaken the former as an endorsement of power for its own sake. Machiavelli's real position was quite different. In the political chaos of early-sixteenth-century Italy, Machiavelli saw the likes of Cesare Borgia as the only hope for revitalizing the spirit of independence among his contemporaries, and so making Italy fit, eventually, for self-governance. However dark his vision of human nature, Machiavelli never ceased to hope that his Italian contemporaries would rise up, expel their French and Spanish conquerors, and restore ancient traditions of liberty and equality. He regarded a period of despotism as a necessary step toward that end, not as a permanent and desirable form of government.

Saint Augustine, who understood that in a fallen world populated by sinful people, a ruler's good intentions do not guarantee that his policies will have good results. Accordingly, Machiavelli insisted that a prince's actions must be judged by their consequences and not by their intrinsic moral quality. He argued that "the necessity of preserving the state will often compel a prince to take actions which are opposed to loyalty, charity, humanity, and religion. . . . So far as he is able, a prince should stick to the path of good but, if the necessity arises, he should know how to follow evil."

On the surface, Machiavelli's two great works of political analysis appear to contradict each other. In his *Discourses*

The Ideal of the Courtier

Far more congenial to contemporary tastes than the shockingly frank political theories of Machiavelli were the guidelines for proper aristocratic conduct offered in *The Book of the Courtier* (1528), by the diplomat and nobleman Baldassare Castiglione. This forerunner of modern handbooks of etiquette stands in sharp contrast to earlier treatises on civic humanism. Whereas Bruni and Alberti taught the sober virtues of strenuous service on behalf of the city-state, Castiglione taught how to attain the elegant and

THE IMPACT OF PERSPECTIVE. Masaccio's painting *The Trinity with the Virgin* illustrates the startling sense of depth made possible by observing the rules of perspective.

exploits celebrated in the French *Song of Roland* (Chapter 8). Yet this work differs radically from previous chivalric epics, not least because it is totally devoid of heroic idealism. Ariosto wrote to make readers laugh and to charm them with descriptions of natural beauties and the passions of lovers. His work embodies the disillusionment of the later Renaissance, and the tendency to seek consolation in the pursuit of pleasure and aesthetic delight.

RENAISSANCE ARTS

Without question, the most enduring legacy of the Italian Renaissance has been the contributions of its artists, particularly those who embraced new techniques and approaches to painting. We have already noted (Chapter 10) the creative and economic opportunities afforded by this medium, which freed artists from having to work on site and on commission: paintings executed on wooden panels are portable—unlike wall paintings—and can be displayed in different settings, reach different markets, and be more widely distributed. To these benefits, the artists of Italy added an important technical ingredient: mastery of a vanishing (one-point) perspective that gave to painting an illusion of three dimensional space. Fifteenth-century artists also experimented with effects of light and shade, and studied intently the anatomy and proportions of the human body.

Meanwhile, increasing private wealth and the growth of lay patronage opened up new markets and created a huge demand for a diverse array of visual narratives: not only religious images, which were as important as ever, but the depiction of classical subjects. Portraiture also came into its own, as princes and merchants alike sought to glorify themselves and their families. The use of oil paints, a medium that had been pioneered in Flanders, further revolutionized fifteenth-century painting styles. Because oil does not dry as quickly as water-based pigments, a painter can work more slowly, taking time with the more difficult parts of a picture and making corrections as he or she goes along.

seemingly effortless skills necessary for advancement in Italy's princely courts. More than anyone else, Castiglione developed and popularized a set of talents now associated with the "Renaissance man": one accomplished in many different pursuits, witty, canny, and stylish. Castiglione also eschewed the misogyny of the humanists by stressing the ways in which court ladies could rise to influence and prominence through the graceful exercise of their womanly powers. Widely read throughout Europe, Castiglione's *Courtier* set the standard for polite behavior into the nineteenth century.

The literature of Renaissance Italy was not entirely devoted to the philosophy of political advancement. Machiavelli himself wrote delightful short stories and an engagingly bawdy play, the *Mandragola*; the great artist Michelangelo (see below) wrote many masterful sonnets; and Ludovico Ariosto (1474–1533), the most eminent of sixteenth-century Italian poets, wrote a lengthy verse narrative called *Orlando Furioso* (The Madness of Roland), a retelling of the heroic

Painting in Florence

In the fifteenth century, the majority of the great painters were Florentines. First among them was the precocious Masaccio (1401–1428) who, although he died at the age of only twenty-seven, inspired the work of artists for the next century. Masaccio's greatness as a painter rested on his

The Blending of Classical and Christian

The paintings known today as *The Birth of Venus* (image A) and *The Madonna of the Pomegranate* (image B) were both executed by Boticelli in Florence between the years 1485–87. Separately and together, they exhibit the artist's signature devotion to blending classical and Christian motifs by using ideas associated with the pagan past to illuminate sacred stories. For example, Neo-platonic philosophers like Ficino taught that all pagan myths prefigure Christian truths—including the story that Aphrodite, goddess of love, was miraculously engendered from the foam of the sea by the god of Time. This also helps to

A. *The Birth of Venus.*

successful employment of one-point perspective and his use of dramatic lighting effects. Both are evident in his painting of the Trinity, where the body of the crucified Christ appears to be thrust forward by the impassive figure of God the Father, while the Virgin's gaze directly engages the viewer.

Masaccio's best-known successor was Sandro Botticelli (1445–1510), who was equally drawn to classical and Christian subjects. Botticelli excels in depicting graceful motion and the sensuous pleasures of nature. He is most famous today for paintings that evoke classical mythology without any overtly Christian frame of reference.

explain the visual reference to a pomegranate in the painting of the Virgin holding the infant Jesus. In Greek mythology, the pomegranate was the fruit whose seeds were eaten by Persephone, daughter of the goddess of fertility, when she was sent to the Underworld to become the bride of Hades. Because she had eaten six of these seeds, Persephone was allowed to return to her mother Demeter for only part of the year; in the winter months, consequently, the Earth becomes less fertile, because Demeter is in mourning for her child.

B. *The Madonna of the Pomegranate.*

Questions for Analysis

1. Scholars have recently argued that *The Birth of Venus* is an allegory of Christian love that also prefigures the Blessed Virgin's immaculate conception and sinless nature. How would you go about proving this? What elements in this painting and in the myth of Aphrodite's birth lend themselves to that interpretation?

2. In what ways can the cyclical story of Jesus' death and resurrection, which Christians celebrate each year, be linked to the Greek myth invoked by *The Madonna of the Pomegranate*?

3. Like many artists, Botticelli used the same models for an array of different pictures. Do you recognize the resemblance between the Virgin and Venus? How does the depiction of the same young woman in these two different contexts underscore the relationship between pagan mythology and Christian sacred history?

For centuries, these were misunderstood as expressions of Renaissance "paganism," but they have more recently been unmasked as Christian allegories whose ancient deities represent aspects of later Christian ideas (see **Interpreting Visual Evidence**).

The most technically adventurous and versitile artist of this period was Leonardo da Vinci (1452–1519). Leonardo personifies our ideal of the Renaissance man: he was a painter, architect, musician, mathematician, engineer, and inventor. The illegitimate son of a notary, Leonardo set up

THE VIRGIN OF THE ROCKS. This painting reveals Leonardo's interest in the variety of human faces and facial expressions, and in natural settings.

about, finally accepting the patronage of the French king, Francis I, under whose auspices he lived and worked until his death.

Leonardo's approach to painting was that it should be the most accurate possible imitation of nature. He based his work on his own detailed observations of a blade of grass, the wing of a bird, a waterfall. He obtained human corpses for dissection and reconstructed in drawing the minutest features of anatomy, carrying this knowledge over to his paintings.

Indeed, Leonardo was convinced of the essential divinity in all living things. It is not surprising, therefore, that he was a vegetarian and that he went to the marketplace to buy caged birds, which he released to their native habitat. *The Virgin of the Rocks* typifies not only his marvelous technical skill but also his passion for science and his belief in the universe as a well-ordered place. The figures are arranged geometrically, with every stone and plant depicted in accurate detail. *The Last Supper*, painted on the refectory walls of a monastery in Milan (and now in an advanced state of decay) is a study of human psychology. A serene Christ, resigned to his terrible fate, has just announced to his disciples that one of them will betray him. The artist succeeds in portraying the mingled emotions of surprise, horror, and guilt on the faces of the disciples as they gradually perceive the meaning of their master's statement. He also implicates the painting's viewers in this dramatic scene, since they too dine alongside Christ, in the very same room.

an artist's shop in Florence by the time he was twenty-five and gained the patronage of the Medici ruler, Lorenzo the Magnificent. But Leonardo had a weakness: he worked slowly, and he had difficulty finishing anything. This naturally displeased Lorenzo and other Florentine patrons, who regarded artists as craftsmen who worked on commission, and on their patrons' time—not their own. Leonardo, however, strongly objected to this view; he considered himself to be an inspired, independent innovator. He therefore left Florence in 1482 and went to work for the court of the Sforza dictators in Milan, where he was given freer rein in structuring his time and work (see page 390). He remained there until the French invasion of 1499; he then wandered

The Venetian and Roman Schools

The innovations of Florentine artists were widely imitated. By the end of the fifteenth century, they had influenced a group of painters active in the wealthy city of Venice, among them Tiziano Vecelli, better known as Titian (c. 1490–1576).

THE LAST SUPPER. This fresco on the refectory wall of the monastery of Santa Marie della Grazie in Milan is a testament to both the powers and limitations of Leonardo's artistry. It skillfully employs the techniques of one-point perspective to create the illusion that Jesus and his disciples are actually dining at the monastery's head table; but because Leonardo had not mastered the techniques of fresco painting, he applied tempera pigments to a dry wall which had been coated with a sealing agent. As a result, the painting's colors began to fade just years after its completion. By the middle of the sixteenth century, it had seriously deteriorated. Large portions of it are now invisible.

DOGE FRANCESCO VENIER (1555). Titian served as the official painter of the Venetian Republic for sixty years. This superb portrait of Venice's ruler shows the artist's mastery of light and color while also displaying the mastery and wealth of his patron.

Leonardo was a naturalist, Michelangelo was an idealist, despite the harsh political and material realities of the conditions in which he worked. He was also a polymath: painter, sculptor, architect, poet—and he expressed himself in all these forms with a similar power. At the center of all of his work—as at the center of Renaissance humanism—is the male figure, the embodied male mind.

Michelangelo's greatest achievements in painting appear in a single location, the Sistine Chapel of the Vatican palace, yet they are products of two different periods in the artist's life and consequently exemplify two different artistic styles and outlooks on the human condition. More famous are the extraordinary frescoes painted on the ceiling from 1508 to 1512, depicting scenes from the book of Genesis. All the panels in this series, including *The Creation of Adam*, exemplify the young artist's commitment to classical artistic principles. Correspondingly, all affirm the sublimity of the Creation and the heroic qualities of humankind. But a quarter of a century later, when Michelangelo returned to work in the Sistine Chapel, both his style and mood had changed dramatically. In the enormous *Last Judgment*, a fresco done for the Chapel's altar wall in 1536, Michelangelo repudiated classical restraint and substituted a style that emphasized tension and distortion to communicate the older man's

Many of Titian's paintings evoke the luxurious, pleasure-loving life of this thriving commercial center. For although they copied Florentine techniques, most Venetian painters showed little of that city's concerns for philosophical issues and religious allegory. Their aim was to appeal to the senses by painting idyllic landscapes and sumptuous portraits of the rich and powerful. In the subordination of form and meaning to color and elegance they may have mirrored the tastes of the men for whom they worked.

Rome, too, became a major artistic center in this era, and a place where the Florentine school exerted a more potent influence. Among its eminent painters was Raffaello Sanzio (1483–1520) or Raphael, a native of Urbino. Although Raphael was influenced by Leonardo, he cultivated a more spiritual and philosophical approach to his subjects, suggestive of Boticelli. As we noted in Chapter 4, his fresco *The School of Athens* depicts both the harmony and the differences of Platonic and Aristotelian thought (see page 114). It also includes a number of Raphael's contemporaries as models. The image of Plato is actually a portrait of Leonardo, while the architect Donato Bramante (c. 1444–1514) stands in for the geometer Euclid, and Michelangelo for the philosopher Heraclitus.

Michelangelo Buonarroti (1475–1564), who spent many decades in Rome, was actually a native of Florence. If

SELF-PORTRAIT OF THE ARTIST AS AN OLD MAN: DETAIL FROM THE LAST JUDGMENT. When Michelangelo returned to the Sistine Chapel to paint this fresco on the wall behind the main altar, he emphasized different aspects of humanity: not the youthful heroism of the new-born Adam, but the grotesque weakness of the aging body. Here, St. Bartholomew holds his own flayed skin (tradition held that he had been skinned alive) – but the face is that of Michelangelo himself.

pessimistic conception of humanity as wracked with fear, guilt, and frailty. He included himself in it: but unlike Raphael's, his self-portrait is a doomed soul whose flayed skin is all that remains of worldly ambition.

Renaissance Sculpture

Sculpture was not a new medium for artists, the way that oil painting was, but it too was an important area of Renaissance innovation. Statues were not only incorporated into columns or doorways or as effigies on tombs; for the first time since late antiquity they became figures "in the round." By freeing sculpture from its bondage to architecture, the Renaissance reestablished it as a separate, secular art form.

The first great master of Renaissance sculpture was Donatello (c. 1386–1466). His bronze statue of David, triumphant over the head of the slain Goliath, is the first free-standing nude of the period. Yet this David is clearly an agile adolescent rather than a muscular Greek athlete—like that of Michelangelo—whose *David*, executed in 1501, was a public expression of Florentine ideals, not merely graceful but heroic. Michelangelo regarded sculpture as the most exalted of the arts because it allowed the artist to imitate God most fully in recreating human forms. Furthermore, in Michelangelo's view, the most God-like sculptor disdained slavish naturalism: anyone can make a plaster cast of a human figure, but only an inspired creative genius can endow his sculpted figures with a sense of life. Accordingly, Michelangelo's sculpture subordinated reality to the force of his imagination and sought to express his ideals in ever more astonishing forms. He also insisted on working in marble—the "noblest" sculptural material—and created a figure twice as large as life. By sculpting a serenely confident young man at the peak of physical

SELF-PORTRAIT OF THE ARTIST AS A YOUNG MAN: DETAIL FROM *THE SCHOOL OF ATHENS.* We have already analyzed aspects of Raphael's famous group portrait of the Greek philosophers, with Plato and Aristotle at their center: see page 114 of Chapter 4. In addition to featuring his own contemporaries as models—including the artists Leonardo and Michelangelo and the architect Bramante—Raphael put himself in the picture, too. ▪ *What messages does this choice convey?*

fitness, Michelangelo celebrated the Florentine republic's own determination in resisting tyrants and upholding ideals of civic justice.

Yet the serenity seen in *David* is no longer prominent in the works of Michelangelo's later life, when, as in his painting, he began to explore the use of anatomical distortion

THE CREATION OF ADAM. This is one of a series of frescoes painted on the ceiling of the Sistine Chapel of the Vatican palace in Rome, executed by Michelangelo over a period of many years and in circumstances of extreme physical hardship. It has since become an iconic image. ▪ *How might it be said to capture Renaissance ideals?*

THE POWER AND VULNERABILITY OF THE MALE BODY. Donatello's *David* (left) was the first free-standing nude executed since antiquity. It shows the Hebrew leader as an adolescent youth, and is a little over 5 feet tall. The *David* by Michelangelo (center) stands thirteen feet high, and was placed prominently in front of Florence's city hall to proclaim the city's power and humanistic values. Michelangelo's *Descent from the Cross* (right), which shows Christ's broken body in the arms of the elderly Nicodemus, was made by the sculptor for his own tomb. (The gospels describe Nicodemus as a Pharisee who became a follower of Jesus and who was present at his death.) ▪ *Why would Michelangelo choose this figure to represent himself?* ▪ *How does his representation of David—and the context in which this figure was displayed—compare to that of Donatello?*

to create effects of emotional intensity. While his statues remained awesome in scale, they also communicate rage, depression, and sorrow. The culmination of this trend is his unfinished but intensely moving *Descent from the Cross*, a depiction of an old man (the sculptor himself) grieving over the distorted, slumping body of the dead Christ.

Renaissance Architecture

To a much greater extent than either sculpture or painting, Renaissance architecture had its roots in the past. The Gothic style pioneered in northern France (Chapter 9) had seldom found a friendly reception in Italy; most of the buildings constructed there during the Middle Ages

were Romanesque in style, and the great architects of the Renaissance generally adopted their building plans from these structures—some of which they believed (mistakenly) to be ancient rather than medieval. They also copied decorative devices from the authentic ruins of ancient Rome.

Renaissance buildings also emphasize geometrical proportion. Italian architects of this era, under the influence of Neoplatonism, concluded that certain mathematical ratios reflect the harmony of the universe. For example, the proportions of the human body serve as the basis for the proportions of the quintessential Renaissance building: St. Peter's Basilica in Rome. Designed by some of the most celebrated architects of the time, including Bramante and Michelangelo, it is still one of the largest buildings in the world. Yet it seems smaller than a Gothic cathedral because

Analyzing Primary Sources

Leonardo da Vinci Applies for a Job

Few sources illuminate the tensions between Renaissance ideals and realities better than the résumé of accomplishments submitted by Leonardo da Vinci to a prospective employer, Ludovico Sforza of Milan. In the following letter, Leonardo explains why he deserves to be appointed chief architect and military engineer in the duke's household administration. He got the job, and moved to Milan in 1481.

1. I have the kind of bridges that are extremely light and strong, made to be carried with great ease, and with them you may pursue, and, at any time, flee from the enemy; . . . and also methods of burning and destroying those of the enemy.

2. I know how, when a place is under attack, to eliminate the water from the trenches, and make endless variety of bridges . . . and other machines. . . .

3. . . . I have methods for destroying every rock or other fortress, even if it were built on rock, etc.

4. I also have other kinds of mortars [bombs] that are most convenient and easy to carry. . . .

5. And if it should be a sea battle, I have many kinds of machines that are most efficient for offense and defense. . . .

6. I also have means that are noiseless to reach a designated area by secret and tortuous mines. . . .

7. I will make covered chariots, safe and unattackable, which can penetrate the enemy with their artillery. . . .

8. In case of need I will make big guns, mortars, and light ordnance of fine and useful forms that are out of the ordinary.

9. If the operation of bombardment should fail, I would contrive catapults, mangonels, trabocchi [trebuchets], and other machines of marvelous efficacy and unusualness. In short, I can, according to each case in question, contrive various and endless means of offense and defense.

10. In time of peace I believe I can give perfect satisfaction that is equal to any other in the field of architecture and the construction of buildings. . . . I can execute sculpture in marble, bronze, or clay, and also in painting I do the best that can be done, and as well as any other, whoever he may be.

Having now, most illustrious Lord, sufficiently seen the specimens of all those who consider themselves master craftsmen of instruments of war, and that the invention and operation of such instruments are no different from those in common use, I shall now endeavor . . . to explain myself to your Excellency by revealing to your Lordship my secrets. . . .

Source: Excerpted from Leonardo da Vinci, *The Notebooks*, in *The Italian Renaissance Reader*, eds. Julia Conaway and Mark Mosa (Harmondsworth: 1987), pp. 195–196.

Questions for Analysis

1. Based on the qualifications highlighted by Leonardo in this letter, what can you conclude about the political situation in Milan and the priorities of its duke? What can you conclude about the state of military technologies in this period and the conduct of warfare?

2. What do you make of the fact that Leonardo mentions his artistic endeavors only at the end of the letter? Does this fact alter your opinion or impression of him? Why or why not?

---

it is built to human scale. The same artful proportions are evident in smaller-scale buildings, too, as in the aristocratic country houses designed by the northern Italian architect Andrea Palladio (1508–1580), who created secular miniatures of ancient temples (such as the Roman Pantheon) to glorify the aristocrats who dwelled within them.

The Waning of the Renaissance

The intensive intellectual and artistic activity that characterizes the Renaissance began to wane toward the end of the fifteenth century. The causes of this decline are varied. The French invasion of 1494 and the incessant warfare that

ST. PETER'S BASILICA, ROME. This eighteenth-century painting shows the massive interior of the Renaissance building. But were it not for the perspective provided by the tiny human figures, the human eye would be fooled into thinking this a much smaller space.

own courts, to patronize the arts, and to adorn their cities with luxurious buildings; but they were puppets of a foreign power and unable to inspire their retinues with a sense of vigorous cultural independence.

To these political disasters was added a waning of Italian prosperity. Italy's virtual monopoly of trade with Asia in the fifteenth century had been one of the chief economic underpinnings for Renaissance patronage, but the gradual shifting of trade routes from the Mediterranean to the Atlantic region (Chapter 11), slowly cost Italy its supremacy as the center of European trade. Warfare also contributed to Italy's economic hardships, as did Spanish financial exactions in Milan and Naples. As Italian wealth diminished, there was less and less of a surplus to support artistic endeavors. But by this time, Renaissance ideas and techniques were spreading from Italy to the rest of Europe; so even as Italy's political and economic power waned, its cultural and intellectual cachet lent it more prominence than it had enjoyed for centuries.

ensued were among the major factors. The French king, Charles VIII, viewed Italy as an attractive target for his expansive dynastic ambitions, and he led an army of 30,000 well-trained troops across the Alps to press his claims to the Duchy of Milan and the Kingdom of the Two Sicilies. Florence swiftly capitulated; within less than a year the French had swept down the peninsula and conquered Naples. By so doing, however, they aroused the suspicions of the rulers of Spain, who also claimed the territory of Sicily. An alliance among Spain, the Papal States, the Holy Roman Empire, Milan, and Venice finally forced Charles to withdraw from Italy.

But the respite was brief. Charles's successor, Louis XII, launched a second invasion, and from 1499 until 1529 warfare in Italy was virtually uninterrupted. Alliances and counteralliances followed each other in bewildering succession, but they managed only to prolong the hostilities. The worst disaster came in 1527, when rampaging troops under the command of the Spanish ruler and Holy Roman emperor, Charles V, sacked the city of Rome, causing enormous destruction. Only in 1529 did Charles finally manage to gain control over most of the Italian peninsula, putting an end to the fighting for a time. Once triumphant, he retained two of the largest portions of Italy for Spain—the Duchy of Milan and the Kingdom of the Two Sicilies—and installed favored princes as the rulers of almost all the other Italian political entities except for Venice and the Papal States. These protégés of the Spanish crown continued to preside over their

THE RENAISSANCE NORTH OF THE ALPS

Contacts between Italy and northern Europe continued throughout the fourteenth and fifteenth centuries. Italian merchants and financiers were familiar figures at northern courts; students from all over Europe studied at Italian universities such as Bologna or Padua; poets (including Geoffrey Chaucer, Chapter 10) and their works traveled to and from Italy; and northern soldiers were frequent participants in Italian wars. Only at the end of the fifteenth century, however, did the new currents of Italian Renaissance learning begin to be exported to Spain and northern Europe.

A variety of explanations have been offered for this delay. Northern European intellectual life in the later Middle Ages was dominated by universities such as Paris, Oxford, and Charles University in Prague, whose curricula focused on the study of philosophical logic and Christian theology. This approach left little room for the study of classical literature. In Italy, by contrast, universities were more often professional schools for law and medicine, and universities themselves exercised much less influence over intellectual life. As a result, a more secular, urban-oriented educational tradition took shape in Italy, within which Renaissance humanism was able to develop. Even in the sixteenth century, northern scholars influenced by Italian Renaissance ideals usually worked outside the university system under the patronage of kings and princes.

Before the sixteenth century, northern rulers were also less interested in patronizing artists and intellectuals than were the city-states and princes of Italy. In Italy, as we may have seen, such patronage was an important arena for competition between political rivals. In northern Europe, however, political units were larger and political rivals were fewer. It was therefore less necessary to use art for political purposes in a kingdom than it was in a city-state. In Florence, a statue erected in a central square would be seen by nearly all the city's residents. In Paris, such a statue would be seen by only a tiny minority of the French king's subjects. But in the sixteenth century, as northern nobles began to spend more time in residence at the royal court, could kings be reasonably certain that their patronage of artists and intellectuals would be noticed by those whom they were trying to impress.

Christian Humanism and the Career of Erasmus

The northern Renaissance was the product of the grafting of certain Italian Renaissance ideals onto preexisting northern traditions. This can be seen very clearly in the case of the most prominent northern Renaissance intellectual movement, Christian humanism. Although they shared the Italian humanists' rejection of scholasticism, northern Christian humanists more often sought ethical guidance from biblical and religious precepts rather than from Cicero or Virgil. Like their Italian counterparts, they sought wisdom from antiquity; but the antiquity they had in mind was Christian rather than classical—the antiquity, that is, of the New Testament and the early Church. Similarly, northern Renaissance artists were inspired by the accomplishments of Italian masters to learn classical techniques. But northern artists depicted classical subject matter far less frequently than did Italians, and almost never portrayed completely nude human figures.

Any discussion of the northern Renaissance must begin with the career of Desiderius Erasmus (c. 1469–1536). The illegitimate son of a priest, Erasmus was born near Rotterdam in the Netherlands. Later, as a result of his wide travels,

THE VILLA ROTUNDA. This country house, designed by Andrea Palladio (1508–1580), mimics the design of Rome's ancient Pantheon, the temple dedicated to "all the gods." But it is a human dwelling, built to human scale.

he became a virtual citizen of all northern Europe. Forced into a monastery against his will when he was a teenager, the young Erasmus found little formal instruction there but plenty of freedom to read what he liked. He devoured all the classics he could get his hands on and the writings of the Church Fathers (Chapter 6). When he was about thirty years old, he obtained permission to leave the monastery and enroll in the University of Paris, where he completed the requirements for the degree of bachelor of divinity.

But Erasmus subsequently rebelled against what he considered the arid learning of Parisian scholasticism. Nor did he ever serve actively as a priest. Instead he made his living from teaching, writing, and the proceeds of various ecclesiastical offices that required no pastoral duties. Ever on the lookout for new patrons, he traveled often to England, stayed once for three years in Italy, and resided in several different cities in Germany and the Netherlands before settling finally, toward the end of his life, in Basel (Switzerland). By means of a voluminous correspondence that he kept up with learned friends, Erasmus became the leader of a humanist coterie. And through the popularity of his numerous publications, he became the arbiter of northern European cultural tastes during his lifetime.

Erasmus's many-sided intellectual activity may be assessed from two different points of view: the literary and the doctrinal. As a Latin prose stylist, Erasmus was unequaled since the days of Cicero. Extraordinarily eloquent and witty, he reveled in tailoring his mode of discourse to fit his subject, creating dazzling verbal effects and coining puns that took on added meaning if the reader knew Greek as well as Latin. Above all, Erasmus excelled in the deft use of irony, poking fun at all and sundry, including himself. For example, in his *Colloquies* (from the Latin for "discussions") he

***ERASMUS* BY HANS HOLBEIN THE YOUNGER.** This is generally regarded as the most evocative portrait of the preeminent Christian humanist.

had a fictional character lament the evil signs of the times: "kings make war, priests strive to line their pockets, theologians invent syllogisms, monks roam outside their cloisters, the commons riot, and Erasmus writes colloquies."

But although Erasmus's urbane Latin style and humor earned him a wide audience on those grounds alone, he intended everything he wrote to promote what he called the "philosophy of Christ." Erasmus believed that the society of his day was caught up in corruption and immorality because people had lost sight of the simple teachings of the Gospels. Accordingly, he offered his contemporaries three different kinds of publication: clever satires meant to show people the error of their ways, serious moral treatises meant to offer guidance toward proper Christian behavior, and scholarly editions of basic Christian texts.

In the first category belong the works of Erasmus that are still widely read today: *The Praise of Folly* (1509), in which he ridiculed scholastic pedantry and dogmatism as well as ignorance and gullibility; and the *Colloquies* (1518), in which he held up contemporary religious practices for examination in a more serious but still pervasively

ironic tone. In such works, Erasmus let fictional characters do the talking; hence his own views can be determined only by inference. But in his second mode Erasmus did not hesitate to speak clearly in his own voice. The most prominent treatises in this second genre are the quietly eloquent *Handbook of the Christian Knight* (1503), which urged the laity to pursue lives of serene inward piety, and the *Complaint of Peace* (1517), which pleaded movingly for Christian pacifism. Erasmus's pacifism was one of his most deeply held values, and he returned to it again and again in his published works.

Despite the success of his writings, Erasmus considered textual scholarship his greatest achievement. Revering the authority of Augustine, Jerome, and Ambrose, he brought out reliable editions of all their works. He also used his extraordinary command of Latin and Greek to produce a more accurate edition of the New Testament. After reading Lorenzo Valla's *Notes on the New Testament* in 1504, Erasmus became convinced that nothing was more imperative than divesting the New Testament of the myriad errors in transcription and translation that had piled up in the course of preceding centuries—for no one could be a good Christian without being certain of exactly what Christ's message really was. Hence he spent ten years studying and comparing all the early Greek biblical manuscripts he could find in order to establish an authoritative text. When it finally appeared in 1516, Erasmus's Greek New Testament, published together with explanatory notes and his own new Latin translation, became one of the most important landmarks of biblical scholarship of all time. In the hands of Martin Luther, it would play a critical role in the early stages of the Reformation (see Chapter 13).

The Influence of Erasmus

One of Erasmus's closest friends, and a close second to him in distinction among Christian humanists, was the Englishman Sir Thomas More (1478–1535). Following a successful career as a lawyer and as speaker of the House of Commons, More was appointed lord chancellor of England in 1529. He was not long in this position, however, before he opposed the king's design to establish a national church under royal control, thus denying the supremacy of the pope (see Chapter 13). In 1534, when More refused to take an oath acknowledging Henry as head of the Church of England, he was thrown into the Tower of London and executed a year later. He is now revered as a Catholic martyr.

Much earlier, however, in 1516, More published the work for which he is best remembered, *Utopia* (Noplace). Purporting to describe an ideal community on an imaginary island, the book is really an Erasmian critique of the glaring abuses of the era—poverty undeserved and wealth unearned, drastic punishments, religious persecution, and the senseless slaughter of war. The inhabitants of Utopia hold all their goods in common, work only six hours a day so that all may have leisure for intellectual pursuits, and practice the natural virtues of wisdom, moderation, fortitude, and justice. Iron is the precious metal "because it is useful," war and monasticism do not exist, and toleration is granted to all who recognize the existence of God and the immortality of the soul. Although More advanced no explicit arguments in his *Utopia* in favor of Christianity, he probably meant to imply that if the Utopians could manage their society so well without the benefit of Christian revelation, Europeans who knew the Gospels ought to be able to do even better.

Erasmus and More head a long list of energetic and eloquent Christian humanists who made signal contributions to the collective enterprise of revolutionizing the study of early Christianity, and their achievements had a direct influence on Martin Luther and other Protestant reformers. Yet very few of them were willing to join Luther

in rejecting the fundamental principles on which the power of the Church was based. Most tried to remain within its fold while still espousing an ideal of inward piety and scholarly inquiry. But as the leaders of the Church grew less and less tolerant of dissent, even mild criticism came to seem like heresy. Erasmus himself died early enough to escape persecution, but several of his less fortunate followers lived on to suffer as victims of the Inquisition.

The Literature of the Northern Renaissance

Although Christian humanism would be severely challenged by the Reformation, the artistic Renaissance in the North continued throughout the sixteenth century. Poets in France and England vied with one another to adapt the elegant lyric forms pioneered by Petrarch, particularly the sonnet. The English poet Edmund Spenser (c. 1552–1599) also drew on the literary innovation of Ariosto's *Orlando Furioso*: his *Faerie Queene* is a similarly long chivalric romance that revels in sensuous imagery. Meanwhile, the more satirical side of Renaissance humanism was embraced by the French writer François Rabelais (*RA-beh-lay*, c. 1494–1553). Like Erasmus, whom he greatly admired, Rabelais began his career in the Church, but soon left the cloister to study medicine. A practicing physician, Rabelais interspersed his professional activities with literary endeavors, the most enduring of which is *Gargantua and Pantagruel*, a series of "chronicles" describing the lives and times of giants whose fabulous size and gross appetites serve as vehicles for much lusty humor. Like Erasmus, too, Rabelais satirized religious ceremonialism, scholasticism, superstition, and bigotry. But unlike Erasmus, who wrote in a highly cultivated classical Latin style comprehensible only to learned readers, Rabelais chose to address a far wider audience by writing in extremely crude French, and by glorifying every human impulse as natural and healthy.

SIR THOMAS MORE BY HANS HOLBEIN THE YOUNGER. Holbein's skill in rendering the gravity and interiority of his subject is matched by his masterful representation of the sumptuous chain of office, furred mantle, and velvet sleeves that indicate the political and professional status of Henry VIII's chancellor.

Northern Architecture and Art

Although many architects in northern Europe continued to build in the flamboyant Gothic style of the later Middle Ages, the classical values of Italian architects can be seen in some of the splendid new castles constructed in France's Loire valley—châteaux too elegant to be defensible—and in the royal palace (now museum) of the Louvre in Paris, which replaced an old twelfth-century fortress. The influence of Renaissance ideals are also visible

THE CHÂTEAU OF CHAMBORD. Built in the early sixteenth century by an Italian architect in the service of King Francis I of France, this magnificent palace in the Loire Valley combines Gothic and Renaissance architectural features.

in the work of the foremost artist of this era, the German Albrecht Dürer (1471–1528). Dürer (*DIRR-er*) was the first northerner to master the techniques of proportion and perspective, and he also shared with contemporary Italians a fascination with nature and the human body. But Dürer never really embraced classical allegory, drawing inspiration instead from more traditional Christian legends and from the self-effacing Christian humanism of Erasmus. Thus Dürer's serenely radiant engraving of Saint Jerome expresses the scholarly absorption that Erasmus may have enjoyed while working quietly in his study.

Indeed, Dürer aspired to immortalize Erasmus in a major portrait, but circumstances prevented him from doing this because the paths of the two men crossed only once; and after Dürer started sketching his hero on that occasion, his work was interrupted by Erasmus's press of business. Instead, the accomplishment of capturing Erasmus's pensive spirit in oils was left to another great northern artist, the German Hans Holbein the Younger (1497–1543, see page 393). As good fortune would have it, during a stay in England, Holbein also painted an extraordinarily acute portrait of Erasmus's friend and kindred spirit Sir Thomas More, which enables us to see clearly why a contemporary called More "a man of . . . sad gravity; a man for all seasons" (see page 394). These two portraits in and of themselves point to a major difference between medieval and Renaissance culture. Whereas the Middle Ages produced

***SAINT JEROME IN HIS STUDY* BY DÜRER.** Jerome, the biblical translator of the fourth century (Chapter 6), was a hero to both Dürer and Erasmus: the paragon of inspired Christian scholarship. Note how the scene exudes contentment, even down to the sleeping lion, which seems more like an overgrown tabby cat than a symbol of Christ.

no convincing naturalistic likenesses of any leading intellectual figures, Renaissance culture's greater commitment to human individuality created the environment in which Holbein was able to make Erasmus and More come to life.

Renaissance Music

Music in western Europe in the fifteenth and sixteenth centuries reached such a high point of development that it constitutes, together with painting and sculpture, one of the most brilliant aspects of Renaissance endeavor. The musical theory of the Renaissance was driven largely by the humanist-inspired (but largely fruitless) effort to recover and imitate classical musical forms and modes. Musical practice, however, showed much more continuity with medieval musical traditions, with an added emphasis on heightened expression and emotional intensity. New musical instruments were developed to add nuance and texture to existing musical forms: the lute, the viol, the violin, and a variety of woodwind and keyboard instruments including the harpsichord. New musical genres also emerged, among them the opera. Most composers of this period were men trained in the service of the Church, but they rarely made sharp distinctions between sacred and secular music. Music was coming into its own as a serious independent art.

During the early fourteenth century, a musical movement called *ars nova* (Latin for "new art") was already flourishing in France, and it naturally spread to Italy during the lifetime of Petrarch. Its outstanding composers were Guillaume de Machaut (c. 1300–1377) and Francesco Landini (c. 1325–1397). The madrigals, ballads, and other songs composed by these musicians testify to a rich medieval tradition of secular music, but the greatest achievement of the period was a highly complicated yet delicate contrapuntal style adapted for the liturgy of the Church. Machaut, indeed, was the first-known composer to provide a polyphonic (harmonized) version of the major sections of the Mass.

In the fifteenth century, the dissemination of this new musical aesthetic combined with a host of French, Flemish, and Italian elements in the multicultural courts of Europe, particularly that of Burgundy. By the beginning of the sixteenth century, Franco-Flemish composers came to dominate many important courts and cathedrals, creating a variety of new genres and styles that bear a close affinity to Renaissance art and poetry. The Flemish composer Roland de Lassus (1532–1594) and the Italian Giovanni Pierluigi da Palestrina (c. 1525–1594) were recognized as masters by their peers, and Palestrina was especially influential because his highly intricate choral music was written under the patronage of the papacy in Rome. Music also flourished in sixteenth-century England, where the Italian madrigal was adapted and enlivened, and where William Byrd (1543–1623) rivaled the great Flemish and Italian composers of the day. Throughout Europe, the general level

After You Read This Chapter

Visit StudySpace for quizzes, additional review materials, and multi-media documents. **wwnorton.com/studyspace**

REVIEWING THE OBJECTIVES

- The Renaissance was an intellectual and cultural movement that coincided with the later Middle Ages but fostered a new outlook on the world. Explain the ways in which this outlook differed.
- The Renaissance began in Italy. Why?
- What was the relationship between Renaissance ideals and Italy's political realities?
- What were the principal features of Renaissance art?
- How were Renaissance ideas adapted in northern Europe?

of musical proficiency was very high: the singing of part-songs was a popular pastime in homes and at informal social gatherings, and the ability to read a part at sight was expected of the educated elite.

CONCLUSION

The ideals of the Renaissance often stand in sharp contrast to the harsh realities alongside which they coexisted, and in which they were rooted. They arose from the calamitous events of the fourteenth century, which had a particularly devastating effect on Italy. Ravaged by the Black Death, abandoned by the papacy, reduced to the status of pawn in other powers' rivalries, Italy was exposed as a mere shadow of what it had been under the Roman Empire. It was therefore to the precedents and glories of the past that Italian intellectuals, artists, and statesmen looked for inspirations, in order to restore its prominence. But to which aspects of the past? Some humanists may have wanted to revive the principles of the Roman Republic, but many of them worked for ambitious despots who modeled themselves on Rome's dictators or on the tyrants of ancient Greece. Artists could thrive in the atmosphere of competition and one-upmanship that characterized Italy's warring principalities and city-states, but they could also find themselves reduced to the status of servants in the households of the wealthy and powerful—or forced to subordinate their artistry to the demands of warfare and espionage. Access to a widening array of classical texts, in Greek as well as Latin, widened the horizons of Renaissance readers; yet women were largely barred from the humanist education that led men to boast of their proximity to God. New critical tools enabled the study of classical texts, but the insistence on a return to the "pure" language of the Roman Empire eventually succeeded in bringing about the death of Latin as a living medium of communication.

Although the Renaissance began in northern Italy, where it filled a cultural and political vacuum, it did not remain confined there. By the end of the fifteenth century, humanist approaches to education and textual criticism had begun to influence intellectual endeavors all over Europe. The techniques of Renaissance artists melded with the artistry of the later Middle Ages in striking ways, while opportunities for patronage expanded along with the demand for artworks and the prestige they lent to their owners. And the theories that undergirded Renaissance politics—civic and princely—were being used to legitimize many different kinds of power, including that of the papacy. All of these trends would be carried forward into the sixteenth century, and would have a role to play in the upheaval that shattered Europe's fragile religious unity and tenuous balance of power. It is to this upheaval, the Reformation, that we turn in Chapter 13.

PEOPLE, IDEAS, AND EVENTS IN CONTEXT

- Why was the ancient past so important to the intellectuals and artists of the **RENAISSANCE**? What was **HUMANISM**, and how did it influence education during this era?
- What were the political and economic underpinnings of the Renaissance? How do the **MEDICI** of Florence and the papacy exemplify new trends in patronage?
- What were some major scholarly achievements of the Renaissance? How did **LORENZO VALLA** and **NICCOLÒ MACHIAVELLI** advance new intellectual and political ideas?
- How do the works of **BOTICELLI, LEONARDO, RAPHAEL,** and **MICHELANGELO** capture Renaissance ideals? Which is the most paradigmatic Renaissance artist, in your opinion, and why?
- How did Christian humanists like **DESIDERIUS ERASMUS** and **THOMAS MORE** apply Renaissance ideas in new ways? How were these ideas expressed in art?

CONSEQUENCES

- The Renaissance is often described as being the antithesis of the Middle Ages, yet it was actually a simultaneous movement. Can you think of other eras when two or more divergent outlooks have coexisted?
- To what extent do the ideals of the Renaissance anticipate those we associate with modernity? To what extent are they more faithful to either the Christian or the classical past?
- Phrases like "Renaissance man" and "a Renaissance education" are still part of our common vocabulary. Given what you have learned in this chapter, how has your understanding of such phrases changed? How would you explain their true meaning to others?

Before
You
Read
This
Chapter

The Age of Dissent and Division, 1500–1600

CORE OBJECTIVES

- **DEFINE** the main premises of Lutheranism.

- **EXPLAIN** why Switzerland emerged as an important Protestant center.

- **IDENTIFY** the ways in which family structures and values changed during the Reformation.

- **UNDERSTAND** the reasons behind England's unusual brand of Protestantism.

- **DESCRIBE** the Catholic Church's response to the challenge of Protestantism.

n the year 1500, Europe's future seemed bright. After two centuries of economic, social, and political turmoil, its economy was expanding, its cities were growing, and the monarchs of France, England, Spain, Scotland, and Poland were all securely established on their thrones. The population was increasing, and governments at every level were extending and deepening their control over people's lives. Europeans had also embarked on a new period of colonial expansion. And although the papacy pursued its territorial wars in Italy, the Church itself had weathered the storms of the Avignon captivity and the Great Schism. Heresies had been suppressed or contained. In the struggle over conciliarism, the papacy had won the support of all major European rulers, which effectively relegated the conciliarists to academic isolation at the University of Paris. Meanwhile, at the local level, the devotion of ordinary Christians was strong and the parish a crucial site of community identity. To be sure, there were some problems. The educational standards of parish clergy were higher than they had ever been, but reformers noted that too many priests were ignorant or neglectful of their spiritual duties. Monasticism, by and large, seemed to have lost its spiritual fire. Religious

399

enthusiasm sometimes led to superstition. Yet on the whole, the Church's problems were manageable.

No one could have predicted that Europe's religious and political coherence would be irreparably shattered in the course of a generation, or that the next century would witness an appallingly destructive series of wars. Nor could anyone have foreseen that the catalyst for these extraordinary events would be a university professor. For it was Martin Luther (1483–1546), a German monk and teacher of theology, who set off the chain reaction we know as the Reformation. Initially intended as a call for another phase in the Church's long history of internal reforms, Luther's teachings would instead launch a religious revolution that would splinter western Christendom into a variety of Protestant ("dissenting") faiths, while prompting the Church of Rome to re-affirm its status as the only true Catholic ("universal) faith through a parallel revolution. At the same time, these movements deepened existing divisions among peoples, rulers, and states while opening up new divisions and points of contention. The result was a profound transformation of the religious, social, and political landscape that affected the lives of everyone in Europe—and everyone in the new European colonies, then and now.

ponent of its principles and practices. Many of his followers were even more radical. The movement that began with Luther therefore went beyond "reformation." It was a frontal assault on religious, political, and social instututions that had been in place for a thousand years.

Luther's Quest for Justice

Although Martin Luther became an inspiration to millions, he was a terrible disappointment to his father. The elder Luther was a Thuringian peasant who had prospered by leasing some mines. Eager to see his clever son rise still further, he sent young Luther to the University of Erfurt to study law. In 1505, however, Martin shattered his hopes by becoming a monk of the Augustinian order. In some sense, though, Luther was a chip off the old block. Throughout his life, he lived simply and expressed himself in the vigorous, earthy vernacular of the German peasantry.

Luther arrived at his new understanding of religious truth by a dramatic conversion experience. As a monk, he zealously pursued all the traditional means for achieving his own salvation. Not only did he fast and pray continu-

MARTIN LUTHER'S CHALLENGE

To explain the impact of Martin Luther's ideas, we must answer three central questions:

1. Why did Luther's theology lead him to break with Rome?
2. Why did large numbers of people rally to his cause?
3. Why did so many German princes and towns impose the new religion within their territories?

As we shall see, those who followed Luther found his message appealing for different reasons. Many peasants hoped that the new religion would free them from the exactions of their lords; towns and princes thought it would allow them to consolidate their political independence; nationalists thought it would liberate Germany from the demands of foreign popes bent on feathering their own nest in central Italy.

But what Luther's followers shared was a conviction that their new understanding of Christianity would lead them to Heaven, whereas the traditional religion of Rome would not. For this reason, *reformation* is a misleading term for the movement they initiated. Although Luther himself began as a reformer seeking to change the Church from within, he quickly developed into an uncompromising op-

MARTIN LUTHER. This late portrait is by Lucas Cranach the Elder (1472–1553), court painter to the electors of Brandenburg and a friend of Luther.

ously but he confessed so often that his exhausted confessor would sometimes jokingly suggest that if he really wanted to do penance he should go out and do something dramatic like committing adultery. Yet, try as he might, Luther could find no spiritual peace because he feared that he could never perform enough good deeds to deserve so great a gift as salvation. But in 1513 he hit upon an insight that changed the course of his life.

Luther's insight was a new understanding of God's justice. For years, he had worried that it seemed unfair for God to issue commandments that he knew human beings could not observe, and then to punish them with eternal damnation. But after becoming a professor of theology at the University of Wittenberg, Luther's further study of the Bible revealed to him that God's justice had nothing to do with his power to punish, but rather with his mercy in saving sinful mortals through faith. As Luther later wrote, "At last, by the mercy of God, I began to understand the justice of God as that by which God makes *us* just, in his mercy and through faith . . . and at this I felt as though I had been born again, and had gone through open gates into paradise." Since this revelation came to Luther in the tower room of his monastery, it is often termed his "tower experience."

After that, everything seemed to fall into place. Lecturing at Wittenberg in the years immediately following, Luther pondered a passage in Saint Paul's Letter to the Romans—"[T]he just shall live by faith" (1:17)—until he reached his central doctrine of "justification by faith alone." Luther concluded that God's justice does not demand endless good works and religious rituals for salvation, because humans can never be saved by their own efforts. Rather, humans are saved by God's grace alone, which God offers as an utterly undeserved gift to those whom he has predestined for salvation. Because this grace comes to humans through the gift of faith, men and women are "justified" (i.e., made worthy of salvation) by faith alone. Those whom God has justified through faith will manifest that fact by performing works of piety and charity, but such works are not what saves them. Piety and charity are merely visible signs of each believer's invisible spiritual state, which is known to God alone.

The essence of this doctrine was not original to Luther. It had been central to the thought of Augustine (see Chapter 6), the patron saint of Luther's own monastic order. During the twelfth and thirteenth centuries, however, theologians such as Peter Lombard and Thomas Aquinas (Chapter 9) had developed a very different understanding of salvation. They emphasized the role that the Church itself (through its sacraments) and the individual believer (through acts of piety and charity) could play in the process of salvation. None of these theologians claimed that a human being could earn his or her way to Heaven by good works alone, but the late medieval Church unwittingly encouraged this misunderstanding by presenting the process of salvation in increasingly quantitative terms—declaring, for example, that by performing a specific action (such as a pilgrimage or a pious donation), a believer could reduce the penance she or he owed to God by a specific number of days.

From the fourteenth century on, popes claimed to dispense such special grace from the so-called Treasury of Merits, a storehouse of surplus good works piled up by Christ and the saints in Heaven. By the late fifteenth century,

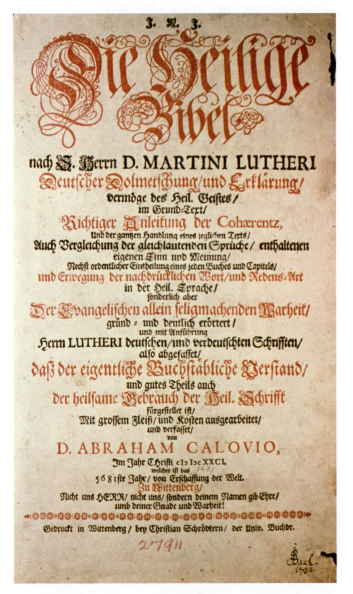

LUTHER'S TRANSLATION OF THE BIBLE. The printing press was instrumental to the rapid dissemination of Luther's messages, as well as those of his supporters and challengers. Also essential was the fact that Luther addressed his audience in plain language, in their native German, and that pamphlets and vernacular Bibles like this one could be rapidly and cheaply mass produced.

popes also began to teach that the dead could receive this grace, too, to speed their way through Purgatory. In both cases, grace was withdrawn from this "Treasury" through indulgences: special remissions of penitential obligations. When indulgences were first conceived, in the eleventh and twelfth centuries, they could be earned only by demanding spiritual exercises, such as joining a crusade (see Chapter 8). By the end of the fifteenth century, however, indulgences were for sale.

To many, this looked like simony: the sin of exchanging God's grace for cash. It had been a practice loudly condemned by Wyclif and his followers (Chapter 10), and it was even more widely criticized by reformers like Erasmus (Chapter 12). But Luther's objections to indulgences had much more radical

SAINT PETER'S BASILICA, ROME. The construction of a new papal palace and monumental church was begun in 1506. This enormous complex replaced a modest, dilapidated Romanesque basilica that had replaced an even older church built on the site of the apostle Peter's tomb. ∎ *How might this building project have been interpreted in different ways, depending on one's attitude toward the papacy?*

consequences, because they rested on a set of theological presuppositions that, taken to their logical conclusion, resulted in dismantling much of contemporary religious practice, not to mention the authority and sanctity of the Church. Luther himself does not appear to have realized this at first. But as the implications of his ideas became clear, he did not withdraw from them. Instead, he pressed on.

The Scandal of Indulgences

Luther developed his ideas as a university professor. But in 1517 he was provoked, by a scandalous abuse of spiritual power, into attacking actual practice more publicly. The worldly bishop Albert of Hohenzollern, youngest brother of the elector of Brandenburg, had sunk himself into debt, and in 1513 he paid a large sum for papal permission to hold the bishoprics of Magdeburg and Halberstadt concurrently—even though, at twenty-three, he was not old enough to be a bishop at all. Moreover, when the prestigious and lucrative archbishopric of Mainz fell vacant in the next year, Albert bought that, too. Obtaining the necessary funds by taking out loans from a German banking firm, he then struck a bargain with Pope Leo X (r. 1513–21): Leo would authorize the sale of indulgences in Albert's ecclesiastical territories with the understanding that half of the income would go to Rome for the building of St. Peter's Basilica, the other half going to Albert.

Luther did not know the sordid details of Albert's bargain, but he did know that a Dominican friar named Tetzel was soon hawking indulgences throughout much of the region, and that Tetzel was deliberately giving people the impression that an indulgence was an automatic ticket to Heaven for oneself or one's loved ones in Purgatory. For Luther, this was doubly offensive: not only was Tetzel violating Luther's conviction that people are saved by faith, not the purchase of grace, he was also misleading people into thinking that if they purchased an indulgence, they no longer needed to confess their sins to a priest. Tetzel was thus putting innocent souls at risk. So on the eve of the feast of All Souls—Hallowe'en night—in 1517, Luther published a list of Ninety-five Theses that he was prepared to debate, all aimed at dismantling the doctrine of indulgences. According to tradition, he nailed this document to the door of the church—and whether or not he did so in fact, the metaphor is clear.

Luther wrote up these points for debate in Latin, not German, and meant them only for academic discussion within the University of Wittenberg. But when some unknown person translated and published them, the hitherto obscure academic suddenly gained widespread notoriety.

POPE LEO X. Raphael's unflinching portrait shows the pope with his nephews: Giulio de' Medici (who would succeed him as pope) and Cardinal de Rossi.

spiritually equal before God, which meant denying that priests, monks, and nuns had any special qualities by virtue of their vocations: hence "the priesthood of all believers."

From these premises a host of practical consequences followed. Because works could not lead to salvation, Luther declared fasts, pilgrimages, and the veneration of relics to be spiritually valueless. He also called for the dissolution of all monasteries and convents. He advocated a demystification of religious rites, proposing the substitution of German and other vernaculars for Latin and calling for a reduction in the number of sacraments from seven to two. In his view, the only true sacraments were baptism and the Eucharist, both of which had been instituted by Christ. (Later, he included penance.) Although Luther continued to believe that Christ was really present in the consecrated bread and wine of the Lord's Supper, he insisted that it was only through the faith of each individual believer that this sacrament could lead anyone to God; it was not a magic trick performed by a priest. To further emphasize that those who served the Church had no supernatural authority, he insisted on calling them "ministers" or "pastors" rather than priests. He also proposed to abolish the entire ecclesiastical hierarchy from popes to bishops on down. Finally, on the principle that no spiritual distinction existed between clergy and laity, Luther argued that ministers could and should marry. In 1525 he himself took a wife, Katharina von Bora, one of a dozen nuns he had helped to escape from a Cistercian convent.

The Break with Rome

Widely disseminated by means of the printing press, Luther's polemical pamphlets of 1520 electrified much of Germany, gaining him passionate popular support and touching off a national religious revolt against the papacy. In highly colloquial German, Luther declared that "if the pope's court were reduced ninety-nine percent it would still be large enough to give decisions on matters of faith"; that "the cardinals have sucked Italy dry and now turn to Germany"; and that, given Rome's corruption, "the reign of Antichrist could not be worse." As word of Luther's defiance spread, his pamphlets became a publishing sensation. Whereas the average press run of a printed book before 1520 had been 1,000 copies, the first run of *To the Christian Nobility* (1520) was 4,000—and it sold out in a few days. Many thousands of copies quickly followed. Even more popular were woodcut illustrations mocking the papacy and exalting Luther. These sold in the tens of thousands and could be readily understood even by the illiterate. (**See Interpreting Visual Evidence.**)

Tetzel and his allies now demanded that Luther withdraw his theses. Rather than backing down, however, Luther became even bolder in his attacks. In 1519, at a public disputation held before throngs in Leipzig, Luther defiantly maintained that the pope and all clerics were merely fallible men, and that the highest authority for an individual's conscience was the truth of Scripture. Pope Leo X responded by charging Luther with heresy; after that Luther had no alternative but to break with the Church entirely.

Luther's year of greatest activity came in 1520 when, in the midst of the crisis caused by his defiance, he composed a series of pamphlets setting forth his three primary premises: justification by faith, the authority of Scripture, and "the priesthood of all believers." We have already examined the meaning of the first premise. By the second he simply meant that the reading of Scripture took precedence over Church traditions—including the teachings of all theologians—and that beliefs (such as Purgatory) or practices (such as prayers to the saints) not explicitly grounded in Scripture could be rejected as human inventions. Luther also declared that Christian believers were

Decoding Printed Propaganda

The printing press has been credited with helping to spread the teachings of Martin Luther and so to securing the success of the Protestant Reformation. But even before Luther's critiques were published, reformers were using the new technology to disseminate images that attacked the corruption of the Church.

After Luther rose to prominence, both his supporters and detractors vied with one another in disseminating propaganda that appealed, visually, to a lay audience and that could be understood even by those who were unable to read.

The first pair of images below is really a single printed artifact datable to around 1500: an early example of a "pop-up" card. It shows Pope Alexander VI (r. 1492–1503) as stately pontiff (image A) whose true identity is concealed by a flap. When the flap is raised (image B), he is revealed as a devil. The Latin texts read: "Alexander VI, *pontifex maximus*" (image A) and "I am the pope" (image B). The other two images represent two sides of the debate as it had developed by 1530, and both do so with reference to the same image: the seven-headed beast mentioned in the

A. Alexander as pontiff.

B. Alexander as a devil.

Bible's Book of Revelation. On the left (image C), a Lutheran engraving shows the papacy as the beast, with seven heads representing seven orders of Catholic clergy. The sign on the cross (referring to the sign hung over the head of the crucified Christ) reads, in German: "For money, a sack full of indulgences." (The Latin words on either side say "Reign of the Devil.") On the right (image D), a Catholic engraving produced in Germany shows Luther as Revelation's beast, with its seven heads labeled: "Doctor–Martin–Luther–Heretic–Hypocrite–Fanatic–Barabbas," the last alluding to the thief who should have been execu-

ted instead of Jesus, according to the Gospels.

Questions for Analysis

1. Given that this attack on Pope Alexander VI precedes Martin Luther's critique of the Church by nearly two decades, what can you conclude about its intended audience? To what extent can it be read as a barometer of popular disapproval? What might have been the reason(s) for the use of the concealing flap?

2. What do you make of the fact that both Catholic and Protestant propa-

gandists were using the same imagery? What do you make of the key differences—for example, the fact that the seven-headed beast representing the papacy sprouts out of an altar in which a Eucharistic chalice is displayed, while the seven-headed Martin Luther is reading a book?

3. All of these printed images also make use of words. What are some of the different relationships between these two media? Would the message of each image be clear without the use of texts? Why or why not?

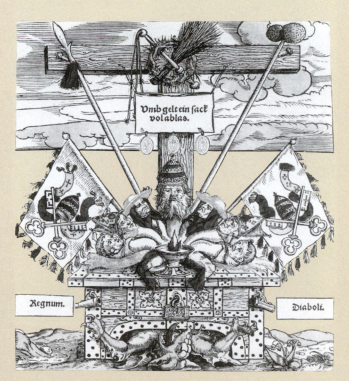

C. The seven-headed papal beast.

D. The seven-headed Martin Luther.

Luther's denunciations reflected widespread public dissatisfaction with the conduct and corruption of the papacy. Pope Alexander VI (r. 1492–1503) had bribed cardinals to gain his office, and had then used the money raised from the papal jubilee of 1500 to support the military campaigns of his illegitimate son. He was also suspected of incest with his own daughter, Lucrezia Borgia. Julius II (r. 1503–13) devoted his reign to enlarging the Papal States in a series of wars; a contemporary remarked of him that he would have gained great glory—if only he had been a secular prince. Leo X (r. 1513–21), Luther's opponent, was a member of the Medici family of Florence. Although not spectacularly immoral, he was a self-indulgent aesthete who, in the words of a modern Catholic historian, "would not have been deemed fit to be a doorkeeper in the house of the Lord had he lived in the days of the apostles." In *The Praise of Folly*, first published in 1511 and frequently reprinted (see Chapter 12), Erasmus declared that if the popes of his day were ever forced to lead Christlike lives, as their office demanded, they would be incapable of it. In *Julius Excluded*, published anonymously in 1517, he went even further, imagining a conversation at the gates of Heaven between Saint Peter and Julius II, in which Peter refuses to admit the pope because he cannot believe that this armored, vainglorious figure could possibly be his own earthly representative.

In Germany, resentment of the papacy ran especially high because there were no special agreements (concordats) limiting papal authority in its principalities, as there were in Spain, France, and England (see Chapter 10). As a result, German princes complained that papal taxes were so high that the country was drained of its wealth. And yet Germans had almost no influence over papal policy. Frenchmen, Spaniards, and Italians dominated the College of Cardinals and the papal bureaucracy, and the popes were now invariably Italian, as they would continue to be until 1978 and the election of John Paul II. As a result, graduates from the rapidly growing German universities almost never found employment in Rome. Instead, many joined the throngs of Luther's supporters to become leaders of the new religious movement.

The Condemnation at Worms

In the year 1520, Pope Leo X issued a papal edict condemning Luther's publications as heretical, and threatening him with excommunication if he did not recant. This edict was of the most solemn kind, known as a *bulla* or "bull," from the lead seal it bore. Luther's reponse was flagrantly defiant: rather than acquiescing to the pope's demand, he

staged a public burning of the document. Thereafter, his heresy confirmed, he was formally given over for punishment to his lay overlord, the elector Frederick "the Wise" of Saxony. Frederick, however, proved a supporter of Luther and a critic of the papacy. Rather than burning Luther at the stake for heresy, Frederick declared that Luther had not yet received a fair hearing. Early in 1521, he therefore brought him to the city of Worms to be examined by a select representative assembly known as a "diet."

At Worms, the diet's presiding officer was the newly elected Holy Roman emperor, Charles V. As a member of the Habsburg family, he had been born and bred in his ancestral holding of Flanders, then part of the Netherlands. By 1521, however, through the unpredictable workings of dynastic inheritance, marriage, election, and luck, he had become not only the ruler of the Netherlands, but also king of Germany and Holy Roman emperor, duke of Austria,

THE EMPEROR CHARLES V. This portrait by the Venetian painter Titian depicts Europe's most powerful ruler sitting quietly in a chair, dressed in simple clothing of the kind worn by judges or bureaucrats. ■ *Why might Charles have chosen to represent himself in this way—rather than in the regalia of his many royal, imperial, and princely offices?*

THE EUROPEAN EMPIRE OF CHARLES V, c. 1550. Charles V ruled a vast variety of widely dispersed territories in Europe and the New World, and as Holy Roman Emperor he was also the titular ruler of Germany. ▪ *What were the main countries and kingdoms under his control?* ▪ *Which regions would have been most threatened by Charles's extraordinary power, and where might the rulers of these regions turn for allies?* ▪ *How might the expansion of the Ottoman Empire have complicated political and religious struggles within Christian Europe?*

duke of Milan, and ruler of the Franche-Comté. And as the grandson of Ferdinand and Isabella on his mother's side, he was also king of Spain; king of Naples, Sicily, and Sardinia; and ruler of all the Spanish possessions in the New World. Governing such an extraordinary combination of territories posed enormous challenges. Charles's empire had no capital and no centralized administrative institutions; it shared no

common language, no common culture, and no geographically contiguous borders. It thus stood completely apart from the growing nationalism of late medieval political life.

Charles recognized the diversity of his empire and tried wherever possible to rule it through local officials and institutions. But he could not tolerate threats to the two fundamental forces that held his empire together: himself

THE WARTBURG, EISENACH (GERMANY). This medieval stronghold became the refuge of Martin Luther after his condemnation at the Diet of Worms in 1520. His room in the castle has since been preserved.

as emperor and Catholicism (as the religion of Rome was coming to be called). Beyond such political calculations, however, Charles was also a faithful and committed servant of the Church, and deeply disturbed by the prospect of heresy within his empire. There was therefore little doubt that the Diet of Worms would condemn Martin Luther for heresy. And when Luther refused to back down, thereby endangering his life, his lord Frederick the Wise once more intervened, this time arranging for Luther to be "kidnapped" and hidden for a year at the elector's castle of the Wartburg, where he was kept out of harm's way.

Thereafter, Luther was never again in mortal danger. Although the Diet of Worms proclaimed him an outlaw, this edict was never enforced. Instead, Charles V left Germany in order to conduct a war with France, and in 1522 Luther returned in triumph to Wittenberg, to find that the changes he had called for had already been put into practice by his university supporters. When several German princes formally converted to Lutheranism, they brought their territories with them. In a little over a decade, a new form of Christianity had been established.

The German Princes and the Lutheran Church

At this point, the last of our three major questions must be addressed: Why did some German princes, secure in their own powers, nonetheless establish Lutheran religious practices within their territories? This is a crucial development, because popular support for Luther would not have been enough to ensure the success of his teachings had they not been embraced by a number of powerful princes and free cities. Indeed, it was only in those territories where rulers formally established Lutheranism that the new religion prevailed. Elsewhere in Germany, Luther's sympathizers were forced to flee, face death, or conform to Catholicism.

The power of individual rulers to determine the religion of their territories reflects developments we noted in Chapter 10. Rulers had long sought to control appointments to Church offices in their own realms, to restrict the flow of money to Rome, and to limit the independence of ecclesiastical courts. The most powerful rulers in western Europe—primarily the kings of France and Spain—had already taken advantage of the continuing struggles between the papacy and the conciliarists to extract such concessions from the embattled popes during the fifteenth century (Chapter 10). But in Germany, as noted above, neither the emperor nor the princes were strong enough to secure special treatment.

This changed as a result of Luther's initiatives. As early as 1520, the Pope's fiery challenger had recognized that he could never hope to institute new religious practices without the strong arms of princes, so he explicitly encouraged them to confiscate the wealth of the Church as an incentive. At first the princes bided their time, but when they realized that Luther had enormous public support and that Charles V would not act swiftly to defend the Catholic faith, several moved to introduce Lutheranism into their territories. Personal piety surely played a role in individual cases, but political and economic considerations were generally more decisive. Protestant princes could consolidate authority by naming their own pastors, cutting off fees to Rome, and curtailing the jurisdiction of Church courts. They could also guarantee that the political and religious boundaries of their territories would now coincide. No longer would a rival ecclesiastical prince (such as a bishop or archbishop) be able to use his spiritual position to undermine a neighboring secular prince's sovereignty.

Similar considerations also moved a number of free cities (independent of territorial princes) to adopt Lutheranism. Town councils and guild masters could thus establish themselves as the supreme governing authorities within their towns, cutting out local bishops or powerful monasteries. Given the added fact that under Lutheranism monasteries and convents could be shut down and their lands appropriated by the newly sovereign secular authorities, the practical advantages of the new faith were overwhelming, quite apart from any considerations of religious zeal.

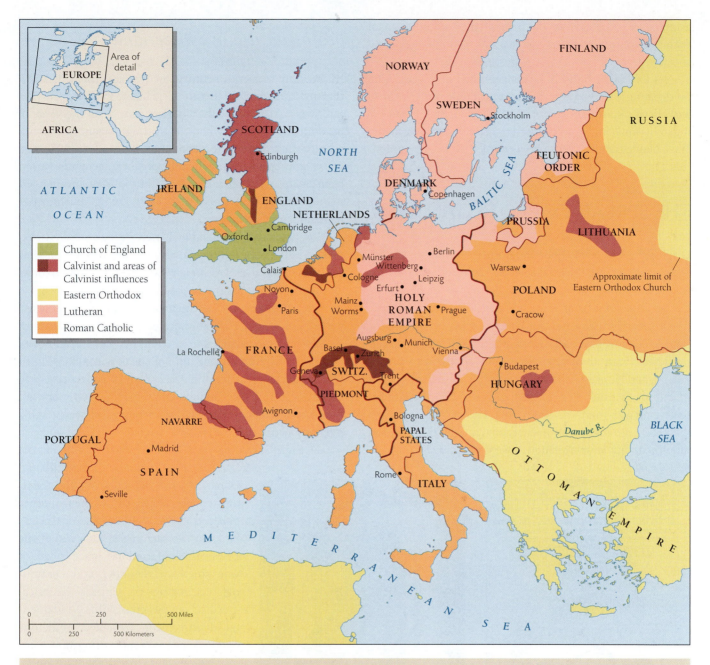

CONFESSIONAL DIFFERENCES, c. 1560. The religious affiliations (confessions) of Europe's territories had become very complicated by the year 1560, roughly a generation after the adoption of Lutheranism in some areas. ▪ *What major countries and kingdoms had embraced Protestantism by 1560?* ▪ *To what extent do these divisions conform to political boundaries, and to what extent would they have complicated the political situation?* ▪ *Why might Lutheranism have spread north into Scandinavia, but not south into Bavaria or west across the Rhine?*

Once safely ensconced in Wittenberg under princely protection, Luther began to express ever more vehemently his own political and social views, which tended toward the strong support of the new political order. In a treatise of 1523, *On Temporal Authority*, he insisted that "godly" (Protestant) rulers must be obeyed in all things and that even "ungodly" ones should never be actively resisted since tyranny "is not to be resisted but endured." In 1525, when

peasants throughout Germany rebelled against their landlords, Luther therefore responded with intense hostility. In his vituperative pamphlet of 1525, *Against the Thievish, Murderous Hordes of Peasants*, he urged readers to hunt the rebels down as though they were mad dogs: to "strike, strangle, stab secretly or in public, and remember that nothing can be more poisonous than a man in rebellion." After the ruthless suppression of this revolt, which may have cost as many as 100,000 lives, the firm alliance of Lutheranism with state power helped preserve and sanction the existing social order.

As for Luther himself, he concentrated in his last years on debating with younger, more radical religious reformers and offering spiritual counsel to all who sought it. Never tiring in his amazingly prolific literary activity, he wrote an average of one treatise every two weeks for twenty-five years.

THE SPREAD OF PROTESTANTISM

Originating as a term applied to Lutherans who "protested" against the German Imperial Diet of 1529, the word *Protestant* was soon applied to a much wider range of dissenting Christianities. Lutheranism itself struck lasting roots only in northern Germany and Scandinavia, where it became the state religion of Denmark, Norway, and Sweden as early as the 1520s. Early Lutheran successes in southern Germany, Poland, and Hungary were eventually rolled back. Elsewhere in Europe, meanwhile, competing forms of Protestantism soon emerged from the seeds that Luther had sown. By the 1550s, Protestantism had become a truly international movement, but an increasingly diverse and divisive one.

Protestantism in Switzerland

In the early sixteenth century, Switzerland was ruled neither by kings nor by territorial princes; instead, prosperous Swiss cities were either independent or on the verge of becoming so. Hence, when the leading citizens of a Swiss municipality decided to adopt Protestant reforms, no one could stop them. Although religious arrangements varied from city to city, three main forms of Protestantism emerged in Switzerland between 1520 to 1550: Zwinglianism, Anabaptism, and Calvinism.

Zwinglianism, founded by Ulrich Zwingli (*TSVING-lee*, 1484–1531) in Zürich, was the most theologically moderate form of the three. Although Zwingli began his career as a Catholic priest, his humanist-inspired study of the Bible convinced him that Catholic theology and practice conflicted with the Gospels. His biblical studies eventually led him also to condemn religious images and hierarchical authority within the Church. But he did not speak out publicly until Luther set the precedent. In 1522, Zwingli began attacking the authority of the Catholic Church in Zürich. Soon all Zürich and much of northern Switzerland had accepted his religious leadership.

Zwingli's reforms closely resembled those of the Lutherans in Germany. Zwingli differed from Luther, however, as to the theology of the Eucharist: whereas Luther believed in the real presence of Christ's body in the sacrament, for Zwingli the Eucharist conferred no grace at all; it was simply a reminder and communal celebration of Christ's historical sacrifice on the cross. This fundamental disagreement prevented Lutherans and Zwinglians from uniting in a common Protestant front. Fighting independently, Zwingli fell in battle against Catholic forces in 1531. Soon thereafter, his movement was absorbed by the more systematic Protestantism of John Calvin (see below).

Before Calvinism prevailed, however, an even more radical form of Protestantism arose in Switzerland and Germany. The first Anabaptists were members of Zwingli's circle in Zürich, but they broke with him around 1525 on the issue of infant baptism. Because Anabaptists were convinced that the sacrament of baptism was only effective

THE ANABAPTISTS' CAGES, THEN AND NOW. After the three Anabaptist leaders of Münster were executed in 1535, their corpses were prominently displayed in cages hung from a tower of the marketplace church. As can be seen from the photo on the right, the bones are gone but the iron cages remain. ▪ *What would be the purpose of keeping these cages on display?*

if administered to willing adults who understood its significance, they required followers who had been baptized as infants to be baptized again as adults (the term *Anabaptism* means "rebaptism"). This doctrine reflected the Anabaptists' fundamental belief that the true church was a small community of believers whose members had to make a deliberate, inspired decision to join it. No other Protestant groups were prepared to go so far in rejecting the medieval Christian view of the Church as a single vast body to which all members of society belonged from birth. In an age when almost everyone assumed that church and state were inextricably connected, Anabaptism was bound to be anathema to the established powers, both Protestant and Catholic. Yet in its first few years the movement did gain numerous adherents in Switzerland and Germany, above all because it appealed to sincere religious piety in calling for pacifism, strict personal morality, and extreme simplicity of worship.

This changed when a group of Anabaptist extremists managed to gain control of the German city of Münster in 1534. These zealots combined sectarianism with millenarianism, the belief that God intends to institute a completely new order of justice and spirituality throughout the world before the end of time. Determined to help God bring about this goal, the extremists attempted to turn Münster into a new Jerusalem. A former tailor named John of Leyden assumed the title "King of the New Temple" and proclaimed himself the successor of the Hebrew king David. Under his leadership, Anabaptist religious practices were made obligatory, private property was abolished, and even polygamy was permitted on the grounds of Old Testament precedents. Such practices were deeply shocking to Protestants and Catholics alike. Accordingly, Münster was besieged and captured by Catholic forces little more than a year after the Anabaptist takeover; and the new "David," together with two of his lieutenants, was put to death by torture.

Thereafter, Anabaptists throughout Europe were ruthlessly persecuted on all sides. The few who survived banded together in the Mennonite sect, named for its founder, the Dutchman Menno Simons (c. 1496–1561). This sect, dedicated to pacifism and the simple "religion of the heart" of original Anabaptism, has continued to exist to the present day and is particularly strong in the central United States.

John Calvin's Reformed Theology

A year after the events in Münster, a twenty-six-year-old Frenchman named John Calvin (1509–1564), published the first version of his *Institutes of the Christian Religion*, the most influential formulation of Protestant theology ever written. Born in Noyon in northern France, Calvin had originally trained for the law, but by 1533 was studying the Greek and Latin classics while living off the income from a priestly benefice. As he later wrote, although he was "obstinately devoted to the superstitions of popery," he experienced a miraculous conversion. He became a Protestant theologian and propagandist, and evenually fled to the Swiss city of Basel to escape persecution.

Although some aspects of Calvin's early career resemble those of Luther, the two men were very different. Luther was an emotionally volatile personality and a lover of controversy. He responded to theological problems as they arose or as the impulse struck him; he never attempted to systematize his beliefs. Calvin, however, was a coolly analytical legalist, who resolved in his *Institutes* to set forth all the principles of Protestantism comprehensively, logically, and systematically. As a result, after several revisions and enlargements (the definitive edition appeared in 1559), Calvin's *Institutes* became the Protestant equivalent of Thomas Aquinas's *Summa Theologiae* (Chapter 9).

Calvin's austere theology started with the omnipotence of God and worked downward. For Calvin, the entire universe depends utterly on the will of the Almighty, who created all things for his greater glory. Because of man's original fall from grace, all human beings are sinners by nature, bound to an evil inheritance they cannot escape. Nevertheless, God (for reasons of his own) has predestined some for eternal salvation and damned all the rest to the torments of Hell. Nothing that human beings may do can alter their fate; all souls are stamped with God's blessing or curse before they are born. Nevertheless, Christians cannot be indifferent to their conduct on earth. If they are among the elect, God will implant in them the desire to live according to his laws. Upright conduct is thus a sign, though not an infallible one, that an individual has been chosen to sit at the throne of glory. Membership in the reformed church (as Calvinist churches are more properly known) is another presumptive sign of election to salvation. But most of all, Calvin urged Christians to conceive of themselves as chosen instruments of God, charged to work actively to fulfill God's purposes on earth. Because sin offends God, Christians should do all they can to prevent it, not because their actions will lead to anyone's salvation (they will not), but simply because God's glory is diminished if sin is allowed to flourish unchecked by the efforts of those whom he has chosen for salvation.

Calvin always acknowledged a great theological debt to Luther, but his religious teachings diverged from those of the Wittenberg reformer in several essentials. First of all, Luther's attitude toward proper Christian conduct in the world was much more passive than Calvin's. For Luther, a Christian should endure the trials of this life through

JOHN CALVIN. This recently discovered portrait by an anonymous artist shows the Protestant reformer as a serene and authoritative figure. It places the grotesque caricature of Calvin (right) in perspective.

CALVIN AS SEEN BY HIS ENEMIES. In this image, which circulated among Calvin's Catholic detractors, the reformer's facial features are a disturbing composite of fish, toad, and chicken.

suffering, whereas for Calvin the world was to be mastered in unceasing labor for God's sake. Calvin's religion was also more legalistic than Luther's. Luther, for example, insisted that his followers attend church on Sunday, but he did not demand that during the remainder of the day they refrain from all pleasure or work. Calvin, however, issued stern strictures against worldliness of any sort on the Sabbath and forbade all sorts of minor self-indulgences, even on non-Sabbath days.

The two men also differed on fundamental matters of church governance and worship. Although Luther broke with the Catholic system of hierarchical church government, Lutheran district superintendents exercised some of the same powers as bishops, including supervision of parish clergy. Luther also retained many features of traditional worship, including altars, music, and ritual. Calvin, however, rejected everything that smacked to him of "popery." Thus he argued for the elimination of all traces of hierarchy within the church. Instead, each congregation should elect its own ministers, and assemblies of ministers and "elders" (laymen responsible for maintaining proper religious conduct among the faithful) were to govern the reformed church as a whole. Calvin also insisted on the utmost simplicity in worship, prohibiting (among much else) vestments, processions, instrumental music, and religious images of any sort, including stained-glass windows. He

also dispensed with all remaining vestiges of Catholic sacramental theology by making the sermon, rather than the Eucharist, the centerpiece of reformed worship.

Calvinism in Geneva

Consistent with his theological convictions, Calvin was intent on putting his religious teachings into practice. Sensing an opportunity in the French-speaking Swiss city of Geneva—then in the throes of political and religious upheaval—he moved there late in 1536 and immediately began preaching and organizing. In 1538, his activities caused him to be expelled by the city council, but in 1541 he returned and brought the city under his sway.

Under Calvin's guidance, Geneva's government became a theocracy. Supreme authority was vested in a "Consistory" composed of twelve lay elders and between ten and twenty pastors, whose weekly meetings Calvin dominated. Aside from passing legislation proposed to it by a congregation of ministers, the Consistory's main function was to supervise morality, both public and private. To this end, Geneva was divided into districts, and a committee of the Consistory visited every household, without prior warning, to check on the behavior of its members. Dancing, card playing, attending the theater, and working or playing on the Sabbath—all were outlawed as works of the devil. Innkeepers were forbidden to allow anyone to consume food or drink without first saying grace, or to permit any patron to stay up after nine o'clock. Murder, treason, adultery, witchcraft, blasphemy, and heresy were all capital crimes. Even penalties for lesser crimes were severe. During the first four years after Calvin gained control in Geneva, there were no fewer than fifty-eight executions in this city with a total population of only 16,000.

As objectionable as such punishments may seem today, Calvin's Geneva was a beacon of light to thousands of Protestants throughout Europe in the mid-sixteenth century. Calvin's disciple John Knox, who brought the reformed religion to Scotland, declared Geneva "the most perfect school of Christ that ever was on earth since the days of the Apostles." Converts such as Knox flocked to Geneva for refuge or instruction and then returned home to become ardent proselytizers for the new religion. Geneva thus became the center of an international movement dedicated to spreading reformed religion to France and the rest of Europe through organized missionary activity and propaganda.

These efforts were remarkably successful. By the end of the sixteenth century, Calvinists were a majority in Scotland (where they were known as Presbyterians) and Holland (where they founded the Dutch Reformed Church). They were also influential in England; although the Church of England adopted reformed theology but not reformed worship (Calvinists there who sought further reforms in worship were known as Puritans). There were also substantial Calvinist minorities in France (where they were called Huguenots), Germany, Hungary, Lithuania, and Poland. God's kingdom on Earth had not yet been fully realized: on his deathbed in 1564, Calvin pronounced the Genevans to still be "a perverse and unhappy nation." But an extraordinary revolution had taken place in the religious life and practices of Europe, and they would soon spread to the New World.

THE DOMESTICATION OF REFORM

Protestantism was a revolutionary movement whose radical claims for the spiritual equality of all true Christian believers had the potential to undermine the political, social, and even gender hierarchies on which European society rested. Luther himself did not anticipate that his ideas might have such implications, and he was genuinely shocked when the rebellious German peasants and the radical Anabaptists at Münster interpreted his teachings in this way. And

Luther was by no means the only staunchly conservative Protestant. None of the prominent early Protestants were social or political radicals. Most Protestant reformers depended on the support of existing social and political leaders: territorial princes, of course, but also the ruling elites of towns. As a result, the Reformation movement was speedily "domesticated," in two senses. Its revolutionary potential was muffled—Luther himself rarely spoke about "the priesthood of all believers" after 1525—and there was an increasing emphasis on the patriarchal family as the central institution of reformed life.

Reform and Discipline

As we have seen, injunctions to lead a more disciplined and godly life had been a frequent message of fifteenth-century religious reform movements. Many of these efforts were actively promoted by princes and town councils, most famously perhaps in Florence, where the Dominican preacher Girolamo Savonarola led the city on an extraordinary but short-lived campaign of puritanism and moral reform between 1494 and 1498. But there are many other examples of rulers legislating against sin. When Desiderius Erasmus called on secular authorities to think of themselves as abbots and of their territories as giant monasteries, he was sounding an already-familiar theme.

Protestant rulers, however, took the need to enforce godly discipline with particular seriousness, because the depravity of human nature was a fundamental tenet of Protestant belief. Like Saint Augustine at the end of the fourth century (Chapter 6), Protestants believed that people would inevitably turn out bad unless they were compelled to be good. It was, therefore, the responsibility of secular and religious leaders to control and punish the behavior of their people, because otherwise their evil deeds would anger God and destroy human society.

Protestant godliness began with the discipline of children. Luther himself wrote two catechisms (instructional tracts) designed to teach children the tenets of their faith and the obligations—toward parents, masters, and rulers—that God imposed on them. Luther also insisted that all children, boys and girls alike, should be taught to read the Bible in their own languages. Schooling thus became a characteristically Protestant preoccupation and rallying cry. Even the Protestant family was designated a "school of godliness," in which fathers were expected to instruct and discipline their wives, their children, and their household servants.

But family life in the early sixteenth century still left much to be desired in the eyes of Protestant reformers. Drunkenness, domestic violence, illicit sexual relations, lewd dancing, and the blasphemous swearing of oaths were frequent topics of reforming discourse. Various methods of discipline were attempted, including private counseling, public confessions of wrongdoing, public penances and shamings, exclusion from church services, and even imprisonment. All these efforts met with varying, but generally modest, success. To create godly Protestant families, and to enforce godly discipline on entire communities, was going to require the active cooperation of godly authorities.

Protestantism, Government, and the Family

The domestication of the Reformation in this sense took place principally in the free towns of Germany and Switzerland—and from there spread westward to the New World. Protestant attacks on monasticism and clerical celibacy found a receptive audience among townsmen who resented the immunity of monastic houses from taxation and regarded clerical celibacy as a subterfuge for the seduction of their own wives and daughters. Protestant emphasis on the depravity of the human will and the consequent need for that will to be disciplined by authority also resonated powerfully with guilds and town governments, which were anxious to maintain and increase the control exercised by urban elites (mainly merchants and master craftsmen) over the apprentices and journeymen who made up the majority of the male population. By eliminating the competing jurisdictional authority of the Catholic Church, Protestantism allowed town governments to consolidate all authority within the city into their own hands.

Meanwhile, Protestantism reinforced the control of individual men over their own households by emphasizing the family as the basic unit of religious education. An all-powerful father figure was expected to assume responsibility for instructing and disciplining his household according to the precepts of reformed religion. At the same time, Protestantism introduced a new religious ideal for women. No longer was the celibate nun the exemplar of female holiness; in her place now stood the married and obedient Protestant "goodwife." As one Lutheran prince wrote in 1527: "Those who bear children please God better than all the monks and nuns singing and praying." To this extent, Protestantism resolved the tensions between piety and sexuality that had long characterized Christian teachings, by declaring the holiness of marital sex.

But this did not promote a new view of women's spiritual potential, nor did it elevate their social and political status; quite the contrary. Luther regarded women as more sexually driven than men and less capable of controlling their sexual desires—despite the fact that Luther confessed himself incapable of celibacy. His opposition to convents allegedly rested on his belief that it was impossible for women to remain chaste, so that sequestering them simply made illicit behavior inevitable. To prevent sin, it was necessary that all women should be married, preferably at a young age, and so placed under the governance of a godly husband.

For the most part, Protestant town governments were happy to cooperate in shutting down convents. The convent's property went to the town, after all. But conflicts did arise between Protestant reformers and town fathers over marriage and sexuality, especially over the reformers' insistence that both men and women should marry young as a restraint on lust. In many German towns, men were traditionally expected to delay marriage until they had achieved the status of a master craftsman—a requirement that had become increasingly difficult to enforce as guilds sought to restrict the number of journeymen permitted to become masters. In theory, then, apprentices and journeymen were not supposed to marry. Instead, they were expected to frequent brothels and taverns, a legally sanctioned outlet for extramarital sexuality long viewed as necessary to men's physical well-being, but that Protestant reformers found morally abhorrent and demanded be abolished.

Towns responded in a variety of ways to these opposing pressures. Some instituted special committees to police public morals, of the sort we have noted in Calvin's Geneva. Some abandoned Protestantism altogether. Others, like Augsburg, flip-flopped back and forth between Protestantism and Catholicism for several decades. Yet regardless of a town's final choice of religious allegiance, by the end of the sixteenth century a revolution had taken place with respect to town governments' attitudes toward public morality. In their competition with each other, neither Catholics nor Protestants wished to be seen as soft on sin. The result, by 1600, was the widespread abolition of publicly licensed brothels, the outlawing of prostitution, and far stricter governmental supervision of many other aspects of private life than had ever been the case in any Western civilization.

The Control of Marriage

Protestantism also increased parents' control over their children's choice of marital partners. The medieval Church defined marriage as a sacrament that did not require the involvement of a priest. The mutual free consent of two individuals, even if given without witnesses or parental approval, was enough to constitute a legally valid marriage in

Competing Viewpoints

Marriage and Celibacy: Two Views

These two selections illustrate the strongly contrasting views on the spiritual value of marriage versus celibacy that came to be embraced by Protestant and Catholic religious authorities. The first selection is part of Martin Luther's more general attack on monasticism, which emphasizes his contention that marriage is the natural and divinely intended state for all human beings. The second selection, from the decrees of the Council of Trent (1545–63), restates traditional Catholic teaching on the holiness of marriage but also emphasizes the spiritual superiority of virginity to marriage as well as the necessity of clerical celibacy.

Luther's Views on Celibacy

Listen! In all my days I have not heard the confession of a nun, but in the light of Scripture I shall hit upon how matters fare with her and know I shall not be lying. If a girl is not sustained by great and exceptional grace, she can live without a man as little as she can without eating, drinking, sleeping, and other natural necessities.

Nor, on the other hand, can a man dispense with a wife. The reason for this is that procreating children is an urge planted as deeply in human nature as eating and drinking. That is why God has given and put into the body the organs, arteries, fluxes, and everything that serves it. Therefore what is he doing who would check this process and keep nature from running its desired and intended course? He is attempting to keep nature from being nature, fire from burning, water from wetting, and a man from eating, drinking, and sleeping.

Source: E. M. Plass, ed., *What Luther Says,* vol. 2 (St. Louis, MO: 1959), pp. 888–89.

Canons on the Sacrament of Matrimony (1563)

Canon 1. If anyone says that matrimony is not truly and properly one of the seven sacraments . . . instituted by Christ the Lord, but has been devised by men in the Church and does not confer grace, let him be anathema [cursed].

Canon 9. If anyone says that clerics constituted in sacred orders or regulars [monks and nuns] who have made solemn profession of chastity can contract marriage . . . and that all who feel that they have not the gift of chastity, even though they have made such a vow, can contract marriage, let him be anathema, since God does not refuse that gift to those who ask for it rightly, neither does *he suffer us to be tempted above that which we are able.*

Canon 10: If anyone says that the married state excels the state of virginity or celibacy, and that it is better and happier to be united in matrimony than to remain in virginity or celibacy, let him be anathema.

Source: H. J. Schroeder, *Canons and Decrees of the Council of Trent* (St. Louis, MO: 1941), pp. 181–82.

Questions for Analysis

1. On what grounds does Luther attack the practice of celibacy? Do you agree with his basic premise?

2. How do the later canons of the Catholic Church respond to Protestant views like Luther's? What appears to be at stake in this defense of marriage and celibacy?

the eyes of the Church. Opposition to this doctrine came from many quarters, especially from families who stood to lose from this *laissez faire* doctrine. Because marriage involved rights of inheritance to property, it was regarded as too important a matter to be left to the choice of adolescents. Instead, parents wanted the power to prevent unsuitable matches and, in some cases, to force their children to accept the marriage arrangements their families might negotiate on their behalf. Protestantism offered an opportunity to achieve such control. Luther had declared marriage to be a purely secular matter, not a sacrament at all, and one that could be regulated however the governing authorities thought best. Calvin largely followed suit, although Calvinist theocracy drew less of a distinction than did Lutheranism between the powers of church and state.

Even Catholicism was eventually forced to give way. Although it never abandoned its insistence that both members of the couple must freely consent to their marriage, by the end of the sixteenth century the Catholic Church required formal public notice of intent to marry and insisted on the presence of a priest at the actual wedding ceremony. Both were efforts to prevent elopements, allowing families time to intervene before an unsuitable marriage was concluded. Individual Catholic countries sometimes went even further in trying to assert parental control over their children's choice of marital partners. In France, for example, although couples might still marry without parental consent, those who did so now forfeited all of their rights to inherit their families' property. In somewhat different ways, both Protestantism and Catholicism thus moved to strengthen the control that parents could exercise over their children—and, in the case of Protestantism, that husbands could exercise over their wives.

THE REFORMATION OF ENGLAND

In England, the Reformation took a rather different course than it did in continental Europe. Although a tradition of popular reform survived into the sixteenth century, the number of dissidents was too small and their influence too limited for Lollardy to play a significant role in paving the way for the ultimate triumph of Protestantism in England (see Chapter 10). Nor was England particularly oppressed by the papal exactions and abuses that roiled Germany. When the sixteenth century began, English monarchs already exercised close control over Church appointments within their kingdom; they also received the lion's share of the papal taxation collected from England. Nor did ecclesiastical

courts inspire any particular resentments. On the contrary, they would continue to function in Protestant England until the eighteenth century. Why, then, did sixteenth-century England become a Protestant country at all?

"The King's Great Matter"

By 1527, King Henry VIII of England had been married for eighteen years to Ferdinand and Isabella's daughter, Catherine of Aragon. Yet all the offspring of this union had died in infancy, with the exception of a daughter, Mary. Because Henry needed a male heir to preserve the peaceful succession to the throne and because Catherine was now past childbearing age, Henry had political reasons to propose a change of wife. He also had more personal motives, having become infatuated with a lady-in-waiting named Anne Boleyn.

Henry therefore appealed to Rome to annul his marriage to Catherine, arguing that because she had previously been married to his older brother Arthur (who had died in adolescence), Henry's marriage to Catherine had

HENRY VIII OF ENGLAND. Hans Holbein the Younger executed several portraits of the English king. This one represents him in middle age, confident of his powers.

Analyzing Primary Sources

The Six Articles of the English Church

Although Henry VIII withdrew the Church of England from obedience to the papacy, he continued to reject most Protestant theology. Some of his advisers, most notably Thomas Cromwell, were committed Protestants; and the king allowed his son and heir, Edward VI, to be raised as a Protestant. But even after several years of rapid (and mostly Protestant) change in the English church, Henry reasserted a set of traditional Catholic doctrines in the Six Articles of 1539. These would remain binding on the Church of England until the king's death in 1547.

First, that in the most blessed sacrament of the altar, by the strength and efficacy of Christ's mighty word, it being spoken by the priest, is present really, under the form of bread and wine, the natural body and blood of our Savior Jesus Christ, conceived of the Virgin Mary, and that after the consecration there remains no substance of bread or wine, nor any other substance but the substance of Christ, God and man;

Secondly, that communion in both kinds is not necessary for salvation, by the law of God, to all persons, and that it is to be believed and not doubted . . . that in the flesh, under the form of bread, is the very blood, and with the blood, under the form of wine, is the very flesh, as well apart as though they were both together;

Thirdly, that priests, after the order of priesthood received as afore, may not marry by the law of God;

Fourthly, that vows of chastity or widowhood by man or woman made to God advisedly ought to be observed by the law of God. . . .

Fifthly, that it is right and necessary that private masses be continued and admitted in this the king's English Church and congregation . . . whereby good Christian people . . . do receive both godly and goodly consolations and benefits; and it is agreeable also to God's law;

Sixthly, that oral, private confession is expedient and necessary to be retained and continued, used and frequented in the church of God.

Source: *Statutes of the Realm,* vol. 3 (London: 1810–28), p. 739 (modernized).

Questions for Analysis

1. Three of these six articles focus on the sacrament of the Mass. Given what you have learned in this chapter, why would Henry have been so concerned about this sacrament? What does this reveal about his values and those of his contemporaries?

2. Given Henry's insistence on these articles, why might he have allowed his son to be raised a Protestant? What does this suggest about the political situation in England?

---

been invalid from the beginning. As Henry's representatives pointed out, the Bible pronounced it "an unclean thing" for a man to take his brother's wife and cursed such a marriage with childlessness (Leviticus 20:31). Even a papal dispensation (which Henry and Catherine had long before obtained for their marriage) could not exempt them from such a clear prohibition, as the marriage's childlessness proved.

Henry's suit put Pope Clement VII (r. 1523–34) in a quandary. Henry was firmly convinced that this Scriptural curse had blighted his chances of perpetuating his lineage; and both Henry and Clement knew that popes in the past had granted annulments to reigning monarchs on far weaker grounds than the ones Henry was alleging. If, however, the pope granted Henry's annulment, he would cast doubt on the validity of all papal dispensations. More seriously, however, he would provoke the wrath of the emperor Charles V, Catherine of Aragon's nephew, whose armies were in firm command of Rome and who at that moment held the pope himself in captivity. Clement was trapped; all he could do was procrastinate and hope that the matter would resolve itself. For two years, he allowed the suit to proceed in England without ever reaching a verdict. Then, suddenly, he transferred the case to Rome, where the legal process began all over again.

Exasperated by these delays, Henry began to increase the pressure on the pope. In 1531 he compelled an assembly of English clergy to declare him "protector and only supreme head" of the Church in England. In 1532 he encouraged

Parliament to produce an inflammatory list of grievances against the English clergy, and used this threat to force them to concede his right as king to approve or disapprove all Church legislation. In January 1533, Henry married Anne Boleyn (already pregnant) even though his marriage to Queen Catherine had still not been annulled. The new archbishop of Canterbury, Thomas Cranmer, provided the required annulment in May, acting on his own authority.

In September, Princess Elizabeth was born; her father, disappointed again in his hopes for a son, refused to attend her christening. Nevertheless, Parliament settled the succession to the throne on the children of Henry and Anne, redirected all papal revenues from England into the king's hands, prohibited appeals to the papal court, and formally declared "the King's highness to be Supreme Head of the Church of England." In 1536, Henry executed his former tutor and chancellor Sir Thomas More (Chapter 12) for his refusal to endorse this declaration of supremacy, and took the first steps toward dissolving England's monasteries. By the end of 1539, the monasteries and convents were gone and their lands and wealth confiscated by the king, who distributed them to his supporters.

These measures broke the bonds that linked the English Church to Rome, but they did not make England a Protestant country. Although certain traditional practices (such as pilgrimages and the veneration of relics) were prohibited, the English Church remained overwhelmingly Catholic in organization, doctrine, ritual, and language. The Six Articles promulgated by Parliament in 1539 at Henry VIII's behest left no room for doubt as to official orthodoxy: oral confession to priests, masses for the dead, and clerical celibacy were all confirmed; the Latin Mass continued; and Catholic Eucharistic doctrine was not only confirmed but its denial made punishable by death. To most English people, only the disappearance of the monasteries and the king's own continuing matrimonial adventures (he married six wives in all) were evidence that their Church was no longer in communion with Rome.

The Reign of Edward VI

For truly committed Protestants, and especially those who had visited Calvin's Geneva, the changes Henry VIII enforced on the English Church did not go nearly far enough. In 1547, the accession of the nine-year-old king Edward VI (Henry's son by his third wife, Jane Seymour) gave them their opportunity to finish the task of reform. Encouraged by the apparent sympathies of the young king, Edward's government moved quickly to reform the creeds and ceremonies of the English Church. Priests were permitted to

marry; English services replaced Latin ones; the veneration of images was discouraged, and the images themselves defaced or destroyed; prayers for the dead were discouraged, and endowments for such prayers were confiscated; and new articles of belief were drawn up, repudiating all sacraments except baptism and communion and affirming the Protestant doctrine of justification by faith alone. Most important, a new prayer book was published to define precisely how the new English-language services of the church were to be conducted. Much remained unsettled with respect to both doctrine and worship; but by 1553, when the youthful Edward died, the English Church appeared to have become a distinctly Protestant institution.

Mary Tudor and the Restoration of Catholicism

Edward's successor, however, was his pious and much older half-sister Mary (r. 1553–58), granddaughter of "the most Catholic monarchs" of Spain, Ferdinand and Isabella (see Chapter 11). Mary speedily reversed her brother's religious policies, restoring the Latin Mass and requiring married priests to give up their wives. She even prevailed on Parliament to vote a return to papal allegiance. Hundreds of Protestant leaders fled abroad, many to Geneva; others, including Archbishop Thomas Cranmer, were burned at the stake for refusing to abjure their Protestantism. News of the martyrdoms spread like wildfire through Protestant Europe. In England, however, Mary's policies sparked relatively little resistance. After two decades of religious upheaval, most English men and women were probably hoping that Mary's reign would bring some stability to their lives.

This, however, Mary could not do. The executions she ordered were insufficient to wipe out religious resistance—instead, Protestant propaganda about "Bloody Mary" caused widespread unease, even among those who welcomed the return of traditional religious forms. Nor could Mary do anything to restore monasticism: too many leading families had profited from Henry VIII's dissolution of the monasteries for this to be reversed. Mary's marriage to her cousin Philip, Charles V's son and heir to the Spanish throne, was another miscalculation. Although the marriage treaty stipulated that in the event of Mary's death Philip could not succeed her, some of her English subjects never trusted him. When the queen allowed herself to be drawn by Philip into a war with France on Spain's behalf—in which England lost Calais, its last foothold on the European continent—many English people became highly disaffected. Ultimately, how-

QUEEN MARY AND QUEEN ELIZABETH. The two daughters of Henry VIII were the first two queens regnant of England: the first women to rule in their own right. Despite the similar challenges they faced, they had strikingly different fates and have been treated very differently in popular histories. ■ *How do these two portraits suggest differences in their personalities and their self-representation as rulers?*

ever, what doomed Mary's policies was simply the accident of biology: Mary was unable to conceive an heir, and when she died after only five years of rule, her throne passed to her Protestant sister, Elizabeth.

The Elizabethan Compromise

The daughter of Henry VIII and Anne Boleyn, Elizabeth (r. 1558–1603) was predisposed in favor of Protestantism by the circumstances of her parents' marriage as well as by her upbringing. But Elizabeth was no zealot, and wisely recognized that supporting radical Protestantism in England might provoke bitter sectarian strife. Accordingly, she presided over what is often known as "the Elizabethan settlement." By a new Act of Supremacy (1559), Elizabeth repealed Mary's Catholic legislation, prohibiting foreign religious powers (i.e., the pope) from exercising any authority within England, and declaring herself "supreme governor" of the English church—a more Protestant title than Henry VIII's "supreme head," insofar as most Protestants believed that Christ alone was the head of the Church. She also adopted many of the Protestant liturgical reforms instituted by her brother, Edward, including a revised version of the prayer book. But she retained vestiges of Catholic practice too, including bishops, church courts, and vestments for the clergy. On most doctrinal matters, including predestination and free will, Elizabeth's Thirty-nine Articles of Faith (approved in 1562) struck a decidedly Protestant, even Calvinist, tone. But the prayer book was more moderate, and on the critical issue of the Eucharist was deliberately ambiguous. By combining Catholic and Protestant interpretations ("This is my body. . . . Do this in remembrance of me") into a single declaration, the prayer book permitted an enormous latitude for competing interpretations of the service by priests and parishioners alike.

Yet religious tensions persisted in Elizabethan England, not only between Protestants and Catholics but also between moderate and more extreme Protestants. The queen's artful fudging of these competing Christianities was by no means a recipe for success. Rather, what preserved "the Elizabethan settlement," and ultimately made England a Protestant country, was the extraordinary length of Queen Elizabeth's reign combined with the fact that for much of that time Protestant England was at war with Catholic Spain. Under Elizabeth, Protestantism and English nationalism gradually fused together into a potent conviction that God himself had chosen England for greatness. After 1588, when English naval forces won an improbable victory over a Spanish Armada (Chapter 11), Protestantism and Englishness became nearly indistinguishable to most of Queen Elizabeth's subjects. Laws against Catholic practices became increasingly severe, and although an English Catholic tradition did survive, its adherents were a persecuted minority. Significant, too, was the situation in Ireland, where the vast majority of the population remained Catholic despite the government's efforts to impose Protestantism on them. By 1603, Irishness was as firmly identified with Catholicism as was Englishness with Protestantism; but it was the Protestants who were in power in both countries.

THE REBIRTH OF THE CATHOLIC CHURCH

So far, our emphasis on the spread of Protestantism has cast the spotlight on dissident reformers such as Luther and Calvin. But there was also a powerful internal reform movement within the Church during the sixteenth century, which resulted in the birth (or rebirth) of a Catholic ("universal") faith. For some, this movement is the "Catholic Reformation"; for others, it is the "Counter-Reformation." Those who prefer the former term emphasize that the Church continued significant reforming movements that can be traced back to the eleventh century (Chapter 8) and which gained new momentum in the wake of the Great Schism (Chapter 10). Others, however, insist that most Catholic reformers of this period were inspired primarily by the urgent need to resist Protestantism and to strengthen the power of the Roman Church in opposition to it.

Catholic Reforms

Even before Luther's challenge to the Church, as we have seen, there was a movement for moral and institutional reform within some religious orders. But while these efforts received strong support from several secular rulers, the papacy showed little interest in them. In Spain, reforming activities directed by Cardinal Francisco Ximenes de Cisneros (1436–1517) led to the imposition of strict rules of behavior and the elimination of abuses prevalent among the clergy. Ximenes (*he-MEN-ez*) also helped to regenerate the spiritual life of the Spanish Church. In Italy, earnest clerics labored to make the Italian Church more worthy of

its calling. Reforming existing monastic orders was a difficult task, not least because the papal court set such a poor example; but Italian reformers did manage to establish several new orders dedicated to high ideals of piety and social service. In northern Europe, Christian humanists such as Erasmus and Thomas More played a role in this Catholic reform movement, not only by criticizing abuses and editing sacred texts but also by encouraging the laity to lead lives of sincere religious piety (Chapter 12).

As a response to the challenges posed by Protestantism, however, these internal reforms proved entirely inadequate. Starting in the 1530s, therefore, a more aggressive phase of reform under a new style of vigorous papal leadership began to gather momentum. The leading Counter-Reformation popes—Paul III (r. 1534–49), Paul IV (r. 1555–59), Pius V (r. 1566–72), and Sixtus V (r. 1585–90)—were the most zealous reformers of the Church since the twelfth century. All led upright lives; some, indeed, were so grimly ascetic that contemporaries longed for the bad old days. As a Spanish councilor wrote of Pius V in 1567, "We should like it even better if the present Holy Father were no longer with us, however great, inexpressible, unparalleled, and extraordinary His Holiness may be." In confronting Protestantism,

THE COUNCIL OF TRENT. This fresco depicts the General Council of the Catholic Church, which met at intervals for nearly twenty years between 1545 and 1563 in the city of Trent (in modern-day Italy) in order to enact significant internal reforms.

however, an excessively holy pope was vastly preferable to a self-indulgent one. And these Counter-Reformation popes were not merely holy men. They were also accomplished administrators who reorganized papal finances and filled ecclesiastical offices with bishops and abbots no less renowned for austerity and holiness than were the popes themselves.

Papal reform efforts intensified at the Council of Trent, a General Council of the entire Church convoked by Paul III in 1545, which met at intervals thereafter until 1563. The decisions taken at Trent (a provincial capital of the Holy Roman Empire, located in modern-day Italy) provided the foundations on which a new Catholic Church would be erected. Although the council began by debating some form of compromise with Protestantism, it ended by reaffirming all of the Catholic tenets challenged by Protestant critics. "Good works" were affirmed as necessary for salvation, and all seven sacraments were declared indispensable means of grace, without which salvation was impossible. Transubstantiation, Purgatory, the invocation of saints, and the rule of celibacy for the clergy were all confirmed as dogmas—essential elements—of the Catholic faith. The Bible (in its imperfect Vulgate form) and the traditions of apostolic teaching were held to be of equal authority as sources of Christian truth. Papal supremacy over every bishop and priest was expressly maintained, and the supremacy of the pope over any Church council was taken for granted outright, signalling a final defeat of the still-active conciliar movement (Chapter 10). The Council of Trent even reaffirmed the doctrine of indulgences that had touched off the Lutheran revolt, although it condemned the worst abuses connected with their sale.

The legislation of Trent was not confined to matters of doctrine. To improve pastoral care of the laity, bishops and priests were forbidden to hold more than one spiritual office. To address the problem of an ignorant priesthood, a theological seminary was to be established in every diocese. The council also suppressed a variety of local religious practices and saints' cults, replacing them with new cults authorized and approved by Rome. To prevent heretical ideas from corrupting the faithful, the council further decided to censor or suppress dangerous books. In 1564, a specially appointed commission published the first Index, an official list of writings that ought not to be read by faithful Catholics. All of Erasmus's works were immediately placed on the Index, even though he had been a chosen champion of the Church against Martin Luther only forty years before. A permanent agency known as the Congregation of the Index was later set up to revise the list, which was maintained until the Index was abolished in 1966 after the Second Vatican Council. It was to become symbolic of the doctrinal intolerance that characterized sixteenth-century Christianity, both in its Catholic and Protestant varieties.

***THE INSPIRATION OF SAINT JEROME* BY GUIDO RENI.** The Council of Trent declared Saint Jerome's Latin translation of the Bible, the Vulgate, to be the official version of the Catholic Church, and in 1592 Pope Clement VIII chose one edition to be authoritative above all others. Since biblical scholars had known since the early sixteenth century that Saint Jerome's translation contained numerous mistakes, Catholic defenders of the Vulgate insisted that even his mistakes had been divinely inspired. ▪ *How does Guido Reni's painting of 1635 attempt to make this point?*

Ignatius Loyola and the Society of Jesus

In addition to the independent activities of popes and the legislation of the Council of Trent, a third main force propelling the Counter-Reformation was the foundation of the Society of Jesus (commonly known as the Jesuits) by Ignatius Loyola (1491–1556). In the midst of a career as a mercenary, this young Spanish nobleman was wounded in battle in 1521, the same year in which Luther defied authority at the Diet of Worms. While recuperating, he turned from the reading of chivalric romances to a romantic vernacular retelling of the life of Jesus—and on the strength

Analyzing Primary Sources

The Demands of Obedience

> *The necessity of obedience in the spiritual formation of monks and nuns can be traced back to the Rule of Saint Benedict in the early sixth century, and beyond. In keeping with the mission of its founder, Ignatius of Loyola (1491–1556) the Society of Jesus brought a new militancy to this old ideal.*

Rules for Thinking with the Church

1. Always to be ready to obey with mind and heart, setting aside all judgment of one's own, the true spouse of Jesus Christ, our holy mother, our infallible and orthodox mistress, the Catholic Church, whose authority is exercised over us by the hierarchy.

2. To commend the confession of sins to a priest as it is practised in the Church; the reception of the Holy Eucharist once a year, or better still every week, or at least every month, with the necessary preparation. . . .

4. To have a great esteem for the religious orders, and to give the preference to celibacy or virginity over the married state. . . .

6. To praise relics, the veneration and invocation of Saints: also the stations, and pious pilgrimages, indulgences, jubilees, the custom of lighting candles in the churches, and other such aids to piety and devotion. . . .

9. To uphold especially all the precepts of the Church, and not censure them in any manner; but, on the contrary, to defend them promptly, with reasons drawn from all sources, against those who criticize them.

10. To be eager to commend the decrees, mandates, traditions, rites, and customs of the Fathers in the Faith or our superiors. . . .

11. That we may be altogether of the same mind and in conformity with the Church herself, if she shall have defined anything to be black which to our eyes appears to be white, we ought in like manner to pronounce it to be black. For we must undoubtingly believe, that the Spirit of our Lord Jesus Christ, and the Spirit of the Orthodox Church His Spouse, by which Spirit we are governed and directed to salvation, is the same. . . .

From the Constitutions of the Jesuit Order

Let us with the utmost pains strain every nerve of our strength to exhibit this virtue of obedience, firstly to the Highest Pontiff, then to the Superiors of the Society; so that in all things . . . we may be most ready to obey his voice, just as if it issued from Christ our Lord . . . leaving any work, even a letter, that we have begun and have not yet finished; by directing to this goal all our strength and intention in the Lord, that holy obedience may be made perfect in us in every respect, in performance, in will, in intellect; by submitting to whatever may be enjoined on us with great readiness, with spiritual joy and perseverance; by persuading ourselves that all things [commanded] are just; by rejecting with a kind of blind obedience all opposing opinion or judgment of our own. . . .

Source: Henry Bettenson, ed., *Documents of the Christian Church,* 2nd ed. (Oxford: 1967), pp. 259–61.

Questions for Analysis

1. How might Loyola's career as a soldier have inspired the language used in his "Rules for Thinking with the Church"?

2. In what ways do these Jesuit principles respond directly to the challenges of Protestant reformers?

---

of this decided to become a spiritual soldier of Christ. For ten months he lived as a hermit in a cave near the town of Manresa, where he experienced ecstatic visions and worked out the principles of his subsequent guidebook, the *Spiritual Exercises.* This manual, completed in 1535 and first published in 1541, offered practical advice on how to master one's will and serve God through a systematic program of meditations on sin and the life of Christ. It eventually became a basic handbook for all Jesuits and has been widely studied by Catholic laypeople as well. Indeed, Loyola's *Spiritual Exercises* ranks alongside Calvin's *Institutes* as the most influential religious text of the sixteenth century.

The Jesuit order originated as a small group of six disciples who gathered around Loyola during his belated career as a student in Paris. They vowed to serve God in poverty, chastity, and missionary work, and were formally constituted by Pope Paul III in 1540; by the time of Loyola's death, the Society of Jesus already numbered some 1,500 members. And it was by far the most militant of the religious orders fostered by the Catholic reform movements of the sixteenth century—not merely a monastic society but a company of soldiers sworn to defend the faith. Their weapons were not bullets and swords but eloquence, persuasion, and instruction in correct doctrines; yet the Society also became accomplished in more worldly methods of exerting influence. Its organization was patterned after that of a military unit, whose commander in chief enforced iron discipline on all members. Individuality was suppressed, and a soldierlike obedience was required from the rank and file. Indeed, the Jesuit general, sometimes known as the "black pope" (from the color of the order's habit), was elected for life and answered only to the pope in Rome, to whom all senior Jesuits took a special vow of strict obedience. As a result of this vow, all Jesuits were held to be at the pope's disposal at all times.

The activities of the Jesuits consisted primarily of proselytizing and establishing schools. As missionaries, the early Jesuits preached to non-Christians in India, China, and Spanish America. One of Loyola's closest associates, Francis Xavier (1506–1552), baptized thousands of native people and traveled thousands of miles in South and East Asia. Yet although Loyola had not at first conceived of his society as a batallion of "shock troops" in the fight against Protestantism, that is what it primarily became. Through preaching and diplomacy—sometimes at the risk of their lives—Jesuits in the second half of the sixteenth century fanned out across Europe in direct confrontation with Calvinists. In many places, the Jesuits were instrumental in keeping rulers and their subjects loyal to Catholicism; in others they met martyrdom; and in some others, notably Poland and parts of Germany and France, they succeeded in regaining territory previously lost to Protestantism. Wherever they were allowed to settle, they set up schools and colleges, on the grounds that only a vigorous Catholicism nurtured by widespread literacy and education could combat Protestantism.

A New Catholic Christianity

The greatest achievement of these reform movements was the revitalization of the Church. Had it not been for such determined efforts, Catholicism would not have swept over

the globe during the seventeenth and eighteenth centuries or reemerged in Europe as a vigorous spiritual force. There were some other consequences, as well. One was the advancement of lay literacy in Catholic countries. Another was the growth of intense concern for acts of charity; because Catholicism continued to emphasize good works as well as faith, charitable activities took on an extremely important role.

There was also a renewed emphasis on the role of religious women. Reformed Catholicism did not exalt marriage as a route to holiness to the same degree as did Protestantism, but it did encourage the piety of a female religious elite. For example, it embraced the mysticism of Saint Teresa of Avila (1515–1582) and established new orders of nuns, such as the Ursulines and the Sisters of Charity. Both Protestants and Catholics continued to exclude women from the priesthood or ministry, but Catholic women could pursue religious lives with at least some degree of independence, and the convent continued to be a route toward spiritual and even political advancement in Catholic countries.

The Reformed Catholic Church did not, however, perpetuate the tolerant Christianity of Erasmus. Instead,

THERESA OF AVILA. Theresa of Avila (1515–1582) was one of many female religious figures who played an important role in the Reformed Catholic Church. She was canonized in 1622. This image is dated 1576. The Latin wording on the scroll unfurled above Theresa's head reads: "I will sing forever of the mercy of the Holy Lord."

Christian humanists lost favor with the papacy, and even scientists such as Galileo were regarded with suspicion (see Chapter 16). Yet contemporary Protestantism was just as intolerant, and even more hostile to the cause of rational thought. Indeed, because Catholic theologians turned for guidance to the scholasticism of Thomas Aquinas, they tended to be much more committed to the dignity of human reason than were their Protestant counterparts, who emphasized the literal interpretation of the Bible and the importance of unquestioning faith. It is no coincidence that René Descartes, one of the pioneers of rational philosophy ("I think, therefore I am"), was educated by Jesuits.

It would be wrong, therefore, to claim that the Protestantism of this era was more forward-looking or progressive than Catholicism. Both were, in fact, products of their time. Each variety of Protestantism responded to specific historical conditions and the needs of specific peoples in specific places, while carrying forward certain aspects of the Christian tradition considered valuable by those communities. The Catholic Church also responded to new spiritual, political, and social realities—to such an extent that it must be regarded as distinct from either the early Church of the later Roman Empire or even the oft-reformed Church of the Middle Ages. That is why the phrase "Roman Catholic Church" has not been used in this book prior to this chapter, because the Roman Catholic Church as we know it emerged for the first time in the sixteenth century. Like Protantism, it is a more modern phenomenon.

CONCLUSION

The Reformation grew out of complex historical processes that we have been tracing in the last few chapters. Foremost among these was the increasing power of Europe's sovereign states (Chapter 10). As we have seen, those German princes who embraced Protestantism were moved to do so by the desire for sovereignty. The kings of Denmark, Sweden, and England followed suit for many of the same reasons. Since Protestant leaders preached absolute obedience to godly rulers, and since the state in Protestant countries assumed direct control of its churches, Protestantism bolstered state power. Yet the power of the state had been growing for a long time prior to this, especially in such countries as France and Spain, where Catholic kings already exercised most of the same rights that were seized by Lutheran German princes and by Henry VIII of England in the course of their own reformations. Those rulers who

After You Read This Chapter

Visit StudySpace for quizzes, additional review materials, and multi-media documents. **wwnorton.com/studyspace**

REVIEWING THE OBJECTIVES

- The main premises of Luther's theology had religious, political, and social implications. What were they?
- Switzerland fostered a number of different Protestant movements. Why was this the case?
- The Reformation had a profound effect on the basic structures of family life and on attitudes toward marriage and morality. Describe these changes.
- The Church of England was established in response to a specific political situation. What was this?
- How did the Catholic Church respond to the challenge of Protestantism?

aligned themselves with Catholicism, then, had the same need to bolster their sovereignty and authority.

Ideas of national identity, too, were already influential and thus available for manipulation by Protestants and Catholics alike. These new religions, in turn, became new sources of identity and disunity. Until the sixteenth century, for example, the peoples in the different regions of Germany spoke such different dialects that they had difficulty understanding each other. But Luther's Bible gained such currency that it eventually became the linguistic standard for all these disparate regions, which eventually began to conceive of themselves as part of a single nation. Yet religion alone could not achieve the political unification of Germany, which did not occur for another three hundred years (see Chapter 21); indeed, it contributed to existing divisions by cementing the opposition of Catholic princes and peoples. Elsewhere in Europe—as in Holland, where Protestants fought successfully against a foreign, Catholic overlord—religion created a shared identity where politics could not. In England, where it is arguable that a sense of nationalism had already been fostered before the Reformation, membership in the Church of England became a new, but not uncontested, attribute of "Englishness."

Ideals characteristic of the Renaissance (Chapter 12) also contributed something to the Reformation and the Catholic responses to it. The criticisms of Christian humanists helped to prepare Europe for the challenges of Lutheranism, and close textual study of the Bible led to the publication of the newer, more accurate editions used by Protestant reformers. For example, Erasmus's improved edition of the Latin New Testament enabled Luther to reach some crucial conclusions concerning the meaning of penance and became the foundation for Luther's own translation of the Bible. Yet Erasmus was no supporter of Lutheran principles and most other Christian humanists followed suit, shunning Protestantism as soon as it became clear to them what Luther was actually teaching. Indeed, in certain basic respects Protestant principles were completely at odds with the principles, politics, and beliefs of most Renaissance humanists, who were staunch supporters of the Catholic Church.

In the New World and Asia, both Protestantism and Catholicism became forces of imperialism and new catalysts for competition. The race to secure colonies and resources now became a race for converts, too, as missionaries of both faiths fanned out over the globe. In the process, the confessional divisions of Europe were mapped onto these regions, often with violent results. Over the course of the ensuing century, newly sovereign nation-states would struggle for hegemony at home and abroad, setting off a series of religious wars that would cause as much destruction as any plague.

PEOPLE, IDEAS, AND EVENTS IN CONTEXT

- How did **MARTIN LUTHER**'s attack on **INDULGENCES** tap into more widespread criticism of the papacy? What role did the printing press and the German vernacular play in the dissemination of his ideas?

- Why did many German principalities and cities rally to Luther's cause? Why did his condemnation at the **DIET OF WORMS** not lead to his execution on charges of heresy?

- How did the Protestant teachings of **ULRICH ZWINGLI**, **JOHN CALVIN**, and the **ANABAPTISTS** differ from one another and from those of Luther?

- What factors made some of Europe's territories more receptive to **PROTESTANTISM** than others? Why, for example, did Switzerland, the Netherlands, and the countries of Scandinavia embrace it?

- How did the **REFORMATION** alter the status and lives of women in Europe? Why did it strengthen male authority in the family?

- Why did **HENRY VIII** break with Rome? How did the **CHURCH OF ENGLAND** differ from other Protestant churches in Europe?

- What decisions were made at the **COUNCIL OF TRENT**? What were the founding principles of **IGNATIUS LOYOLA**'s **SOCIETY OF JESUS**, and what was its role in the **COUNTER-REFORMATION** of the **CATHOLIC CHURCH**?

CONSEQUENCES

- Our study of Western civilizations has shown that reforming movements are nothing new: Christianity has been continuously reformed throughout its long history. What made this Reformation so different?

- Was a Protestant break with the Catholic Church inevitable? Why or why not?

- The political, social, and religious structures put in place during the Reformation continue to shape our lives in such profound ways that we scarcely notice them—or we assume them to be inevitable and natural. In your view, what is the most far-reaching consequence of this age of dissent and division, and why? In what ways has it formed your own values and assumptions?

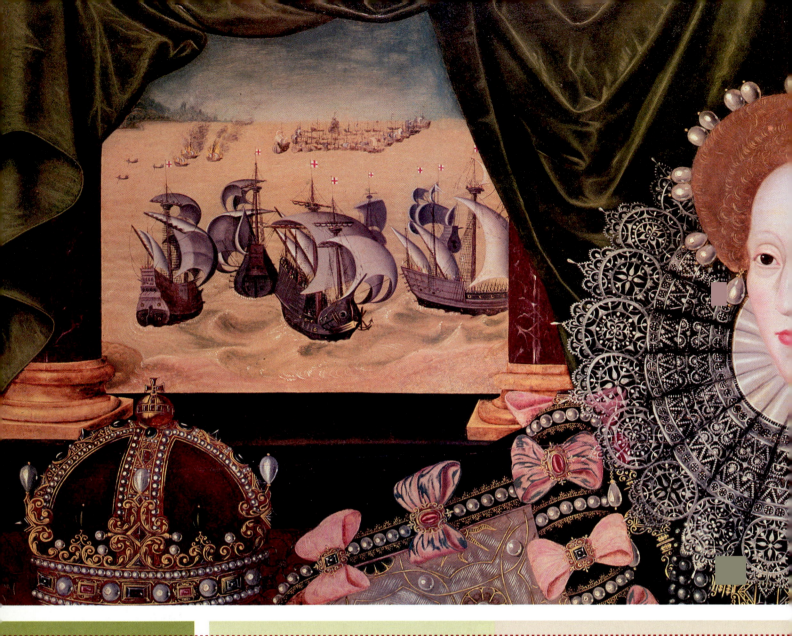

Before You Read This Chapter

Religion, Warfare, and Sovereignty: 1540–1660

CORE OBJECTIVES

- **UNDERSTAND** the ways in which early modern religious and political conflicts were intertwined.

- **TRACE** the main phases of religious warfare on the Continent.

- **IDENTIFY** the causes for Spain's decline and France's rise to power.

- **EXPLAIN** the origins and significance of the English Civil War.

- **DESCRIBE** some of the ways that intellectuals and artists responded to the challenges of this era.

In the early spring of 1592, a new play was mounted at the Rose Theatre, one of the enclosed places of entertainment recently constructed in London's suburbs. It was the prequel to two vastly popular plays that had already chronicled the dynastic wars that divided England in the fifteenth century, when English losses in the Hundred Years' War gave way to civil wars at home. The play, *The First Part of Henry VI*, was intended to explore the origins of those wars during the reign of the child-king who had suceeded the heroic Henry V, and it completed a trilogy that launched an ambitious young playwright called Will Shakespeare. Civil strife was a hot topic in the sixteenth century. Shakspeare's England was much more peaceful and unified than almost any other country in Europe, but that unity was fragile. It had been shattered numerous times because of ongoing religious divisions, and it was only now being maintained by a growing sense of national identity. Shakespeare's early plays promoted that identity by celebrating the superiority of the average Englishman over his European neighbors, who were often represented as either ridiculous or villainous. So in this new play the most interesting and ultimately dangerous character is the French heroine Joan of Arc, whose fervent Catholic faith turns out to be a mask for witchcraft. In Shakespeare's version of her legend, Joan actually attempts to be released from the tortures of the stake by claiming to be pregnant, and dies calling on her demon familiars to rescue her from the flames.

Shakespeare's plays, like many other products of contemporary popular culture, reveal the profound tensions that fractured the kingdoms and communities of Europe in the century after the Reformation. Martin Luther's call for universal access to the Bible had not resulted in a unified interpretation of the Christian faith; nor did his dream of a "priesthood of all believers" topple the clerical hierarchy of the Roman Church. Instead, Europe's religious divisions multiplied, often crystallizing along political lines. By the time of Luther's death in 1546, a clear pattern had already emerged. With only rare exceptions, Protestantism triumphed in areas where those in power stood to gain by rejecting the Church's hold over them; meanwhile, Catholicism prevailed in territories whose rulers had forged close political alliances with Rome. In both cases, Protestants and Catholics clung to the same belief in the mutual interdependence of religion and politics, an old certainty that had also undergirded the civilization of ancient Rome (Chapter 5) and most other Western civilizations before it.

Because many Europeans continued to believe that the proper role of the state was to enforce "true religion" on those subject to its authority, most sixteenth-century rulers were convinced that religious pluralism could bring only chaos and disloyalty. Ironically, then, Catholics and Protestants were united in one conviction: that western Europe had to return to a single religious faith enforced by properly constituted political authorities. What they could not agree on was *which* faith—and which authorities. The result was a brutal series of wars whose reverberations continue to be felt in many regions of Europe and in her former colonies. Vastly expensive and destructive, these wars affected everyone in Europe, from peasants to princes. Yet it would be misleading to suggest that they were caused by religious differences alone. Regional tensions, dynastic politics, and nascent nationalist tendencies were also potent contributors to the violence into which Europe was plunged and were therefore staple elements of Shakespeare's dramatic histories. Together, these forces of division and disorder brought into question the very survival of the political order that had emerged in the twelfth and thirteenth centuries (Chapter 9). Faced with the prospect of political collapse, those who still held power a century later were forced to embrace, gradually and grudgingly, a notion that had seemed impossible: religious tolerance was the only way to preserve political, social, and economic order.

SOURCES OF TENSION AND UNREST

The troubles that engulfed Europe during the long, traumatic century between 1540 and 1660 caught contemporaries unaware. Most of Europe had enjoyed steady economic growth since the middle of the fifteenth century, and the colonization of the Americas seemed certain to be the basis of greater prosperity to come. Political trends too seemed auspicious, because most western European governments were becoming more efficient and and effective. By the middle of the sixteenth century, however, there were warning signs.

The Price Revolution

The first of these warning signs was economic: an unprecedented inflation in prices that had begun in the latter half of the sixteenth century. Nothing like it had ever happened before, at least not on this scale, even during the Roman Empire's turbulent third century (Chapter 6). In Flanders, the cost of wheat tripled between 1550 and 1600, grain prices in Paris quadrupled, and the overall cost of living in England more than doubled. The twentieth century would see much more dizzying inflations than this, but in the sixteenth century the skyrocketing of prices was a terrifying novelty, what most historians describe as the "price revolution."

Two developments in particular underlay the soaring prices. The first was demographic. Starting in the later fifteenth century, Europe's population began to grow again after the plague-induced decline of the fourteenth century (Chapter 10); roughly estimated, Europe had about 50 million people around 1450, and 90 million around 1600. Because Europe's food supply remained more or less constant, owing to the lack of any noteworthy breakthroughs in agricultural technology analogous to those of the eleventh century (Chapter 8), food prices were driven sharply higher by greater demand. At the same time, wages stagnated or even declined. As a result, workers around 1600 were paying a higher percentage of their wages to buy food, even though basic nutritional levels were declining.

Population trends explain much, but since Europe's population did not increase nearly so rapidly in the second half of the sixteenth century as did prices, other explanations for the great inflation are necessary. Foremost among these is the enormous influx of bullion from Spanish America. From 1556 to 1560, roughly 10 million ducats' worth of silver passed through the Spanish entry port of harvests drove grain prices out of reach, some of the poor starved to death. The picture that emerges is one of the rich getting richer and the poor getting poorer—splendid feasts enjoyed amid the most appalling misery.

The price revolution also placed new pressures on the sovereign states of Europe. Since inflation depressed the real value of money, fixed incomes from taxes and tolls yielded less and less income. Thus, merely to keep their revenues constant, governments were forced to raise taxes. But to compound this problem, most states still needed more real income because they were engaging in more wars; and warfare was becoming increasingly expensive. The only recourse, then, was to raise taxes precipitously, which aroused great resentment. Hence governments faced continuous threats of defiance and even armed resistance. Although prices rose less rapidly after 1600, as population growth slowed and the flood of silver from America began to slow down, the period from 1600 to 1660 was one of economic stagnation rather than growth. A few areas—notably Holland—bucked the trend, and the rich were usually able to hold their own, but the poor as a group made no advances because the relationship of prices to wages remained fixed, to their disadvantage. Indeed, the lot of the poor in many places deteriorated further because the mid-seventeenth century saw particularly destructive wars in which helpless civilians were plundered by rapacious tax collectors or looting soldiers, or sometimes both. The Black Death also returned, wreaking havoc in London and elsewhere during the 1660s.

Political and Religious Instability

Compounding these economic problems were the disunities inherent in major European monarchies. Most had grown during the later Middle Ages by absorbing or colonizing smaller, traditionally autonomous, territories—sometimes by conquest, but more often through marriage alliances or inheritance arrangements among ruling families (a policy known as "dynasticism"). At first, some degree of provincial autonomy was usually preserved in these newly absorbed territories. But in the period we are now examining, governments began making ever-greater financial claims on all their subjects while trying to enforce religious uniformity. As a result, rulers often rode roughshod over the rights of these traditionally autonomous provinces.

At the same time, claims to the sovereignty—the unity, autonomy, and authority—of these states were increasingly made on the basis of religious uniformity. Rulers on both sides felt that religious minorities, if allowed to flourish in

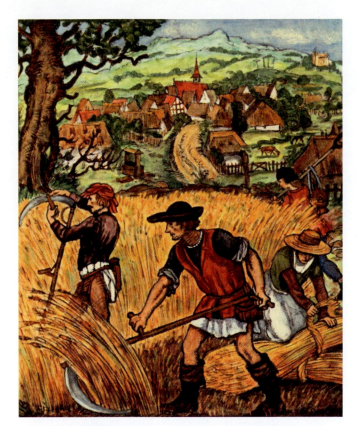

PEASANTS HARVESTING WHEAT, SIXTEENTH CENTURY. The inflation that swept through Europe in the late sixteenth century affected poorer workers most acutely, as the abundant labor supply dampened wages while at the same time the cost of food rose because of poor harvests.

Seville. Between 1576 and 1580 that figure doubled, and between 1591 and 1595 it more than quadrupled. Most of this silver was used by the Spanish crown to pay its foreign creditors and its armies abroad; as a result, this bullion quickly circulated throughout Europe, where much of it was minted into coins. This dramatic increase in the volume of money in circulation fueled the spiral of rising prices. "I learned a proverb here," said a French traveler in Spain in 1603: "everything costs a lot, except silver."

Aggressive entrepreneurs and large-scale farmers profited most from the changed economic circumstances, while the masses of laboring people were hurt the most. Landlords benefited from the rising prices of agricultural produce, and merchants from the increasing demand for luxury goods. But laborers were caught in a squeeze because wages rose far more slowly than prices, owing to the presence of a more than adequate labor supply. Moreover, because the cost of food staples rose at a sharper rate than the cost of most other items of consumption, poor people had to spend an ever-greater percentage of their paltry incomes on necessities. When disasters such as wars or bad their realms, would inevitably engage in sedition; nor were they always wrong, since militant Calvinists and Jesuits were indeed dedicated to subverting constituted powers in areas where their parties had not yet triumphed. Thus states tried to extirpate all potential religious resistance but, in the process, sometimes provoked civil wars in which each side tended to assume there could be no victory until the other was exterminated. And of course, civil wars could become international in scope if foreign powers chose to aid their embattled religious allies elsewhere.

Regionalism, economic grievances, and religious animosities were thus compounded into a volatile and destructive mixture. Nor was that all, since most governments seeking money and/or religious uniformity tried to rule with a firmer hand than before and thus increasingly provoked armed resistance from subjects seeking to preserve traditional liberties. As a result, the long century between 1540 and 1660 was one of the most turbulent in all of European history.

A CENTURY OF RELIGIOUS WARS

The greatest single cause of warfare during this period was religious conflict. These "wars of religion" are usually divided into four phases:

1. a series of regional wars in Germany from the 1540s to 1555
2. the French wars of religion from 1562 until 1598
3. the simultaneous revolts of the (Protestant) Dutch against the (Catholic) Spanish Habsburg Empire between 1566 and 1609
4. the Thirty Years' War that devasted German-speaking lands again, between 1618 and 1648.

Regional Warfare in Germany

Wars between Catholics and Protestant rulers in Germany began in the 1540s, less than a generation after Lutheranism first took hold there. The Holy Roman emperor, Charles V (Chapter 13), was also king of Spain and a devout supporter of the Church. His goal was therefore to reestablish Catholic unity in Germany by launching a military campaign against several German princes who had instituted Lutheran worship in their territories. But despite several notable victories, Charles's efforts to defeat the Protestant

princes failed. In part, this was because he was also involved in wars against France, but primarily it was because the Catholic princes of Germany worked against him, fearing that any suppression of Protestant princes might also suppress their own independence. As a result, the Catholic princes' support for the foreign-born Charles was only lukewarm; at times, they even joined with Protestants in battle against the emperor.

This regional warfare sputtered on and off until a compromise settlement was reached via the Peace of Augsburg in 1555. Its governing principle was *cuius regio, eius religio*: "as the ruler, so the religion." This meant that in those principalities where Lutherans ruled, Lutheranism would be the sole state religion; but where Catholic princes ruled, the people of their territories would also be Catholic. For better and for worse, the Peace of Augsburg was a historical

THE EMPEROR CHARLES V BY TITIAN. Charles V's attempts to enforce Catholicism in his German territories failed. In 1555, the Peace of Augsburg recognized the existence of both Protestant and Catholic territories, with the faith of each determined by the religion of the ruler. ▪ *How does this portrait of Charles compare to that on page 406 (Chapter 13)?* ▪ *How might changing historical circumstances account for these different representations of the same ruler?*

milestone. For the first time since Luther had been excommunicated, on the one hand, Catholic rulers were forced to acknowledge the legality of Protestantism. But on the other hand, the peace set a dangerous precedent because it established the principle that no sovereign state could tolerate religious diversity. Moreover, it excluded Calvinism entirely, and thus spurred German Calvinists to become aggressive opponents of the status quo.

The French Wars of Religion

From the 1560s on, Europe's religious wars became far more brutal, partly because the combatants had become more intransigent (with Calvinists and Jesuits taking the lead on their respective sides), and partly because these later wars were aggravated by regional, political, and dynastic animosities. For example, Calvin's Geneva bordered on France; and because Calvin himself was a Frenchman, Calvinist missionaries made considerable headway there after 1541, when he took power. But their concentration in the southern part of the country reflected long-standing hosilities that reached back to the ravages of northern French "crusaders" against Albigensian "heretics" during the thirteenth century (Chapter 9). Also assisting the Calvinist cause was the conversion of many aristocratic Frenchwomen, who in turn won over their husbands, many of whom maintained large private armies. The foremost example of these was Jeanne d'Albret, queen of Navarre, who converted her husband, the prominent aristocrat Antoine de Bourbon, and her brother-in-law, the prince of Condé.

Within two decades, Calvinists—known in France as Huguenots (*YOO-guh-nohs*), for reasons that remain obscure—made up between 10 and 20 percent of France's population. Although they lived uneasily alongside their Catholic neighbors, there was no open warfare until 1562, when the reigning king died unexpectedly, leaving a young child as his heir. This spurred a struggle between two factions within the regency government which formed along religious lines: the Huguenots, led by the prince of Condé, and the Catholics, led by the duke of Guise. And since both Catholics and Protestants believed that a kingdom could have only one *roi, foi,* and *loi* ("king," "faith," and "law"), this political struggle turned into a religious war. Soon all France was aflame. Rampaging mobs, often incited by members of the clergy, used this opportunity to settle local scores. Although the Huguenots were not numerous enough to gain a victory, they were too strong to be defeated, especially in their stronghold of southern France. Hence warfare dragged on for a decade until a truce was arranged in 1572. This truce required the young Huguenot leader, Prince Henry of Navarre, to marry the Catholic sister of the reigning French king.

But this compromise was defeated by the powerful dowager queen of France, Catherine de' Medici, scion of the Florentine family that was closely aligned with the papacy (Chapter 13). Instead of honoring the truce, she plotted with members of the Catholic faction to kill all the Huguenot leaders while they were assembled in Paris for her daugher's wedding to Henry of Navarre. In the early morning of St. Bartholomew's Day (August 24), most of these leaders were murdered in their beds, while thousands of other Protestants were slaughtered in the streets or drowned in the Seine by Catholic mobs. When word of the Parisian massacre spread to the provinces, some 10,000 more Huguenots were killed. Henry of Navarre escaped, along with his new bride; but now the conflict entered a new and even more bitter phase.

HENRY IV OF FRANCE. The rule of Henry of Navarre (r. 1589–1610) initiated the Bourbon dynasty that would rule France until 1792, and ended the bitter civil war between Catholic and Huguenot factions.

Catherine's death in 1589 enabled Henry of Navarre to be crowned king as Henry IV, but peace was not restored until he renounced his Protestant faith in order to placate France's Catholic majority. In 1598, however, he offered limited religious freedom to the Huguenots by issuing the Edict of Nantes. This edict recognized Catholicism as the official religion of the kingdom, but allowed Huguenot aristocrats to hold Protestant services privately in their homes, while other Huguenots were allowed to worship in certain specified places at certain times. The Huguenot party was also permitted to fortify some towns, especially in the south and west, for their own military defense. Huguenots were further guaranteed the right to hold public office and to enter universities and hospitals.

The Edict of Nantes did not guarantee absolute freedom of worship, but it was still a major stride in the direction of tolerance. Unfortunately, however, the effect was to divide the kingdom into separate religious enclaves. In southern and western France, Huguenots came to have their own law courts, staffed by their own judges. They also received substantial powers of self-government, because it was presumed on all sides that the members of one religious group could not be ruled equitably by the adherents of a competing religion. Because of its regional character, the edict also represented a concession to the long-standing traditions of provincial autonomy within the kingdom of France. In some ways, indeed, Huguenot areas became a confederacy within the state, thus raising the fear that the kingdom might once again crumble into its constituent parts, as had happened during the Hundred Years' War. On its own terms, however, the Edict of Nantes was a success. France began to recover from decades of devastation, and peace was maintained even after Henry IV was assassinated by a Catholic in 1610.

The Revolt of the Netherlands

Bitter warfare also broke out between Catholics and Protestants in the Low Countries, where regional resentments exacerbated religious animosities. For almost a century, the territories comprising much of the modern-day Netherlands and Belgium had been ruled by the Habsburg family of Holy Roman emperors, who also ruled Spain. The southern Netherlands in particular had prospered greatly from this, through trade and manufacture: their inhabitants generated the greatest per capita wealth of all Europe, and their metropolis of Antwerp was northern Europe's leading commercial and financial center. Moreover, the half-century rule of Charles V had been successful here. Charles had

been born in the Flemish city of Ghent, and had a strong rapport with his subjects, whom he allowed a large measure of self-government.

But a year after the Peace of Augsburg in 1555, Charles V retired to a monastery and ceded all of his vast territories outside of the Holy Roman Empire and Hungary to his son Philip II (r. 1556–98). Unlike Charles, Philip had been born in Spain and, thinking of himself as a Spaniard, made Spain his residence and the focus of his policy. He viewed the Netherlands primarily as a source of income necessary for pursuing Spanish imperial conquests in the New World. The better to exploit the region's wealth, Philip therefore tried to tighten control over the Netherlands. This aroused the resentment of the region's fiercely independent cities and of the local magnates who had dominated the government under Charles V. A religious storm was also brewing. French Calvinists were beginning to

THE NETHERLANDS AFTER 1609. ▪ *What were the two main divisions of the Netherlands?* ▪ *Which was Protestant, and which was Catholic?* ▪ *How could William the Silent and his allies use the geography of the northern Netherlands against the Spanish?* ▪ *Why were the southern provinces of the Netherlands wealthier than the northern ones?*

PROTESTANTS RANSACKING A CATHOLIC CHURCH IN THE NETHERLANDS.
Protestant destruction of religious images provoked a stern response from Phillip II.
■ *Why would Protestants have smashed statuary and other devotional artifacts?*

Yet the tide turned quickly. The exiled William converted openly to Protestantism and sought help from religious allies in France, Germany, and England; meanwhile, organized bands of Protestant privateers harassed Spanish shipping on the Netherlandish coast. Alva's tyranny also advanced William's cause, especially when the hated Spanish governor attempted to levy a devastating sales tax. In 1572, William was able to seize the northern Netherlands, even though the north until then had been predominantly Catholic. Thereafter, geography played a major role in determining the outcome of the conflict. Spanish armies repeatedly attempted to win back the north, but they were stopped by a combination of impassable rivers and dikes that could be opened to flood out the invaders. Although William was assassinated by a Catholic in 1584, his son continued to lead the resistance until the Spanish crown finally agreed to recognize the independence of a northern Dutch Republic in 1609. Meanwhile, the pressures of war and persecution had made the whole north Calvinist, whereas the south—which remained under Spanish control—returned to Catholicism.

stream into the southern Netherlands, intent on making converts. Within decades, there were more Calvinists in Antwerp than in Geneva. To Philip, an ardent supporter of the Catholic Church, this was intolerable. As he declared to the pope, "Rather than suffer the slightest harm to the true religion and service of God, I would lose all my states and even my life a hundred times over, because I am not and will not be the ruler of heretics."

Worried by the growing tensions, a group of Catholic aristocrats appealed to Philip to allow toleration for Calvinists within the Netherlands. They were led by William of Orange, known as "William the Silent" because he was so successful at hiding his religious and political leanings. But before Philip could respond, radical Protestant mobs began ransacking Catholic churches throughout the country, desecrating altars, smashing statuary, and shattering stained-glass windows. Local troops brought the situation under control, but Philip nonetheless decided to dispatch an army of 10,000 Spanish soliders, led by the duke of Alva, to wipe out Protestantism in the Netherlands. Alva's rule as governor quickly became a reign of terror. Operating under martial law, his "Council of Blood" examined some 12,000 people on charges of heresy or sedition, of whom 9,000 were convicted and thousands executed. William fled the country, and all hope for peace in the Netherlands seemed lost.

England and the Spanish Armada

Religious strife could spark civil war, as in France, or political rebellion, as in the Netherlands. But it could also provoke warfare between sovereign states, as in the struggle between England and Spain. As we noted in Chapter 13, the Catholic queen Mary of England (r. 1553–58), herself the granddaughter of Ferdinand and Isabella of Spain, had married her cousin Philip II of Spain in 1554. After her death, Philip appears to have extended a marriage proposal to her half-sister, the Protestant queen Elizabeth (r. 1558–1603), and to have been rejected. Adding to the animosity created by religious differences and dynastic politics was the fact that English economic interests were directly opposed to those of Spain. English seafarers and traders were steadily making inroads into Spanish naval and commercial networks and were also engaged in lucrative trade with the Spanish Netherlands. But the greatest source of antagonism lay in the Atlantic, where English privateers, with the tacit consent of Queen Elizabeth, began attacking Spanish treasure ships. Taking as an excuse the Spanish oppression of Protestants in the Netherlands, English sea captains such as Sir Francis Drake and Sir John Hawkins plundered Spanish vessels on the high seas. In a particularly dramatic exploit lasting from 1577 to 1580, prevailing winds and lust for treasure propelled Drake all the way around the world, to return with stolen Spanish treasure worth twice as much as Queen Elizabeth's annual revenue.

All this would have been sufficient provocation for Spain to retaliate against England, but Philip resolved to invade the island only after the English openly allied with Dutch rebels in 1585. Even then, Philip moved slowly. Finally, in 1588 he dispatched an enormous fleet, confidently called the "Invincible Armada," to invade insolent England. After an initial standoff in the English Channel, however, the smaller English warships, more agile and armed with longer-range guns, outmaneuvered the Spanish fleet, while English fireships set some Spanish galleons ablaze and forced the rest to break formation. A fierce "Protestant wind" did the rest. After a disastrous circumnavigation of the British Isles and Ireland, the shattered Spanish flotilla limped home with almost half its ships lost. Elizabeth quickly took credit for her country's miraculous escape.

THE "ARMADA PORTRAIT" OF ELIZABETH. This is one of several portraits that commemorated the defeat of the Spanish Armada in 1588. Through the window on the left (the queen's right hand), an English flotilla sails serenely on sunny seas; on the right, Spanish ships are wrecked by a "Protestant wind." Elizabeth's right hand rests protectively—and commandingly—on the globe. ▪ *How would you "read" this image?*

Although the war with Spain dragged on until 1604, the fighting was just lively enough to foster feelings of English nationalism and Protestant fervor.

The Thirty Years' War

With the promulgation of the French Edict of Nantes in 1598, the peace between England and Spain of 1604, and the truce between Spain and the Dutch republic of 1609, religious warfare in northwestern Europe came briefly to an end. But in 1618 a major new war broke out in Germany. Because this struggle raged more or less incessantly until 1648, it is known as the Thirty Years' War, and it eventually encompassed Spain and France as well, becoming an international struggle in which the initial religious provocations were all but forgotten.

After the Peace of Augsburg in 1555, the balance of powers between Protestant and Catholic territories within the Holy Roman Empire had remained largely undisturbed. In 1618, however, the Catholic Habsburg prince who ruled Poland, Austria, and Hungary was elected king of Protestant Bohemia, prompting a rebellion among the Bohemian aristocracy. When this same prince, Ferdinand, became Holy Roman Emperor a year later, German Catholic forces were sent to crush the rebellion. Within a decade, then, a German imperial Catholic league seemed close to extirpating Protestantism throughout Germany. But this threatened the political autonomy of all German princes, Catholic and Protestant alike. So when the Lutheran king of Sweden, Gustavus Adolphus, championed the Protestant cause in 1630, he was welcomed by several German Catholic princes, too.

To make matters still more complicated, the Swedish king's Protestant army was secretly subsidized by Catholic France, whose policy was then dictated by Cardinal Richelieu (*RIH-shlyuh*, 1585–1642). Sweden had French support because Richelieu was determined to prevent France from being surrounded by a strong Habsburg alliance on the north, east, and south. Something of a military genius, Gustavus Adolphus began routing the Habsburgs. But when Gustavus died in battle in 1632, Cardinal Richelieu found himself having to conduct the war himself; in 1635, France openly declared

Analyzing Primary Sources

The Devastation of the Thirty Years' War

The author of the following excerpt, Hans Jakob Christoph von Grimmelshausen (1621–1676), barely survived the horrors of the Thirty Years' War. His parents were killed, probably when he was thirteen years old, and he himself was kidnapped the following year and forced into the army. By age fifteen, he was a soldier. His darkly satiric masterpiece, Simplicissimus (The Simpleton), *drew heavily on these experiences. Although technically a fictional memoir, it portrays with brutal accuracy the terrible realities of this era.*

lthough it was not my intention to take the peaceloving reader with these troopers to my dad's house and farm, seeing that matters will go ill therein, yet the course of my history demands that I should leave to kind posterity an account of what manner of cruelties were now and again practised in this our German war: yes, and moreover testify by my own example that such evils must often have been sent to us by the goodness of Almighty God for our profit. For, gentle reader, who would ever have taught me that there was a God in Heaven if these soldiers had not destroyed my dad's house, and by such a deed driven me out among folk who gave me all fitting instruction thereupon? . . .

The first thing these troopers did was, that they stabled their horses: thereafter each fell to his appointed task: which task was neither more nor less than ruin and destruction. For though some began to slaughter and to boil and to roast so that it looked as if there should be a merry banquet forward, yet others there were who did but storm through the house above and below stairs. Others stowed together great parcels of cloth and apparel and all manner of household stuff, as if they would set up a frippery market. All that they had no mind to take with them they

cut in pieces. Some thrust their swords through the hay and straw as if they had not enough sheep and swine to slaughter: and some shook the feathers out of the beds and in their stead stuffed in bacon and other dried meat and provisions as if such were better and softer to sleep upon. Others broke the stove and the windows as if they had a never-ending summer to promise. Houseware of copper and tin they beat flat, and packed such vessels, all bent and spoiled, in with the rest. Bedsteads, tables, chairs, and benches they burned, though there lay many cords of dry wood in the yard. Pots and pipkins must all go to pieces, either because they would eat none but roast flesh, or because their purpose was to make there but a single meal.

Our maid was so handled in the stable that she could not come out, which is a shame to tell of. Our man they laid bound upon the ground, thrust a gag into his mouth, and poured a pailful of filthy water into his body: and by this, which they called a Swedish draught, they forced him to lead a party of them to another place where they captured men and beasts, and brought them back to our farm, in which company were my dad, my mother, and our Ursula.

And now they began: first to take the flints out of their pistols and in place of them to jam the peasants' thumbs in and so to torture the poor rogues as if they

had been about the burning of witches: for one of them they had taken they thrust into the baking oven and there lit a fire under him, although he had as yet confessed no crime: as for another, they put a cord round his head and so twisted it tight with a piece of wood that the blood gushed from his mouth and nose and ears. In a word each had his own device to torture the peasants, and each peasant his several tortures.

Source: Hans Jakob Christoph von Grimmelshausen, *Simplicissimus*, trans. S. Goodrich (New York: 1995), pp. 1–3, 8–10, 32–35.

Questions for Analysis

1. The first-person narrator here recounts the atrocities committed "in this our German war," in which both perpetrators and victims are German. How believable is this description? What lends it credibility?

2. Why might Grimmelshausen have chosen to publish his account as a satirical fiction, rather than as a straightforward historical narrative or autobiography? How would this choice affect a reader's response to scenes such as this?

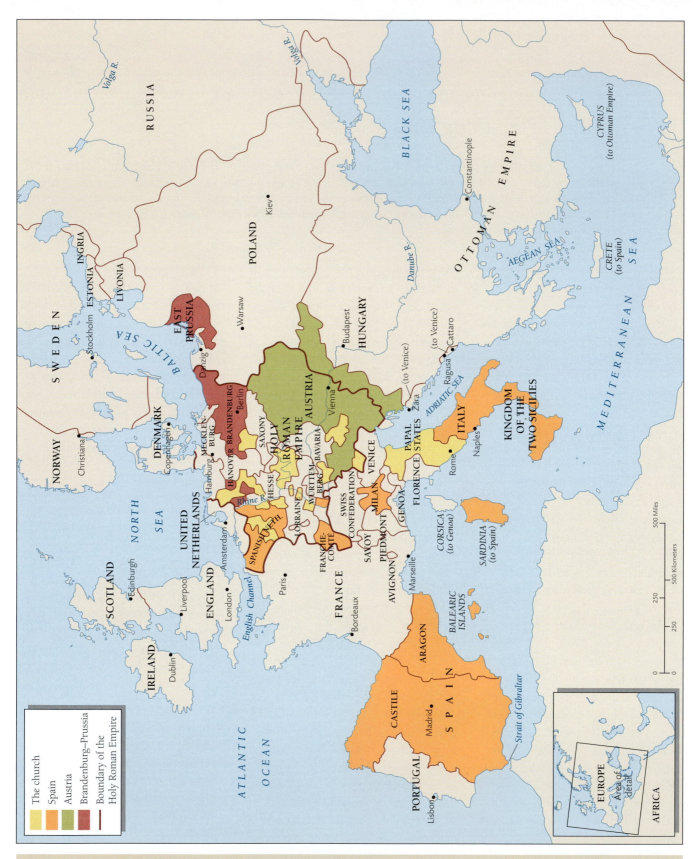

EUROPE AT THE END OF THE THIRTY YEARS' WAR. This map shows the fragile political checkerboard that resulted from Peace of Westphalia in 1648. ■ *When you compare this map to the map on page 407 in Chapter 13, what are the most significant territorial changes between 1550 and 1648?* ■ *Which regions would have been weakened or endangered by this arrangement?* ■ *Which would be in a strong position to dominate Europe?*

itself for Sweden and against Austria and Spain. In the middle lay Germany, a helpless battleground.

Germany suffered more from warfare in the terrible years between 1618 and 1648 than than at any time until the twentieth century. Several German cities were besieged and sacked nine or ten times over, and soldiers from all nations, who often had to sustain themselves by plunder, gave no quarter to defenseless civilians. With plague and disease adding to the toll of outright butchery, some parts of Germany lost more than half their populations. Most horrifying was the loss of life in the final four years of the war, when the carnage continued unabated even after peace negotiators arrived at broad areas of agreement.

The eventual adoption of the Peace of Westphalia in 1648 was a watershed in European history. It marked the emergence of France as the predominant power on the Continent, a position it would hold for the next two centuries. The greatest losers in the conflict (aside from the millions of German victims) were the Austrian Habsburgs, who were forced to surrender all the territory they had gained and to abandon their hopes of using the office of Holy Roman Emperor to dominate central Europe. Spain became increasingly relegated to the margins of Europe, and Germany remained a volatile checkerboard of Protestant and Catholic principalities.

DIVERGENT POLITICAL PATHS: SPAIN AND FRANCE

The long century of war between 1540 and 1648 decisively altered the balance of power among the major kingdoms of western Europe. Germany emerged from the Thirty Years' War a devastated and exhausted land. Spain, too, was crippled by its unremitting military exertions. The French monarchy, by contrast, steadily increased its power. By 1660, France had become the most powerful country on the European mainland. In England, meanwhile, a bloody civil war had broken out between the king and his critics in Parliament, culminating in an unprecedented event: the legal execution of a reigning monarch by his own parliamentary government.

The Decline of Spain

The story of Spain's fall from grandeur unfolds almost as relentlessly as a Greek tragedy. In 1600, the Spanish Empire—comprising all of the Iberian Peninsula (including Portugal, which had been annexed by Phillip II in 1580), half of Italy, half of the Netherlands, all of Central and South America, and the Philippine Islands in the Pacific Ocean—was the mightiest power not just in Europe but in the world. Yet only a half century later, this empire was beginning to fall apart.

Spain's greatest underlying weakness was economic. At first this may seem odd considering that in 1600, as in the three or four previous decades, huge amounts of American silver were being unloaded at the harbor of Seville. Yet as contemporaries themselves recognized, the New World that Spain had conquered was now conquering Spain. Lacking both agricultural and mineral resources of its own, Spain desperately needed to develop industries and a balanced trading pattern, as some of its Atlantic rivals were doing. But the Spanish nobility prized honor and chivalric ideals over practical business affairs. They used imperial silver to buy manufactured goods from other parts of Europe and, as a result, had no incentive to develop industries and exports of their own. When the river of silver began to abate, Spain was plunged into debt.

Meanwhile, the crown's commitment to supporting the Catholic Church and maintaining Spain's international dominance meant the continuance of costly wars. Even in the relatively peaceful year of 1608, about 4 million ducats—out of a total revenue of 7 million—were spent on military ventures. Spain's involvement in the Thirty Years' War was the last straw. In 1643, French troops inflicted a stunning defeat on the famed Spanish infantry at Rocroi in nothern France, the first time that a Spanish army had been overcome in battle since the reign of Ferdinand and Isabella (Chapter 11).

By then, two of Spain's Iberian territories were in open revolt. The governing power of Spain lay entirely in Castile, which had emerged as the dominant power after the marriage of Isabella to Ferdinand of Aragon in 1469. Castile became even more dominant when it took over Portugal in 1580. In the absence of any great financial hardships, semi-autonomous Catalonia (historically, an independent part of Aragon) also endured Castilian hegemony. But in 1640, when the strains of warfare induced Castile to limit Catalan liberties and to raise more money and men for combat, Catalonia revolted and drove out its Castilian governors. When the Portuguese learned of the Catalan uprising, they revolted as well, followed by southern Italians who rose up against Castilian viceroys in Naples and Sicily in 1647. It was only by chance that Spain's greatest external enemies, France and England, could not act in time to take advantage of its plight. This gave the Castilian government time to put down the Italian revolts; by 1652 it had also brought Catalonia to heel. But Portugal retained its independence, and Spain's isolation after the Peace of Westphalia further increased.

THE BATTLE OF ROCROI, 1643. Spain's defeat by the French at Rocroi was the first time the Spanish army had lost a land battle since the reign of Ferdinand and Isabella (Chapter 11), and was yet another contributing factor to the decline of Spanish power during the Thirty Years' War. This painting shows the victorious French general, the duke d'Enghien, surveying the battlefield from afar.

The Growth of France

A comparison of the fortunes of Spain and France in the first half of the seventeenth century shows some striking similarities between the two countries. Both were of almost identical territorial extent, and both had been created by the same process of accretion and conquest over the course of the previous centuries (Chapters 9 and 10). Just as the Castilian crown had gained Aragon, Catalonia, Granada, and then Portugal, so the kingdom of France had grown by adding such diverse territories as Languedoc, Provence, Burgundy, and Brittany. Since the inhabitants of all these territories cherished traditions of local independence, and since French and Spanish monarchs were determined to govern their provinces ever more firmly—especially when costs of the Thirty Years' War made ruthless tax collecting an urgent necessity—a direct confrontation between the central government and the provinces became inevitable in both cases.

The fact that France emerged powerfully from this while Spain did not can be attributed in part to France's greater natural resources and the greater prestige of the French monarchy. Most subjects of the French king, including those from the outlying provinces, were loyal to him. Certainly they had excellent reason to be so during the reign of Henry IV. Having established religious peace by the Edict of Nantes, the affable Henry declared that there should be a chicken in every French family's pot each Sunday, and therefore set out to restore the prosperity of a country devastated by civil war. And France had enormous economic resiliency, owing primarily to its extremely rich and varied agricultural productivity. Unlike Spain, which had to import food, France was able to feed itself; and Henry's finance minister, the duke of Sully, quickly ensured that it did just that. Among other things, Sully distributed free copies of a guide to recommended farming techniques and financed the rebuilding or construction of roads, bridges, and canals to facilitate the flow of goods. Henry IV, meanwhile, ordered the construction of royal factories to manufacture luxury goods such as crystal, glass, and tapestries while supporting the growth of silk, linen, and woolen cloth industries in many different parts of the country. Henry's patronage also allowed the explorer Samuel de Champlain to claim parts of Canada as France's first foothold in the New World.

Cardinal Richelieu on the Common People of France

Armand Jean du Plessis, duke of Richelieu and cardinal of the Roman Catholic Church, was the effective ruler of France from 1624 until his death in 1642. His Political Testament was assembled after his death from historical sketches and memoranda of advice which he prepared for King Louis XIII, the ineffectual monarch whom he ostensibly served. This book was eventually published in 1688, during the reign of Louis XIV.

All students of politics agree that when the common people are too well off it is impossible to keep them peaceable. The explanation for this is that they are less well informed than the members of the other orders in the state, who are much more cultivated and enlightened, and so if not preoccupied with the search for the necessities of existence, find it difficult to remain within the limits imposed by both common sense and the law.

It would not be sound to relieve them of all taxation and similar charges, since in such a case they would lose the mark of their subjection and consequently the awareness of their station. Thus being free from paying tribute, they would consider themselves exempted from obedience. One should compare them with mules, which being accustomed to work, suffer more when long idle than when kept busy. But just as this work should be reasonable, with the burdens placed upon these animals proportionate to their strength, so it is likewise with the burdens placed upon the people. If they are not moderate, even when put to good public use, they are certainly unjust. I realize that when a king undertakes a program of public works it is correct to say that what the people gain from it is returned by paying the *taille* [a heavy tax imposed on the peasantry]. In the same fashion it can be maintained that what a king takes from the people returns to them, and that they advance it to him only to draw upon it for the enjoyment of their leisure and their investments, which would be impossible if they did not contribute to the support of the state.

Source: *The Political Testament of Cardinal Richelieu*, trans. Henry Bertram Hill (Madison, WI: 1961), pp. 31–32.

Questions for Analysis

1. According to Cardinal Richelieu, why should the state work to subjugate the common people? What assumptions about the nature and status of "common people" underlie this argument?

2. What theory of "the state" emerges from this argument? What is the relationship between the king and the state, and between the king and the people, according to Richelieu?

Cardinal Richelieu

Henry IV's reign can be counted as one of the most benevolent and effective in France's history. Far less benevolent was that of Henry's de facto successor, Cardinal Richelieu. The real king of France, Henry's son Louis XIII (r. 1610–43), came to the throne at the age of nine. But his reign was dominated by Richelieu, his chief minister of state. It was Richelieu who centralized royal power at home and expanded French influence abroad. For example, when Huguenots rebelled against certain restrictions that been placed on them by the Edict of Nantes, Richelieu amended the edict to revoke their political and military rights altogether. He then moved to gain more income for the crown by ending the semi-autonomy of Burgundy, the Dauphiné, and Provence so that he could introduce direct royal taxation in all three areas. Later, to make sure taxes were efficiently collected, Richelieu instituted a new system of local government by royal officials who were expressly commissioned to put down provincial resistance. By these and other methods Richelieu made the French monarchy more powerful than any in Europe and managed to double the crown's income during his rule. He also engaged in ambitious foreign wars against the Habsburgs of Austria and Spain, as we have seen. Yet increased centralization and France's costly involvement in the Thirty Years' War would lead to increased internal pressures in the years after Richelieu's death.

The Fronde

An immediate reaction to French governmental control was the series of uncoordinated revolts known collectively the *Fronde* (from the French word for "slingshot") which occured in 1643. Louis XIII had just been succeeded by the five-year-old Louis XIV, whose regents were his mother, Anne of Austria, and her paramour, Cardinal Mazarin. Both were foreigners—Anne was a Habsburg and Mazarin was an Italian adventurer named Giulio Mazarini—and many of their subjects, including some extremely powerful nobles, hated them. Popular resentments were greater still because the costs of the ongoing Thirty Years' War were now combined with several consecutive years of bad harvests. So when cliques of nobles expressed their disgust for Mazarin, they found much popular support throughout the country.

France did not, however, come close to falling apart. Neither the aristocratic leaders of the Fronde nor the commoners who joined them in revolt claimed to be resisting the young king; their targets were the alleged corruption and mismanagement of Mazarin. Some of the rebels, it is true, insisted that part of Mazarin's fault lay in his pursuit of Richelieu's centralizing, antiprovincial policy. But most were aristocrats who wanted to become part of this centralizing process. Thus when Louis XIV began to rule in his own right in 1651, and pretexts for revolt against corrupt ministers no longer existed, the opposition was soon silenced. Yet Louis XIV remembered the turbulence of the Fronde for the rest of his life, and resolved never to let his aristocracy or his provinces get out of hand. Pursuing this policy, he became the most effective absolute monarch in Europe (see Chapter 15).

MONARCHY AND CIVIL WAR IN ENGLAND

The power of Louis XIV in France stands in stark contrast to the challenges faced by his older contemporary, King Charles I of England. Of all the revolts that shook mid-seventeenth-century Europe, the most radical in its consequences was the English Civil War. The causes of this conflict were similar to those that sparked rebellions in Spain and France: hostilities between the component parts of a composite kingdom; religious animosities between Catholics and Protestants and within the ruling (Protestant) camp; struggles for power among competing factions of aristocrats at court; and a fiscal system that could not keep pace with the increasing costs of government, much less those of war. But in England, these conflicts led to the unprecedented deposition and execution of the king (1649), an eleven-year "interregnum" during which England was ruled as a parliamentary republic (1649–60), and ultimately to the restoration of the monarchy under conditions designed to safeguard Parliament's place in government up to the present day.

The Origins of the English Civil War

The chain of events leading to war between royalist and Parliamentary forces in 1642 can be traced to the last decades of Queen Elizabeth's reign. During the 1590s, the expenses of war with Spain, together with a rebellion in Ireland, widespread crop failures, and the inadequacies of the antiquated English taxation system, drove the queen's government deeply into debt. Factional disputes around the court also became more bitter as courtiers, anticipating the aging queen's death, jockeyed for position under her presumed successor, the Scottish king James Stuart (James VI). Only on her deathbed, however, did the queen finally confirm that her throne should go to her Scottish cousin. As a result, neither James nor his new English subjects knew very much about each other when he took the throne at the end of 1603, ruling England as James I.

The relationship did not begin well. James's English subjects looked down on the Scots whom he brought with him to London. Although English courtiers were pleased to accept their new king's generosity to themselves, they resented the grants he made to his Scottish supporters, whom they blamed, quite unreasonably, for the crown's indebtedness. James, meanwhile, saw that to resolve his debts he had to have more revenue. But rather than bargain with parliamentary representatives for increased taxation, he chose to lecture them on the prerogatives of kingship, comparing kings to gods on earth: "As it is atheism and blasphemy to dispute what God can do, so it is presumption and high contempt in a subject to dispute what a king can do." When this approach failed, James raised what revenues he could without parliamentary approval, imposing new tolls on trade and selling trading monopolies to favored courtiers. These measures aroused further resentments against the king and so made voluntary grants of taxation from Parliament even less likely.

James was more adept with respect to religious policy. Scotland had been a firmly Calvinist country since the 1560s. England, too, was a Protestant country, but of a very different kind, since the Church of England retained many of the rituals, hierarchies, and doctrines of the medieval Church (Chapter 13). A significant number of English

Protestants wanted to bring their church more firmly into line with Calvinist principles, but others resisted such efforts and labeled their Calvinist opponents "Puritans." As king, James was compelled to mediate these conflicts. By and large, he did so successfully. In Scotland, he convinced the reformed (Calvinist) church to retain its bishops, and in England, he encouraged Calvinist doctrine while resisting any alterations to the religious tenets articulated in the English Prayer Book and the Thirty-Nine Articles of the Faith. Only in Ireland, which remained overwhelmingly Catholic, did James stir up future trouble. By encouraging the "plantation" of more than 8,000 Scottish Calvinists in the northern province of Ulster, he undermined the property rights of Irish Catholics and created religious animosities that have lasted to the present day.

The Reign of Charles Stuart

This state of affairs became volatile in 1625, when James was succeeded by his surviving son, Charles. Charles almost immediately launched a new war with Spain, exacerbating his financial problems. He then alarmed his Protestant subjects by marrying Henrietta Maria, the Catholic daughter of France's Louis XIII. The situation became truly dangerous, however, when Charles and his archbishop of Canterbury, William Laud, began to favor the most anti-Calvinist elements in the English church, thus threatening the forthrightly Calvinist church in Scotland. The Scots rebelled, and in 1640 a Scottish army marched south into England to demand the withdrawal of Charles's "Catholicizing" reforms.

To meet the Scottish threat, Charles was forced to summon the English Parliament, something he (like his father) had avoided doing. Relations between the king and Parliament had broken down severely in the late 1620s, when Charles responded to Parliament's refusal to grant him additional funds by demanding forced loans from his subjects—and punishing those who refused by forcing them to lodge soldiers in their homes, or throwing them into prison without trial. In response, Parliament had forced the king to accept the Petition of Right in 1628, which declared all taxes not voted by Parliament illegal, condemned the quartering of soldiers in private houses, and prohibited arbitrary imprisonment and martial law in time of peace. Angered rather than chastened by the Petition of Right, Charles resolved to rule without Parliament, funding his government during the 1630s with a variety of levies and fines imposed without parliamentary consent.

When the Scottish invasion forced Charles to summon a new Parliament, therefore, its representatives

were determined to impose a series of radical reforms on the king's government before they would even consider granting him funds to raise an army against the Scots. Charles initially cooperated with these reforms, even allowing Parliament to execute his chief minister. But it soon became clear that parliamentary leaders had no intention of fighting the Scots, but actually shared with them a common Calvinist outlook. In 1642, Charles attempted to break this stalemate by marching his guards into the House of Commons and attempting to arrest its leaders. When he failed in this, he withdrew from London to raise his own army. Parliament responded by summoning its own force and voting the taxation to pay for it. By the end of 1642, open warfare had erupted between the

CHARLES I. King Charles of England was a connoisseur of the arts and a patron of artists. He was adept at using portraiture to convey the magnificence of his tastes and the grandeur of his conception of kingship. ▪ *How does this portrait by Anthony Van Dyck compare to the engravings of the "martyred" king on page 444 in* Interpreting Visual Evidence?

Debating the English Civil War

> The English Civil War raised fundamental questions about political rights and responsibilities. Many of these are addressed in the two excerpts below. The first comes from a lengthy debate held within the General Council of Cromwell's army in October of 1647. The second is taken from the speech given by King Charles, moments before his execution in 1649.

The Army Debates, 1647

Colonel Rainsborough: Really, I think that the poorest man that is in England has a life to live as the greatest man, and therefore truly, sir, I think it's clear, that every man that is to live under a government ought first by his own consent to put himself under that government, and I do think that the poorest man in England is not at all bound in a strict sense to that government that he has not had a voice to put himself under ... insomuch that I should doubt whether I was an Englishman or not, that should doubt of these things.

General Ireton: Give me leave to tell you, that if you make this the rule, I think you must fly for refuge to an absolute natural right, and you must deny all civil right, and I am sure it will come to that in the consequence.... For my part, I think it is no right at all. I think that no person has a right to an interest or share in the disposing of the affairs of the kingdom, and in determining or choosing those that shall determine what laws we shall be ruled by here, no person has a right to this that has not a permanent fixed interest in this kingdom, and those persons together are properly the represented of this kingdom who, taken together, and consequently are to make up the representers of this kingdom....

We talk of birthright. Truly, birthright there is.... [M]en may justly have by birthright, by their very being born in England, that we should not seclude them out of England. That we should not refuse to give them air and place and ground, and the freedom of the highways and other things, to live amongst us, not any man that is born here, though he in birth or by his birth there come nothing at all that is part of the permanent interest of this kingdom to him. That I think is due to a man by birth. But that by a man's being born here he shall have a share in that power that shall dispose of the lands here, and of all things here, I do not think it is a sufficient ground.

Source: *Divine Right and Democracy: An Anthology of Political Writing in Stuart England*, ed. David Wootton (New York: 1986), pp. 286–87 (language modernized).

English king and the English government—something inconceivable in France, where the king and the government were inseparable.

Arrayed on the king's side were most of England's aristocrats and largest landowners, who were almost all loyal to the established Church of England, despite their opposition to some of Charles's own religious innovations. The parliamentary forces were made up of smaller landholders, tradesmen, and artisans, many of whom were Puritan sympathizers. The king's royalist supporters were commonly known by the aristocratic name of Cavaliers. Their opponents, who cut their hair short in contempt for the fashionable custom of wearing curls, were derisively called Roundheads. At first the Cavaliers, having obvious advantages of military experience, won most of the victories. In 1644, however, the parliamentary army was effectively reorganized, and afterward the fortunes of battle shifted. The royalist forces were badly beaten, and in 1646 the king was compelled to surrender. Soon thereafter, the episcopal hierarchy was abolished and a Calvinist-style church was mandated throughout England and Wales.

The struggle might have ended here had not a quarrel developed within the parliamentary party. The majority of its members were ready to restore Charles to the throne as a limited monarch, under an arrangement whereby a uniformly Calvinist faith would be imposed on both Scotland and England as the state religion. But a radical minority of Puritans, commonly known as Independents, distrusted

Charles I on the Scaffold, 1649

I think it is my duty, to God first, and to my country, for to clear myself both as an honest man, a good king, and a good Christian.

I shall begin first with my innocence. In truth I think it not very needful for me to insist long upon this, for all the world knows that I never did begin a war with the two Houses of Parliament, and I call God to witness, to whom I must shortly make an account, that I never did intend to incroach upon their privileges. . . .

As for the people—truly I desire their liberty and freedom as much as anybody whatsoever. But I must tell you that their liberty and freedom consists in having of government those laws by which their lives and goods may be most their own. It is not for having share in government. That is nothing pertaining to them.

A subject and a sovereign are clean different things, and therefore, until they do that—I mean that you do put the people in that liberty as I say—certainly they will never enjoy themselves.

Sirs, it was for this that now I am come here. If I would have given way to an arbitrary way, for to have all laws changed according to the power of the sword, I needed not to have come here. And therefore I tell you (and I pray God it be not laid to your charge) that I am the martyr of the people.

Source: Brian Tierney, Donald Kagan, and L. Pearce Williams, eds., *Great Issues in Western Civilization* (New York: 1967), pp. 46–47.

Questions for Analysis

1. What fundamental issues are at stake in both of these excerpts? How do the debaters within the parliamentary army (first excerpt) define "natural" and "civil" rights?

2. How does Charles defend his position? What is his theory of kingship, and how does it compare to that of Cardinal Richelieu (page 439)? How does it conflict with the ideas expressed in the army's debate?

3. It is interesting that none of the participants in these debates seems to have recognized the implications their arguments might have for the political rights of women. Why would that have been the case?

Charles and insisted on religious toleration for themselves and all other Protestants. Their leader was Oliver Cromwell (1599–1658), who had risen to command the Roundhead army, which he had reconstituted as "the New Model Army." Ultimately, he became the new leader of Parliament, too.

The Fall of Charles Stuart and the Commonwealth

Taking advantage of the dissension within the ranks of his opponents, Charles renewed the war in 1648 but, after a brief campaign, was forced to surrender. Cromwell was now resolved to end the life of "that man of blood" and, ejecting all the moderates from Parliament by force, he obliged this "Rump" (remaining) Parliament to put the king on trial and eventually to condemn him to death for treason against his own subjects. Charles Stuart was publicly beheaded on 30 January 1649: the first time in history that a reigning king had been legally deposed and executed by his own government. Europeans reacted to his death with horror, astonishment, or rejoicing, depending on their own political convictions (see **Interpreting Visual Evidence** on page 444).

A short time later, Parliament's hereditary House of Lords was abolished and England was declared a Commonwealth, an English translation of the Latin *res publica*. But founding a republic was far easier than maintaining

The Execution of a King

This allegorical engraving (image A) accompanied a pamphlet called *Eikon Basilike* ("The Kingly Image"), which began to circulate in Britain just weeks after the execution of King Charles I. It purported to be an autobiographical account of the king's last days and a justification of his royal policies. It was intended to arouse widespread sympathy for the king and his exiled heir, Charles II, and it succeeded admirably: the cult of Charles "King and Martyr" became increasingly popular. Here, the Latin inscription on the shaft of light suggests that Charles' piety will beam "brighter through the shadows," while the scrolls at the left proclaim that "virtue grows beneath weight" and "unmoved, triumphant." Charles' earthly crown (on the floor at his side) is "splendid and heavy," while the crown of thorns he grasps is "bitter and light" and the heavenly crown is "blessed and eternal." Even people who could not read these and other Latin mottoes would have known that Charles' last words were: "I shall go from a corruptible to an incorruptible Crown, where no disturbance can be."

At the same time, broadsides showing the moment of execution (image B) circulated in various European countries with explanatory captions. This one was

A. King Charles I as a martyr.

one. Technically, the Rump Parliament continued as the legislative body; but Cromwell, with the army at his command, possessed the real power and soon became exasperated by the legislators' attempts to enrich themselves by confiscating their opponents' property. In 1653, he marched a detachment of troops into the Rump Parliament. The Commonwealth thus ceased to exist and was soon replaced by the "Protectorate," a thinly disguised autocracy established under a constitution drafted by officers of the army. Called the Instrument of Government, this text is the nearest approximation to a written constitution England has ever had. Extensive powers were given to Cromwell as Lord Protector for life, and his office was made hereditary. At first, a new Parliament exercised limited authority to make laws and levy taxes, but in 1655 Cromwell abruptly dismissed its members. Thereafter the government became a virtual dictatorship, with Cromwell wielding a sovereignty more absolute than any previous English monarch ever dreamed of claiming. Many intellectuals noted the similarities between these events and those that had given rise to the Principate of Augustus after the death of Julius Caesar (Chapter 5).

printed in Germany, and there are almost identical versions surviving from the Netherlands. It shows members of the crowd fainting and turning away at the sight of blood spurting from the king's neck, while the executioner holds up the severed head.

B. The execution of Charles I.

The Restoration of the Monarchy

Given the choice between a Puritan military dictatorship and the old royalist regime, most of England opted for the latter. Years of unpopular Calvinist austerities—such as the prohibition of any public recreation on Sundays and the closing of London's theaters—had made most people long for the milder Church of England, and for monarchy. So not long after Cromwell's death in 1658, one of his generals seized power and called for the election of a new Parliament, which met in the spring of 1660. Almost overnight, England was a monarchy again and Charles I's exiled son, Charles II, was proclaimed its king and recalled from the court of his cousin, Louis XIV.

Charles II (r. 1660–85) restored bishops to the Church of England but he did not return to the provocative religious policies of his father. Quipping that he did not wish to "resume his travels," Charles agreed to respect Parliament and to observe the Petition of Right that had so enraged his father. He also accepted all the legislation passed by Parliament immediately before the outbreak of civil war

OLIVER CROMWELL AS PROTECTOR OF THE COMMONWEALTH.
This coin, minted in 1658, shows the Lord Protector wreathed with laurel garlands like a classical hero or a Roman consul, but it also proclaims him to be "by the Grace of God Protector of the Commonwealth." ▪ *What mixed messages does this coin convey?*

faith as an adequate foundation for universal philosophical conclusions, for even Christians now disagreed about the fundamental truths of the faith. Political allegiances were similarly under threat, as intellectuals and common people alike began to assert a right to resist princes with whom they disagreed on matters of religion. Even morality and custom were beginning to seem arbitrary and detached from the natural ordering of the world.

Europeans responded to this pervasive climate of doubt in a variety of ways, ranging from radical skepticism to authoritarian assertions of ecclesiastical control and political absolutism. What united their responses, however, was a sometimes desperate search for new foundations on which to construct some measure of certainty in the face of intellectual, religious, and political challenges.

Witchcraft and the Power of the State

Adding to Europeans' fears was the conviction of many that witchcraft was a new and increasing threat to their world. Although the belief that certain individuals could heal or harm through the practice of magic had always been widespread, it was not until the late fifteenth century that authorities began to insist that such powers could derive only from some kind of satanic bargain. Once this belief became widely accepted, judicial officers became much more active in seeking out suspected witches for prosecution. In 1484, Pope Innocent VIII had ordered papal inquisitors to use all means at their disposal to detect and eliminate witchcraft, even condoning the torture of suspected witches. Predictably, torture increased the number of accused witches who "confessed" to their alleged crimes; and as more accused witches "confessed," more and more witches were "discovered," tried, and executed—even in realms like England and Scotland where torture was not legal and where the Inquisition of the Roman Catholic Church did not operate.

In considering the rash of witchcraft persecutions that swept early modern Europe, then, we need to keep two facts in mind. First of all, witchcraft trials were by no means limited to Catholic countries. Protestant reformers believed in the insidious powers of Satan just as much as Catholics did, if not more so. Both Luther and Calvin urged that accused witches be tried more peremptorily and sentenced with less leniency than ordinary criminals, a recommendation that their followers heeded. Second, it was only when religious authorities' efforts to detect witchcraft were backed by the coercive powers of secular governments that the fear of witches could translate into imprisonment and execution. It was therefore through this fundamental agreement between Catholics and Protestants, and with the complicity of secular

in 1642, including the requirement that Parliament be summoned at least once every three years. England thus emerged from its civil war as a limited monarchy, in which power was exercised by "the king in Parliament." It remains a constitutional monarchy to this day.

THE PROBLEM OF DOUBT AND THE QUEST FOR CERTAINTY

Between 1540 and 1660, Europeans were forced to confront a world in which all that they had once taken for granted was suddenly cast into doubt. Vast new continents had been discovered in the Americas, populated by millions of people whose very existence compelled Europeans to rethink some of their most basic ideas about humanity and human nature. Equally disorienting, the religious uniformity of medieval Europe, although never absolute, had been shattered to an unprecedented extent by the Reformation and the religious wars that arose from it. In 1540, it was still possible to imagine that these religious divisions might be temporary. By 1660, it was clear they would be permanent. No longer, therefore, could Europeans regard revealed religious states, that this witch craze could claim tens of thousands of victims, of whom the vast majority were women.

The final death toll will never be known, but in the 1620s there were, on average, 100 burnings a year in the German cities of Würzburg and Bamberg; around the same time, it was said that the town square of Wolfenbüttel "looked like a little forest, so crowded were the stakes." When accusations of witchcraft diminished in Europe, they became endemic in some European colonies, as at the English settlement of Salem, Massachusetts.

This witch mania reflects the fears that early modern Europeans held about the adequacy of traditional remedies (such as prayers, relics, and holy water) to combat the evils of their world, another consequence of religious dissent and uncertainty. It also reflects their growing conviction that only the state had the power to protect them. One of the most striking features of the mania for hunting down witches is the extent to which these prosecutions, in both Catholic and Protestant countries, were state-sponsored processes, carried out by secular authorities claiming to act as the protectors of society against the spiritual and temporal evils that assailed it. Even in Catholic countries, where witchcraft prosecutions were sometimes begun in Church courts, these cases would be transferred to the state's courts for final judgment and punishment, because Church courts were forbidden to impose capital penalties. In most Protestant countries, where ecclesiastical courts had been abolished (only England retained them), the entire process of detecting, prosecuting, and punishing suspected witches was carried out under the supervision of the state. In both Catholic and Protestant countries, the result of these witchcraft trials was thus a considerable increase in the scope of the state's powers to regulate the lives of its subjects.

The Search for a Source of Authority

The crisis of Europe's "iron century"—the name given to the sixteenth century by some contemporary intellectuals—was fundamentally a crisis of authority, with far-reaching implications. Attempts to reestablish some foundation for a new authority therefore took many forms. For the French nobleman Michel de Montaigne (1533–1592), who wrote during the height of the French wars of religion, the result was a searching skepticism about the possibilities of any certain knowledge whatsoever. The son of a Catholic father and a Huguenot mother of Jewish ancestry, the well-to-do Montaigne retired from a legal career at the age of thirty-eight to devote himself to a life of reflection. The *Essays* that resulted were a new literary form originally conceived as "experiments" (the French *essai* means "attempt"). Because they are beautifully composed as well as searchingly reflective, Montaigne's *Essays* are among the most enduring classics of European literature and thought.

Although the range of subjects covered by the *Essays* is wide, two main themes are dominant. One is constant questioning. Making his motto *Que sais-je?* ("What do I know?"), Montaigne decided that he knew very little for certain. According to him, "it is folly to measure truth and error by our own capacities" because our capacities are severely limited. As he maintained in one of his most famous essays, "On Cannibals," what may seem indisputably true and moral to one nation may seem absolutely false to another because "everyone gives the title of barbarism to everything that is not of his usage." From this Montaigne's second main principle followed: the need for moderation. Because all people think they know the perfect religion and the perfect government, yet few agree on what that perfection might be, Montaigne concluded that no religion or government is really perfect, and consequently no belief is worth fighting or dying for. Instead, people should accept the teachings of religion on faith, and obey the governments

ALLEGED "WITCHES" WORSHIPING THE DEVIL IN THE FORM OF A GOAT. This is one of the earliest visual conceptions, dating from around 1460, of witchcraft's reliance on satanic support. In the background, other witches ride bareback on flying demons.

Montaigne on Skepticism and Faith

The Essays *of Michel de Montaigne (1533–1592) reflect the sincerity of his own attempts to grapple with the contradictions of his time, even if he could not resolve those contradictions. Here, he discusses the relationship between human knowledge and the teachings of religious authorities.*

Perhaps it is not without reason that we attribute facility in belief and conviction to simplicity and ignorance, for . . . the more a mind is empty and without counterpoise, the more easily it gives beneath the weight of the first persuasive argument. That is why children, common people, women, and sick people are most subject to being led by the ears. But then, on the other hand, it is foolish presumption to go around disdaining and condemning as false whatever does not seem likely to us; which is an ordinary vice in those who think they have more than common ability. I used to do so once. . . . But reason has taught me that to condemn a thing thus, dogmatically, as false and impossible, is to assume the advantage of knowing the bounds and limits of God's will and of the power of our mother Nature, and that there is no more notable folly in the world than to reduce these things to the measure of our capacity and competence. . . .

It is a dangerous and fateful presumption, besides the absurd temerity that it implies, to disdain what we do not comprehend. For after you have established, according to your fine understanding, the limits of truth and falsehood, and it turns out that you must necessarily believe things even stranger than those you deny, you are obliged from then on to abandon these limits. Now what seems to me to bring as much disorder into our consciences as anything, in these religious troubles that we are in, is this partial surrender of their beliefs by Catholics. It seems to them that they are being very moderate and understanding when they yield to their opponents some of the articles in dispute. But, besides the fact that they do not see what an advantage it is to a man charging you for you to begin to give ground and withdraw, and how much that encourages him to pursue his point, those articles which they select as the most trivial are sometimes very important. We must either submit completely to the authority of our ecclesiastical government, or do without it completely. It is not for us to decide what portion of obedience we owe it.

Source: *Montaigne: Selections from the Essays,* trans. and ed. Donald M. Frame (Arlington Heights, IL: 1971), pp. 34–38.

Questions for Analysis

1. Why does Montaigne say that human understanding is limited? How do his assumptions compare to those of Richelieu (page 439)?

2. What does Montaigne mean by the "partial surrender" of belief? If a Catholic should place his faith in the Church, what then is the purpose of human intellect?

---

constituted to rule over them, without resorting to fanaticism in either sphere.

Although Montaigne's writings seem modern in many ways—that is, familiar—he was very much a man of his time, and also the product of a long philosophical tradition reaching back to antiquity (Chapters 3 and 4). At heart, he was a Stoic: in a world governed by unpredictable fortune, he believed that the best human strategy was to face the good and the bad with steadfastness and dignity. And indeed, the wide circulation of Montaigne's *Essays* actually helped to combat the fanaticism and religious intolerance of his own and subsequent ages.

Another attempt to resolve the problem of doubt was offered by the French philosopher Blaise Pascal (1623–1662). Pascal began his career as a mathematician and scientist. But at age thirty he abandoned science after a profound conversion experience. This led him to embrace an extreme form of puritanical Catholicism known as Jansenism (after its Flemish founder, Cornelius Jansen). From then until his death he worked on a highly ambitious philosophical-religious project meant to establish the truth of Christianity by appealing simultaneously to intellect and emotion.

After his premature death, the results of this effort were published as a series of "Thoughts" (*Pensées*). In this collection of intellectual fragments, Pascal argues that faith alone can resolve the contradictions of the world and that "the heart has its reasons of which reason itself knows nothing." Pascal's *Pensées* express the author's own terror, anguish, and awe in the face of evil and uncertainty, but present that awe as evidence for the existence of God. Pascal's hope was that, on this foundation, some measure of confidence in humanity and its capacity for self-knowledge could be rediscovered, thus avoiding both the dogmatism and the extreme skepticism that were so prominent in seventeenth-century society.

Theories of Absolute Government

Montaigne's contemporary, the French lawyer Jean Bodin (1530–1596), took a more active approach to the problem of uncertain authority. He wanted to resolve the disorders of the day by reestablishing the powers of the state on new and more secure foundations. Like Montaigne, Bodin was particularly troubled by the upheavals caused by the religious wars in France; he had witnessed the St. Bartholomew's Day Massacre of 1572. But he was resolved to offer a practical, political solution to such turbulence. In his monumental *Six Books of the Commonwealth* (1576), he developed a theory of absolute state sovereignty. According to Bodin, the state arises from the needs of collections of families and, once constituted, should brook no opposition to its authority because maintaining order is its paramount duty. For Bodin, sovereignty was "the most high, absolute, and perpetual power over all subjects," which could make and enforce laws without the consent of those governed by the state—precisely what Charles I of England would have argued, and precisely what his Puritan subjects disputed. Although Bodin acknowledged the possibility of government by the aristocracy or even by a democracy, he assumed that the powerful nation-states of his day would have to be ruled by monarchs, and insisted that such monarchs should in no way be limited—whether by legislative and judicial bodies, or even by laws made by their own predecessors. Bodin maintained that every subject must trust in the ruler's "mere and frank good will." Even if the ruler proved a tyrant, Bodin insisted that the subject had no right to resist, for any resistance would open the door "to a licentious anarchy which is worse than the harshest tyranny in the world."

Like Bodin, Thomas Hobbes (1588–1679) was moved by the turmoil of the English Civil War to advance a new political theory in his treatise *Leviathan* (1651). Yet Hobbes's formulation differs from that of Bodin in several respects. Whereas Bodin assumed that absolute sovereign power should be vested in a monarch, Hobbes argued that any form of government capable of protecting its subjects' lives and property might act as sovereign and hence all-powerful. And whereas Bodin defined his state as "the lawful government of families" and hence did not believe that the state could abridge private property rights because families could not exist without property, Hobbes's state existed to rule over atomistic individuals and was thus licensed to trample over both liberty and property if the government's own survival was at stake.

But the most fundamental difference between Bodin and Hobbes lay in the latter's uncompromisingly pessimistic view of human nature. Hobbes posited that the "state of nature" that existed before government was "war of all against all." Because man naturally behaves as "a wolf" toward other men, human life without government is necessarily "solitary, poor, nasty, brutish, and short." To escape such consequences, people must therefore surrender their liberties to a sovereign ruler in exchange for his obligation to keep the peace. Having traded away their liberties, subjects have no right to win them back, and the sovereign may rule as he likes—free to oppress his subjects in any way other than to kill them, an act that would negate the very purpose of his rule, which is to preserve his people's lives.

THE ART OF BEING HUMAN

Doubt and uncertainty were also primary themes in the profusion of literature and art produced in this era. Moved by the ambiguities and ironies of existence and the horrors of war and persecution, writers and artists sought to find redemptive qualities in human suffering and hardship.

The Adventures of Don Quixote

A timeless example of this artistic response is the satirical novel *Don Quixote*, which its author, Miguel de Cervantes (1547–1616), composed largely in prison. It recounts the adventures of an idealistic Spanish gentleman, Don Quixote of La Mancha, who becomes deranged by his constant reading of chivalric romances. His mind filled with all kinds of fantastic adventures, he sets out at the age of fifty on the slippery road of knight-errantry, imagining windmills to be glowering giants and flocks of sheep to be armies of infidels. In his distorted world view he mistakes inns for castles and serving girls for courtly ladies. His sidekick, Sancho Panza, is his exact opposite: a plain, practical man with his feet on the ground, content with modest bodily pleasures. Yet Cervantes does not suggest that realism is categorically preferable to "quixotic" idealism. Rather, these two men represent different facets of human nature. On the one hand, *Don Quixote* is a devastating satire on the anachronistic chivalric mentality that was already hastening Spain's decline. On the other, it is a sincere celebration of the human capacity for optimism and goodness.

English Playwrights and Poets

In the late sixteenth century, the emergence of public playhouses made drama an especially effective mass medium for the expression of opinions, the dissemination of ideas, and the articulation of national identies. This was especially so in England during the last two decades of Elizabeth's reign and that of her successor, James. Among the large number of playwrights at work in London during this era, the most noteworthy are Christopher Marlowe (1564–1593), Ben Jonson (c. 1572–1637), and William Shakespeare (1564–1616). Marlowe, who may have been a spy for Elizabeth's government and who was mysteriously murdered in a tavern brawl before he reached the age of thirty, was extremely popular in his own day. In plays such as *Tamburlaine*—about the life of the Mongolian emperor Timur the Lame (Chapter 11)—and *Doctor Faustus*, Marlowe created vibrant heroes who pursue larger-than-life ambitions only to be felled by their own human limitations. In contrast to the heroic tragedies of Marlowe, Ben Jonson wrote dark comedies that expose human vices and foibles. In the particularly bleak *Volpone*, Jonson shows people behaving like deceitful and lustful animals. In the later *Alchemist*, he balances an attack on pseudo-scientific quackery with admiration for resourceful lower-class characters who cleverly take advantage of their supposed betters.

William Shakespeare was born into the family of a tradesman in the provincial town of Stratford-upon-Avon, where he attained a modest education before moving to London around the age of twenty. There he found employment in the theater as an actor and playwright, a "maker of plays." He eventually earned a reputation as a poet, too, but it was his success at the box office that enabled him to retire, rich, to his native Stratford about twenty-five years later. Shakespeare composed or collaborated in the writing of an unknown number of plays, of which some forty survive in whole or in part. They have since become a kind of secular English Bible, and owe their longevity to the author's unrivaled gifts of verbal expression, humor, and psychological insight.

Shakespeare's dramas fall thematically into three groups. Those written during the playwright's early years

reflect the political, religious, and social upheavals of the late sixteenth century. As we have already seen, these include many history plays which recount episodes from England's medieval past and the struggles that established the Tudor dynasty of Elizabeth's grandfather, Henry VII. They also include the lyrical tragedy *Romeo and Juliet* and a number of comedies, including *A Midsummer Night's Dream*, *Twelfth Night*, *As You Like It*, and *Much Ado about Nothing*. Most explore fundamental problems of identity, honor and ambition, love and friendship.

The plays from Shakespeare's second period are, like other contemporary artworks, characterized by a troubled searching into the mysteries and meaning of human existence. They showcase the perils of indecisive idealism (*Hamlet*) and the abuse of power (*Measure for Measure*), culminating in the searing tragedies of *Macbeth* and *King Lear*. Those plays composed at the end of his career emphasize the possibilities of reconciliation and peace, even after

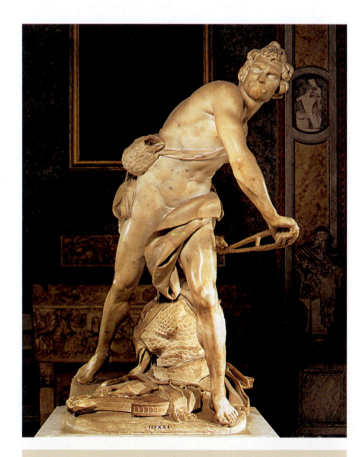

DAVID BY BERNINI (1598–1680). Whereas the earlier conceptions of David by the Renaissance sculptors Donatello and Michelangelo were serene and dignified (see page 389), the Baroque sculptor Bernini chose to portray his young hero at the peak of physical exertion. ■ *Can you discern the influence of Hellenistic sculpture (Chapter 4, pages 135–136) in this work?* ■ *What are some shared characteristics?*

VIEW OF TOLEDO BY EL GRECO. This is one of many landscape portraits representing the hilltop city that became the artist's home in later life. Its supple "Mannerist" style almost defies historical periodization.

years of misunderstanding and sorrow: *A Winter's Tale*, *Cymbeline*, and finally *The Tempest*, an extended reflection on the paradoxical relationship between the weakness of human nature and the power of the human artist.

Though less versatile than Shakespeare, the Puritan poet John Milton (1608–1674) is considered to be his equal in the grandeur of his artistic vision. The leading publicist of Oliver Cromwell's regime, Milton wrote the official defense of the beheading of Charles I as well as a number of treatises justifying Puritan ideologies. But he loved the Greek and Latin classics at least as much as the Bible. He wrote a pastoral elegy, *Lycidas*, mourning (in classical terms) the loss of a dear friend. And later, when forced into retirement by the accession of Charles II, Milton (now blind) embarked on a classical epic based on Genesis, *Paradise Lost*. Setting out to "justify the ways of God to man," Milton first plays "devil's advocate" by creating the compelling character of Satan, who defies God with boldness and subtlety. Indeed, the eloquence of Satan is never quite counterbalanced by the supposed hero, Adam, who learns to accept the human lot of moral responsibility and suffering.

The Artistry of Southern Europe

The ironies and tensions inherent in human existence were also explored in the visual arts. In Italy and Spain, many painters of the sixteenth century cultivated a highly

dramatic and emotionally compelling style sometimes known as "Mannerism." The most unusual of these artists was El Greco ("the Greek," c. 1541–1614), a pupil of the Venetian master Tintoretto (1518–1594). Born Domenikos Theotokopoulos on the Greek island of Crete, El Greco absorbed some of the stylized elongation characteristic of Byzantine icon painting (Chapter 7) before traveling to Italy. He eventually settled in Spain. Many of his paintings were too strange to be greatly appreciated in his own day and even now appear so *avant garde* as to be almost surreal. His *View of Toledo*, for example, is a transfigured landscape, mysteriously lit from within. Equally amazing are his swirling Biblical scenes and the stunning portraits of gaunt, dignified saints who radiate austerity and spiritual insight.

The dominant artistic style of southern Europe in the seventeenth century was that of the Baroque, a school whose name has become a synonym for elaborate, highly wrought sculpture and architecural details. The Baroque style originated in Rome during the Counter-Reformation and promoted a glorified Catholic worldview. Its most imaginative and influential figure was the architect and sculptor Gianlorenzo Bernini (1598–1680), a frequent employee of the papacy who created a magnificent celebration of papal grandeur in the sweeping colonnades leading up to St. Peter's Basilica. Breaking with the serene Renaissance classicism of Palladio (Chapter 13), Bernini's architecture retained such classical elements as columns and domes

THE MAIDS OF HONOR (LAS MERINAS) BY DIEGO VELÁZQUEZ. The artist himself (at left) is shown working at his easel and gazing out at the viewer—or at the subjects of his double portrait, the Spanish king and queen, depicted in a distant mirror. But the real focus of the painting is the delicate, impish princess in the center, flanked by two young ladies-in-waiting, a dwarf, and another royal child. Courtiers in the background look on.

but combined them in ways meant to express aggressive restlessness and power. Bernini was also one of the first to experiment with church facades built "in depth"—that is, with frontages not conceived as continuous surfaces but instead jutting out at odd angles and thus seeming to invade the open space in front of them. The purpose of these innovations was to pull the viewer into the work of art. This was also the aim of Bernini's sculpture, which drew inspiration from the restless motion and artistic bravado of Hellenistic statuary (Chapter 4).

Although the Baroque movement began in Rome and was originally expressed in three dimensions, characteristics of this style can also be found in painting. Many consider its greatest master to be the Spanish painter Diego Velázquez (1599–1660). Unlike Bernini, however, Velázquez was a court painter in Madrid, not a servant of the Church. And although many of his canvases display a Baroque attention to motion and drama, his most characteristic work is more restrained and conceptually thoughtful. An example is *The Maids of Honor*, completed around 1656 and a masterpiece of self-referentiality. It shows the artist himself at work on a double portrait of the Spanish king and queen, but the scene is dominated by the children and servants of the royal family.

Dutch Painting in the Golden Age

Southern Europe's main rival for artistic laurels was the Netherlands, where three exemplary but dissimilar painters explored the theme of the greatness and wretchedness of man to the fullest. Peter Bruegel the Elder (*BROY-ghul*, c. 1525–1569) exulted in portraying the busy, elemental life of the peasantry. Most famous in this respect are his rollicking *Peasant Wedding* and *Peasant Wedding Dance* and his spacious *Harvesters*, in which guzzling and snoring field hands are taking a well-deserved break from their heavy labors under the noon sun. Such vistas celebrate the uninterrupted rhythms of life; but late in his career Bruegel became appalled by the intolerance and bloodshed he witnessed during the Calvinist riots and the Spanish repression of the Netherlands, expressing his criticism in an understated yet searing manner. From a distance, *The Massacre of the Innocents* looks like a snug scene of Flemish village life. In fact, however, soldiers are methodically breaking into homes and slaughtering helpless infants, just as Herod's soldiers once did. The artist—alluding to a Gospel message unheeded by warring Catholics and Protestants alike—seems to be saying "as it happened in the time of Christ, so it happens now."

SELF-PORTRAITS. Self-portraits became common during the sixteenth and seventeenth centuries, reflecting the intense introspection of the period. Left: Rembrandt painted more than sixty self-portraits; this one, dating from around 1660, captures the artist's creativity, theatricality (note the costume), and honesty of self-examination. Right: Judith Leyster (1609–1660) was a contemporary of Rembrandt who pursued a successful career during her early twenties, before she married. Respected in her own day, she was all but forgotten for centuries thereafter but is once against the object of much attention.

THE MASSACRE OF THE INNOCENTS BY BRUEGEL (c. 1525–1569). This painting shows how effectively art can be used as a means of political and social commentary. Here, Bruegel depicts the suffering of the Netherlands at the hands of the Spanish in his own day, with reference to the Biblical story of Herod's slaughter of Jewish children after the birth of Jesus—thereby collapsing these two historical incidents.

THE HORRORS OF WAR BY RUBENS (1577–1640). In his old age, Rubens took a far more critical view of war than he had done for most of his earlier career. Here, the war-god Mars casts aside his mistress Venus, goddess of love, and threatens humanity with death and destruction.

Vastly different from Bruegel was the Netherlandish painter Peter Paul Rubens (1577–1640). Since the Baroque was an international movement closely linked to the spread of the Counter-Reformation, it should offer no surprise that Baroque style was extremely well represented in just that part of the Netherlands which, after long warfare, had been retained by Spain and reintroduced to the Catholic faith. Indeed, Rubens of Antwerp was a far more typical Baroque artist than Velázquez of Madrid, painting literally thousands of robust canvases that glorified resurgent Catholicism or exalted second-rate aristocrats by portraying them as epic heroes dressed in bearskins. Even when Rubens's intent was not overtly propagandistic, he customarily reveled in the sumptuous extravagance of the Baroque style; he is most famous today for the pink and rounded flesh of his well-nourished nudes. But unlike a host of lesser Baroque artists, Rubens was not lacking in subtlety or depth. Although he celebrated martial valor for most of his career, his late *The Horrors of War* movingly portrays what he himself called "the grief of unfortunate Europe,

which, for so many years now, has suffered plunder, outrage, and misery."

In some ways a blend of Bruegel and Rubens, Rembrandt van Rijn (*vahn-REEN*, 1606–1669) defies all attempts at easy characterization. Living across the border from the Spanish Netherlands in the staunchly Calvinistic Dutch Republic, Rembrandt belonged to a society that was too austere to tolerate the unbuckled realism of Brueghel or the fleshy pomposity of Rubens. Yet Rembrandt managed to put both realistic and Baroque traits to new uses. In his early career he gained fame and fortune as a painter of biblical scenes and was also active as a portrait painter who knew how to flatter his subjects—to the great advantage of his purse. But gradually his prosperity waned, and as personal tragedies mounted in his middle and declining years, the painter's art gained in dignity, subtlety, and mystery. His later portraits, including several self-portraits, are highly introspective and suggest that only part of the story is being told. Equally compelling are explicitly philosophical paintings such as *Aristotle Contemplating the Bust of Homer*,

After You Read This Chapter

Visit StudySpace for quizzes, additional review materials, and multi-media documents. **wwnorton.com/studyspace**

REVIEWING THE OBJECTIVES

- Religious and political conflicts have always been intertwined, but the combination was especially deadly in the era between 1540 and 1660. Why was this?

- Although the religious warfare of this period seems almost continuous, it took distinctive forms in France, the Netherlands, and Germany. Explain why.

- What factors led to the decline of Spain as Europe's dominant power, and to the rise of France?

- The main causes of the English Civil War can be traced back to the reign of Elizabeth I and her successor, James Stuart of Scotland. What were the main sources of disagreement between the Stuart monarchy and Parliament?

- Intellectuals and artists responded to the challenges of this era in creative ways. Identify some of the major figures and ideas that emerged from this period of crisis.

in which the philosopher seems spellbound by the radiance of the epic poet, and *The Polish Rider*, in which realistic and symbolic elements merge to portray a pensive young man setting out fearlessly into a perilous world. Equally fearless is the frank gaze of Rembrandt's slightly younger contemporary, Judith Leyster (1609–1660), who looks out of her own self-portrait with a refreshingly optimistic and good-humored expression.

CONCLUSION

Between 1540 and 1660, Europe was racked by a combination of religious war, political rebellion, and economic crisis that undermined confidence in traditional structures of social, religious, and political authority. The result was fear, skepticism, and a search for new foundations on which to rebuild Europe. For artists and intellectuals, the period proved to be one of the most creative epochs in the history of Western civilizations. But for common people, the century was one of extraordinary suffering.

By 1660, after a hundred years of destructive efforts to restore the religious unity of Europe through war, a de facto religious toleration among states was beginning to emerge as the only way to preserve political order. But within states, toleration was still very limited. In territories where religious rivalries ran too deep to be overcome, therefore, rulers began to discover that loyalty to the state could override even religious divisions among their subjects. The end result of this century of crises was thus to strengthen Europeans' reliance on in the state's capacity to heal their wounds and right their wrongs, with religion relegated more and more to the private sphere of individual conscience. In the following centuries, this new confidence in the state as an autonomous moral agent acting in accordance with its own "reasons of state" and for its own purposes, would prove a powerful challenge to the traditions of limited consensual government that had emerged from the Middle Ages.

PEOPLE, IDEAS, AND EVENTS IN CONTEXT

- What were the main sources of instability in Europe during the sixteenth century? How did the **PRICE REVOLUTION** exacerbate these?

- How did the **EDICT OF NANTES** challenge the doctrine *CUIUS REGIO, EIUS RELIGIO* ("as the ruler, so the religion") established by the **PEACE OF AUGSBURG**?

- What were the initial causes of the **THIRTY YEARS' WAR**? Why did Sweden and France become involved in it?

- Describe the political configuration of Europe after the **PEACE OF WESTPHALIA**. Why did Spain's power decline while France emerged as dominant? How did the policies of **CARDINAL RICHELIEU** strengthen the power of the French monarchy?

- What factors led to the **ENGLISH CIVIL WAR** and the execution of **CHARLES I**?

- In what ways did the **WITCH CRAZE** of early modern Europe reveal the religious and social tensions of the sixteenth and seventeenth centuries?

- How did **MONTAIGNE** and **PASCAL** respond to the problem of authority? What were the differences between **JEAN BODIN**'s theory of absolute sovereignty and that of **THOMAS HOBBES**?

CONSEQUENCES

- The period between 1540 and 1660 is considered to be one of the most turbulent in Europe's history, but it also has deep roots in the more distant past of Western civilizations. How far back would you trace the origins of this "perfect storm"?

- The execution of King Charles I of England was a watershed event, and yet the English monarchy itself survived this crisis. How would you account for this remarkable fact? In what ways did the concept of English kingship have to change in order for this to happen?

- In your view, do the various artistic movements of this era seem especially modern? Or are they better understood as comparable to the movements responding to the Black Death (Chapter 10) or to the artistic innovations characteristic of the Renaissance (Chapter 12)? What elements make a work of art seem "modern"?

STORY LINES

- After the devastation caused by the crisis of the seventeenth century, European rulers sought stability in the centralization of government authority and by increasing their own power at the expense of other groups and institutions in society, such as the nobility and the church.

- Population growth, increased agricultural productivity, and innovations in business practices created new wealth and new incentives for economic development and colonial expansion to other continents. All of these processes favored European powers with access to Atlantic trade, especially France and Britain, who opened up profitable trading networks to the Americas and the Caribbean.

- Within Europe, only a few European powers continued to pursue expansionist foreign policies. Others sought stability through treaties that aimed at an international balance of powers.

CHRONOLOGY

1600s	British and French establish colonies in North America and the Caribbean and outposts in Africa and India
1500s–1800s	Europeans engage in African slave trade from Africa to the Caribbean, Brazil, and North America
1643–1715	Louis XIV of France
1685	Revocation of the Edict of Nantes
1688	Glorious Revolution in England
1689–1725	Peter the Great of Russia's reign
1702–1713	War of the Spanish Succession
1713	Treaty of Utrecht
1740–1780	Maria Theresa of Austria's reign
1740–1786	Frederick the Great of Prussia's reign
1756–1763	The Seven Years' War
1762–1796	Catherine the Great of Russia's reign
1772–1795	Partition of Poland
1775–1783	United States Independence

Absolutism and Empire, 1660–1789

CORE OBJECTIVES

- **DEFINE** *absolutism* and understand its central principles as a theory of government.

- **IDENTIFY** the absolutist monarchs who were most successful in imposing their rule in Europe between 1600 and 1800.

- **EXPLAIN** the alternatives to absolutism that emerged, most notably in England.

- **DESCRIBE** the eighteenth-century commercial revolution in Europe.

- **UNDERSTAND** the new economic and cultural linkages between Europe and the Atlantic world that emerged as a result of colonial expansion and the slave trade in the seventeenth and eighteenth centuries.

In the mountainous region of south-central France known as the Auvergne in the 1660s, the marquis of Canillac had a notorious reputation. His noble title gave him the right to collect minor taxes on special occasions, but he insisted that these small privileges be converted into annual tributes. To collect these payments, he housed twelve accomplices in his castle that he called his apostles. Their other nicknames—one was known as Break Everything—gave a more accurate sense of their activities in the local villages. The marquis imprisoned those who resisted and forced their families to buy their freedom. In an earlier age, the marquis might have gotten away with this profitable arrangement. In 1662, however, he ran up against the authority of a king, Louis XIV, who was determined to demonstrate that the power of the central monarch was absolute. The marquis was brought up on charges before a special court of judges from Paris. He was found guilty and forced to pay a large fine. The king confiscated his property and had the marquis's castle destroyed.

Louis XIV's special court in the Auvergne heard nearly a thousand civil cases over four months in 1662. It convicted 692 people, and many of them, like the marquis of Canillac, were noble. The verdicts were an extraordinary example of Louis XIV's ability to project his authority into the remote corners of his realm and to do so in a way that diminished the power of other elites. During his long reign (1643–1715), Louis XIV systematically pursued such a policy on many fronts, asserting his power over the nobility, the clergy, and the provincial courts. Increasingly, these elites were forced to look to the crown to guarantee their interests, and their own power became more closely connected with the sacred aura of the monarchy itself. Louis XIV's model of kingship was so successful that it became known as absolute monarchy. In recognition of the success and influence of Louis XIV's political system, the period from around 1660 (when the English monarchy was restored and Louis XIV began his personal rule in France) to 1789 (when the French Revolution erupted) is traditionally known as the age of absolutism. This is a crucial period in the development of the modern, centralized, bureaucratic state.

Absolutism was a political theory that encouraged rulers to claim complete sovereignty within their territories. An absolute monarch could make law, dispense justice, create and direct a bureaucracy, declare war, and levy taxation, without the approval of any other governing body. Assertions of absolute authority were buttressed by claims that rulers governed by divine right, just as fathers ruled over their households. After the chaos of the previous century, many Europeans came to believe that it was only by exalting the sovereignty of absolute rulers that order could be restored to European life.

European monarchs also successfully projected their power abroad during this period. By 1660, the French, Spanish, Portuguese, English, and Dutch had all established important colonies in the Americas and in Asia. These colonies created important trading networks that brought profitable new consumer goods such as sugar, tobacco, and coffee to a wide public in Europe, while also encouraging the spread of slavery to produce these goods. Rivalry among colonial powers to control the trade in slaves and consumer goods was intense. In the eighteenth century, Europe's wars were driven by colonial considerations and imperial conflicts, as global commerce assumed a growing role in the European economy.

Absolutism was not the only political theory used by European governments during this period. England, Scotland, the Dutch Republic, Switzerland, Venice, Sweden, and Poland-Lithuania were all either limited monarchies, or republics. In Russia, an extreme autocracy emerged that gave the tsar a degree of control over his subjects' lives and property far beyond anything imagined by western European absolutists. Even in Russia, however, absolutism was never unlimited in practice. Even the most absolute

monarchs could rule effectively only with the consent of their subjects (particularly the nobility). When serious opposition erupted, even absolutists were forced to back down. In 1789, when an outright political revolution occurred, the entire structure of absolutism came crashing to the ground.

THE APPEAL AND JUSTIFICATION OF ABSOLUTISM

Absolutism's promise of stability, prosperity, and order was an appealing alternative to the disorder of the "iron century" that preceded it. Louis XIV was profoundly disturbed by an aristocratic revolt that occurred while he was still a child. When marauding Parisians entered his bedchamber one night in 1651, Louis saw the intrusion as a horrid affront not only to his own person but to the majesty of the French state he personified. Such experiences convinced him that he must rule assertively and without limitation if France was to survive as a great European state.

Absolutist monarchs sought control of the state's armed forces and its legal system and demanded the right to collect and spend the state's financial resources at will. To achieve these goals, they also needed to create an efficient, centralized bureaucracy that owed its allegiance directly to the monarch. Creating and sustaining such a bureaucracy was expensive but essential to the larger absolutist goal of weakening the special interests that hindered the free exercise of royal power. The nobility and the clergy, with their traditional legal privileges; the political authority of semi-autonomous regions; and representative assemblies such as parliaments, diets, or estates general were all obstacles—in the eyes of absolutists—to strong, centralized monarchical government. The history of abolutism is a history of attempts by aspiring absolutists to bring such institutions to heel.

In most Protestant countries, the power of the church had already been subordinated to the the state when the age of absolutism began. In France, Spain, and Austria, however, where Roman Catholicism remained the state religion, absolutist monarchs now devoted considerable attention to bringing the church and its clergy under royal control. These efforts built on agreements that the French and Spanish monarchies extracted from the papacy during the fifteenth and sixteenth centuries, but they went much further in consolidating the king's authority over the church. In Austria, Joseph II (1741–1790) closed hundreds of monasteries, drastically limited the number of monks and nuns permitted to live in contemplative orders, and ordered that the education of priests be placed under government supervision. Even Charles III, the devout Spanish king who ruled from 1759 to 1788, pressed successfully for a papal concordat granting him control over ecclesiastical appointments and the right to nullify any papal bull affecting Spain.

The most important potential opponents of royal absolutism were not churchmen, however, but nobles. Monarchs dealt with this threat in various ways. Louis XIV deprived the French nobility of political power in the provinces but increased their social prestige by making them live at his lavish court at Versailles. Peter the Great of Russia (1689–1725) forced his nobles into lifelong government service. Later in the century, Catherine II of Russia (1762–1796) struck a bargain whereby in return for vast estates and a variety of privileges (including exemption from taxation) the Russian nobility virtually surrendered the administrative and political power of the state into the empress's hands. In Prussia, the army was staffed by nobles, as was generally the case in Spain, France, and England. But in eighteenth-century Austria, the emperor Joseph II (1765–1790) denied the nobility exemption from taxation and blurred the distinctions between nobles and commoners.

Struggles between monarchs and nobles frequently affected relations between local and central government. In France, the requirement that nobles live at the king's court undermined the provincial institutions that the nobility used to exercise their power. In Spain, the monarchy, based in Castile, battled the independent-minded nobles of Aragon and Catalunya. Prussian rulers asserted control over formerly "free" cities by claiming the right to police and tax their inhabitants. The Habsburg emperors tried, unsuccessfully, to suppress the largely autonomous nobility of Hungary. Rarely, however, was the path of confrontation between crown and nobility successful in the long run. The most effective absolutist monarchies of the eighteenth century continued to trade privileges for allegiance, so that nobles came to see their own interests as tied to those of the crown. For this reason, cooperation more often characterized the relations between kings and nobles during the eighteenth-century "old regime" (*ancien régime*) than did conflict.

THE ABSOLUTISM OF LOUIS XIV

In Louis XIV's state portrait, it is almost impossible to discern the human being behind the facade of the absolute monarch, dressed in his coronation robes and surrounded by the symbols of his authority. That facade was artfully constructed by Louis, who recognized, more fully than any other early modern ruler, the importance of theater to effective kingship. Louis and his successors deliberately staged theatrical demonstrations of their sovereignty to enhance their position as rulers endowed with godlike powers.

Performing Royalty at Versailles

Louis's most elaborate exhibitions of his sovereignty took place at his palace at Versailles (*vuhr-SY*), the town outside of Paris to which he moved his court. The palace and its grounds became a stage for Louis's performance of his daily rituals and demonstrations of royal power. The main facade of the palace was a third of a mile in length. Inside, tapestries and paintings celebrated French military victories and royal triumphs; mirrors reflected shimmering light throughout the building. In the vast gardens outside, statues of the Greek god Apollo, god of the sun, recalled Louis's claim to be the "Sun King" of France. Noblemen vied to attend him when he arose from bed, ate his meals (usually stone cold after having traveled the distance of several city blocks from kitchen to table), strolled in his gardens (even the way the king walked was choreographed by the royal dancing master), or rode to the hunt. As the home of the Sun King, Louis's court was the epicenter of his gleaming royal resplendence. France's leading nobles were required to reside with him at Versailles for a portion of the year; the splendor of Louis's court was deliberately calculated to blind them to the possibility of disobedience while raising their prestige by associating them with himself. Instead of plotting some minor treason on his estate, a marquis could instead enjoy the pleasure of knowing that on the morrow he would be privileged to engage the king in two or three minutes of conversation as the royal party made its way through the vast palace halls. At the same time, the almost impossibly detailed rules of etiquette at court left these privileged nobles in constant suspense, forever fearful of offending the king by committing some trivial violation of proper manners.

Of course, the nobility did not surrender their social and political power entirely under the absolutist system. The social order defended by the monarchy was still a hierarchical one, and the nobility retained enormous privileges and rights over local peasants within their jurisdiction. The absolutist system may have forced the nobility to depend on the crown to defend their privileges, but it did not seek to undermine their superior place in society. In this sense, the relationship between Louis XIV and the nobility was more of a negotiated settlement than a complete victory of

Competing Viewpoints

Absolutism And Patriarchy

These selections show how two political theorists justified royal absolutism by deriving it from the absolute authority of a father over his household. Bishop Jacques-Benigne Bossuet (1627–1704) was a famous French preacher who served as tutor to the son of King Louis XIV of France before becoming bishop of Meaux. Sir Robert Filmer (1588–1653) was an English political theorist. Filmer's works attracted particular attention in the 1680s, when John Locke directed the first of his Two Treatises of Government to refuting Filmer's views on the patriarchal nature of royal authority.

Bossuet on the Nature of Monarchical Authority

There are four characteristics or qualities essential to royal authority. First, royal authority is sacred; Secondly, it is paternal; Thirdly, it is absolute; Fourthly, it is subject to reason. . . . All power comes from God. . . . Thus princes act as ministers of God, and his lieutenants on earth. It is through them that he exercises his empire. . . . In this way . . . the royal throne is not the throne of a man, but the throne of God himself. . . .

We have seen that kings hold the place of God, who is the true Father of the human race. We have also seen that the first idea of power that there was among men, is that of paternal power; and that kings were fashioned on the model of fathers. Moreover, all the world agrees that obedience, which is due to public power, is only found . . . in the precept which obliges one to honor his parents. From all this it appears that the name "king" is a father's name, and that goodness is the most natural quality in kings. . . .

Royal authority is absolute. In order to make this term odious and insupportable, many pretend to confuse absolute government and arbitrary government. But nothing is more distinct, as we shall make clear when we speak of justice. . . . The prince need account to no one for what he ordains. . . . Without this absolute authority, he can neither do good nor suppress evil: his power must be such that no one can hope to escape him. . . . [T]he sole defense of individuals against the public power must be their innocence. . . .

One must, then, obey princes as if they were justice itself, without which there is neither order nor justice in affairs. They are gods, and share in some way in divine independence. . . . It follows from this that he who does not want to obey the prince . . . is condemned irremissibly to death as an enemy of public peace and of human society. . . . The prince can correct himself when he knows that he has done badly; but against his authority there can be no remedy. . . .

Source: Jacques-Benigne Bossuet, *Politics Drawn from the Very Words of Holy Scripture*, trans. Patrick Riley (Cambridge: 1990), pp. 46–69 and 81–83.

---

the king over other powerful elites. Louis XIV understood this, and in a memoir that he prepared for his son on the art of ruling he wrote, "The deference and the respect that we receive from our subjects are not a free gift from them but payment for the justice and the protection that they expect from us. Just as they must honor us, we must protect and defend them." In their own way, absolutists depended on the consent of those they ruled.

Administration and Centralization

Louis defined his responsibilities in absolutist terms: to concentrate royal power so as to produce domestic tranquillity. While coopting the nobility into his own theater of royalty, he also recruited the upper bourgeoisie as royal administrators and especially as intendants, responsible for

Filmer on the Patriarchal Origins of Royal Authority

The first government in the world was monarchical, in the father of all flesh, Adam being commanded to multiply, and people the earth, and to subdue it, and having dominion given him over all creatures, was thereby the monarch of the whole world; none of his posterity had any right to possess anything, but by his grant or permission, or by succession from him. . . . Adam was the father, king and lord over his family: a son, a subject, and a servant or a slave were one and the same thing at first. . . .

I cannot find any one place or text in the Bible where any power . . . is given to a people either to govern themselves, or to choose themselves governors, or to alter the manner of government at their pleasure. The power of government is settled and fixed by the commandment of "honour thy father"; if there were a higher power than the fatherly, then this commandment could not stand and be observed. . . .

All power on earth is either derived or usurped from the fatherly power, there being no other original to be found of any power whatsoever. For if there should be granted two sorts of power without any subordination of one to the other, they would be in perpetual strife which should be the supreme, for two supremes cannot agree. If the fatherly power be supreme, then the power of the people must be subordinate and depend on it. If the power of the people be supreme, then the fatherly power must submit to it, and cannot be exercised without the licence of the people, which must quite destroy the frame and course of nature. Even the power which God himself exercises over mankind is by right of fatherhood: he is both the king and father of us all. As God has exalted the dignity of earthly kings . . . by saying they are gods, so . . . he has been pleased . . . [t]o humble himself by assuming the title of a king to express his power, and not the title of any popular government.

Source: Robert Filmer, "Observations upon Aristotle's Politiques" (1652), in *Divine Right and Democracy: An Anthology of Political Writing in Stuart England,* ed. David Wootton (Harmondsworth: 1986), pp. 110–118.

Questions for Analysis

1. Bossuet's definition of *absolutism* connected the sacred power of kings with the paternal authority of fathers within the household. What consequences does he draw from defining the relationship between king and subjects in this way?

2. What does Filmer mean when he says, "All power on earth is either derived or usurped from the fatherly power"? How many examples does he give of paternal or monarchical power?

3. Bossuet and Filmer make obedience the basis for order and justice in the world. What alternative political systems did they most fear?

administering the thirty-six *generalités* into which France was divided. Intendants usually served outside the region where they were born and were thus unconnected with the local elites over whom they exercised authority. They held office at the king's pleasure and were clearly his men. Other administrators, often from families newly ennobled as a reward for their service, assisted in directing affairs of state from Versailles. These men were not actors in the theater of Louis the Sun King; rather, they were the hardworking assistants of Louis the royal custodian of his country's welfare.

Louis's administrators devoted much of their time and energy to collecting the taxes necessary to finance the large standing army on which his aggressive foreign policy depended. Absolutism was fundamentally an approach to government by which ambitious monarchs could increase their own power through conquest and display. As such, it

The Performance and Display of Absolute Power at the Court of Louis XIV

Historians studying the history of absolutism and the court of Louis XIV in particular have emphasized the Sun King's brilliant use of symbols and display to demonstrate his personal embodiment of sovereignty. Royal portraits, such as that painted by Hyacinthe Rigaud in 1701, vividly illustrate the degree to which Louis's power was based on a studied performance. His pose, with his exposed and shapely calf, was an important indication of power and virility, necessary elements of legitimacy for a hereditary monarch. In the elaborate rituals of court life at Versailles, Louis often placed his own body at the center of attention, performing in one instance as the god Apollo in a ballet before his assembled courtiers. His movements through the countryside, accompanied by a retinue of soldiers, servants, and aristocrats, were another occasion for highly stylized ritual demonstrations of his quasi-divine status. Finally, of course, the construction of his palace at Versailles, with its symmetrical architecture and its sculpted gardens, was a demonstration that his power extended over the natural world as easily as it did over the lives of his subjects.

Questions for Analysis

1. Who was the intended audience for the king's performance of absolute sovereignty?

2. Who were Louis's primary competitors in this contest for eminence through the performance of power?

3. What possible political dangers might lay in wait for a regime that invested so heavily in the sumptuous display of semi-divine authority?

A. Hyacinthe Rigaud's 1701 portrait of Louis XIV.

B. Louis XIV as the Sun King.

C. *The Royal Procession of Louis XIV* by Adam Franz van der Meulen.

D. Louis XIV arrives at the Palace of Versailles.

was enormously expensive. In addition to the *taille*, or land tax, which increased throughout the seventeenth century, Louis's government introduced a *capitation* (a head tax) and pressed successfully for the collection of indirect taxes on salt (the *gabelle*), wine, tobacco, and other goods. Because the nobility was exempt from the *taille*, its burden fell most heavily on the peasantry, whose local revolts Louis easily crushed.

Regional opposition was curtailed, but not eliminated, during Louis's reign. By removing the provincial nobility to Versailles, Louis cut them off from their local sources of power and influence. To restrict the powers of regional parlements, Louis decreed that members of any parlement that refused to approve and enforce his laws would be summarily exiled. The Estates-General, the national French representative assembly last summoned in 1614, did not meet at all during Louis's reign. It would not meet again until 1789.

Louis XIV's Religious Policies

Both for reasons of state and of personal conscience, Louis was determined to impose religious unity on France, regardless of the economic and social costs.

Although the vast majority of the French population was Roman Catholic, French Catholics were divided between Quietists, Jansenists, Jesuits, and Gallicans. Quietists preached retreat into personal mysticism, emphasizing a direct relationship between God and the individual human heart. Such doctrine, dispensing as it did with the intermediary services of the church, was suspect in the eyes of absolutists wedded to the doctrine of *un roi, une loi, une foi* ("one king, one law, one faith"). Jansenism—a movement named for its founder Cornelius Jansen, a seventeenth-century bishop of Ypres—held to an Augustinian doctrine of predestination that could sound and look surprisingly like a kind of Catholic Calvinism. Louis vigorously persecuted Quietists and Jansenists, offering them a choice between recanting and prison and exile. Instead, he supported the Jesuits in their efforts to create a Counter-Reformation Catholic Church in France. Louis's support for the Jesuits upset the traditional Gallican Catholics of France, however, who desired a French church independent of papal, Jesuit, and Spanish influence. As a result of this dissension among Catholics, the religious aura of Louis's kingship diminished during the course of his reign.

Against the Protestant Huguenots, however, Louis waged unrelenting war. Protestant churches and schools were destroyed, and Protestants were banned from many professions, including medicine and printing. In 1685, Louis revoked the Edict of Nantes, the legal foundation of the toleration Huguenots had enjoyed since 1598. Protestant clerics were exiled, laymen were sent to the galleys as slaves, and their children were forcibly baptized as Catholics. Many families converted, but 200,000 Protestant refugees fled to England, Holland, Germany, and America, bringing with them their professional and artisanal skills. This was an enormous loss to France. Among many other examples, the silk industries of Berlin and London were established by Huguenots fleeing Louis XIV's persecution.

Colbert and Royal Finance

Louis's drive to unify and centralize France depended on a vast increase in royal revenues engineered by Jean Baptiste Colbert, the king's finance minister from 1664 until his death in 1683. Colbert tightened the process of tax collection and eliminated wherever possible the practice of tax farming (which permitted collection agents to retain for themselves a percentage of the taxes they gathered for the king). When Colbert assumed office, only about 25 percent of the taxes collected throughout the kingdom reached the treasury. By the time he died, that figure had risen to 80 percent. Under Colbert's direction, the state sold public offices, including judgeships and mayoralties, and guilds purchased the right to enforce trade regulations. Colbert also tried to increase the nation's income by controlling and regulating foreign trade. As a confirmed mercantilist (see **Analyzing Primary Sources** on page 465), Colbert believed that France's wealth would increase if its imports were reduced and its exports increased. He therefore imposed tariffs on foreign goods imported into France while using state money to promote the domestic manufacture of formerly imported goods, such as silk, lace, tapestries, and glass. He was especially anxious to create domestic industries capable of producing the goods France would need for war. To encourage domestic trade, he improved France's roads, bridges, and waterways.

Despite Colbert's efforts to increase crown revenues, his policies ultimately foundered on the insatiable demands of Louis XIV's wars (see page 469). Colbert himself foresaw this result when he lectured the king in 1680: "Trade is the source of public finance and public finance is the vital nerve of war. . . . I beg your Majesty to permit me only to say to him that in war as in peace he has never consulted the amount of money available in determining his expenditures." Louis, however, paid him no heed. By the end of Louis's reign, his aggressive foreign policy lay in ruins and his country's finances had been shattered by the unsustainable costs of war.

Analyzing Primary Sources

Mercantilism and War

Jean-Baptiste Colbert (1619–1683) served as Louis XIV's finance minister from 1664 until his death. He worked assiduously to promote commerce, build up French industry, and increase exports. However much Colbert himself may have seen his economic policies as ends in themselves, to Louis they were always means to the end of waging war. Ultimately, Louis's wars undermined the prosperity that Colbert tried so hard to create. This memorandum, written to Louis in 1670, illustrates clearly the mercantilist presumptions of self-sufficiency on which Colbert operated: every item needed to build up the French navy must ultimately be produced in France, even if it could be acquired at less cost from elsewhere.

nd since Your Majesty has wanted to work diligently at reestablishing his naval forces, and since afore that it has been necessary to make very great expenditures, since all merchandise, munitions and manufactured items formerly came from Holland and the countries of the North, it has been absolutely necessary to be especially concerned with finding within the realm, or with establishing in it, everything which might be necessary for this great plan.

To this end, the manufacture of tar was established in Médoc, Auvergne, Dauphiné, and Provence; iron cannons, in Burgundy, Nivernois, Saintonge and Périgord; large anchors in Dauphiné, Nivernois, Brittany, and Rochefort; sailcloth for the Levant, in Dauphiné; coarse muslin, in Auvergne; all the implements for pilots and others, at Dieppe and La Rochelle; the cutting of wood suitable for vessels, in Burgundy, Dauphiné, Brittany, Normandy, Poitou, Saintonge, Provence, Guyenne, and the Pyrenees; masts, of a sort once unknown in this realm, have been found in Provence, Languedoc, Auvergne, Dauphiné, and in the Pyrenees. Iron, which was obtained from Sweden and Biscay, is currently manufactured in the realm. Fine hemp for ropes, which came from Prussia and from Piedmont, is currently obtained in Burgundy, Mâconnais, Bresse, Dauphiné; and markets for it have since been established in Berry and in Auvergne, which always provides money in these provinces and keeps it within the realm.

In a word, everything serving for the construction of vessels is currently established in the realm, so that Your Majesty can get along without foreigners for the navy and will even, in a short time, be able to supply them and gain their money in this fashion. And it is with this same objective of having everything necessary to provide abundantly for his navy and that of his subjects that he is working at the general reform of all the forests in his realm, which, being as carefully preserved as they are at present, will abundantly produce all the wood necessary for this.

Source: Charles W. Cole, *Colbert and a Century of French Mercantilism*, 2 vols. (New York: 1939), p. 320.

Questions for Analysis

1. Why would Colbert want to manufacture materials for supplying the navy within France rather than buying them from abroad?

2. From this example, does Colbert see the economy as serving any other interest other than that of the state?

3. Was there a necessary connection between mercantilism and war?

ALTERNATIVES TO ABSOLUTISM

Although absolutism was the dominant model for seventeenth- and eighteenth-century European monarchs, it was by no means the only system by which Europeans governed themselves. A republican oligarchy continued to rule in Venice. In The Netherlands, the territories that had won their independence from Spain during the early seventeenth century combined to form the United Provinces, the only truly new country to take shape in Europe during the early modern era. The Spanish wars created a deep distrust among the Dutch toward monarchs of any stripe. As a result, although Holland dominated the United Provinces, its House of Orange, which had led the wars for independence, never attempted to transform the new country from a republic into a monarchy. Even after 1688, when William of Orange also became King William III of England, the United Provinces remained a republic.

Limited Monarchy: The Case of England

While the powers of representative assemblies were being undermined across much of Europe, the English Parliament was the longest-surviving such body in Europe. English political theorists had long seen their government as a mixed monarchy, composed of monarchical, noble, and nonnoble elements. During the seventeenth century, these traditions came under threat, first through Charles I's attempts to rule without Parliament and then during Oliver Cromwell's dictatorial Protectorate. The restoration of the monarchy in 1660 resolved the question of whether England would in future be a republic or a monarchy, but the sort of monarchy England would become remained an open question.

THE REIGN OF CHARLES II

Despite the fact that he was the son of the beheaded and much-hated Charles I, Charles II (1660–1685) was initially welcomed by most English men and women. He declared limited religious toleration for Protestant "dissenters" (Protestants who were not members of the official Church of England). He promised to observe the Magna Carta and the Petition of Right, declaring, with characteristic good humor, that he did not wish to "resume his travels." The unbuttoned moral atmosphere of his court, with its risqué plays, dancing, and sexual licentiousness, reflected a public desire to forget the restraints of the Puritan past. Some critics suggested that Charles, "that known enemy to virginity and chastity," took his role as the father of his country rather too seriously, but in fact he produced no legitimate heir and only a single illegitimate son to vie for the throne.

Having grown up an exile in France, Charles was an admirer of all things French. During the 1670s, however, he began openly to model his kingship on the absolutism of Louis XIV. As a result, the great men of England soon came to be publically divided between Charles's supporters (called by their opponents "Tories," a popular nickname for Irish Catholic bandits) and his opponents (called by their opponents "Whigs," a nickname for Scottish Presbyterian rebels). Both sides feared absolutism, just as both sides feared a return to the bad old days of the 1640s, when resistance to the crown had led to civil war and ultimately to republicanism. What they could not agree on was which possibility frightened them more.

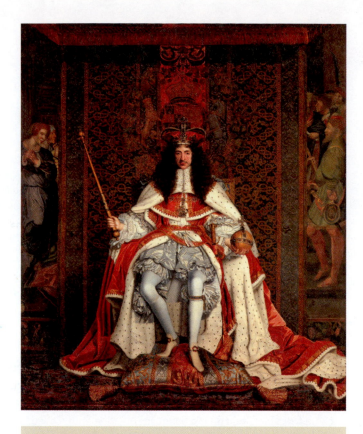

CHARLES II OF ENGLAND (1660–1685) IN HIS CORONATION ROBES. This full frontal portrait of the monarch, holding the symbols of his rule, seems to confront the viewer personally with the overwhelming authority of the sovereign's gaze. Compare this classic image of the absolutist monarch with the very different portraits of William and Mary, who ruled after the Glorious Revolution of 1688 (page 467). ■ *What had changed between 1660, when Charles II came to the throne, and 1688, when the more popular William and Mary became the rulers of England?*

Religion also remained a divisive issue. Charles was sympathetic to Roman Catholicism, even to the point of a deathbed conversion in 1685. During the 1670s, he briefly suspended civil penalties against Catholics and Protestant dissenters by asserting his right as king to ignore Parliamentary legislation. The resulting public outcry compelled him to retreat, but this controversy, together with rising opposition to Charles's ardently Catholic brother James as the heir to the throne, led to a series of Whig electoral victories between 1679 and 1681. When a group of radical Whigs attempted to exclude James by law from succeeding his brother on the throne, however, Charles stared the opposition down in the so-called Exclusion Crisis. Thereafter, Charles found that his rising revenues from customs duties, combined with a secret subsidy from Louis XIV, enabled him to govern without relying on Parliament for money.

Charles further alarmed Whig politicians by executing several of them on charges of treason and by remodeling local government to make it more amenable to royal control. Charles died in 1685 with his power enhanced, but he left behind a political and religious legacy that was to be the undoing of his less able and adroit successor.

THE REIGN OF JAMES II

James II was the very opposite of his worldly brother. A zealous Catholic convert, he alienated his Tory supporters, who were close to the established Church of England, by suspending the laws preventing Catholics and Protestant dissenters from holding political office. James flaunted his own Roman Catholicism, openly declaring his wish that his subjects convert and publicly parading papal legates through the streets of London. When, in June 1688, he ordered all Church of England clergymen to read his decree of religious toleration from their pulpits, seven bishops refused and were promptly imprisoned. At their trial, however, they were declared not guilty of sedition, to the enormous satisfaction of the Protestant English populace.

The trial of the bishops was one event that brought matters to a head. The other was the unexpected birth of a son in 1688 to James and his second wife, Mary of Modena. This child, who was to be raised a Catholic, replaced James's much older Protestant daughter Mary Stuart as heir to the thrones of Scotland and England. So unexpected was this birth that there were widespread rumors that the child was not in fact James's son at all but had been smuggled into the royal bedchamber in a warming pan.

With the birth of the "warming-pan baby," events moved swiftly toward a climax. A delegation of Whigs and Tories crossed the channel to Holland to invite Mary Stuart and her Protestant husband, William of Orange, to cross to England with an invading army to preserve Protestantism and English liberties by summoning a new Parliament. As the leader of a continental coalition then at war with France, William also welcomed the opportunity to make England an ally against Louis XIV's expansionist foreign policy.

THE GLORIOUS REVOLUTION

William and Mary's invasion became a bloodless coup (although James is reputed to have suffered a nosebleed at the moment of crisis). James fled the country, and Parliament declared the throne vacant, clearing the way for William and Mary to succeed him as joint sovereigns. The Bill of Rights, passed by Parliament and accepted by the new king and queen in 1689, reaffirmed English civil liberties, such as trial by jury, habeas corpus (a guarantee that no

WILLIAM AND MARY. In 1688, William of Orange and his wife, Mary Stuart, became Protestant joint rulers of England, in a bloodless coup that took power from her father, the Catholic James II. Compare this contemporary print with the portraits of Louis XIV (page 462) and Charles II (page 466). ▪ *What relationship does it seem to depict between the royal couple and their subjects?* ▪ *What is the significance of the gathered crowd in the public square in the background?* ▪ *How is this different from the spectacle of divine authority projected by Louis XIV or the image of Charles II looking straight at the viewer?*

one could be imprisoned unless charged with a crime), and the right to petition the monarch through Parliament. The Bill of Rights also declared that the monarchy was subject to the law of the land. The Act of Toleration, also passed in 1689, granted Protestant dissenters the right to worship freely, though not to hold political office. And in 1701, the Act of Succession ordained that every future English monarch must be a member of the Church of England. Queen Mary died childless, and the throne passed from William to Mary's Protestant sister Anne (1702–1714) and then to George, elector of the German principality of Hanover and the Protestant great-grandson of James I. In 1707, the formal Act of Union between Scotland and England ensured that the Catholic heirs of King James II would in future have no more right to the throne of Scotland than they did to the throne of England.

The English soon referred to the events of 1688 and 1689 as the "Glorious Revolution," because it firmly established England as a mixed monarchy governed by the "king in Parliament." Although William and Mary and their successors continued to exercise a large measure of executive power, after 1688 no English monarch attempted to govern without Parliament, which has met annually from that time on. Parliament, and especially the House of Commons, also strengthened its control over taxation and expenditure. Protestants in particular celebrated the Glorious Revolution as another sign of God's special favor to England, noting the favorable (Protestant) winds that blew William and Mary so speedily to England and kept King James's fleet from mounting an effective resistance.

Yet 1688 was not all glory. It was a revolution that consolidated the position of large property holders, whose control over local government had been threatened by Charles II and James II. It thus restored the status quo on behalf of a wealthy class of magnates that would soon become even wealthier from government patronage and the profits of war. It also brought misery to the Catholic minority in Scotland and to the Catholic majority in Ireland. After 1690, when King William won a decisive victory over James II's forces at the Battle of the Boyne, power in Ireland would lie firmly in the hands of a "Protestant Ascendancy," whose dominance over Irish society would last until modern times.

JOHN LOCKE AND THE CONTRACT THEORY OF GOVERNMENT

The Glorious Revolution was the product of unique circumstances, but it also reflected antiabsolutist theories of politics that were taking shape in the late seventeenth century in response to the ideas of writers such as Bodin, Hobbes, Filmer, and Bossuet. Chief among these opponents of absolutism was the Englishman John Locke (1632–1704), whose *Two Treatises of Government* were written before the revolution but published for the first time in 1690.

Locke maintained that humans had originally lived in a state of nature characterized by absolute freedom and equality, with no government of any kind. The only law was the law of nature (which Locke equated with the law of reason), by which individuals enforced for themselves their natural rights to life, liberty, and property. Soon, however, humans began to perceive that the inconveniences of the state of nature outweighed its advantages. Accordingly, they agreed first to establish a civil society based on absolute equality and then to set up a government to arbitrate the disputes that might arise within this civil society. But they did not make government's powers absolute. All powers not expressly surrendered to the government were reserved to the people themselves; as a result, governmental authority was both contractual and conditional. If a government

JOHN LOCKE.

exceeded or abused the authority granted to it, society had the right to dissolve it and create another.

Locke condemned absolutism in every form. He denounced absolute monarchy, but he was also critical of claims for the sovereignty of parliaments. Government, he argued, had been instituted to protect life, liberty, and property; no political authority could infringe these natural rights. The law of nature was therefore an automatic and absolute limitation on every branch of government.

In the late eighteenth century, Locke's ideas would resurface as part of the intellectual background of both the American and French revolutions. Between 1690 and 1720, however, they served a far less radical purpose. The landed magnates who replaced James II with William and Mary read Locke as a defense of their conservative revolution. Rather than protecting their liberty and property, James II had threatened both; hence the magnates were entitled to overthrow the tyranny he had established and replace it with a government that would defend their interests by preserving these natural rights. English government after 1689 would be dominated by Parliament; Parliament in turn was controlled by a landed aristocracy who were firm in the defence of their common interests.

During the beginning of the eighteenth century, then, both France and Britain had solved the problem of political dissent and social disorder in their own way. The emergence of a stable constitutional monarchy in England after

1688 contrasted vividly with the absolutist system developed by Louis XIV, but both systems worked well enough to contain the immediate threat to royal authority posed by a powerful class of landed nobles. Domestic stability was no guarantee of international peace, however, and the period from 1661, when Louis XIV assumed personal rule, to his death in 1715, was marked by almost constant warfare.

WAR AND THE BALANCE OF POWER, 1661–1715

Louis XIV's foreign policy reflected his belief that military victories abroad were necessary to reinforce the glory of his realm and the power that he wielded at home. Louis's wars sought to meet the threat posed by the Habsburg powers in Spain, the Spanish Netherlands, and the Holy Roman Empire and to promote his own dynastic interests. Through a series of campaigns in the Low Countries, Louis expanded his territory, eventually taking Strasbourg (1681), Luxembourg (1684), and Cologne (1688). In response, William of Orange (1672–1702) organized the League of Augsburg, which over time included Holland, England, Spain, Sweden, Bavaria, Saxony, the Rhine Palatinate, and the Austrian Habsburgs. The resulting Nine Years' War extended from Ireland to India to North America (where it was known as King William's War).

The League of Augsburg reflected the emergence of a new diplomatic goal in western and central Europe: the preservation of a balance of power. This goal would animate European diplomacy for the next two hundred years, until the balance of power system collapsed with the outbreak of the First World War. The main proponents of balance of power diplomacy were England, the United Provinces (Holland), Prussia, and Austria. By 1697, the league forced Louis XIV to make peace, because France was exhausted by war and famine. Louis gave back much of his recent gains but kept Strasbourg and the surrounding territory of Alsace. He was nevertheless looking at the real prize: a French claim to succeed to the throne of Spain and so control the Spanish Empire in the Americas, Italy, the Netherlands, and the Philippines.

The War of the Spanish Succession

In the 1690s it became clear that King Charles II of Spain (1665–1700) would soon die without a clear heir, and both Louis XIV of France and Leopold I of Austria (1658–1705)

were interested in promoting their own relatives to succeed him. Either solution would have upset the balance of power in Europe, and several schemes to divide the Spanish realm between French and Austrian candidates were discussed. Meanwhile, King Charles II's advisers sought to avoid partition by passing the entire Spanish Empire to a single heir: Louis XIV's grandson, Philip of Anjou. Philip was to renounce any claim to the French throne in becoming king of Spain, but the terms of this will were kept secret. When Charles II died, Philip V (1700–1746) was proclaimed king of Spain, and Louis XIV rushed troops into the Spanish Netherlands, while also sending French merchants into Spanish America and withdrawing his recognition of William of Orange as king of England.

THE TREATY OF UTRECHT, 1713. This illustration from a French royal almanac depicts the treaty that ended the War of Spanish Succession and reshaped the balance of power in western Europe in favor of Britain and France.

The resulting war, known as the War of the Spanish Succession, pitted England, the United Provinces, Austria, and Prussia against France, Bavaria, and Spain. Although William of Orange died in 1702, just as the war was beginning, his generals led an extraordinary march deep into the European Continent, inflicting a devastating defeat on the French and their Bavarian allies at Blenheim (1704). Soon after, the English captured Gibraltar, establishing a commercial foothold in the Mediterranean. By 1709, France was on the verge of defeat, but when they met the British at the battle of Malplaquet in present-day Belgium they inflicted twenty-four thousand casualties before retreating from the field. Meanwhile, the costs of the campaign created a chorus of complaints from English and Dutch merchants, who feared the damage that was being done to trade and commerce. Queen Anne of England (Mary's sister and William's successor) gradually grew disillusioned with the war, and her government sent out peace feelers to France.

The Treaty of Utrecht

In 1713 the war finally came to an end with the Treaty of Utrecht. Its terms were reasonably fair to all sides. Philip V, Louis XIV's grandson, remained on the throne of Spain and retained Spain's colonial empire intact. In return, Louis agreed that France and Spain would never be united under the same ruler. Austria gained territories in the Spanish Netherlands and Italy, including Milan and Naples. The Dutch were guaranteed protection of their borders against future invasions by France, but the French retained both Lille and Strasbourg. The biggest winner by far was Great Britain, as the combined kingdoms of England and Scotland were known after 1707. The British kept Gibraltar and Minorca in the Mediterranean and also acquired large chunks of French territory in the New World, including Newfoundland, mainland Nova Scotia, the Hudson Bay, and the Caribbean island of St. Kitts. Even more valuable, however, Britain also extracted from Spain the right to transport and sell African slaves in Spanish America. As a result, the British were now poised to become the principal slave merchants and the dominant colonial and commercial power of the eighteenth-century world.

The Treaty of Utrecht reshaped the balance of power in western Europe in fundamental ways. Spain's collapse was already precipitous; by 1713 it was complete. Spain would remain the "sick man of Europe" for the next two centuries. Holland's decline was more gradual, but by 1713, its greatest days were also over. In the Atlantic world, Britain and France were now the dominant powers. Although they would duel for another half century for control of North America, the balance of colonial power tilted decisively in Britain's favor after Utrecht. Within Europe, the myth of French military supremacy had been shattered. Britain's navy, not France's army, would rule the new imperial and commercial world of the eighteenth century.

THE REMAKING OF CENTRAL AND EASTERN EUROPE

The decades between 1680 and 1720 were also decisive in reshaping the balance of power in central and eastern Europe. As Ottoman power waned, the Austro-Hungarian Empire of the Habsburgs emerged as the dominant power in central and southeastern Europe. To the north, Brandenburg-Prussia was also a rising power. The most dramatic changes, however, occurred in Russia, which emerged from a long war with Sweden as the dominant power in the Baltic Sea and would soon threaten the combined kingdom of Poland-Lithuania.

MARIA THERESA OF AUSTRIA AND HER FAMILY. A formidable and capable ruler who fought to maintain Austria's dominance in central Europe against the claims of Frederick the Great of Prussia, Maria Theresa had sixteen children, including Marie Antoinette, later queen of France as wife of Louis XVI. ■ *Why did she emphasize her role as mother in a royal portrait such as this one, rather than her other undeniable political skills?* ■ *How does this compare to the portraits of William and Mary or of Louis XIV elsewhere in this chapter?*

EUROPE AFTER THE TREATY OF UTRECHT (1713). ▪ *What were the major Habsburg Dominions?* ▪ *What geographical disadvantage faced the kingdom of Poland as Brandenburg-Prussia grew in influence and ambition?* ▪ *How did the balance of power change in Europe as a result of the Treaty of Utrecht?*

The Habsburg Empire

In 1683, the Ottoman Turks launched their last assault on Vienna. Only the arrival of seventy thousand Polish troops saved the Austrian capital from capture. Thereafter, Ottoman power in southeastern Europe declined rapidly. By 1699, Austria had reconquered most of Hungary from the Ottomans; by 1718, it controlled all of Hungary and also Transylvania and Serbia. In 1722, Austria acquired the territory of Silesia from Poland. With Hungary now a buffer state between Austria and the Ottomans, Vienna emerged as one of the great cultural and political capitals of

eighteenth-century Europe, and Austria became one of the arbiters of the European balance of power.

Although the Austrian Habsburgs retained their title as Holy Roman emperors and after 1713 also held lands in the Netherlands and Italy, their real power lay in Austria, Bohemia, Moravia, Galicia, and Hungary. These territories were geographically contiguous, but they were deeply divided by ethnicity, religion, and language. Despite the centralizing efforts of a series of Habsburg rulers, their empire would remain a rather loose confederation of distinct territories.

In Bohemia and Moravia, the Habsburgs encouraged landlords to produce crops for export by forcing peasants to

PRUSSIANS SWEARING ALLEGIANCE TO THE GREAT ELECTOR AT KÖNIGSBERG, 1663. The occasion on which the Prussian estates first acknowledged the overlordship of their ruler. This ceremony marked the beginning of the centralization of the Prussian state.

Austria, Prussia was a composite state made up of several geographically divided territories acquired through inheritance by the Hohenzollern family. Their two main holdings were Brandenburg, centered on its capital city, Berlin, and the duchy of East Prussia. Between these two territories lay Pomerania (claimed by Sweden) and an important part of the kingdom of Poland, including the port of Gdansk (Danzig). The Hohenzollerns' aim was to unite their state by acquiring these intervening territories. Over the course of more than a century of steady state building, they finally succeeded in doing so. In the process, Brandenburg-Prussia became a dominant military power and a key player in the balance-of-power diplomacy of the mid-eighteenth century.

The foundations for Prussian expansion were laid by Frederick William, the "Great Elector" (1640–1688). He obtained East Prussia from Poland in exchange for help in a war against Sweden. Behind the Elector's diplomatic triumphs lay his success in building an army and mobilizing the resources to pay for it. He gave the powerful nobles of his territories (known as *Junkers*) the right to enserf their peasants and guaranteed them immunity from taxation. In exchange, they staffed the officer corps of his army and supported his highly autocratic taxation system. Secure in their estates and made increasingly wealthy in the grain trade, the Junkers surrendered management of the Prussian state to the Elector's newly reformed bureaucracy, which set about its main task: increasing the size and strength of the Prussian army.

By supporting Austria in the War of the Spanish Succession, the Great Elector's son, Frederick I (1688–1713) earned the right to call himself king of Prussia from the Austrian emperor. He too was a crafty diplomat, but his main attention was devoted to developing the cultural life of his new royal capital, Berlin. His son, Frederick William I (1713–1740) focused, like his grandfather, on building the army. During his reign, the Prussian army grew from thirty thousand to eighty-three thousand men, becoming the fourth largest army in Europe, after France, Austria, and Russia. To support his army, Frederick William I increased taxes and shunned the luxuries of court life. For him, the theater of absolutism was not the palace but the office, where he

provide three days of unpaid work per week to their lords. In return, the landed elites of these territories permitted the emperors to reduce the political independence of their traditional legislative estates. In Hungary, however, the powerful and independent nobility resisted such compromises. Habsburg efforts to administer Hungary through the army and to impose Catholic religious uniformity also met with stiff resistance. As a result, Hungary would remain a semi-autonomous region within the empire whose support the Austrians could never take for granted.

After 1740, the empress Maria Theresa (1740–1780) and her son Joseph II (1765–1790; from 1765 until 1780 the two were co-rulers) pioneered a new style of "enlightened absolutism" within their empire: centralizing the administration in Vienna, increasing taxation, creating a professional standing army, and tightening their control over the church while creating a statewide system of primary education, relaxing censorship, and instituting a new, more liberal criminal code. But in practice, Habsburg absolutism, whether enlightened or not, was always limited by the diversity of its imperial territories and by the weakness of its local governmental institutions.

The Rise of Brandenburg-Prussia

After the Ottoman collapse, the main threat to Austria came from the rising power of Brandenburg-Prussia. Like personally supervised his army and the growing bureaucracy that sustained it.

A hard, unimaginative man, Frederick William I had little use for his son Frederick, whose passion was not the army but the flute and who admired French culture as much as his father disdained it. It is not surprising that young Frederick rebelled. In 1730, when he was eighteen, he ran away from court with a friend. Apprehended, the companions were returned to the king, who executed his son's friend before Frederick's eyes. The grisly lesson took. Although Frederick never gave up his love of music and literature, he thereafter bound himself to his royal duties, living in accordance with his own image of himself as "first servant of the state" and earning history's title of Frederick the Great.

Frederick William I had made Prussia a strong state. Frederick the Great (1740–1786) raised his country to the status of a major power. As soon as he became king in 1740, Frederick mobilized the army his father had never taken into battle and occupied the Austrian province of Silesia. Prussia had no conceivable claim to Silesia, but the territory was both rich and poorly defended, and so Frederick seized it with French support. The new Habsburg empress, Maria Theresa, counterattacked; but despite the support of both Britain and Hungary, she was unable to recover Silesia. Emboldened, Frederick spent the rest of his reign consolidating his gains in Silesia and extending his control over the Polish territories that lay between Prussia and Brandenburg. Through relentless diplomacy and frequent war, Frederick transformed Prussia by 1786 into a powerful, contiguous territorial kingdom.

To ensure a united domestic front against Prussia's enemies, Frederick was careful to cultivate Junker support for his policies. His father had recruited civil servants according to merit rather than birth, but Frederick relied on the Junker nobility to staff the army and his expanding administration. Remarkably, Frederick's strategy worked. His nobility remained loyal, and Frederick fashioned the most professional and efficient bureaucracy in Europe.

Like his contemporary Joseph II of Austria, Frederick was an enlightened absolutist. He supervised a series of social reforms, prohibited the judicial torture of accused criminals, abolished the bribing of judges, and established a system of elementary schools. Although strongly anti-Semitic, he encouraged religious toleration toward Christians and declared that he would happily build a mosque in Berlin if he could find enough Muslims to fill it. On his own royal estates he abolished capital punishment, curtailed the forced labor services of his peasantry, and granted them long leases on the land they worked. He encouraged scientific forestry and the cultivation of new crops. He cleared new lands in Silesia and brought in thousands of immigrants to cultivate them. When wars ruined their farms, he supplied his peasants with new livestock and tools. But he never attempted to extend these reforms to the estates of the Prussian nobility. To have done so would have alienated the very group on whom Frederick's rule depended.

THE CITY OF STETTIN UNDER SIEGE BY THE GREAT ELECTOR FREDERICK WILLIAM IN THE WINTER OF 1677–78 (c. 1680). This painting depicts the growing sophistication and organization of military operations under the Prussian monarchy. Improvements in artillery and siege tactics forced cities to adopt new defensive strategies, especially the zone of battlements and protective walls that became ubiquitous in central Europe during this period. ▪ *How might these developments have shaped the layout of Europe's growing towns and cities?* ▪ *How might this emphasis on the military and its attendant bureaucracy have affected the relationship between the monarchy and the nobility or between the king and his subjects?*

AUTOCRACY IN RUSSIA

An even more dramatic transformation took place in Russia under Tsar Peter I (1672–1725). Peter's accomplishments alone would have earned him his title of "Great." But his imposing height—he was six feet eight inches tall—as well as his mercurial personality—jesting one moment, raging the next—certainly added to the outsize impression he made on his contemporaries. Peter was not the first tsar to bring his country into contact with western Europe, but his policies were decisive in making Russia a great European power.

The Early Years of Peter's Reign

Since 1613 Russia had been ruled by members of the Romanov Dynasty, who had attempted to restore political stability after the chaotic "time of troubles" that followed the death of the bloodthirsty, half-mad tsar Ivan the Terrible in 1584. The Romanovs faced a severe threat to their rule between 1667 and 1671, when a Cossack leader (the Russian Cossacks were semi-autonomous bands of peasant cavalrymen) named Stenka Razin led a rebellion in southeastern Russia. This uprising found widespread support, not only from oppressed serfs but also from non-Russian tribes in the lower Volga region who longed to cast off the domination of Moscow. Ultimately Tsar Alexis I (1654–1676) and the Russian nobility were able to defeat Razin's zealous but disorganized bands of rebels, slaughtering more than a hundred thousand of them in the process.

Like Louis XIV of France, Peter came to the throne as a young boy, and his minority was marked by political dissension and court intrigue. In 1689, however, at the age of seventeen, he overthrew the regency of his half-sister Sophia and assumed personal control of the state. Determined to make Russia into a great military power, the young tsar traveled to Holland and England during the 1690s to study shipbuilding and to recruit skilled foreign workers to help him build a navy. While he was abroad, however, his elite palace guard (the *streltsy*) rebelled, attempting to restore Sophia to the throne. Peter quickly returned home from Vienna and crushed the rebellion with striking savagery. About twelve hundred suspected conspirators were summarily executed, many of them gibbeted outside the walls of the Kremlin, where their bodies rotted for months as a graphic reminder of the fate awaiting those who dared challenge the tsar's authority.

The Transformation of the Tsarist State

Peter is most famous as the tsar who attempted to westernize Russia by imposing a series of social and cultural reforms on the traditional Russian nobility: ordering noblemen to cut off their long beards and flowing sleeves; publishing a book of manners that forbade spitting on the floor and eating with one's fingers; encouraging polite conversation between the sexes; and requiring noblewomen to appear, together with men, in Western garb at weddings, banquets, and other public occasions. The children of Russian nobles were sent to western European courts for their education. Thousands of western European experts were brought to Russia to staff the new schools and academies Peter built; to design the new buildings he constructed; and to serve in the tsar's army, navy, and administration.

PETER THE GREAT CUTS THE BEARD OF AN OLD BELIEVER. This woodcut depicts the Russian emperor's enthusiastic policy of westernization, as he pushed everybody in Russia who was not a peasant to adopt Western styles of clothes and grooming. The Old Believer (a member of a religious sect in Russia) protests that he has paid the beard tax and should therefore be exempt.
■ *Why would an individual's choices about personal appearance be so politically significant in Peter's Russia?* ■ *What customs were the target of Peter's reforms?*

These measures were important, but the tsar was not primarily motivated by a desire to modernize or westernize Russia. Peter's policies transformed Russian life in fundamental ways, but his real goal was to make Russia a great military power, not to remake Russian society. His new taxation system (1724), for example, which assessed taxes on individuals rather than on households, rendered many of the traditional divisions of Russian peasant society obsolete. It was created, however, to raise more money for war. His Table of Ranks, imposed in 1722, had a similar impact on the nobility. By insisting that all nobles must work their way up from the (lower) landlord class to the (higher) administrative class and to the (highest) military class, Peter reversed the traditional hierarchy of Russian noble society, which had valued landlords by birth above administrators and soldiers who had risen by merit. But he also created a powerful new incentive to lure his nobility into administrative and military service to the tsar.

As autocrat of all the Russias, Peter the Great was the absolute master of his empire to a degree unmatched else-where in Europe. After 1649, Russian peasants were legally the property of their landlords; by 1750, half were serfs and the other half were state peasants who lived on lands owned by the tsar himself. State peasants could be conscripted to serve as soldiers in the tsar's army, workers in his factories (whose productive capacity increased enormously during Peter's reign), or as forced laborers in his building projects. Serfs could also be taxed by the tsar and summoned for military service, as could their lords. All Russians, of whatever rank, were expected to serve the tsar, and all Russia was considered in some sense to belong to him.

To further consolidate his power, Peter replaced the Duma—the nation's rudimentary national assembly—with a hand-picked senate, a group of nine administrators who supervised military and civilian affairs. In religious matters, he took direct control over the Russian Orthodox Church by appointing an imperial official to manage its affairs. To cope with the demands of war, he also fashioned a new, larger, and more efficient administration, for which he recruited both nobles and nonnobles. But rank in the

THE GROWTH OF RUSSIAN EMPIRE. ▪ *How did Peter the Great expand the territory controlled by Russia?* ▪ *What neighboring dynasties would have been the most affected by Russian expansion?* ▪ *How did the emergence of a bigger, more powerful Russia affect the European balance of power?*

new bureaucracy did not depend on birth. One of his principal advisers, Alexander Menshikov, began his career as a cook and finished as a prince. This degree of social mobility would have been impossible in any contemporary western European country. Instead, noble status depended on governmental service, with all nobles expected to participate in Peter's army or administration. Peter was not entirely successful in enforcing this requirement, but the administrative machinery he devised furnished Russia with its ruling class for the next two hundred years.

Peter's Foreign Policy

The goal of Peter's foreign policy was to secure year-round ports for Russia on the Black Sea and the Baltic Sea. In the Black Sea, his enemy was the Ottomans. Here, however, he had little success; although he captured the port of Azov in 1696, he was forced to return it in 1711. Russia would not secure its position in the Black Sea until the end of the eighteenth century. In the north, however, Peter achieved much more. In 1700, he began what would become a twenty-one-year war with Sweden, then the dominant power in the Baltic Sea. By 1703, Peter had secured a foothold on the Gulf of Finland and immediately began to build a new capital city there, which he named St. Petersburg. After 1709, when Russian armies, supported by Prussia, decisively defeated the Swedes at the battle of Poltava, work on Peter's new capital city accelerated. An army of serfs was now conscripted to build the new city, whose centerpiece was a royal palace designed to imitate and rival Louis XIV's Versailles.

The Great Northern War with Sweden ended in 1721 with the Peace of Nystad. This treaty marks a realignment of power in eastern Europe comparable to that effected by the Treaty of Utrecht in the West. Sweden lost its North Sea territories to Hanover and its Baltic German territories to Prussia. Its eastern territories, including the entire Gulf of Finland, Livonia, and Estonia, passed to Russia. Sweden was now a second-rank power in the northern European world. Poland-Lithuania survived but faced the expanding power of Prussia in the West and the expanding power of Russia in the East. It too was a declining power; by the end of the eighteenth century, the kingdom would disappear altogether, its territories swallowed up by its more powerful neighbors. The victors at Nystad were the Prussians and the Russians. These two powers secured their position along the Baltic coast, positioning themselves to take advantage of the lucrative eastern European grain trade with western Europe.

Peter's victory came at enormous cost. Direct taxation increased 500 percent during his reign, and his army in the 1720s numbered more than three hundred thousand men. Peter made Russia a force to be reckoned with on the European scene; but in so doing, he also aroused great resentment, especially among his nobility. Peter's only son and heir, Alexis, became the focus for conspiracies against the tsar, until finally Peter had him arrested and executed in 1718. As a result, when Peter died in 1725, he left no son to succeed him. A series of ineffective tsars followed, mostly creatures of the palace guard, under whom the resentful nobles reversed many of Peter the Great's reforms. In 1762, however, the crown passed to Catherine the Great, a ruler whose ambitions and determination were equal to those of her great predecessor.

Catherine the Great and the Partition of Poland

Catherine was a German who came to the throne in 1762 on the death of her husband, the weak (and possibly mad) Tsar Peter III, who was deposed and executed in a palace coup

CATHERINE THE GREAT.

that Catherine herself may have helped arrange. Although she cultivated an image of herself as an enlightened ruler (she corresponded with French philosophers, wrote plays, and began to compose a history of Russia), Catherine was determined not to lose the support of the nobility who had placed her on the throne. As a result, her efforts at social reform did not extend much beyond the founding of hospitals and orphanages and the creation of an elementary school system for the children of the provincial nobility. Like her contemporary enlightened absolutists Joseph of Austria and Frederick the Great of Prussia, she too summoned a commission, in 1767, to codify and revise Russian law. But few of its radical proposals (which included the abolition of capital punishment, an end to judicial torture, and prohibitions on the selling of serfs) were ever implemented. Any possibility such measures might have been enforced ended in 1773–1775, when a massive peasant revolt led by a Cossack named Emelyan Pugachev briefly threatened Moscow itself. Catherine responded to the uprising by further centralizing her own government and by tightening aristocratic control over the peasantry.

Catherine's greatest achievements were gained through war and diplomacy. In 1769, she renewed Peter the Great's push to secure a warm-water port on the Black Sea. In the resulting war with the Ottoman Turks (which ended in 1774), Russia won control over the northern coast of the Black Sea, secured the independence of Crimea (which Russia would annex in 1783), and obtained safe passage for Russian ships through the Bosporus and into the Mediterranean Sea. In the course of this campaign, Russia also won control over several Ottoman provinces along the Danube River.

Russia's gains in the Balkans alarmed Austria, however, which now found itself with the powerful Russian Empire on its southern doorstep. Prussia too was threatening to become involved in the war as an ally of the Ottomans. Frederick the Great's real interests, however, lay much closer to home. To preserve the peace among Russia, Prussia, and Austria, he proposed instead a partition of Poland. Russia would abandon its Danubian conquests and, in return, would acquire the grain fields of eastern Poland, along with a population of 1 to 2 million Poles. Austria would take Galicia, acquiring 2.5 million Poles. Prussia, meanwhile, would take the coastal regions of Poland, including the port of Gdansk (Danzig), that separated Brandenburg and Pomerania from East Prussia. As a result of this agreement, finalized in 1772, Poland lost about 30 percent of its territory and about half of its population.

Poland was now paying the price for its political conservatism. Alone among the major central European powers, the Polish nobility had successfully opposed any move toward monarchical centralization as a threat to its liberties,

among which was the right of every individual noble to veto any measure proposed in the Polish representative assembly, the Diet. To make matters worse, Polish aristocrats were also quite prepared to accept bribes from foreign powers in return for their vote in elections for the Polish king. In 1764, Catherine the Great had intervened in this way to secure the election of one of her former lovers, Stanislaus Poniatowski, as the new king of Poland. In 1772, King Stanislaus reluctantly accepted the partition of his country because he was too weak to resist it. In 1788, however, he took advantage of a new Russo-Turkish war to try to strengthen his control over what remained of his kingdom. In May 1791 a new constitution was adopted that established a much stronger

DIVIDING THE ROYAL SPOILS. A contemporary cartoon showing the monarchs of Europe at work carving up a hapless Poland. Note there is little reference here to the people who lived in the Polish territories that were being divided up between Russia, Prussia, and the Habsburg Empire. All three of these realms already contained people who spoke different languages and practiced different religions. The result of such expansion was to increase the linguistic and cultural diversity of these kingdoms. ■ *How might this have complicated the internal politics of these monarchies?* ■ *What long-term consequences might one expect from such multiethnic or multireligious societies?*

monarchy than had previously existed. But it was too late. In January 1792 the Russo-Turkish war ended, and Catherine the Great pounced. Together the Russians and Prussians took two more enormous bites out of Poland in 1793, destroying the new constitution in the process. A final swallow by Russia, Austria, and Prussia in 1795 left nothing of Poland or Lithuania at all.

COMMERCE AND CONSUMPTION

Despite the increased military power of Russia, Prussia, and Austria, the balance of power within Europe was shifting steadily toward the West during the eighteenth century. The North Atlantic economies in particular were growing more rapidly than those anywhere else in Europe. As a result, France and Britain were becoming preponderant powers both in Europe and the wider world.

Economic Growth in Eighteenth-Century Europe

The reasons for this rapid economic and demographic growth in northwestern Europe are complex. In Britain and Holland, new, more intensive agricultural systems produced more food per acre. Combined with improved transportation, the new farming methods resulted in fewer famines and a better-nourished population. New crops, especially maize and potatoes (both introduced to Europe from the Americas), also helped increase the supply of food. Although famines became less common and less widespread, infectious disease continued to kill half of all Europeans before the age of twenty. Even here, however, some progress was being made. Plague was ceasing to be a major killer, as a degree of immunity (perhaps the result of a genetic mutation) began to emerge within the European population. Together with a better diet, improved sanitation may also have played some role in reducing the infection rates from typhoid, cholera, smallpox, and measles.

Northwestern Europe was also becoming increasingly urbanized. Across Europe as a whole the total number of urban dwellers did not change markedly between 1600 and 1800. At both dates, approximately two hundred cities in Europe had a population of over ten thousand. What did change was, first, the fact that these cities were increasingly concentrated in northern and western Europe and, second, the extraordinary growth of the very largest cities. Patterns of trade and commerce had much to do with these shifts. Cities such as Hamburg in Germany,

Liverpool in England, Toulon in France, and Cadíz in Spain grew by about 250 percent between 1600 and 1750. Amsterdam, the hub of early modern international commerce, increased from 30,000 in 1530 to 200,000 by 1800. Naples, the busy Mediterranean port, went from a population of 300,000 in 1600 to nearly half a million by the late eighteenth century. Even more spectacular population growth occurred in the administrative capitals of Europe. London grew from 674,000 in 1700 to 860,000 a century later. Paris went from 180,000 people in 1600 to more than 500,000 in 1800. Berlin grew from a population of 6,500 in 1661 to 140,000 in 1783.

The rising prosperity of northwestern Europe depended on developments in trade and manufacturing as well as agriculture. Spurred by improvements in transportation, entrepreneurs began to promote the production of textiles in the countryside. They distributed ("put out") wool and flax to rural workers who would card, spin, and weave it into cloth on a piece-rate basis. The entrepreneur then collected and sold the finished cloth in a market that extended from local towns to international exporters. For country dwellers, this system (sometimes called *protoindustrialization*) provided welcome employment during otherwise slack seasons of the agricultural year. For the merchant-entrepreneurs who administered it, the system allowed them to avoid expensive guild restrictions in the towns and to reduce their levels of capital investment, thus reducing their overall costs of production. Urban cloth workers suffered, but the system led nonetheless to markedly increased employment and to much higher levels of industrial production, not only for textiles but also for iron, metalworking, and even toy and clock making.

The role of cities as manufacturing centers also continued to grow during the eighteenth century. In northern France, many of the million or so men and women employed in the textile trade lived and worked in Amiens, Lille, and Rheims. The rulers of Prussia made it their policy to develop Berlin as a manufacturing center, taking advantage of an influx of French Protestants to establish a silk-weaving industry there and constructing canals to link the city with Breslau and Hamburg. Most urban manufacturing took place in small shops employing from five to twenty journeymen working under a master. But the scale of such enterprise was growing and becoming more specialized, as workshops began to group together to form a single manufacturing district in which several thousand workers might be employed to produce the same product.

Techniques in some crafts remained much as they had been for centuries. In others, however, inventions changed the pattern of work as well as the nature of the product. Knitting frames, simple devices to speed the manufacture of textile goods, made their appearance in Britain and Holland.

POPULATION GROWTH c. 1600. ▪ *Where did the population grow more rapidly?* ▪ *Why were the largest gains in population on the coasts?* ▪ *How did urbanization affect patterns of life and trade?*

Wire-drawing machines and slitting mills, the latter enabling nail makers to convert iron bars into rods, spread from Germany into Britain. Techniques for printing colored designs directly on calico cloth were imported from Asia. New and more efficient printing presses appeared, first in Holland and then elsewhere. The Dutch even invented a machine called a "camel," with which the hulls of ships could be raised in the water so that they could be more easily repaired.

Workers did not readily accept innovations of this kind. Labor-saving machines threw people out of work. Artisans, especially those organized into guilds, were by nature conservative, anxious to protect not only their rights but also the secrets of their trade. Often, therefore, governments would intervene to block the widespread use of machines if they threatened to increase unemployment or in some other way to create unrest. States might also intervene to protect the interests of their powerful commercial and financial backers. On behalf of domestic textile manufacturers and importers of Indian goods, both Britain and France outlawed calico printing for a time. Mercantilist doctrines could also impede innovation. In both Paris and Lyons, for example, the use of indigo dyes was banned because they were manufactured abroad. But the pressures for economic innovation were irresistable, because behind them lay an insatiable eighteenth-century appetite for goods.

A World of Goods

In the eighteenth century, for the first time, a mass market for consumer goods emerged in Europe, and especially in northwestern Europe. Houses became larger, particularly in towns; but even more strikingly, the houses of middling ranks were now stocked with hitherto uncommon luxuries such as sugar, tobacco, tea, coffee, chocolate, newspapers, books, pictures, clocks, toys, china, glassware, pewter, silver plate, soap, razors, furniture (including beds with mattresses, chairs, and chests of drawers), shoes, cotton cloth, and spare clothing. Demand for such products consistently outstripped the supply, causing prices for these items to rise faster than the price of foodstuffs throughout the century. But the demand for them continued unabated. Such goods were indulgences, of course, but they were also repositories of value in which families could invest their surplus cash, knowing that they could pawn them in hard times if cash were needed.

The exploding consumer economy of the eighteenth century spurred demand for manufactured goods of all sorts. But it also encouraged the provision of services. In eighteenth-century Britain, the service sector was the fastest-growing part of the economy, outstripping both agriculture and manufacturing. Almost everywhere in urban Europe, the eighteenth century was the golden age of the small shopkeeper. People bought more prepared foods and more ready-made (as opposed to personally tailored) clothing. Advertising became an important part of doing business, helping create demand for new products and shaping popular taste for changing fashions. Even political allegiances could be expressed through consumption when people purchased plates and glasses commemorating favorite rulers or causes.

The result of all these developments was a European economy vastly more complex, more specialized, more integrated, more commercialized, and more productive than anything the world had seen before.

COLONIZATION AND TRADE IN THE SEVENTEENTH CENTURY

Many of the new consumer goods that propelled the economy of eighteenth-century Europe, including such staples as sugar, tobacco, tea, coffee, chocolate, china, and cotton cloth, were the products of Europe's growing colonial empires in Asia, Africa, and the Americas. The economic history of these empires is part of a broader pattern of accelerating global connection beginning in the late fifteenth century that witnessed an extraordinary exchange of peoples, plants, animals, diseases, goods, and culture between the African and Eurasian land mass on the one hand, and the Americas, Australia, and the Pacific Islands on the other. Historians refer to this as the "Columbian exchange"—a reference to Columbus's voyage in 1492—and many see it as a fundamental turning point in human history and in the history of the earth's ecology. The exchange brought new agricultural products to Europe—such as cane sugar, tobacco, corn, and the potato—and new domesticated animals to the Americas and Australia, transforming agriculture on both sides of the Atlantic and the Pacific Oceans, and reshaping the landscape itself. The transfer of human populations in the form of settlers, merchants, and slaves accelerated the process of cultural change for many

TOPSY-TURVY WORLD BY JAN STEEN. This Dutch painting depicts a household in the throes of the exploding consumer economy that hit Europe in the eighteenth century. Consumer goods ranging from silver and china to clothing and furniture cluttered the houses of ordinary people as never before.

peoples, even as other groups saw their cultures wiped out through violence or forced resettlement. The accompanying transfer of disease agents, meanwhile, had devastating effects—some historians suggest that between 50 and 90 percent of the pre-Columbian population of the Americas died from communicable diseases brought from Europe such as smallpox, cholera, influenza, typhoid, and measles.

Europe's growing colonial empires between the fifteenth and eighteenth centuries were thus a part of a series of fundamental changes that transformed people's lives, and their relation to their environment over the long term in many parts of the world. Europe's growing wealth during this period had complex causes, but it is impossible to imagine the prosperity of the eighteenth century without understanding this history of colonialism.

Spanish Colonialism

After the exploits of the conquistadors, the Spanish established colonial governments in Peru and in Mexico, which they controlled from Madrid. In keeping with the doctrines of mercantilism, the Spanish government allowed only Spanish merchants to trade with their American colonies, requiring all colonial exports and imports to pass through a single Spanish port (first Seville, then later the more navigable port of Cadíz), where they were registered at the government-operated customs house. During the sixteenth century, this system worked reasonably well. The Spanish colonial economy was dominated by mining; the lucrative market for silver in East Asia even made it profitable to establish an outpost in Manila, where Spanish merchants exchanged Asian silk for South American bullion. But Spain also took steps to promote farming and ranching in Central and South America and established settlements in Florida and California.

Throughout this empire, a relatively small number of Spaniards had conquered complex and highly populous Native American societies. To rule these new territories, the Spanish replaced existing elites with Spanish administrators and churchmen. By and large, they did not attempt to uproot or eliminate existing native cultures but focused on controlling and exploiting native labor for their own profit, above all in extracting mineral resources. The native peoples of Spanish America already lived, for the most part, in large, well-organized villages and towns. The Spanish collected tribute from these communities and attempted to convert them to Catholicism but did not attempt to change their basic patterns of life.

The result was widespread cultural assimilation between the Spanish colonizers and the native populations, combined with a relatively high degree of intermarriage between them. Out of this reality emerged a complex and distinctive system of racial and social castes, with Spaniards at the top, peoples of mixed descent (combinations of Spanish, African, and Native American) in the middle, and nontribal American Indians at the bottom. In theory, these racial categories corresponded with class distinctions, but in practice race and class did not always coincide, and race itself was often a social fiction. Individuals of mixed descent who prospered economically often found ways to establish their "pure" Spanish ancestry by adopting the social practices that characterized elite (that is, Spanish) status. Spaniards always remained at the top of the social hierarchy, however, even when they fell into poverty.

The wealth of Spain's colonial trade tempted the merchants of other countries to win a share of the treasure for themselves. Probably the boldest challengers were the English, whose leading buccaneer was the sea dog Sir Francis Drake. Three times Drake raided the east and west coasts of Spanish America. In 1587 he attacked the Spanish fleet at its anchorage in Cadíz harbor; and in 1588 he played a key role in defeating the Spanish Armada. His career illustrates the mixture of piracy and patriotism that characterized England's early efforts to break into the colonial trade. Until the 1650s, however, the English could only dent the lucrative Spanish trade in bullion, hides, silks, and slaves.

French Colonialism

French colonial policy matured under Louis XIV's mercantilist finance minister, Jean Baptiste Colbert, who regarded overseas expansion as an integral part of state economic policy. Realizing the profits to be made in responding to Europe's growing demand for sugar, he encouraged the development of sugar-producing colonies in the West Indies, the largest of which was Saint-Domingue (present-day Haiti). Sugar, virtually unknown in Christian Europe during the Middle Ages, became a popular luxury item in the late fifteenth century. It took the slave plantations of the Caribbean to turn sugar into a mass-market product. By 1750, slaves in Saint-Domingue produced 40 percent of the world's sugar and 50 percent of its coffee, exporting more sugar than Jamaica, Cuba, and Brazil combined. France also dominated the interior of the North American continent, where French traders brought furs to the American Indians and missionaries preached Christianity in a vast territory that stretched from Quebec to Louisiana. The financial returns from North America were never large, however. Furs, fish, and tobacco were exported to European markets but never matched the profits from the Caribbean

ILLINOIS INDIANS TRADING WITH FRENCH SETTLERS. This engraving from Nicholas De Fer's 1705 map of the Western Hemisphere illustrates the economic interdependence that developed between early French colonies and the native peoples of the surrounding region. ■ *How did this differ from relations between Native Americans and English agricultural communities on the Atlantic coast?*

sugar colonies or from the trading posts that the French maintained in India.

Like the Spanish colonies, the French colonies were established and administered as direct crown enterprises. French colonial settlements in North America were conceived mainly as military outposts and trading centers, and they were overwhelmingly populated by men. The elite of French colonial society were military officers and administrators sent from Paris. Below their ranks were fishermen, fur traders, small farmers, and common soldiers who constituted the bulk of French settlers in North America. Because the fishing and the fur trades relied on cooperative relationships with native peoples, a mutual economic interdependence grew up between the French colonies and the peoples of the surrounding region. Intermarriage, especially between French traders and native women, was common. These North American colonies remained dependent on the wages and supplies sent to them from the mother country. Only rarely did they become truly self-sustaining economic enterprises.

The phenomenally successful sugar plantations of the Caribbean had their own social structure, with slaves at the bottom, people of mixed African and European descent forming a middle layer, and wealthy European plantation owners at the top, controlling the lucrative trade with the outside world. Well over half of the sugar and coffee sent to France was resold and sent elsewhere to markets throughout Europe. Because the monarchy controlled the prices that colonial plantation owners could charge French merchants for their goods, traders in Europe who bought the goods for resale abroad could also make vast fortunes. Historians estimate that as many as a million of the twenty-five million inhabitants of France in the eighteenth century lived off the money flowing through this colonial trade, making the slave colonies of the Caribbean a powerful force for economic change in France.

English Colonialism

England's own American colonies had no significant mineral wealth. As a result, English colonists sought profits by establishing agricultural settlements in North America and the Caribbean basin. Their first permanent, though ultimately unsuccessful, colony was founded in 1607 at Jamestown, Virginia. Over the next forty years, eighty thousand English emigrants would sail to more than twenty autonomous settlements in the New World. Many of these early settlers were driven by religious motives. The Pilgrims who landed at Plymouth, Massachusetts, in 1620 were one of many dissident groups, both Protestant and Catholic, that sought to escape the English government's religious intolerance by emigrating to North America. Strikingly, however, English colonists showed little interest in trying to convert Native American peoples to Christianity. Missionizing played a much larger role in Spanish efforts to colonize Central and South America and French efforts to penetrate the North American hinterlands.

These English colonies did not begin as crown enterprises as in the Spanish or French empires. Instead they were private ventures, either proprietary (as in Maryland and Pennsylvania) or joint-stock companies (as in Virginia and the Massachusetts Bay colony). Building on their experience in Ireland, English colonists established planned settlements known as plantations, in which they attempted to replicate as many features of English life as possible. Geography also contributed to the English settlement patterns, as the rivers and bays of the northeast Atlantic coast provided the first locations for colonists. Aside from the Hudson, however, there were no great rivers to lead colonists very far inland, and the English colonies clung to the coast and to each other.

Once they realized the profits to be made in colonial trade, however, the governments of both Oliver Cromwell

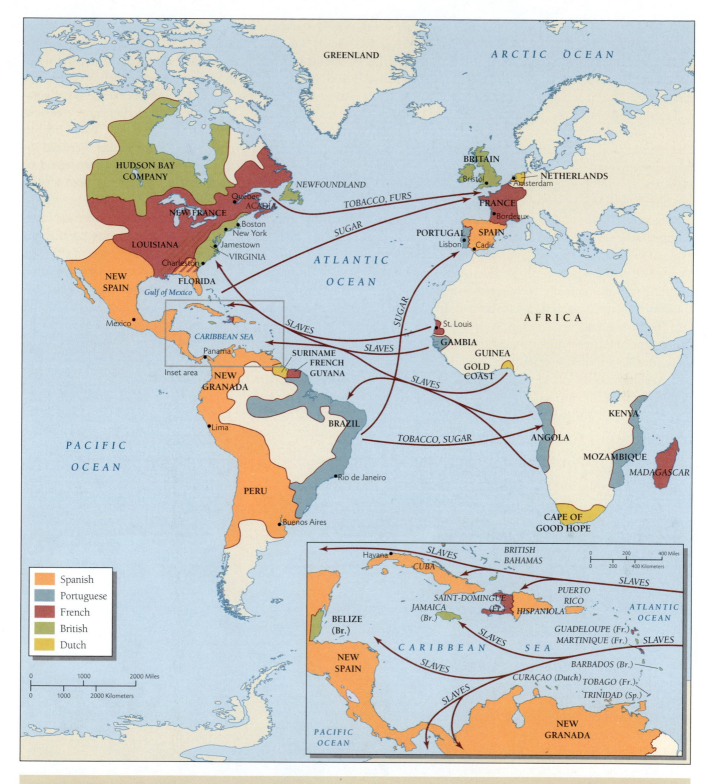

The following labels appear on the map:

GREENLAND

ARCTIC OCEAN

HUDSON BAY COMPANY

NEWFOUNDLAND

Quebec · ACADIA

NEW FRANCE

Boston
New York

LOUISIANA

Jamestown
Charleston · VIRGINIA

NEW SPAIN

FLORIDA

Gulf of Mexico

Mexico ·

Inset area

Panama ·

NEW GRANADA

SURINAME FRENCH GUYANA

CARIBBEAN SEA

· Lima

PERU

BRAZIL

Rio de Janeiro ·

Buenos Aires ·

PACIFIC OCEAN

ATLANTIC OCEAN

TOBACCO, FURS

SUGAR

SUGAR

SLAVES

SLAVES

SLAVES

TOBACCO, SUGAR

BRITAIN
Bristol

NETHERLANDS
Amsterdam

FRANCE
· Bordeaux

PORTUGAL   SPAIN
Lisbon ·   Cadiz ·

AFRICA

St. Louis

GAMBIA

GUINEA

GOLD COAST

ANGOLA

KENYA

MOZAMBIQUE

MADAGASCAR

CAPE OF GOOD HOPE

Legend:
- Spanish
- Portuguese
- French
- British
- Dutch

Scale: 1000, 2000 Miles / 1000, 2000 Kilometers

Inset map labels:
Havana · CUBA SLAVES BRITISH BAHAMAS
BELIZE (Br.)
JAMAICA (Br.) SAINT-DOMINGUE (Fr.) HISPANIOLA PUERTO RICO
NEW SPAIN
CARIBBEAN SEA
GUADELOUPE (Fr.)
MARTINIQUE (Fr.) SLAVES
SLAVES
BARBADOS (Br.)
CURAÇAO (Dutch) TOBAGO (Fr.)
TRINIDAD (Sp.)
ATLANTIC OCEAN
PACIFIC OCEAN
NEW GRANADA
SLAVES

THE ATLANTIC WORLD. ■ *What products did French and British colonies in North America provide to the European market in the eighteenth century?* ■ *Which colonies were most dependent on slave labor?* ■ *What products did they produce?* ■ *Why were European governments so concerned with closely controlling the means by which certain products traveled from the colonies to European ports?*

and Charles II began to intervene in their management. Mercantilist-inspired navigation acts, passed in 1651 and 1660 decreed that exports from English colonies to the mother country be carried in English ships and forbade the direct exporting of "enumerated" products, such as sugar and tobacco, directly from the colonies to foreign ports. The English sugar-producing colonies competed directly with the French, and during the eighteenth century, profits from the tiny islands of Jamaica and Barbados were worth more than all of British imports from China and India combined. Tobacco, which was first brought to Europe by the Spaniards, became profitable as smoking caught on in Europe in the seventeenth century, popularized by English explorers who learned about it from Native Americans in Virginia. Governments at first joined the church in condemning it, but eventually encouraged its production and consumption, realizing the profits to be made from the trade.

The early English colonies in North America relied on fishing and the fur trade for their exports, but they soon grew into agricultural communities populated by small- and medium-scale landholders for whom the key to wealth was control over land. In part this reflected the kinds of people recruited by the private colonial enterprises for settlement in North America. But the focus on agriculture also resulted from the demographic catastrophe that struck the native populations of the Atlantic seaboard during the second half of the sixteenth century. European diseases—brought by Spanish armies and by the French, British, and Portuguese fisherman who frequented the rich fishing banks off the New England coast—had already decimated the native peoples of eastern North America even before the first European colonists set foot there. By the early seventeenth century, a great deal of rich agricultural land had been abandoned simply because there were no longer enough native farmers to till it—one reason that many native groups initially welcomed the new arrivals.

Unlike the Spanish, English colonists along the Atlantic seaboard had neither the need nor the opportunity to control a large native labor force. What they wanted, rather, was complete and exclusive control over native lands. To this end, the English colonists soon set out to eliminate, through expulsion and massacre, the indigenous peoples of their colonies. There were exceptions—in the Quaker colony of Pennsylvania, colonists and Native Americans maintained friendly relations for more than half a century. In the Carolinas, on the other hand, there was widespread enslavement of native peoples, either for sale to the West Indies or, from the 1690s, to work on the rice plantations along the coast. Elsewhere, however, attempts to enslave the native peoples of North American failed. When English planters looked for bond laborers, they either recruited indentured servants from England (most of whom would be freed after a specified period of service) or purchased African captives (who would usually be enslaved for life).

In contrast to the Spanish and French colonies, intermarriage between English colonists and native populations was rare. Instead, a rigid racial division emerged that distinguished all Europeans from all Native Americans and Africans. Intermarriage between natives and Africans was relatively common, but between the English and the native peoples of the colonies an unbridgeable gulf developed.

Dutch Colonialism

Until the 1670s, the Dutch controlled the most prosperous commercial empire of the seventeenth century. Although some Dutch settlements were established, including one at the Cape of Good Hope in modern-day South Africa, Dutch

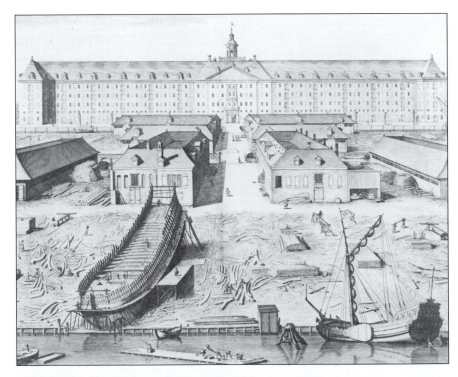

THE DUTCH EAST INDIA COMPANY WAREHOUSE AND TIMBER WHARF AT AMSTERDAM. The substantial warehouse, the stockpiles of lumber, and the company ship under construction in the foreground illustrate the degree to which overseas commerce could stimulate the economy of the mother country.

colonialism generally followed the "fort and factory" model established by the Portuguese in Asia. In Southeast Asia, the Dutch East India Company, founded in 1602, seized control of Sumatra, Borneo, and the Moluccas (Spice Islands), driving Portuguese traders from an area they had previously dominated and establishing a Dutch monopoly within Europe over pepper, cinnamon, nutmeg, mace, and cloves. The Dutch also secured an exclusive right to trade with Japan and maintained military and trading outposts in China and India as well. In the Western Hemisphere, however, their achievements were less spectacular. After a series of trade wars with England, in 1667 they formally surrendered their colony of New Amsterdam (subsequently renamed New York), retaining only Surinam (off the northern coast of South America) and Curaçao and Tobago (in the West Indies). Although the Dutch dominated the seventeenth-century slave trade with Africa, they lost this position to the British after 1713.

***THE DEFENSE OF CADÍZ AGAINST THE ENGLISH* BY FRANCISCO ZURBARAN.** The rivalry between European powers that played out over the new colonial possessions further proved the decline of Spain, which lost the island of Jamaica and ships in the harbor of Cadíz to the English in the 1650s.

The Dutch also pioneered new financial mechanisms for investing in colonial enterprises. One of the most important of these was the joint-stock company, of which the Dutch East India Company was among the first. Such companies raised cash by selling shares in their enterprise to investors. Even though the investors might not take any role in managing the company, they were joint owners of the business and therefore entitled to a share in the profits. Initially, the Dutch East India Company intended to pay off its investors ten years after its founding, but the directors soon recognized the impossibility of this plan. By 1612, the company's assets—ships, wharves, warehouses, and cargoes—were scattered around the globe. Moreover, its commercial prospects were continuing to improve. The directors therefore urged investors anxious to realize their profits to sell their shares on the Amsterdam stock exchange to other investors, thereby ensuring the continued operation of their enterprise and, in the process, establishing a method of continuous business financing that would soon spread elsewhere in Europe.

Colonial Rivalries

The fortunes of these colonial empires changed dramatically in the course of the seventeenth and early eighteenth centuries. Spain proved unable to defend its early monopoly over colonial trade, and in 1650 the Spanish suffered a crippling blow when they were forced to surrender Jamaica and several treasure ships lying off of the Spanish harbor of Cadíz. By 1700, although Spain still possessed a colonial empire, it lay at the mercy of its more dynamic rivals. Portugal, too, found it impossible to prevent foreign penetration of its colonial empire. In 1703, the English signed a treaty with Portugal allowing English merchants to export woolens duty free into Portugal and allowing Portugal to ship its wines duty free into England. Access to Portugal also led British merchants to trade with the Portuguese colony of Brazil, an important sugar producer and the largest of all the American markets for African slaves. In the eighteenth century, English merchants would dominate these Brazilian trade routes.

The 1713 Treaty of Utrecht opened a new era of colonial rivalries. The biggest losers were the Dutch, who gained only a guarantee of their own borders, and the Spanish, who were forced to concede to Britain the right to market slaves in the Spanish colonies. The winners were the British (who acquired large chunks of territory in North America) and to a lesser extent, the French, who retained Quebec and other territories in North America, as well as their foothold in India. The eighteenth century would witness a continuing struggle between Britain and France for control over the expanding commerce that now bound the European economy to the Americas and to Asia.

THE TRIANGULAR TRADE IN SUGAR AND SLAVES

During the eighteenth century, European colonial trade came to be dominated by trans-Atlantic routes that developed in response to the increased demand for sugar and tobacco and the corresponding market for slaves to produce these goods on American and Caribbean plantations. In this "triangular" trade, naval superiority gave Britain a decisive advantage over its French, Spanish, Portuguese, and Dutch rivals. Typically, a British ship might begin its voyage from New England with a consignment of rum and sail to Africa, where the rum would be exchanged for a cargo of slaves. From the west coast of Africa the ship would then cross the South Atlantic to the sugar colonies of Jamaica or Barbados, where slaves would be traded for molasses. It would then make the final leg of the journey back to New England, where the molasses would be made into rum. A

variant triangle might see cheap manufactured goods move from England to Africa, where they would be traded for slaves. Those slaves would then be shipped to Virginia and exchanged for tobacco, which would be shipped to England and processed there for sale throughout Europe.

The cultivation of New World sugar and tobacco depended on slave labor. As European demand for these products increased, so too did the traffic in enslaved Africans. At the height of the Atlantic slave trade in the eighteenth century, seventy-five to ninety thousand Africans were shipped across the Atlantic yearly: at least six million in the eighteenth century, out of a total of over eleven million for the entire history of the trade. About 35 percent went to English and French Caribbean plantations, 5 percent (roughly five hundred thousand) to North America, and the rest to the Portuguese colony of Brazil and to the Spanish colonies in Central and South America. By the 1780s, there were more than five hundred thousand slaves on the largest French plantation island, Saint-Domingue, and at least two hundred thousand on its English counterpart, Jamaica.

Although run as a monopoly by various governments in the sixteenth and early seventeenth centuries, the slave trade in the eighteenth century was open to private entre-

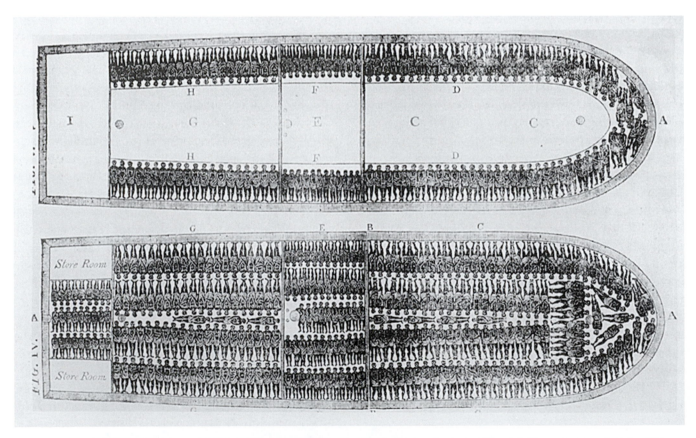

HOW SLAVES WERE STOWED ABOARD SHIP DURING THE MIDDLE PASSAGE. Men were "housed" on the right; women on the left; children in the middle. The human cargo was jammed onto platforms six feet wide without sufficient headroom to permit an adult to sit up. This diagram is from evidence gathered by English abolitionists and depicts conditions on the Liverpool slave ship *Brookes*.

preneurs who operated ports on the West African coast. These traders exchanged Indian cloth, metal goods, rum, and firearms with African slave merchants in return for their human cargo, who would then be packed by the hundreds into the holds of slave ships for the gruesome Middle Passage across the Atlantic (so called to distinguish it from the slave ship's voyage from Europe to Africa, and then from the colonies back to Europe). Shackled belowdecks without sanitary facilities, the captive men, women, and children suffered horribly. The mortality rate, however, remained at about 10 or 11 percent, not much higher than the rate for a normal sea voyage of a hundred days or more. Since traders had to invest as much as £10 per slave in their enterprise, they were generally anxious to ensure that their consignment would reach its destination in good enough shape to be sold for a profit.

The Commercial Rivalry between Britain and France

British dominance of the slave trade gave it decisive advantages in its colonial struggles with France. As one Englishman wrote in 1749, the slave trade had provided "an unexhastible fund of wealth to this nation." But even apart from the slave trade, the value of colonial commerce was increasing dramatically during the eighteenth century. French colonial trade, valued at 25 million livres in 1716, rose to 263 million livres in 1789. In England, during roughly the same period, foreign trade increased in value from £10 million to £40 million, the latter amount more than twice that for France.

The growing value of colonial commerce tied the interests of governments and transoceanic merchants together in an increasingly tight embrace. Merchants engaged in the colonial trade depended on their governments to protect and defend their overseas investments; but governments depended in turn on merchants and their financial backers to build the ships and sustain the trade on which national power depended. In the eighteenth century, even the ability to wage war rested largely (and increasingly) on a government's ability to borrow the necessary funds from wealthy investors and then to pay back those debts, with interest, over time. As it did in commerce, so too in finance, Britain came to enjoy a decisive advantage in this respect over France. The Bank of England, founded in the 1690s, managed the English national debt with great success, providing the funds required for war by selling shares to investors, then repaying those investors at moderate rates of interest. In contrast, chronic governmental indebtedness forced the French crown to borrow at ruinously high rates of interest,

provoking a series of fiscal crises that in 1789 finally led to the collapse of the French monarchy.

War and Empire in the Eighteenth-Century World

After 1713, western Europe remained largely at peace for a generation. In 1740, however, that peace was shattered when Frederick the Great of Prussia took advantage of the accession of a woman, the empress Maria Theresa, to the throne of Austria to seize the Austrian province of Silesia (discussed earlier in this chapter). In the resulting War of the Austrian Succession, France and Spain fought on the side of Prussia, hoping to reverse some of the losses they had suffered in the Treaty of Utrecht. As they had done since the 1690s, Britain and the Dutch Republic sided with Austria. Like those earlier wars, this war quickly spread beyond the frontiers of Europe. In India, the British East India Company lost control over the coastal area of Madras to its French rival; but in North America, British colonists from New England captured the important French fortress of Louisbourg on Cape Breton Island, hoping to put a stop to French interference with their fishing and shipping. When the war finally ended in 1748, Britain recovered Madras and returned Louisbourg to France.

Eight years later, these colonial conflicts reignited when Prussia once again attacked Austria. This time, however, Prussia allied itself with Great Britain. Austria found support from both France and Russia. In Europe, the Seven Years' War (1756–1763) ended in stalemate. In India and North America, however, the war had decisive consequences. In India, mercenary troops employed by the British East India Company joined with native allies to eliminate their French competitors. In North America (where the conflict was known as the French and Indian War), British troops captured both Louisbourg and Quebec and also drove French forces from the Ohio River Valley and the Great Lakes. By the Treaty of Paris in 1763, which brought the Seven Years' War to an end, France formally surrendered both Canada and India to the British. Six years later, the French East India Company was dissolved.

The American Revolution

Along the Atlantic seaboard, however, the rapidly growing British colonies were beginning to chafe at rule from London. To recover some of the costs of the Seven Years'

War and to pay for the continuing costs of protecting its colonial subjects, the British Parliament imposed a series of new taxes on its American colonies. These taxes were immediately unpopular. Colonists complained that because they had no representatives in Parliament, they were being taxed without their consent—a fundamental violation of their rights as British subjects. They also complained that British restrictions on colonial trade, particularly the requirement that certain goods pass first through British ports before being shipped to the Continent, were strangling American livelihoods and making it impossible to pay even the king's legitimate taxes.

The British government, led since 1760 by the young and inexperienced King George III, responded to these complaints with a badly calculated mixture of vacillation and force. Various taxes were imposed and then withdrawn in the face of colonial resistance. In 1773, however, when East India Company tea was dumped in Boston Harbor by rebellious colonials objecting to the customs duties that had been imposed on it, the British government closed the port of Boston and curtailed the colony's representative institutions. These "Coercive Acts" galvanized the

support of the other American colonies for Massachusetts. In 1774, representatives from all the American colonies met at Philadelphia to form the Continental Congress to negotiate with the crown over their grievances. In April 1775, however, local militiamen at Lexington and Concord clashed with regular British troops sent to disarm them. Soon thereafter, the Continental Congress began raising an army, and an outright rebellion erupted against the British government.

On July 4, 1776, the thirteen colonies formally declared their independence from Great Britain. During the first two years of the war, it seemed unlikely that such independence would ever become a reality. In 1778, however, France, anxious to undermine the colonial hegemony Great Britain had established since 1713, joined the war on the side of the Americans. Spain entered the war in support of France, hoping to recover Gibraltar and Florida (the latter lost in 1763 to Britain). In 1780, Britain also declared war on the Dutch Republic for continuing to trade with the rebellious colonies. Now facing a coalition of its colonial rivals, Great Britain saw the war turn against it. In 1781, combined land and sea operations by French and American troops

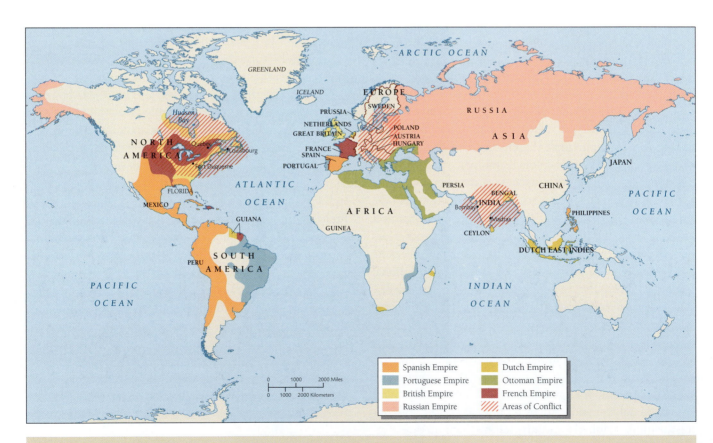

THE SEVEN YEARS' WAR, 1756–1763. ▪ *What continents were involved in the Seven Years' War?* ▪ *What was the impact of naval power on the outcome of the war?* ▪ *What were the consequences for the colonies involved in the conflict?*

Analyzing Primary Sources

The American Declaration of Independence

The Declaration of Independence, issued from Philadelphia on July 4, 1776, is perhaps the most famous single document of American history. But its familiarity does not lesssen its interest as a piece of political philosophy. The indebtedness of the document's authors to the ideas of John Locke will be obvious from the selections here. But Locke, in turn, drew many of his ideas about the contractual and conditional nature of human government from the conciliarist thinkers of the fifteenth and early sixteenth centuries. The appeal of absolutism notwithstanding, the declaration shows how vigorous the medieval tradition of contractual, limited government remained at the end of the eighteenth century.

 hen in the course of human events, it becomes necessary for one people to dissolve the political bonds which have connected them with another, and to assume among the powers of the earth the separate and equal station to which the Laws of Nature and of Nature's God entitle them, a decent respect to the opinions of mankind requires that they should declare the causes which impel them to the separation. . . . We hold these truths to be self-evident, that all men are created equal, that they are endowed by their Creator with certain unalienable rights, that among these are Life, Liberty and the pursuit of Happiness. . . . That to secure these rights, Governments are instituted among men, deriving their just powers from the consent of the governed. . . . That whenever any form of Government becomes destructive of these ends, it is the Right of the People to alter or to abolish it, and to institute new Government, laying its foundation upon such principles and organizing its power in such form, as to them shall seem most likely to effect their Safety and Happiness. Prudence, indeed, will dictate that Governments long established should not be changed for light and transient causes; and accordingly all experience has shown, that mankind are more disposed to suffer, while evils are sufferable, than to right themselves by abolishing the forms to which they are accustomed. But when a long train of abuses and usurpations, pursuing invariably the same Object, evinces a design to reduce them under absolute despotism, it is their right, it is their duty, to throw off such Government, and to provide new Guards for their future security. . . . Such has been the patient sufferance of these Colonies; and such is now the necessity which constrains them to alter their former Systems of Government. . . .

Questions for Analysis

1. Who are "the people" mentioned in the first sentence of this selection? Are the rights of "the people" the same as individual rights? How did the authors of this declaration come to think of themselves as the representatives of such a body?

2. What is the purpose of government, according to this document? Who gets to decide if the government is doing its job?

3. How would Robert Filmer or Bossuet have viewed such a declaration? How might John Locke have defended it?

---

forced the surrender of the main British army at Yorktown in Virginia. As the defeated British soldiers surrendered their weapons, their band played a song titled "The World Turned Upside Down."

Negotiations for peace began soon after the defeat at Yorktown but were not concluded until September 1783. The Treaty of Paris left Great Britain in control of Canada and Gibraltar. Spain retained its possessions west of the Mississippi River and recovered Florida. The United States gained its independence; its western border was fixed on the Mississippi River, and it secured valuable fishing rights off the eastern coast of Canada. France gained only the satisfaction of defeating its colonial rival; but even that satisfaction was short lived. Six years later, the massive debts France had incurred in supporting the American Revolution helped bring about another, very different kind of revolution in France that would permanently alter the history of Europe.

CONCLUSION

Seen in this light, the American War of Independence was the final military conflict in a century-long struggle between Great Britain and France for colonial dominance. But the consequences of Britain's defeat in 1783 were far less significant than might have been expected. Even after American independence, Great Britain would remain the most important trading partner for its former American colonies, while elsewhere around the globe, the commercial dominance Britain had already established would continue to grow. The profits of slavery certainly helped fuel the eighteenth-century British economy; by the end of the century, however, British trade and manufacturing had reached such high levels of productivity that even the abolition of the slave trade (in 1808) and of slavery itself (in 1833) did not impede its continuing growth.

The economic prosperity of late-eighteenth-century Britain was mirrored to some degree throughout northwestern Europe. Improved transportation systems, more reliable food supplies, and growing quantities of consumer goods brought improved standards of living to large numbers of Europeans, even as the overall population of Europe was rising faster after 1750 than it had ever done before. Population growth was especially rapid in the cities, where a new urban

SEVENTEENTH- AND EIGHTEENTH-CENTURY WARS

Glorious Revolution	1688–1689
War of the League of Augsburg	1689–1697
War of the Spanish Succession	1702–1713
Seven Years' War	1756–1763
American Revolution	1775–1783
The Russo-Turkish War	1787–1792

After You Read This Chapter

Visit StudySpace for quizzes, additional review materials, and multi-media documents. **wwnorton.com/studyspace**

REVIEWING THE OBJECTIVES

- Absolutist rulers claimed a monopoly of power and authority within their realms. What did they do to achieve this goal?
- Monarchies in both western and eastern Europe adopted the absolutist system, but they faced different challenges. How did the absolutist monarchies in eastern Europe differ from their counterparts in western Europe?
- England developed an alternative to absolutism by the end of the seventeenth century. What was it?
- The commercial revolution of the eighteenth century resulted in major changes in the European economy. What were they?
- Colonial expansion in the Atlantic world and the African slave trade connected Africa and the Americas with Europe in new ways. Who profited most from the Atlantic's new political and economic relationships?

middle class was emerging whose tastes drove the market for goods and whose opinions were reshaping the world of ideas.

But the prosperity of late-eighteenth-century Europe remained very unevenly distributed. In the cities, rich and poor lived separate lives in separate neighborhoods. In the countryside, regions bypassed by the developing commercial economy of the period continued to suffer from hunger and famine, just as they had done in the sixteenth and seventeenth centuries. In eastern Europe the contrasts between rich and poor were even more extreme, as many peasants fell into a new style of serfdom that would last until the end of the nineteenth century. War too remained a fact of European life, bringing death and destruction to hundreds of thousands of people across the continent and around the world—yet another consequence of the worldwide reach of these European colonial empires.

Political change was more gradual. Throughout Europe, the powers of governments steadily increased. Administrators became more numerous, more efficient, and more demanding, partly to meet the mounting costs of war but also because governments were starting to take on a much wider range of responsibilities for the welfare of their subjects. Despite the increasing scope of government, however, the structure and principles of government changed relatively little. Apart from Great Britain and the Dutch Republic, the great powers of eighteenth-century Europe were still governed by rulers who styled themselves as absolutist monarchs in the mold of Louis XIV. By 1789, however, the European world was a vastly different place than it had been a century before, when the Sun King had dominated European politics. The full extent of those differences was about to be revealed.

PEOPLE, IDEAS, AND EVENTS IN CONTEXT

- What did **LOUIS XIV** of France, **PETER THE GREAT** of Russia, **FREDERICK THE GREAT** of Prussia, and **MARIA THERESA** of Austria have in common? How did they deal with those who resisted their attempts to impose absolutist rule?
- What limits to royal power were recognized in Great Britain as a result of the **GLORIOUS REVOLUTION**?
- What does the **TREATY OF UTRECHT** (1713) tell us about the diminished influence of Spain and the corresponding rise of Britain as a European power?
- How did European monarchies use the economic theory known as **MERCANTILISM** to strengthen the power and wealth of their kingdoms?
- What was the **COLUMBIAN EXCHANGE**? What combination of demographic, cultural, and ecological transformations are contained within this idea?
- How did the **COMMERCIAL REVOLUTION** change social life in Europe?
- What was the **TRIANGULAR TRADE** and how was it related to the growth of commerce in the Atlantic world during this period?
- What debt does the American **DECLARATION OF INDEPENDENCE** owe to the ideas of the English political thinker **JOHN LOCKE**?

CONSEQUENCES

- Was any European monarch's power ever really *absolute*?
- What do you suppose had more effect on the lives of ordinary Europeans: the rise of absolutist regimes or the commercial revolution of the eighteenth century?
- In a world in which a British merchant's fortune depended on the price of molasses in Boston, the demand for African slaves in Jamaica, and the price of rum in Senegal, could one already speak of *globalization*?

Before You Read This Chapter

The New Science of the Seventeenth Century

Doubt thou the stars are fire,
Doubt that the sun doth move,
Doubt truth to be a liar,
But never doubt I love.

SHAKESPEARE, HAMLET, II.2

CORE OBJECTIVES

- **DEFINE** *scientific revolution* and explain what is meant by *science* in this historical context.

- **UNDERSTAND** the older philosophical traditions that were important for the development of new methods of scientific investigation in the seventeenth century.

- **IDENTIFY** the sciences that made important advances during this period and understand what technological innovations encouraged a new spirit of investigation.

- **EXPLAIN** the differences between the Ptolemaic view of the universe and the new vision of the universe proposed by Nicolas Copernicus.

- **UNDERSTAND** the different definitions of scientific method that emerged from the work of Francis Bacon and René Descartes.

"Doubt thou the stars are fire" and "that the sun doth move." Was Shakespeare alluding to controversial ideas about the cosmos that contradicted the teachings of medieval scholars? *Hamlet* (c. 1600) was written more than fifty years after Copernicus had suggested, in his treatise *On the Revolutions of the Heavenly Spheres* (1543), that the sun did not move and that the earth did, revolving around the sun. Shakespeare probably knew of such theories, although they circulated only among small groups of learned Europeans. As Hamlet's love-torn speech to Ophelia makes clear, they were considered conjecture—or strange mathematical hypotheses. These theories were not exactly new—a heliocentric universe had been proposed as early as the second century B.C.E. by ancient Greak astronomers.

493

But they flatly contradicted the consensus that had set in after Ptolemy proposed an earth-centered universe in the second century C.E., and to Shakespeare's contemporaries, they defied common sense and observation. Learned philosophers, young lovers, shepherds, and sailors alike could watch the sun and the stars move from one horizon to the other each day and night, or so they thought.

Still, a small handful of thinkers did doubt. Shakespeare was born in 1564, the same year as Galileo. By the time the English playwright and the Italian natural philosopher were working, the long process of revising knowledge about the universe, and discovering a new set of rules that explained how the universe worked was under way. By the end of the seventeenth century a hundred years later, the building blocks of the new view had been put in place. This intellectual transformation brought sweeping changes to European philosophy and to Western views of the natural world and of humans' place in it.

Science entails at least three things: a body of knowledge, a method or system of inquiry, and a community of practitioners and the institutions that support them and their work. The *scientific revolution* of the seventeenth century (usually understood to have begun in the mid-sixteenth century and culminated in 1687 with Newton's *Principia*) involved each of these three realms. As far as the content of knowledge is concerned, the scientific revolution saw the emergence and confirmation of a heliocentric (sun-centered) view of the planetary system, which displaced the earth—and humans—from the center of the universe. Even more fundamental, it brought a new mathematical physics that described and confirmed such a view. Second, the scientific revolution established a method of inquiry for understanding the natural world: a method that emphasized the role of observation, experiment, and the testing of hypotheses. Third, *science* emerged as a distinctive branch of knowledge. During the period covered in this chapter, people referred to the study of matter, motion, optics, or the circulation of blood as natural philosophy (the more theoretical term), experimental philosophy, medicine, and—increasingly—science. The growth of societies and institutions dedicated to what we now commonly call scientific research was central to the changes at issue here. Science required not only brilliant thinkers but patrons, states, and communities of researchers; the scientific revolution was thus embedded in other social, religious, and cultural transformations.

The scientific revolution was not an organized effort. Brilliant theories sometimes led to dead ends, discoveries were often accidental, and artisans grinding lenses for telescopes played a role in the advance of knowledge just as surely as did great abstract thinkers. Educated women also claimed the right to participate in scientific debate, but their efforts were met with opposition or indifference. Old and new worldviews often overlapped as individual thinkers struggled to reconcile their discoveries with their faith or to make their theories (about the earth's movements, for instance) fit with received wisdom. Science was slow to work its way into popular understanding. It did not necessarily undermine religion, and it certainly did not intend to; figures like Isaac Newton thought their work confirmed and deepened their religious beliefs. In short, change came slowly and fitfully. But as the new scientific method began to produce radical new insights into the workings of nature, it eventually came to be accepted well beyond the small circles of experimenters, theologians, and philosophers with whom it began.

THE INTELLECTUAL ORIGINS OF THE SCIENTIFIC REVOLUTION

The scientific revolution marks one of the decisive breaks between the Middle Ages and the modern world. For all its novelty, however, it was rooted in earlier developments. Medieval artists and intellectuals had been observing and illustrating the natural world with great precision since at least the twelfth century. Medieval sculptors carved plants and vines with extraordinary accuracy, and fifteenth-century painters and sculptors devoted the same careful attention to the human face and form. Nor was the link between observation, experiment, and invention new to the sixteenth century. The magnetic compass had been known in Europe since the thirteenth century; gunpowder since the early fourteenth; printing, which permeated the intellectual life of the period and opened new possibilities—disseminating ideas quickly, collaborating more easily, buying books, and building libraries—since the middle of the fifteenth. "Printing, firearms, and the compass," wrote Francis Bacon, "no empire, sect or star appears to have exercised a greater power and influence on human affairs than these three mechanical discoveries." A fascination with light, which was a powerful symbol of divine illumination for medieval thinkers, encouraged the study of optics and, in turn, new techniques for grinding lenses. Lens grinders laid the groundwork for the seventeenth-century inventions of the telescope and microscope, creating reading glasses along the way. Astrologers were also active in the later Middle Ages, charting the heavens in the firm belief that the stars controlled the fates of human beings.

Behind these efforts to understand the natural world lay a nearly universal conviction that the natural world had been created by God. Religious belief spurred scientific study. One school of thinkers (the Neoplatonists) argued that nature was a book written by its creator to reveal the ways of God to humanity. Convinced that God's perfection must be reflected in nature, Neoplatonists searched for the ideal and perfect structures they believed must lie behind the "shadows" of the everyday world. Mathematics, particularly geometry, were important tools in this quest. The mathematician and astronomer Johannes Kepler, for example, was deeply influenced by Neoplatonism.

Renaissance humanism also helped prepare the grounds for the scientific revolution. The humanists' educational program placed a low value on natural philosophy, directing attention instead toward the recovery and study of classical antiquity. Humanists revered the authority of the ancients. Yet the energies the humanists poured into recovering, translating, and understanding classical texts (the source of conceptions of the natural world) made many of those important works available for the first time, and to a wider audience. Previously, Arabic sources had provided Europeans with the main route to ancient Greek learning; Greek classics were translated into Arabic and then picked up by late medieval scholars in Spain and Sicily. The humanists' return to the texts themselves—and the fact that the new texts could be more easily printed and circulated—encouraged new study and debate. Islamic scholars knew Ptolemy better than did Europeans until the humanist scholar and printer Johannes Regiomontanus recovered and prepared a new summary of Ptolemy's work. The humanist rediscovery of works by Archimedes—the great Greek mathematician who had proposed that the natural world operated on the basis of mechanical forces, like a great machine, and that these forces could be described mathematically—profoundly impressed important late-sixteenth- and seventeenth-century thinkers, including the Italian scientist Galileo, and shaped mechanical philosophy in the 1600s.

The Renaissance also encouraged collaboration between artisans and intellectuals. Twelfth- and thirteenth-century thinkers had observed the natural world, but they rarely tinkered with machines and they had little contact with the artisans who developed expertise in constructing machines for practical use. During the fifteenth century, however, these two worlds began to come together. Renaissance artists such as Leonardo da Vinci were accomplished craftsmen; they investigated the laws of perspective and optics, they worked out geometric methods for supporting the weight of enormous architectural domes, they studied the human body, and they devised new and more effective weapons for war. The Renaissance brought a vogue for alchemy and astrology; wealthy amateurs built observatories and measured the courses of the stars. These social and intellectual developments laid the groundwork for the scientific revolution.

What of the voyages of discovery? Sixteenth-century observers often linked the exploration of the globe to new knowledge of the cosmos. An admirer wrote to Galileo that he had kept the spirit of exploration alive: "The memory of Columbus and Vespucci will be renewed through you, and with even greater nobility, as the sky is more worthy than the earth." The parallel does not work quite so neatly. Columbus had not been driven by an interest in science.

PTOLEMAIC ASTRONOMICAL INSTRUMENTS. Armillary sphere, 1560s, built to facilitate the observation of planetary positions relative to the earth, in support of Ptolemy's theory of an earth-centered universe. In the sphere, seven concentric rings rotated about different axes. When the outermost ring was set to align with a north–south meridian, and the next was set to align with the celestial pole (the North Star, or the point around which the stars seem to rotate), one could determine the latitude of the place where the instrument was placed. The inner rings were used to track the angular movements of the planets, key measurements in validating the Ptolemaic system. ▪ *What forms of knowledge were necessary to construct such an instrument?* ▪ *How do they relate to the breakthrough that is known as the scientific revolution?*

Moreover, it took centuries for European thinkers to process the New World's implications for different fields of study, and the links between the voyages of discovery and breakthroughs in science were largely indirect. The discoveries made the most immediate impact in the field of natural history, which was vastly enriched by travelers' detailed accounts of the flora and fauna of the Americas. Finding new lands and cultures in Africa and Asia and the revelation of the Americas, a world unknown to the ancients and unmentioned in the Bible, also laid bare gaps in Europeans' inherited body of knowledge. In this sense, the exploration of the New World dealt a blow to the authority of the ancients.

In sum, the late medieval recovery of ancient texts long thought to have been lost, the expansion of print culture and reading, the turmoil in the church and the fierce wars and political maneuvering that followed the Reformation, and the discovery of a new world across the oceans to explore and exploit all shook the authority of older ways of thinking. What we call the scientific revolution was part of the intellectual excitement that surrounded these challenges, and, in retrospect, the scientific revolution enhanced and confirmed the importance of these other developments.

THE COPERNICAN REVOLUTION

Medieval cosmologists, like their ancient counterparts and their successors during the scientific revolution, wrestled with the contradictions between ancient texts and the evidence of their own observations. Their view of an earth-centered universe was particularly influenced by the teachings of Aristotle (384–322 B.C.E.), especially as they were systematized by Ptolemy of Alexandria (100–178 C.E.). In fact, Ptolemy's vision of an earth-centered universe contradicted an earlier proposal by Aristarchus of Samos (310–230 B.C.E.), who had deduced that the earth and other planets revolve around the sun. Like the ancient Greeks, Ptolemy's medieval followers used astronomical observations to support their theory, but the persuasiveness of the model for medieval scholars also derived from the ways that it fit with their Christian beliefs (see Chapter 4). According to Ptolemy, the heavens orbited the earth in a carefully organized hierarchy of spheres. Earth and the heavens were fundamentally different, made of different matter and subject to different laws of motion. The sun, moon, stars, and planets were formed of an unchanging (and perfect) quintessence or ether. The earth, by contrast, was composed of four elements (earth, water, fire, and air), and each of these elements had its natural place: the heavy elements (earth and water) toward the center and the lighter ones farther out. The heavens—first the planets, then the stars—traced perfect circular paths around the stationary earth. The motion of these celestial bodies was produced by a prime mover, whom Christians identified as God. The view fit Aristotelian physics, according to which objects could move only if acted on by an external force, and it fit with a belief that each fundamental element of the universe had a natural place. Moreover, the view both followed from and confirmed belief in the purposefulness of God's universe.

By the late Middle Ages astronomers knew that this cosmology, called the "Ptolemaic system," did not correspond exactly to what many had observed. Orbits did not conform to the Aristotelian ideal of perfect circles. Planets, Mars in particular, sometimes appeared to loop backward before continuing on their paths. Ptolemy had managed to account for these orbital irregularities, but with complicated mathematics. By the early fifteenth century, the efforts to make the observed motions of the planets fit into the model of perfect circles in a geocentric (earth-centered) cosmos had produced astronomical charts that were mazes of complexity. Finally, the Ptolemaic system proved unable to solve serious difficulties with the calendar. That practical crisis precipitated Nicolaus Copernicus's intellectual leap forward.

By the early sixteenth century the old Roman calendar was significantly out of alignment with the movement of the heavenly bodies. The major saints' days, Easter, and the other holy days were sometimes weeks off where they should have been according to the stars. Catholic authorities tried to correct this problem, consulting mathematicians and astronomers all over Europe. One of these was a Polish church official and astronomer, Nicolaus Copernicus (1473–1543). Educated in Poland and northern Italy, he was a man of diverse talents. He was trained in astronomy, canon law, and medicine. He read Greek. He was well versed in ancient philosophy. He was also a careful mathematician and a devout Catholic, who did not believe that God's universe could be as messy as the one in Ptolemy's model. His proposed solution, based on mathematical calculations, was simple and radical: Ptolemy was mistaken; the earth was neither stationary nor at the center of the planetary system; the earth rotated on its axis and orbited with the other planets around the sun. Reordering the Ptolemaic system simplified the geometry of astronomy and made the orbits of the planets comprehensible.

Copernicus was in many ways a conservative thinker. He did not consider his work to be a break with either the church or with the authority of ancient texts. He believed, rather, that he had restored a pure understanding of God's design, one that had been lost over the centuries.

Still, the implications of his theory troubled him. His ideas contradicted centuries of astronomical thought, and they were hard to reconcile with the observed behavior of objects on earth. If the earth moved, why was that movement imperceptible? Copernicus calculated the distance from the Earth to the Sun to be at least six million miles. Even by Copernicus's very low estimate, the earth was hurtling around the sun at the dizzying rate of many thousands of miles an hour. How did people and objects remain standing? (The earth is actually about ninety-three million miles from the sun, moving through space at sixty-seven thousand miles an hour and spinning on its axis at about a thousand miles an hour!)

Copernicus was not a physicist. He tried to refine, rather than overturn, traditional Aristotelian physics, but

his effort to reconcile that physics with his new model of a sun-centered universe created new problems and inconsistencies that he could not resolve. These frustrations and complications dogged Copernicus's later years, and he hesitated to publish his findings. Just before his death, he consented to the release of his major treatise, *On the Revolutions of the Heavenly Spheres* (*De Revolutionibus*), in 1543. To fend off scandal, the Lutheran scholar who saw his manuscript through the press added an introduction to the book declaring that Copernicus's system should be understood as an abstraction, a set of mathematical tools for doing astronomy and not a dangerous claim about the nature of heaven and earth. For decades after 1543, Copernicus's ideas were taken in just that sense—as useful but not realistic mathematical hypotheses. In the long run, however, as one historian puts it, Copernicanism represented the first "serious and systematic" challenge to the Ptolemaic conception of the universe.

TYCHO'S OBSERVATIONS AND KEPLER'S LAWS

Within fifty years, Copernicus's cosmology was revived and modified by two astronomers also critical of the Ptolemaic model of the universe: Tycho Brahe (*TI-koh BRAH-hee*, 1546–1601) and Johannes Kepler (1571–1630). Each was considered the greatest astronomer of his day. Tycho was born into the Danish nobility but he abandoned his family's military and political legacy to pursue his passion for astronomy. He was hotheaded as well as talented; at twenty he lost part of his nose in a duel. Like Copernicus he sought to correct the contradictions in traditional astronomy. Unlike Copernicus, who was a theoretician, Tycho championed observation and believed careful study of the heavens would unlock the secrets of the universe. He first made a name for himself by observing a completely new star, a "nova," that flared into sight in 1572. The Danish king Friedrich II, impressed by Tycho's work, granted him the use of a small island, where he built a castle specially designed to house an observatory. For over twenty years, Tycho meticulously charted the movements of each significant object in the night sky, compiling the finest set of astronomical data in Europe.

Tycho was not a Copernican. He suggested that the planets orbited the sun and the whole system then orbited a stationary earth. This picture of cosmic order, though clumsy, seemed to fit the observed evidence better than the Ptolemaic system, and it avoided the upsetting physical

NICOLAUS COPERNICUS. This anonymous portrait of Copernicus characteristically blends his devotion and his scientific achievements. His scholarly work (behind him in the form of an early planetarium) is driven by his faith (as he turns toward the image of Christ triumphant over death). ■ *What relationship between science and religion is evoked by this image?*

Astronomical Observations and the Mapping of the Heavens

One (often-repeated) narrative about the scientific revolution is that it marked a crucial break separating modern science from an earlier period permeated by an atmosphere of superstition and theological speculation. In fact, medieval scholars tried hard to come up with empirical evidence for beliefs that their faith told them must be true, and without these traditions of observation, scientists like Copernicus would never have been led to propose alternative cosmologies (see "Ptolemaic Astronomical Instruments" on page 495).

The assumption, therefore, that the "new" sciences of the seventeenth century marked an extraordinary rupture with a more ignorant or superstitious past is thus not entirely correct. It would be closer to the truth to suggest that works such as that of Copernicus or Galileo provided a new context for assessing the relationship between observations and knowledge that came from other sources. Printed materials provided opportunities for early modern scientists to learn as much from each other as from more ancient sources.

The illustrations here are from scientific works on astronomy both before and after the appearance of Coperni-

A. The Ptolemaic universe, as depicted in Peter Apian, *Cosmographia* (1540).

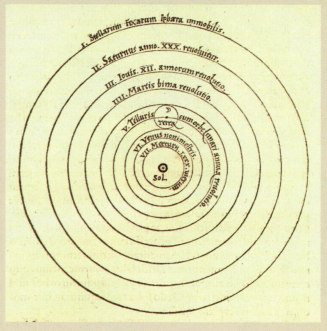

B. The Copernican universe (1543).

and theological implications of the Copernican model. In the late 1590s, Tycho moved his work and his huge collection of data to Prague, where he became court astronomer to the Holy Roman emperor Rudolph II. In Prague he was assisted by a young mathematician from a troubled family, Johannes Kepler. Kepler was more impressed with the Copernican model than was Tycho, and Kepler combined study of Copernicus's work with his own interest in mysticism, astrology, and the religious power of mathematics.

Kepler believed that everything in creation, from human souls to the orbits of the planets, had been created according to mathematical laws. Understanding those laws would thus allow humans to share God's wisdom and penetrate the inner secrets of the universe. Mathematics was

cus's work. All of them were based on some form of observation and claimed to be descriptive of the existing universe. Compare the abstract illustrations of the Ptolemaic (image A) and Copernican (image B) universes with Tycho Brahe's (image C) attempt to reconcile heliocentric observations with geocentric assumptions, or with Galileo's illustration of sunspots (image D) observed through a telescope.

Questions for Analysis

1. What do these illustrations tell us about the relationship between knowledge and observation in sixteenth- and seventeenth-century science? What kinds of knowledge were necessary to produce these images?

2. Are the illustrations A and B intended to be visually accurate, in the sense that they represent what the eye sees?

Can one say the same of D? What makes Galileo's illustration of the sunspots different from the others?

3. Are the assumptions about observation contained in Galileo's drawing of sunspots (D) applicable to other sciences such as biology or chemistry? How so?

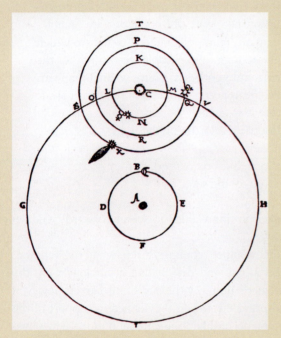

C. Tycho Brahe's universe (c. 1572, A, earth; B, moon; C, sun).

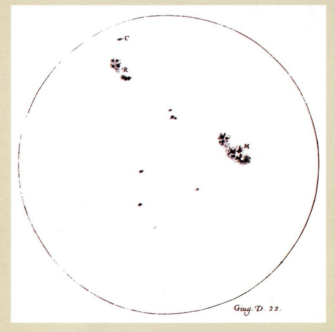

D. Galileo's sunspots, as observed through a telescope (1612).

God's language. Kepler's search for the pattern of mathematical perfection took him through musical harmonies, nested geometric shapes inside the planets' orbits, and numerical formulas. After Tycho's death, Kepler inherited Tycho's position in Prague, as well as his trove of observations and calculations. That data demonstrated to Kepler that two of Copernicus's assumptions about planetary mo-

tion simply did not match observations. Copernicus, in keeping with Aristotelian notions of perfection, had believed that planetary orbits were circular. Kepler calculated that the planets traveled in elliptical orbits around the sun; this finding became his First Law. Copernicus held that planetary motion was uniform; Kepler's Second Law stated that the speed of the planets varied with their distance from the sun. Kepler also argued that magnetic forces between the sun and the planets kept the planets in orbital motion, an insight that paved the way for Newton's law of universal gravitation formulated nearly eighty years later, at the end of the seventeenth century.

Each of Kepler's works, beginning with *Cosmographic Mystery* in 1596 and continuing with *Astronomia Nova* in 1609 and *The Harmonies of the World* in 1619, revised and augmented Copernicus's theory. His version of Copernicanism fit with remarkable accuracy the best observations of the time (which were Tycho's). Kepler's search for rules of motion that could account for the earth's movements in its new position was also significant. More than Copernicus, Kepler broke down the distinction between the heavens and the earth that had been at the heart of Aristotelian physics.

NEW HEAVENS, NEW EARTH, AND WORLDLY POLITICS: GALILEO

Kepler had a friend deliver a copy of *Cosmographic Mystery* to the "mathematician named Galileus Galileus," then teaching mathematics and astronomy at Padua, near Venice. Galileo (1564–1642) thanked Kepler in a letter that nicely illustrates the Italian's views at the time (1597).

> So far I have only perused the preface of your work, but from this I gained some notion of its intent, and I indeed congratulate myself of having an associate in the study of Truth who is a friend of Truth. . . . I adopted the teaching of Copernicus many years ago, and his point of view enables me to explain many phenomena of nature which certainly remain inexplicable according to the more current hypotheses. I have written many arguments in support of him and in refutation of the opposite view—which, however, so far I have not dared to bring into the public light. . . . I would certainly dare to publish my reflections at once if more people like you existed; as they don't, I shall refrain from doing so.

Kepler replied, urging Galileo to "come forward!" Galileo did not answer.

At Padua, Galileo couldn't teach what he believed; Ptolemic astronomy and Aristotelian cosmology were the established curriculum. By the end of his career, however, Galileo had provided powerful evidence in support of the Copernican model and laid the foundation for a new physics. What was more, he wrote in the vernacular (Italian) as well as in Latin. Kepler may have been a "friend of Truth," but his work was abstruse and bafflingly mathematical. (So was Copernicus's.) By contrast, Galileo's writings were widely translated and widely read, raising awareness of changes in natural philosophy across Europe.

Ultimately, Galileo made the case for a new relationship between religion and science, challenging in the process some of the most powerful churchmen of his day. His discoveries made him the most famous scientific figure of his time, but his work put him on a collision course with Aristotelian philosophy and the authority of the Catholic Church.

TYCHO BRAHE, 1662. This seventeenth-century tribute shows the master astronomer in his observatory. ▪ *How much scientific knowledge does one need to understand this image?* ▪ *Is this image, which celebrates science and its accomplishments itself, a scientific statement?* ▪ *What can one learn about seventeenth-century science from such imagery?*

Galileo became famous by way of discoveries with the telescope. In 1609 he heard reports from Holland of a lens grinder who had made a spyglass that could magnify very distant objects. Excited, Galileo quickly devised his own telescope; trained it first on earthly objects to demonstrate that it worked; and then, momentously, pointed it at the night sky. Galileo studied the moon, finding on it mountains, plains, and other features of an earth-like landscape. His observations suggested that celestial bodies resembled the earth, a view at odds with the conception of the heavens as an unchanging sphere of heavenly perfection, inherently and necessarily different from the earth. He saw moons orbiting Jupiter, evidence that earth was not at the center of all orbits. He saw spots on the sun. Galileo published these results, first in *The Starry Messenger* (1610) and then in *Letters on Sunspots* in 1613. *The Starry Messenger,* with its amazing reports of Jupiter's moons, was short, aimed to be read by many, and bold. It only hinted at Galileo's Copernicanism, however. The *Letters on Sunspots* declared it openly.

A seventeenth-century scientist needed powerful and wealthy patrons. As a professor of mathematics, Galileo chafed at the power of university authorities who were subject to church control. Princely courts offered an inviting alternative. The Medici family of Tuscany, like others, burnished its reputation and bolstered its power by surrounding itself with intellectuals as well as artists. Persuaded he would be freer at its court than in Padua, Galileo took a position as tutor to the Medicis and flattered and successfully cultivated the family. He addressed *The Starry Messenger* to them. He named the newly discovered moons of Jupiter "the Medicean stars." He was rewarded with the title of chief mathematician and philosopher to Cosimo de' Medici, the grand duke of Tuscany. Now well positioned in Italy's networks of power and patronage, Galileo was able to pursue his goal of demonstrating that Copernicus's heliocentric (sun-centered) model of the planetary system was correct.

This pursuit, however, was a high-wire act, for he could not afford to antagonize the Catholic Church. In 1614, however, an ambitious and outspoken Dominican monk denounced Galileo's ideas as dangerous deviations from biblical teachings. Other philosophers and churchmen began to ask Galileo's patrons, the Medicis, whether their court mathematician was teaching heresy.

Disturbed by the murmurings against Copernicanism, Galileo penned a series of letters to defend himself, by addressing the relationship between natural philosophy and religion. *Analyzing Primary Sources* on Galileo (see page 502) argued that one could be a sincere Copernican and a sincere Catholic. The church, Galileo said, did the sacred work of teaching scripture and saving souls. Accounting for the workings of the physical world was a task better left to natural philosophy, grounded in observation and mathematics. For the church to take a side in controversies over natural science might compromise the church's spiritual authority and credibility. Galileo envisioned natural philosophers and theologians as partners in a search for truth, but with very different roles. In a brilliant rhetorical moment, he quoted Cardinal Baronius in suppport of his own argument: the purpose of the Bible was to "teach us how to go to heaven, not how heaven goes."

Nevertheless, in 1616, the church moved against Galileo. The Inquisition ruled that Copernicanism was "foolish and absurd in philosophy and formally heretical." Copernicus's *De Revolutionibus* was placed on the Index of Prohibited Books, and Galileo was warned not to teach Copernicanism.

For a while, he did as he was asked. But when his Florentine friend and admirer Maffeo Barberini was elected pope as Urban VIII in 1623, Galileo believed the door to

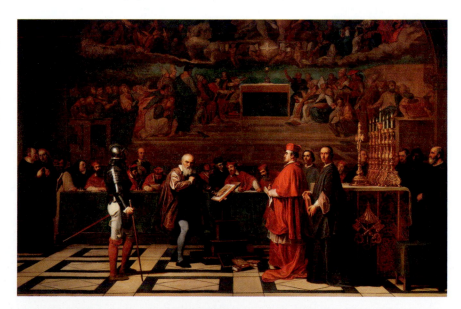

GALILEO GALILEI BEFORE THE INQUISITION BY FRANCOIS RICHARD FLEURY. This nineteenth-century painting of Galileo before the Holy Office dramatizes the conflict between science and religion and depicts the Italian natural philosopher as defiant. In fact, Galileo submitted but continued his work under house arrest and published, secretly, in the Netherlands. ■ *Would Galileo himself have subscribed to the message of this much later painting, that religion and science were opposed to one another?*

Galileo on Nature, Scripture, and Truth

One of the clearest statements of Galileo's convictions about religion and science comes from his 1615 letter to the grand duchess Christina, mother of Galileo's patron, Cosimo de' Medici, and a powerful figure in her own right. Galileo knew that others objected to his work. The church had warned him that Copernicanism was inaccurate and impious; it could be disproved scientifically, and it contradicted the authority of those who interpreted the Bible. Thoroughly dependent on the Medicis for support, he wrote to the grand duchess to explain his position. In this section of the letter, Galileo sets out his understanding of the parallel but distinct roles of the church and natural philosophers. He walks a fine line between acknowledging the authority of the church and standing firm in his convictions.

Possibly because they are disturbed by the known truth of other propositions of mine which differ from those commonly held, and therefore mistrusting their defense so long as they confine themselves to the field of philosophy, these men have resolved to fabricate a shield for their fallacies out of the mantle of pretended religion and the authority of the Bible. . . .

Copernicus never discusses matters of religion or faith, nor does he use arguments that depend in any way upon the authority of sacred writings which he might have interpreted erroneously. He stands always upon physical conclusions pertaining to the celestial motions, and deals with them by astronomical and geometrical demonstrations, founded primarily upon sense experiences and very exact observations. He did not ignore the Bible, but he knew very well that if his doctrine were proved, then it could not contradict the Scriptures when they were rightly understood. . . .

I think that in discussions of physical problems we ought to begin not from the authority of scriptural passages, but from sense-experiences and necessary demonstrations; for the holy Bible and the phenomena of nature proceed alike from the divine Word, the former as the dictate of the Holy Ghost and the latter as the observant executrix of God's commands. It is necessary for the Bible, in order to be accommodated to the understanding of every man, to speak many things which appear to differ from the absolute truth so far as the bare meaning of the words is concerned. But Nature, on the other hand, is inexorable and immutable; she never transgresses the laws imposed upon her, or cares a whit whether her abstruse reasons and methods of operation are understandable to men. For that reason it appears that nothing physical which sense-experience sets before our eyes, or which necessary demonstrations prove to us, ought to be called in question (much less condemned) upon the testimony of biblical passages which may have some different meaning beneath their words. For the Bible is not chained in every expression to conditions as strict as those which govern all physical effects; nor is God any less excellently revealed in Nature's actions than in the sacred statements of the Bible. . . .

Source: Galileo, "Letter to the Grand Duchess Christina," in *The Discoveries and Opinions of Galileo Galilei*, ed. Stillman Drake (Garden City, NY: 1957), pp. 177–183.

Questions for Analysis

1. How does Galileo deal with the contradictions between the evidence of his senses and biblical teachings?

2. For Galileo, what is the relationship between God, man, and nature?

3. Why did Galileo need to defend his views in a letter to Christina de' Medici?

Copernicanism was (at least half) open. He drafted one of his most famous works, *A Dialogue Concerning the Two Chief World Systems* published in 1632. The *Dialogue* was a hypothetical debate between supporters of the old Ptolemaic system, represented by a character he named Simplicio (simpleton) on the one hand and proponents of the new astronomy on the other. Throughout, Galileo gave the best lines to the Copernicans. At the very end, however, to satisfy the letter of the Inquisition's decree, he had them capitulate to Simplicio.

The Inquisition banned the *Dialogue* and ordered Galileo to stand trial in 1633. Pope Urban, provoked by Galileo's scorn and needing support from church conservatives during a difficult stretch of the Thirty Years' War, refused to protect his former friend. The verdict of the secret trial shocked Europe. The Inquisition forced Galileo to repent his Copernican position, banned him from working on or even discussing Copernican ideas, and placed him under house arrest for life. According to a story that began to circulate shortly afterward, as he left the court for house arrest he stamped his foot and muttered defiantly, looking down at the earth: "Still, it moves."

The Inquisition could not put Galileo off his life's work. He refined the theories of motion he had begun to develop early in his career. He proposed an early version of the theory of inertia, which held that an object's motion stays the same until an outside force changed it. He calculated that objects of different weights fall at almost the same speed and with a uniform acceleration. He argued that the motion of objects follows regular mathematical laws. The same laws that govern the motions of objects on earth (which could be observed in experiments) could also be observed in the heavens—again a direct contradiction of Aristotelian principles and an important step toward a coherent physics based on a sun-centered model of the universe. Compiled under the title *Two New Sciences* (1638), this work was smuggled out of Italy and published in Protestant Holland.

Among Galileo's legacies, however, was exactly the rift between religion and science that he had hoped to avoid. Galileo believed that Copernicanism and natural philosophy in general need not subvert theological truths, religious belief, or the authority of the church. But his trial seemed to show the contrary, that natural philosophy and church authority could not coexist. Galileo's trial silenced Copernican voices in southern Europe, and the church's leadership retreated into conservative reaction. It was therefore in northwest Europe that the new philosophy Galileo had championed would flourish.

METHODS FOR A NEW PHILOSOPHY: BACON AND DESCARTES

As the practice of the new sciences became concentrated in Protestant northwest Europe, new thinkers began to spell out standards of practice and evidence. Sir Francis Bacon and René Descartes (*deh-KAHRT*) loomed especially large in this development: setting out methods or the rules that should govern modern science. Bacon (1561–1626) lived at roughly the same time as Kepler and Galileo—and Shakespeare; Descartes (1596–1650) was slightly younger. Both Bacon and Descartes came to believe that theirs was

an age of profound change, open to the possibility of astonishing discovery. Both were persuaded that knowledge could take the European moderns beyond the ancient authorities. Both set out to formulate a philosophy to encompass the learning of their age.

"Knowledge is power." The phrase is Bacon's and captures the changing perspective of the seventeenth century and its new confidence in the potential of human thinking. Bacon trained as a lawyer, served in Parliament and, briefly, as lord chancellor to James I of England. His abiding

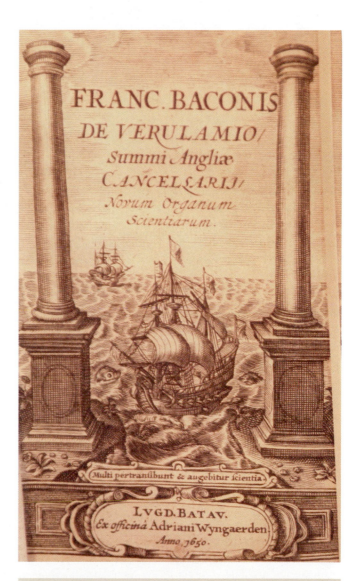

FRONTSPIECE TO BACON'S *NOVUM ORGANUM* (1620). The illustration suggests that scientific work is like a voyage of discovery, similar to a ship setting out through uncharted waters. Is it a voyage of conquest? Compare this image with the fanciful image of Tycho Brahe at work in his observatory (page 500).

■ *What metaphors and allegorical imagery did scientists use during this period to characterize the significance of their work?*

Competing Viewpoints

The New Science and The Foundations of Certainty

Francis Bacon (1561–1626) and René Descartes (1596–1650) were both enthusiastic supporters of science in the seventeenth century, but they differed in their opinions regarding the basis for certainty in scientific argumentation. Bacon's inductive method emphasized the gathering of particular observations about natural phenomena, which he believed could be used as evidence to support more general conclusions about causes, regularity, and order in the natural world. Descartes, on the other hand, defended a deductive method: he believed that certainty could be built only by reasoning from first principles that one knew to be true and was less certain of the value of evidence that came from the senses alone.

Aphorisms From *Novum Organum*

XXXI

It is idle to expect any advancement in science from the superinducing and engrafting of new things upon old. We must begin anew from the very foundations, unless we would revolve forever in a circle with mean and contemptible progress...

XXXVI

One method of delivery alone remains to us which is simply this: we must lead men to the particulars themselves, and their series and order; while men on their side must force themselves for a while to lay their notions by and begin to familiarize themselves with facts...

XLV

The human understanding of its own nature is prone to suppose the existence of more order and regularity in the world than it finds. And though there be many things in nature which are singular and unmatched, yet it devises for them parallels and conjugates and relatives which do not exits. Hence the fiction that all celestial bodies move in perfect circles. ...Hence too the element of fire with its orb is brought in, to make up the square with the other three which the sense perceives... And so on of other dreams. And these fancies affect not dogmas only, but simple notion also...

XCV

Those who have handled sciences have been either men of experiment or men of dogmas. The men of experiment are like the ant, they only collect and use; the reasoners resemble spiders, who make cobwebs out of their own substance. But the bee takes a middle course: it gathers its material from the flowers of the garden and of the field, but transforms and digests it by a power of its own. Not unlike this is the true business of philosophy; for it neither relies solely or chiefly on the powers of the mind, nor does it take the matter which it gathers from natural history and mechanical experiments and lay it up in the memory whole . . . but lays it up in the understanding altered and digested. Therefore, from a closer and purer league between these two faculties, the experimental and the rational (such as has never yet been made), much may be hoped...

Source: Michel R. Matthews, ed., *The Scientific Background to Modern Philosophy:* Selected Readings (Indianapolis, IN: 1989), pp. 47–48, 50–52.

From *A Discourse on Method*

[J]ust as a great number of laws is often a pretext for wrong-doing, with the result that a state is much better governed when, having only a few, they are strictly observed; so also I came to believe that in the place of the great number of precepts that go to make up logic, the following four would be sufficient for my purposes, provided that I took a firm but unshakeable decision never once to depart from them.

The first was never to accept anything as true that I did not *incontrovertibly* know to be so; that is to say, carefully to avoid both *prejudice* and premature conclusions; and to include nothing in my judgments other than that which presented itself to my mind so *clearly* and *distinctly*, that I would have no occasion to doubt it.

The second was to divide all the difficulties under examination into as many parts as possible, and as many as were required to solve them in the best way.

The third was to conduct my thoughts in a given order, beginning with the *simplest* and most easily understood objects, and gradually ascending, as it were step by step, to the knowledge of the most *complex;* and *positing* an order even on those which do not have a natural order of precedence.

The last was to undertake such complete enumerations and such general surveys that I would be sure to have left nothing out.

The long chain of reasonings, every one simple and easy, which geometers habitually employ to reach their most difficult proofs had given me cause to suppose that all those things which fall within the domain of human understanding follow on from each other in the same way, and that as long as one stops oneself taking anything to be true that is not true and sticks to the right order so as to deduce one thing from another, there can be nothing so remote that one cannot eventually reach it, nor so hidden that one cannot discover it. . . .

[B]ecause I wished . . . to concentrate on the pursuit of truth, I came to think that I should . . . reject as completely false everything in which I could detect the least doubt, in order to see if anything thereafter remained in my belief that was completely indubitable. And so, because our senses sometimes deceive us, I decided to suppose that nothing was such as they lead us to imagine it to be. And because there are men who make mistakes in reasoning, even about the simplest elements of geometry, and commit logical fallacies, I judged that I was as prone to error as anyone else, and I rejected as false all the reasoning I had hitherto accepted as valid proof. Finally, considering that all the same thoughts which we have while awake can come to us while asleep without any one of them then being true, I resolved to pretend that everything that had ever entered my head was no more true than the illusions of my dreams. But immediately afterwards I noted that, while I was trying to think of all things being false in this way, it was necessarily the case that I, who was thinking them, had to be something; and observing this truth: *I am thinking therefore I exist,* was so secure and certain that it could not be shaken by any of the most extravagant suppositions of the sceptics, I judged that I could accept it without scruple, as the first principle of the philosophy I was seeking.

Source: René Descartes, *A Discourse on the Method,* trans. Ian Maclean (New York: 2006), pp. 17–18, 28.

Questions for Analysis

1. Descartes's idea of certainty depended on a "long chain of reasonings" that departed from certain axioms that could not be doubted and rejected evidence from the senses. What science provided him with the model for this idea of certainty? What was the first thing that he felt he could be certain about? Did he trust his senses?

2. Bacon's idea of certainty pragmatically sought to combine the benefits of sensory knowledge and experience (gathered by "ants") with the understandings arrived at through reason (cobwebs constructed by "spiders"). How would Descartes have responded to Bacon's claims? According to Bacon, was Descartes an ant or a spider?

3. What do these two thinkers have in common?

concern was with the assumptions, methods, and practices that he believed should guide natural philosophers and the progress of knowledge. The authority of the ancients should not constrain the ambition of modern thinkers. Deferring to accepted doctrines could block innovation or obstruct understanding. "There is but one course left . . . to try the whole thing anew upon a better plan, and to commence a total reconstruction of sciences, arts, and all human knowledge, raised upon the proper foundations." To pursue knowledge did not mean to think abstractly and leap to conclusions; it meant observing, experimenting, confirming ideas, or demonstrating points. If thinkers will be "content to begin with doubts," Bacon wrote, "they shall end with certainties." We thus associate Bacon with the gradual separation of scientific investigation from philosophical argument.

Bacon advocated an *inductive* approach to knowledge: amassing evidence from specific observations to draw general conclusions. In Bacon's view, many philosophical errors arose from beginning with assumed first principles. The traditional view of the cosmos, for instance, rested on the principles of a prime mover and the perfection of circular motion. The inductive method required accumulating data (as Tycho had done, for example) and then, after careful review and experiment, drawing appropriate conclusions. Bacon argued that knowledge was best tested through the cooperative efforts of researchers performing experiments that could be repeated and verified. The knowledge thus gained would be predictable and useful to philosophers and artisans alike, contributing to a wide range of endeavors from astronomy to shipbuilding.

Bacon's vision of science and progress is vividly illustrated by two images. The first, more familiar, is the title page of Bacon's *Novum Organum* (1620) with its bold ships sailing out beyond the Strait of Gibraltar, formerly the limits of the West, into the open sea, in pursuit of unknown but great things to come. The second is Bacon's description of an imagined factory of discovery, "Solomon's house," at end of his utopian *New Atlantis* (1626). Inside the factory, "sifters" would examine and conduct experiments, passing on findings to senior researchers who would draw conclusions and develop practical applications.

René Descartes was French, though he lived all over Europe. He was intellectually restless as well; he worked in geometry, cosmology, optics, and physiology—for a while dissecting cow carcasses daily. He was writing a (Copernican) book on physics when he heard of Galileo's condemnation in 1633, a judgement that impressed on him the dangers of "expressing judgements on this world." Descartes's *The Discourse on Method* (1637), for which he is best known, began simply as a preface to three essays on optics, geometry, and meteorology. It is personal, recounting Descartes's dismay at the "strange and unbelievable" theories he encountered in his traditional education. His first response, as he described it, was to systematically doubt everything he had ever known or been taught. Better to clear the slate, he believed, than to build an edifice of knowledge on received assumptions. His first rule was "never to receive anything as a truth which [he] did not clearly know to be such." He took the human ability to think as his point of departure, summed up in his famous and enigmatic, *Je pense, donc je suis,* later translated into Latin as *cogito ergo sum* and in English as "I think, therefore I am." As the phrase suggests, Descartes's doubting led

FROM RENÉ DESCARTES, *L'HOMME* (1729; ORIGINALLY PUBLISHED AS *DE HOMINI*, 1662).
Descartes's interest in the body as a mechanism led him to suppose that physics and mathematics could be used to understand all aspects of human physiology, and his work had an important influence on subsequent generations of medical researchers. In this illustration, Descartes depicts the optical properties of the human eye. ■ *How might such a mechanistic approach to human perception have been received by proponents of Baconian science, who depended so much on the reliability of human observations?*

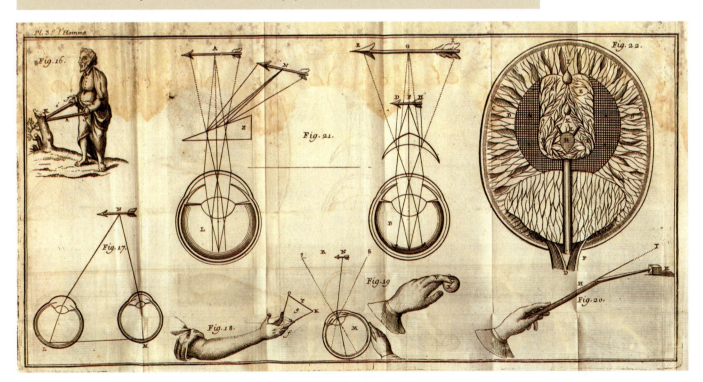

(quickly, by our standards) to self-assurance and truth: the thinking individual existed, reason existed, God existed. For Descartes, then, doubt was a ploy, or a piece that he used in an intellectual chess game to defeat skepticism. Certainty, not doubt, was the centerpiece of the philosophy he bequeathed to his followers.

Descartes, like Bacon, sought a "fresh start for knowledge" or the rules for understanding of the world as it was. Unlike Bacon, Descartes emphasized *deductive* reasoning, proceeding logically from one certainty to another. "So long as we avoid accepting as true what is not so," he wrote in *Discourse on Method*, "and always preserve the right order of deduction of one thing from another, there can be nothing too remote to be reached in the end, or too well hidden to be discovered." For Descartes, mathematical thought expressed the highest standards of reason, and his work contributed greatly to the authority of mathematics as a model for scientific reasoning.

Descartes made a particularly forceful statement for *mechanism*, a view of the world shared by Bacon and Galileo and one that came to dominate seventeenth-century scientific thought. As the name suggested, mechanical philosophy proposed to consider nature as a machine. It rejected the traditional Aristotelian distinction between the works of humans and those of nature and the view that nature, as God's creation, necessarily belonged to a different—and higher—order. In the new picture of the universe that was emerging from the discoveries and writings of the early seventeenth century, it seemed that all matter was composed of the same material and all motion obeyed the same laws. Descartes sought to explain everything, including the human body, mechanically. As he put it firmly, "There is no difference between the machines built by artisans and the diverse bodies that nature alone composes." Nature operated according to regular and predictable laws and was thus accessible to human reason. The belief guided, indeed inspired, much of the scientific experiment and argument of the seventeenth century.

The Power of Method and the Force of Curiosity: Seventeenth-Century Experimenters

For nearly a century after Bacon and Descartes, most of England's natural philosophers were Baconian, and most of their colleagues in France, Holland, and elsewhere in northern Europe were Cartesians (followers of Descartes). The English Baconians concentrated on performing experiments in many different fields, producing results that could then be debated and discussed. The Cartesians turned instead toward mathematics and logic. Descartes himself pioneered analytical geometry. Blaise Pascal (1623–1662) worked on probability theory and invented a calculating machine before applying his intellectual skills to theology. The Cartesian thinker Christian Huygens (1629–1695) from Holland combined mathematics with experiments to understand problems of impact and orbital motion. The Dutch Cartesian Baruch Spinoza (1632–1677) applied geometry to ethics and believed he had gone beyond Descartes by proving that the universe was composed of a single substance that was both God and nature.

English experimenters pursued a different course. They began with practical research, putting the alchemist's tool, the laboratory, to new uses. They also sought a different kind of conclusion: empirical laws or provisional generalizations based on evidence rather than absolute statements of deductive truth. Among the many English laboratory scientists of the era were the physician William Harvey (1578–1657), the chemist Robert Boyle (1627–1691), and the inventor and experimenter Robert Hooke (1635–1703).

Harvey's contribution was enormous: he observed and explained that blood circulated through the arteries, heart, and veins. To do this he was willing to dissect living animals (vivisection) and experiment on himself. Boyle performed experiments and established a law (known as Boyle's law) showing that at a constant temperature the volume of a gas decreases in proportion to the pressure placed on it. Hooke introduced the microscope to the experimenter's tool kit. The compound microscope had been invented in Holland early in the seventeenth century. But it was not until the 1660s that Hooke and others demonstrated its potential by using it to study the cellular structure of plants. Like the telescope before it, the microscope revealed an unexpected dimension of material phenomena. Examining even the most ordinary objects revealed detailed structures of perfectly connected smaller parts and persuaded many that with improved instruments they would uncover even more of the world's intricacies.

The microscope also provided what many regarded as new evidence of God's existence. The way each minute structure of a living organism, when viewed under a microscope, corresponded to its purpose testified not only to God's existence but to God's wisdom as well. The mechanical philosophy did not exclude God but in fact could be used to confirm his presence. If the universe was a clock, after all, there must be a clockmaker. Hooke himself declared that only imbeciles would believe that what they saw under the microscope was "the production of chance" rather than of God's creation.

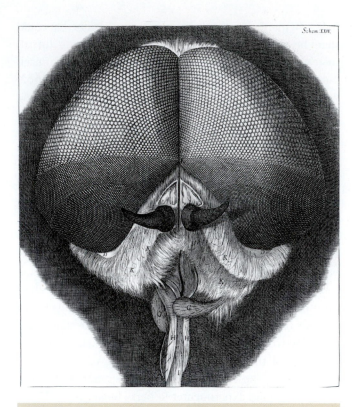

ROBERT HOOKE'S *MICROGRAPHIA*. Hooke's diagram of a fly's eye as seen through a microscope seemed to reveal just the sort of intricate universe the mechanists predicted. ▪ *Compare this image with that of Galileo's sunspots. What do these two images have in common?*

The State, Scientific Academies, and Women Scientists

Seventeenth-century state building (see Chapter 14) helped secure the rise of science. In 1660, England's monarchy was restored after two decades of revolution and civil war. The newly crowned King Charles II granted a group of natural philosophers and mathematicians a royal charter (1662) to establish the Royal Society of London, for the "improvement of natural knowledge" and committed to experimentation and collaborative work among natural philosophers. The founders of the Royal Society, in particular Boyle, believed it could serve a political as well as an intellectual purpose. The Royal Society would pursue Bacon's goal of collective research in which members would conduct formal experiments, record the results, and share them with other members. These members would in turn study the methods, reproduce the experiment, and assess the outcome. The enterprise would give England's natural philosophers a common sense of purpose and a system to reach

reasoned, gentlemanly agreement on "matters of fact." By separating systematic scientific research from the dangerous language of politics and religion that had marked the civil war, the Royal Society could also help restore a sense of order and consensus to English intellectual life.

The society's journal, *Philosophical Transactions,* reached out to professional scholars and experimenters throughout Europe. Similar societies began to appear elsewhere. The French Academy of Sciences was founded in 1666 and was also tied to seventeenth-century state building, in this case Bourbon absolutism (see Chapter 15). Royal societies, devoted to natural philosophy as a collective enterprise, provided a state (or princely) sponsored framework for science and an alternative to the important but uncertain patronage of smaller nobles or to the religious (and largely conservative, Aristotelian) universities. Scientific societies reached rough agreement about what constituted legitimate research. They established the modern scientific custom of crediting discoveries to those who were first to publish results. They enabled information and theories to be exchanged more easily across national boundaries, although philosophical differences among Cartesians, Baconians, and traditional Aristotelians remained very difficult to bridge. Science began to take shape as a discipline.

The early scientific academies did not have explicit rules barring women, but with few exceptions they contained only male members. This did not mean that women did not practice science, though their participation in scientific research and debate remained controversial. In some cases, the new science could itself become a justification for women's inclusion, as when the Cartesian philospher François Poullain de la Barre used anatomy to declare in 1673 that "the mind has no sex." Since women possessed the same physical senses as men and the same nervous systems and brains, Poullain asked, Why should they not equally occupy the same roles in society? In fact, historians have discovered more than a few women who taught at European universities in the sixteenth and seventeenth centuries, above all in Italy. Elena Cornaro Piscopia received her doctorate of philosophy in Padua in 1678, the first woman to do so. Laura Bassi became a professor of physics at the University of Bologna after receiving her doctorate there in 1733, and based on her exceptional contributions to mathematics she became a member of the Academy of Science in Bologna. Her papers—including titles such as "On the Compression of Air" (1746), "On the Bubbles Observed in Freely Flowing Fluid" (1747), "On Bubbles of Air That Escape from Fluids" (1748)—gained her a stipend from the academy.

Italy appears to have been an exception in allowing women to get formal recognition for their education and

FROM MARIA SYBILLA MERIAN, *METAMORPHOSIS OF THE INSECTS OF SURINAM* (1705). Merian, the daughter of a Frankfurt engraver, learned in her father's workshop the skills necessary to become an important early entymologist and scientific illustrator, and conducted her research on two continents.

The construction of observatories in private residences enabled some women living in such homes to work their way into the growing field of astronomy. Between 1650 and 1710, 14 percent of German astronomers were women, the most famous of whom was Maria Winkelmann (1670–1720). Winkelmann had worked with her husband, Gottfried Kirch, in his observatory, and when he died she had already done significant work, discovering a comet and preparing calendars for the Berlin Academy of Sciences. When Kirch died, she petitioned the academy to take her husband's place in the prestigious body, but was rejected. Gottfried Leibniz, the academy's president, explained that "Already during her husband's lifetime the society was burdened with ridicule because its calendar was prepared by a woman. If she were now to be kept on in such capacity, mouths would gape even wider." In spite of this rejection, Winkelmann continued to work as an astronomer, training both her son and two daughters in the discipline.

Like Winkelmann, the entymologist Maria Sibylla Merian (1647–1717) also made a career based on observation. And like Winkelmann, Merian was able to carve out a space for her scientific work by exploiting the precedent of guild women who learned their trade in family workshops. Merian was the daughter of an engraver and illustrator in Frankfurt, and she served as an informal apprentice to her father before beginning her own career as a scientific illustrator, specializing in detailed engravings of insects and plants. Traveling to the Dutch colony of Surinam, Merian supported herself and her two daughters by selling exotic insects and animals she collected and brought back to Europe. She fought the colony's sweltering climate and malaria to publish her most important scientific work, *Metamorphosis of the Insects of Surinam*, which detailed the life cycles of Surinam's insects in sixty ornate illustrations. Merian's *Metamorphosis* was well received in her time; in fact, Peter I of Russia proudly displayed Merian's portrait and books in his study.

research in established institutions. Elsewhere, elite women could educate themselves by associating with learned men. The aristocratic Margaret Cavendish (1623–1673), a natural philosopher in England, gleaned the information necessary to start her career from her family and their friends, a network that included Thomas Hobbes and, while in exile in France in the 1640s, René Descartes. These connections were not enough to overcome the isolation she felt working in a world of letters that was still largely the preserve of men, but this did not prevent her from developing her own speculative natural philosophy and using it to critique those who would exclude her from scientific debate. The "tyrannical government" of men over women, she wrote, "hath so dejected our spirits, that we are become so stupid, that beasts being but a degree below us, men use us but a degree above beasts. Whereas in nature we have as clear an understanding as men, if we are bred in schools to mature our brains."

"AND ALL WAS LIGHT": ISAAC NEWTON

Sir Isaac Newton's work marks the culmination of the scientific revolution. Galileo, peering through his telescope in the early 1600s, had come to believe that the earth and the heavens were made of the same material. Galileo's experiments with pendulums aimed to discover the laws of motion, and he proposed theories of inertia. It was Newton who articulated those laws and presented a coherent, unified vision of how the universe worked. All bodies in the universe, Newton said, whether on earth or in the heavens, obeyed the same basic laws. One set of forces and one pattern, which could be expressed mathematically, explained why planets orbited in ellipses and why (and at what speed) apples fell from trees. An Italian mathematician later commented that Newton was the "greatest and most fortunate of mortals"—because there was only one universe, and he had discovered its laws.

Isaac Newton (1642–1727) was born on Christmas Day to a family of small landowners. His father died before his birth, and it fell to a succession of relatives, family friends, and schoolmasters to spot, then encourage, his genius. In 1661 he entered Trinity College in Cambridge University, where he would remain for the next thirty-five years, first as a student, then as the Lucasian Professor of Mathematics. The man who came to represent the personification of modern science was reclusive, secretive about his findings, and obsessive. During his early work with optics he experimented with his own eyes, pressing them to see how

different shapes would change the effects of light and then, intrigued by what he found, inserting a very thick needle "betwixt my eye and the bone as neare to the backside of my eye as I could" to actually curve his eyeball. (Please do not try this at home.)

Newton's first great burst of creativity came at Cambridge, in the years from 1664 to 1666, "the prime of my age for invention." During these years Newton broke new ground in three areas. The first was optics. Descartes believed that color was a secondary quality produced by the speed of particulate rotation but that light itself was white. Newton, using prisms he had purchased at a local fair, showed that white light was composed of different-colored rays. The second area in which Newton produced innovative work during these years was in mathematics. In a series of brilliant insights, he invented both integral calculus and differential calculus, providing mathematical tools to model motion in space. The third area of his creative genius involved his early works on gravity. Newton later told different versions of the same story: the idea about gravity had come to him when he was in a "contemplative mood" and was "occasioned by the fall of an apple." Why did the apple "not go sideways or upwards, but constantly to the earth's center?" "Assuredly the reason is, that the earth draws it. There must be a drawing power in matter." Voltaire, the eighteenth-century French essayist, retold the story to dramatize Newton's simple brilliance. But the theory of gravity rested on mathematical formulations, it was far from simple, and it would not be fully worked out until *Principia,* more than twenty years later.

Newton's work on the composite nature of white light led him to make a reflecting telescope, which used a curved mirror rather than lenses. The telescope earned him election to the Royal Society (in 1672) and drew him out of his sheltered obscurity at Cambridge. Encouraged by the Royal Society's support, he wrote a paper describing his theory of optics and allowed it to be published in *Philosophical Transactions.* Astronomers and scientists across Europe applauded the work. Robert Hooke, the Royal Society's curator of experiments, did not. Hooke was unpersuaded by Newton's mode of argument; he found Newton's claims that science had to be mathematical both dogmatic and high-handed; and he objected—in a series of sharp exchanges with the reclusive genius—that Newton had not provided any physical explanation for his results. Stung by the conflict with Hooke and persuaded that few natural philosophers could understand his theories, Newton withdrew to Cambridge and long refused to share his work. Only the patient effort of friends and fellow scientists like the astronomer Edmond Halley (1656–1742), already well known for his astronomical observations in the Southern Hemisphere

NEWTON EXPERIMENTING WITH LIGHT. Newton showed that what seemed to be a single ray of light could be broken down into many different ones.

and the person for whom Halley's Comet is named, convinced Newton to publish again.

Newton's *Principia Mathematica* (Mathematical Principles of Natural Philosophy) was published in 1687. It was prompted by a visit from Halley, in which the astronomer asked Newton for his ideas on a question being discussed at the Royal Society: was there a mathematical basis for the elliptical orbits of the planets? Halley's question inspired Newton to expand calculations he had made earlier into an all-encompassing theory of celestial—and terrestrial—dynamics. Halley not only encouraged Newton's work but supervised and financed its publication (though he had less money than Newton); and on several occasions he had to persuade Newton, enraged again by reports of criticism from Hooke and others, to continue with the project and to commit his findings to print.

Principia was long and difficult—purposefully so, for Newton said he did not want to be "baited by little smatterers in mathematics." Its central proposition was that gravitation was a universal force and one that could be expressed mathematically. Newton built on Galileo's work on inertia, Kepler's findings concerning the elliptical orbits of planets, the work of Boyle and Descartes, and even his rival Hooke's work on gravity. He once said, "If I have seen further, it is by standing on the shoulders of giants." But Newton's universal theory of gravity, although it drew on work of others before him, formulated something entirely new. His synthesis offered a single, descriptive account of mass and motion. "All bodies whatsoever are endowed with a principle of mutual gravitation." The law of gravitation was stated in a mathematical formula; supported by observation and experience; and, literally, universal.

The scientific elite of Newton's time was not uniformly persuaded. Many mechanical philosophers, particularly Cartesians, objected to the prominence in Newton's theory of forces acting across empty space. Such attractions smacked of mysticism (or the occult); they seemed to lack any driving mechanism. Newton responded to these criticisms in a note added to the next edition of the *Principia* (*General Scholium*, 1713). He did not know what *caused* gravity, he said, and he did not "feign hypotheses." "For whatever is not deduced from the phenomena must be called hypothesis," he wrote, and has "no place in the experimental philosophy." For Newton, certainty and objectivity lay in the precise mathematical characterization of phenomena—"the mathematization of the universe," as one historian puts it. Science could not, and need not, always uncover causes. It did describe natural phenomena and accurately predict the behavior of objects as confirmed by experimentation.

Other natural philosophers immediately acclaimed Newton's work for solving long-standing puzzles. Thinkers

NEWTON AND SATIRE. The English artist and satirist William Hogarth mocking both philosophy and "Newton worship" in 1763. The philosophers' heads are being weighed on a scale that runs from "absolute gravity" to "absolute levity" or "stark fool."

persuaded that the Copernican version of the universe was right had been unable to piece together the physics of a revolving earth. Newton made it possible to do so. Halley provided a poem to accompany the first edition of *Principia*. "No closer to the gods can any mortal rise," he wrote, of the man with whom he had worked so patiently. Halley did have a financial as well as an intellectual interest in the book, and he also arranged for it to be publicized and reviewed in influential journals. John Locke (whose own *Essay Concerning Human Understanding* was written at virtually the same time, in 1690) read *Principia* twice and summarized it in French for readers across the Channel. By 1713 pirated editions of *Principia* were being published in Amsterdam for distribution throughout Europe. By the time Newton died, in 1727, he had become an English national hero and was given a funeral at Westminster Abbey. The poet Alexander Pope expressed the awe that Newton inspired in some of his contemporaries in a famous couplet:

Nature and nature's law lay hid in night;
God said, "Let Newton be!" and all was light.

Analyzing Primary Sources

Newton on the Purposes of Experimental Philosophy

When Newton added his General Scholium to the second edition of Principia *in 1713, he was seventy-one, president of the Royal Society, and widely revered. Responding to continental critics, he set out his general views on science and its methods, arguing against purely deductive reasoning and reliance on hypotheses about ultimate causes.*

 itherto we have explained the phenomena of the heavens and of our sea by the power of gravity, but have not yet assigned the cause of this power. This is certain, that it must proceed from a cause that penetrates to the very centres of the sun and planets, without suffering the least diminution of its force; that operates not according to the quantity of the surfaces of the particles on which it acts (as mechanical causes used to do), but according to the quantity of the solid matter which they contain, and propagates its virtue on all sides to immense distances, decreasing always as the inverse square of the distances. . . . [H]itherto I have not been able to discover the cause of those properties of gravity from phenomena, and I frame no hypothesis; for whatever is not deduced from the phenomena is to be called an hypothesis and hypotheses, whether metaphysical or physical, whether of occult qualities or mechanical, have no place in experimental philosophy. In this philosophy particular propositions are inferred from the phenomena, and afterwards rendered general by induction. . . . And to us it is enough that gravity does really exist, and acts according to the laws which we have explained, and abundantly serves to account for all the motions of the celestial bodies, and of our sea.

Source: Michael R. Matthews, ed., *The Scientific Background to Modern Philosophy: Selected Readings* (Indianapolis, IN: 1989), p. 152.

Questions for Analysis

1. Why did Isaac Newton declare that "hypotheses, whether metaphysical or physical, whether of occult qualities or mechanical, have no place in experimental philosophy"?

2. Is Newton's thinking similar to Bacon's or does he argue in ways similar to Descartes?

Voltaire, the French champion of the Enlightenment (discussed in the next chapter), was largely responsible for Newton's reputation in France. In this he was helped by a woman who was a brilliant mathematician in her own right, Emilie du Châtelet. Du Châtelet co-authored a book with Voltaire introducing Newton to a French audience; and she translated *Principia*, a daunting scientific and mathematical task and one well beyond Voltaire's mathematical abilities. Newton's French admirers and publicists disseminated Newton's findings. In their eyes Newton also represented a cultural transformation, a turning point in the history of knowledge.

Science and Cultural Change

From the seventeenth century on, science stood at the heart of what it meant to be "modern." It grew increasingly central to the self-understanding of Western culture, and scientific and technological power became one of the justifications for the expansion of Western empires and the subjugation of other peoples. For all these reasons, the scientific revolution was and often still is presented as a thorough-going break with the past, a moment when Western culture was recast. But, as one historian has written, "no house is ever built of entirely virgin materials, according to a plan bearing no resemblance to old patterns, and no body of culture is able to wholly reject its past. Historical change is not like that, and most 'revolutions' effect less sweeping changes than they advertise or than are advertised for them."

To begin with, the transformation we have canvassed in this chapter involved elite knowledge. Ordinary people inhabited a very different cultural world. Second, natural philosophers' discoveries—Tycho's mathematics and Galileo's observations, for instance—did not undo the authority of the ancients in one blow. They did not seek to do so. Third, science did not subvert religion. Even when traditional concepts collapsed in the face of new discoveries, natural philosophers seldom gave up on the project of restoring a picture of a divinely ordered universe. Mechanists argued that the intricate universe revealed by the discoveries of Copernicus, Kepler, Galileo, Newton, and others was evidence of God's guiding presence. Robert Boyle's will provided the funds for a lecture series on the "confutation of atheism" by scientific means. Isaac Newton was happy to have his work contribute to that project. "Nothing," he wrote to one of the lecturers in 1692, "can rejoice me more than to find [*Principia*] usefull for that purpose." The creation of "the Sun and Fixt stars," "the motion which the Planets now have could not spring from any naturall cause alone but were imprest with a divine Agent." Science was thoroughly compatible with belief in God's providential design, at least through the seventeenth century.

The greatest scientific minds were deeply committed to beliefs that do not fit present-day notions of science. Newton, again, is the most striking case in point. The great twentieth-century economist John Maynard Keynes was one of the first to read through Newton's private manuscripts. On the three hundredth anniversary of Newton's birth (the celebration of which was delayed because of the Second World War), Keynes offered the following reappraisal of the great scientist:

I believe that Newton was different from the conventional picture of him . . . .

In the eighteenth century and since, Newton came to be thought of as the first and greatest of the modern age of scientists, a rationalist, one who taught us to think on the lines of cold and untinctured reason.

I do not see him in this light. I do not think that any one who has pored over the contents of that box which he packed up when he finally left Cambridge in 1696 and which, though partly dispersed, have come down to us, can see him like that. Newton was not the first of the age of reason. He was the last of the magicians, the last of the Babylonians and Sumerians, the last great mind

ESTABLISHMENT OF THE ACADEMY OF SCIENCES AND FOUNDATION OF THE OBSERVATORY, 1667. The 1666 founding of the Academy of Sciences was a measure of the new prestige of science and the potential value of research. Louis XIV sits at the center, surrounded by the religious and scholarly figures who offer the fruits of their knowledge to the French state. ▪ *What was the value of science for absolutist rulers like Louis?*

which looked out on the visible and intellectual world with the same eyes as those who began to build our intellectual inheritance rather less than 10,000 years ago.

Like his predecessors, Newton saw the world as a God's message to humanity, a text to be deciphered. Close reading and study would unlock its mysteries. This same impulse led Newton to read accounts of magic, investigate alchemist's claims that base metals could be turned into gold, and to immerse himself in the writings of the church fathers and in the Bible, which he knew in intimate detail. If these activities sound unscientific from the perspective of the present, it is because the strict distinction between rational inquiry and belief in the occult or religious traditions simply did not exist in his time. Such a distinction is a product of the long history of scientific developments after the eighteenth century. Newton, then, was the last representative of an older tradition, and also, quite unintentionally, the first of a new one.

What, then, did the scientific revolution change? Seventeenth-century natural philosophers had produced new answers to fundamental questions about the physical world. Age-old questions about astronomy and physics had been recast and, to some extent (although it was not yet clear to what extent), answered. In the process there had developed a new approach to amassing and integrating information in a systematic way, an approach that helped yield more insights into the workings of nature as time went on. In this period, too, the most innovative scientific work moved out of the restrictive environment of the church and the universities. Natural philosophers began talking to and working with each other in lay organizations that developed standards of research. England's Royal Society spawned imitators in Florence and Berlin and later in Russia. The French Royal Academy of Sciences had a particularly direct relationship with the monarchy and the French state. France's statesmen exerted control over the academy and sought to share in the rewards of any discoveries its members made.

New, too, were beliefs about the purpose and methods of science. The practice of breaking a complex problem down into parts made it possible to tackle more and different questions in the physical sciences. Mathematics assumed a more central role in the new science. Finally,

After You Read This Chapter

Visit StudySpace for quizzes, additional review materials, and multi-media documents. **wwnorton.com/studyspace**

REVIEWING THE OBJECTIVES

- The scientific revolution marked a shift toward new forms of explanation in descriptions of the natural world. What made the work of scientists during this period different from earlier forms of knowledge or research?

- The scientific revolution nevertheless depended on earlier traditions of philosophical thought. What earlier traditions proved important in fostering a spirit of scientific investigation?

- Astronomical observations played a central role in the scientific revolution. What technological innovations made new astronomical work possible and what conclusions did astronomers reach using these new technologies?

- Central to the scientific revolution was the rejection of the Ptolemaic view of the universe and its replacement by the Copernican model. What was this controversy about?

- Francis Bacon and René Descartes had contrasting ideas about scientific method. What approach to science did each of these natural philosophers defend?

rather than simply confirming established truths, the new methods were designed to explore the unknown and provide means to discover new truths. As Kepler wrote to Galileo, "How great a difference there is between theoretical speculation and visual experience, between Ptolemy's discussion of the Antipodes and Columbus's discovery of the New World." Knowledge itself was reconceived. In the older model, to learn was to read: to reason logically, to argue, to compare classical texts, and to absorb a finite body of knowledge. In the newer one, to learn was to discover, and what could be discovered was boundless.

CONCLUSION

The pioneering natural philosophers remained circumspect about their abilities. Some sought to lay bare the workings of the universe; others believed humans could only catalog and describe the regularities observed in nature. By unspoken but seemingly mutual agreement, the question of first causes was left aside. The new science did not say *why*, but *how*. Newton, for one, worked toward explanations that would reveal the logic of creation laid out in mathematics. Yet in the end, he settled for theories explaining motions and relationships that could be observed and tested.

The eighteenth-century heirs to Newton were much more daring. Laboratory science and the work of the scientific societies largely stayed true to the experimenters' rules and limitations. But as we will see in the next chapter, the natural philosophers who began investigating the human sciences cast aside some of their predecessors' caution. Society, technology, government, religion, even the individual human mind seemed to be mechanisms or parts of a larger nature waiting for study. The scientific revolution overturned the natural world as it had been understood for a millennium; it also inspired thinkers more interested in revolutions in society.

PEOPLE, IDEAS, AND EVENTS IN CONTEXT

- How did the traditions of **NEOPLATONISM** and **RENAISSANCE HUMANISM** contribute to a vision of the physical world that encouraged scientific investigation and explanation?
- In what way did the work of **NICOLAS COPERNICUS, TYCHO BRAHE, JOHANNES KEPLER,** and **GALILEO GALILEI** serve to undermine the intellectual foundations of the **PTOLEMAIC SYSTEM?** Why did their work largely take place outside of the traditional centers of learning in Europe, such as universities?
- What differences in scientific practice arose from **FRANCIS BACON'S** emphasis on observation and **RENÉ DESCARTES'S** insistence that knowledge could only be derived from unquestionable first principles?
- What were **ISAAC NEWTON'S** major contributions to the scientific revolution? Why have some suggested that Newton's interests and thinking were not all compatible with modern conceptions of scientific understanding?
- What was important about the establishment of institutions such as the British **ROYAL SOCIETY** or the French **ACADEMY OF SCIENCES** for the development of scientific methods and research?
- What prevented women from entering most of Europe's scientific academies? How did educated women such as **LAURA BASSI, MARGARET CAVENDISH, MARIA WINKELMANN,** and **MARIA SYBILLA MERIAN** gain the skills necessary to participate in scientific work?

CONSEQUENCES

- What long-term social and cultural developments since the medieval period may have encouraged the intellectual openness that was necessary for the ideas of the scientific revolution to take root and flourish?
- How revolutionary was the "scientific revolution" really? Can one really point to this as a period of intellectual or cultural rupture?

STORY LINES

- In the eighteenth century, intellectuals in Britain, France, and (later) elsewhere in Europe sought to answer questions about the nature of good government, morality, and the social order by applying principles of rational argument and empirical investigation. In doing so, they questioned the value of many traditional institutions and insisted that an "enlightened" use of human reason could solve social problems more efficiently than age-old customs or beliefs.

- As a cultural movement, the Enlightenment influenced the beliefs of many more people than did the scientific revolution of the previous century. By this time, more people could read, a larger amount of printed material was in circulation, and Enlightenment authors made a concerted effort to write in ways that a broader audience could understand.

CHRONOLOGY

1734	Voltaire (1694–1778), *Philosophical Letters*
1748	Baron Montesquieu (1689–1755), *The Spirit of Laws*
1748	David Hume (1711–1776), *A Treatise of Human Nature*, 1739–1740, and *Enquiries Concerning Human Understanding*
1751–1772	Denis Diderot (1713–1784), *Encyclopedia*
1762	Jean-Jacques Rousseau (1712–1778), *The Social Contract* and *Emile*
1770	Guillaume Thomas François Raynal (1713–1796), *Philosophical and Political History of European Settlements and Trade in the Two Indies*
1776	Adam Smith (1723–1790), *Inquiry into Nature and Causes of the Wealth of Nations*
1792	Mary Wollstonecraft (1759–1797), *A Vindication of the Rights of Woman*

Before You Read This Chapter

The Enlightenment

n 1762, the *Parlement* (law court) of Toulouse, in France, convicted Jean Calas of murdering his son. Calas was Protestant in a region where Catholic–Protestant tensions ran high. Witnesses claimed that the young Calas had wanted to break with his family and convert to Catholicism, and they convinced the magistrates that Calas had killed his son to prevent this conversion. French law stipulated the punishment. Calas was tortured twice: first to force a confession and, next, as a formal part of certain death sentences, to identify his alleged accomplices. His arms and legs were slowly pulled apart, gallons of water were poured down his throat, and his body was publicly broken on the wheel, which meant that each of his limbs was smashed with an iron bar. Then the executioner cut off his head. Throughout the trial, torture, and execution, Calas maintained his innocence. Two years later, the *Parlement* reversed its verdict, declared Calas not guilty, and offered the family a payment in compensation.

François Marie Arouet, also known as Voltaire, was one of those appalled by the verdict and punishment. At the time of the case, Voltaire was the most famous Enlightenment thinker in Europe. Well connected and a prolific writer, Voltaire took up his pen to clear Calas's name; he contacted friends, hired lawyers for the family, and wrote briefs, letters, and essays to bring the case to the public eye. Calas's case exemplified nearly everything Voltaire opposed in his culture. Intolerance, ignorance, and what Voltaire throughout his life called religious "fanaticism" and "infâmy" had made a travesty of justice. "Shout everywhere, I beg you, for Calas and against fanaticism, for it is *l'infâme* that has caused their misery," he wrote to his friend Jean Le Rond d'Alembert, a fellow Enlightenment thinker. Torture demonstrated the power of the courts but could not uncover the truth. Legal procedures that included secret interrogations, trials behind closed doors, summary judgment (Calas was executed the day after being convicted, with no review by a higher court), and barbaric punishments defied reason, morality, and human dignity. Any criminal, however wretched, "is a man," wrote Voltaire, "and you are accountable for his blood."

Voltaire's comments on the Calas case illustrate the classic concerns of the Enlightenment: the dangers of arbitrary and unchecked authority, the value of religious toleration, and the overriding importance of law, reason, and human dignity in all affairs. He borrowed most of his arguments from others—from his predecessor the Baron de Montesquieu and from the Italian writer Cesare Beccaria, whose *On Crimes and Punishments* appeared in 1764. Voltaire's reputation did not rest on his originality as a philosopher. It came from his effectiveness as a writer and advocate, his desire and ability to reach a wide audience. In this, too, he was representative of the Enlightenment project.

THE FOUNDATIONS OF THE ENLIGHTENMENT

The Enlightenment lasted for most of the eighteenth century. Not every important thinker who lived and worked during these years rallied to the Enlightenment banner. Some, such as the Italian philosopher of history G. B. Vico (1668–1744), opposed almost everything the Enlightenment stood for. Others, most notably Jean-Jacques Rousseau, accepted certain Enlightenment values but sharply rejected others. Patterns of Enlightenment thought varied from country to country, and they changed everywhere over the course of the century. Many eighteenth-century thinkers nonetheless shared the sense of living in an exciting new intellectual environment in which the "party of humanity" would prevail over superstition and traditional thought.

Enlightenment writings shared several basic characteristics. They were marked, first, by a confidence in the powers of human reason. This self-assurance stemmed from the accomplishments of the scientific revolution. Even when the details of Newton's physics were poorly understood, his methods provided a model for scientific inquiry into other phenomena. Nature operated according to laws that could be grasped by study, observation, and thought. The work of the extraordinary Scottish writer David Hume (*A Treatise of Human Nature,* 1739–1740, and the *Enquiries Concerning Human Understanding,* 1748) provided the most direct bridge from science to the Enlightenment. Newton had refused hypotheses, or speculation about ultimate causes, arguing for the precise description of natural phenom-

THE CRUEL DEATH OF CALAS. This print, reproduced in a pamphlet that circulated in Britain in the late eighteenth century, portrayed the French Protestant Jean Calas as a martyr to his beliefs and directly implicated the Roman Catholic Church in the cruelty of his execution by placing an enthusiastic priest prominently at the scene. The pamphlet may also have sought to reinforce anti-French sentiments among an increasingly nationalistic British population. ▪ *How might Enlightenment authors have used such a scene to promote their message of toleration?* ▪ *How might church officials have responded to such attacks?*

ena (see Chapter 16). Hume took this same rigor and skepticism to the study of morality, the mind, and government, often using Newtonian language or drawing analogies to scientific laws. Hume criticized the "passion for hypotheses and systems" that dominated much philisophical thinking. Experience and careful observation, he argued, usually did not support the premises on which those systems rested.

Embracing human understanding and the exercise of human reason also required confronting the power of Europe's traditional monarchies and the religious institutions that supported them. "Dare to know!" the German philosopher Immanuel Kant challenged his contemporaries in his classic 1784 essay "What Is Enlightenment?" For Kant, the Enlightenment represented a declaration of intellectual independence. (He also called it an awakening and credited Hume with rousing him from his "dogmatic slumber.") Kant likened the intellectual history of humanity to the growth of a child. Enlightenment, in this view, was an escape from humanity's "self-imposed immaturity" and a long overdue break with humanity's self-imposed parental figure, the Catholic Church. Coming of age meant the "determination and courage to think without the guidance of someone else," as an individual. Reason required autonomy, or freedom from tradition and well-established authorities.

Despite their declarations of independence from the past, Enlightenment thinkers recognized a great debt to their immediate predecessors. Voltaire called Bacon, Newton, and John Locke his "Holy Trinity." Indeed, much of the eighteenth-century Enlightenment consisted of translating, republishing, and thinking through the implications of the great works of the seventeenth century. Enlightenment thinkers drew heavily on Locke's studies of human knowledge, especially his *Essay Concerning Human Understanding* (1690), which was even more influential than his political philosophy. Locke's theories of how humans acquire knowledge gave education and environment a critical role in shaping human character. All knowledge, he argued, originates from sense perception. The human mind at birth is a "blank tablet" (in Latin, *tabula rasa*). Only when an infant begins to experience things, to perceive the external world with its senses, does anything register in its mind. Locke's starting point, which became a central premise for those who followed, was the goodness and perfectibility of humanity. Building on Locke, eighteenth-century thinkers made education central to their project, because education promised that social progress could be achieved through individual moral improvement. It is worth noting that Locke's theories had potentially more radical implications: if all humans were capable of reason, education might be able to level hierarchies of status, sex, or race. As we will see, only a few Enlightenment thinkers made such egali-

tarian arguments. Still, optimism and a belief in universal human progress constituted a second defining feature of nearly all Enlightenment thinking.

Third, Enlightenment thinkers sought nothing less than the organization of all knowledge. The *scientific method,* by which they meant the empirical observation of particular phenomena to arrive at general laws, offered a way to pursue research in all areas—to study human affairs as well as natural ones. Thus they collected evidence to learn the laws governing the rise and fall of nations, and they compared governmental constitutions to arrive at an ideal and universally applicable political system. As the English poet Alexander Pope stated in his *Essay on Man* (1733), "the science of human nature [may be] like all other sciences

VOLTAIRE'S *CANDIDE.* Voltaire's best-selling novel gently mocked the optimism of some Enlightenment thinkers. The young Candide's tutor, Pangloss, insisted on repeating that "this is the best of all possible worlds," even as he; Candide; and Candide's love, the beautiful Cunegonde, suffered terrible accidents and misfortune. In the scene shown here Candide is kicked out of the castle by Cunegonde's father, with "great kicks in the rear" after they have been caught kissing behind a screen. This mix of serious message and humorous delivery was quite common in Enlightenment literature. ▪ *How might this combination of humor and philosophic meditation have been received by the educated middle-class audience that made up the readership of works such as* **Candide***?*

reduced to a few clear points," and Enlightenment thinkers became determined to learn exactly what those few clear points were. They took up a strikingly wide array of subjects in this systematic manner: knowledge and the mind, natural history, economics, government, religious beliefs, customs of indigenous peoples in the New World, human nature, and sexual (or what we would call gender) and racial differences.

Historians have called the Enlightenment a "cultural project," emphasizing Enlightenment thinkers' interest in practical, applied knowledge and their determination to spread knowledge and to promote free public discussion. They intended, as Denis Diderot (*deed-ROH*) wrote, "to change the common way of thinking" and to advance the cause of "enlightenment" and humanity. Although they shared many of their predecessors' theoretical concerns, they wrote in a very different style and for a much larger audience. Hobbes and Locke had published treatises for small groups of learned seventeenth-century readers. Voltaire, in contrast, wrote plays, essays, and letters; Rousseau composed music, published his *Confessions,* and wrote novels that moved his readers to tears; Hume wrote history for a wide audience. A British aristocrat or a governor in the North American colonies would have read Locke. But a middle-class woman might have read Rousseau's fiction, and shopkeepers and artisans could become familiar with popular Enlightenment-inspired pamphlets. Among the elite, newly formed "academies" sponsored prize essay contests, and well-to-do women and men discussed affairs of state in salons. In other words, the intellectual achievements of the Enlightenment were absorbed by a much broader portion of European society in the course of the eighteenth century. This was possible because of cultural developments that included the expansion of literacy, growing markets for printed material, new networks of readers, and new forms of intellectual exchange. Taken together, these developments marked the emergence of what some historians call the first "public sphere."

THE WORLD OF THE *PHILOSOPHES*

Enlightenment thought was European in a broad sense, including southern and eastern Europe as well as Europe's colonies in the New World. British thinkers played a—perhaps *the*—key role. France, however, provided the stage for some of the most widely read Enlightenment books and the most closely watched battles. For this reason, Enlightenment thinkers, regardless of where they lived, are often called by the French word *philosophes.* Yet hardly any of the *philosophes,* with the exceptions of David Hume and Immanuel Kant, were philosophers in the sense of being highly original abstract thinkers. Especially in France, Enlightenment thinkers shunned forms of expression that might seem incomprehensible, priding themselves instead on their clarity and style. *Philosophe,* in French, simply meant "a free thinker," a person whose reflections were unhampered by the constraints of religion or dogma in any form.

Voltaire

At the time, the best known of the *philosophes* was Voltaire, born François Marie Arouet (1694–1778). As Erasmus two centuries earlier had embodied Christian humanism, Voltaire virtually personified the Enlightenment, commenting on an enormous range of subjects in a wide variety of literary forms. Educated by the Jesuits, he emerged quite young as a gifted and sharp-tongued writer. His gusto for provocation landed him in the Bastille (a notorious prison in Paris) for libel and soon afterward in temporary exile in England. In his three years there, Voltaire became an admirer of British political institutions, British culture, and British science; above all, he became an extremely persuasive convert to the ideas of Newton, Bacon, and Locke. His single greatest accomplishment may have been popularizing Newton's work in France and more generally championing the cause of British empiricism and the scientific method against the more Cartesian French.

Voltaire's *Philosophical Letters* (*Letters on the English Nation*), published after his return in 1734, made an immediate sensation. Voltaire's themes were religious and political liberty, and his weapons were comparisons. His admiration for British culture and politics became a stinging critique of France—and other absolutist countries on the Continent. He praised British open-mindedness and empiricism: the country's respect for scientists and its support for research. He considered the relative weakness of the British aristocracy a sign of Britain's political health. Unlike the French, the British respected commerce and people who engage in it, Voltaire wrote. The British tax system was rational, free of the complicated exemptions for the privileged that were ruining French finances. The British House of Commons represented the middle classes and, in contrast with French absolutism, brought balance to British government and checked arbitrary power. In one of the book's more incendiary passages, he argued that in Britain, violent revolution had actually produced political moderation and stability: "[T]he idol of arbitrary power was drowned in seas of blood. . . . The English nation is the only nation in the world that has succeeded in moderating the power of its kings by resisting them." Of all Britain's reputed virtues, religious toleration loomed largest of all. Britain, Voltaire argued, brought together citizens of different religions in a harmonious and productive culture. In this and other instances, Voltaire oversimplified: British Catholics, Dissenters, and Jews did not have equal civil rights. Yet the British policy of "toleration" did contrast with Louis XIV's intolerance of Protestants. Revoking the Edict of Nantes (1685) had stripped French Protestants of civil rights and had helped create the atmosphere in which Jean Calas—and others—were persecuted.

Of all forms of intolerance Voltaire opposed religious bigotry most, and with real passion he denounced religious fraud, faith in miracles, and superstition. His most famous battle cry was "Écrasez l'infâme!" (Crush this infamous thing), by which he meant all forms of repression, fanaticism, and bigotry. "The less superstition, the less fanaticism; and the less fanaticism, the less misery." He did not oppose religion per se; rather he sought to rescue morality, which he believed to come from God, from

dogma—elaborate ritual, dietary laws, formulaic prayers—and from a powerful church bureaucracy. He argued for common sense and simplicity, persuaded that these would bring out the goodness in humanity and establish stable authority. "The simpler the laws are, the more the magistrates are respected; the simpler the religion will be, the more one will revere its ministers. Religion can be simple. When enlightened people will announce a single God, rewarder and avenger, no one will laugh, everyone will obey."

Voltaire relished his position as a critic, and it never stopped him from being successful. He was regularly exiled from France and other countries, his books banned and burned. As long as his plays attracted large audiences, however, the French king felt he had to tolerate their author. Voltaire had an attentive international public, including Frederick of Prussia, who invited him to his court at Berlin, and Catherine of Russia, with whom he corresponded about reforms she might introduce in Russia. When he died in 1778, a few months after a triumphant return to Paris, he was possibly the best-known writer in Europe.

Montesquieu

The Baron de Montesquieu (*mahn-tuhs-KYOO,* 1689–1755) was a very different kind of Enlightenment figure. Montesquieu was born to a noble family. He inherited both an estate and, since state offices were property that passed from father to son, a position as magistrate in the *Parlement,* or law court, of Bordeaux. He was not a stylist or a provocateur like Voltaire but a relatively cautious jurist, though he did write a satirical novel, *The Persian Letters* (1721), published anonymously (to protect his reputation) in Amsterdam as a young man. The novel was composed as letters from two Persian visitors to France. The visitors detailed the odd religious superstitions they witnessed, compared manners at the French court with those in Turkish harems, and likened French absolutism to their own brands of *despotism,* or the abuse of government authority. *The Persian Letters* was an immediate best-seller, which inspired many imitators, as other authors used the formula of a foreign observer to criticize contemporary French society.

Montesquieu's serious treatise *The Spirit of Laws* (1748) may have been the most influential work of the Enlightenment. It was a groundbreaking study in what we would call comparative historical sociology and very Newtonian in its careful, empirical approach. Montesquieu asked about the structures that shaped law. How had different environments, histories, and religious traditions combined to create such a variety of governmental institutions? What were the different forms of government: what spirit

VOLTAIRE AND FRANKLIN, 1778. Voltaire blesses the grandson of Benjamin Franklin, who stands in the background. The two Enlightenment thinkers met in Paris shortly before Voltaire's death.

characterized each, and what were their respective virtues and shortcomings? Montesquieu suggested that there were three forms of government: republics, monarchies, and despotisms. A republic was governed by many—either an elite aristocracy or the people as a whole. The soul of a republic was virtue, which allowed individual citizens to transcend their particular interests and rule in accordance with the common good. In a monarchy, on the other hand, one person ruled in accordance with the law. The soul of a monarchy, wrote Montesquieu, was honor, which gave individuals an incentive to behave with loyalty toward their sovereign. The third form of government, despotism, was rule by a single person unchecked by law or other powers. The soul of despotism was fear, since no citizen could feel secure and punishment took the place of education. Lest this seem abstract, Montesquieu devoted two chapters to the French monarchy, in which he spelled out what he saw as a dangerous drift toward despotism in his own land. Like other Enlightenment thinkers, Montesquieu admired the British system and its separate and balanced powers—executive, legislative, and judicial—which guaranteed liberty in the sense of freedom from the absolute power of any single governing individual or group. His idealization of "checks and balances" had formative influence on Enlightenment political theorists and members of the governing elites, particularly those who wrote the United States Constitution in 1787.

Diderot and the Encyclopedia

Voltaire's and Montesquieu's writings represent the themes and style of the French Enlightenment. But the most remarkable French publication of the century was a collective one: the *Encyclopedia*. The *Encyclopedia* claimed to summarize all the most advanced contemporary philosophical, scientific, and technical knowledge, making it available to any reader. In terms of sheer scope, this was the grandest statement of the *philosophes'* goals. It demonstrated how scientific analysis could be applied in nearly all realms of thought. It aimed to reconsider an enormous range of traditions and institutions and to put reason to the task of bringing happiness and progress to humanity. The guiding spirit behind the venture was Denis Diderot. Diderot was helped by the Newtonian mathematician Jean Le Rond d'Alembert (1717–1783) and other leading men of letters, including Voltaire and Montesquieu. The *Encyclopedia* was published, in installments, between 1751 and 1772; by the time it was completed, it ran to seventeen large volumes of text and eleven more of illustrations, and contained over seventy-one thousand articles. A collaborative project, it helped create the *philosophes'* image as the "party of humanity."

Diderot commissioned articles on science and technology, showing how machines worked and illustrating new industrial processes. The point was to demonstrate how the everyday applications of science could promote progress and alleviate all forms of human misery. Diderot turned the same methods to matters of politics and the foundations of the social order, including articles on economics, taxes, and the slave trade. Censorship made it difficult to write openly antireligious articles. Diderot, therefore, thumbed his nose at religion in oblique ways; at the entry on the Eucharist, the reader found a terse cross-reference: "See *cannibalism*." Gibes like this aroused storms of controversy when the early volumes of the *Encyclopedia* appeared. The French government revoked the publishing permit for the *Encyclopedia*, declaring in 1759 that the encyclopedists were trying to "propagate materialism" (which meant atheism) "to destroy Religion, to inspire a spirit of independence, and to nourish the corruption of morals." The volumes sold remarkably well despite such bans and their hefty price. Purchasers belonged to the elite: aristocrats, government officials, prosperous merchants, and a scattering of members of the higher clergy. That elite, though, stretched across Europe, including its overseas colonies.

MONTESQUIEU. The French baron's *The Spirit of Laws* (1748) was probably the most influential single text of the Enlightenment. Montesquieu's suggestion that liberty could best be preserved in a government whose powers were divided between executive, legislative, and judicial functions had a notable influence on the authors of the United States Constitution.

TECHNOLOGY AND INDUSTRY. This engraving, from the mining section, is characteristic of Diderot's *Encyclopedia*. The project aimed to detail technological changes, manufacturing processes, and forms of labor—all in the name of advancing human knowledge.

ship, and Great Britain also produced important Enlightenment thinkers: the historian Edward Gibbon and the Scottish philosophers David Hume and Adam Smith. The *philosophes* considered Thomas Jefferson and Benjamin Franklin part of their group. Despite stiffer resistance from religious authorities, stricter state censors, and smaller networks of educated elites, the Enlightenment flourished across central and southern Europe. Frederick II of Prussia housed Voltaire during one of his exiles from France, though the *philosophe* quickly wore out his welcome. Frederick also patronized a small but unusually productive group of Enlightenment thinkers. Northern Italy was an important center of Enlightenment thought. Enlightenment thinkers across Europe raised similar themes: humanitarianism, or the dignity and worth of all individuals; religious toleration; and liberty.

Although the French *philosophes* sparred with the state and the church, they sought political stability and reform. Montesquieu, not surprising in light of his birth and position, hoped that an enlightened aristocracy would press for reforms and defend liberty against a despotic king. Voltaire, persuaded that aristocrats would represent only their particular narrow interests, looked to an enlightened monarch for leadership. Neither was a democrat, and neither conceived of reform from below. Still, their widely read writings were subversive. Their satires of absolutism and, more broadly, arbitrary power, stung. By the 1760s the French critique of despotism provided the language in which many people across Europe articulated their opposition to existing regimes.

Among the most influential writers of the entire Enlightenment was the Italian (Milanese) jurist Cesare Beccaria (1738–1794). Beccaria's *On Crimes and Punishments* (1764) sounded the same general themes as did the French *philosophes*—a critique of arbitrary power and respect for reason and human dignity—and it provided Voltaire with most of his arguments in the Calas case. Beccaria also proposed concrete legal reforms. He attacked the prevalent view that punishments should represent society's vengeance on the criminal. The only legitimate rationale for punishment was to maintain social order and to prevent other crimes. Beccaria argued for the greatest possible leniency compatible with deterrence; respect for individual dignity dictated that humans should punish other humans no more than is absolutely necessary. Above all, Beccaria's book eloquently opposed torture and the death penalty. The spectacle of public execution, which sought to dramatize the power of the state and the horrors of hell, dehumanized the victim, judge, and spectators. In 1766, a few years after the Calas case, another French trial provided an example of what horrified Beccaria and the *philosophes*. A nineteen-year-old French nobleman, convicted of blasphemy, had his tongue cut out and his hand cut off before he was burned at the stake. Since the court discovered the blasphemer had read Voltaire, it ordered the *Philosophical Dictionary* burned along with the body. Sensational cases such as this one helped publicize Beccaria's work, and *On Crimes and Punishments* was quickly translated into a dozen languages. Owing primarily to its

INTERNATIONALIZATION OF ENLIGHTENMENT THEMES: HUMANITARIANISM AND TOLERATION

The party of humanity was international. French became the lingua franca of much Enlightenment discussion, but "French" books were often published in Switzerland, Germany, and Russia. As we have seen, Enlightenment thinkers admired British institutions and British scholar-

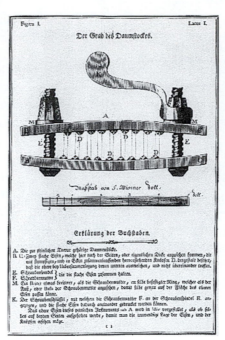

INSTRUMENTS OF TORTURE. A man being stretched on the rack (left) and a thumbscrew (right), both from an official Austrian government handbook. By 1800, Beccaria's influence had helped phase out the use of such instruments.

influence, most European countries by around 1800 abolished torture, branding, whipping, and mutilation and reserved the death penalty for capital crimes.

Humanitarianism and reason also counseled religious toleration. Enlightenment thinkers spoke almost as one on the need to end religious warfare and the persecution of heretics and religious minorities. It is important, though, to differentiate between the church as an institution and dogma, against which many Enlightenment thinkers rebelled, and as religious belief, which most accepted. Only a few Enlightenment thinkers, notably Paul Henri d'Holbach (1723–1789), were atheists, and an only a slightly greater number were avowed agnostics. Many (Voltaire, for instance) were deists, holding a religious outlook that saw God as a "divine clockmaker" who, at the beginning of time, constructed a perfect timepiece and then left it to run with predictable regularity. Enlightenment inquiry proved compatible with very different stances on religion.

Enlightenment support for toleration was limited. Most Christians saw Jews as heretics and Christ killers. And although Enlightenment thinkers deplored persecution, they commonly viewed Judaism and Islam as backward religions, mired in superstition and obscurantist ritual. One of the few Enlightenment figures to treat Jews sympathetically was the German *philosophe* Gotthold Lessing (1729–1781). Lessing's extraordinary play *Nathan the Wise* (1779) takes place in Jerusalem during the Fourth Crusade and begins with a pogrom—or violent, orchestrated attack—in which the wife and children of Nathan, a Jewish merchant, are murdered. Nathan survives to become a sympathetic and wise father figure. He adopts a Christian-born daughter and raises her with three religions: Christianity, Islam, and Judaism. At several points, authorities ask him to choose the single true religion. Nathan shows none exists. The three great monotheistic religions are three versions of the truth. Religion is authentic, or true, only insofar as it makes the believer virtuous.

Lessing modeled his hero on his friend Moses Mendelssohn (1729–1786), a self-educated rabbi and bookkeeper (and the grandfather of the composer Felix Mendelssohn). Moses Mendelssohn moved—though with some difficulty—between the Enlightenment circles of Frederick II and the Jewish community of Berlin. Mendelssohn unsuccessfully tried to avoid religion as a subject. Repeatedly attacked and invited to convert to Christianity, he finally took up the question of Jewish identity. In a series of writings, the best-known of which is *On the Religious Authority of Judaism* (1783), he defended Jewish communities against anti-Semitic policies and Jewish religion against Enlightenment criticism. At the same time, he also promoted reform within the Jewish community, arguing that his community had special reason to embrace the broad Enlightenment project: religious faith should be voluntary, states should promote tolerance, humanitarianism would bring progress to all.

Economics, Government, and Administration

Enlightenment ideas had a very real influence over affairs of state. The *philosophes* defended reason and knowledge for humanitarian reasons. But they also promised to make nations stronger, more efficient, and more prosperous. Beccaria's proposed legal reforms were a good case in point; he sought to make laws not simply more just but also more effective. In other words, the Enlightenment spoke to individuals but also to states. The *philosophes* addressed issues of liberty and rights but also took up matters of administration, tax collection, and economic policy.

The rising fiscal demands of eighteenth-century states and empires made these issues newly urgent. Which eco-

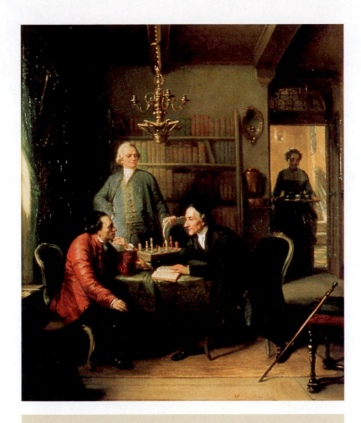

LESSING AND MENDELSSOHN. This painting of a meeting between the *philosophe* Gotthold Lessing (standing) and his friend Moses Mendelssohn (seated right) emphasizes the personal nature of their intellectual relationship, which transcended their respective religious backgrounds (Christian and Jewish, respectively). The Enlightenment's atmosphere of earnest discussion is invoked both by the open book before them and the shelf of reading material behind Lessing. Compare this image of masculine discussion (note the role of the one woman in the painting) with the image of the aristocratic salon on page 538 and the coffeehouse on page 540. ▪ *What similarities and differences might one point to in these various illustrations of the Enlightenment public sphere?*

(1723–1790), and especially from Smith's landmark treatise *Inquiry into the Nature and Causes of the Wealth of Nations* (1776). Smith disagreed with the physiocrats on the value of agriculture, but he shared their opposition to mercantilism. For Smith, the central issues were the productivity of labor and how labor was used in different sectors of the economy. Mercantile restrictions—such as high taxes on imported goods, one of the grievances of the colonists throughout the American empires—did not encourage the productive deployment of labor and thus did not create real economic health. For Smith, general prosperity could best be obtained by allowing the famous "invisible hand" to guide economic activity. Individuals, in other words, should pursue their own interests without competition from state-chartered monopolies or legal restraints. As Smith wrote in his earlier *Theory of Moral Sentiments* (1759), self-interested individuals could be "led by an invisible hand . . . without knowing it, without intending it, [to] advance the interest of the society."

The Wealth of Nations spelled out, in more technical and historical detail, the different stages of economic development, how the invisible hand actually worked, and the beneficial aspects of competition. Its perspective owed much to Newton and to the Enlightenment's idealization of both nature and human nature. Smith wanted to follow what he called, in classic Enlightenment terms, the "obvious and simple system of natural liberty." Smith thought of himself as the champion of justice against state-sponsored economic privilege and monopolies. He was also a theorist of human feelings as well as of market forces. Smith emerged as the most influential of the new eighteenth-century economic thinkers. In the following century, ironically, his work and his followers became the target of reformers and critics of the new economic world.

nomic resources were most valuable to states? Enlightenment economic thinkers such as the physiocrats argued that long-standing mercantilist policies were misguided. By the eighteenth century, *mercantilism* had become a term for a very wide range of policies based on government regulation of trade (see Chapter 15). The physiocrats, most of them French, held that real wealth came from the land and agricultural production. More important, they advocated simplifying the tax system and following a policy of laissez-faire, which comes from the French expression *laissez faire la nature* ("let nature take its course"), letting wealth and goods circulate without government interference.

The now-classic expression of laissez-faire economics, however, came from the Scottish economist Adam Smith

EMPIRE AND ENLIGHTENMENT

Smith's *Wealth of Nations* formed part of a debate about the economics of empire: *philosophes* and statesmen alike asked how the colonies could be profitable, and to whom. The colonial world loomed large in Enlightenment thinking in several other ways. Enlightenment thinkers saw the Americas through a highly idealized vision, as an uncorrupted territory where humanity's natural simplicity was expressed in the lives of native peoples. In comparison, Europe and Europeans appeared decadent or corrupt. Second, Europeans' colonial activities—especially, by the eighteenth century, the slave trade—could not help but

The Impact of the New World on Enlightenment Thinkers

The Abbé Guillaume Thomas François Raynal (1713–1796) was a clergyman and intellectual who moved in the inner circles of the Enlightenment. As a senior cleric he had access to the royal court; as a writer and intellectual he worked with the encyclopedists and other authors who criticized France's institutions, including the Catholic Church of which Raynal himself was a part. Here he tries to offer a perspective on the profound effects of discovering the Americas and ends by asking whether particular historical developments and institutions lead to the betterment of society.

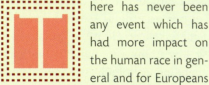 here has never been any event which has had more impact on the human race in general and for Europeans in particular, as that of the discovery of the New World, and the passage to the Indies around the Cape of Good Hope. It was then that a commercial revolution began, a revolution in the balance of power, and in the customs, the industries and the government of every nation. It was through this event that men in the most distant lands were linked by new relationships and new needs. The produce of equatorial regions were consumed in polar climes. The industrial products of the north were transported to the south; the textiles of the Orient became the luxuries of Westerners; and everywhere men mutually exchanged their opinions, their laws, their customs, their illnesses, and their medicines, their virtues and their vices. Everything changed, and will go on changing. But will the changes of the past and those that are to come be useful to humanity? Will they give man one day more peace, more happiness, or more pleasure? Will his condition be better, or will it be simply one of constant change?

Source: Abbé Guillaume Thomas François Raynal, *Philosophical and Political History of European Settlements and Trade in the Two Indies* (1770), as cited in Dourinda Outram, *The Enlightenment* (Cambridge: 1995), p. 73.

Questions for Analysis

1. Why does Raynal attribute such significance to the voyages of exploration that connected Europe to the Americas and to Africa and Asia? Which peoples were changed by these voyages?

2. Why is Raynal concerned with people's conduct and happiness, rather than, say, the wealth of states?

3. Is Raynal clear about whether the changes he enumerates are a gain or a loss for humanity?

raise pressing issues about humanitarianism, individual rights, and natural law. The effects of colonialism on Europe were a central Enlightenment theme.

Smith wrote in *The Wealth of Nations* that the "discovery of America, and that of a passage to the East Indies by the cape of Good Hope are the two greatest and most important events recorded in the history of mankind. What benefits, or what misfortunes to mankind may hereafter result from those great events," he continued, "no human wisdom can foresee." Smith's language was nearly identical to that of a Frenchman, the Abbé Guillaume Thomas François Raynal. Raynal's massive *Philosophical and Political History of European Settlements and Trade in the Two Indies* (1770), a co-authored work like the *Encyclopedia*, was one of the most widely read works of the Enlightenment, going through twenty printings and at least forty pirated editions. Raynal drew his inspiration from the *Encyclopedia* and aimed at nothing less than a total history of colonization: customs and civilizations of indigenous peoples, natural history, exploration, and commerce in the Atlantic world and India.

Raynal also asked whether colonization had made humanity happier, more peaceful, or better. The question was fully in the spirit of the Enlightenment. So was the answer: Raynal believed that industry and trade brought improvement and progress. Like other Enlightenment writers, however, he and his co-authors considered natural simplicity an antidote to the corruptions of their culture. They sought out and idealized what they considered examples of "natural" humanity, many of them in the New World. For example, they wrote that what Europeans considered savage life might be "a hundred times preferable to that of societies corrupted by despotism" and lamented the loss of humanity's "natural liberty." They condemned the tactics of the Spanish in Mexico and Peru, of the Portuguese in Brazil, and of the British in North America. They echoed Montesquieu's theme that good government required checks and balances against arbitrary authority. In the New World, they argued, Europeans found themselves with virtually unlimited power, which encouraged them to be arrogant, cruel, and despotic. In a later edition, after the outbreak of the American Revolution, the book went even further, drawing parallels between exploitation in the colonial world and inequality at home: "We are mad in the way we act with our colonies, and inhuman and mad in our conduct toward our peasants," asserted one author. Eighteenth-century radicals repeatedly warned that overextended empires sowed seeds of decadence and corruption at home.

Slavery and the Atlantic World

Discussing Europe's colonies and economies inevitably raised the issue of slavery. The sugar islands of the Caribbean were among the most valued possessions of the colonial world and the sugar trade one of the leading sectors of the Western economy. The Atlantic slave trade reached its peak in the eighteenth century. European slave traders sent at least one million Africans into New World slavery in the late seventeenth century, and at least six million in the eighteenth century. On this topic, however, even thinkers as radical as Raynal and Diderot hesitated, and their hesitations are revealing about the tensions in Enlightenment thought. Enlightenment thinking began with the premise that individuals could reason and govern themselves. Individual moral freedom lay at the heart of what the Enlightenment considered to be a just, stable, and harmonious society. Slavery defied natural law and natural freedom. Montesquieu, for instance, wrote that civil law created chains, but natural law would always break them. Nearly all Enlightenment thinkers condemned slavery in the metaphorical sense. That the "mind should break free of its chains" and that "despotism enslaved the king's subjects" were phrases that echoed through much eighteenth-century writing. It was common for the central characters of eighteenth-century fiction, such as Voltaire's hero Candide, to meet enslaved people, learning compassion as part of their moral education. Writers dealt more gingerly, however, with the actual enslavement and slave labor of Africans.

Some Enlightenment thinkers skirted the issue of slavery. Others reconciled principle and practice in different ways. Smith condemned slavery as uneconomical. Voltaire, quick to expose his contemporaries' hypocrisy, wondered whether Europeans would look away if Europeans—rather than Africans—were enslaved. Voltaire, however, did not question his belief that Africans were inferior peoples. Montesquieu (who came from Bordeaux, one of the central ports for the Atlantic trade) believed that slavery debased master and slave alike. But he also argued that all societies balanced their systems of labor in accordance with their different needs, and slave labor was one such system. Finally, like many Enlightenment thinkers, Montesquieu defended property rights, including those of slaveholders.

The *Encyclopedia's* article on the slave trade did condemn the slave trade in the clearest possible terms, as a violation of self-government. Humanitarian antislavery movements, which emerged in the 1760s, advanced similar arguments. From deploring slavery to imagining freedom for slaves, however, proved a very long step, and one that few were willing to take. In the end, the Enlightenment's environmental determinism—the belief that environment shaped character—provided a common way of postponing the entire issue. Slavery corrupted its victims, destroyed their natural virtue, and crushed their natural love of liberty. Enslaved people, by this logic, were not ready for freedom. It was characteristic for Warville de Brissot's Society of the Friends of Blacks to call for abolition of the slave trade and to invite Thomas Jefferson, a slaveholder, to join the organization. Only a very few advocated abolishing slavery, and they insisted that emancipation be gradual. The debate about slavery demonstrated that different currents in Enlightenment thought could lead to very different conclusions.

Exploration and the Pacific World

The Pacific world also figured prominently in Enlightenment thinking. Systematically mapping new sections of the Pacific was among the crucial developments of the age, and one with a tremendous impact on the public imagination. These explorations were also scientific missions, sponsored as part of the Enlightenment project of expanding scientific knowledge. In 1767 the French government sent Louis-Anne de Bougainville (1729–1811) to the South Pacific in search of a new route to China, new lands suitable for colonization, and new spices for the ever lucrative trade. They sent along scientists and artists to record his findings. Like many other explorers, Bougainville found none of what he sought, but his travel accounts—above all his fabulously lush descriptions of the earthly paradise of Nouvelle-Cythère, or Tahiti—captured the attention and imaginations of many at home. The British captain James Cook (1728–1779), who followed Bougainville, made two trips into the South Pacific (1768–1771 and 1772–1775),

Analyzing Primary Sources

Slavery and the Enlightenment

The encyclopedists made an exhaustive and deliberate effort to comment on every institution, trade, and custom in Western culture. The project was conceived as an effort to catalog, analyze, and improve each facet of society. Writing in an age of burgeoning maritime trade and expanding overseas empires, they could not, and did not wish to, avoid the subject of slavery. These were their thoughts on plantation slavery, the African slaves who bore its brunt, and broader questions of law and liberty posed by the whole system.

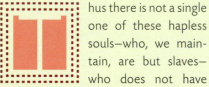hus there is not a single one of these hapless souls—who, we maintain, are but slaves—who does not have the right to be declared free, since he has never lost his freedom; since it was impossible for him to lose it; and since neither his ruler nor his father nor anyone else had the right to dispose of his freedom; consequently, the sale of his person is null and void in and of itself: this Negro does not divest himself, indeed cannot under any condition divest himself of his natural rights; he carries them everywhere with him, and he has the right to demand that others allow him to enjoy those rights. Therefore, it is a clear case of inhumanity on the part of the judges in those free countries to which the slave is shipped, not to free the slave instantly by legal declaration, since he is their brother, having a soul like theirs.

Source: From *Encyclopédie,* Vol. 16 (1765), as cited in David Brion Davis, *The Problem of Slavery in Western Culture* (Ithaca, NY: 1966), p. 416.

Questions for Analysis

1. What arguments against slavery does the *Encyclopedia* article present? What "natural rights" were violated by the practice, according to this view?

2. The enslavement of conquered peoples was historically an ancient and well-established custom, approved by civil and religious authorities. Even some Enlightenment figures, such as Thomas Jefferson, were slave owners. How did some Enlightenment *philosophes* use universal ideas of freedom to argue against custom in regard to slavery and other questions?

---

with impressive results. He charted the coasts of New Zealand and New Holland and added the New Hebrides and Hawaii to European maps. He explored the outer limits of the Antarctic continent, the shores of the Bering Sea, and the Arctic Ocean. The artists and scientists who accompanied Cook and Bougainville vastly expanded the boundaries of European botany, zoology, and geology. Their drawings—such as Sydney Parkinson's extraordinary portraits of the Maori and William Hodge's portraits of Tahitians—appealed to a wide public. So did the accounts of dangers overcome and peoples encountered. A misguided attempt to communicate with South Pacific islanders, perhaps with the intention of conveying them to Europe, ended in the grisly deaths of Cook and four royal marines on Hawaii in late January 1779, which surely added to European readers' fascination with his travels. Large numbers of people in Europe avidly read travel accounts of these voyages. When Cook and Bougainville brought Pacific islanders to the metropolis they attracted large crowds. Joshua Reynolds painted portraits of the islanders.

THE IMPACT OF THE SCIENTIFIC MISSIONS

Back in Europe, Enlightenment thinkers drew freely on reports of scientific missions. Since they were already committed to understanding human nature and the origins of society and to studying the effects of the environment on character and culture, stories of new peoples and cultures were immediately fascinating. In 1772 Diderot, one of many eager readers of Bougainville's accounts, published his own reflections on the cultural significance of those accounts, the *Supplément au Voyage de Bougainville.* For Diderot, the Tahitians were the original human beings and, unlike the inhabitants of the New World, were virtually free of European influence. They represented humanity in its natural state, Diderot believed, uninhibited about sexuality and free of religious dogma. Their simplicity exposed the hypocrisy and rigidity of overcivilized Europeans. Others considered the indigenous peoples of the Pacific akin to the classical civilizations of Greeks and Romans, associating Tahitian women, for instance, with Venus, the Roman goddess of love. All these views said more about Europe and European utopias than about indigenous cultures in the Pacific. Enlightenment thinkers found it impossible to see other peoples as anything other than primitive versions of Europeans. Even these views, however, marked a change from former times. In earlier periods Europeans had understood the world as divided between Christendom and heathen others. In sum, during the eighteenth century a religious understanding of Western identity was giving way to more secular and historical conceptions.

One of the most important scientific explorers of the period was the German scientist Alexander von Humboldt. Humboldt spent five years in Spanish America, aiming to do nothing less than assess the civilization and natural resources of the continent. He went equipped with the most advanced scientific instruments Europe could provide. Between 1814 and 1819, Humboldt produced an impressive multivolume *Personal Narratives of Travels* much like the lavishly illustrated reports by Cook and Bougainville. The expense bankrupted him, sending him to the Prussian court in search of financial support. Humboldt's investigations provide an important link between the Enlightenment and nineteenth-century science. Humboldt, in good Enlightenment fashion, attempted to demonstrate that climate and physical environment determined which forms of life would survive in any given region. These investigations would continue in nineteenth-century discussions of evolutionary change. Charles Darwin referred to Humboldt as "the greatest scientific traveler who ever lived," and the German scientist's writing inspired Darwin's voyage to the Galapagos Islands off the coast of Ecuador.

Thus Europeans who looked outward did so for a variety of reasons and reached very different conclusions. For some Enlightenment thinkers and rulers, scientific reports from overseas fitted into a broad inquiry about civilization and human nature. That inquiry at times encouraged self-criticism and at others simply shored up Europeans' sense

MAORIS IN A WAR CANOE NEAR LOOKOUT POINT. This copy of an illustration by Sidney Parkinson, who accompanied James Cook's explorations, is typical of the images of the South Pacific that may have circulated in Europe in the late eighteenth century.
■ *What questions might have been prompted among Enlightenment thinkers by an increased awareness of different cultures throughout the globe?*

of their superiority. These themes reemerged during the nineteenth century, when new empires were built and the West's place in the world was reassessed.

THE RADICAL ENLIGHTENMENT

How revolutionary was the Enlightment? Enlightenment thought did undermine central tenets of eighteenth-century culture and politics. It had wide resonance, well beyond a small group of intellectuals. Yet Enlightenment thinkers did not hold to any single political position. Even the most radical among them disagreed on the implications of their thought. Jean-Jacques Rousseau and Mary Wollstonecraft provide good examples of such radical thinkers.

The World of Rousseau

Jean-Jacques Rousseau (*roo-SOH,* 1712–1778) was an "outsider" who quarreled with the other *philosophes* and contradicted many of their assumptions. He shared the *philosophes'* search for intellectual and political freedom, attacked inherited privilege, and believed in the good of humanity and the possibility of creating a just society. Yet he introduced other strains into Enlightenment thought, especially morality

The Europeans Encounter the Peoples of the Pacific in the Eighteenth Century

When European explorers set out to map the Pacific, they brought with them artists to paint the landscapes and peoples they encountered. Later, other artists produced engravings of the original paintings and these engravings were made available to a wider public. In this way, even people of modest means or only limited literacy could learn something about the different cultures and peoples that were now in more regular contact with European commerce elsewhere in the world.

These artists documented what they saw, but their vision was also shaped by the ideas that they brought with them and by the classical European styles of portraiture and landscape painting that they had been trained to produce. On the one hand, their images sometimes emphasized the exotic or essentially different quality of life in the Pacific. At the same time, the use of conventional poses in the portraiture or in the depiction of human forms suggested hints of a developing understanding of the extent to which Europeans and people elsewhere in the world shared essential

A. *Portrait of Omai* by Joshua Reynolds (c. 1774).

B. "Omiah [*sic*] the Indian from Otaheite, presented to their Majesties at Kew," 1774

and what was then called "sensibility," or the cult of feeling. Rousseau's interest in emotions led him to develop a more complicated portrait of human psychology than that of Enlightenment writers, who emphasized reason as the most important attribute of human beings. He was also considerably more radical than his counterparts, one of the first to talk about popular sovereignty and democracy. He was surely the most utopian, which made his work popular at the time and has opened it to different interpretations since. In the late eighteenth century he was the most influential and most often cited of the *philosophes*, the thinker who brought the Enlightenment to a larger audience.

Rousseau's milestone and difficult treatise on politics, *The Social Contract*, began with a now famous paradox: "Man was born free, and everywhere he is in chains." How had humans freely forged these chains? To ask this was to reformulate the key questions of seventeenth- and eighteenth-century thought. What were the origins of government? Was government's authority legitimate? If not, Rousseau asked, how could it become so? Rousseau argued that in the state of nature, all men had been equal. (On women, men, and nature, see pages 536–537.) Social inequality, anchored in private property, profoundly corrupted "the social contract," or the formation of government. Under conditions

C. *View of the Inside of a House in the Island of Ulietea, with the Representation of a Dance to the Music of the Country*, engraving after Sydney Parkinson, 1773.

voyage to the Pacific in 1768 (image C). The two artists had never visited the South Pacific, and their image is noteworthy for the way that the bodies of the islanders were rendered according to the classical styles of European art (see also the image on page 529).

Questions for Analysis

1. Does the Reynolds portrait, in its choice of posture and expression, imply that Europeans and the peoples of the Pacific might share essential traits? What uses might Enlightenment thinkers have made of such a universalist implication?

2. How might a contemporary person in Britain have reacted to the portrait of Omai kneeling before the king?

3. Do you think image C is an accurate representation of life in the South Pacific? What purpose did such imaginary and idyllic scenes serve for their audience in Europe?

human characteristics. This ambiguity was typical of Enlightenment political and social thought, which sought to uncover universal human truths, while at the same time, remaining deeply interested and invested in exploring the differences they observed in peoples from various parts of the globe.

The first two images depict a Tahitian named Omai, who came to Britain as a crew member on a naval vessel in July 1774. Taken three days later to meet King George III and Queen Charlotte at Kew (image B), he became a celebrity in England and had his portrait drawn by Joshua Reynolds, a famous painter of the period (image A). The third image is an engraving by two Florentine artists after a drawing by Sydney Parkinson, who was with James Cook on his first

of inequality, governments and laws represented only the rich and privileged. They became instruments of repression and enslavement. Legitimate governments could be formed, Rousseau argued. "The problem is to find a form of association . . . in which each, while uniting himself with all, may still obey himself alone, and remain as free as before." Freedom did not mean the absence of restraint, it meant that equal citizens obeyed laws they had made themselves. Rousseau hardly imagined any social leveling, and by *equality* he meant only that no one would be "rich enough to buy another, nor poor enough to have to sell oneself."

Rousseau believed that legitimate authority arose from the people alone. His argument has three parts. First, sovereignty belonged to the people alone. This meant sovereignty should not be divided among different branches of government (as suggested by Montesquieu), and it emphatically could not be usurped by a king. In the late seventeenth century, Locke had spelled out the people's right to rebel against a tyrannical king. Rousseau argued that a king never became sovereign to begin with since the people could not legitimately delegate their sovereignty to any person or body. Second, exercising sovereignty transformed the nation. Rousseau argued that when individual citizens formed a "body politic," that body became more than just the sum of its parts. He offered what was to many an appealing image of a regenerated and more powerful nation, in which citizens were bound by mutual obligation rather than coercive laws and united in equality rather than divided and weakened by privilege. Third, the national community would be united by what Rousseau called the "general will." This term is notoriously difficult. Rousseau proposed it as a way to understand the common interest, which rose above particular individual demands. The general will favored equality; that made it general, and in principle at least equality guaranteed that citizens' common interests would be represented in the whole.

Rousseau's lack of concern for balancing private interests against the general will leads some political theorists to consider him authoritarian, coercive, or moralistic. Others interpret the general will as one expression of his utopianism. In the eighteenth century, *The Social Contract* was the least understood of Rousseau's works. Yet it provided influential radical arguments and, more important, extraordinarily powerful images and phrases, which were widely cited during the French Revolution.

Rousseau was better known for his writing on education and moral virtue. His widely read novel *Emile* (1762) tells the story of a young man who learns virtue and moral autonomy in the school of nature rather than in the academy. Rousseau disagreed with other *philosophes'* emphasis on reason, insisting instead that "the first impulses of nature are always right." Children should not be forced to reason early in life. Books, which "teach us only to talk about things we do not know," should not be central to learning until adolescence. Emile's tutor thus walked him through the woods, studying nature and its simple precepts, cultivating his conscience and, above all, his sense of independence. "Nourished in the most absolute liberty, the greatest evil he can imagine is servitude."

Such an education aimed to give men moral autonomy and make them good citizens. Rousseau argued that women should have very different educations. "All education of women must be relative to men, pleasing them, being useful to them, raising them when they are young and caring for them when they are old, advising them, consoling them, making their lives pleasant and agreeable, these have been the duties of women since time began." Women were to be useful socially as mothers and wives. In *Emile*, Rousseau laid out just such an education for Emile's wife-to-be, Sophie. At times, Rousseau seemed convinced that women "naturally" sought out such a role: "Dependence is a natural state for women, girls feel themselves made to obey." At other moments he insisted that girls needed to be disciplined and weaned from their "natural" vices.

Rousseau's conflicting views on female nature provide a good example of the shifting meaning of *nature,* a concept central to Enlightenment thought. Enlightenment thinkers used nature as a yardstick against which to measure society's shortcomings. "Natural" was better, simpler, uncorrupted. What, though, was nature? It could refer to the physical world. It could refer to allegedly primitive societies. Often, it was a useful invention.

Rousseau's novels sold exceptionally well, especially among women. *Julie* (subtitled *La nouvelle Héloïse*), published just after *Emile*, went through seventy editions in three decades. *Julie* tells the story of a young woman who falls in love with one man but dutifully obeys her father's order to marry another. At the end, she dies of exposure after rescuing her children from a cold lake—a perfect example of domestic and maternal virtue. What appealed to the public, was the love story, the tragedy, and Rousseau's conviction that humans were ruled by their hearts as much as their heads, that passion was more important than reason. Rousseau's novels became part of a larger cult of *sensibilité* ("feeling") in middle-class and aristocratic circles, an emphasis on

ENLIGHTENMENT EDUCATION AS ILLUSTRATED IN *EMILE*. These colored engravings from Rousseau's influential novel depict Emile's studies in the great outdoors as opposed to the classroom.

Analyzing Primary Sources

Rousseau's Social Contract (1762)

Jean-Jacques Rousseau (1712–1778) was one of the most radical Enlightenment thinkers. In his works he suggested that humans needed not only a clearer understanding of natural laws but also a much closer relationship with nature itself and a thorough reorganization of society. He believed that a sovereign society, formed by free association of equal citizens without patrons or factions, was the clearest expression of natural law. This society would make laws and order itself by the genuinely collective wisdom of its citizens. Rousseau sets out the definition of his sovereign society and its authority in the passages reprinted here.

Book I, Chapter 6

"To find a form of association that defends and protects the person and possessions of each associate with all the common strength, and by means of which each person, joining forces with all, nevertheless obeys only himself, and remains as free as before." Such is the fundamental problem to which the social contract furnishes the solution.

Book II, Chapter 4

What in fact is an act of sovereignty? It is not an agreement between a superior and an inferior, but an agreement between the body and each of its members, a legitimate agreement, because it is based upon the social contract; equitable, because it is common to all; useful, because it can have no other purpose than the general good; and reliable, because it is guaranteed by the public force and the supreme power. As long as the subjects are only bound by agreements of this sort, they obey no one but their own will, and to ask how far the respective rights of the sovereign and citizens extend is to ask to what point the latter can commit themselves to each other, one towards all and all towards one.

Source: Jean-Jacques Rousseau, *Rousseau's Political Writings,* trans. Julia Conaway Bondanella, eds. Allan Ritter and Julia Conaway Bondanella (New York: 1988), pp. 92–103.

Questions for Analysis

1. What was the goal of political association according to Rousseau?

2. How did Rousseau claim to overcome the tension between the need for some form of social constraint and the desire to preserve liberty?

3. What is more important for Rousseau: equality or liberty?

---

spontaneous expressions of feeling, and a belief that sentiment was an expression of authentic humanity. Thematically, this aspect of Rousseau's work contradicted much of the Enlightenment's cult of reason. It is more closely related to the concerns of nineteenth-century romanticism.

How did Rousseau's ideas fit into Enlightenment views on gender? As we have seen, Enlightenment thinkers considered education key to human progress. Many lamented the poor education of women, especially because, as mothers, governesses, and teachers, many women were charged with raising and teaching children. What kind of education, however, should girls receive? Here, again, Enlightenment thinkers sought to follow the guidance of nature, and they produced scores of essays and books in philosophy, history, literature, and medicine, discussing the nature or character of the sexes. Were men and women different? Were those differences natural, or had they been created by custom and tradition? Humboldt and Diderot wrote essays on the nature

of the sexes; scientific travel literature reported on the family structures of indigenous peoples in the Americas, the South Pacific, and China. Histories of civilization by Adam Smith among many others commented on family and gender roles at different stages of history. Montesquieu's *The Spirit of Laws* included an analysis of how the different stages of government affected women. To speculate on the subject, as Rousseau did, was a common Enlightenment exercise.

Some disagreed with his conclusions. Diderot, Voltaire, and the German thinker Theodor Von Hippel, among many others, deplored legal restrictions on women. Rousseau's prescriptions for women's education drew especially sharp criticism. The English writer and historian Catherine Macaulay set out to refute his points. The Marquis de Condorcet argued on the eve of the French Revolution that the Enlightenment promise of progress could not be fulfilled unless women were educated—and Condorcet was virtually alone in asserting that women should be granted political rights.

The World of Wollstonecraft

Rousseau's sharpest critic was the British writer Mary Wollstonecraft (1759–1797). Wollstonecraft published her best known work, *A Vindication of the Rights of Woman,* in 1792, during the French Revolution. Her argument, however, was anchored in Enlightenment debates and needs to be understood here. Wollstonecraft shared Rousseau's political views and admired his writing and influence. Like Rousseau and her countryman Thomas Paine, a writer who supported the American and French revolutions, Wollstonecraft was a republican. She called monarchy "the pestiferous purple which renders the progress of civilization a curse, and warps the understanding." She spoke even more forcefully than Rousseau against inequality and the artificial distinctions of rank, birth, or wealth. Believing that equality laid the basis for virtue, she contended, in classic Enlightenment language, that the society should seek "the perfection of our nature and capability of happiness." She argued more forcefully than any other Enlightenment thinker that (1) women had the same innate capacity for reason and self-government as men, (2) *virtue* should mean the same thing for men and women, and (3) relations between the sexes should be based on equality.

Wollstonecraft did what few of her contemporaries even imagined. She applied the radical Enlightenment critique of monarchy and inequality to the family. The legal inequalities of marriage law, which among other things deprived married women of property rights, gave husbands "despotic" power over their wives. Just as kings cultivated their subjects' deference, so culture, she argued, cultivated women's weakness. "Civilized women are . . . so weakened by false refinement, that, respecting morals, their condition is much below what it would be were they left in a state nearer to nature." Middle-class girls learned manners, grace, and seductiveness to win a husband; they were trained to be dependent creatures. "My own sex, I hope, will excuse me, if I treat them like rational creatures instead of flattering their *fascinating* graces, and viewing them as if they were in a state of perpetual childhood, unable to stand alone. I earnestly wish to point out in what true dignity and human happiness consists—I wish to persuade women to endeavor to acquire strength, both of mind and body." A culture that encouraged feminine weakness produced women who were childish, cunning, cruel—and vulnerable. Here Wollstonecraft echoed common eighteenth-century themes. The scheming aristocratic women in Choderlos de Laclos's *Dangerous Liaisons,* written in the 1780s, were meant to illustrate the same points. To Rousseau's specific prescriptions for female education,

which included teaching women timidity, chasteness, and modesty, Wollstonecraft replied that Rousseau wanted women to use their reason to "burnish their chains rather than to snap them." Instead, education for women had to promote liberty and self-reliance.

Wollstonecraft was a woman of her time. She argued for the common humanity of men and women but believed that they had different duties and that women's foremost responsibility was mothering and educating children. Like many of her fellow Enlightenment thinkers, Wollstonecraft believed that a natural division of labor existed and that it would ensure social harmony. "Let there be no coercion *established* in society, and the common law of gravity prevailing, the sexes will fall into their proper places." Like others, she wrote about middle-class women, for whom education and property were issues. She was considered scandalously radical for merely hinting that women might have political rights.

The Enlightenment as a whole left a mixed legacy on gender, one that closely paralleled that on slavery. Enlightenment writers developed and popularized arguments about natural rights. They also elevated natural differences to a higher plane by suggesting that nature should dictate different, and quite possibly unequal, social roles. Mary Wollstonecraft and Jean-Jacques Rousseau shared a radical opposition to despotism and slavery, a moralist's vision of a corrupt society, and a concern with virtue and community. Their divergence

MARY WOLLSTONECRAFT. The British writer and radical suggested that Enlightenment critiques of monarchy could also be applied to the power of fathers within the family.

on gender is characteristic of Enlightenment disagreements about nature and its imperatives and a good example of different directions in which the logic of Enlightenment thinking could lead.

THE ENLIGHTENMENT AND EIGHTEENTH-CENTURY CULTURE

The Book Trade

What about the social structures that produced these debates and received these ideas? To begin with, the Enlightenment was bound up in a much larger expansion of printing and print culture. From the early eighteenth century on, book publishing and selling flourished, especially in Britain, France, the Netherlands, and Switzerland. National borders, though, mattered very little. Much of the book trade was both international and clandestine. Readers bought books from stores, by subscription, and by special mail order from book distributors abroad. Cheaper printing and better distribution also helped multiply the numbers of journals, some specializing in literary or scientific topics and others quite general. They helped bring daily newspapers, which first appeared in London in 1702, to Moscow, Rome, and cities and towns throughout Europe. By 1780, Britons could read 150 different magazines, and 37 English towns had local newspapers. These changes have been called a "revolution in communication," and they form a crucial part of the larger picture of the Enlightenment.

Governments did little to check this revolutionary transformation. In Britain, the press encountered few restrictions, although the government did use a stamp tax on printed goods to raise the price of newspapers or books and discourage buyers. Elsewhere, laws required publishers to apply in advance for the license or privilege (in the sense of "private right") to print and sell any given work. Some regimes granted more permissions than others. The French government, for instance, alternately banned and tolerated different volumes of the *Encyclopedia,* depending on the subjects covered in the volume, the political climate in the capital, and economic considerations. In practice, publishers frequently printed books without advance permission, hoping that the regime would not notice, but bracing themselves for fines, having their books banned, and finding their privileges temporarily revoked. Russian, Prussian, and Austrian censors tolerated much less dissent; but those governments also sought to stimulate publishing and, to a certain degree, permitted public discussion. Vienna housed an important publishing empire during the reigns of Joseph and Maria Theresa. Catherine of Russia encouraged the development of a small publishing enterprise which, by 1790, was issuing 350 titles a year. In the smaller states of Germany and Italy, governed by many local princes, it was easier to find progressive local patrons, and English and French works also circulated widely through those regions. That governments were patrons as well as censors of new scholarship illustrates the complex relationship between the age of absolutism and the Enlightenment.

As one historian puts it, censorship only made banned books expensive, keeping them out of the hands of the poor. Clandestine booksellers, most near the French border in Switzerland and the Rhineland, smuggled thousands of books across the border to bookstores, distributors, and private customers. What did readers want, and what does this tell us about the reception of the Enlightenment? Many clandestine dealers specialized in what they called "philosophical books," which meant subversive literature of all kinds: stories of languishing in prison, gossipy memoirs of life at the court, pornographic fantasies (often about religious and political figures), and tales of crime and criminals. A book smuggler would have carried several copies of *The Private Lives of Louis XIV* or *The Black Gazette;* Voltaire's comments on *Encyclopedia;* and, less frequently, Rousseau's *Social Contract.* Much of this flourishing eighteenth-century "literary underground," as the historian Robert Darnton calls it, echoed the radical Enlightenment's themes, especially the corruption of the aristocracy and the monarchy's degeneration into despotism. Less explicitly political writings, however, such as Raynal's *History,* Rousseau's novels, travel accounts, biographies, and futuristic fantasies such as Louis Sebastien Mercier's *The Year 2440* proved equally popular. Even expensive volumes like the *Encyclopedia* sold remarkably well, testifying to a keen public interest. It is worth underscoring that Enlightenment work circulated in popular form, and that Rousseau's novels sold as well as his political theory.

High Culture, New Elites, and the Public Sphere

The Enlightenment was not simply embodied in books; it was produced in networks of readers and new forms of sociability and discussion. Eighteenth-century elite or "high" culture was small in scale but cosmopolitan and very literate, and it took discussion seriously. A new elite joined together members of the nobility and wealthy people from the middle classes. Among the institutions that produced this new elite were learned societies: the American Philosophical

Competing Viewpoints

Rousseau and His Readers

Jean-Jacques Rousseau's writings provoked very different responses from eighteenth-century readers—women as well as men. Many women readers loved his fiction and found his views about women's character and prescriptions for their education inspiring. Other women disagreed vehemently with his conclusions. In the first excerpt here, from Rousseau's novel Emile (1762), the author sets out his views on a woman's education. He argues that her education should fit with what he considers her intellectual capacity and her social role. It should also complement the education and role of a man. The second selection is an admiring response to Emile from Anne-Louise-Gennaine Necker, or Madame de Staël (1766–1817), a well-known French writer and literary critic. While she acknowledged that Rousseau sought to keep women from participating in political discussion, she also thought that he had granted women a new role in matters of emotion and domesticity. The third excerpt is from Mary Wollstonecraft, who shared many of Rousseau's philosophical principles but sharply disagreed with his assertion that women and men should have different virtues and values. She believed that women like Madame de Staël were misguided in embracing Rousseau's ideas.

Rousseau's Emile

Researches into abstract and speculative truths, the principles and axioms of sciences—in short, everything which tends to generalize our ideas—is not the proper province of women; their studies should be relative to points of practice; it belongs to them to apply those principles which men have discovered.... All the ideas of women, which have not the immediate tendency to points of duty, should be directed to the study of men, and to the attainment of those agreeable accomplishments which have taste for their object; for as to works of genius, they are beyond their capacity; neither have they sufficient precision or power of attention to succeed in sciences which require accuracy; and as to physical knowledge, it belongs to those only who are most active, most inquisitive, who comprehend the greatest variety of objects....

She must have the skill to incline us to do everything which her sex will not enable her to do herself, and which is necessary or agreeable to her; therefore she ought to study the mind of man thoroughly, not the mind of man in general, abstractedly, but the dispositions of those men to whom she is subject either by the laws of her country or by the force of opinion. She should learn to penetrate into the real sentiments from their conversation, their actions, their looks and gestures. She should also have the art, by her own conversation, actions, looks, and gestures, to communicate those sentiments which are agreeable to them without seeming to intend it. Men will argue more philosophically about the human heart; but women will read the heart of men better than they.... Women have most wit, men have most genius; women observe, men reason. From the concurrence of both we derive the clearest light and the most perfect knowledge which the human mind is of itself capable of attaining.

Source: Jean-Jacques Rousseau, Emile (1762), as cited in Mary Wollstonecraft, A Vindication of the Rights of Woman (New York: 1992), pp. 124–125.

Society of Philadelphia, British literary and philosophical societies, and the Select Society of Edinburgh. Such groups organized intellectual life outside of the universities, and they provided libraries, meeting places for discussion, and journals that published members' papers or organized debates on issues from literature and history to economics and ethics. Elites also met in "academies," financed by governments to advance knowledge, whether through research into the natural sciences (the Royal Society of London, and the French Academy of Science, both founded in 1660), promoting the national language (the Académie Française, or French Academy of Literature), or safeguarding traditions in the arts (the various academies of painting). The Berlin Royal Academy, for instance, was founded in 1701 to demonstrate the Prussian state's commitment to learning. Members included scholars in residence, corresponding

Madame De Staël

Though Rousseau has endeavoured to prevent women from interfering in public affairs, and acting a brilliant part in the theatre of politics; yet in speaking of them, how much has he done it to their satisfaction! If he wished to deprive them of some rights foreign to their sex, how has he for ever restored to them all those to which it has a claim! And in attempting to diminish their influence over the deliberations of men, how sacredly has he established the empire they have over their happiness! In aiding them to descend from an usurped throne, he has firmly seated them upon that to which they were destined by nature; and though he be full of indignation against them when they endeavour to resemble men, yet when they come before him with all the *charms, weaknesses, virtues,* and *errors* of their sex, his respect for their *persons* amounts almost to adoration.

Source: Cited in Mary Wollstonecraft, *A Vindication of the Rights of Woman* (New York: 1992), pp. 203–204.

Mary Wollstonecraft

Rousseau declares that a woman should never, for a moment, feel herself independent, that she should be governed by fear to exercise her *natural* cunning, and made a coquettish slave in order to render her a more alluring object of desire, a *sweeter* companion to man, whenever he chooses to relax himself. He carries the arguments, which he pretends to draw from the indications of nature, still further, and insinuates that truth and fortitude, the corner stones of all human virtue, should be cultivated with certain restrictions, because, with respect to the female character, obedience is the grand lesson which ought to be impressed with unrelenting rigour.

What nonsense! When will a great man arise with sufficient strength of mind to puff away the fumes which pride and sensuality have thus spread over the subject! If women are by nature inferior to men, their virtues must be the same in quality, if not in degree, or virtue is a relative idea; consequently, their conduct should be founded on the same principles, and have the same aim.

Source: Cited in Susan Bell and Karen Offen, eds., *Women, the Family, and Freedom: The Debate in Documents,* Vol. 1, *1750–1880* (Stanford, CA: 1983), p. 58.

Questions for Analysis

1. Why did Rousseau seek to limit the sphere of activities open to women in society? What capacities did he feel they lacked? What areas of social life did he feel women were most suited for?

2. Did Madame de Staël agree with Rousseau that women's social roles were essentially different from men's roles in society?

3. What is the basis for Mary Wollstonecrafts's disagreement with Rousseau?

4. Why did gender matter to Enlightenment figures such as Rousseau, de Staël, and Wollstonecraft?

---

members in other countries, and honorary associates, so the academy's reach was quite broad; and the Prussian government made a point of bringing in scholars from other countries. Particularly under Frederick II, who was eager to sponsor new research, the Berlin Academy flourished as a center of Enlightenment thinking. The academy's journal published members' papers every year, in French, for a European audience. In France, provincial academies played much the same role. Works such as Rousseau's *Discourse on the Origins of Inequality* were entered in academy-sponsored essay contests. Academy members included government and military officials, wealthy merchants, doctors, noble landowners, and scholars. Learned societies and academies both brought together different social groups (most from the elite); and in so doing, they fostered a sense of common purpose and seriousness.

SALONS

Salons did the same but operated informally. Usually they were organized by well-connected and learned aristocratic women. The prominent role of women distinguished the salons from the academies and universities. Salons brought together men and women of letters with members of the aristocracy for conversation, debate, drink, and food. Rousseau loathed this kind of ritual and viewed salons as a sign of superficiality and vacuity in a privileged and overcivilized world. Thomas Jefferson thought the influence of women in salons had put France in a "desperate state." Some of the salons reveled in parlor games. Others, such as the one organized in Paris by Madame Necker, wife of the future French reform minister, lay quite close to the halls of power and served as testing ground for new policy ideas. Madame Marie-Thérèse Geoffrin, another celebrated French *salonière*, became an important patron of the *Encyclopedia* and exercised influence in placing scholars in academies. Moses Mendelssohn held an open house for intellectuals in Berlin.

Salons in London, Vienna, Rome, and Berlin worked the same way; and like academies, they promoted among their participants a sense of belonging to an active, learned elite.

Scores of similar societies emerged in the eighteenth century. Masonic lodges, organizations with elaborate secret rituals whose members pledged themselves to the regeneration of society, attracted a remarkable array of aristocrats and middle-class men. Mozart, Frederick II, and Montesquieu were Masons. Behind their closed doors, the lodges were egalitarian. They pledged themselves to a common project of rational thought and benevolent action, and to banishing religion and social distinction—at least from their ranks.

Other networks of sociability were less exclusive. Coffeehouses multiplied with the colonial trade in sugar, coffee, and tea, and they occupied a central spot in the circulation of ideas. A group of merchants gathering to discuss trade, for instance, could turn to politics; and the many newspapers lying about the café tables provided a ready-to-hand link between their smaller discussions and news and debates elsewhere.

A READING IN THE SALON OF MADAME GEOFFRIN, 1755. Enlightenment salons encouraged a spirit of intellectual inquiry and civil debate, at least among educated elites. Such salon discussions were notable for the extent to which women helped organize and participate in the conversations. This fact led Rousseau to attack the salons for encouraging unseemly posturing and promiscuity between the sexes, which he believed were the antithesis of rational pursuits. In this painting, Madame Geoffrin, a famed hostess, (at left in gray) presides over a discussion of a learned work. Note the bust of Voltaire in the background, the patron saint of rationalist discourse. ▪ *What developments were required for this notion of free public discussion among elites to become more general in society?* ▪ *Would Enlightenment thinkers favor such developments? (Compare with images on pages 525 and 540).*

The philosopher Immanuel Kant remarked that a sharper public consciousness seemed one of the hallmarks of his time. "If we attend to the course of conversation in mixed companies consisting not merely of scholars and subtle reasoners but also of business people or women, we notice that besides storytelling or jesting they have another entertainment, namely, arguing." The ability to think critically and speak freely, without deferring to religion or tradition, was a point of pride, and not simply for intellectuals. Eighteenth-century cultural changes—the expanding networks of sociability, the flourishing book trade, the new genres of literature, and the circulation of Enlightenment ideas—widened the circles of reading and discussion, expanding what some historians and political theorists call the *public sphere*. That, in turn, began to change politics. Informal deliberations, debates about how to regenerate the nation, discussions of civic virtue, and efforts to forge a consensus played a crucial role in moving politics beyond the confines of the court.

The eighteenth century gave birth to the very idea of public opinion. A French observer described the changes this way: "In the last thirty years alone, a great and important revolution has occurred in our ideas. Today, public opinion has a preponderant force in Europe that cannot be resisted." Few thought the "public" involved more than the elite. Yet by the late eighteenth century, European governments recognized the existence of a civic-minded group that stretched from salons to coffeehouses, academies, and circles of government and to which they needed, in some measure, to respond.

Middle-Class Culture and Reading

Enlightenment fare constituted only part of the new cultural interests of the eighteenth-century middle classes. Lower down on the social scale, shopkeepers, small merchants, lawyers, and professionals read more and more different kinds of books. Instead of owning one well-thumbed Bible to read aloud, a middle-class family would buy and borrow books to read casually, pass on, and discuss. This literature consisted of science, history, biography, travel literature, and fiction. A great deal of it was aimed at middle-class women, among the fastest-growing groups of readers in the eighteenth century. Etiquette books sold very well; so did how-to manuals for the household. Scores of books about the manners, morals, and education of daughters, popular versions of Enlightenment treatises on education and the mind, illustrate close parallels between the intellectual life of the high Enlightenment and everyday middle-class reading matter.

The rise of a middle-class reading public, much of it female, helps account for the soaring popularity and production of novels, especially in Britain. Novels were the single most popular new form of literature in the eighteenth century. A survey of library borrowing in late-eighteenth-century Britain, Germany, and North America showed that 70 percent of books taken out were novels. For centuries, Europeans had read romances such as tales of the knights of the Round Table. Novels, though, did not treat quasimythical subjects, the writing was less ornate, and the setting and situations were literally closer to home. The novel's more recognizable, nonaristocratic characters seemed more relevant to common middle-class experience. Moreover, examining emotion and inner feeling also linked novel writing with a larger eighteenth-century concern with personhood and humanity. As we have seen, classic Enlightenment writers like Voltaire, Goethe, and Rousseau wrote very successful novels; and those should be understood alongside the *Pamela* or *Clarissa* of Samuel Richardson (1689–1761), the *Moll Flanders* or *Robinson Crusoe* of Daniel Defoe (1660–1731), and the *Tom Jones* of Henry Fielding (1707–1754).

Many historians have noted that women figured prominently among fiction writers. In seventeenth-century France the most widely read authors of romances had been Madeleine de Scudéry and the countess de La Fayette. Later, in England, Fanny Burney (1752–1840), Ann Radcliffe (1764–1823), and Maria Edgeworth (1767–1849) all wrote extremely popular novels. The works of Jane Austen (1775–1817), especially *Pride and Prejudice* and *Emma,* are to many readers the height of a novelist's craft. Women writers, however, were not the only ones to write novels, nor were they alone in paying close attention to the domestic or private sphere. Their work took up central eighteenth-century themes of human nature, morality, virtue, and reputation. Their novels, like much of the nonfiction of the period, explored those themes in domestic as in public settings.

Popular Culture: Urban and Rural

How much did books and print culture touch the lives of the common people? Literacy rates varied dramatically by gender, social class, and region, but were generally higher in northern than in southern and eastern Europe. It is not surprising that literacy ran highest in cities and towns—higher, in fact, than we might expect. In early eighteenth-century Paris, 85 percent of men and 60 percent of women could read. Well over half the residents of poorer Parisian neighborhoods, especially small shopkeepers, domestic servants and valets, and artisans, could read and sign their names. Even the illiterate, however, lived in a culture of print. They saw one-page newspapers and broadsides or fly-sheets posted on streets and tavern walls and regularly heard them read aloud. Moreover, visual material—inexpensive woodcuts especially, but also prints, drawings, satirical cartoons—figured as prominently as text in much popular reading material. By many measures, then, the circles of reading and discussion were even larger than literacy rates might suggest, especially in cities.

To be sure, poorer households had few books on their shelves, and those tended to be religious texts: an abridged Bible, *The Pilgrim's Progress,* or an illustrated prayer book bought or given on some special occasion and read aloud repeatedly. But popular reading was boosted by the increasing availability of new materials. From the late seventeenth century on, a French firm published a series of inexpensive small paperbacks, the so-called blue books, which itinerant peddlers carried from cities to villages in the countryside for a growing popular market. The blue library included traditional popular literature. That meant short catechisms, quasireligious tales of miracles, and stories of the lives of the saints, which the church hoped would provide religious instruction. It also included almanacs, books on astrology, and manuals of medical cures for people or farm animals.

In the eighteenth century, book peddlers began to carry abridged and simple novels and to sell books on themes popular in the middle classes, such as travel and history. Books provided an incentive to read.

Neither England nor France required any primary schooling, leaving education to haphazard local initiatives. In central Europe, some regimes made efforts to develop state-sponsored education. Catherine of Russia summoned an Austrian consultant to set up a system of primary schools, but by the end of the eighteenth century only twenty-two thousand of a population of forty million had attended any kind of schools. In the absence of primary schooling, most Europeans were self-taught. The varied texts in the peddler's cart—whether religious, political propaganda, or entertainment—attest to a widespread and rapidly growing popular interest in books and reading.

Like its middle-class counterpart, popular culture rested on networks of sociability. Guild organizations offered discussion and companionship. Street theater and singers mocking local political figures offered culture to people from different social classes. The difficulties of deciphering popular culture are considerable. Most testimony comes to us from outsiders who regarded the common people as hopelessly superstitious and ignorant. Still, historical research has begun to reveal new insights. It has shown, first, that popular culture did not exist in isolation. Particularly in the countryside, market days and village festivals brought social classes together, and popular entertainments reached a wide social audience. Folktales and traditional songs resist pigeonholing as either elite, middle-class, or popular culture, for they passed from one cultural world to another, being revised and reinterpreted in the process. Second, oral and literate culture overlapped. In other words, even people who could not read often had a great deal of "book knowledge": they argued seriously about points from books and believed that books conferred authority. A group of villagers, for instance, wrote this eulogy to a deceased friend: "he read his life long, and died without ever knowing how to read." The logic and worldview of popular culture needs to be understood on its own terms.

It remains true that the countryside, especially in less economically de-

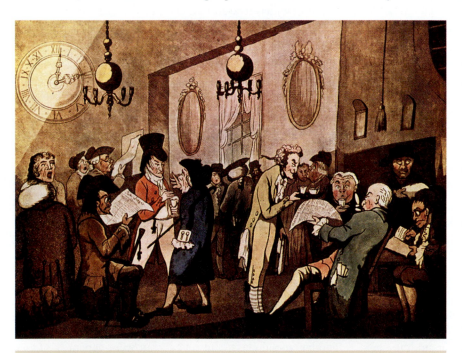

A COFFEEHOUSE IN LONDON, 1798. Coffeehouses served as centers of social networks and hubs of opinion contributing to a public consciousness that was new to the Enlightenment. This coffeehouse scene illustrates a mixing of classes, lively debate, and a burgeoning culture of reading. Compare this image with that of the aristocratic salon on page 538 and the meeting of Mendelssohn and Lessing on page 525. ▪ *How were coffeehouses different from aristocratic salons or the middle-class drawing room discussion between the two German thinkers?* ▪ *Can they all be seen as expressions of a new kind of "public sphere" in eighteenth-century Europe?*

veloped regions, was desperately poor. Life there was far more isolated than in towns. A yawning chasm separated peasants from the world of the high Enlightenment. The *philosophes*, well established in the summits of European society, looked at popular culture with distrust and ignorance. They saw the common people of Europe much as they did indigenous peoples of other continents. They were humanitarians, critical thinkers, and reformers; they were not democrats. The Enlightenment, while well entrenched in eighteenth-century elite culture, nonetheless involved changes that reached well beyond elite society.

Eighteenth-Century Music

European elites sustained other forms of high culture. English gentlemen who read scientific papers aloud in clubs also commissioned architects to design classical revival country houses for the weekends. Royal courts underwrote the academies of painting, which upheld aristocratic taste and aesthetics; Austrian salons that hosted discussions of Voltaire also staged performances of Mozart. We have already noted that the *philosophes'* work crossed genres, from political theory to fiction. Rousseau not only wrote discourses and novels but composed music and wrote an opera. A flourishing musical culture was one of the most important features of the eighteenth century.

BACH AND HANDEL

The early eighteenth century brought the last phase of Baroque music, culminating in the work of Johann Sebastian Bach (1685–1750) and George Frideric Handel (1685–1759). Bach was a deeply pious man, a devout Protestant, whose life was entirely unaffected by the secularism of the Enlightenment. A church musician in Leipzig for most of his adult life, he wrote music for every Sunday and holiday service, music of such intensity that the listener feels the salvation of the world hanging on every note. He also wrote concertos and suites for orchestra as well as subtle and complex fugues for piano and organ.

Handel, in contrast, was a publicity-seeking cosmopolitan who sought out large, secular audiences. Born in Brandenburg-Prussia, he studied composition in Italy and eventually established himself as a celebrity composer in London, known for his oratorios (musical dramas performed in concert, without staging) composed in English. Handel's greatest oratorio, *Messiah*, is still sung widely throughout the English-speaking world every Christmas; its stirring "Hallelujah" chorus remains the most popular choral piece in the classical repertoire.

HAYDN AND MOZART

If Bach and Handel were the last (and the greatest) composers of Baroque music, the Austrians Joseph Haydn (1732–1809) and Wolfgang Amadeus Mozart (1756–1791) were the leading representatives of the Classical style, which transformed musical culture in Europe in the second half of the eighteenth century. Classicism in music sought to organize itself around the principles of order, clarity, and symmetry, and its practitioners developed new forms of composition for pursuing these goals, including the string quartet and, most enduringly, the symphony, sometimes called a novel in music. Following their taste for order, nearly all Classical composers wrote their symphonies in four movements, and the first movement is usually in sonata form, characterized by the successive presentation of musical themes, their development, and their recapitulation.

Mozart wrote forty-one symphonies, and his last three (especially Symphony no. 41, known as the *Jupiter* Symphony) are often said to be unequaled in their grace, variety, and technical perfection. He was a child prodigy of astounding talents and celebrity who died at thirty-five after a career of extraordinary productivity and financial instability. His inability to secure steady employment from a wealthy patron in spite of his well-known genius illustrated

MOZART'S LAST PORTRAIT, 1789. Like the composer's famous *Requiem*, this portrait, painted by Mozart's brother-in-law Joseph Lange, was left unfinished at Mozart's death.

the challenges that faced even the most talented of artists in the eighteenth century. Contrary to myth he was not buried in a pauper's grave, but was buried after a simple and cheap funeral in keeping with his Masonic principles and Enlightenment opposition to Catholic ritual.

Joseph Haydn knew much better than Mozart how to appeal to a patron, and he spent the bulk of his career in the service of a wealthy aristocratic family that maintained its own private orchestra. Only toward the end of his life, in 1791, did Haydn strike out on his own by traveling to London where he supported himself handsomely by writing for a paying public. Eighteenth-century London was one of the rare places with a commercial market for culture—later, entrepreneurial opportunities for musicians would open up elsewhere, and in the nineteenth century serious music would leave the aristocratic salon for urban concert halls all over Europe. Haydn furthered this development with his last twelve symphonies (he wrote over a hundred), performed to great acclaim in London.

THE MAGIC FLUTE, 1793. Mozart's opera opened in 1791, just before the extraordinary young composer died. The opera has been noted for its use of masonic symbols and its endorsement of Enlightenment models of authority, though most people today treasure it less for its obscure political meanings than for its delightful music.

OPERA

Opera flourished in the eighteenth century. Developed as a musical form in Italy during the seventeenth century by Baroque composers such as Claudio Monteverdi (1567–1643), opera's combination of theater and music spread rapidly throughout Europe in the space of a single generation. During the classical period, opera's popularity grew due to the spectacles organized by Christoph Willibald von Gluck. Gluck insisted that the text was as important as the music, and he simplified arias and emphasized dramatic action. The much beloved operas of Mozart—including *The Marriage of Figaro, Don Giovanni,* and *The Magic Flute*—remain the most popular operas of the Classical period today.

The Marriage of Figaro, indeed, followed a classic eighteenth-century path to popularity. The author of the play

After You Read This Chapter

REVIEWING THE OBJECTIVES

- Many eighteenth-century thinkers used the term *Enlightenment* to describe what their work offered to European society. Who were they, and what did they mean by the term?
- Enlightenment ideas spread rapidly throughout Europe and in European colonies. How did this expanded arena for public discussion shape the development of Enlightenment thought?
- Enlightenment debates were shaped by the availability of new information about peoples and cultures in different parts of the globe. How did Enlightenment thinkers incorporate this new information into their thought?
- Enlightenment thinkers were often critical of widely held cultural and political beliefs. What was radical about the Enlightenment?
- The Enlightenment took place in an expanded sphere of public discussion and debate. How broad was the audience for Enlightenment thought, and how important was this audience for our understanding of the period?

was born Pierre Caron, the son of a watchmaker. Caron rose to become watchmaker to the king, bought a noble office, married well, took the name Pierre Augustin de Beaumarchais, and wrote several comedies in an Enlightenment tone satirizing the French nobility. *Figaro* ran into trouble with French censors, but like so many other banned works, the play sold well. It was translated into Italian, was set to music by Mozart, and played to appreciative elite audiences from Paris to Prague. Satire, self-criticism, the criticism of hierarchy, optimism and social mobility, and a cosmopolitan outlook supported by what was in many ways a traditional society—all of these are key to understanding eighteenth-century culture as well as the Enlightenment.

CONCLUSION

The Enlightenment arose from the scientific revolution, from the new sense of power and possibility that rational thinking made possible, and from the rush of enthusiasm for new forms of inquiry. Enlightenment thinkers scrutinized a remarkably wide range of topics: human nature, reason, understanding, religion, belief, law, the origins of government, economics, new forms of technology, and social practices—such as marriage, child-rearing, and education. In doing so, they made many of their contemporaries (and sometimes, even themselves) uncomfortable. Ideas with radical or even subversive implications circulated in popular forms from pamphlets and journalism to plays and operas. The intellectual movement that lay behind the Enlightenment thus had broad consequences for the creation of a new kind of elite, based not on birth but on the acquisition of knowledge and the encouragement of open expression and debate. A new sphere of public opinion had come into existence, one that would have profound consequences in the nineteenth and twentieth centuries.

The Atlantic revolutions (the American Revolution of 1776, the French Revolution of 1789, and the Latin American upheavals of the 1830s) were steeped in the language of the Enlightenment. The constitutions of the new nations formed by these revolutions made reference to the fundamental assumptions of Enlightenment liberalism: on the liberty of the individual conscience and the freedom from the constraints imposed by religious or government institutions. Government authority could not be arbitrary; equality and freedom were natural; and humans sought happiness, prosperity, and the expansion of their potential. These arguments had been made tentatively earlier, and even after the Atlantic revolutions their aspirations were only partially realized. But when the North American colonists declared their independence from Britain in 1776, they called such ideas "self-evident truths." That bold declaration marked both the distance traveled since the late seventeenth century and the self-confidence that was the Enlightenment's hallmark.

PEOPLE, IDEAS, AND EVENTS IN CONTEXT

- Who were the **PHILOSOPHES**? What gave them such faith in **REASON**?
- What did **DAVID HUME** owe to **ISAAC NEWTON**? What made his work different from that of the famous physicist?
- What did **VOLTAIRE** admire about the work of **FRANCIS BACON** and **JOHN LOCKE**? What irritated Voltaire about French society?
- What was **MONTESQUIEU**'s contribution to theories of government?
- What made **DENIS DIDEROT**'s *ENCYCLOPEDIA* such a definitive statement of the Enlightenment's goals?
- What influence did **CESARE BECCARIA** have over legal practices in Europe?
- What contributions did **ADAM SMITH** make to economic theory?
- What was radical about **JEAN-JACQUES ROUSSEAU**'s views on education and politics?
- What does the expansion of the **PUBLIC SPHERE** in the eighteenth century tell us about the effects of the Enlightenment?

CONSEQUENCES

- If humans were as rational as Enlightenment thinkers said they were, why did they need Enlightenment *philosophes* to tell them how to live? How might a *philosophe* have answered this question?
- Did increases in literacy, the rise of print culture, and the emergence of new forms of intellectual sociability such as salons, reading societies, and coffeehouses really make public opinion more rational?

STORY LINES

- The French Revolution of 1798–1799 overthrew Louis XVI and created a government committed in principle to the rule of law, the liberty of the individual, and an idea of the nation as a sovereign body of citizens. These political changes also opened the way for the expression of a wide variety of social grievances by peasants, laborers, women, and other social groups in Europe.

- The French Revolution encouraged the spread of democratic ideas, but it also led to an increase in the power of centralized nation-states in Europe. The pressures of the revolutionary wars led governments to develop larger national bureaucracies, modern professional armies, new legal codes, and new tax structures.

- The French Revolution was part of a broader set of changes which rocked the Atlantic world at the end of the eighteenth century. Along with the Haitian Revolution and the American Revolution, this wave of cataclysmic change reshaped the political order of Europe and the Americas.

CHRONOLOGY

May 1789	The Estates General meets
June 1789	The Tennis Court Oath
July 1789	The Fall of the Bastille
September 1792	First French Republic
January 1793	Execution of King Louis XIV
September 1793– July 1794	The Terror
1798–1799	Napoleon's invasion of Egypt
January 1804	Haitian independence
1804	Napoleon crowned Emperor
1804	Civil code
1808	Invasion of Spain
1812	Invasion of Russia
1814–1815	Napoleon's abdication and defeat

The French Revolution

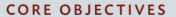
When a crowd of Parisians attacked the antiquated and nearly empty royal prison known as the Bastille on July 14, 1789, they were doing several things all at once. On the one hand, the revolt was a popular expression of support for the newly created National Assembly. This representative body had only weeks earlier declared an intention to put an end to absolutism in France by writing a constitution that made the nation, rather than the king, the sovereign authority in the land. But the Parisians in the street on July 14 did not express themselves like members of the National Assembly, who spoke the language of the Enlightenment. The actions of the revolutionary crowd were an expression of violent anger at the king's soldiers, who they feared might turn their guns on the city in a royal attempt to restore order by force. When the governor of the Bastille prison opened fire on the attackers, killing as many as a hundred, they responded with redoubled fury. By the end of the day, the prison had fallen, and the governor's battered body was dragged to the square before the city hall, where he was beheaded. Among the first to meet such an end as a consequence of revolution in France, he would not be the last.

This tension between noble political aspirations and cruel violence lies at the heart of the French Revolution. The significance of this contradiction was not lost on the millions of people throughout Europe who watched in astonishment as France was engulfed in turmoil in the 1790s. In 1789, one European out of every five lived in France, a kingdom that many considered to be the center of European culture. Other kingdoms were not immune to the same social and political tensions that divided the French. Aristocrats across Europe and the colonies resented monarchical inroads on their ancient freedoms. Members of the middle classes chafed under a system of official privilege that they increasingly saw as unjust and outmoded. Peasants fiercely resented the endless demands of central government on their limited resources. Nor were resentments focused exclusively on absolutist monarchs. Bitter resentments and tensions existed between country and city dwellers, between rich and poor, overprivileged and underprivileged, slave and free. The French Revolution was the most dramatic and tumultuous expression of all of these conflicts.

This age of revolution opened on the other side of the Atlantic ocean. The American Revolution of 1776 was a crisis of the British Empire, linked to a long series of conflicts between England and France over colonial control of North America. It led to a major crisis of the old regime in France. Among "enlightened" Europeans, the success with which citizens of the United States had thrown off British rule and formed a republic based on Enlightenment principles was a source of tremendous optimism. Change would come, many believed. Reform was possible. The costs would be modest.

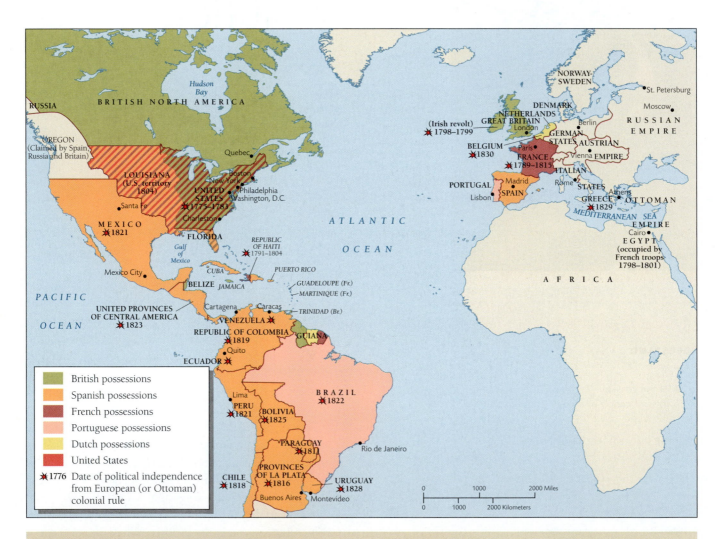

THE ATLANTIC REVOLUTIONS. The Atlantic revolutions shook nations and empires on both sides of the ocean, challenging the legitimacy of Europe's dynastic realms, lending further support to notions of popular sovereignty and forcing contemporaries to rethink the meanings of citizenship in a context of intense political and economic struggle. ▪ *How many of these struggles took place within Europe?* ▪ *How many appear to have taken place on the periphery of the Atlantic world?* ▪ *What circumstances may have made it more difficult for such revolutionary movements to develop within Europe itself?*

The French Revolution did not live up to these expectations, though change certainly did come. By any measure, the accomplishments of the revolutionary decade were extraordinary: it successfully proved that the residents of an old monarchy in the heart of Europe could come together to constitute themselves as citizens of a new political idea, the nation. Freed from the shackles of tradition, revolutionaries in France posed new questions about the role of women in public life, about the separation of church and state, about the rights of Jews and other minorities. A slave revolt in the French colonies convinced the revolutionaries that the new liberties they defended so ardently also belonged to African slaves, though few had suggested such a thing at the outset. Meanwhile, the European wars precipitated by the revolution marked the first time that entire populations were mobilized as part of a new kind of devastating international conflict, the first "total wars." In other words, in spite of the optimism of those who began the revolution in 1789, it quickly became something much more costly, complex, and violent. Its effects were to resonate throughout Europe for the next half a century.

THE FRENCH REVOLUTION: AN OVERVIEW

The term *French Revolution* is a shorthand for a complex series of events between 1789 and 1799. (Napoleon ruled from 1799 to 1814–1815.) To simplify, those events can be divided into four stages. In the first stage, running from 1788 to 1792, the struggle was constitutional and relatively peaceful. An increasingly bold elite articulated its grievances against the king. Like the American revolutionaries, French elites refused taxation without representation; attacked despotism, or arbitrary authority; and offered an Enlightenment-inspired program to rejuvenate the nation. Reforms, many of them breathtakingly wide ranging, were instituted—some accepted or even offered by the king, and others passed over his objections. The peaceful, constitutional phase did not last. Unlike the American Revolution, the French Revolution did not stabilize around one constitution or one set of political leaders, for many reasons.

Reforms met with resistance, dividing the country. The threat of dramatic change within one of the most powerful countries in Europe created international tensions. In 1792, these tensions exploded into war, and the crises of war, in turn, spelled the end of the Bourbon monarchy and the beginning of the republic. The second stage of the revolution, which lasted from 1792 to 1794, was one of acute crisis, consolidation, and repression. A ruthlessly centralized government mobilized all the country's resources to fight the foreign enemy as well as counterrevolutionaries at home, to destroy traitors and the vestiges of the Old Regime.

The Terror, as this policy was called, did save the republic, but it exhausted itself in factions and recriminations and collapsed in 1794. In the third phase, from 1794 to 1799, the government drifted. France remained a republic. It continued to fight with Europe. Undermined by corruption and division, the state fell prey to the ambitions of a military leader, Napoleon Bonaparte. Napoleon's rule, punctuated by astonishing victories and catastrophes, stretched from 1799 to 1815. It began as a republic, became an empire, and ended—after a last hurrah—in the muddy fields outside the Belgian village of Waterloo. After Napoleon's final defeat, the other European monarchs restored the Bourbons to the throne. That restoration, however, would be short lived, and the cycle of revolution and reaction continued into the nineteenth century.

THE COMING OF THE REVOLUTION

What were the long-term causes of the revolution in France? Historians long ago argued that the causes and outcomes should be understood in terms of class conflict. According to this interpretation, a rising bourgeoisie, or middle class, inspired by Enlightenment ideas and by its own self-interest, overthrew what was left of the aristocratic order. This interpretation drew on the writings of the nineteenth-century philosopher Karl Marx and on much twentieth-century sociology.

Historians have substantially modified this bold thesis. To be sure, the origins of the revolution lie in eighteenth-century French society. Yet that society was not simply divided between a bourgeois class and the aristocracy. Instead, it was increasingly dominated by a new elite or social group that brought together aristocrats, officeholders, professionals, and—to a lesser degree—merchants and businessmen. To understand the revolution, we need to understand this new social group and its conflicts with the government of Louis XVI.

French society was divided into Three Estates. (An individual's *estate* marked his standing, or status, and it determined legal rights, taxes, and so on.) The First Estate comprised all the clergy; the Second Estate, the nobility. The Third Estate, by far the largest, included everyone else, from wealthy lawyers and businessmen to urban laborers and poor peasants. Within the political and social elite of the country, a small but powerful group, these legal distinctions often seemed artificial. To begin with, in the upper reaches of society, the social boundaries between nobles and wealthy commoners were ill-defined. Noble title was accessible to those who could afford to buy an ennobling office. For example, close to fifty thousand new nobles were created between 1700 and 1789. The nobility depended on a constant infusion of talent and economic power from the wealthy social groups of the Third Estate.

To preserve their elite status, aristocrats spoke of a distinction between the nobility of the sword and of the robe, the former supposedly of a more ancient and distinguished lineage derived from military service, the latter aristocrats because they had purchased administrative or judicial office (hence the robe).

Nevertheless, wealth did not take predictable forms. Most noble wealth was proprietary—that is, tied to land, urban properties, purchased offices, and the like. Yet noble families did not disdain trade or commerce, as historians long thought. In fact, noblemen financed most industry, and they also invested heavily in banking and such enterprises as ship owning, the slave trade, mining, and metallurgy. Moreover, the very wealthy members of the Third Estate also preferred to invest in secure, proprietary holdings. Thus, throughout the century, much middle-class wealth was

transformed into noble wealth, and a significant number of rich bourgeois became noblemen. Wealthy members of the bourgeoisie themselves did not see themselves as a separate class. They thought of themselves as different from—and often opposed to—the common people, who worked with their hands, and they identified with the values of a nobility to which they frequently aspired.

There were, nonetheless, important social tensions. Less prosperous lawyers—and there were an increasing number of them—were jealous of the privileged position of a favored few in their profession. Over the course of the century the price of offices rose, making it more difficult to buy one's way into the nobility, and creating tensions between middling members of the Third Estate and the very rich in trade and commerce who, by and large, were the only group able to afford to climb the social ladder. Less wealthy nobles resented the success of rich, upstart commoners whose income allowed them to live in luxury. In sum, several fault lines ran through the elite and the middle classes. All these social groups could nonetheless join in attacking a government and an economy that were not serving their interests.

The Enlightenment had changed public debate (see Chapter 17). Although ideas did not cause the revolution, they played a critical role in articulating grievances. The political theories of Locke, Voltaire, and Montesquieu could appeal to both discontented nobles and members of

PREREVOLUTIONARY PROPAGANDA. Political cartoons in late-eighteenth-century France commonly portrayed the Third Estate as bearing the burden of taxation while performing the bulk of the nation's productive work. ▪ *Would one expect the nobility or the clergy to defend their status on the basis of their usefulness to society?* ▪ *Can one detect the power of certain Enlightenment ideas behind these forms of social critique?* ▪ *Which ones?* ▪ *How might an opponent of Enlightenment thought have confronted such arguments?*

the middle class. Voltaire was popular because of his attacks on noble privileges; Locke and Montesquieu gained widespread followings because of their defense of private property and limited sovereignty. Montesquieu's ideas appealed to the noble lawyers and officeholders who dominated France's powerful law courts, the *parlements*. They read his doctrine of checks and balances as support for their argument that parlements could provide a check to the despotism of the king's government. When conflicts arose, noble leaders presented themselves as defenders of the nation threatened by the king and his ministers.

The campaign for change was also fueled by economic reformers. The "physiocrats" urged the government to simplify the tax system and free the economy from mercantilist regulations. They advocated an end to price controls in the grain trade, which had been imposed to keep the cost of bread low. Such interventions, they argued, interfered with the natural workings of the market.

In the countryside, peasants were caught in a web of obligations to landlords, church, and state: a tithe, or levy, on farm produce owed to the church; fees for the use of a landlord's mill or wine press; fees to the landlord; and fees when land changed hands. In addition, peasants paid a disproportionate share of both direct and indirect taxes—the most onerous of which was the salt tax—levied by the government. (For some time the production of salt had been a state monopoly; every individual was required to buy at least seven pounds a year from the government works. The result was a commodity whose cost was often as much as fifty or sixty times its actual value.) Further grievances stemmed from the requirement to maintain public roads (the corvée) and from the hunting privileges that nobles for centuries had regarded as the distinctive badge of their order.

Social and economic conditions deteriorated on the eve of the revolution. A general price increase during much of the eighteenth century, which permitted the French economy to expand by providing capital for investment, created hardship for the peasantry and for urban tradesmen and laborers. Their plight deteriorated further at the end of the 1780s, when poor harvests sent bread prices sharply higher. In 1788 families found themselves spending more than 50 percent of their income on bread, which made up the bulk of their diet. The following year the figure rose to as much as 80 percent. Poor harvests reduced demand for manufactured goods, and contracting markets in turn created unemployment. Many peasants left the countryside for the cities, hoping to find work there—only to discover that urban unemployment was far worse than that in rural areas. Evidence indicates that between 1787 and 1789 the unemployment rate in many parts of urban France was as high as 50 percent.

Failure and Reform

An inefficient tax system further weakened the country's financial position. Taxation was tied to differing social standings and varied from region to region—some areas were subject to a much higher rate than others. Special exemptions made the task of collectors more difficult. The financial system, already burdened by debts incurred under Louis XIV, all but broke down completely under the increased expenses brought on by French participation in the American Revolution. The cost of servicing the national debt in the 1780s consumed 50 percent of the nation's budget.

Problems with the economy reflected weaknesses in France's administrative structure, ultimately the responsibility of the country's absolutist monarch, Louis XVI (1774–1792).

LOUIS XVI. The last prerevolutionary French king, who was to lose his life in the Terror, combined in his person a strong attachment to the monarchy's absolutist doctrine with an inability to find workable solutions to the financial crisis facing his government. His royal portrait mimicked the forms of spectacular display that proved so useful to Louis XIV in shoring up the power of the monarchy. ▪ *What made this display so much less potent in the late eighteenth century?* ▪ *What caused the monarchy to lose its aura?*

Analyzing Primary Sources

What is the Third Estate? (1789)

The Abbé Emmanuel-Joseph Sieyès (1748–1836) was, by virtue of his office in the church, a member of the First Estate of the Estates General. Nevertheless, his political savvy led him to be elected as a representative of the Third Estate from the district of Chartres. Sieyès was a formidable politician as well as a writer. His career during the revolution, which he ended by assisting Napoleon's seizure of power, began with one of the most important radical pamphlets of 1789. In What is the Third Estate?, Sieyès posed fundamental questions about the rights of the estate, which represented the great majority of the population and helped provoke its secession from the Estates General.

he plan of this book is fairly simple. We must ask ourselves three questions.

1. What is the Third Estate? *Everything.*

2. What has it been until now in the political order? *Nothing.*

3. What does it want to be? *Something.*

It suffices to have made the point that the so-called usefulness of a privileged order to the public service is a fallacy; that without help from this order, all the arduous tasks in the service are performed by the Third Estate; that without this order the higher posts could be infinitely better filled; that they ought to be the natural prize and reward of recognized ability and service; and that if the privileged have succeeded in usurping all well-paid and honorific posts, this is both a hateful iniquity towards the generality of citizens and an act of treason to the commonwealth.

Who is bold enough to maintain that the Third Estate does not contain within itself everything needful to constitute a complete nation? It is like a strong and robust man with one arm still in chains. If the privileged order were removed, the nation would not be something less but something more. What then is the Third Estate? All; but an "all" that is fettered and oppressed. What would it be without the privileged order? It would be all; but free and flourishing. Nothing will go well without the Third Estate; everything would go considerably better without the two others.

Source: Emmanuel-Joseph Sieyès, *What is the Third Estate?*, trans. M. Blondel, ed. S. E. Finer (London: 1964), pp. 53–63.

Questions for Analysis

1. How might contemporaries have viewed Sieyès's argument that the Three Estates should be evaluated according to their usefulness to the "commonwealth"?

2. Was Sieyès's language—accusing the privileged orders of "treason" and arguing for their "removal"—an incitement to violence?

3. What did Sieyès mean by the term *nation*? Could one speak of France as a nation in these terms before 1789?

Louis wished to improve the lot of the poor, abolish torture, and shift the burden of taxation onto the richer classes, but he lacked the ability to accomplish these tasks. He appointed reformers like Anne-Robert-Jacques Turgot, a physiocrat, and Jacques Necker, a Swiss Protestant banker, as finance ministers, only to arouse the opposition of traditionalists at court. When he pressed for new taxes to be paid by the nobility, he was defeated by the provincial parlements, who defended the aristocracy's immunity from taxation. He allowed his wife, the young but strong-willed Marie Antoinette—daughter of Austria's Maria Theresa—a free hand to dispense patronage among her friends. The result was constant intrigue and frequently reshuffled alliances at Versailles. By 1788, a weak monarch, together with a chaotic financial situation and severe social tensions, brought absolutist France to the edge of political disaster.

THE DESTRUCTION OF THE OLD REGIME

The fiscal crisis precipitated the revolution. In 1787 and 1788 the king's principal ministers, Charles de Calonne and Loménie de Brienne, proposed new taxes to meet the growing deficit, notably a stamp duty and a direct tax on the annual produce of the land.

Hoping to persuade the nobility to agree to these reforms, the king summoned an Assembly of Notables from among the aristocracy. This group insisted that any new tax scheme must be approved by the Estates General, the representative body of the Three Estates of the realm, and that the king had no legal authority to arrest and imprison arbitrarily. These proposed constitutional changes echoed the English aristocrats of 1688 and the American revolutionaries of 1776.

Faced with economic crisis and financial chaos, Louis XVI summoned the Estates General (which had not met since 1614) to meet in 1789. His action appeared to many as the only solution to France's deepening problems. Long-term grievances and short-term hardships produced bread riots across the country in the spring of 1789. Fear that the forces of law and order were collapsing and that the common people might take matters into their own hands spurred the Estates General. Each of the three orders elected its own deputies—the Third Estate indirectly through local assemblies. These assemblies were charged as well with the responsibility of drawing up lists of grievances (*cahiers des doléances*) further heightening expectations for fundamental reform.

The delegates of the Third Estate, though elected by assemblies chosen in turn by artisans and peasants, represented the outlook of an elite. Only 13 percent were men of business. About 25 percent were lawyers; 43 percent were government officeholders of some sort.

By tradition, each estate met and voted as a body. In the past, this had generally meant that the First Estate (the clergy) had combined with the Second (the nobility) to defeat the Third. Now the Third Estate made it clear it would not tolerate such an arrangement. The Third's interests were articulated most memorably by the Abbé Emmanuel

THE TENNIS COURT OATH BY JACQUES LOUIS DAVID (1748–1825). In June 1789, the members of the Third Estate, now calling themselves the National Assembly, swear an oath not to disband until France had a constitution. In the center stands Jean Bailly, president of the new assembly. The Abbé Sieyès is seated at the table. In the foreground, a clergyman, an aristocrat, and a member of the Third Estate embrace in a symbol of national unity. The single deputy who refused to take the oath sits at right, his hands clasped against his chest. ▪ *What is the significance of this near unanimity expressed in defiance of the king?* ▪ *What options were available to those who did not support this move?*

Sieyès, a radical member of the clergy. "What is the Third Estate?" asked Sieyès, in his famous pamphlet of January 1789. Everything, he answered, and pointed to eighteenth-century social changes to bolster his point. In early 1789, Sieyès's views were still unusually radical. But the leaders of the Third Estate agreed that the three orders should sit together and vote as individuals. More important, they insisted that the Third Estate should have twice as many members as the First and Second.

The king first opposed "doubling the Third" and then changed his position. His unwillingness to take a strong stand on voting procedures cost him support he might otherwise have obtained from the Third Estate. Shortly after the Estates General opened at Versailles in May 1789, the Third Estate, angered by the king's attitude, took the revolutionary step of leaving the body and declaring itself the National Assembly. Locked out of the Estates General meeting hall on June 20, the Third Estate and a handful of sympathetic nobles and clergymen moved to a nearby indoor tennis court.

Here, under the leadership of the volatile, maverick aristocrat Mirabeau and the radical clergyman Sieyès, they bound themselves by a solemn oath not to separate until they had drafted a constitution for France. This Tennis Court Oath, sworn on June 20, 1789, can be seen as the beginning of the French Revolution. By claiming the authority to remake the government in the name of the people, the National Assembly was asserting its right to act as the highest sovereign power in the nation. On June 27 the king virtually conceded this right by ordering all the delegates to join the National Assembly.

First Stages of the French Revolution

The first stage of the French Revolution extended from June 1789 to August 1792. In the main, this stage was moderate, its actions dominated by the leadership of liberal nobles and men of the Third Estate. Yet three events in the summer and fall of 1789 furnished evidence that their leadership would be challenged.

POPULAR REVOLTS

From the beginning of the political crisis, public attention was high. It was roused not merely by interest in political reform but also by the economic crisis that, as we have seen, brought the price of bread to astronomical heights. Many believed that the aristocracy and the king were conspiring to punish the Third Estate by encouraging scarcity and high prices. Rumors circulated in Paris during the lat-

ter days of June 1789 that the king's troops were mobilizing to march on the city. The electors of Paris (those who had voted for the Third Estate—workshop masters, artisans, and shopkeepers) feared not only the king but also the Parisian poor, who had been parading through the streets and threatening violence. The common people would soon be referred to as sans-culottes (sahn koo-LAWTS). The term, which translates to "without breeches," was an antiaristocratic badge of pride: a man of the people wore full-length trousers rather than aristocratic breeches with stockings and gold-buckled shoes. Led by the electors, the people formed a provisional municipal government and organized a militia of volunteers to maintain order. Determined to obtain arms, they made their way on July 14 to the Bastille, an ancient fortress where guns and ammunition were stored. Built in the Middle Ages, the Bastille had served as a prison for many years but was no longer much used. Nevertheless, it symbolized hated royal authority. When crowds demanded arms from its governor, he procrastinated and then, fearing a frontal assault, opened fire, killing ninety-eight of the attackers. The crowd took revenge, capturing the fortress (which held only seven prisoners—five common criminals and two people confined for mental incapacity) and decapitating the governor. Similar groups took control in other cities across France. The fall of the Bastille was the first instance of the people's role in revolutionary change.

The second popular revolt occurred in the countryside. Peasants, too, expected and feared a monarchical and aristocratic counterrevolution. Rumors flew that the king's armies were on their way, that Austrians, Prussians, or "brigands" were invading. Frightened and uncertain, peasants and villagers organized militias; others attacked and burned manor houses, sometimes to look for grain but usually to find and destroy records of manorial dues. This "Great Fear," as historians have labeled it, compounded the confusion in rural areas. The news, when it reached Paris, convinced deputies at Versailles that the administration of rural France had simply collapsed.

The third instance of popular uprising, the "October Days of 1789," was brought on by economic crisis. This time Parisian women from the market district, angered by the soaring price of bread and fired by rumors of the king's continuing unwillingness to cooperate with the assembly, marched to Versailles on October 5 and demanded to be heard. Not satisfied with its reception by the assembly, the crowd broke through the gates to the palace, calling for the king to return to Paris from Versailles. On the afternoon of the following day the king yielded and returned to Paris, accompanied by the crowd and the National Guard.

Each of these popular uprisings shaped the political events unfolding at Versailles. The storming of the Bastille

WOMEN OF PARIS LEAVING FOR VERSAILLES, OCTOBER 1789. A crowd of women, accompanied by Lafayette and the National Guard, marched to Versailles to confront the king about shortages and rising prices in Paris. ▪ *Did the existence of the National Assembly change the meaning of such popular protests?*

persuaded the king and nobles to agree to the creation of the National Assembly. The Great Fear compelled the most sweeping changes of the entire revolutionary period. In an effort to quell rural disorder, on the night of August 4 the assembly took a giant step toward abolishing all forms of privilege. It eliminated the church tithe (tax on the harvest), the labor requirement known as the corvée, the nobility's hunting privileges, and a wide variety of tax exemptions and monopolies. In effect, these reforms obliterated the remnants of feudalism. One week later, the assembly abolished the sale of offices, thereby sweeping away one of the fundamental institutions of the Old Regime. The king's return to Paris during the October Days of 1789 undercut his ability to resist further changes.

THE NATIONAL ASSEMBLY AND THE RIGHTS OF MAN

The assembly issued its charter of liberties, the Declaration of the Rights of Man and of the Citizen, in September 1789. It declared property to be a natural right, along with liberty, security, and "resistance to oppression." It declared freedom of speech, religious toleration, and liberty of the press inviolable. All citizens were to be treated equally before the law. No one was to be imprisoned or punished without due process of law. Sovereignty resided in the people, who could depose officers of the government if they abused their powers. These were not new ideas; they represented the outcome of Enlightenment discussions and revolutionary debates and deliberations. The Declaration became the

preamble to the new constitution, which the assembly finished in 1791.

Whom did the Declaration mean by "man and the citizen"? The constitution distinguished between "passive" citizens, guaranteed rights under law, and "active" citizens, who paid a certain amount in taxes and could thus vote and hold office. About half the adult males in France qualified as active citizens. Even their power was curtailed, because they could vote only for "electors," men whose property ownership qualified them to hold office. Later in the revolution, the more radical republic abolished the distinction between active and passive, and the conservative regimes reinstated it. Which men could be trusted to participate in politics and on what terms was a hotly contested issue.

Also controversial were the rights of religious minorities. The revolution gave full civil rights to Protestants, though in areas long divided by religious conflict those rights were challenged by Catholics. The revolution did, hesitantly, give civil rights to Jews, a measure that sparked protest in areas of eastern France. Religious toleration, a central theme of the Enlightenment, meant ending persecution; it did not mean that the regime was prepared to accommodate religious difference. The assembly abolished serfdom and banned slavery in continental France. It remained silent on colonial slavery, and although delegations pressed the assembly on political rights for free people of color, the assembly exempted the colonies from the constitution's provisions. Events in the Caribbean, as we will see, later forced the issue.

The rights and roles of women became the focus of sharp debate, as revolutionaries confronted demands that working women participate in guilds or trade organizations, and laws on marriage, divorce, poor relief, and education were reconsidered. The Englishwoman Mary Wollstonecraft's milestone book *A Vindication of the Rights of Woman* (see Chapter 17) was penned during the revolutionary debate over national education. Should girls be educated? To what end? Wollstonecraft, as we have seen, argued strongly that reforming education required forging a new concept of independent and equal womanhood. Even Wollstonecraft, however, only hinted at political representation, aware that such an idea would "excite laughter."

Only a handful of thinkers broached the subject of women in politics: the aristocratic Enlightenment thinker the Marquis de Condorcet and, from another shore, Marie

DECLARATION OF THE RIGHTS OF MAN (1789). Presented as principles of natural law inscribed on stone, this print gives a good indication of how the authors of the Declaration wished it to be perceived by the French people. Over the tablets is a beneficent and all-seeing deity accompanied by two female allegorical figures representing strength and virtue on one side and the French nation on the other. Two armed soldiers wear the uniform of the newly created National Guard. The image's symbols refer to Masonic lore (the triangle or pyramid with an eye at the center, the snake grasping its tail), and a set of historical references from the Roman Republic: a Phrygian cap, used by Romans as a symbol of liberty, is mounted on a spear emerging from a bundle of sticks. This bundle was known as a *faisceau*, and was carried in ancient Rome by magistrates as symbols of their authority. ▪ *Given the absence of any monarchical symbolism or references to the Catholic Church, why was it important for the authors to come up with an alternative set of historical references?*

Beginning with the proposition that "social distinctions can only be based on the common utility," she declared that women had the same rights as men, including resistance to authority, participation in government, and naming the fathers of illegitimate children. This last demand offers a glimpse of the shame, isolation, and hardship faced by an unmarried woman.

De Gouges's demand for equal rights was unusual, but many women nevertheless participated in the everyday activities of the revolution, joining clubs, demonstrations, and debates and making their presence known, sometimes forcefully. Women artisans' organizations had a well-established role in municipal life, and they used the revolution as an opportunity to assert their rights to produce and sell goods. Market women were familiar public figures, often central to the circulation of news and spontaneous popular demonstrations (the October Days are a good example). Initially, the regime celebrated the support of women "citizens," and female figures were favorite symbols for liberty, prudence, and the bounty of nature in revolutionary iconography. When the revolution became more radical, however, some revolutionaries saw autonomous political activity by women's organizations as a threat to public order, and in 1793 the revolutionaries shut down the women's political clubs. Even so, many ordinary women were able to make use of the revolution's new legislation on marriage (divorce was legalized in 1792) and inheritance to support claims for relief from abusive husbands or absent fathers, claims that would have been impossible under the prerevolutionary legislation.

THE NATIONAL ASSEMBLY AND THE CHURCH

In November 1789 the National Assembly decided to confiscate all church lands to use them as collateral for issuing interest-bearing notes known as *assignats*. The assembly hoped that this action would resolve the economy's inflationary crisis, and eventually these notes circulated widely as paper money. In July 1789, the assembly enacted the Civil Constitution of the Clergy, bringing the church under state authority. The new law forced all bishops and priests to swear allegiance to the state, which henceforth paid their salaries. The aim was to make the Catholic Church of France a national institution, free from interference from Rome.

These reforms were bitterly divisive. Many people resented the privileged status of the church, and its vast monastic land holdings. On the other hand, for centuries the parish church had been a central institution in small towns and villages, providing poor relief and other services, in addition to baptisms and marriages. The Civil Constitution of the Clergy sparked fierce resistance in some parts of rural France. When the pope threatened to excommunicate

Gouze, the self-educated daughter of a butcher. Gouze became an intellectual and playwright and renamed herself Olympe de Gouges. Like many "ordinary" people, she found in the explosion of revolutionary activity the opportunity to address the public by writing speeches, pamphlets, or newspapers. She composed her own manifesto, the *Declaration of the Rights of Woman and the Citizen* (1791).

Analyzing Primary Sources

Declaration of the Rights of Man and of the Citizen

One of the first important pronouncements of the National Assembly after the Tennis Court Oath was the Declaration of the Rights of Man and of the Citizen. *The authors drew inspiration from the American Declaration of Independence, but the language is even more heavily influenced by the ideals of French Enlightenment philosophers, particularly Rousseau. Following are the* Declaration's *preamble and some of its most important principles.*

he representatives of the French people, constituted as the National Assembly, considering that ignorance, disregard, or contempt for the rights of man are the sole causes of public misfortunes and the corruption of governments, have resolved to set forth, in a solemn declaration, the natural, inalienable, and sacred rights of man, so that the constant presence of this declaration may ceaselessly remind all members of the social body of their rights and duties; so that the acts of legislative power and those of the executive power may be more respected . . . and so that the demands of the citizens, grounded henceforth on simple and incontestable principles, may always be directed to the maintenance of the constitution and to the welfare of all. . . .

Article 1. Men are born and remain free and equal in rights. Social distinctions can be based only on public utility.

Article 2. The aim of every political association is the preservation of the natural and imprescriptible rights of man. These rights are liberty, property, security, and resistance to oppression.

Article 3. The source of all sovereignty resides essentially in the nation. No body, no individual can exercise authority that does not explicitly proceed from it.

Article 4. Liberty consists in being able to do anything that does not injure another; thus the only limits upon each man's exercise of his natural laws are those that guarantee enjoyment of these same rights to the other members of society.

Article 5. The law has the right to forbid only actions harmful to society. No action may be prevented that is not forbidden by law, and no one may be constrained to do what the law does not order.

Article 6. The law is the expression of the general will. All citizens have the right to participate personally, or through representatives, in its formation. It must be the same for all, whether it protects or punishes. All citizens, being equal in its eyes, are equally admissable to all public dignities, positions, and employments, according to their ability, and on the basis of no other distinction than that of their virtues and talents. . . .

Article 16. A society in which the guarantee of rights is not secured, or the separation of powers is not clearly established, has no constitution.

Source: Declaration of the Rights of Man and of the Citizen, as cited in K. M. Baker, ed., *The Old Regime and the French Revolution* (Chicago: 1987), pp. 238–239.

Questions for Analysis

1. Who is the Declaration addressed to? Is it just about the rights of the French or do these ideas apply to all people?

2. What gave a group of deputies elected to advise Louis XVI on constitutional reforms the right to proclaim themselves a National Assembly? What was revolutionary about this claim to represent the French nation?

3. Article 6, which states that "law is the expression of general will," is adapted from Rousseau's *Social Contract.* Does the Declaration give any indication of how the "general will" can be known?

---

priests who signed the Civil Constitution, he raised the stakes: allegiance to the new French state meant damnation. Many people, especially peasants in the deeply Catholic areas of western France, were driven into open revolt.

The National Assembly made a series of economic and governmental changes with lasting effects. To raise money, it sold off church lands, although few of the genuinely needy could afford to buy them. To encourage the growth of economic enterprise, it abolished guilds. To rid the country of local aristocratic power, it reorganized local governments, dividing France into eighty-three equal departments. These measures aimed to defend individual liberty and freedom from customary privilege. Their principal beneficiaries were, for the most part, members of the elite, people on their way up under the previous regime who were able to take advantage of the opportunities, such as buying land or being elected to office, that the new one offered. In this realm as elsewhere, the social changes of the revolution endorsed changes already under way in the eighteenth century.

A NEW STAGE: POPULAR REVOLUTION

In the summer of 1792, the revolution's moderate leaders were toppled and replaced by republicans, who repudiated the monarchy and claimed to rule on behalf of a sovereign people. Why this abrupt and drastic change? Was the revolution blown off course? These are among the most difficult questions about the French Revolution. Historians have focused on three factors to explain the revolution's radical turn: changes in popular politics, a crisis of leadership, and international polarization.

First, the revolution politicized the common people, especially in cities. Newspapers filled with political and social commentary multiplied, freed from censorship. From 1789 forward, a wide variety of political clubs became part of daily political life. Some were formal, almost like political parties, gathering members of the elite to debate issues facing the country and influence decisions in the assembly. Other clubs opened their doors to those excluded from formal politics, and they read aloud from newspapers and discussed the options facing the country, from the provisions of the constitution to the trustworthiness of the king and his ministers. This political awareness was heightened by nearly constant shortages and fluctuating prices. Prices particularly exasperated the working people of Paris who had eagerly awaited change since their street demonstrations of 1789. Urban demonstrations, often led by women, demanded cheaper bread; political leaders in clubs and newspapers called for the government to control rising inflation. Club leaders spoke for men and women who felt cheated by the constitution.

A second major reason for the change of course was a lack of effective national leadership. Louis XVI remained a weak monarch. He was forced to support measures personally distasteful to him, in particular the Civil Constitution of the Clergy. He was sympathetic to the plottings of the queen, who was in contact with her brother Leopold II of Austria. Urged on by Marie Antoinette, Louis agreed to attempt an escape from France in June 1791, hoping to rally foreign support for counterrevolution. The members of the royal family managed to slip past their palace guards in Paris, but they were apprehended near the border at Varennes and brought back to the capital. The constitution of 1791 declared France a monarchy, but after the escape to Varennes, Louis was little more than a prisoner of the assembly.

The Counterrevolution

The third major reason for the dramatic turn of affairs was war. From the outset of the revolution, men and women across Europe had been compelled, by the very intensity of events in France, to take sides in the conflict. In the years immediately after 1789, the revolution in France won the enthusiastic support of a wide range of thinkers. The British poet William Wordsworth, who later became disillusioned, recalled his initial mood: "Bliss was it in that dawn to be alive." His sentiments were echoed across the Continent by poets and philosophers, including the German Johann Gottfried von Herder, who declared the revolution the most important historical moment since the Reformation. In Britain, the Low Countries, western Germany, and Italy, "patriots" proclaimed their allegiance to the new revolution.

Others opposed the revolution from the start. Exiled nobles, who fled France for sympathetic royal courts in Germany and elsewhere, did all they could to stir up counterrevolutionary sentiment. In Britain the conservative cause was strengthened by the publication in 1790 of Edmund Burke's *Reflections on the Revolution in France*. A Whig politician who had sympathized with the American revolutionaries, Burke deemed the revolution in France a monstrous crime against the social order (see page 558).

Burke's famous book aroused some sympathy for the counterrevolutionary cause, but active opposition came slowly. The first European states to express public concern about events in revolutionary France were Austria and Prussia, declaring in 1791 that order and the rights of the monarch of France were matters of "common interest to all sovereigns of Europe." The leaders of the French assembly pronounced the declaration an affront to national sovereignty. Nobles who had fled France played into their hands with plots and pronouncements against the government. Oddly, perhaps, both supporters and opponents of the Revolution in France believed war would serve their cause. The National Assembly's leaders expected an aggressive policy to shore up the people's loyalty and bring freedom to the rest of Europe. Counterrevolutionaries hoped the intervention of Austria and Prussia would undo all that had happened since 1789. Radicals, suspicious of aristocratic leaders and the king, believed that war would expose traitors with misgivings about the revolution and flush out those who sympathized with the king and European tyrants. On April 20, 1792, the assembly declared war against Austria and Prussia. Thus began the war that would keep the Continent in arms for a generation.

As the radicals expected, the French forces met serious reverses. By August 1792 the allied armies of Austria

Analyzing Primary Sources

Social Grievances on the Eve of the Revolution (1789)

During the elections to the Estates General, communities drew up "notebooks of grievances" to be presented to the government. The following comes from a rural community, Lignère la Doucelle.

For a long time now, the inhabitants have been crushed beneath the excessive burden of the multiplicity of taxes that they have been obliged to pay. Their parish is large and spread out, but it is a hard land with many uncultivated areas, almost all of it divided into small parcels. There is not one single farm of appreciable size, and these small properties are occupied either by the poor or by people who are doing so poorly that they go without bread every other day. They buy bread or grain nine months of the year. No industries operate in this parish, and from the time they began complaining, no one has ever listened. The cry of anguish echoed all to the way to the ministry after having fruitlessly worn out their intendants. They have always seen their legitimate claims being continuously denied, so may the fortunate moment of equality revive them.

* * *

That all lords, country gentlemen, and others of the privileged class who, either directly or through their proxies, desire to make a profit on their wealth, regardless of the nature of that wealth, pay the same taxes as the common people.

* * *

That the seigneur's mills not be obligatory, allowing everyone to choose where he would like to mill his grain.

* * *

That the children of common people living on a par with nobles be admitted for military service, as the nobility is.

That the king not bestow noble titles upon someone and their family line, but that titles be bestowed only upon those deserving it.

That nobility not be available for purchase or by any fashion other than by the bearing of arms or other service rendered to the State.

* * *

That church members be only able to take advantage of one position. That those who are enjoying more than one be made to choose within a fixed time period.

That future abbeys all be placed into the hands of the king, that His Majesty benefit from their revenue as the head abbots have been able to.

That in towns where there are several convents belonging to the same order, there be only one, and the goods and revenue of those that are to be abolished go to the profit of the crown.

That the convents where there are not normally twelve residents be abolished.

That no tenth of black wheat be paid to parish priests, priors or other beneficiaries, since this grain is only used to prepare the soil for the sowing of rye.

That they also not be paid any tenths of hemp, wool, or lamb. That in the countryside they be required to conduct burials and funerals free of charge. That the ten sous for audit books, insinuations, and the 100 [sous] collected for the parish be abolished.

* * *

That grain be taxed in the realm at a fixed price, or rather that its exportation abroad be forbidden except in the case where it would be sold at a low price.

Source: Armand Bellée, ed., *Cahiers de plaintes & doléances des paroisses de la province du Maine pour les Etats-généraux de 1789*, vol. 2 (Le Mans: 1881–1892), pp. 578–582.

Questions for Analysis

1. Do these grievances reflect the interests of only one social group or can one hear demands being made from different groups within this rural community?

2. What do you think were the main problems faced by this community?

3. How did the revolutionaries receive these grievances?

Debating the French Revolution: Edmund Burke and Thomas Paine

> *The best-known debate on the French Revolution set the Irish-born conservative Edmund Burke against the British radical Thomas Paine. Burke opposed the French Revolution from the beginning. His* Reflections on the Revolution in France *was published early, in 1790, when the French king was still securely on the throne. Burke disagreed with the premises of the revolution. Rights, he argued, were not abstract and "natural" but the results of specific historical traditions. Remodeling the French government without reference to the past and failing to pay proper respect to tradition and custom had, in his eyes, destroyed the fabric of French civilization.*
>
> *Thomas Paine was one of many to respond to Burke.* The Rights of Man *(1791–1792) defended the revolution and, more generally, conceptions of human rights. In the polarized atmosphere of the revolutionary wars, simply possessing Paine's pamphlet was cause for imprisonment in Britain.*

Edmund Burke

You will observe, that from the Magna Charta to the Declaration of Rights, it has been the uniform policy of our constitution to claim and assert our liberties, as an entailed inheritance derived to us from our forefathers. . . . We have an inheritable crown; an inheritable peerage; and a house of commons and a people inheriting privileges, franchises, and liberties, from a long line of ancestors. . . .

You had all these advantages in your ancient states, but you chose to act as if you had never been moulded into civil society, and had every thing to begin anew. You began ill, because you began by despising every thing that belonged to you. . . . If the last generations of your country appeared without much luster in your eyes, you might have passed them by, and derived your claims from a more early race of ancestors. . . . Respecting your forefathers, you would have been taught to respect yourselves. You would not have chosen to consider the French as a people of yesterday, as a nation of low-born servile wretches until the emancipating year of 1789. . . . [Y]ou would not have been content to be represented as a gang of Maroon slaves, suddenly broke loose from the house of bondage, and therefore to be pardoned for your abuse of liberty to which you were not accustomed and ill fitted. . . .

. . . The fresh ruins of France, which shock our feelings wherever we can turn our eyes, are not the devastation of civil war; they are the sad but instructive monuments of rash and ignorant council in time of profound peace. They are the display of inconsiderate and presumptuous, because unresisted and irresistible authority. . . .

Nothing is more certain, than that of our manners, our civilization, and all the good things which are connected with manners, and with civilization, have, in this European world of ours, depended upon two principles; and were indeed the result of both combined; I mean the spirit of a gentleman, and the spirit of religion. The nobility and the clergy, the one by profession, the other by patronage, kept learning in existance, even

and Prussia had crossed the frontier and were threatening to capture Paris. Many, including soldiers, believed that the military disasters were evidence of the king's treason. On August 10, Parisian crowds, organized by their radical leaders, attacked the royal palace. The king was imprisoned and a second and far more radical revolution began.

The French Republic

From this point, the country's leadership passed into the hands of the more egalitarian leaders of the Third Estate. These new leaders were known as Jacobins, the name of a political club to which many of them belonged. Although

in the midst of arms and confusions. . . . Learning paid back what it received to nobility and priesthood. . . . Happy if they had all continued to know their indissoluble union, and their proper place.

Happy if learning, not debauched by ambition, had been satisfied to continue the instructor, and not aspired to be the master! Along with its natural protectors and guardians, learning will be cast into the mire, and trodden down under the hoofs of a swinish multitude.

Source: Edmund Burke, *Reflections on the Revolution in France (1790)* (New York: 1973), pp. 45, 48, 49, 52, 92.

Thomas Paine

Mr. Burke, with his usual outrage, abuses the *Declaration of the Rights of Man*. . . . Does Mr. Burke mean to deny that man has any rights? If he does, then he must mean that there are no such things as rights any where, and that he has none himself; for who is there in the world but man? But if Mr. Burke means to admit that man has rights, the question will then be, what are those rights, and how came man by them originally?

The error of those who reason by precedents drawn from antiquity, respecting the rights of man, is that they do not go far enough into antiquity. They stop in some of the intermediate stages of an hundred or a thousand years, and produce what was then a rule for the present day. This is no authority at all. . . .

To possess ourselves of a clear idea of what government is, or ought to be, we must trace its origin. In doing this, we shall easily discover that governments must have arisen either *out* of the people, or *over* the people. Mr. Burke has made no distinction. . . .

What were formerly called revolutions, were little more than a change of persons, or an alteration of local circumstances. They rose and fell like things of course, and had nothing in their existance or their fate that could influence beyond the spot that produced them. But what we now see in the world, from the revolutions of America and France, is a renovation of the natural order of things, a system of principles as universal as truth and the existance of man, and combining moral with political happiness and national prosperity.

Source: Thomas Paine, *The Rights of Man* (New York: 1973), pp. 302, 308, 383.

Questions for Analysis

1. How does Burke define *liberty*? Why does he criticize the revolutionaries for representing themselves as slaves freed from bondage?

2. What does Paine criticize about Burke's emphasis on history? According to Paine, what makes the French Revolution different from previous changes of regime in Europe?

3. How do these two authors' attitudes about the origins of human freedoms shape their understandings of the revolution?

their headquarters were in Paris, their membership extended throughout France. Their members included large numbers of professionals, government officeholders, and lawyers; but they proclaimed themselves spokesmen for the people and the nation. An increasing number of artisans joined Jacobin clubs as the movement grew, and other, more democratic clubs expanded as well.

The National Convention, elected by free white men, became the effective governing body of the country for the next three years. It was elected in September 1792, at a time when enemy troops were advancing, spreading panic. Rumors flew that prisoners in Paris were plotting to aid the enemy. They were hauled from their cells, dragged before hastily convened tribunals, and killed. The "September

Massacres" killed more than a thousand "enemies of the Revolution" in less than a week. Similar riots engulfed Lyons, Orléans, and other French cities.

The newly elected convention was far more radical than its predecessor, and its leadership was determined to end the monarchy. On September 21, the convention declared France a republic. In December it placed the king on trial, and in January 1793 he was condemned to death by a narrow margin. The heir to the grand tradition of French absolutism met his end bravely as "citizen Louis Capet," beheaded by the guillotine. Introduced as a swifter and more humane form of execution, the frightful mechanical headsman came to symbolize revolutionary fervor.

The convention took other radical measures. It confiscated the property of enemies of the revolution, breaking up some large estates and selling them on easier terms to less-wealthy citizens. It abruptly canceled the policy of compensating nobles for their lost privileges. It repealed primogeniture, so that property would not be inherited exclusively by the oldest son but would be divided in substantially equal portions among all immediate heirs. It abolished slavery in French colonies (discussed later). It set maximum prices for grain and other necessities. In an astonishing effort to root out Christianity from everyday life, the convention adopted a new calendar. The calendar year began with the birth of the republic (September 22, 1792) and divided months in such a way as to eliminate the Catholic Sunday.

Most of this program was a hastily improvised response to crisis and political pressure from the common people in the cities and their leaders. In the three years after 1790, prices had risen staggeringly: wheat by 27 percent, beef by 136 percent, potatoes by 700 percent. While the government imposed its maximums in Paris, small vigilante militias, representing the sans-culottes, attacked those they considered hoarders and profiteers.

THE EXECUTION OF LOUIS XVI. The execution of Louis XVI shocked Europe, and even committed revolutionaries in France debated the necessity of such a dramatic act. The entire National Convention (a body of over seven hundred members) acted as jury, and although the assembly was nearly unanimous in finding the king guilty of treason, a majority of only one approved the final death sentence. Those who voted for Louis XVI's execution were known forever after as "regicides." ▪ *What made this act necessary from the point of view of the most radical of revolutionaries?* ▪ *What made it repugnant from the point of view of the revolution's most heated enemies?*

The convention also reorganized its armies, with astonishing success. By February 1793, Britain, Holland, Spain, and Austria were in the field against the French. Britain came into the war for strategic and economic reasons: they feared a French threat to Britain's growing global power. The allied coalition, though united only in its desire to contain France, was nevertheless a formidable force. To counter it, the revolutionary government mustered all men capable of bearing arms. The revolution flung fourteen hastily drafted armies into battle under the leadership of newly promoted, young, and inexperienced officers. What they lacked in training and discipline they made up for in organization, mobility, flexibility, courage, and morale. In 1793–1794, the French armies preserved their homeland. In 1794–1795, they occupied the Low Countries; the Rhineland; and parts of Spain, Switzerland, and Savoy. In 1796, they invaded and occupied key parts of Italy and broke the coalition that had arrayed itself against them.

The Reign of Terror

In 1793, however, those victories lay in a hard-to-imagine future. France was in crisis. In 1793, the convention drafted a new democratic constitution based on male suffrage. That constitution never took effect—suspended indefinitely by wartime emergency. Instead, the convention prolonged its own life year after year and increasingly delegated its responsibilities to a group of twelve leaders, the Committee of Public Safety. The committee's ruthlessness had two purposes: to seize control of the revolution and to prosecute all the revolution's enemies—"to make terror the order of the day." The Terror lasted less than two years but left a bloody and authoritarian legacy.

Perhaps the three best-known leaders of the radical revolution were Jean Paul Marat, Georges Jacques Danton, and Maximilien Robespierre, the latter two members of the Committee of Public Safety. Marat was educated as a physician and by 1789 had already earned enough distinction in that profession to be awarded an honorary degree by St. Andrews University in Scotland. Marat opposed nearly all of his moderate colleagues' assumptions, including their admiration for Great Britain, which Marat considered corrupt and despotic. Persecuted by powerful factions in the constituent assembly who feared his radicalism, he was forced to take refuge in unsanitary sewers and dungeons. He persevered as the editor of the popular news sheet *The Friend of the People.* Exposure to infection left him with a chronic and painful skin disease, from which baths provided the only relief. In the summer of 1793, at the height of the crisis of the revolution, he was stabbed in his bath

by Charlotte Corday, a young royalist, and thus became a revolutionary martyr.

Danton, like Marat, was a popular political leader, well known in the more plebian clubs of Paris. Elected a member of the Committee of Public Safety in 1793, he had much to do with organizing the Terror. As time went on, however, he wearied of ruthlessness and displayed a tendency to compromise, which gave his opponents in the convention their opportunity. In April 1794, Danton was sent to the guillotine. On mounting the scaffold he is reported to have said, "Show my head to the people; they do not see the like every day."

The most famous of the radical leaders was Maximilien Robespierre. Born of a family reputed to be of Irish descent, Robespierre trained in law and quickly became a modestly successful lawyer. His eloquence and his consistent, or ruthless, insistence that leaders respect the "will of the people" eventually won him a following in the Jacobin club. Later, he became president of the National Convention and a member of the Committee of Public Safety. Though he

THE DEATH OF MARAT. This painting by the French artist David immortalized Marat. The note in the slain leader's hand is from Charlotte Corday, his assassin. ▪ *Why was it important to represent Marat as a martyr?*

had little to do with starting the Terror, he was nevertheless responsible for enlarging its scope. "The Incorruptible," he came to represent ruthlessness justified as virtue and necessary to revolutionary progress.

The two years of the radical Republic (August 1792–July 1794) brought dictatorship, centralization, suspension of any liberties, and war. The committee faced foreign enemies and opposition from both the political right and left at home. In June 1793, responding to an escalating crisis, leaders of the "Mountain," a party of radicals allied with Parisian artisans, purged moderates from the conven-

tion. Rebellions broke out in the provincial cities of Lyons, Bordeaux, and Marseilles, mercilessly repressed by the committee and its local representatives. The government also faced counterrevolution in the western region known as the Vendée, where movements enlisted peasants and artisans, who believed their local areas were being invaded and who fought for their local priest or against the summons from the revolutionaries' conscription boards. By the summer, the forces in the Vendée posed a serious threat to the convention. Determined to stabilize France, whatever the cost, the committee redeployed its forces, defeated the counterrevolutionaries, and launched murderous campaigns of pacification—torching villages, farms, and fields and killing all who dared oppose them and many who did not.

During the period of the Terror, from September 1793 to July 1794, the most reliable estimates place the number of deaths at close to 40,000 to about 16,500 from actual death sentences, with the rest resulting from extra-judicial killings and deaths in prison. Approximately 300,000 were incarcerated between March 1793 and August 1794. These numbers, however, do not include the pacification of the Vendée and rebellious cities in the Rhone Valley, which took more than 100,000 lives. Few victims of the Terror were aristocrats. Many more were peasants or laborers accused of hoarding, treason, or counterrevolutionary activity. Anyone who appeared to threaten the republic, no matter what his or her social or economic position, was at risk. When some time later the Abbé Sieyès was asked what he had done to distinguish himself during the Terror, he responded dryly, "I lived."

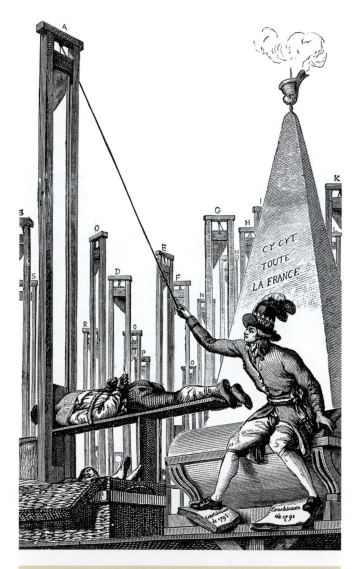

ROBESPIERRE GUILLOTINING THE EXECUTIONER. The original caption for this 1793 engraving read "Robespierre guillotines the executioner after having had all the French guillotined." In fact, Robespierre himself was guillotined after his fall from power in July 1794. ▪ *What made the struggle for power and authority among revolutionaries so merciless and uncompromising?*

The Legacy of the Second French Revolution

The "second" French Revolution affected the everyday life of French men, women, and children in a remarkably direct way. Workers' trousers replaced the breeches that had been a sartorial badge of the middle classes and the nobility. A red cap, said to symbolize freedom from slavery, became popular headgear, wigs vanished. Men and women addressed each other as "citizen" or "citizeness." Public life was marked by ceremonies designed to dramatize the break with the Old Regime and celebrate new forms of fraternity. In the early stages of the revolution, these festivals seem to have captured genuine popular enthusiasm for new ways of living and thinking. Under the Committee of Public Safety, they became didactic and hollow.

The radical revolution of 1792–1793 also dramatically reversed the trend toward decentralization and democracy. The assembly replaced local officials, some of them still royalist in sympathy, with "deputies on mission," whose task was to conscript troops and generate patriotic fervor. When these deputies appeared too eager to act independently, they were replaced by "national agents," with instructions to report directly to the committee. In another effort to stabilize authority, the assembly closed down all the women's political clubs, decreeing them a political and social danger. Ironically, those who claimed to govern in the name of the people found the popular movement threatening.

Finally, the revolution eroded the strength of those traditional institutions—church, guild, parish—that had for centuries given people a common bond. In their place now stood patriotic organizations and a culture that insisted on loyalty to one national cause. Those organizations had first emerged with the election campaigns, meetings, and pamphlet wars of 1788 and the interest they heightened. They included the political clubs and local assemblies, which at the height of the revolution (1792–1793) met every day of the week and offered an apprenticeship in politics. The army of the republic become the premier national institution.

On the one hand, the revolution divided France, mobilizing counterrevolutionaries as well as revolutionaries. At the same time, the revolution, war, and culture of sacrifice forged new bonds. The sense that the rest of Europe, carrying what the verses of the *Marseillaise,* the most famous anthem of the revolution, called the "blood-stained flag of tyranny," sought to crush the new nation and its citizens unquestionably strengthened French national identity.

PATRIOTIC WOMEN'S CLUB. The members of this patriotic club wear constitutional bonnets to show their support for the revolution and the reforms of the convention. ▪ *What can one conclude about the atmosphere in Paris during the revolution from the existence of such associations?*

FROM THE TERROR TO BONAPARTE: THE DIRECTORY

The Committee of Public Safety might have saved France from enemy armies but could not save itself. Inflation became catastrophic. The long string of military victories convinced growing numbers that the committee's demands for continuing self-sacrifice and Terror were no longer justified. By July 1794, the committee was virtually without allies. On July 27 (9 Thermidor, according to the new calendar), Robespierre was shouted down while attempting to speak on the floor of the convention. The following day, along with twenty-one other conspirators, he met his death by guillotine.

Ending the Terror did not immediately bring moderation. Vigilante groups of royalists hunted down Jacobins. The repeal of price controls, combined with the worst winter in a century caused widespread misery. Other measures that had constituted the Terror were gradually repealed. In 1795 the National Convention adopted a new and more conservative constitution. It granted suffrage to all adult male

citizens who could read and write. Yet it set up indirect elections: citizens voted for electors, who in turn chose the legislative body. Wealthy citizens thus held authority. Eager to avoid personal dictatorship, it vested executive authority in a board of five men known as the Directory, chosen by the legislative body. The new constitution included not only a bill of rights but also a declaration of the duties of the citizen.

The Directory lasted longer than its revolutionary predecessors. It still faced discontent on both the radical left and the conservative right. On the left, the Directory repressed radical movements to abolish private property and parliamentary-style government, including one led by the radical "Gracchus Babeuf." Dispatching threats from the right proved more challenging. In 1797 the first free elections held in France as a republic returned a large number of monarchists to the councils of government, alarming politicians who had voted to execute Louis XVI. Backed by the army, the Directory annulled most of the election results. After two years of more uprisings and purges, and with the country still plagued by severe inflation, the Directors grew desperate. This time they called for help from a brilliant young general named Napoleon Bonaparte.

Bonaparte's first military victory had come in 1793, with the recapture of Toulon from royalist and British forces, and had earned him promotion from captain to brigadier general at the age of twenty-four. After the Terror, he was briefly arrested for his Jacobin associations. But he proved his usefulness to the Directory in October 1795 when he put down an uprising with "a whiff of grapeshot," saving the

FRANCE AND ITS SISTER REPUBLICS. ▪ *The French revolutionaries, fighting against the conservative monarchs of Europe, conquered and annexed large sections of what three countries?* ▪ *Who were potential supporters of the French Revolution in areas outside France during the Napoleanic Era?* ▪ *Who was most likely to oppose it in these areas?*

Map legend:
- French Republic, 1792
- Annexed to France, 1792–1795
- Sister republics

the leading Director, that former revolutionary champion of the Third Estate, the Abbé Sieyès. On November 9, 1799 (18 Brumaire), Bonaparte was declared a "temporary consul." He was the answer to the Directory's prayers: a strong, popular leader who was not a king. Sieyès declared that Bonaparte would provide "Confidence from below, authority from above." With those words Sieyès pronounced the end of the revolutionary period.

NAPOLEON AND IMPERIAL FRANCE

Few figures in Western history have compelled the attention of the world as Napoleon Bonaparte did during the fifteen years of his rule in France. Few men lived on with such persistence as myth, not just in their own countries, but across the West. Why? For the great majority of ordinary Europeans, memories of the French Revolution were dominated by those of the Napoleonic wars, which devastated Europe, convulsed its politics, and traumatized its peoples for a generation.

And yet, Bonaparte's relationship to the revolution was not simple. His regime consolidated some of the revolution's political and social changes but sharply repudiated others. He presented himself as the son of the revolution, but he also borrowed freely from very different regimes, fashioning himself as the heir to Charlemagne or to the Roman Empire. His regime remade revolutionary politics and the French state; offered stunning examples of the new kinds of warfare; and left a legacy of conflict and legends of French glory that lingered in the dreams, or nightmares, of Europe's statesmen and citizens for more than a century.

Consolidating Authority: 1799–1804

Bonaparte's early career reinforced the claim that the revolution rewarded the efforts of able men. The son of a provincial Corsican nobleman, he attended the École Militaire in Paris. In prerevolutionary France he would have been unable to rise beyond the rank of major, which required buying a regimental command. The revolution, however, abolished the purchase of military office, and Bonaparte quickly became a general. Here, then, was a man who had risen from obscurity because of his own gifts, which he lent happily to the service of France's revolution.

Once in power, however, Bonaparte showed less respect for revolutionary principles. After the coup of 1799, he assumed the title of "first consul." A new constitution

new regime from its opponents. Promoted, he won a string of victories in Italy, forcing Austria to withdraw (temporarily) from the war. He attempted to defeat Britain by attacking British forces in Egypt and the Near East, a campaign that went well on land but ran into trouble at sea, where the French fleet was defeated by Admiral Horatio Nelson (Abukir Bay, 1798). Bonaparte found himself trapped in Egypt by the British and unable to win a decisive victory.

It was at this point that the call came from the Directory. Bonaparte slipped away from Egypt and appeared in Paris, already having agreed to participate in a coup d'état with established universal white male suffrage and set up two legislative bodies. Elections, however, were indirect, and the power of the legislative bodies sharply curbed. "The government?" said one observer. "There is Bonaparte." Bonaparte instituted what has since become a common authoritarian device, the plebiscite, which put a question directly to popular vote. This allows the head of state to bypass politicians or legislative bodies who might disagree with him—as well as permitting local officials to tamper with ballot boxes. In 1802, flush with victory abroad, he asked the legislature to proclaim him consul for life. When the senate refused to do so, Bonaparte's Council of State stepped in, offered him the title, and had it ratified by plebiscite. Throughout, his regime retained the appearance of consulting with the people, but its most important feature was the centralization of authority.

That authority came from reorganizing the state, and on this score Bonaparte's accomplishments were extraordinary and lasting. Bonaparte's regime confirmed the abolition of privilege, thereby promising "careers open to talent." Centralizing administrative departments, he accomplished what no recent French regime had yet achieved: an orderly and generally fair system of taxation. More efficient tax collection and fiscal management also helped halt the inflationary spiral that had crippled the revolutionary governments, although Bonaparte's regime relied heavily on resources from areas he had conquered to fund his military ventures. As we have seen, earlier revolutionary regimes began to reorganize France's administration—abolishing the ancient fiefdoms with their separate governments, legal codes, privileges, and customs—setting up a uniform system of departments. Bonaparte continued that work, pressing it further and putting an accent on centralization. He replaced elected officials and local self-government with centrally appointed prefects and subprefects, who answered directly to the Council of State in Paris. The prefects wielded considerable power, much more than any elected representative: they were in charge of everything from collecting statistics and reporting on the economy and the population to education, roads, and public works. With more integrated administration, in which the different branches were coordinated (and supervised from above), a more professional bureaucracy, and more rational and efficient taxation (though the demands of war strained the system), Napoleon's state marked the transition from Bourbon absolutism to the modern state.

Law, Education, and a New Elite

Napoleon's most significant contribution to modern state building was the promulgation of a new legal code in 1804.

Each revolutionary regime had taken up the daunting task of modernizing the laws; each had run out of time. Napoleon tolerated no delays, and threw himself into the project, pressing his own ideas and supervising half the meetings. The Napoleonic Code, as the civil code came to be called, pivoted on two principles that had remained significant through all the constitutional changes since 1789: uniformity and individualism. It cleared through the thicket of contradictory legal traditions that governed the ancient provinces of France, creating one uniform law. It confirmed the abolition of feudal privileges of all kinds: not only noble and clerical privileges but the special rights of craft guilds, municipalities, and so on. It set the conditions for exercising property rights: the drafting of contracts, leases, and stock companies. The code's provisions on the family, which Napoleon developed personally, insisted on the importance of paternal authority and the subordination of women and children. In 1793, during the most radical period of the revolution, men and women had been declared "equal in marriage"; now Napoleon's code affirmed the "natural supremacy" of the husband. Married women could not sell property, run a business, or have a profession without their husbands' permission. Fathers had the sole right to control their children's financial affairs, consent to their marriages, and (under the ancient right to correction) to imprison them for up to six months without showing cause. Divorce remained legal, but under unequal conditions; a man could sue for divorce on the grounds of adultery, but a woman could do so only if her husband moved his "concubine" into the family's house. Most important to the common people, the code prohibited paternity suits for illegitimate children.

In all, Napoleon developed seven legal codes covering commercial law, civil law and procedures, crime, and punishment. Like the civil code, the new criminal code consolidated some of the gains of the revolution, treating citizens as equals before the law and outlawing arbitrary arrest and imprisonment. Yet it, too, reinstated brutal measures that the revolutionaries had abolished, such as branding and cutting off the hands of parricides. The Napoleonic legal regime was more egalitarian than law under the Old Regime but no less concerned with authority.

Napoleon also rationalized the educational system. He ordered the establishment of lycées (high schools) in every major town to train civil servants and army officers and a school in Paris to train teachers. To supplement these changes, Napoleon brought the military and technical schools under state control and founded a national university to supervise the entire system. It is not surprising that he built up a new military academy. He reorganized and established solid financing for the premier schools of higher education: the

Representing the People during the French Revolution

From the moment the population of Paris came to the assistance of the beleaguered National Assembly in July 1789, representations of "the people" in the French Revolution took on an overwhelming significance. Building a new government that was committed to an idea of popular sovereignty meant that both the revolution's supporters and its opponents were deeply invested in shaping perceptions of the people. And of course, Article III of the Declaration of the Rights of Man ("The principle of sovereignty resides essentially in the na-

tion") meant that any individual, group, or institution that could successfully claim to represent the will of the people could wield tremendous power, so long as others accepted that claim.

Of course, revolutionary crowds did not always conform to the images of them that circulated so widely in prints and paintings during the period 1789–1799. Some were spontaneous, and others were organized; some were made up of recognizable social and professional groups with clear political goals, and others were a hodgepodge of conflicting and even inarticulate aspirations. Many were nonviolent; some were exceedingly

threatening and murderous. All politicians sought to use them to support their political programs, and many learned to fear their unpredictable behavior.

These four images give a sense of the competing visions of the people that appeared in the public realm during the French Revolution. The first (image A) shows the killing of Foulon, a royal official who was lynched and beheaded by an enthusiastic crowd barely a week after the fall of the Bastille because he was suspected of conspiring to starve the Parisian population as punishment for their rebellion against the king. The second (image B) shows a more care-

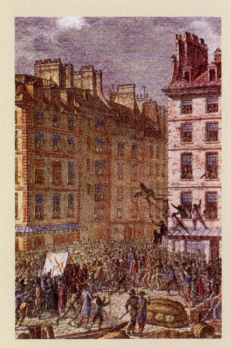

A. The punishment of Foulon (revolutionary print, 1789).

B. *The Festival of Federation*, by Charles Thévenin, 1790.

fully choreographed representation of the people during the Festival of Federation, organized in July 1790 by the revolutionary government to commemorate the first anniversary of the fall of the Bastille. Finally, the last two documents show contrasting images of the revolutionary *sans-culottes,* the working-class revolutionaries who supported the government during the Terror in 1792–1794. The first (image C), a sympathetic portrait of a sans-culottes as a virtuous and self-sacrificing working man, standing with an eye to the future, seems completely incongruous when paired with the British satirist James Gilray's portrait of a cannibalistic sans-culottes family (image D), drawn literally "without pants," feasting on the bodies of their victims after a hard day's work.

Questions for Analysis

1. Image A depicts an event from July 1789—that is, before the August publication of the Declaration of the Rights of Man. How does this image portray the crowd's vengeance on Foulon? What possible political messages are contained in this image?

2. Image B, on the other hand, chooses to display the people celebrating their own birth as a political body, by convening on the anniversary of the fall of the Bastille. What emotions is this painting designed to invoke and how is it related to more disturbing images such as Image A?

3. How are the positive and negative portrayals of sans-culottes as political actors (Images C and D) constructed? Can one imagine a painting of a worker like Image C being produced before 1789? What does Image D tell us about how the revolution was viewed from Britain?

C. *A Sans-Culotte* by Louis-Léopold Boilly, 1792.

D. A family of sans-culotts [sic] refreshing after the fatigues of the day. (British Satirical Cartoon by James Gilray, 1793).

polytechnic (for engineers) and the normal (for teachers), to which students would be admitted based on examinations and from which would issue the technical, educational, and political elites of the country. Like almost all his reforms, this one reinforced reforms introduced during the revolution, and it intended to abolish privilege and create "careers open to talent." Napoleon also embraced the burgeoning social and physical sciences of the Enlightenment. He sponsored the Institute of France, divided into four sections, or academies: fine arts, sciences, humanities, and language (the famous Académie française). These academies dated back to the age of absolutism—now they were coordinated and put on a new footing. They acquired under Napoleon the character that they have preserved to this day: centralized, meritocratic, and geared to serving the state.

Who benefited from these changes? Like Bonaparte's other new institutions, the new schools helped confirm the power of a new elite. The new elite included businessmen, bankers, and merchants but was still composed primarily of powerful landowners. What was more, at least half of the fellowships to the high schools went to the sons of military officers and high civil servants. Finally, like most of Bonaparte's reforms, changes in education aimed to strengthen the empire: "My object in establishing a teaching corps is to have a means of directing political and moral opinion," Napoleon said bluntly.

Bonaparte's early measures were ambitious. To win support for them, he made allies without regard for their past political affiliations. He admitted back into the country exiles of all political stripes. His two fellow consuls were a regicide of the Terror and a bureaucrat of the Old Regime. His minister of police had been an extreme radical republican; his minister of foreign affairs was the aristocrat and opportunist Charles Talleyrand. The most remarkable act of political reconciliation came in 1801, with Bonaparte's concordat with the pope, an agreement that put an end to more than a decade of hostility between the French state and the Catholic Church. Although it shocked anticlerical revolutionaries, Napoleon, ever the pragmatist, believed that reconciliation would create domestic harmony and international solidarity. The agreement gave the pope the right to depose French bishops and to discipline the French clergy. In return, the Vatican agreed to forgo any claims to church lands expropriated by the revolution. That property would remain in the hands of its new middle-class rural and urban proprietors. The concordat did not revoke the principle of religious freedom established by the revolution, but it did win Napoleon the support of conservatives who had feared for France's future as a godless state.

Such political balancing acts increased Bonaparte's general popularity. Combined with early military suc-cesses (peace with Austria in 1801 and with Britain in 1802), they muffled any opposition to his personal ambitions. He had married Josephine de Beauharnais, a Creole from Martinique and an influential mistress of the revolutionary period. Josephine had given the Corsican soldier-politician legitimacy and access among the revolutionary elite early in his career. Neither Bonaparte nor his ambitious wife were content to be first among equals, however; and in December of 1804, he finally cast aside any traces of republicanism. In a ceremony that evoked the splendor of medieval kingship and Bourbon absolutism, he crowned himself Emperor Napoleon I in the Cathedral of Notre Dame in Paris. Napoleon did much to create the modern state, but he did not hesitate to proclaim his links to the past.

In Europe as in France: Napoleon's Empire

The nations of Europe had looked on—some in admiration, others in horror, all in astonishment—at the phenomenon that was Napoleon. Austria, Prussia, and Britain led two coalitions against revolutionary France in 1792–1795 and in 1798, and both were defeated. After Napoleon came to power in 1799, the alliance split. Russia and Austria withdrew from the fray in 1801, and even the intransigent British were forced to make peace the following year.

By 1805 the Russians, Prussians, Austrians, and Swedes had joined the British in an attempt to contain France. Their efforts were to no avail. Napoleon's military superiority led to defeats, in turn, of all the continental allies. Napoleon was a master of well-timed, well-directed shock attacks on the battlefield: movement, regrouping, and pressing his advantage. He led an army that had transformed European warfare; first raised as a revolutionary militia, it was now a trained conscript army, loyal, well supplied by a nation whose economy was committed to serving the war effort, and led by generals promoted largely on the basis of talent. This new kind of army inflicted crushing defeats on his enemies. The battle of Austerlitz, in December 1805, was a triumph for the French against the combined forces of Austria and Russia and became a symbol of the emperor's apparent invincibility. His subsequent victory against the Russians at Friedland in 1807 only added to his reputation.

Out of these victories Napoleon created his new empire and affiliated states. To the southeast, the empire included Rome and the pope's dominions, Tuscany, and the Dalmatian territories of Austria (now the coastline of Croatia). To the east Napoleon's rule extended over a federation of German states known as the Confederation of the Rhine and a section of Poland. These new states were presented as France's gift of independence to patriots elsewhere in Europe, but in practice they served as a military buffer against renewed expansion by Austria. The empire itself was ringed by the allied kingdoms of Italy, Naples, Spain, and Holland, whose thrones were occupied by Napoleon's brothers, brothers-in-law, and trusted generals.

The empire brought the French Revolution's practical consequences—a powerful, centralizing state and an end to old systems of privilege—to Europe's door-step, applying to the empire principles that had already transformed France. Administrative modernization, which meant overhauling the procedures, codes, and practices of the state, was the most powerful feature of changes introduced. The empire changed the terms of government service (careers open to talent), handing out new titles and recruiting new men for the civil service and the judiciary. It ended the nobility's monopoly on the officer corps. The new branches of government hired engineers, mapmakers, surveyors, and legal consultants. Public works and education were reorganized. Prefects in the outer reaches of the empire, as in France, built roads, bridges, dikes (in Holland), hospitals, and prisons; they reorganized universities and built observatories. In the empire and some of the satellite

NAPOLEON'S EUROPEAN EMPIRE AT ITS HEIGHT. At the height of his power in 1812, Napoleon controlled most of Europe, ruling either directly or through dependent states and allies. ▪ *Compared to the map on page 564, by what means had Napoleon expanded French control on continental Europe?* ▪ *Which major countries remained outside of French control?* ▪ *Which areas felt the most long-lasting impact of Napoleon's reign?*

kingdoms, tariffs were eliminated, feudal dues abolished, new tax districts formed, and plentiful new taxes collected to support the new state.

In the realm of liberty and law, Napoleon's rule eliminated feudal and church courts and created a single legal system. The Napoleonic Code was often introduced, but not always or entirely. (In southern Italy measures against the Catholic Church were deemed too controversial.) Reforms eliminated many inequalities and legal privileges. The Duchy of Warsaw in Poland ended serfdom but offered no land reform, so former serfs became impoverished tenants. In most areas, the empire gave civil rights to Protestants and Jews. In Rome, the conquering French opened the gates of the Jewish ghetto—and made Jews subject to conscription. In some areas, Catholic monasteries, convents, and other landholdings were broken up and sold, almost always to wealthy buyers. In the empire as in France, and under Napoleon as during the revolution, many who benefited were the elite: people and groups already on their way up and with the resources to take advantage of opportunities.

In government, the regime sought a combination of legal equality (for men) and stronger state authority. The French and local authorities created new electoral districts, expanded the suffrage, and wrote constitutions, but newly elected representative bodies were dismissed if they failed to cooperate, few constitutions were ever fully applied, and political freedoms were often fleeting. Napoleon's regime referred to revolutionary principles to anchor its legitimacy, but authority remained its guiding light. All governmental direction emanated from Paris and therefore from Napoleon.

Finally, in the empire as in France, Napoleon displayed his signature passions. The first of these was an Enlightenment zeal for accumulating useful knowledge. The empire gathered statistics as never before, for it was important to know the resources—including population—that a state had at its disposal. That spirit had been evident already in Bonaparte's extraordinary 1798 excursion into Egypt. He took hundreds of scholars and artists along with the army, founded the Egyptian institute in Cairo, and sent researchers off to make a systematic inventory of the country (its geology, rivers, minerals, antiquities, animal life) and to conduct archaeological expeditions to Upper Egypt, where they sketched the pyramids and excavated what would turn out to be the Rosetta stone (see Chapter 20). Napoleon's second passion was cultivating his relationship to imperial glories of the past. He poured time and energy into (literally) cementing his image for posterity. The Arc de Triomphe in Paris, designed to imitate the Arc of Constantine in Rome, is the best example; but Napoleon also ordered work to be undertaken to restore ruins in Rome, to make the Prado Palace in Madrid a museum, and to renovate and preserve the Alhambra in Granada.

Such were Napoleon's visions of his legacy and himself. How did others see him? Europe offered no single reaction. Some countries and social groups collaborated enthusiastically, some negotiated, some resisted. Napoleon's image as a military hero genuinely inspired young men from the elite, raised in a culture that prized military honor. By contrast, Catholic peasants in Spain fought him from the beginning. In many small principalities previously ruled by princes—the patchwork states of Germany, for example, and the repressive kingdom of Naples—reforms that provided for more efficient, less corrupt administration, a workable tax structure, and an end to customary privilege were welcomed by most of the local population. Yet the Napoleonic presence proved a mixed blessing. Vassal states contributed heavily to the maintenance of the emperor's military power. The French levied taxes, drafted men, and required states to support occupying armies. In Italy, the policy was called "liberty and requisitions"; and

NAPOLEON ON HORSEBACK AT THE ST. BERNARD PASS BY JACQUES LOUIS DAVID, 1801. David painted many episodes of the revolution: the Tennis Court Oath, the death of Marat, and the rise and rule of Napoleon. Here Napoleon heroically leads his troops over the Alps into Italy to attack Austrian troops.

the Italians, Germans, and Dutch paid an especially high price for reforms—in terms of economic cost and numbers of men recruited. From the point of view of the common people, the local lord and priest had been replaced by the French tax collector and army recruiting board.

It is telling that even Napoleon's enemies came to believe that the upstart emperor represented the wave of the future, particularly in regard to the reorganization of the state. Though they fought Napoleon, Prussian and Austrian administrators set about instituting reforms that resembled his: changing rules of promotion and recruitment, remodeling bureaucracies, redrawing districts, eliminating some privileges, and so on. Many who came of age under Napoleon's empire believed that, for better or worse, his empire was modern.

THE RETURN TO WAR AND NAPOLEON'S DEFEAT: 1806–1815

Napoleon's boldest attempt at consolidation, a policy banning British goods from the Continent, was a dangerous failure. Britain had bitterly opposed each of France's revolutionary regimes since the death of Louis XVI; now it tried to rally Europe against Napoleon with promises of generous financial loans and trade. Napoleon's Continental System, established in 1806, sought to starve Britain's trade and force its surrender. The system failed for several reasons. Throughout the war Britain retained control of the seas. The British naval blockade of the Continent, begun in 1807, effectively countered Napoleon's system. While the French Empire strained to transport goods and raw materials overland to avoid the British blockade, the British successfully developed a lively trade with South America. A second reason for the failure of the system was its internal tariffs. Europe divided into economic camps, at odds with each other as they tried to subsist on what the Continent alone could produce and manufacture. Finally, the system hurt the Continent more than Britain. Stagnant trade in Europe's ports and unemployment in its manufacturing centers eroded public faith in Napoleon's dream of a working European empire.

The Continental System was Napoleon's first serious mistake. His ambition to create a European empire, modeled on Rome and ruled from Paris, was to become a second cause of his decline. The symbols of his empire—reflected in painting, architecture, and the design of furniture and clothing—were deliberately Roman in origin. Where early revolutionaries referred to the Roman Rebublic for their imagery, Napoleon looked to the more ostentatious style of the Roman emperors. In 1809 he divorced the empress Josephine and ensured himself a successor of royal blood by marrying a Habsburg princess, Marie Louise—the great-niece of Marie-Antionette. Such actions lost Napoleon the support of revolutionaries, former Enlightenment thinkers, and liberals across the Continent.

Over time, the bitter tonic of defeat began to have an effect on Napoleon's enemies, who changed their own approach to waging war. After the Prussian army was humiliated at Jena in 1806 and forced out of the war, a whole generation of younger Prussian officers reformed their military and their state by demanding rigorous practical training for commanders and a genuinely national army made up of patriotic Prussian citizens rather than well-drilled mercenaries.

The myth of Napoleon's invincibility worked against him as well, as he took ever greater risks with France's military and national fortunes. Russian numbers and Austrian artillery inflicted horrendous losses on the French at Wagram in 1809, although these difficulties were forgotten

NAPOLEON ON THE BATTLEFIELD OF EYLAU. Amid bitter cold and snow, Napoleon engaged with the Russian army in February 1807. Although technically a victory for the French, it was only barely that, with the French losing at least ten thousand men and the Russians twice as many. This painting, characteristic of Bonaparte propaganda, emphasizes not the losses but the emperor's saintlike clemency—even enemy soldiers reach up toward him.

in the glow of victory. Napoleon's allies and supporters shrugged off the British admiral Horatio Nelson's victory at Trafalgar in 1805 as no more than a temporary check to the emperor's ambitions. But Trafalgar broke French naval power in the Mediterranean and led to a rift with Spain, which had been France's equal partner in the battle and suffered equally in the defeat. In the Caribbean, too, Napoleon was forced to cut growing losses (see page 573).

A crucial moment in Napoleon's undoing came with his invasion of Spain in 1808. Napoleon overthrew the Spanish king, installed his own brother on the throne, and then imposed a series of reforms similar to those he had instituted elsewhere in Europe. Napoleon's blow against the Spanish monarchy weakened its hold on its colonies across the Atlantic, and the Spanish crown never fully regained its grip (see Chapter 20). But in Spain itself, Napoleon reckoned without two factors that led to the ultimate failure of his mission: the presence of British forces and the determined resistance of the Spanish people, who detested Napoleon's interference in the affairs of the church. The peninsular wars, as the Spanish conflicts were called, were long and bitter. The smaller British force learned how to concentrate a devastating volume of gunfire on the French pinpoint attacks on the open battlefield and laid siege to French garrison towns. The Spanish quickly began to wear down the French invaders through guerrilla warfare. Terrible atrocities were committed by both sides; the French military's torture and execution of Spanish guerrillas and civilians was immortalized by the Spanish artist Francisco Goya (1746–1828) with sickening accuracy in his prints and paintings. Though at one point Napoleon himself took charge of his army, he could not achieve anything more than temporary victory. The Spanish campaign was the first indication that Napoleon could be beaten, and it encouraged resistance elsewhere.

The second, and most dramatic stage in Napoleon's downfall began with the disruption of his alliance with Russia. As an agricultural country, Russia had suffered a severe economic crisis when it was no longer able to trade its surplus grain for British manufactures. The consequence was that Tsar Alexander I began to wink at trade with Britain and to ignore or evade the protests from Paris. By 1811 Napoleon decided that he could no longer endure this flouting of their agreement. He collected an army of six hundred thousand and set out for Russia in the spring of 1812. Only a third of the soldiers in this "Grande Armée" were French; nearly as many were Polish or German, joined by soldiers and adventurers from the rest of France's client states. It was the grandest of Napoleon's imperial expeditions, an army raised from across Europe and sent to punish the autocratic tsar. The invasion ended in disaster. The Russians refused to make a stand, drawing the French farther and farther into the heart of their country. Just before Napoleon reached the ancient Russian capital of Moscow, the Russian army drew the French forces into a bloody, seemingly pointless battle in the narrow streets of a town called Borodino, where both sides suffered terrible losses of men and supplies, harder on the French who were now so far from home. After the battle, the Russians permitted Napoleon to occupy Moscow. But on the night of his entry, Russian partisans put the city to the torch, leaving little but the blackened walls of the Kremlin palaces to shelter the French troops.

Hoping that the tsar would eventually surrender, Napoleon lingered amid the ruins for more than a month. On October 19 he finally ordered the homeward march. The delay was a fatal blunder. Long before he had reached the border, the terrible Russian winter was on his troops. Frozen streams, mountainous drifts of snow, and bottomless mud slowed the retreat almost to a halt. To add to the miseries of frostbite, disease, and starvation, mounted

THE 3RD OF MAY, 1808 BY FRANCISCO GOYA. This painting of the execution of Spanish rebels by Napoleon's army as it marched through Spain is one of the most memorable depictions of a nation's martyrdom.

Cossacks rode out of the blizzard to harry the exhausted army. Each morning the miserable remnant that pushed on left behind circles of corpses around the campfires of the night before. Temperatures dropped to -27°F. On December 13 a few thousand broken soldiers crossed the frontier into Germany—a fragment of the once proud Grande Armée. Nearly three hundred thousand of its soldiers and untold thousands of Russians lost their lives in Napoleon's Russian adventure.

After the retreat from Russia, the anti-Napoleonic forces took renewed hope. United by a belief that they might finally succeed in defeating the emperor, Prussia, Russia, Austria, Sweden, and Britain renewed their attack. Citizens of many German states in particular saw this as a war of liberation, and indeed most of the fighting took place in Germany. The climax of the campaign occurred in October 1813 when, at what was thereafter known as the Battle of the Nations, fought near Leipzig, the allies dealt the French a resounding defeat. Meanwhile, allied armies won significant victories in the Low Countries and Spain. By the beginning of 1814, they had crossed the Rhine into France. Left with an army of inexperienced youths, Napoleon retreated to Paris, urging the French people to resist despite constant setbacks at the hands of the larger invading armies. On March 31, Tsar Alexander I of Russia and King Frederick William III of Prussia made their triumphant entry into Paris. Napoleon was forced to abdicate unconditionally and was sent into exile on the island of Elba, off the Italian coast.

Napoleon was back on French soil in less than a year. In the interim the allies had restored the Bourbon dynasty to the throne, in the person of Louis XVIII, brother of Louis XVI. Despite his administrative abilities, Louis could not fill the void left by Napoleon's abdication. It was no surprise that, when the former emperor staged his escape from Elba, his fellow countrymen once more rallied to his side. By the time Napoleon reached Paris, he had generated enough support to cause Louis to flee the country. The allies, meeting in Vienna to conclude peace treaties with the French, were stunned by the news of Napoleon's return. They dispatched a hastily organized army to meet the emperor's typically bold offensive push into the Low Countries. At the battle of Waterloo, fought over three bloody days from June 15 to 18, 1815, Napoleon was stopped by the forces of his two most persistent enemies, Britain and Prussia, and suffered his final defeat. This time the allies took no chances and shipped their prisoner off to the bleak island of St. Helena in the South Atlantic. The once-mighty emperor, now the exile Bonaparte, lived out a dreary existence writing self-serving memoirs until his death in 1821.

Liberty, Politics, and Slavery: The Haitian Revolution

In the French colonies across the Atlantic, the revolution took a different course, with wide-ranging ramifications. The Caribbean islands of Guadeloupe, Martinique, and St. Domingue occupied a central role in the eighteenth-century French economy because of the sugar trade. Their planter elites had powerful influence in Paris. The French National Assembly (like its American counterpart) declined to discuss the matter of slavery in the colonies, unwilling to encroach on the property rights of slave owners and fearful of losing the lucrative sugar islands to their British or Spanish rivals should discontented slave owners talk of independence from France. (Competition between the European powers for the islands of the Caribbean was intense; that islands would change hands was a real possibility.) French men in the National Assembly also had to consider the question of rights for free men of color, a group that included a significant number of wealthy owners of property (and slaves).

St. Domingue had about forty thousand whites of different social classes, thirty thousand free people of color, and five hundred thousand slaves, most of them recently enslaved in West Africa. In 1790, free people of color from St. Domingue sent a delegation to Paris, asking to be seated by the assembly, underscoring that they were men of property and, in many cases, of European ancestry. The assembly refused. Their refusal sparked a rebellion among free people of color in St. Domingue. The French colonial authorities repressed the movement quickly—and brutally. They captured Vincent Ogé, a member of the delegation to Paris and one of the leaders of the rebellion, and publicly executed him and his allies by breaking on the wheel and decapitation. Radical deputies, in Paris, including Robespierre, expressed outrage but could do little to change the assembly's policy.

In August 1791 the largest slave rebellion in history broke out in St. Domingue. How much that rebellion owed to revolutionary propaganda is unclear; like many rebellions during the period, it had its own roots. The British and the Spanish invaded, confident they could crush the rebellion and take the island. In the spring of 1792, the French government, on the verge of collapse and war with Europe, scrambled to win allies in St. Domingue by making free men of color citizens. A few months later (after the revolution of August 1792), the new French Republic dispatched commissioners to St. Domingue with troops and instructions to hold the island. There they faced a combination of different forces: Spanish and British troops, defiant St. Domingue

Analyzing Primary Sources

Two Letters from Napoleon

Napoleon placed his brothers on the thrones of different vassal states in conquered territories throughout Europe. The first excerpt here is from a letter to his brother Eugène, head of one of the new Italian states, in which Napoleon explains how Italy's lucrative silk trade was to be diverted to damage English commercial interests and bolster the French Empire. It provides a revealing glimpse of Napoleon's vision of a united Europe, with the other countries' futures tied to France's.

On March 1, 1815, Napoleon landed in the south of France, having escaped from his exile on the island of Elba. The restored Bourbon king abdicated, and Napoleon ruled for a hundred more days, until his defeat at the battle of Waterloo in June. The second selection is excerpted from a proclamation, addressed to the sovereigns of Europe, explaining the emperor's return. It is an excellent illustration of Napoleon's self-image, his rhetoric, and his belief that he represented the force of history itself.

Letter to Prince Eugène, August 23, 1810

 have received your letter of August 14. All the raw silk from the Kingdom of Italy goes to England, for there are no silk factories in Germany. It is therefore quite natural that I should wish to divert it from this route to the advantage of my French manufacturers: otherwise my silk factories, one of the chief supports of French commerce, would suffer substantial losses. I cannot agree with your observations. My principle is *France first.* You must never lose sight of the fact that, if English commerce is supreme on the high seas, it is due to her sea power: it is therefore to be expected that, as France is the strongest land power, she should claim commercial supremacy on the continent: it is indeed our only hope. And isn't it better for Italy to come to the help of France, in such an important matter as this, than to be covered with Customs Houses? For it would be short-sighted not to recognise that Italy owes her independence to France; that it was won by French blood and French victories; that it must not be misused; and that nothing could be more unreasonable than to start calculating what commercial advantages France gets out of it.

Piedmont and Parma produce silk too; and there also I have prohibited its export to any country except France. It is no use for Italy to make plans that leave French prosperity out of account; she must face the fact that the interests of the two countries hang together. Above all, she must be careful not to give France any reason for annexing her; for if it paid France to do this, who could stop her? So make this your motto too—*France first.*

planters, and slaves in rebellion. In this context, the local French commissioners reconsidered their commitment to slavery; in 1793 they promised freedom to slaves who would join the French. A year later, the assembly in Paris extended to slaves in all the colonies a liberty that had already been accomplished in St. Domingue, by the slave rebellion.

Emancipation and war brought new leaders to the fore, chief among them a former slave, Toussaint Bréda, later Toussaint L'Ouverture (*too-SAN LOO-vehr-tur*), meaning "the one who opened the way." Over the course of the next five years, Toussaint and his soldiers, now allied with the French army, emerged victorious over the French planters, the British (in 1798), and the Spanish (in 1801). Toussaint also broke the power of his rival generals in both the mulatto and former slave armies, becoming the statesman of the revolution. In 1801, Toussaint set up a constitution, swearing allegiance to France but denying France any right to interfere in St. Domingue affairs. The constitution abolished slavery, reorganized the military, established Christianity as the state religion (this entailed a rejection of vodoun, a blend of Christian and various West and Central African traditions), and made Toussaint governor for life. It was an extraordinary moment in the revolutionary period: the formation of an authoritarian society but also an utterly unexpected symbol of the universal potential of revolutionary ideas.

Toussaint's accomplishments, however, put him on a collision course with the other French general he admired

Circular Letter to the Sovereigns of Europe, April 4, 1815

Monsieur, My Brother,

You will have learnt, during the course of last month, of my landing again in France, of my entry into Paris, and of the departure of the Bourbon family. Your Majesty must by now be aware of the real nature of these events. They are the work of an irresistible power, of the unanimous will of a great nation conscious of its duties and of its rights. A dynasty forcibly reimposed upon the French people was no longer suitable for it: the Bourbons refused to associate themselves with the natural feelings or the national customs; and France was forced to abandon them. The popular voice called for a liberator. The expectation which had decided me to make the supreme sacrifice was in vain. I returned; and from the place where my foot first touched the shore I was carried by the affection of my subjects into the bosom of my capital.

My first and heartfelt anxiety is to repay so much affection by the maintenance of an honourable peace. The re-establishment of the Imperial throne was necessary for the happiness of Frenchmen: my dearest hope is that it may also secure repose for the whole of Europe. Each national flag in turn has had its gleam of glory: often enough, by some turn of fortune, great victories have been followed by great defeats.... I have provided the world in the past with a programme of great contests; it will please me better in future to acknowledge no rivalry but that of the advocates of peace, and no combat but a crusade for the felicity of mankind. It is France's pleasure to make a frank avowal of this noble ideal. Jealous of her independence, she will always base her policy upon an unqualified respect for the independence of other peoples....

Monsieur my Brother,
Your good Brother,
Napoleon

Source: K. M. Baker, ed., *The Old Regime and the French Revolution* (Chicago: 1987), pp. 419–420, 426–427.

Questions for Analysis

1. What does the 1810 letter reveal about Napoleon's vision of the European economy? Does his view differ substantially from the mercantilist doctrine of the prerevolutionary monarchy?

2. In his 1815 address to the monarchs of Europe can one still detect certain aspects of revolutionary rhetoric in Napoleon's words, even as he harnessed this rhetoric to his project of reestablishing the empire after his 1814 defeat?

3. Who in France (or in Europe as a whole) might still have supported Napoleon in 1815? Who would have celebrated his downfall?

---

and whose career was remarkably like his own: Napoleon Bonaparte. St. Domingue stood at the center of Bonaparte's vision of an expanded empire in the New World, an empire that would recoup North American territories France had lost under the Old Regime and pivot around the lucrative combination of the Mississippi, French Louisiana, and the sugar and slave colonies of the Caribbean. In January 1802, Bonaparte dispatched twenty thousand troops to bring the island under control. Toussaint, captured when he arrived for discussions with the French, was shipped under heavy guard to a prison in the mountains of eastern France, where he died in 1803. Fighting continued in St. Domingue, however, with fires now fueled by Bonaparte's decree reestablishing slavery where the convention had abolished it.

The war turned into a nightmare for the French. Yellow fever killed thousands of French troops, including one of Napoleon's best generals and brother-in-law. Armies on both sides committed atrocities. By December 1803, the French army had collapsed. Napoleon scaled back his vision of an American empire and sold the Louisiana territories to Thomas Jefferson. "I know the value of what I abandon . . . I renounce it with the greatest regret," he told an aide. In St. Domingue, a general in the army of former slaves, Jean-Jacques Dessalines, declared the independent state of Haiti in 1804.

The Haitian Revolution remained, in significant ways, an anomaly. It was the only successful slave revolution in history and by far the most radical of the revolutions that

TOUSSAINT L'OUVERTURE. A portrait of L'Ouverture, leader of what would become the Haitian Revolution, as a general.

occurred in this age. It suggested that the emancipatory ideas of the revolution and Enlightenment might apply to non-Europeans and enslaved peoples—a suggestion that residents of Europe attempted to ignore but one that struck home with planter elites in North and South America. Combined with later rebellions in the British colonies, it contributed to the British decision to end slavery in 1838. And it cast a long shadow over nineteenth-century slave societies from the southern United States to Brazil. The Napoleonic episode, then, had wide-ranging effects across the Atlantic: in North America, the Louisiana purchase; in the Caribbean, the Haitian Revolution; in Latin America, the weakening of Spain and Portugal's colonial empires.

CONCLUSION

The tumultuous events in France formed part of a broad pattern of late-eighteenth-century democratic upheaval. The French Revolution was the most violent, protracted, and contentious of the revolutions of the era; but the dynamics of revolution were much the same everywhere. One of the most important developments of the French Revolution was the emergence of a popular movement,

After You Read This Chapter

Visit StudySpace for quizzes, additional review materials, and multi-media documents. **wwnorton.com/studyspace**

REVIEWING THE OBJECTIVES

- The French Revolution resulted both from an immediate political crisis and long-term social tensions. What was this crisis, and how did it lead to popular revolt against the monarchy?
- The revolutionaries in the National Assembly in 1789 set out to produce a constitution for France. What were their political goals, and what was the reaction of monarchs and peoples elsewhere in Europe?
- After 1792, a more radical group of revolutionaries seized control of French state. How did they come to power, and how were their political goals different from their predecssors?
- Napoleon's career began during the revolution. What did he owe to the revolution, and what was different about his regime?
- Three major revolutions took place in the Atlantic world at the end of the eighteenth century: the American Revolution, the French Revolution, and the Haitian Revolution. What was similar about these revolutions? What was different?

which included political clubs representing people previously excluded from politics, newspapers read by and to the common people, and political leaders who spoke for the sans-culottes. In the French Revolution as in other revolutions, the popular movement challenged the early and moderate revolutionary leadership, pressing for more radical and democratic measures. And as in other revolutions, the popular movement in France was defeated, and authority was reestablished by a quasi-military figure. Likewise, the revolutionary ideas of liberty, equality, and fraternity were not specifically French; their roots lay in the social structures of the eighteenth century and in the ideas and culture of the Enlightenment. Yet French armies brought them, literally, to the doorsteps of many Europeans.

What was the larger impact of the revolution and the Napoleonic era? Its legacy is partly summed up in three key concepts: liberty, equality, and nation. Liberty meant individual rights and responsibilities and, more specifically, freedom from arbitrary authority. By equality, as we have seen, the revolutionaries meant the abolition of legal distinctions of rank among European men. Though their concept of equality was limited, it became a powerful mobilizing force in the nineteenth century. The most important legacy of the revolution may have been the new term *nation*. Nationhood was a political concept. A nation was formed of citizens, not a king's subjects; it was ruled by law and treated citizens as equal before the law; sovereignty did not lie in dynasties or historic fiefdoms but in the nation of citizens. This new form of nation gained legitimacy when citizen armies repelled attacks against their newly won freedoms; the victories of "citizens in arms" lived on in myth and history and provided the most powerful images of the period. As the war continued, military nationhood began to overshadow its political cousin. By the Napoleonic period, this shift became decisive; a new political body of freely associated citizens was most powerfully embodied in a centralized state, its army and a kind of citizenship defined by individual commitment to the needs of the nation at war. This understanding of national identity spread throughout Europe in the coming decades.

PEOPLE, IDEAS, AND EVENTS IN CONTEXT

- Why was **LOUIS XVI** forced to convene the **ESTATES GENERAL** in 1789?
- What argument did **ABBÉ SIEYÈS** make about the role of the **THIRD ESTATE**?
- What made the **TENNIS COURT OATH** a revolutionary act?
- What was the role of popular revolt (the attack on the **BASTILLE**, the **GREAT FEAR**, the **OCTOBER DAYS**) in the revolutionary movements of 1789?
- What was the connection between the French Revolution with the **SLAVE REVOLT IN SAINT-DOMINGUE** that began in 1791?
- What was the **DECLARATION OF THE RIGHTS OF MAN AND OF THE CITIZEN**?
- What was the **CIVIL CONSTITUTION OF THE CLERGY**?
- What circumstances led to the abolition of the monarchy in 1792?
- Why did the **JACOBINS** in the **NATIONAL CONVENTION** support a policy of **TERROR**?
- What were **NAPOLEON'S** most significant domestic accomplishments in France? What significance did **NAPOLEON'S MILITARY CAMPAIGNS** have for other parts of Europe and for the French Empire?
- What was the significance of the **HAITIAN REVOLUTION** of 1804?

CONSEQUENCES

- Was the French Revolution a success? Why or why not?
- Who benefited from the French Revolution? Who suffered the most from its consequences?
- In what ways do you think the French Revolution would have an impact on nineteenth-century history?

STORY LINES

- Industrialization put Europe on the path to a new form of economic development, based on the concentration of labor and production in areas with easy access to new sources of energy. This led to rapid growth of new industrial cities and the development of new transportation links to connect industrial centers to growing markets.

- Industrialization created new social groups in society, defined less by their status at birth than by their place in the new economy. Workers faced new kinds of discipline in the workplace, and women and children entered the new industrial workforce in large numbers. A new elite, made up of businessmen, entrepreneurs, bankers, engineers, and merchants, emerged as the primary beneficiaries of industrialization.

- Countryside population increases spurred migration to cities where laborers and the middle classes did not mix socially. They adopted different dress, speech, leisure activities, and had significantly different opportunities when it came to marriage, sex, family life, and the raising of children.

CHRONOLOGY

1780s	Industrialization begins in Britain
1825	First railroad in Britain
1830s	Industrialization begins in France and Belgium
1845–1849	Irish Potato Famine
1850s	Industrialization begins in Prussia and German states of central Europe
1861	Russian tsar emancipates the serfs

The Industrial Revolution and Nineteenth-Century Society

The French Revolution transformed the political landscape of Europe suddenly and dramatically. More gradual, but just as consequential for the modern world, was the economic transformation that began in Europe in the 1780s. Following the development of mechanized industry and the emergence of large-scale manufacturing in the British textile trade, industrialization spread to the European Continent and eventually to North America. This "Industrial Revolution" led to the proliferation of more capital-intensive enterprises, new ways of organizing human labor, and the rapid growth of cities. It was made possible by new sources of energy and power, which led to faster forms of mechanized transportation, higher productivity, and the emergence of large consumer markets for manufactured goods. In turn, these interrelated developments triggered social and cultural changes with revolutionary consequences for Europeans and their relationship to the rest of the world.

Of all the changes, perhaps the most revolutionary came at the very root of human endeavor: new forms of energy. Over the space of two or three generations, a society and an economy that had drawn on water, wind, and wood for most of its energy needs came to depend on machines driven by steam engines and coal. In 1800, the world produced ten million tons of coal. In 1900, it produced one billion: a hundred times more. The Industrial Revolution brought the beginning of the fossil-fuel age, altering as it did so the balance of humanity and the environment.

Mechanization made possible enormous gains in productivity in some sectors of the economy, but to focus only on mechanization can be misleading. The new machines were limited to a few sectors of the economy, especially at the outset, and did not always lead to a dramatic break with older techniques. Above all, technology did not dispense with human toil. Historians emphasize that the Industrial Revolution intensified human labor—carrying water on iron rails, digging trenches, harvesting cotton, sewing by hand, or pounding hides—much more often than it eased it. One historian has suggested that we would do better to speak of the "industrious revolution." This revolution did not lie solely in machines but in a new economic system based on mobilizing capital and labor on a much larger scale. The industrious economy redistributed wealth and power, creating new social classes and producing new social tensions.

It also prompted deep-seated cultural shifts. The English critic Raymond Williams has pointed out that in the eighteenth century, *industry* referred to a human quality: a hardworking woman was "industrious," an ambitious clerk showed "industry." By the middle of the nineteenth century, industry had come to mean an economic system, one that followed its own logic and worked on its own—seemingly independent of humans. This is our modern understanding of the term, and it was born in the early nineteenth century. As the Industrial Revolution altered the foundations of the economy, it also changed the very assumptions with which people approached economics and the ways in which they regarded the role of human beings in the economy. These new assumptions could foster a sense of power but also anxieties about powerlessness.

The dramatic changes of the late eighteenth and early nineteenth centuries emerged out of earlier developments. Overseas commercial exploration opened new territories to European trade. India, Africa, and the Americas had already been brought into the web of the European economy. Expanding trade networks created new markets for goods and sources for raw materials, and the need to organize commerce over long distances fostered financial innovations and sophisticated credit schemes for managing risk. These developments paved the way for industrialization. Within Europe, the commercialization of agriculture and the spread of handicraft manufacturing in rural areas also changed the economy in ways that anticipated later industrial developments. A final factor seems to have been population growth, which began to accelerate in the eighteenth century. Because these earlier developments did not affect all areas in Europe the same way, industrialization did not always follow the same pattern across the Continent. It happened first in Great Britain, and that is where we will begin.

THE INDUSTRIAL REVOLUTION IN BRITAIN, 1760–1850

Great Britain in the eighteenth century had a fortunate combination of natural, economic, and cultural resources. It was a small and secure island nation with a robust empire and control over crucial lanes across the oceans. It had ample supplies of coal, rivers, and a well-developed network of canals.

ENCLOSED FIELDS IN CENTRAL BRITAIN. The large, uniform, square fields in the background of this photograph are fields that were enclosed from smaller holdings and common lands in the 1830s. They contrast with the smaller and older strip fields in the foreground. The larger enclosed fields were more profitable for their owners, who benefited from legislation that encouraged enclosure, but the process created hardship for the village communities that depended on the use of these lands for their survival.
■ *What circumstances made enclosure possible?* ■ *What connection have historians made between enclosure and early industrialization?*

In addition, agriculture in Britain was already more thoroughly commercialized than elsewhere. British agriculture had been transformed by a combination of new techniques, new crops, and by the "enclosure" of fields and pastures, which turned small holdings, and in many cases commonly held lands, into large fenced tracts that were privately owned and individually managed by commercial landlords. The British Parliament encouraged enclosure with a series of bills in the second half of the eighteenth century. Commercialized agriculture was more productive and yielded more food for a growing and increasingly urban population. The concentration of property in fewer hands drove small farmers off the land, sending them to look for work in other sectors of the economy. Last, commercialized

agriculture produced higher profits, wealth that would be invested in industry.

A key precondition for industrialization, therefore, was Britain's growing supply of available capital, in the forms of private wealth and well-developed banking and credit institutions. London had become the leading center for international trade, and the city was a headquarters for the transfer of raw material, capital, and manufactured products throughout the world. This capital was readily available to underwrite new economic enterprises and eased the transfer of money and goods—importing, for instance, silks from the East or Egyptian and North American cottons.

Social and cultural conditions also encouraged investment in enterprises. In Britain far more than on the

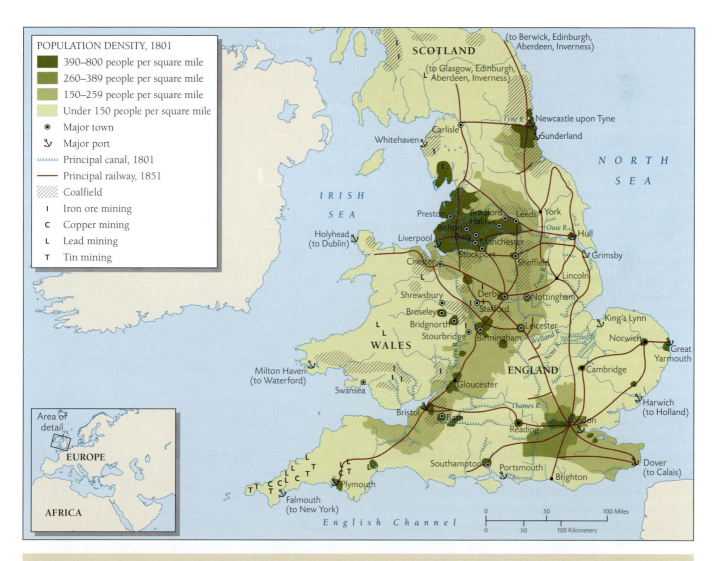

THE FIRST INDUSTRIAL NATION. Large-scale mechanization of industry developed first in Britain. ▪ *The accumulation of large deposits of what two natural resources caused urban growth outside of London?* ▪ *What new forms of transportation were critical for moving natural resources to market?* ▪ *What else was necessary for industrialization to develop as it did?*

Continent, the pursuit of wealth was perceived to be a worthy goal. European nobility cultivated the notion of gentlemanly conduct, in part to hold the line against those moving up from below. British aristocrats respected commoners with a talent for making money and did not hesitate to invest themselves. Their scramble to enclose their lands reflected a keen interest in commercialization and investment. Outside the aristocracy, an even lower barrier separated merchants from the rural gentry. Many of the entrepreneurs of the early Industrial Revolution came from the small gentry or independent farmer class. Eighteenth-century Britain was not by any means free of social snobbery: lords looked down on bankers and bankers looked down on craft workers. But a lord's disdain might well be tempered by the fact that his own grandfather had worked in the counting house.

Growing domestic and international markets made eighteenth-century Britain prosperous. The British were voracious consumers. The court elite followed and bought up yearly fashions, and so did most of Britain's landed and professional society. "Nature may be satisfied with little," one London entrepreneur declared. "But it is the wants of fashion and the desire of novelties that causes trade." The country's small size and the fact that it was an island encouraged the development of a well-integrated domestic market. Unlike continental Europe, Britain did not have a system of internal tolls and tariffs, so goods could be moved freely to wherever they might fetch the best price. A constantly improving transportation system boosted that freedom of movement. So did a favorable political climate. Some members of Parliament were businessmen themselves; others were investors. And both groups were eager to encourage by legislation the construction of canals, the establishment of banks, and the enclosure of common lands.

Foreign markets promised even greater returns than domestic ones, though with greater risks. British foreign policy responded to its commercial needs. At the end of every major eighteenth-century war, Britain wrested overseas territories from its enemies. At the same time, Britain penetrated hitherto unexploited territories, such as India and South America. In 1759, over one-third of all British exports went to the colonies; by 1784, if we include the former colonies in North America, that figure had increased to one half. Production for export rose by 80 percent between 1750 and 1770; production for domestic consumption gained just 7 percent over the same period. The British possessed a merchant marine capable of transporting goods around the world and a navy practiced in the art of protecting its commercial fleets. By the 1780s, Britain's markets, together with its fleet and its established position at the center of world commerce, gave its entrepreneurs unrivaled opportunities for trade and profit.

Innovation in the Textile Industries

The Industrial Revolution began with dramatic technological leaps in a few industries, the first of which was cotton textiles. The industry was already long established. Tariffs prohibiting imports of East Indian cottons, which Parliament had imposed to protect British woolen goods, had spurred the manufacture of British cotton. British textile manufacturers imported raw materials from India and the American South and borrowed patterns from Indian spinners and weavers. What, then, were the revolutionary breakthroughs?

In 1733, John Kay's invention of the flying shuttle speeded the process of weaving. The task of spinning thread, however, had not kept up. A series of comparatively simple mechanical devices eliminated this spinning-to-weaving bottleneck. The most important device was the spinning jenny, invented by James Hargreaves, a hand-

COTTON SPINNING, 1861. An illustration from a series showing spinning at Walter Evans and Company, cotton manufacturers in Derby, England. ■ *Why did textile factories prefer female employees?*

loom weaver, in 1764. The spinning jenny was a compound spinning wheel capable of producing sixteen threads at once—though the threads were not strong enough to be used for the longitudinal fibers, or warp, of cotton cloth. The invention of the water frame by Richard Arkwright, a barber, in 1769, made it possible to produce both warp and woof (latitudinal fibers) in great quantity. In 1799 Samuel Compton invented the spinning mule, which combined the features of both the jenny and the frame. All of these important technological changes were accomplished by the end of the eighteenth century.

A jenny could spin from six to twenty-four times more yarn than a hand spinner. By the end of the eighteenth century, a mule could produce two to three hundred times more. Just as important, the new machines made better-quality—stronger and finer—thread. These machines revolutionized production across the textile industry. Last, the cotton gin, invented by the American Eli Whitney in 1793, mechanized the process of separating cotton seeds from the fiber, thereby speeding up the production of cotton and reducing its price. The supply of cotton fibers could now expand to keep pace with rising demand from cotton cloth manufacturers. This cotton gin had many effects, including, paradoxically, making slavery more profitable in the United States. The cotton-producing slave plantations in the American South became enmeshed in the lucrative trade with manufacturers who produced cotton textiles in the northern United States and England.

The first textile machines were inexpensive enough to be used by spinners in their own cottages. But as machines grew in size and complexity, they were housed instead in workshops or mills located near water that could be used to power the machines. Eventually, the further development of steam-driven equipment allowed manufacturers to build mills wherever they could be used. Frequently, those mills went up in towns and cities in the north of England, away from the older commercial and seafaring centers, but nearer to the coal fields that provided fuel for new machines. From 1780 on, British cotton textiles flooded the world market. In 1760, Britain imported 2.5 million pounds of raw cotton; in 1787, 22 million pounds; in 1837, 366 million pounds. By 1815, the export of cotton textiles amounted to 40 percent of the value of all domestic goods exported from Great Britain. Although the price of manufactured cotton goods fell dramatically, the market expanded so rapidly that profits continued to increase.

Behind these statistics lay a revolution in clothing and consumption. Cotton in the form of muslins and calicos was fine enough to appeal to wealthy consumers. Cotton was also light and washable. For the first time, ordinary people could have sheets, table linens, curtains, and underwear.

(Wool was too scratchy.) As one writer commented in 1846, the revolution in textiles had ushered in a "brilliant transformation" in dress. "Every woman used to wear a blue or black dress that she kept ten years without washing it for fear that it would fall to pieces. Today her husband can cover her in flower-printed cotton for the price of a day's wages."

The explosive growth of textiles also prompted a debate about the benefits and tyranny of the new industries. The British Romantic poet William Blake famously wrote in biblical terms of the textile mills' blight on the English countryside:

> And did the Countenance Divine
> Shine forth upon our clouded hills?
> And was Jerusalem builded here
> Among these dark Satanic mills?

By the 1830s, the British House of Commons was holding hearings on employment and working conditions in factories, recording testimony about working days that stretched from 3:00 A.M. to 10:00 P.M., the employment of very small children, and workers who lost hair and fingers in the mills' machinery. Women and children counted for roughly two-thirds of the labor force in textiles. The principle of regulating any labor (and emphatically that of adult men), however, was controversial. Only gradually did a series of factory acts prohibit hiring children under age nine and limit the labor of workers under age eighteen to ten hours a day.

Coal and Iron

Meanwhile, decisive changes were transforming the production of iron. As in the textile industry, many important technological changes came during the eighteenth century. A series of innovations (coke smelting, rolling, and puddling) enabled the British to substitute coal (which they had in abundance) for wood (which was scarce and inefficient) to heat molten metal and make iron. The new "pig iron" was higher quality and could be used in building an enormous variety of iron products: machines, engines, railway tracks, agricultural implements, and hardware. Those iron products became, literally, the infrastructure of industrialization. Britain found itself able to export both coal and iron to rapidly expanding markets around the industrializing regions of the world. Between 1814 and 1852, exports of British iron doubled, rising to over one million tons of iron, more than half of the world's total production.

Rising demand for coal required mining deeper veins. In 1711, Thomas Newcomen had devised a cumbersome

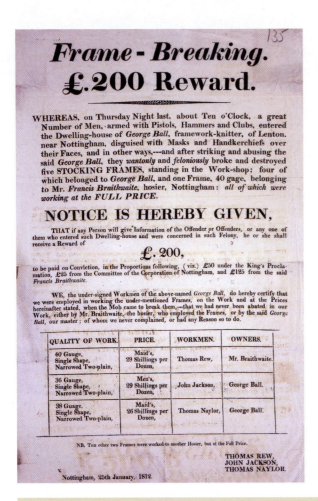

NED LUDD AND THE LUDDITES. In 1811 and 1812, in northern England, bands of working men who resented the adoption of new mechanical devices in the weaving industries attacked several establishments and destroyed the frames used to weave cloth. The movement took the name Luddites from Ned Ludd, a man who had broken the frames belonging to his employer in 1779. His mythological presence in the movement is depicted in the illustration at the right. Although their anger was directed at the machines, the real target of their resentment may have been a new pricing scheme imposed on them by the merchants who bought finished work. The debate about prices is a central part of the poster on the left, which offers a reward for information leading to the conviction of frame breakers. The poster is signed by several workers of the establishment, who published the price they received for each piece of clothing and their lack of complaints about their employer. ■ *How might the need to adjust to the price fluctuations of a market economy have been perceived by weavers accustomed to getting fixed prices for their goods?*

but remarkably effective steam engine for pumping water from mines. Though it was immensely valuable to the coal industry, its usefulness in other industries was limited by the amount of fuel it consumed. In 1763, James Watt improved on Newcomen's machine, and by 1800, Watt and his partner, Matthew Boulton, had sold 289 engines for use in factories and mines. Watt and Boulton made their fortune from their invention's efficiency; they earned a regular percentage of the increased profits from each mine that operated an engine.

Steam power was still energy consuming and expensive and so only slowly replaced traditional water power.

Even in its early form, however, the steam engine decisively transformed the nineteenth-century world with one application: the steam-driven locomotive. Railroads revolutionized industry, markets, public and private financing, and ordinary people's conceptions of space and time.

THE COMING OF RAILWAYS

Transportation had improved during the years before 1830, but moving heavy materials, particularly coal, remained a problem. It is significant that the first modern railway, built in England in 1825, ran from the Durham coal field of

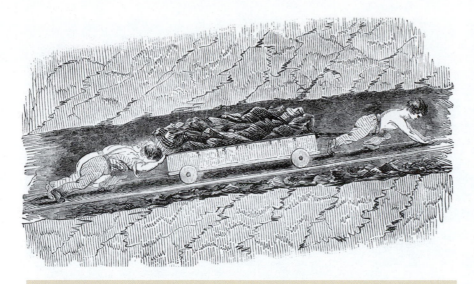

Stockton to Darlington, near the coast. Coal had traditionally been hauled short distances via tramways, or tracks along which horses pulled coal carts. The locomotives on the Stockton-Darlington line traveled at fifteen miles per hour, the fastest rate at which machines had yet moved goods overland. Soon they would move people as well, transforming transportation in the process.

Building railways became a massive enterprise and a risky but potentially profitable opportunity for investment. No sooner did the first combined passenger and goods service open in 1830, operating between Liverpool and Manchester, England, than plans were formulated and money pledged to extend rail systems throughout Europe, the Americas, and beyond. In 1830, there were no more than a few dozen miles of railway in the world. By 1840, there were over forty-five hundred miles; by 1850, over twenty-three thousand. British engineers, industrialists, and investors were quick to realize the global opportunities available in constructing railways overseas; a large part of Britain's industrial success in the later nineteenth century came through building other nations' infrastructures. The English contractor Thomas Brassey, for instance, built railways in Italy, Canada, Argentina, India, and Australia.

Throughout the world, a veritable army of construction workers built the railways. In Britain, they were called "navvies," derived from *navigator*, a term first used for the construction workers on Britain's eighteenth-century canals. Navvies were a rough lot, living with a few women in temporary encampments as they migrated across the countryside. Often they were immigrant workers and faced local hostil-

ity. A sign posted by local residents outside a mine in Scotland in 1845 warned the Irish navvies to get "off the ground and out of the country" in a week or else be driven out "by the strength of our armes and a good pick shaft." Later in the century railway building projects in Africa and the Americas were lined with camps of immigrant Indian and Chinese laborers, who also became targets of nativist (a term that means "opposed to foreigners") anger.

The magnitude of the navvies' accomplishment was extraordinary. In Britain and in much of the rest of the world, mid-nineteenth-century railways were constructed almost entirely without the aid of machinery. An assistant engineer on the London-to-Birmingham line calculated that the labor involved was the equivalent of lifting twenty-five billion cubic feet of earth and stone one foot high. He compared this feat with building the Great Pyramid, a task he estimated had involved the hoisting of some sixteen billion tons. The building of the pyramid, however, had required over two hundred thousand men and had taken twenty years. The construction of the London-to-Birmingham railway was accomplished by twenty thousand men in less than five years. If we translated this into individual terms, a navvy was expected to move an average of twenty tons of earth per day. Railways were produced by toil as much as

MANCHESTER TO LIVERPOOL, LATE NINETEENTH CENTURY. Lower-class passengers, physically separated from their social superiors, are packed into the rear of the train.

BARRY DOCK AND ISLAND, WALES, 1895. The convergence of coal, steam power, railways, and maritime shipping were at the center of industrialization in Britain. ■ *In what way did the circular relationship between coal and iron production and the larger transportation revolution associated with the construction of railroads and later, steamships, help sustain the initial growth associated with industrial development?*

by technology, by human labor as much as by engineering; they illustrate why some historians prefer to use the term *industrious* revolution.

Steam engines, textile machines, new ways of making iron, and railways—all these were interconnected. Changes in one area endorsed changes in another. Pumps run by steam engines made it possible to mine deeper veins of coal; steam-powered railways made it possible to transport coal. Mechanization fueled the production of iron for machines and the mining of coal to run steam engines. The railway boom multiplied the demand for iron products: rails, locomotives, carriages, signals, switches, and the iron to make all of these. Building railroads called for engineering expertise: scaling mountains, designing bridges and tunnels. Railway construction, which required capital investment beyond the capacity of any single individual, forged new kinds of public and private financing. The scale of production expanded and the tempo of economic activity quickened, spurring the search for more coal, the production of more iron, the mobilization of more capital, and the recruitment of more labor. Steam and speed were becoming the foundation of the economy and of a new way of life.

THE INDUSTRIAL REVOLUTION ON THE CONTINENT

Continental Europe followed a different path. Eighteenth-century France, Belgium, and Germany did have manufacturing districts in regions with raw materials, access to markets, and long-standing traditions of craft and skill. Yet for a variety of reasons, changes along the lines seen in Britain did not occur until the 1830s. Britain's transportation system was highly developed; those of France and Germany were not. France was far larger than England: its rivers more difficult to navigate; its seaports, cities, and coal deposits farther apart. Much of central Europe was divided into small principalities, each with its own tolls and tariffs, which complicated the transportation of goods over any considerable distance. The Continent had fewer raw materials, coal in particular, than Britain. The abundance and cheapness of wood discouraged exploration that might have resulted in new discoveries of coal. It also meant that coal-run steam engines were less economical on the Continent. Capital, too, was less readily available. Early British industrialization was underwritten by private wealth; this was less feasible elsewhere. Different patterns of landholding formed obstacles to the commercialization of agriculture. In the East, serfdom was a powerful disincentive to labor-saving innovations. In the West, especially in France, the large number of small peasants, or farmers, stayed put on the land.

The wars of the French Revolution and Napoleon disrupted economies. During the eighteenth century, the population had grown and mechanization had begun in a few key industries. The ensuing political upheaval and the financial strains of warfare did virtually nothing to help economic development. Napoleon's Continental System and British destruction of French merchant shipping hurt commerce badly. The ban on British-shipped cotton stalled the growth of cotton textiles for decades, though the armies' greater demand for woolen cloth kept that sector of textiles humming. Iron processing increased to satisfy the military's rising needs, but techniques for making iron remained largely unchanged. Probably the revolutionary change most beneficial to industrial advance in Europe was the removal of previous restraints on the movement of capital and labor—for example, the abolition of craft guilds and the reduction of tariff barriers across the Continent.

After 1815, a number of factors combined to change the economic climate. In those regions with a well-established commercial and industrial base—the northeast of France, Belgium, and swaths of territory across the Rhineland, Saxony, Silesia, and northern Bohemia (see map on page 591)—population growth further boosted economic development. Rising population did not by itself produce industrialization, however: in Ireland, where other necessary factors were absent, more people meant less food.

Transportation improved. The Austrian Empire added over thirty thousand miles of roads between 1830 and 1847; Belgium almost doubled its road network in the same period; France built not only new roads but two thousand miles of canals. These improvements, combined with the construction of railroads in the 1830s and 1840s, opened up new markets and encouraged new methods of manufacturing. In many of the Continent's manufacturing regions, however, industrialists continued to tap large pools of skilled but inexpensive labor. Thus older methods of putting out industry and handwork persisted alongside new-model factories longer than in Britain.

In what other ways was the continental model of industrialization different? Governments played a considerably more direct role in industrialization. France and Prussia granted subsidies to private companies that built railroads. After 1849, the Prussian state took on the task itself, as did Belgium and, later, Russia. In Prussia, the state also operated a large proportion of that country's mines. Governments on the Continent provided incentives for industrialization. Limited-liability laws, to take the most important example, allowed investors to own shares in a corporation or company without becoming liable for the company's debts—and they enabled enterprises to recruit investors to put together the capital for railroads, other forms of industry, and commerce.

Mobilizing capital for industry was one of the challenges of the century. In Great Britain, overseas trade had created well-organized financial markets; on the Continent, capital was dispersed and in short supply. New joint-stock investment banks, unlike private banks, could sell bonds to and take deposits from individuals and smaller companies. They could offer start-up capital in the form of long-term, low-interest commercial loans to aspiring entrepreneurs. The French Crédit Mobilier, for instance, founded in 1852 by the wealthy and well-connected Périere brothers, assembled enough capital to finance insurance companies; the Parisian bus system; six municipal gas companies; transatlantic shipping; enterprises in other European countries; and, with the patronage of the state, the massive railroad-building spree of the 1850s. The Crédit Mobilier

SILK WEAVERS OF LYONS, 1850. The first significant working-class uprisings in nineteenth-century France occurred in Lyons in 1831 and 1834. Note the domestic character of the working conditions.

Competing Viewpoints

The Factory System, Science, and Morality: Two Views

Reactions to the Industrial Revolution and the factory system it produced ranged from celebration to horror. Dr. Andrew Ure, a Scottish professor of chemistry, was fascinated with these nineteenth-century applications of Enlightenment science. He believed that the new machinery and its products would create a new society of wealth, abundance, and, ultimately, stability through the useful regimentation of production.

Friedrich Engels (1820–1895) was one of the many socialists to criticize Dr. Ure as shortsighted and complacent in his outlook. Engels was himself part of a factory-owning family and so was able to examine the new industrial cities at close range. He provides a classic nineteenth-century analysis of industrialization. The Condition of the Working Class in England is compellingly written, angry, and revealing about middle-class concerns of the time, including female labor.

Dr. Andrew Ure (1835)

This island [Britain] is preeminent among civilized nations for the prodigious development of its factory wealth, and has been therefore long viewed with a jealous admiration by foreign powers. This very pre-eminence, however, has been contemplated in a very different light by many influential members of our own community, and has even been denounced by them as the certain origin of innumerable evils to the people, and of revolutionary convulsions to the state. . . .

The blessings which physico-mechanical science has bestowed on society, and the means it has still in store for ameliorating the lot of mankind, has been too little dwelt upon; while, on the other hand, it has been accused of lending itself to the rich capitalists as an instrument for harassing the poor, and of exacting from the operative an accelerated rate of work. It has been said, for example, that the steam-engine now drives the power-looms with such velocity as to urge on their attendant weavers at the same rapid pace; but that the hand-weaver, not being subjected to this restless agent, can throw his shuttle and move his treddles at his convenience. There is, however, this difference in the two cases, that in the factory, every member of the loom is so adjusted, that the driving force leaves the attendant nearly nothing at all to do, certainly no muscular fatigue to sustain, while it produces for him good, unfailing wages, besides a healthy workshop *gratis*: whereas the non-factory weaver, having everything to execute by muscular exertion, finds the labour irksome, makes in consequence innumerable short pauses, separately of little account, but great when added together; earns therefore proportionally low wages, while he loses his health by poor diet and the dampness of his hovel.

Source: Andrew Ure, *The Philosophy of Manufacturers: Or, An Exposition of the Scientific, Moral and Commercial Economy of the Factory System of Great Britain, 1835,* as cited in J. T. Ward, *The Factory System,* vol. 1 (New York: 1970), pp. 140–141.

---

collapsed in scandal, but the revolution in banking was well under way.

Finally, continental Europeans actively promoted invention and technological development. They were willing for the state to establish educational systems whose aim, among others, was to produce a well-trained elite capable of assisting in the development of industrial technology. In sum, what Britain had produced almost by chance, the Europeans began to reproduce by design.

Industrialization after 1850

Until 1850 Britain remained the preeminent industrial power. Between 1850 and 1870, however, France, Germany, Belgium, and the United States emerged as challengers to the power and place of British manufacturers. The British iron industry remained the largest in the world (in 1870 Britain still produced half the world's pig iron), but it grew more slowly than did its counterparts in France

Friedrich Engels (1844)

Histories of the modern development of the cotton industry, such as those of Ure, Baines, and others, tell on every page of technical innovations.... In a well-ordered society such improvements would indeed be welcome, but social war rages unchecked and the benefits derived from these improvements are ruthlessly monopolized by a few persons.... Every improvement in machinery leads to unemployment, and the greater the technical improvement the greater the unemployment. Every improvement in machinery affects a number of workers in the same way as a commercial crisis and leads to want, distress, and crime....

Let us examine a little more closely the process whereby machine-labour continually supersedes hand-labour. When spinning or weaving machinery is installed practically all that is left to be done by the hand is the piecing together of broken threads, and the machine does the rest. This task calls for nimble fingers rather than muscular strength. The labour of grown men is not merely unnecessary but actually unsuitable.... The greater the degree to which physical labour is displaced by the introduction of machines worked by water- or steam-power, the fewer grown men need be employed. In any case women and children will work for lower wages than men and, as has already been observed, they are more skillful at piecing than grown men. Consequently it is women and children who are employed to do this work.... When women work in factories, the most important result is the dissolution of family ties. If a woman works for twelve or thirteen hours a day in a factory and her husband is employed either in the same establishment or in some other works, what is the fate of the children? They lack parental care and control.... It is not difficult to imagine that they are left to run wild.

Source: Friedrich Engels, *The Condition of the Working Class in England in 1844,* trans. and eds. W. O. Henderson and W. H. Chaloner (New York: 1958), pp. 150–151, 158, 160.

Questions for Analysis

1. According to Andre Ure, why was industrialization good for Britain? How can the blessings of "physico-mechanical science" lead to the improvement of humanity?

2. What criticism did Engels level at Ure and other optimists on industrialization? Why did Engels think conditions for workers were getting worse instead of better?

2. What consequences do these two writers see for society in the wake of technological change? What assumptions do they make about the relationship between economic development and the social order?

or Germany. Most of continental Europe's gains came as a result of continuing changes in those areas we recognize as important for sustained industrial growth: transport, commerce, and government policy. The spread of railways encouraged the free movement of goods. International monetary unions were established and restrictions removed on international waterways such as the Danube. Free trade went hand in hand with removing guild barriers to entering trades and ending restrictions on practicing business. Guild control over artisanal production was abolished in Austria in 1859 and in most of Germany by the mid-1860s. Laws against usury, most of which had ceased to be enforced, were officially abandoned in Britain, Holland, Belgium, and in many parts of Germany. Governmental regulation of mining was surrendered by the Prussian state in the 1850s, freeing entrepreneurs to develop resources as they saw fit. Investment banks continued to form, encouraged by an increase in the money supply and an easing of credit after the California gold fields opened in 1849.

The first phase of the Industrial Revolution, one economic historian reminds us, was confined to a narrow set of industries and can be summed up rather simply: "cheaper and better clothes (mainly made of cotton), cheaper and better metals (pig iron, wrought iron, and steel) and faster travel (mainly by rail)." The second half of the century brought changes farther afield and in areas where Great Britain's early advantages were no longer decisive. Transatlantic cable (starting in 1865) and the telephone (invented in 1876) laid the ground for a revolution in communications. New chemical processes, dyestuffs, and pharmaceuticals emerged. So did new sources of energy: electricity, in which the United States and Germany led both invention and commercial development; and oil, which was being refined in the 1850s and widely used by 1900. Among the early exploiters of Russian oil discoveries were the Swedish Nobel brothers and the French Rothschilds. The developments that eventually converged to make the automobile came primarily from Germany and France. The internal combustion engine, important because it was small, efficient, and could be used in a very wide variety of situations, was developed by Carl Benz and Gottlieb Daimler in the 1880s. The removable pneumatic tire was patented in 1891 by Edouard Michelin, a painter who had joined with his engineer brother in running the family's small agricultural-equipment business. These developments are discussed fully in Chapter 23, but their pioneers' familiar names illustrate how industry and invention had diversified over the course of the century.

In eastern Europe, the nineteenth century brought different patterns of economic development. Spurred by the ever-growing demand for food and grain, large sections of eastern Europe developed into concentrated, commercialized agriculture regions that played the specific role of exporting food to the West. Many of those large agricultural enterprises were based on serfdom and remained so, in the face of increasing pressure for reform, until 1850. Peasant protest and liberal demands for reform only gradually chipped away at the nobility's determination to hold on to its privilege and system of labor. Serfdom was abolished in most parts of eastern and southern Europe by 1850 and in Poland and Russia in the 1860s.

Although industry continued to take a back seat to agriculture, eastern Europe had several important manufacturing regions. In the Czech region of Bohemia, textile industries, developed in the eighteenth century, continued to thrive. By the 1830s, there were machine-powered Czech cotton mills and iron works. In Russia, a factory industry producing coarse textiles—mostly linens—had grown up around Moscow. At mid-century, Russia was purchasing 24 percent of the total British machinery exports to mechanize its own mills. Many who labored in Russian industry actually remained serfs until the 1860s—about 40 percent of them employed in mines. Of the over eight hundred thousand Russians engaged in manufacturing by 1860, however, most were employed in small workshops of about forty persons.

By 1870, then, the core industrial nations of Europe included Great Britain, France, Germany, Italy, the Netherlands, and Switzerland. Austria stood at the margins. Russia, Spain, Bulgaria, Greece, Hungary, Romania, and Serbia formed the industrial periphery—and some regions of these nations seemed virtually untouched by the advance of industry. What was more, even in Great Britain, the most fully industrialized nation, agricultural laborers still constituted the single largest occupational category in 1860 (although they formed only 9 percent of the overall population). In Belgium, the Netherlands, Switzerland, Germany, France, Scandinavia, and Ireland, 25 to 50 percent of the population still worked on the land. In Russia, the number was 80 percent. *Industrial,* moreover, did not mean automation or machine production, which long remained confined to a few sectors of the economy. As machines were introduced in some sectors to do specific tasks, they usually intensified the tempo of handwork in other sectors. Thus even in the industrialized regions, much work was still accomplished in tiny workshops—or at home.

Industry and Empire

From an international perspective, nineteenth-century Europe was the most industrial region of the world. Europeans, particularly the British, jealously guarded their international advantages. They preferred to do so through financial leverage. Britain, France, and other European nations gained control of the national debts of China, the Ottoman Empire, Egypt, Brazil, Argentina, and other non-European powers. They also supplied large loans to other states, which bound those nations to their European investors. If the debtor nations expressed discontent, as Egypt did in the 1830s when it attempted to establish its own cotton textile industry, they confronted financial pressure and shows of force. Coercion, however, was not always necessary or even one-sided. Social change in other empires—China, Persia, and the Mughal Empire of India, for example—made those empires newly vulnerable and created new opportunities for the European powers and their local partners. Ambitious local elites often reached agreements with Western governments

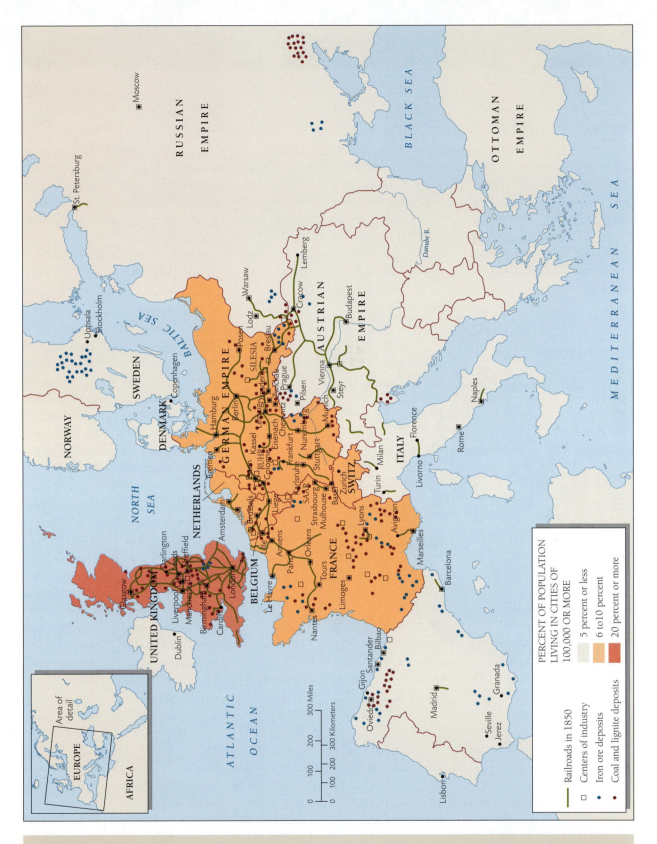

PERCENT OF POPULATION
LIVING IN CITIES OF
100,000 OR MORE

5 percent or less
6 to10 percent
20 percent or more

—— Railroads in 1850
☐ Centers of industry
• Iron ore deposits
• Coal and lignite deposits

THE INDUSTRIAL REVOLUTION. Rapid industrial growth depended on a circular network of relationships. ■ *According to the map key, what elements made up the circular networks of relationships?* ■ *How were these elements connected, and how might they have reinforced one another, contributing to rapid growth?* ■ *Why do you think the percentage of populations living in cities was so much greater in the United Kingdom?*

Interpreting Visual Evidence

Learning to Live in a Global Economy

The commercial networks of the Atlantic world were already well established before the Industrial Revolution, and Europeans were also trading widely with South and East Asia before the end of the eighteenth century. Nevertheless, the advent of an industrial economy in Europe at the beginning of the nineteenth century created such a demand for raw materials and such a need for new markets abroad that it became profitable for manufacturers and merchants to ship much larger amounts of goods over long distances than ever before. As different industrialized regions in Europe became more and more dependent on overseas markets, people in Europe came to be aware of the extent to which their own activities were linked to other parts of the world. Awareness of these linkages did not always mean that they possessed complete or accurate information about the people who produced the cotton that they wore, or who purchased the manufactured goods that they made, but the linkages stimulated their imagination and changed their consciousness of their place in the world.

This awareness is well-illustrated in the cartoons shown here, which come from the British illustrated news in the 1850s and 1860s. The first (image A) depicts John Bull (representing British textile manufacturers) looking on as U.S. cotton suppliers fight one another during the Civil War in the United States. He states, "Oh! If you two like fighting better than business, I shall deal at the other shop." In the background, an Indian cotton merchant is happy to have him as a customer.

The second cartoon (image B) depicts the ways that the increasingly

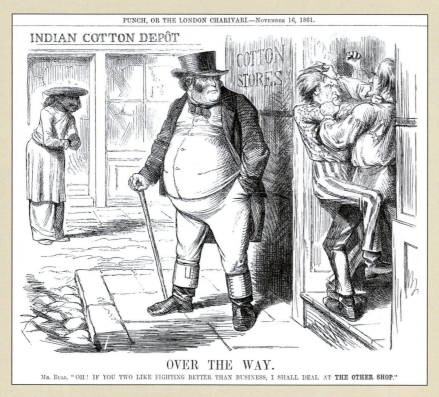

PUNCH, OR THE LONDON CHARIVARI.—November 16, 1861.

INDIAN COTTON DEPÔT

COTTON STORES

OVER THE WAY.

Mr. Bull. "OH! IF YOU TWO LIKE FIGHTING BETTER THAN BUSINESS, I SHALL DEAL AT THE OTHER SHOP."

A. John Bull and cotton merchants.

or groups such as the British East India Company. These trade agreements transformed regional economies on terms that sent the greatest profits to Europe after a substantial gratuity to the Europeans' local partners. Where agreements could not be made, force prevailed, and Europe took territory and trade by conquest (see Chapter 22).

Industrialization tightened global links between Europe and the rest of the world, creating new networks of trade and interdependence. To a certain extent, the world economy divided between the producers of manufactured goods—Europe itself—and suppliers of the necessary raw materials and buyers of finished goods—everyone else.

interconnected global economy might stimulate a new kind of political awareness. Emperor Napoleon III has placed a French worker in irons for participating in a revolutionary movement. The worker compares his situation to an African slave seated next to him, saying, "Courage, my friend! Am I not a man and a brother?" On the wall behind the two men a poster refers to the Portuguese slave trade—Napoleon III himself came to power by overthrowing the Second Republic in France, a government that had abolished the slave trade in French territories.

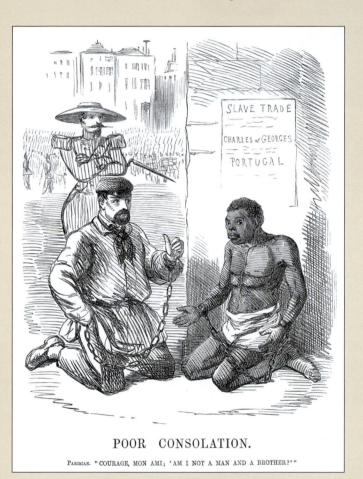

POOR CONSOLATION.

Parisian. "COURAGE, MON AMI; 'AM I NOT A MAN AND A BROTHER?'"

B. Increasing global awarness in France.

Questions for Analysis

1. What constellation of private and national interests were at play in the relationships portrayed in image A? What significance might contemporaries have attached to the possibility that the British may have chosen to buy their cotton from an Asian source "over the way" rather than from North America?

2. In image B, what is the message of the cartoon's suggestion that the slave and the worker might discover their equality only in the fact that they are both in chains? What was at stake in comparing a worker to a slave in mid-nineteenth-century Europe? Why does the caption read "Poor Consolation?"

3. How does the racial imagery of these images relate to their intended message?

Cotton growers in the southern United States, sugar growers in the Caribbean, and wheat growers in Ukraine accepted their arrangements with the industrialized West and typically profited by them. If there were disputes, however, those suppliers often found that Europe could look elsewhere for the same goods or dictate the terms of trade down the business end of a bank ledger or a cannon barrel.

In 1811 Britain imported 3 percent of the wheat it consumed. By 1891, that portion had risen to 79 percent. Why? In an increasingly urban society, fewer people lived off the land. The commercialization of agriculture, which began

BRITISH CLIPPER SHIPS IN CALCUTTA HARBOR, 1860. Calcutta, a long-established city on the eastern coast of India, was one of the hubs of the British Empire—a center for trade in cotton, jute, opium, and tea. The dazzling new clipper ships, first built in the 1830s and 1840s, were very fast and central to the global economy of the nineteenth century. ▪ *What was the significance of this trade for the Indian economy?* ▪ *Could Indian merchants compete on equal terms with U.S. cotton producers in 1860?*

was 480 million. (Over the same span of time, world population went from about 900 million to 1.6 billion.) Britain, with its comparatively high standard of living, saw its population rise from 16 to 27 million. Increases, however, came in the largely rural regions as well. In Russia, the population rose from 39 to 60 million during the same period.

Population

This population explosion did not occur because people were living longer—declines in mortality were not observable on a large scale until late in the nineteenth century, when improvements in hygiene and medicine had significant impact on the number of people who survived childhood to reach adulthood. Even in 1880, the average male life expectancy at birth in Berlin was no more than thirty years (in rural districts nearby it was forty-three). Population growth in the nineteenth century resulted from increasing fertility—there were simply more babies being born. Men and women married earlier, which raised the average number of children born to each woman and increased the size of families. Peasants tended to set up households at a younger age. The spread of rural manufacturing allowed couples in the countryside to marry and set up households—even before they inherited any land. Not only did the age of marriage fall but more people married. And because population growth increased the proportion of young and fertile people, the process reinforced itself in the next generation, setting the stage for a period of prolonged growth.

early in Britain, had taken even firmer hold elsewhere, turning new regions—Australia, Argentina, and North America (Canada and the United States)—into centers of grain and wheat production. New forms of transportation, finance, and communication made it easier to shuttle commodities and capital through international networks. Those simple percentages, in other words, dramatize the new interdependence of the nineteenth century; they illustrate as well as any statistics can how ordinary Britons' lives—like their counterparts' in other nations—were embedded in an increasingly global economy.

THE SOCIAL CONSEQUENCES OF INDUSTRIALIZATION

We have mentioned population growth as one factor in industrial development, but it deserves treatment on its own terms. By any measure, the nineteenth century constituted a turning point in European demographic history. In 1800 the population of Europe as a whole was estimated roughly at 205 million. By 1850, it had risen to 274 million; by 1900, 414 million; on the eve of the First World War it

Life on the Land: The Peasantry

Even as the West grew more industrial, the majority of people continued to live on the land. Conditions in the countryside were harsh. Peasants—as farmers of humble origin were called in Europe—still did most of their sowing and harvesting by hand. Millions of tiny farms produced, at most, a bare subsistence living, and families wove, spun, made knives, and sold butter to make ends meet. The average daily diet for an entire family in a good year might amount to no more than two or three pounds of bread—

a total of about three thousand calories daily. By many measures, living conditions for rural inhabitants of many areas in Europe grew worse in the first half of the nineteenth century, a fact of considerable political importance in the 1840s. Rising population put more pressure on the land. Small holdings and indebtedness were chronic problems in regions where peasants scraped by on their own lands. Over the course of the century some thirty-seven million people—most of them peasants—left Europe, eloquent testimony to the bleakness of rural life. They settled in the United States, South America, northern Africa, New Zealand, Australia, and Siberia. In many cases, governments encouraged emigration to ease overcrowding.

The most tragic combination of famine, poverty, and population in the nineteenth century came to Ireland in the Great Famine of 1845–1849. Potatoes, which had come to Europe from the New World, fundamentally transformed the diets of European peasants, providing much more nutrition for less money than corn and grain. They also grew more densely, an enormous advantage for peasants scraping a living from small plots of land. Nowhere did they become more important than in Ireland, where the climate and soil made growing grain difficult and both overpopulation and poverty were rising. When a fungus hit the potato crop—first in 1845 and again, fatally, in 1846 and 1847—no alternate foods were at hand. At least 1 million Irish died of starvation; of dysentery from spoiled foods; or of fever, which spread through villages and the overcrowded poorhouses. Before the famine, tens of thousands of Irish were already crossing the Atlantic to North America; they accounted for one-third of all voluntary migration to the New World. In the ten years after 1845, 1.5 million people left Ireland for good. The potato blight also struck in Germany, Scotland, and the Netherlands, but with less catastrophic results. Europe had known deadly famines for centuries. The tragic Irish famine came late, however, at a time when many thought that starvation was receding into the past, and it illustrated just how vulnerable the nineteenth-century countryside remained to bad harvests and shortages.

Changes in the land depended partly on particular governments. States sympathetic to commercial agriculture made it easier to transfer land, eliminate small farms, and create larger estates. In Britain, over half the total area of the country, excluding wasteland, was composed of estates of a thousand acres or more. In Spain, the fortunes of large-scale commercial agriculture fluctuated with changes in the political regime: in 1820, the liberal regime passed legislation encouraging the free transfer of land; when absolutism was restored in 1823 the law was repealed. In Russia some of the largest landowners possessed over half a million acres. Until the emancipation of the serfs in the 1860s, landowners claimed the labor of dependent peasant populations for as much as several days per week. But the system of serfdom gave neither landowners nor serfs much incentive to improve farming techniques.

IRISH POTATO FAMINE, 1845–1849. The Irish potato famine was widely held by many in Ireland to have human as well as natural causes. Historians have noted that food exports from Ireland continued and may have even increased for some products during the famine, as merchants sought higher prices abroad. The cartoon at left depicts armed soldiers keeping starving Irish Catholic families at bay as sacks of potatoes are loaded on to a ship owned by a prosperous Irish Protestant trader. At right, an 1848 engraving from the *Illustrated London News* depicts an impoverished tenant family being evicted from their cottage by their landlord for nonpayment of rent. Thousands of such evictions took place, adding to the misery of the tenant farmers, who were thus unable to plant new crops after losing the potato harvest to blight.

Thomas Malthus on Population and Poverty

Thomas Malthus's enormously influential Essay on the Principle of Population *(1798) marked a shift away from Enlightenment optimism about the "perfectibility of society" and a break with a long tradition of considering a large population to be a sign of economic strength. The English cleric (1766–1834) argued that hopes for prosperity ran up against a simple and grim law of nature: population grew more rapidly than food supply. Famine, disease, poverty, infant malnutrition—Malthus considered all of these inevitable, indeed "positive," checks on population. Governments could do nothing to alleviate poverty, he argued; instead the poor had to exercise "moral restraint," postpone marriage, and have fewer children.*

 say, that the power of population is indefinitely greater than the power in the earth to produce subsistence for man.

Population, when unchecked, increases in a geometrical ratio. Subsistence increases only in an arithmetical ratio. A slight acquaintance with numbers will shew the immensity of the first power in comparison of the second.

By that law of our nature which makes food necessary to the life of man, the effects of these two unequal powers must be kept equal.

This implies a strong and constantly operating check on population from the difficulty of subsistence. This difficulty must fall somewhere and must necessarily be severely felt by a large portion of mankind.

Through the animal and vegetable kingdoms, nature has scattered the seeds of life abroad with the most profuse and liberal hand. She has been comparatively sparing in the room and the nourishment necessary to rear them. The germs of existence contained in this spot of earth, with ample food, and ample room to expand in, would fill millions of worlds in the course of a few thousand years. Necessity, that imperious all pervading law of nature, restrains them within the prescribed bounds. The race of plants and the race of animals shrink under this great restrictive law. And the race of man cannot, by any efforts of reason, escape from it. Among plants and animals its effects are waste of seed, sickness, and premature death. Among mankind, misery and vice. The former, misery, is an absolutely necessary consequence of it. Vice is a highly probable consequence, and we therefore see it abundantly prevail, but it ought not, perhaps, to be called an absolutely necessary consequence. The ordeal of virtue is to resist all temptation to evil.

This natural inequality of the two powers of population and of production in the earth, and that great law of our nature which must constantly keep their effects equal, form the great difficulty that to me appears insurmountable in the way to the perfectibility of society. All other arguments are of slight and subordinate consideration in comparison of this. I see no way by which man can escape from the weight of this law which pervades all animated nature. No fancied equality, no agrarian regulations in their utmost extent, could remove the pressure of it even for a single century. And it appears, therefore, to be decisive against the possible existence of a society, all the members of which should live in ease, happiness, and comparative leisure; and feel no anxiety about providing the means of subsistence for themselves and families.

Consequently, if the premises are just, the argument is conclusive against the perfectibility of the mass of mankind.

Source: Thomas Malthus, *An Essay on the Principle of Population*, ed. Philip Appleman, Norton Critical Edition, 2nd ed. (New York: 2004), pp. 19–20.

Questions for Analysis

1. What assumptions about human behavior are contained in Malthus's argument that population will always increase more quickly than the available food supply? What are the possible checks on population growth that he considers? Why does he say that "misery" is "a necessary consequence" and "vice" only "highly probable"? Why does he conclude from this that society will never be "perfectible"?

2. The history of the Industrial Revolution and population growth in Europe in the nineteenth century seemed to prove that Malthus's belief in the ecological constraints on population growth were ill-founded. What events that he could not have predicted changed the equilibrium between subsistence and population during this period?

3. Compare Malthus's views expressed here with the documents on page 598 concerning the 1846 potato famine. Can one see the influence of his ideas in those documents?

European serfdom, which bound hundreds of thousands of men, women, and children to particular estates for generations, made it difficult to buy and sell land freely and created an obstacle to the commercialization of agriculture. Yet the opposite was also the case. In France, peasant landholders who had benefited from the French Revolution's sale of lands and laws on inheritance stayed in the countryside, continuing to work their small farms. Although French peasants were poor, they could sustain themselves on the land. This had important consequences. France suffered less agricultural distress, even in the 1840s, than did other European countries; migration from country to city was slower than in the other nations; far fewer peasants left France for other countries.

Industrialization came to the countryside in other forms. Improved communication networks not only afforded rural populations a keener sense of events and opportunities elsewhere but also made it possible for governments to intrude into the lives of these men and women to a degree previously impossible. Central bureaucracies now found it easier to collect taxes from the peasantry and to conscript sons of peasant families into armies. Some rural cottage industries faced direct competition from factory-produced goods, which meant less work or lower piece rates and falling incomes for families, especially during winter months. In other sectors of the economy, industry spread out into the countryside, making whole regions producers of shoes, shirts, ribbons, cutlery, and so on in small shops and workers' homes. Changes in the market could usher in prosperity, or they could bring entire regions to the verge of starvation.

Vulnerability often led to political violence. Rural rebellions were common in the early nineteenth century. In southern England in the late 1820s, small farmers and day laborers joined forces to burn barns and haystacks, protesting the introduction of threshing machines, a symbol of the new agricultural capitalism. They masked and otherwise disguised themselves, riding out at night under the banner of their mythical leader, "Captain Swing." Their raids were preceded by anonymous threats, such as the one received by a large-scale farmer in the county of Kent: "Pull down your threshing machine or else [expect] fire without delay. We are five thousand men [a highly inflated figure] and will not be stopped." In the southwest of France, peasants,

AGRICULTURAL DISTURBANCES. Violence erupted in southern England in 1830 in protest against the introduction of threshing machines. As in the Luddite disturbances, the Captain Swing riots took aim at the changes brought about by the integration of rural communities into the expanding market economy.

at night and in disguise, attacked local authorities who had barred them from collecting wood in the forests. Since forest wood was in demand for new furnaces, the peasants' traditional gleaning rights had come to an end. Similar rural disturbances broke out across Europe in the 1830s and 1840s: insurrections against landlords; against tithes, or taxes to the church; against laws curtailing customary rights; against unresponsive governments. In Russia, serf uprisings were a reaction to continued bad harvests and exploitation.

Many onlookers considered the nineteenth-century cities dangerous seedbeds of sedition. Yet conditions in the countryside and frequent flareups of rural protest remained the greatest source of trouble for governments, and rural politics exploded, as we will see, in the 1840s. Peasants were land poor, deep in debt, and precariously dependent on markets. More important, however, a government's inability to contend with rural misery made it look autocratic, indifferent, or inept—all political failings.

The Urban Landscape

The growth of cities was one of the most important facts of nineteenth-century social history, and one with significant cultural reverberations. Over the course of the nineteenth century, as we have seen, the overall population of Europe

Competing Viewpoints

The Irish Famine: Interpretations and Responses

When the potato blight appeared for the second year in a row in 1846, famine came to Ireland. The first letter excerpted here is from Father Theobald Mathew, a local priest, to Charles Edward Trevelyan, the English official in charge of Irish relief. While Father Mathew attributes the potato blight to "divine providence," he also worries that businessmen opposed to government intervention in a free market will let the Irish starve.

The second and third excerpts are from letters that Trevelyan wrote to other British officials concerned with the crisis. Trevelyan makes clear that, although he does not want the government to bear responsibility for starving its people, he believes that the famine will work to correct "social evils" in Ireland, by which he means everything from families having too many children to farmers failing to plant the right crops. In the nineteenth century, reactions to food crises were reshaped by the rise of new economic doctrines, changing social assumptions, and the shifting relationship between religion and government. These letters provide good examples of those changes and how they affected government officials.

The Reverend Theobald Mathew to Trevelyan

Cork, 7 August 1846.

Divine providence, in its inscrutable ways, has again poured out upon us the viol [*sic*] of its wrath. A blot more destructive than the simoom of the desert has passed over the land, and the hopes of the poor potato-cultivators are totally blighted, and the food of a whole nation has perished. On the 27th of last month I passed from Cork to Dublin, and this doomed plant bloomed in all the luxuriance of an abundant harvest. Returning on the 3rd instant, I beheld, with sorrow, one wide waste of putrefying vegetation. In many places the wretched people were seated on the fences of their decaying gardens, wringing their hands and wailing bitterly the destruction that had left them foodless.

It is not to harrow your benevolent feelings, dear Mr. Trevelyan, I tell this tale of woe. No, but to excite your sympathy in behalf of our miserable peasantry. It is rumoured that the capitalists in the corn and flour trade are endeavoring to induce government not to protect the people from famine, but to leave them at their mercy. I consider this a cruel and unjustifiable interference.

Trevelyan to Routh

Treasury, 3 February 1846.

That indirect permanent advantages will accrue to Ireland from the scarcity and the measures taken for its relief, I entertain no doubt; but if we were to pursue these incidental objects to the neglect of any of the precautions immediately required to save the people from actual starvation, our responsibility would be fearful indeed. Besides, the greatest improvement of all which could take place in Ireland would be to teach the people to depend upon themselves for developing the resources of their country, instead of having recourse to the assistance of the government on every occasion. Much has been done of late years to put this important matter on its proper footing; but if a firm stand is not made against the prevailing disposition to take advantage of this crisis to break down all barriers, the true permanent interest of the country will, I am convinced, suffer in a manner which will be irreparable in our time.

Trevelyan to Lord Monteagle

To the Right Hon. Lord Monteagle.

My Dear Lord,

I need not remind your lordship that the ability even of the most powerful government is extremely limited in dealing with a social evil of this description. It forms no part of the functions of government to provide supplies of food or to increase the productive powers of the land. In the great institution of the business of society, it falls to the share of government to protect the merchant and the agriculturist in the free exercise of their respective employments; but

not itself to carry on those employments; and the condition of a community depends upon the result of the efforts which each member of it makes in his private and individual capacity. . . .

I must give expression to my feelings by saying that I think I see a bright light shining in the distance through the dark cloud which at present hangs over Ireland. A remedy has been already applied to that portion of the maladies of Ireland which was traceable to political causes, and the morbid habits which still to a certain extent survive are gradually giving way to a more healthy action. The deep and inveterate root of social evil remains, and I hope I am not guilty of irreverence in thinking that, this being altogether beyond the power of man, the cure has been applied by the direct stroke of an all-wise providence in a manner as unexpected and unthought of as it is likely to be effectual. God grant that we may rightly perform our part and not turn into a curse what was intended for a blessing. The ministers of religion and especially the pastors of the Roman Catholic Church, who possess the largest share of influence over the people of Ireland, have well performed their part; and although few indications appear from any proceedings which have yet come before the public that the landed proprietors have even taken the first step of preparing for the conversion of the land now laid down to potatoes to grain cultivation, I do not despair of seeing this class in society still taking the lead which their position requires of them, and preventing the social revolution from being so extensive as it otherwise must become.

Believe me, my dear lord,
yours very sincerely,
C. E. Trevelyan.
Treasury, 9 October 1846.

Source: Noel Kissane, *The Irish Famine: A Documentary History* (Dublin: 1995), pp. 17, 47, 50–51.

Questions for Analysis

1. Reverend Mathew's letter suggests that although the potato blight seems to be an act of God, the response to the crisis by those in government and in commerce plays a role in determining who has enough to eat. What relationship between hunger and the market does Mathew fear most?

2. What are the stakes in the crisis for Trevelyan, as the English official responsible for relief of the food shortage? What interests does he appear to serve and in what order of preference? What exactly is the responsibility of the government in the face of such an emergency, according to his view?

3. Do Mathew and Trevelyan agree on the relationship that should exist between the government and the economy? What accounts for their difference of opinion? Are the religious values of the reverend and the economic calculations of the official compatible with one another?

doubled. The percentage of that population living in cities tripled—that is, urban populations rose sixfold. In mining and manufacturing areas or along newly built railway lines, it sometimes seemed that cities (like Manchester, Birmingham, and Essen) sprang up from nowhere. Sometimes the rates of growth were dizzying. Between 1750 and 1850, London (Europe's largest city) grew from 676,000 to 2.3 million. The population of Paris went from 560,000 to 1.3 million, adding 120,000 new residents between 1841 and 1846 alone! Berlin, which like Paris became the hub of a rapidly expanding railway system, nearly tripled in size during the first half of the century. Such rapid expansion was almost necessarily unplanned and brought in its wake new social problems.

Almost all nineteenth-century cities were overcrowded and unhealthy, their largely medieval infrastructures strained by the burden of new population and the demands of industry. Construction lagged far behind population growth, and working men and women who had left families behind in the country often lived in temporary lodging houses. The poorest workers dwelt in wretched basement or attic rooms, often without any light or drainage. A local committee appointed to investigate conditions in the British manufacturing town of Huddersfield—by no means the worst of that country's urban centers—reported that there were large areas without paving, sewers, or drains, "where garbage and filth of every description are left on the surface to ferment and rot; where pools of stagnant water are almost constant; where dwellings adjoining are thus necessarily caused to be of an inferior and even filthy description; thus where disease is engendered, and the health of the whole town perilled."

Governments gradually adopted measures in an attempt to cure the worst of these ills, if only to prevent the spread of catastrophic epidemics. Legislation was designed to rid cities of their worst slums by tearing them down and to improve sanitary conditions by supplying both water and drainage. Yet by 1850, these projects had only just begun. Paris, perhaps better supplied with water than any other European city, had enough for no more than two baths per person per year; in London, human waste remained uncollected in 250,000 domestic cesspools; in Manchester, fewer than one-third of the dwellings were equipped with toilets of any sort.

Industry and Environment in the Nineteenth Century

The Industrial Revolution began many of the environmental changes of the modern period. Nowhere were those changes more visible than in the burgeoning cities. Dickens's description of the choking air and polluted water of "Coketown," the fictional city in *Hard Times* (1854) is deservedly well known:

VIEW OF LONDON WITH SAINT PAUL'S CATHEDRAL IN THE DISTANCE BY WILLIAM HENRY CROME. Despite the smog-filled skies and intense pollution, many entrepreneurs and politicians celebrated the new prosperity of the Industrial Revolution. As W. P. Rend, a Chicago businessman, wrote in 1892, "Smoke is the incense burning on the altars of industry. It is beautiful to me. It shows that men are changing the merely potential forces of nature into articles of comfort for humanity."

It was a town of red brick, or of brick that would have been red if the smoke and ashes had allowed it. . . . It was a town of machines and tall chimneys, out of which interminable serpents of smoke trailed themselves forever and ever, and never got uncoiled. It had a black canal in it, and a river that ran purple with ill-smelling dye, and vast piles of building full of windows where there was a rattling and a trembling all day long.

Wood-fired manufacturing and heating for homes had long spewed smoke across the skies, but the new concentration of industrial activity and the transition to coal made the air measurably worse. In London especially, where even homes switched to coal early, smoke from factories, railroads, and domestic chimneys hung heavily over the city; and the last third of the century brought the most intense pollution in its history. Over all of England, air pollution took an enormous toll on health, contributing to the bronchitis and tuberculosis that accounted for 25 percent of British deaths. The coal-rich and industrial regions of North America (especially Pittsburgh) and central Europe were other concentrations of pollution; the Ruhr in particular by the end of the century had the most polluted air in Europe.

Toxic water—produced by industrial pollution and human waste—posed the second critical environmental hazard in urban areas. London and Paris led the way in building municipal sewage systems, though those emptied into the Thames and the Seine. Cholera, typhus, and tuberculosis were natural predators in areas without adequate sewage facilities or fresh water. The Rhine River, which flowed through central Europe's industrial heartland and intersected with the Ruhr, was thick with detritus from coal mining, iron processing, and the chemical industry. Spurred by several epidemics of cholera, in the late nineteenth century the major cities began to purify their water supplies; but conditions in the air, rivers, and land continued to worsen until at least the mid-twentieth century.

The Social Question

Against the backdrop of the French Revolution of 1789 and subsequent revolutions in the nineteenth century (as we will see in the following chapters), the new "shock" cities of the nineteenth century and their swelling multitudes posed urgent questions. Political leaders, social scientists, and public health officials across all of Europe issued thousands of reports—many of them several volumes long—on criminality, water supply, sewers, prostitution, tuberculosis and cholera, alcoholism, wet nursing, wages, and unemployment. Radicals and reformers grouped all these issues under a broad heading known as "the social question." Governments, pressed by reformers and by the omnipresent rumblings of unrest, felt they had to address these issues before complaints swelled into revolution. They did so, in the first social engineering: police forces, public health, sewers and new water supplies, inoculations, elementary schools, Factory Acts (regulating work hours), poor laws (outlining the conditions of receiving relief), and new urban regulation and city planning. Central Paris, for instance, would be almost entirely redesigned in the nineteenth century—the crowded, medieval, and revolutionary poor neighborhoods gutted; markets rebuilt; streets widened and lit (see Chapter 21). From the 1820s on, the social question hung over Europe like a cloud, and it formed part of the backdrop to the revolutions of 1848 (discussed in Chapter 21). Surveys and studies, early social science, provided direct inspiration for novelists such as Honoré de Balzac, Charles Dickens, and Victor Hugo. In his novel *Les Misérables* (1862), Hugo even used the sewers of Paris as a central metaphor for the general condition of urban existence. Both Hugo and Dickens wrote sympathetically of the poor, of juvenile delinquency, and of child labor; revolution was never far from their minds. The French writer Balzac had little sympathy for the poor, but he shared his fellow writers' views on the corruption of modern life. His *Human Comedy* (1829–55) was a series of ninety-five novels and stories, including *Eugenie Grandet, Old Goriot, Lost Illusions,* and *A Harlot High and Low.* Balzac was biting in his observations about ruthless and self-promoting young men and about the cold calculations behind romantic liaisons. And he was but one of many writers to use prostitution as a metaphor for what he considered the deplorable materialism and desperation of his time.

Sex in the City

Prostitution flourished in nineteenth-century cities; in fact it offers a microcosm of the nineteenth-century urban economy. At mid-century the number of prostitutes in Vienna was estimated to be fifteen thousand; in Paris, where prostitution was a licensed trade, fifty thousand; in London, eighty thousand. London newspaper reports of the 1850s cataloged the elaborate hierarchies of the vast underworld of prostitutes and their customers. Those included entrepreneurs with names like Swindling Sal who ran lodging houses; the pimps and "fancy men" who managed the trade of prostitutes on the street; and the relatively few "prima donnas" or courtesans who enjoyed the protection of rich, upper-middle-class lovers, who entertained lavishly and whose wealth allowed them to move on the fringes of more respectable high society. The heroines of Alexandre Dumas's novel *La Dame aux Camélias* and of Giuseppe Verdi's opera *La Traviata* (The Lost One) were modeled on these women. Yet the vast majority of prostitutes were not courtesans but rather women (and some men) who worked long and dangerous hours in port districts of cities or at lodging houses in the overwhelmingly male working-class neighborhoods. Most prostitutes were young women who had just arrived in the city or working women trying to manage during a period of unemployment. Single women in the cities were very vulnerable to sexual exploitation. Many were abandoned by their partners if they became pregnant, others faced the danger of rape by their employers. Such experiences—abandonment and rape—could lead to prostitution since women in these circumstances were unlikely to secure "respectable" employment.

THE MIDDLE CLASSES

Nineteenth-century novelists such as Charles Dickens and William Thackeray in Britain, Victor Hugo and Honoré Balzac in France, and Theodor Fontane in Germany painted a sweeping portrait of middle-class society in the nineteenth century. Their novels are peopled with characters from all walks of life—journalists, courtesans, small-town mayors, mill owners, shopkeepers, aristocrats, farmers, laborers, and students. The plots of these stories explore the ways that older hierarchies of rank, status, and privilege were gradually giving way to a new set of gradations based on wealth and social class. In this new world, money trumped birth, and social mobility was an accepted fact rather than something to be hidden. One of Thackeray's characters observes caustically that "Ours is a ready-money society. We live among bankers and city big-wigs . . . and every man, as he talks to you, is jingling his guineas in his pocket." Works of literature need to be approached cautiously, for their characters express their authors' points of view. Still, literature and art offer an extraordinary source of social historical detail and insight. And we can safely say that the rising visibility of the middle classes and their new political and social power—lamented by some writers but hailed by others—were central facts of nineteenth-century society.

Who were the middle classes? (Another common term for this social group, the *bourgeoisie*, originally meant city [*bourg*] dweller.) Its ranks included shopkeepers and their households, the families of laywers, doctors, and other professionals, as well as well-off factory owners who might aspire to marry their daughters to titled aristocrats. At the lower end of the social scale the middle classes included the families of salaried clerks and office workers for whom white-collar employment offered hope of a rise in status.

Movement within middle-class ranks was often possible in the course of one or two generations. Very few, however, moved from the working class into the middle class. Most middle-class success stories began in the middle class itself, with the children of relatively well-off farmers, skilled artisans, or professionals. Upward mobility was almost impossible without education, and education was a rare, though not unattainable, luxury for working-class children. Careers open to talents, that goal achieved by the French Revolution, frequently meant opening jobs to middle-class young men who could pass exams. The examination system was an important path upward within government bureaucracies.

The journey from middle class to aristocratic, landed society was equally difficult. In Britain, mobility of this sort was easier to achieve than on the Continent. Sons from wealthy upper-middle-class families, if they were sent to elite schools and universities and if they left the commercial or industrial world for a career in politics, might actually move up. William Gladstone, son of a Liverpool merchant, attended the exclusive educational preserves of Eton (a private boarding school) and Oxford University, married into the aristocratic Grenville family, and became prime minister of England. Yet Gladstone was an exception to the rule, even in Britain, and most upward mobility was much less spectacular.

Nevertheless, the European middle class helped sustain itself with the belief that it was possible to get ahead by means of intelligence, pluck, and serious devotion to work. The Englishman Samuel Smiles, in his extraordinarily successful how-to-succeed book *Self-Help* (1859), preached a gospel dear to the middle class: "The spirit of self-help is the root of all genuine growth in the individual." As Smiles also suggested, those who succeeded were obliged to follow middle-class notions of respectability. The middle-classes' claim to political power and cultural influence rested on arguments that they constituted a new and deserving social

***THE LEGISLATIVE BELLY* BY HONORE DAUMIER, 1834.** Daumier's caricatures of bourgeois politicians mock the close link between politics and a prosperous elite made up of men of property.

elite, superior to the common people yet sharply different from the older aristocracy, and the rightful custodians of the nation's future. Thus middle-class respectability, like a code, stood for many values. It meant financial independence, providing responsibly for one's family, avoiding gambling and debt. It suggested merit and character as opposed to aristocratic privilege and hard work as opposed to living off noble estates. Respectable middle-class gentlemen might be wealthy, but they should live modestly and soberly, avoiding conspicuous consumption, lavish dress, womanizing, and other forms of dandyish behavior associated with the aristocracy. Of course, these were aspirations and codes, not social realities. They nonetheless remained key to the middle-class sense of self and understanding of the world.

Private Life and Middle-Class Identity

Family and home played a central role in forming middle-class identity. Few themes were more common in nineteenth-century fiction than men and women pursuing mobility and status by or through marriage. Families served intensely practical purposes: sons, nephews, and cousins were expected to assume responsibility in family firms when it came their turn; wives managed accounts; and parents-in-law provided business connections, credit, inheritance, and so on. The family's role in middle-class thought, however, did not arise only from these practical considerations; family was part of a larger worldview. A well-governed household offered a counterpoint to the business and confusion of the world, and families offered continuity and tradition in a time of rapid change.

Gender and the Cult of Domesticity

There was no single type of middle-class family or home. Yet many people held powerful convictions about how a respectable home should be run. According to advice manuals, poetry, and middle-class journals, wives and mothers were supposed to occupy a "separate sphere" of life, in which they lived in subordination to their spouses. "Man for the field and woman for the hearth; man for the sword and for the needle she. . . . All else confusion," wrote the British poet Alfred Lord Tennyson in 1847. These prescriptions were directly applied to young people. Boys were educated in secondary schools; girls at home. This nineteenth-century conception of separate spheres needs to be understood in relation to much longer-standing traditions of paternal authority, which were codified in law. Throughout Europe, laws subjected women to their husbands' authority. The Napoleonic Code, a model for other countries after 1815, classified women, children, and the mentally ill together as legally incompetent. In Britain, a woman transferred all her property rights to her husband on marriage. Although unmarried women did enjoy a degree of legal independence in France and Austria, laws generally assigned them to the "protection" of their fathers. Gender relations in the nineteenth century rested on this foundation of legal inequality. Yet the idea or doctrine of separate spheres was meant to underscore that men's and women's spheres complemented each other. Thus, for instance, middle-class writings were full of references to spiritual equality between men and women; and middle-class people wrote, proudly, of marriages in which the wife was a "companion" and "helpmate."

It is helpful to recall that members of the middle class articulated their values in opposition to aristocratic customs on the one hand and the lives of the common people on the other. They argued, for instance, that middle-class marriages did not aim to found aristocratic dynasties and were not arranged to accumulate power and privilege; instead they were to be based on mutual respect and division of responsibilities. A respectable middle-class woman should be free from the unrelenting toil that was the lot of a woman of the people. Called in Victorian Britain the "angel in the house," the middle-class woman was responsible for the moral education of her children. It was understood that being a good wife and mother was a demanding task, requiring an elevated character. This belief, sometimes called the "cult of domesticity," was central to middle-class Victorian thinking about women. Home life, and by extension the woman's role in that life, were infused with new meaning. As one young woman put it after reading a popular book on female education, "What an important sphere a woman fills! How thoroughly she ought to be qualified for it—I think hers the more honourable employment than a man's." In sum, the early nineteenth century brought a general reassessment of femininity. The roots of this reassessment lay in early-nineteenth-century religion and efforts to moralize society, largely to guard against the disorders of the French and Industrial Revolutions.

As a housewife, a middle-class woman had the task of keeping the household functioning smoothly and harmoniously. She maintained the accounts and directed the activities of the servants. Having at least one servant was a mark of middle-class status; and in wealthier families governesses and nannies cared for children, idealized views of motherhood notwithstanding. The middle classes, however, included many gradations of wealth, from a well-housed banker with a governess and five servants to a village preacher with one. Moreover, the work of running and maintaining a home was enormous. Linens and clothes had to be made and mended. Only the wealthy had the luxury of running water, and others had to carry and heat water for cooking, laundry, and cleaning. Heating with coal and lighting with kerosene involved hours of cleaning, and so on. If the "angel in the house" was a cultural ideal, it was partly because she had real economic value.

Outside the home, women had very few respectable options for earning a living. Unmarried women might act as companions or governesses—the British novelist

ILLUSTRATION FROM A VICTORIAN BOOK ON MANNERS.
Advice books such as this were very popular in the nineteenth century—a mark, perhaps, of preoccupation with status and the emergence of new social groups. ■ *Why would people be concerned about "respectability" in an age of greater social mobility?*

Marriage, Sexuality, and the Facts of Life

In the nineteenth century sexuality became the subject of much anxious debate, largely because it raised other issues: the roles of men and women, morality, and social respectability. Doctors threw themselves into the discussion, offering their expert opinions on the health (including the sexual lives) of the population. Yet doctors did not dictate people's private lives. Nineteenth-century men and women responded to what they experienced as the facts of life more than to expert advice. The first document provides an example of medical knowledge and opinion in 1870. The second offers a glimpse of the daily realities of family life in 1830.

A French Doctor Denounces Contraception

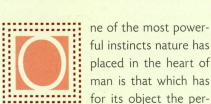 One of the most powerful instincts nature has placed in the heart of man is that which has for its object the perpetuation of the human race. But this instinct, this inclination, so active, which attracts one sex towards the other, is liable to be perverted, to deviate from the path nature has laid out. From this arises a number of fatal aberrations which exercise a deplorable influence upon the individual, upon the family and upon society. . . .

We hear constantly that marriages are less fruitful, that the increase of population does not follow its former ratio. I believe that this is mainly attributable to genesiac frauds. It might naturally be supposed that these odious calculations of egotism, these shameful refinements of debauchery, are met with almost entirely in large cities, and among the luxurious classes, and that small towns and country places yet preserve that simplicity of manners attributed to primitive society, when the *pater familias* was proud of exhibiting his numerous offspring. Such, however, is not the case, and I shall show that those who have an unlimited confidence in the patriarchal habits of our country people are deeply in error. At the present time frauds are practiced by all classes. . . .

The laboring classes are generally satisfied with the practice of Onan [withdrawal]. . . . They are seldom familiar with the sheath invented by Dr. Condom, and bearing his name.

Among the wealthy, on the other hand, the use of this preservative is generally known. It favors frauds by rendering them easier; but it does not afford complete security. . . .

Case X.—This couple belongs to two respectable families of vintners. They are both pale, emaciated, downcast, sickly. . . .

They have been married for ten years; they first had two children, one immediately after the other, but in order to avoid an increase of family, they have had recourse to conjugal frauds. Being both very amorous, they have found this practice very convenient to satisfy their inclinations. They have employed it to such an extent, that up to a few months ago, when their health began to fail, the husband had intercourse with his wife habitually two and three times in twenty-four hours.

The following is the condition of the woman: She complains of continual pains in the lower part of the abdomen and kidneys. These pains disturb the functions of the stomach and render her nervous. . . . By the touch we find a very intense heat, great sensibility to pressure, and all the signs of a chronic metritis. The patient attributes positively her present state to the too frequent approaches of her husband.

Charlotte Brontë's heroine Jane Eyre did so and led a generally miserable life until "rescued" by marriage to her difficult employer. But nineteenth-century convictions about women's moral nature, combined as they were with middle-class aspirations to political leadership, encouraged middle-class wives to undertake voluntary charitable work or to campaign for social reform. In Britain and the United States, women played an important role in the struggle to abolish the slave trade and slavery in the British Empire. Many of these movements also drew on the energies of religious, especially Protestant, organizations, committed to the eradication of social evils and moral improvement.

The husband does not attempt to exculpate himself, as he also is in a state of extreme suffering. It is not in the genital organs, however, that we find his disorder, but in the whole general nervous system; his history will find its place in the part of this work relative to general disturbances. . . .

Source: Louis-François-Etienne Bergeret, *The Preventive Obstacle, or Conjugal Onanism*, trans. P. de Marmon (New York: 1870), pp. 3–4, 12, 20–22, 25, 56–57, 100–101, 111–113. Originally published in Paris in 1868.

Death in Childbirth (1830)

Mrs. Ann B. Pettigrew was taken in Labour after returning from a walk in the garden, at 7 o'clock in the evening of June 30, 1830. At 40 minutes after 11 o'clock, she was delivered of a daughter. A short time after, I was informed that the Placenta was not removed, and, at 10 minutes after 12 was asked into the room. I advanced to my dear wife, and kissing her, asked her how she was, to which she replied, I feel very badly. I went out of the room, and sent for Dr. Warren.

I then returned, and inquired if there was much hemorrhage, and was answered that there was. I then asked the midwife (Mrs. Brickhouse) if she ever used manual exertion to remove the placenta. She said she had more than fifty times. I then, fearing the consequences of hemorrhage, observed, Do, my dear sweet wife, permit Mrs. Brickhouse to remove it: To which she assented. . . .

After the second unsuccessful attempt, I desired the midwife to desist. In these two efforts, my dear Nancy suffered exceedingly and frequently exclaimed: "O Mrs Brickhouse you will kill me," and to me, "O I shall die, send for the Doctor." To which I replied, "I have sent."

After this, my feelings were so agonizing that I had to retire from the room and lay down, or fall. Shortly after which, the midwife came to me and, falling upon her knees, prayed most fervently to God and to me to forgive her for saying that she could do what she could not. . . .

The placenta did not come away, and the hemorrhage continued with unabated violence until five o'clock in the morning, when the dear woman breathed her last 20 minutes before the Doctor arrived.

So agonizing a scene as that from one o'clock, I have no words to describe. O My God, My God! have mercy on me. I am undone forever. . . .

Source: Cited in Erna Olafson Hellerstein, Leslie Parker Hume, and Karen M. Offen, eds., *Victorian Women: A Documentary Account of Women's Lives in Nineteenth-Century England, France, and the United States.* (Stanford, CA: 1981) pp. 193–94, 219–20.

Questions for Analysis

1. The French doctor states that the impulse to have sexual relations is "one of the most powerful instincts" given to humans by nature, while simultaneously claiming that this natural instinct is "liable to be perverted." What does this reveal about his attitude toward "nature"?

2. What does he mean by "genesiac frauds"? Who is being deceived by this fraud? What consequences for individuals and for society as a whole does the doctor fear from this deception?

3. What does the story of Mrs. Pettigrew's death reveal about the dangers of childbirth and the state of obstetric medicine in the nineteenth century?

Throughout Europe, a wide range of movements to improve conditions for the poor in schools and hospitals, for temperance, against prostitution, or for legislation on factory hours were often run by women. Florence Nightingale, who went to the Crimean Peninsula in Russia to nurse British soldiers fighting there in the 1850s, remains the most famous of those women, whose determination to right social wrongs compelled them to defy conventional notions of woman's "proper" sphere. Equally famous—or infamous, at the time—was the French female novelist George Sand (1804–1876), whose real name was Amandine Aurore Dupin Dudevant. Sand dressed like a man and smoked cigars, and her novels often told the tales of independent women thwarted by convention and unhappy marriage.

Queen Victoria, who came to the British throne in 1837, labored to make her solemn public image reflect contemporary feminine virtues of moral probity and dutiful domesticity. Her court was eminently proper, a marked contrast to that of her uncle George IV, whose cavalier ways had set the style for high life a generation before. Though possessing a bad temper, Victoria trained herself to curb it in deference to her ministers and her public-spirited, ultrarespectable husband, Prince Albert of Saxe-Coburg. She was a successful queen because she embodied the traits important to the middle class, whose triumph she seemed to epitomize and whose habits of mind we have come to call Victorian. Nineteenth-century ideas about gender had an impact on masculinity as well as femininity. Soon after the revolutionary and Napoleonic period, men began to dress in sober, practical clothing—and to see as effeminate or dandyish the wigs, ruffled collars, and tight breeches that had earlier been the pride of aristocratic masculinity.

"Passionlessness": Gender and Sexuality

Victorian ideas about sexuality are among the most remarked-on features of nineteenth-century culture. They have become virtually synonymous with anxiety, prudishness, and ignorance. An English mother counseling her daughter about her wedding night is said to have told her to "lie back and think of the empire." Etiquette apparently required that piano legs be covered. Many of these anxieties and prohibitions, however, have been caricatured. More recently, historians have tried to disentangle the teachings or prescriptions of etiquette books and marriage manuals from the actual beliefs of men and women. Equally important, they have sought to understand each on its own terms. Beliefs about sexuality followed from convictions, described earlier, concerning separate spheres. Indeed, one of the defining aspects of nineteenth-century ideas about men and women is the extent to which they rested on scientific arguments about nature. Codes of morality and methods of science combined to reinforce the certainty that specific characteristics were inherent to each sex. Men and women had different social roles, and those differences were rooted in their bodies. The French social thinker Auguste Comte provides a good example: "Biological philosophy teaches us that, through the whole animal scale, and while the specific type is preserved, radical differences, physical and moral, distinguish the sexes." Comte also spelled out the implications of biological difference: "[T]he equality of the sexes, of which so much is said, is incompatible with all social existence. . . . The economy of the human family could never be inverted without an entire change in our cerebral organism." Women were unsuited for higher education because their brains were smaller or because their bodies were fragile. "Fifteen or 20 days of 28 (we may say nearly always) a woman is not only an invalid, but a wounded one. She ceaselessly suffers from love's eternal wound," wrote the well-known French author Jules Michelet about menstruation.

Finally, scientists and doctors considered women's alleged moral superiority to be literally embodied in an absence of sexual feeling, or "passionlessness." Scientists and doctors considered male sexual desire natural, if not admirable—an unruly force that had to be channeled. Many governments legalized and regulated prostitution—which included the compulsory examination of women for venereal disease—precisely because it provided an outlet for male sexual desire. Doctors disagreed about female sexuality, but the British doctor William Acton stood among those who asserted that women functioned differently:

> I have taken pains to obtain and compare abundant evidence on this subject, and the result of my inquiries I may briefly epitomize as follows:— I should say that the majority of women (happily for society) are not very much troubled with sexual feeling of any kind. What men are habitually, women are only exceptionally.

Like other nineteenth-century men and women, Acton also believed that more open expressions of sexuality were disreputable and, also, that working-class women were less "feminine."

Convictions like these reveal a great deal about Victorian science and medicine, but they did not necessarily dictate people's intimate lives. As far as sexuality was concerned, the absence of any reliable contraception mattered more in people's experiences and feelings than sociologists' or doctors' opinions. Abstinence and withdrawal were the only common techniques for preventing pregnancy. Their effectiveness was limited, since until the 1880s doctors continued to believe that a woman was most fertile during and around her menstrual period. Midwives and prostitutes knew of other forms of contraception and abortifacients (all of them dangerous and most ineffective), and surely some middle-class women did as well, but such information was not respectable middle-class fare. Concretely, then, sexual intercourse was directly related to the very real dangers of frequent pregnancies. In England, one in a hundred childbirths ended in the death of the mother; at a time when a woman might become pregnant eight or nine times in her life, this was a sobering prospect. Those dangers varied with social class, but even among wealthy and better-cared-for women, they took a real toll. It is not surprising that middle-class women's diaries and letters are full of their anticipations of childbirth, both joyful and anxious. Queen Victoria, who bore nine children, declared that childbirth was the "shadow side" of marriage—and she was a pioneer in using anesthesia!

Middle-Class Life in Public

The public life of middle-class families literally reshaped the nineteenth-century landscape. Houses and their furnishings were powerful symbols of material security. Solidly built, heavily decorated, they proclaimed the financial worth and social respectability of those who dwelt within. In provincial cities they were often freestanding villas. In London, Paris, Berlin, and Vienna, they might be in rows of five- or six-story townhouses or large apartments. Whatever particular shape they took, they were built to last a long time. The rooms were certain to be crowded with furniture, art objects, carpets, and wall hangings. The size of the rooms, the elegance of the furniture, the number of servants—all depended, of course, on the extent of one's income. A bank clerk did not live as elegantly as a bank director. Yet they shared many standards and aspirations, and those common values helped bind them to the same class, despite the differences in their material way of life.

As cities grew, they became increasingly segregated. Middle-class people lived far from the unpleasant sights and smells of industrialization. Their residential areas, usually built to the west of the cities, out of the path of the prevailing breeze and therefore of industrial pollution, were havens from congestion. The public buildings in the center, many constructed during the nineteenth century, were celebrated as signs of development and prosperity. The middle classes increasingly managed their cities' affairs, although members of the aristocracy retained considerable power, especially in central Europe. And it was these new middle-class civic leaders who provided new industrial cities with many of their architectural landmarks: city halls, stock exchanges, museums, opera houses, outdoor concert halls, and department stores. One historian has called these buildings the new cathedrals of the industrial age; projects intended to express the community's values and represent public culture, they were monuments to social change.

The suburbs changed as well. The advent of the railways made outings to concerts, parks, and bathing spots popular. They made it possible for families of relatively moderate means to take one- or two-week-long trips to the

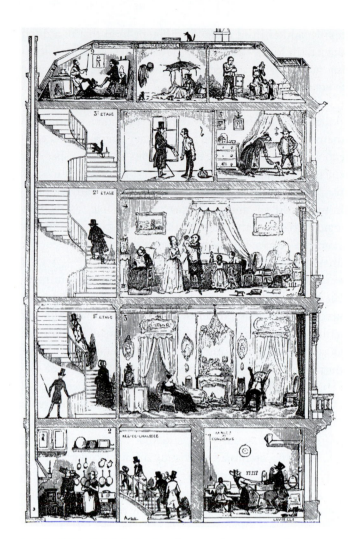

APARTMENT LIVING IN PARIS. This print shows that on the Continent rich and poor often lived in the same buildings, the rich on the lower floors, the poor at the top. This sort of residential mixing was less common in Britain.

mountains or to the seashore. New resorts opened, offering racetracks, mineral springs baths, and cabanas on the beach. Mass tourism would not come until the twentieth century. But the now-familiar Impressionist paintings of the 1870s and 1880s testify to something that was dramatically new in the nineteenth century: a new range of middle-class leisures.

Working-Class Life

Like the middle class, the working class was divided into various subgroups and categories, determined in this case by skill, wages, gender, and workplace. Workers' experiences varied, depending on where they worked, where they lived, and, above all, how much they earned. A skilled textile worker lived a life far different from that of a ditch digger, the former able to afford the food, shelter, and clothing necessary for a decent existence, the latter barely able to scrape by.

Some movement from the ranks of the unskilled to the skilled was possible, if children were provided, or provided themselves, with at least a rudimentary education. Yet education was considered by many parents a luxury, especially since children could be put to work at an early age to supplement a family's meager earnings. Downward mobility from skilled to unskilled was also possible, as technological change—the introduction of the power loom, for example—drove highly paid workers into the ranks of the unskilled and destitute.

Working-class housing was unhealthy and unregulated. In older cities single-family dwellings were broken up into apartments, often of no more than one room per family. In new manufacturing centers, rows of tiny houses, located close by smoking factories, were built back to back, thereby eliminating any cross-ventilation or space for gardens. Crowding was commonplace. A newspaper account from the 1840s noted that in Leeds, a textile center in northern Britain, an ordinary worker's house contained no more than 150 square feet, and that in most cases those houses were "crammed almost to suffocation with human beings both day and night."

Household routines, demanding in the middle classes, were grinding for the poor. The family remained a survival network, in which everyone played a crucial role. In addition to working for wages, wives were expected to house, feed, and clothe the family on the very little money different members of the family earned. A good wife was able to make ends meet even in bad times. Working women's daily lives involved constant rounds of carrying and boiling water, cleaning, cooking, and doing laundry—in one- and two-room crowded, unventilated, poorly lit apartments. Families could not rely on their own gardens to help supply them with food. City markets catered to their needs for cheap goods, but these were regularly stale, nearly rotten, or dangerously adulterated. Formaldehyde was added to milk to prevent spoilage. Pounded rice was mixed into sugar. Fine brown earth was introduced into cocoa.

WORKING WOMEN IN THE INDUSTRIAL LANDSCAPE

Few figures raised more public anxiety and outcry in the nineteenth century than the working woman. Contemporaries worried out loud about the "promiscuous mixing of the sexes" in crowded and humid workshops. Nineteenth-century writers, starting in England and France, chronicled what they considered to be the economic and moral horrors of female labor: unattended children running in the streets, small children caught in accidents at the mills or the mines, pregnant women hauling coal, or women laboring alongside men in shops.

Women's work was not new, but industrialization made it more visible. Both before and after the Industrial Revolution labor was divided by gender, but as employers implemented new manufacturing processes, ideas about which jobs were appropriate for women shifted. In traditional textile production, for example, women spun and men operated the looms. In industrial textile factories, on the other hand, employers preferred women and children, both because they were considered more docile and less likely to make trouble and because it was believed that their smaller hands were better suited to the intricate job of tying threads on the power looms. Manufacturers sought to recruit women mill hands from neighboring villages, paying good wages by comparison with other jobs open to women. Most began to work at the age of ten or eleven, and when they had children they either put their children out to a wet nurse, brought them to the mills, or continued to work doing piecework at home. This transformation of the gendered structure of work caused intense anxiety in the first half of the nineteenth century and is one of the reasons that the emerging labor movement began to include calls for excluding women from the workplace in their programs.

Most women did not work in factories, however, and continued to labor at home or in small workshops—"sweatshops," as they came to be called—for notoriously low wages paid not by the hour but by the piece for each shirt stitched or each matchbox glued. The greatest number of unmarried working-class women worked less visibly in domestic service, a job that brought low wages and, to judge by the testimony of many women, coercive sexual relationships with male employers or their sons. Domestic service, however, provided room and board. In a time when a single woman simply could not survive on her own wages, a young woman who had just arrived in the city had few choices: marriage, which was unlikely to happen right away; renting a room in a boardinghouse, many of which were often centers of prostitution; domestic service; or living with someone. How women balanced the demands for money and the time for household work varied with the number and age of their children. Mothers were actually more likely to work when their children were very small, for there were more mouths to feed and the children were not yet old enough to earn wages.

Poverty, the absence of privacy, and the particular vulnerabilities of working-class women made working-class sexuality very different from its middle-class counterpart.

Illegitimacy rose dramatically between 1750 and 1850. In Frankfurt, Germany, for example, where the illegitimacy rate had been a mere 2 percent in the early 1700s, it reached 25 percent in 1850. In Bordeaux, France, in 1840, one-third of the recorded births were illegitimate. Reasons for this increase are difficult to establish. Greater mobility and urbanization meant weaker family ties, more opportunities for young men and women, and more vulnerabilities. Premarital sex was an accepted practice in preindustrial villages, but because of the social controls that dominated village life, it was almost always followed by marriage. These controls were weaker in the far more anonymous setting of a factory town or commercial city. The economic uncertainties of the early industrial age meant that a young working-man's promise of marriage based on his expectation of a job might frequently be difficult to fulfill. Economic vulnerability drove many single women into temporary relationships that produced children and a continuing cycle of poverty and abandonment. Historians have shown, however, that in the city as in the countryside, many of these temporary relationships became enduring ones: the parents of illegitimate children would marry later. Again, nineteenth-century writers dramatized what they considered the disreputable sexuality of the "dangerous classes" in the cities. Some of them attributed illegitimacy, prostitution, and so on to the moral weakness of working-class people, others to the systematic changes wrought by industrialization. Both sides, however, overstated the collapse of the family and the destruction of traditional morality. Working-class families transmitted expectations about gender roles and sexual behavior: girls should expect to work, daughters were responsible for caring for their younger siblings as well as for earning wages, sexuality was a fact of life, midwives could help desperate pregnant girls, marriage was an avenue to respectability, and so on. The gulf that separated these expectations and codes from those of middle-class women was one of the most important factors in the development of nineteenth-century class identity.

A Life Apart: "Class Consciousness"

The new demands of life in an industrial economy created common experiences and difficulties. The factory system denied skilled workers the pride in craft they had previously enjoyed. Stripped of the protections of guilds and apprenticeships and prevented from organizing by legislation in France, Germany, and Britain in the first half of the nineteenth century, workers felt vulnerable in the face of their socially and politically powerful employers. Factory hours were long—usually twelve to fourteen hours. Textile mills were unventilated, and minute particles of lint lodged in workers' lungs. Machines were unfenced and posed dangers to child workers. British physicians cataloged the toll that long hours tending machines took on children, including spinal curvature and bone malformations. Children were also employed in large numbers in mines—over fifty thousand worked in British mines in 1841.

Factories also imposed new routines and disciplines. Artisans in earlier times worked long hours for little pay, but they set their own schedules and controlled the pace of work, moving from their home workshops to their small garden plots as they wished. In a factory all hands learned the discipline of the clock. To increase production, the factory system encouraged the breaking down of the manufacturing process into specialized steps, each with its own time. Workers began to see machinery itself as the tyrant that changed

CAPITAL AND LABOUR. In its earliest years, the British magazine *Punch*, though primarily a humorous weekly, manifested a strong social conscience. This 1843 cartoon shows the capitalists enjoying the rewards of their investments while the workers shiver in cold and hunger. ■ *How would a defender of the new industrial order respond to this cartoon?* ■ *What is the significance of the image on the top right, showing a scene from the British Empire?*

their lives and bound them to industrial slavery. A radical working-class song written in Britain in the 1840s expressed the feeling:

> There is a king and a ruthless king;
> Not a king of the poet's dream;
> But a tyrant fell, white slaves know well,
> And that ruthless king is steam.

Yet the defining feature of working-class life was vulnerability—to unemployment, sickness, accidents in dangerous jobs, family problems, and spikes in the prices of food. Seasonal unemployment, high in almost all trades, made it impossible to collect regular wages. Markets for manufactured goods were small and unstable, producing cyclical economic depressions; when those came, thousands of workers found themselves laid off with no system of unemployment insurance to sustain them. The early decades of industrialization were also marked by several severe agricultural depressions and economic crises. During the crisis years of the 1840s, half the working population of Britain's industrial cities was unemployed. In Paris, eighty-five thousand went on relief in 1840. Families survived by working several small jobs, pawning their possessions, and getting credit from local wineshops and grocery stores. The chronic insecurity of working-class life helped fuel the creation of workers' self-help societies, fraternal associations, and early socialist organizations. It also meant that economic crises could have explosive consequences (see Chapter 20).

By mid-century, various experiences were beginning to make working people conscious of themselves as different from and in opposition to the middle classes. Changes in the workplace—whether the introduction of machines and factory labor, speedups, subcontracting to cheap labor, or the loss of guild protections—were part of the picture. The social segregation of the rapidly expanding nineteenth-century cities also contributed to the sense that working people lived a life apart. Class differences seemed embedded in a very wide array of everyday experiences and beliefs: work, private life, expectations for children, the roles of men and women, and definitions of respectability. Over the course of the nineteenth century all of these different experiences gave concrete, specific meaning to the word *class*.

CONCLUSION

Why did the Industrial Revolution occur at this moment in human history? Why did it begin in Europe? Why did it not occur in other regions in the world with large populations

After You Read This Chapter

Visit StudySpace for quizzes, additional review materials, and multi-media documents. **wwnorton.com/studyspace**

REVIEWING THE OBJECTIVES

- The Industrial Revolution in Europe began in northern Great Britain. What circumstances made this process of economic development begin there?
- Certain industries were particularly suitable for the kinds of technological developments that encouraged industrialization. What were these industries and where did they exist in Europe?
- Industrial development changed the nature of work and production in significant ways. What were these changes, and how did they change the relations between laborers and their employers, or local producers and wider markets?
- Industrialization had social effects far beyond the factories. What larger changes in European society were associated with the Industrial Revolution?
- A large and diverse group of middle-class people emerged in Europe as a result of the social changes brought on by industrialization. What kinds of people qualified as middle-class during the nineteenth century and how were they different from other social groups?

and advanced technologies, such as China or India? These fundamental questions remain subject to serious debate among historians. One school of explanations focuses on the fact that the mechanization of industry occurred first in northern Europe, and seeks to explain the Industrial Revolution's origins in terms of this region's vibrant towns, its well-developed commercial markets, and the presence of a prosperous land-owning elite that had few prejudices against entrepreneurial activity. These historians have suggested that industrialization is best understood as a process rooted in European culture and history.

More recently, however, historians with a more global approach have argued that it may be incorrect to assert that industrialization developed as it did because of the advantages enjoyed by a central, European, core. Instead, they have explored the possibility that the world's economies constituted a larger interlocking system that had no definitive center until *after* the take-off of European industrialization. Before that period, when it came to agricultural practices, ecological constraints, population densities, urbanization, and technological development, *many* global regions were not so different from the western European model. In the end, suggest these historians, Europe was able to move more quickly to industrial production because their economies were better positioned to mobilize the resources available to them on the periphery of their trading sphere. The access enjoyed by European traders to agricultural products from slave-owning societies in the Americas helped them escape the ecological constraints imposed by their own intensely farmed lands, and made the move to an industrial economy possible. Contingent factors—such as patterns of disease and epidemic or the location of coal fields—may have also played a role.

There is less debate about the consequences of the Industrial Revolution within Europe. New forms of industrial production created a new economy and changed the nature of work for both men and women. Industrialization changed the landscape of Europe and changed the structures of families and the private lives of people in both the cities and the countryside. Industrialization created new forms of wealth along with new kinds of poverty. It also fostered an acute awareness of the disparity between social groups. In the eighteenth century, that disparity would have been described in terms of birth, rank, or privilege. In the nineteenth century, it was increasingly seen in terms of class. Both champions and critics of the new industrial order spoke of a "class society." The identities associated with class were formed in the crowded working-class districts of the new cities, in experiences of work, and in the new conditions of respectability that determined life in middle-class homes. These new identities would be sharpened in the political events to which we now turn.

PEOPLE, IDEAS, AND EVENTS IN CONTEXT

- Why was **ENCLOSURE** an important factor in the Industrial Revolution?
- What was the **FLY SHUTTLE** or the **SPINNING JENNY**? What was the **COTTON GIN**? What effect did these machines have on industrial development?
- What was the significance of **EUROPEAN EMPIRE** and overseas expansion for industrialization?
- How did industrialization affect **POPULATION GROWTH** in Europe? What effects did it have on the **PEASANTRY**? On **URBAN POPULATIONS**?
- What **ENVIRONMENTAL CHANGES** were associated with the use of new sources of fuel such as coal or the construction of large and concentrated centers of industrial manufacture?
- What was the **IRISH POTATO FAMINE** and how was it related to the economic developments of nineteenth-century Europe? What might **THOMAS MALTHUS** have thought about the potato famine?

CONSEQUENCES

- What might the changes associated with the Industrial Revolution have done to people's conceptions of time and space? How might they have perceived their lives against what they knew of the experience of their parent's generation or what they anticipated for their children?
- What did the Industrial Revolution do for European nation-states?

Rulers of Principal States

THE CAROLINGIAN DYNASTY

Pepin of Heristal, Mayor of the Palace, 687–714
Charles Martel, Mayor of the Palace, 715–741
Pepin III, Mayor of the Palace, 741–751; King, 751–768
Charlemagne, King, 768–814; Emperor, 800–814
Louis the Pious, Emperor, 814–840

West Francia

Charles the Bald, King, 840–877; Emperor, 875–877
Louis II, King, 877–879
Louis III, King, 879–882
Carloman, King, 879–884

Middle Kingdoms

Lothair, Emperor, 840–855
Louis (Italy), Emperor, 855–875
Charles (Provence), King, 855–863
Lothair II (Lorraine), King, 855–869

East Francia

Ludwig, King, 840–876
Carloman, King, 876–880
Ludwig, King, 876–882
Charles the Fat, Emperor, 876–887

HOLY ROMAN EMPERORS

Saxon Dynasty

Otto I, 962–973
Otto II, 973–983
Otto III, 983–1002
Henry II, 1002–1024

Franconian Dynasty

Conrad II, 1024–1039
Henry III, 1039–1056
Henry IV, 1056–1106
HenryV, 1106–1125
Lothair II (Saxony), 1125–1137

Hohenstaufen Dynasty

Conrad III, 1138–1152
Frederick I (Barbarossa), 1152–1190
Henry VI, 1190–1197
Philip of Swabia, 1198–1208 ⎫
Otto IV (Welf), 1198–1215 ⎭ Rivals

Frederick II, 1220–1250
Conrad IV, 1250–1254

Interregnum, 1254–1273

Emperors from Various Dynasties

Rudolf I (Habsburg), 1273–1291
Adolf (Nassau), 1292–1298
Albert I (Habsburg), 1298–1308
Henry VII (Luxemburg), 1308–1313
Ludwig IV (Wittelsbach), 1314–1347
Charles IV (Luxemburg), 1347–1378
Wenceslas (Luxemburg), 1378–1400
Rupert (Wittelsbach), 1400–1410
Sigismund (Luxemburg), 1410–1437

Habsburg Dynasty

Albert II, 1438–1439
Frederick III, 1440–1493

Maximilian I, 1493–1519
Charles V, 1519–1556
Ferdinand I, 1556–1564
Maximilian II, 1564–1576
Rudolf II, 1576–1612
Matthias, 1612–1619
Ferdinand II, 1619–1637
Ferdinand III, 1637–1657

Leopold I, 1658–1705
Joseph I, 1705–1711
Charles VI, 1711–1740
Charles VII (not a Habsburg), 1742–1745
Francis I, 1745–1765
Joseph II, 1765–1790
Leopold II, 1790–1792
Francis II, 1792–1806

RULERS OF FRANCE FROM HUGH CAPET

Capetian Dynasty

Hugh Capet, 987–996
Robert II, 996–1031
Henry I, 1031–1060
Philip I, 1060–1108
Louis VI, 1108–1137
Louis VII, 1137–1180
Philip II (Augustus), 1180–1223
Louis VIII, 1223–1226
Louis IX (St. Louis), 1226–1270
Philip III, 1270–1285
Philip IV, 1285–1314
Louis X, 1314–1316
Philip V, 1316–1322
Charles lV, 1322–1328

Valois Dynasty

Philip VI, 1328–1350
John, 1350–1364
Charles V, 1364–1380
Charles VI, 1380–1422
Charles VII, 1422–1461
Louis XI, 1461–1483
Charles VIII, 1483–1498
Louis XII, 1498–1515
Francis I, 1515–1547

Henry II, 1547–1559
Francis II, 1559–1560
Charles IX, 1560–1574
Henry III, 1574–1589

Bourbon Dynasty

Henry IV, 1589–1610
Louis XIII, 1610–1643
Louis XIV, 1643–1715
Louis XV, 1715–1774
Louis XVI, 1774–1792

After 1792

First Republic, 1792–1799
Napoleon Bonaparte, First Consul, 1799–1804
Napoleon I, Emperor, 1804–1814
Louis XVIII (Bourbon dynasty), 1814–1824
Charles X (Bourbon dynasty), 1824–1830
Louis Philippe, 1830–1848
Second Republic, 1848–1852
Napoleon III, Emperor, 1852–1870
Third Republic, 1870–1940
Pétain regime, 1940–1944
Provisional government, 1944–1946
Fourth Republic, 1946–1958
Fifth Republic, 1958–

RULERS OF ENGLAND

Anglo-Saxon Dynasty

Alfred the Great, 871–899
Edward the Elder, 899–924
Ethelstan, 924–939
Edmund I, 939–946
Edred, 946–955
Edwy, 955–959
Edgar, 959–975

Edward the Martyr, 975–978
Ethelred the Unready, 978–1016
Canute, 1016–1035 (Danish Nationality)
Harold I, 1035–1040
Hardicanute, 1040–1042
Edward the Confessor, 1042–1066
Harold II, 1066

House of Normandy

William I (the Conqueror), 1066–1087
William II, 1087–1100
Henry I, 1100–1135
Stephen, 1135–1154

House of Plantagenet

Henry II, 1154–1189
Richard I, 1189–1199
John, 1199–1216
Henry III, 1216–1272
Edward I, 1272–1307
Edward II, 1307–1327
Edward III, 1327–1377
Richard II, 1377–1399

House of Lancaster

Henry IV, 1399–1413
Henry V, 1413–1422
Henry VI, 1422–1461

House of York

Edward IV, 1461–1483
Edward V, 1483
Richard III, 1483–1485

House of Tudor

Henry VII, 1485–1509
Henry VIII, 1509–1547
Edward VI, 1547–1553
Mary, 1553–1558
Elizabeth I, 1558–1603

House of Stuart

James I, 1603–1625
Charles I, 1625–1649

Commonwealth and Protectorate, 1649–1659

House of Stuart Restored

Charles II, 1660–1685
James II, 1685–1688
William III and Mary II, 1689–1694
William III alone, 1694–1702
Anne, 1702–1714

House of Hanover

George I, 1714–1727
George II, 1727–1760
George III, 1760–1820
George IV, 1820–1830
William IV, 1830–1837
Victoria, 1837–1901

House of Saxe-Coburg-Gotha

Edward VII, 1901–1910
George V, 1910–1917

House of Windsor

George V, 1917–1936
Edward VIII, 1936
George VI, 1936–1952
Elizabeth II, 1952–

RULERS OF AUSTRIA AND AUSTRIA-HUNGARY

*Maximilian I (Archduke), 1493–1519
*Charles V, 1519–1556
*Ferdinand I, 1556–1564
*Maximilian II, 1564–1576
*Rudolf II, 1576–1612
*Matthias, 1612–1619
*Ferdinand II, 1619–1637
*Ferdinand III, 1637–1657
*Leopold I, 1658–1705
*Joseph I, 1705–1711
*Charles VI, 1711–1740
Maria Theresa, 1740–1780

*Joseph II, 1780–1790
*Leopold II, 1790–1792
*Francis II, 1792–1835 (Emperor of Austria as Francis I
    after 1804)
Ferdinand I, 1835–1848
Francis Joseph, 1848–1916 (after 1867 Emperor of Austria
    and King of Hungary)
Charles I, 1916–1918 (Emperor of Austria and King of
    Hungary)
Republic of Austria, 1918–1938 (dictatorship after 1934)
Republic restored, under Allied occupation, 1945–1956
Free Republic, 1956–

*also bore title of Holy Roman Emperor

RULERS OF PRUSSIA AND GERMANY

*Frederick I, 1701–1713
*Frederick William I, 1713–1740
*Frederick II (the Great), 1740–1786
*Frederick William II, 1786–1797
*Frederick William III,1797–1840
*Frederick William IV, 1840–1861
*William I, 1861–1888 (German Emperor after 1871)
Frederick III, 1888

*Kings of Prussia

*William II, 1888–1918
Weimar Republic, 1918–1933
Third Reich (Nazi Dictatorship), 1933–1945
Allied occupation, 1945–1952
Division into Federal Republic of Germany in west and
    German Democratic Republic in east, 1949–1991
Federal Republic of Germany (united), 1991–

RULERS OF RUSSIA

Ivan III, 1462–1505
Vasily III, 1505–1533
Ivan IV, 1533–1584
Theodore I, 1534–1598
Boris Godunov, 1598–1605
Theodore II,1605
Vasily IV, 1606–1610
Michael, 1613–1645
Alexius, 1645–1676
Theodore III, 1676–1682
Ivan V and Peter I, 1682–1689
Peter I (the Great), 1689–1725
Catherine I, 1725–1727
Peter II, 1727–1730

Anna, 1730–1740
Ivan VI, 1740–1741
ElIzabeth, 1741–1762
Peter III, 1762
Catherine II (the Great), 1762–1796
Paul, 1796–1801
Alexander I,1801–1825
Nicholas I, 1825–1855
Alexander II,1855–1881
Alexander III, 1881–1894
Nicholas II, 1894–1917
Soviet Republic, 1917–1991
Russian Federation, 1991–

RULERS OF UNIFIED SPAIN

Ferdinand { and Isabella, 1479–1504
          { and Philip I, 1504–1506
          { and Charles I, 1506–1516
Charles I (Holy Roman Emperor Charles V), 1516–1556
Philip II, 1556–1598
Philip III, 1598–1621
Philip IV, 1621–1665
Charles II, 1665–1700
Philip V, 1700–1746
Ferdinand VI, 1746–1759
Charles III, 1759–1788
Charles IV, 1788–1808

Ferdinand VII, 1808
Joseph Bonaparte, 1808–1813
Ferdinand VII (restored), 1814–1833
Isabella II, 1833–1868
Republic, 1868–1870
Amadeo, 1870–1873
Republic, 1873–1874
Alfonso XII, 1874–1885
Alfonso XIII, 1886–1931
Republic, 1931–1939
Fascist Dictatorship, 1939–1975
Juan Carlos I, 1975–

RULERS OF ITALY

Victor Emmanuel II, 1861–1878
Humbert I, 1878–1900
Victor Emmanuel III, 1900–1946

Fascist Dictatorship, 1922-1943 (maintained in northern
   Italy until 1945)
Humbert II, May 9–June 13, 1946
Republic, 1946–

PROMINENT POPES

Silvester I, 314–335
Leo I, 440–461
Gelasius I, 492–496
Gregory I, 590–604
Nicholas I, 858–867
Silvester II, 999–1003
Leo IX, 1049–1054
Nicholas II, 1058–1061
Gregory VII, 1073–1085
Urban II, 1088–1099
Paschal II, 1099–1118
Alexander III, 1159–1181
Innocent III, 1198–1216
Gregory IX, 1227–1241
Innocent IV, 1243–1254
Boniface VIII, 1294–1303
John XXII, 1316–1334
Nicholas V, 1447–1455
Pius II, 1458–1464

Alexander VI, 1492–1503
Julius II, 1503–1513
Leo X, 1513–1521
Paul III, 1534–1549
Paul IV, 1555–1559
Sixtus V, 1585–1590
Urban VIII, 1623–1644
Gregory XVI, 1831–1846
Pius IX, 1846–1878
Leo XIII, 1878–1903
Pius X, 1903–1914
Benedict XV, 1914–1922
Pius XI, 1922–1939
Pius XII, 1939–1958
John XXIII, 1958–1963
Paul VI, 1963–1978
John Paul I, 1978
John Paul II, 1978–2005
Benedict XVI 2005–

Further Readings

CHAPTER 10

Allmand, Christopher T., ed. *Society at War: The Experience of England and France During the Hundred Years' War.* Edinburgh, 1973. An outstanding collection of documents.

————. *The Hundred Years' War: England and France at War, c. 1300–c. 1450.* Cambridge and New York, 1988. Still the best analytic account of the war; after a short narrative, the book is organized topically.

Boccaccio, Giovanni. *The Decameron.* Trans. Mark Musa and P. E. Bondanella. New York, 1977.

Bynum, Caroline Walker. *Holy Feast and Holy Fast: The Religious Significance of Food to Medieval Women.* Berkeley and Los Angeles, 1988. One of the most influential and important works of scholarship published in the late twentieth century.

Chaucer, Geoffrey. *The Canterbury Tales.* Trans. Nevill Coghill. New York, 1951. A modern English verse translation, lightly annotated.

Cohn, Samuel K., Jr. *Lust for Liberty: The Politics of Social Revolt in Medieval Europe, 1200–1425. Italy, France, and Flanders.* Cambridge, MA, 2006. An important new study.

Cole, Bruce. *Giotto and Florentine Painting, 1280–1375.* New York, 1976. A clear and stimulating introduction.

Crummey, Robert O. *The Formation of Muscovy, 1304–1613.* New York, 1987. The standard account.

Dobson, R. Barrie. *The Peasants' Revolt of 1381,* 2d ed. London, 1983. A comprehensive source collection, with excellent introductions to the documents.

Dyer, Christopher. *Standards of Living in the Later Middle Ages: Social Change in England, c. 1200–1520.* Cambridge and New York, 1989. Detailed but highly rewarding.

Froissart, Jean. *Chronicles.* Trans. Geoffrey Brereton. Baltimore, MD, 1968. A selection from the most famous contemporary account of the Hundred Years' War to about 1400.

Hobbins, Daniel, ed. and trans. *The Trial of Joan of Arc.* Cambridge, MA, 2007. A new and excellent translation of the transcripts of Joan's trial.

Horrox, Rosemary, ed. *The Black Death.* New York, 1994. A fine collection of documents reflecting the impact of the Black Death, especially in England.

John Hus at the Council of Constance. Trans. M. Spinka, New York, 1965. The translation of a Czech chronicle with an expert introduction and appended documents.

Jordan, William Chester. *The Great Famine: Northern Europe in the Early Fourteenth Century.* Princeton, NJ, 1996. An outstanding social and economic study.

Keen, Maurice, ed. *Medieval Warfare: A History.* Oxford and New York, 1999. The most attractive introduction to this important subject. Lively and well illustrated.

Kempe, Margery. *The Book of Margery Kempe.* Trans. Barry Windeatt. New York, 1985. A fascinating personal narrative by an early-fifteenth-century Englishwoman who hoped she might be a saint.

Lerner, Robert E. *The Heresy of the Free Spirit in the Later Middle Ages,* 2d ed. Notre Dame, IN, 1991. A revealing study of a heretical movement that hardly existed at all.

Lewis, Peter S. *Later Medieval France: The Polity.* London, 1968. Still fresh and suggestive after forty years. A masterwork.

Memoirs of a Renaissance Pope: The Commentaries of Pius II. Abridged ed. Trans. F. A. Gragg, New York, 1959. Remarkable insights into the mind of a particularly well-educated mid-fifteenth-century pope.

Nicholas, David. *The Transformation of Europe, 1300–1600.* Oxford and New York, 1999. The best textbook presently available.

Oakley, Francis C. *The Western Church in the Later Middle Ages.* Ithaca, NY, 1979. The best book by far on the history of conciliarism, the late medieval papacy, Hussitism, and the efforts at institutional reform during this period. On popular piety, see Swanson.

Shirley, Janet, trans. *A Parisian Journal, 1405–1449.* Oxford, 1968. A marvelous panorama of Parisian life recorded by an eyewitness.

Sumption, Jonathan. *The Hundred Years' War.* Vol. 1: *Trial by Battle.* Vol. 2: *Trial by Fire.* Philadelphia, 1999. The first two volumes of a massive narrative history of the war, carrying the story up to 1369.

Swanson, R. N. *Religion and Devotion in Europe, c. 1215–c. 1515.* Cambridge and New York, 1995. An excellent study of late-medieval popular piety; an excellent complement to Oakley.

Vaughan, Richard. *Valois Burgundy.* London, 1975. A summation of the author's four-volume study of the Burgundian dukes.

Ziegler, Philip. *The Black Death.* New York, 1969. A popular account, but reliable and engrossing.

CHAPTER 11

Abu-Lughod, Janet L. *Before European Hegemony: The World System A.D. 1250–1350.* Oxford and New York, 1989. A study of the trading links among Europe, the Middle East, India, and China, with special attention to the role of the Mongol Empire; extensive bibliography.

Allsen, Thomas T. *Culture and Conquest in Mongol Eurasia.* Cambridge and New York, 2001. A synthesis of the author's earlier studies, emphasizing Mongol involvement in the cultural and commercial exchanges that linked China, Central Asia, and Europe.

Amitai-Preiss, Reuven, and David O. Morgan, eds. *The Mongol Empire and Its Legacy.* Leiden, 1999. A collection of essays that represents some of the new trends in Mongol studies.

Christian, David. *A History of Russia, Central Asia and Mongolia.* Vol. 1, *Inner Eurasia from Prehistory to the Mongol Empire.* Oxford, 1998. The authoritative English-language work on the subject.

Coles, Paul. *The Ottoman Impact on Europe.* London, 1968. An excellent introductory text, still valuable despite its age.

Fernández-Armesto, Felipe. *Before Columbus: Exploration and Colonisation from the Mediterranean to the Atlantic, 1229–1492.* London, 1987. An indispensible study of the medieval background to the sixteenth-century European colonial empires.

——. *Columbus.* Oxford and New York, 1991. An excellent biography that stresses the millenarian ideas that underlay Columbus's thinking.

Flint, Valerie I. J. *The Imaginative Landscape of Christopher Columbus.* Princeton, NJ, 1992. A short, suggestive analysis of the intellectual influences that shaped Columbus's geographical ideas.

Goffman, Daniel. *The Ottoman Empire and Early Modern Europe.* Cambridge and New York, 2002. A revisionist account that presents the Ottoman Empire as a European state.

The History and the Life of Chinggis Khan: The Secret History of the Mongols. Trans. Urgunge Onon. Leiden, 1997. A newer version of *The Secret History,* now the standard English version of this important Mongol source.

Inalcik, Halil. *The Ottoman Empire: The Classical Age, 1300–1600.* London, 1973. The standard history by the dean of Turkish historians.

——, ed. *An Economic and Social History of the Ottoman Empire, 1300–1914.* Cambridge, 1994. An important collection of essays, spanning the full range of Ottoman history.

Jackson, Peter. *The Mongols and the West, 1221–1410.* Harlow, UK, 2005. A well-written survey that emphasizes the interactions among the Mongol, Latin Christian, and Muslim worlds.

Kafadar, Cemal. *Between Two Worlds: The Construction of the Ottoman State.* Berkeley and Los Angeles, 1995. An important study of Ottoman origins in the border regions between Byzantium, the Seljuk Turks, and the Mongols.

Larner, John. *Marco Polo and the Discovery of the World.* New Haven, CT, 1999. A study of the influence of Marco Polo's *Travels* on Europeans.

Morgan, David. *The Mongols.* 2d ed. Oxford, 2007. An accessible introduction to Mongol history and its sources, written by a noted expert on medieval Persia.

Parker, Geoffrey. *The Military Revolution: Military Innovation and the Rise of the West (1500–1800).* 2d ed. Cambridge and New York, 1996. A work of fundamental importance for understanding the global dominance achieved by early modern Europeans.

Phillips, J. R. S. *The Medieval Expansion of Europe.* 2d ed. Oxford, 1998. An outstanding study of the thirteenth- and fourteenth-century background to the fifteenth-century expansion of Europe. Important synthetic treatment of European relations with the Mongols, China, Africa, and North America. The second edition includes a new introduction and a bibliographical essay; the text is the same as in the first edition (1988).

Phillips, William D., Jr., and Carla R. Phillips. *The Worlds of Christopher Columbus.* Cambridge and New York, 1991. The first book to read on Columbus: accessible, engaging, and scholarly. Then read Fernández-Armesto's biography.

Ratchnevsky, Paul. *Genghis Khan: His Life and Legacy.* Trans. Thomas Nivison Haining. Oxford, 1991. An English translation and abridgment of a book first published in German in 1983. The author was one of the greatest Mongol historians of his generation.

Rossabi, M. *Khubilai Khan: His Life and Times.* Berkeley, CA, 1988. The standard English biography.

Russell, Peter. *Prince Henry "The Navigator": A Life.* New Haven, CT, 2000. A masterly biography by a great historian who has spent a lifetime on the subject. The only book one now needs to read on Prince Henry.

Saunders, J. J. *The History of the Mongol Conquests.* London, 1971. Still the standard English-language introduction; somewhat more positive about the Mongols' accomplishments than is Morgan.

Scammell, Geoffrey V. *The First Imperial Age: European Overseas Expansion, 1400–1715.* London, 1989. A useful introductory survey, with a particular focus on English and French colonization.

The Book of Prophecies, Edited by Christopher Columbus. Trans. Blair Sullivan, ed. Roberto Rusconi. Berkeley and Los Angeles, 1996. After his third voyage, from which Columbus was returned to Spain in chains, he compiled a book of quotations from various sources selected to emphasize the millenarian implications of his discoveries; a fascinating insight into the mind of the explorer.

The Four Voyages: Christopher Columbus. Trans. J. M. Cohen. New York, 1992. Columbus's own self-serving account of his four voyages to the Indies.

Mandeville's Travels. Ed. M. C. Seymour. Oxford, 1968. An edition of the *Book of Marvels* based on the Middle English version popular in the fifteenth century.

The Secret History of the Mongols. Trans. F. W. Cleaves. Cambridge, MA, 1982.

The Secret History of the Mongols and Other Pieces. Trans. Arthur Waley. London, 1963. The later Chinese abridgment of the Mongol original.

The Travels of Marco Polo, trans. R. E. Latham. Baltimore, MD, 1958. The most accessible edition of this remarkably interesting work.

CHAPTER 12

Alberti, Leon Battista. *The Family in Renaissance Florence (Della Famiglia).* Trans. Renée Neu Watkins. Columbia, SC, 1969.

Baxandall, Michael. *Painting and Experience in Fifteenth-Century Italy.* Oxford, 1972. A classic study of the perceptual world of the Renaissance.

Brucker, Gene. *Florence, the Golden Age, 1138–1737.* Berkeley and Los Angeles, CA, 1998. The standard account.

Bruni, Leonardo. *The Humanism of Leonardo Bruni: Selected Texts.* Trans. Gordon Griffiths, James Hankins, and David Thompson.

Binghamton, NY, 1987. Excellent translations, with introductions, to the Latin works of a key Renaissance humanist.

Burke, Peter. *The Renaissance*. New York, 1997. A brief introduction by an influential modern historian.

Burkhardt, Jacob. *The Civilization of the Renaissance in Italy*. Many editions. The nineteenth-century work that first crystallized an image of the Italian Renaissance, and with which scholars have been wrestling ever since.

Cassirer, Ernst, et al., eds. *The Renaissance Philosophy of Man*. Chicago, 1948. Important original works by Petrarch, Ficino, and Pico della Mirandola, among others.

Castiglione, Baldassare. *The Book of the Courtier*. Many editions. The translations by C. S. Singleton (New York, 1959) and by George Bull (New York, 1967) are both excellent.

Cellini, Benvenuto. *Autobiography*. Trans. George Bull. Baltimore, MD, 1956. This Florentine goldsmith (1500–1571) is the source for many of the most famous stories about the artists of the Florentine Renaissance.

Cochrane, Eric, and Julius Kirshner, eds. *The Renaissance*. Chicago, 1986. An outstanding collection, from the University of Chicago Readings in Western Civilization series.

Erasmus, Desiderius. *The Praise of Folly*. Trans. J. Wilson. Ann Arbor, MI, 1958.

Fox, Alistair. *Thomas More: History and Providence*. Oxford, 1982. A balanced account of a man too easily idealized.

Grafton, Anthony, and Lisa Jardine. *From Humanism to the Humanities: Education and the Liberal Arts in Fifteenth- and Sixteenth-Century Europe*. London, 1986. An account that presents Renaissance humanism as the elitist cultural program of a self-interested group of pedagogues.

Grendler, Paul, ed. *Encyclopedia of the Renaissance*. New York, 1999. A valuable reference work.

Hale, John R. *The Civilization of Europe in the Renaissance*. New York, 1993. A synthetic volume summarizing the life's work of a major Renaissance historian.

Hankins, James. *Plato in the Italian Renaissance*. Leiden and New York, 1990. A definitive study of the reception and influence of Plato on Renaissance intellectuals.

———, ed. *Renaissance Civic Humanism: Reappraisals and Reflections*. Cambridge and New York, 2000. An excellent collection of scholarly essays reassessing republicanism in the Renaissance.

Jardine, Lisa. *Worldly Goods*. London, 1996. A revisionist account that emphasizes the acquisitive materialism of Italian Renaissance society and culture.

Kanter, Laurence, Hilliard T. Goldfarb, and James Hankins. *Botticelli's Witness: Changing Style in a Changing Florence*. Boston, 1997. This catalog for an exhibition of Botticelli's works, at the Gardner Museum in Boston, offers an excellent introduction to the painter and his world.

King, Margaret L. *Women of the Renaissance*. Chicago, 1991. Deals with women in all walks of life and in a variety of roles.

Kristeller, Paul O. *Eight Philosophers of the Italian Renaissance*. Stanford, 1964. An admirably clear and accurate account that fully appreciates the connections between medieval and Renaissance thought.

———. *Renaissance Thought: The Classic, Scholastic, and Humanistic Strains*. New York, 1961. Very helpful in defining the main trends of Renaissance thought.

Lane, Frederic C. *Venice: A Maritime Republic*. Baltimore, MD, 1973. An authoritative account.

Machiavelli, Niccolò. *The Discourses* and *The Prince*. Many editions. These two books must be read together if one is to understand Machiavelli's political ideas properly.

Martines, Lauro. *Power and Imagination: City-States in Renaissance Italy*. New York, 1979. Insightful account of the connections among politics, society, culture, and art.

More, Thomas. *Utopia*. Many editions.

Murray, Linda. *High Renaissance and Mannerism*. London, 1985. The place to begin a study of fifteenth- and sixteenth-century Italian art.

Olson, Roberta, *Italian Renaissance Sculpture*. New York, 1992. The most accessible introduction to the subject.

Perkins, Leeman L. *Music in the Age of the Renaissance*. New York, 1999. A massive new study that needs to be read in conjunction with Reese.

Rabelais, François. *Gargantua and Pantagruel*. Trans. J. M. Cohen. Baltimore, MD, 1955. A robust modern translation.

Reese, Gustave. *Music in the Renaissance*, rev. ed. New York, 1959. A great book; still authoritative, despite the more recent work by Perkins, which supplements but does not replace it.

Rice, Eugene F., Jr., and Anthony Grafton. *The Foundations of Early Modern Europe, 1460–1559*, 2d ed. New York, 1994. The best textbook account of its period.

Rowland, Ingrid D. *The Culture of the High Renaissance: Ancients and Moderns in Sixteenth-Century Rome*. Cambridge and New York, 2000. Beautifully written examination of the social, intellectual, and economic foundations of the Renaissance in Rome.

CHAPTER 13

Bainton, Roland. *Erasmus of Christendom*. New York, 1969. Still the best biography in English of the Dutch reformer and intellectual.

———. *Here I Stand: A Life of Martin Luther*. Nashville, TN, 1950. Although old and obviously biased in Luther's favor, this remains an absorbing and dramatic introduction to Luther's life and thought.

Benedict, Philip. *Christ's Churches Purely Reformed: A Social History of Calvinism*. New Haven, CT, 2002. A wide-ranging recent survey of Calvinism in both western and eastern Europe.

Bossy, John. *Christianity in the West, 1400–1700*. Oxford and New York, 1985. A brilliant, challenging picture of the changes that took place in Christian piety and practice as a result of the sixteenth-century reformations.

Bouwsma, William J. *John Calvin: A Sixteenth-Century Portrait*. Oxford and New York, 1988. The best biography of the magisterial reformer.

Collinson, Patrick. *The Religion of Protestants: The Church in English Society, 1559–1625*. Oxford, 1982. A great book by a noted historian of early English Protestantism.

Dixon, C. Scott, ed. *The German Reformation: The Essential Readings*. Oxford, 1999. A collection of important recent articles.

Duffy, Eamon. *The Stripping of the Altars: Traditional Religion in England, c. 1400–c. 1550*. A brilliant study of religious exchange at the parish level.

Hillerbrand, Hans J., ed. *The Protestant Reformation*. New York, 1967. Source selections are particularly good for illuminating the political consequences of Reformation theological ideas.

John Calvin: Selections from His Writings, ed. John Dillenberger. Garden City, NY, 1971. A judicious selection, drawn mainly from Calvin's *Institutes*.

Loyola, Ignatius. *Personal Writings*. Trans. by Joseph A. Munitiz and Philip Endean. London and New York, 1996. An excellent collection that includes Loyola's autobiography, his spiritual diary, and some of his letters, as well as his *Spiritual Exercises*.

Luebke, David, ed. *The Counter-Reformation: The Essential Readings*. Oxford, 1999. A collection of nine important recent essays.

MacCulloch, Diarmaid. *Reformation: Europe's House Divided, 1490–1700*. London and New York, 2003. A definitive new survey; the best single-volume history of its subject in a generation.

Martin Luther: Selections from His Writings, ed. John Dillenberger. Garden City, NY, 1961. The standard selection, especially good on Luther's theological ideas.

McGrath, Alister E. *Reformation Thought: An Introduction*. Oxford, 1993. A useful explanation, accessible to non-Christians, of the theological ideas of the major Protestant reformers.

Mullett, Michael A. *The Catholic Reformation*. London, 2000. A sympathetic survey of Catholicism from the mid-sixteenth to the eighteenth century that presents the mid-sixteenth-century Council of Trent as a continuation of earlier reform efforts.

Oberman, Heiko A. *Luther: Man between God and the Devil*. Trans. by Eileen Walliser-Schwarzbart. New Haven, CT, 1989. A biography stressing Luther's preoccupations with sin, death, and the devil.

O'Malley, John W. *The First Jesuits*. Cambridge, MA, 1993. A scholarly account of the origins and early years of the Society of Jesus.

———. *Trent and All That: Renaming Catholicism in the Early Modern Era*. Cambridge, MA, 2000. Short, lively, and with a full bibliography.

Pettegree, Andrew, ed. *The Reformation World*. New York, 2000. An exhaustive multi-author work representing the most recent thinking about the Reformation.

Pelikan, Jaroslav. *Reformation of Church and Dogma, 1300–1700*. Vol. 4 of *A History of Christian Dogma*. Chicago, 1984. A masterful synthesis of Reformation theology in its late-medieval context.

Roper, Lyndal. *The Holy Household: Women and Morals in Reformation Augsburg*. Oxford, 1989. A pathbreaking study of Protestantism's effects on a single town, with special attention to its impact on attitudes toward women, the family, and marriage.

Shagan, Ethan H. *Popular Politics and the English Reformation*. Cambridge, 2002. Argues that the English Reformation reflects an ongoing process of negotiation, resistance, and response.

Tracy, James D. *Europe's Reformations, 1450–1650*. 2d ed. Lanham, MD, 2006. An outstanding survey, especially strong on Dutch and Swiss developments, but excellent throughout.

Williams, George H. *The Radical Reformation*. 3d ed. Kirksville, MO, 1992. Originally published in 1962, this is still the best book on Anabaptism and its offshoots.

CHAPTER 14

Bonney, Richard. *The European Dynastic States, 1494–1660*. Oxford and New York, 1991. An excellent survey of continental Europe during the "long" sixteenth century.

Briggs, Robin. *Early Modern France, 1560–1715*, 2d ed. Oxford and New York, 1997. Updated and authoritative, with new bibliographies.

———. *Witches and Neighbors: The Social and Cultural Context of European Witchcraft*. New York, 1996. An influential recent account of Continental witchcraft.

Cervantes, Miguel de. *Don Quixote*. Trans. Edith Grossman. New York, 2003. A splendid new translation.

Clarke, Stuart. *Thinking with Demons: The Idea of Witchcraft in Early Modern Europe*. Oxford and New York, 1999. By placing demonology into the context of sixteenth- and seventeenth-century intellectual history, Clarke makes sense of it in new and exciting ways.

Cochrane, Eric, Charles M. Gray, and Mark A. Kishlansky. *Early Modern Europe: Crisis of Authority*. Chicago, 1987. An outstanding source collection from the University of Chicago Readings in Western Civilization series.

Held, Julius S., and Donald Posner. *Seventeenth- and Eighteenth-Century Art: Baroque Painting, Sculpture, Architecture*. New York, 1971. The most complete and best-organized introductory review of the subject in English.

Hibbard, Howard. *Bernini*. Baltimore, MD, 1965. The basic study in English of this central figure of Baroque artistic activity.

Hirst, Derek. *England in Conflict, 1603–1660: Kingdom, Community, Commonwealth*. Oxford and New York, 1999. A complete revision of the author's *Authority and Conflict* (1986), this is an up-to-date and balanced account of a period that has been a historical battleground over the past twenty years.

Hobbes, Thomas. *Leviathan*. Ed. Richard Tuck. 2d ed. Cambridge and New York, 1996. The most recent edition, containing the entirety of *Leviathan*, not just the first two parts.

Holt, Mack P. *The French Wars of Religion, 1562–1629*. Cambridge and New York, 1995. A clear account of a confusing time.

Kors, Alan Charles, and Edward Peters. *Witchcraft in Europe, 400–1700: A Documentary History*, 2d ed. Philadelphia, 2000. A superb collection of documents, significantly expanded in the second edition, with up-to-date commentary.

Kingdon, Robert. *Myths about the St. Bartholomew's Day Massacres, 1572–1576*. Cambridge, MA, 1988. A detailed account of this pivotal moment in the history of France.

Levack, Brian P. *The Witch-Hunt in Early Modern Europe*, 2d ed. London and New York, 1995. The best account of the persecution of suspected witches; coverage extends from Europe in 1450 to America in 1750.

Levin, Carole. *The Heart and Stomach of a King: Elizabeth I and the Politics of Sex and Power*. Philadelphia, 1994. A provocative argument for the importance of Elizabeth's gender for understanding her reign.

Limm, Peter, ed. *The Thirty Years' War*. London, 1984. An outstanding short survey, followed by a selection of primary-source documents.

Lynch, John. *Spain, 1516–1598: From Nation-State to World Empire*. Oxford and Cambridge, MA, 1991. The best book in English on Spain at the pinnacle of its sixteenth-century power.

MacCaffrey, Wallace. *Elizabeth I.* New York, 1993. An outstanding traditional biography by an excellent scholar.

Martin, Colin, and Geoffrey Parker. *The Spanish Armada.* London, 1988. Incorporates recent discoveries from undersea archaeology with more traditional historical sources.

Martin, John Rupert. *Baroque.* New York, 1977. A thought-provoking, thematic treatment, less a survey than an essay on the painting, sculpture, and architecture of the period.

Mattingly, Garrett. *The Armada.* Boston, 1959. A great narrative history that reads like a novel; for more recent work, however, see Martin and Parker.

Parker, Geoffrey. *The Dutch Revolt*, 2d ed. Ithaca, NY, 1989. The standard survey in English on the revolt of the Netherlands.

———. *Philip II.* Boston, 1978. A fine biography by an expert in both the Spanish and the Dutch sources.

———, ed. *The Thirty Years' War*, rev. ed. London and New York, 1987. A wide-ranging collection of essays by scholarly experts.

Pascal, Blaise. *Pensées* (French-English edition). Ed. H. F. Stewart. London, 1950.

Quint, David. *Montaigne and the Quality of Mercy: Ethical and Political Themes in the "Essais."* Princeton, NJ, 1999. A fine treatment that presents Montaigne's thought as a response to the French wars of religion.

Roberts, Michael. *Gustavus Adolphus and the Rise of Sweden.* London, 1973. Still the authoritative English-language account.

Russell, Conrad. *The Causes of the English Civil War.* Oxford, 1990. A penetrating and provocative analysis by one of the leading "revisionist" historians of the period.

Tracy, James D. *Holland under Habsburg Rule, 1506–1566: The Formation of a Body Politic.* Berkeley and Los Angeles, CA, 1990. A political history and analysis of the formative years of the Dutch state.

Van Gelderen, Martin. *Political Theory of the Dutch Revolt.* Cambridge, 1995. A fine book on a subject whose importance is too easily overlooked.

CHAPTER 15

Beik, William. *Louis XIV and Absolutism.* New York, 2000. A helpful short examination of the French king, the theory of absolutism, and the social consequences of absolutist rule. Supplemented by translated documents from the period.

Jones, Colin. *The Great Nation: France From Louis XV to Napoleon.* New York, 2002. An excellent and readable scholarly account that argues that the France of Louis XV in the eighteenth century was even more dominant than the kingdom of Louis XIV in the preceding century.

Kishlansky, Mark A. *A Monarchy Transformed: Britain, 1603–1714.* London, 1996. An excellent survey that takes seriously its claims to be a "British" rather than merely an "English" history.

Klein, Herbert S. *The Atlantic Slave Trade.* Cambridge and New York, 1999. An accessible survey by a leading quantitative historian.

Koch, H. W. *A History of Prussia.* London, 1978. Still the best account of its subject.

Lewis, William Roger, gen. ed. *The Oxford History of the British Empire.* Vol. I: *The Origins of Empire: British Overseas Enterprise to the Close of the Seventeenth Century*, ed. Nicholas Canny. Vol. II: *The Eighteenth Century*, ed. Peter J. Marshall. Oxford and New York, 1998. A definitive, multiauthor account.

Locke, John. *Two Treatises of Government.* Ed. Peter Laslett. Rev. ed. Cambridge and New York, 1963. Laslett has revolutionized our understanding of the historical and ideological context of Locke's political writings.

Miller, John, ed. *Absolutism in Seventeenth-Century Europe.* London, 1990. An excellent, multiauthor survey, organized by country.

Monod, Paul K. *The Power of Kings: Monarchy and Religion in Europe, 1589–1715.* New Haven, Conn. 1999. A study of the seventeenth century's declining confidence in the divinity of kings.

Quataert, Donald. *The Ottoman Empire, 1700–1822.* Cambridge and New York, 2000. Well balanced and intended to be read by students.

Riasanovsky, Nicholas V., and Steinberg, Mark D. *A History of Russia.* 7th ed. Oxford and New York, 2005. Far and away the best single-volume textbook on Russian history: balanced, comprehensive, intelligent, and with full bibliographies.

Saint-Simon, Louis. *Historical Memoirs.* Many editions. The classic source for life at Louis XIV's Versailles.

Thomas, Hugh. *The Slave Trade: The History of the Atlantic Slave Trade, 1440–1870.* London and New York, 1997. A survey notable for its breadth and depth of coverage and for its attractive prose style.

Tracy, James D. *The Rise of Merchant Empires: Long-Distance Trade in the Early Modern World, 1350–1750.* Cambridge and New York, 1990. Important collection of essays by leading authorities.

White, Richard. *It's Your Misfortune and None of My Own: A History of the American West.* Norman, Okla., 1991. An outstanding textbook with excellent introductory chapters on European colonialism in the Americas.

CHAPTER 16

Biagioli, Mario. *Galileo, Courtier.* Chicago, 1993. Emphasizes the importance of patronage and court politics in Galileo's science and career.

Cohen, I. B. *The Birth of a New Physics.* New York, 1985. Emphasizes the mathematical nature of the revolution; unmatched at making the mathematics understandable.

Dear, Peter. *Revolutionizing the Sciences: European Knowledge and Its Ambitions, 1500–1700.* Princeton, N.J., 2001. Among the best short histories.

Drake, Stillman. *Discoveries and Opinions of Galileo.* Garden City, N.Y., 1957. The classic translation of Galileo's most important papers by his most admiring modern biographer.

Feingold, Mardechai, *The Newtonian Moment: Isaac Newton and the Making of Modern Culture.* New York, 2004. An engaging essay on the dissemination of Newton's thought, with excellent visual material.

Gaukroger, Stephen. *Descartes: An Intellectual Biography.* Oxford, 1995. Detailed and sympathetic study of the philosopher.

Gleick, James. *Isaac Newton.* New York, 2003. A vivid and well-documented brief biography.

Grafton, Anthony. *New Worlds, Ancient Texts: The Power of Tradition and the Shock of Discovery.* Cambridge, Mass., 1992. Accessible essay by one of the leading scholars of early modern European thought.

Hall, A. R. *The Revolution in Science, 1500–1750.* New York, 1983. Revised version of a 1954 classic.

Jones, Richard Foster. *Ancients and Moderns: A Study of the Rise of the Scientific Movement in Early Modern England.* Berkeley, Calif., 1961. Still a persuasive study of the scientific revolutionaries' attempts to situate their work in relation to that of the Greeks.

Koestler, Arthur. *The Sleepwalkers: A History of Man's Changing Vision of the Universe.* London, 1958. A readable classic.

Kuhn, Thomas. *The Structure of Scientific Revolutions.* Chicago, 1962. A classic and much-debated study of how scientific thought changes.

Pagden, Anthony, *European Encounters with the New World.* New Haven, Conn., and London, 1993. Subtle and detailed on how European intellectuals thought about the lands they saw for the first time.

Scheibinger, Londa. *The Mind Has No Sex? Women in the Origins of Modern Science.* Cambridge, Mass., 1989. A lively and important recovery of the lost role played by women mathematicians and experimenters.

Shapin, Steven. *The Scientific Revolution.* Chicago, 1996. Engaging, accessible, and brief—organized thematically.

———, and Simon Schaffer. *Leviathan and the Air Pump.* Princeton, N.J., 1985. A modern classic, on one of the most famous philosophical conflicts in seventeenth-century science.

Stephenson, Bruce. *The Music of the Heavens: Kepler's Harmonic Astronomy.* Princeton, N.J., 1994. An engaging and important explanation of Kepler's otherworldly perspective.

Thoren, Victor. *The Lord of Uranibourg: A Biography of Tycho Brahe.* Cambridge, 1990. A vivid reconstruction of the scientific revolution's most flamboyant astronomer.

Westfall, Richard. *The Construction of Modern Science.* Cambridge, 1977.

Westfall, Richard. *Never at Rest: A Biography of Isaac Newton.* Cambridge, 1980. The standard work.

Wilson, Catherine. *The Invisible World: Early Modern Philosophy and the Invention of the Microscope.* Princeton, N.J., 1995. An important study of how the "microcosmic" world revealed by technology reshaped scientific philosophy and practice.

Zinsser, Judith P. *La Dame d'Esprit: A Biography of the Marquise Du Châtelet.* New York, 2006. An excellent cultural history. To be issued in paper as *Emilie du Châtelet: Daring Genius of the Enlightenment* (2007).

CHAPTER 17

Baker, Keith. *Condorcet: From Natural Philosophy to Social Mathematics.* Chicago, 1975. An important reinterpretation of Condorcet as a social scientist.

Bell, Susan, and Karen Offen, eds. *Women, the Family, and Freedom: The Debate in Documents.* Vol. 1, *1750–1880.* Stanford, Calif., 1983. An excellent introduction to Enlightenment debates about gender and women.

Blum, Carol. *Rousseau and the Republic of Virtue: The Language of Politics in the French Revolution.* Ithaca and London, 1986.

Fascinating account of how eighteenth-century readers interpreted Rousseau.

Buchan, James. *The Authentic Adam Smith: His Life and Ideas.* New York, 2006.

Calhoun, Craig, ed. *Habermas and the Public Sphere.* Cambridge, Mass., 1992. Calhoun's introduction is a good starting point for Habermas's argument.

Cassirer, E. *The Philosophy of the Enlightenment.* Princeton, N.J., 1951.

Chartier, Roger. *The Cultural Origins of the French Revolution.* Durham, N.C., 1991. Looks at topics from religion to violence in everyday life and culture.

Darnton, Robert. *The Business of Enlightenment: A Publishing History of the* Encyclopédie, *1775–1800.* Cambridge, Mass., 1979. Darnton's work on the Enlightenment offers a fascinating blend of intellectual, social, and economic history. See his other books as well: *The Literary Underground of the Old Regime* (Cambridge, Mass., 1982); *The Great Cat Massacre and Other Episodes in French Cultural History* (New York, 1984); and *The Forbidden Best Sellers of Revolutionary France* (New York and London, 1996).

Davis, David Brion. *The Problem of Slavery in Western Culture.* New York, 1988. A Pulitzer Prize–winning examination of a central issue as well as a brilliant analysis of different strands of Enlightenment thought.

Gay, Peter. *The Enlightenment: An Interpretation.* Vol. 1, *The Rise of Modern Paganism.* Vol. 2, *The Science of Freedom.* New York, 1966–1969. Combines an overview with an interpretation. Emphasizes the *philosophes'* sense of identification with the classical world and takes a generally positive view of their accomplishments. Includes extensive annotated bibliographies.

Gray, Peter. *Mozart.* New York, 1999. Brilliant short study.

Goodman, Dena. *The Republic of Letters: A Cultural History of the French Enlightenment.* Ithaca, N.Y., 1994. Important in its attention to the role of literary women.

Hazard, Paul. *The European Mind: The Critical Years (1680–1715).* New Haven, Conn., 1953. A basic and indispensable account of the changing climate of opinion that preceded the Enlightenment.

Hildesheimer, Wolfgang. *Mozart.* New York, 1982. An exceptionally literate and thought-provoking biography.

Israel, Jonathan Irvine. *Radical Enlightenment: Philosophy and the Making of Modernity, 1650–1750.* New York, 2001. Massive and erudite, a fresh look at the international movement of ideas.

Israel, Jonathan Irvine. *Enlightenment Contested: Philosophy, Modernity, and the Emancipation of Man, 1670–1752.* New York, 2006. Massive and erudite, a fresh look at the international movement of ideas.

Munck, Thomas. *The Enlightenment: A Comparative Social History 1721–1794.* London, 2000. An excellent recent survey, especially good on social history.

Outram, Dorinda. *The Enlightenment.* Cambridge, 1995. An excellent short introduction and a good example of new historical approaches.

Porter, Roy. *The Creation of the Modern World: The Untold Story of the British Enlightenment.* New York, 2000.

Rendall, Jane. *The Origins of Modern Feminism: Women in Britain, France and the United States, 1780–1860.* New York, 1984. A very basic survey.

Sapiro, Virginia. *A Vindication of Political Virtue: The Political Theory of Mary Wollstonecraft.* Chicago, 1992. A subtle and intelligent analysis for more advanced readers.

Shklar, Judith. *Men and Citizens: A Study of Rousseau's Social Theory.* London, 1969.

Shklar, Judith. *Montesquieu.* Oxford, 1987. Shklar's studies are brilliant and accessible.

Taylor, Barbara. *Mary Wollstonecraft and the Feminist Imagination.* Cambridge and New York, 2003. Fascinating study that sets Wollstonecraft in the radical circles of eighteenth-century England.

Venturi, Franco. *The End of the Old Regime in Europe, 1768–1776: The First Crisis.* Trans. R. Burr Litchfield. Princeton, N.J., 1989.

Venturi, Franco. *The End of the Old Regime in Europe, 1776–1789.* Princeton, N.J. 1991. Both detailed and wide-ranging, particularly important on international developments.

Watt, Ian P. *The Rise of the Novel.* London, 1957. The basic work on the innovative qualities of the novel in eighteenth-century England.

CHAPTER 18

Applewhite, Harriet B., and Darline G. Levy, eds. *Women and Politics in the Age of the Democratic Revolution.* Ann Arbor, Mich., 1990. Essays on France, Britain, the Netherlands, and the United States.

Bell, David A. *The First Total War: Napoleon's Europe and the Birth of Warfare as We Know It.* Boston and New York, 2007. Lively and concise study of the "cataclysmic intensification" of warfare.

Blackburn, Robin. *The Overthrow of Colonial Slavery.* London and New York, 1988. A longer view of slavery and its abolition.

Blanning, T. C. W. *The French Revolutionary Wars, 1787–1802.* Oxford, 1996. On the revolution and war.

Blum, Carol. *Rousseau and the Republic of Virtue: The Language of Politics in the French Revolution.* Ithaca, N.Y., 1986. Excellent on how Rousseau was read by the revolutionaries.

Cobb, Richard. *The People's Armies.* New Haven, Conn., 1987. Brilliant and detailed analysis of the popular militias.

Cole, Juan. *Napoleon's Egypt: Invading the Middle East.* New York, 2007. Readable history by a scholar familiar with sources in Arabic as well as European languages.

Connelly, Owen. *The French Revolution and Napoleonic Era.* 3rd ed. New York, 2000. Accessible, lively, one-volume survey.

Darnton, Robert, *The Forbidden Best-Sellers of Pre-Revolutionary France.* New York, 1995. One of Darnton's many imaginative studies of subversive opinion and books on the eve of the revolution.

Doyle, William. *Origins of the French Revolution.* New York, 1988. A revisionist historian surveys recent research on the political and social origins of the revolution and identifies a new consensus.

———. *Oxford History of the French Revolution.* New York, 1989.

Dubois, Laurent. *Avengers of the New World. The Story of the Haitian Revolution.* Cambridge, Mass., 2004. Now the best and most accessible study.

———, and John D. Garrigus. *Slave Revolution in the Caribbean, 1789–1804: A Brief History with Documents.* New York, 2006. A particularly good collection.

Englund, Steven. *Napoleon, A Political Life.* Cambridge, Mass., 2004. Prize-winning biography, both dramatic and insightful.

Forrest, Alan. *The French Revolution and the Poor.* New York, 1981. A moving and detailed social history of the poor, who fared little better under revolutionary governments than under the Old Regime.

Furet, Francois. *Revolutionary France, 1770–1880.* Trans. Antonia Nerill. Cambridge, Mass., 1992. Overview by the leading revisionist.

Geyl, Pieter. *Napoleon: For and Against.* Rev. ed. New Haven, Conn., 1964. The ways in which Napoleon was interpreted by French historians and political figures.

Hunt, Lynn. *The French Revolution and Human Rights.* Boston, 1996. A collection of documents.

———. *Politics, Culture, and Class in the French Revolution.* Berkeley, Calif., 1984. An analysis of the new culture of democracy and republicanism.

Hunt, Lynn, and Jack R. Censer. *Liberty, Equality, Fraternity: Exploring the French Revolution.* University Park, Pa., 2001. Two leading historians of the revolution have written a lively, accessible study, with excellent documents and visual material.

Landes, Joan B. *Women and the Public Sphere in the Age of the French Revolution.* Ithaca, N.Y., 1988. On gender and politics.

Lefebvre, Georges. *The Coming of the French Revolution.* Princeton, N.J., 1947. The classic Marxist analysis.

Lewis, G., and C. Lucas. *Beyond the Terror: Essays in French Regional and Social History, 1794–1815.* New York, 1983. Shifts focus to the understudied period after the Terror.

O'Brien, Connor Cruise. *The Great Melody: A Thematic Biography of Edmund Burke.* Chicago, 1992. Passionate, partisan, and brilliant study of Burke's thoughts about Ireland, India, America, and France.

Palmer, R. R. *The Age of the Democratic Revolution: A Political History of Europe and America, 1760–1800.* 2 vols. Princeton, N.J., 1964. Impressive for its scope; places the French Revolution in the larger context of a worldwide revolutionary movement.

———, and Isser Woloch. *Twelve Who Ruled: The Year of the Terror in the French Revolution.* Princeton, N.J. 2005. The terrific collective biography of the Committee of Public Safety, now updated.

Schama, Simon. *Citizens: A Chronicle of the French Revolution.* New York, 1989. Particularly good on art, culture, and politics.

Soboul, Albert. *The Sans-Culottes: The Popular Movement and Revolutionary Government, 1793–1794.* Garden City, N.Y., 1972. Dated, but a classic.

Sutherland, D. M. G. *France, 1789–1815: Revolution and Counterrevolution.* Oxford, 1986. An important synthesis of work on the revolution, especially in social history.

Thompson, J. M. *Robespierre and the French Revolution.* London, 1953. An excellent short biography.

Tocqueville, Alexis de. *The Old Regime and the French Revolution.* Garden City, N.Y., 1955. Originally written in 1856, this remains a provocative analysis of the revolution's legacy.

Trouillot, Michel Rolph. *Silencing the Past.* Boston, 1995. Essays on the Haitian revolution.

Woloch, Isser. *The New Regime: Transformations of the French Civic Order, 1789–1820.* New York, 1994. The fate of revolutionary civic reform.

Woolf, Stuart. *Napoleon's Integration of Europe.* New York, 1991. Technical but very thorough.

CHAPTER 19

Berg, Maxine. *The Age of Manufactures: Industry, Innovation, and Work in Britain, 1700–1820.* Oxford, 1985. Good on new scholarship and on women.

Bridenthal, Renate, Claudia Koonz, and Susan Stuard, eds. *Becoming Visible: Women in European History.* 2d ed. Boston, 1987. Excellent, wide-ranging introduction.

Briggs, Asa. *Victorian Cities.* New York, 1963. A survey of British cities, stressing middle-class attitudes toward the new urban environment.

Cameron, R. E. *France and the Industrial Development of Europe.* Princeton, 1968. Valuable material on the Industrial Revolution outside Britain.

Chevalier, Louis. *Laboring Classes and Dangerous Classes during the First Half of the Nineteenth Century.* New York, 1973. An important, though controversial, account of crime, class, and middle-class perceptions of life in Paris.

Cipolla, Carlo M., ed. *The Industrial Revolution, 1700–1914.* New York, 1976. A collection of essays that emphasizes the wide range of industrializing experiences in Europe.

Cott, Nancy. *The Bonds of Womanhood: "Woman's Sphere" in New England, 1780–1935.* New Haven, Conn., and London, 1977. One of the most influential studies of the paradoxes of domesticity.

Davidoff, Leonore, and Catherine Hall. *Family Fortunes: Men and Women of the English Middle Class, 1780–1850.* Chicago, 1985. A brilliant and detailed study of the lives and ambitions of several English families.

Ferguson, Niall. *The Cash Nexus: Money and Power in the Modern World, 1700–2000* (New York, 2001). A very stimulating and fresh overview of the period.

———. "The European Economy, 1815–1914." In *The Nineteenth Century,* ed. T. C. W. Blanning. Oxford and New York, 2000. A very useful short essay.

Gay, Peter. *The Bourgeois Experience: Victoria to Freud.* New York, 1984. A multivolume, path-breaking study of middle-class life in all its dimensions.

———. *Schnitzler's Century: The Making of Middle-Class Culture, 1815–1914.* New York and London, 2002. A synthesis of some of the arguments presented in *The Bourgeois Experience.*

Hellerstein, Erna, Leslie Hume, and Karen Offen, eds. *Victorian Women: A Documentary Account.* Stanford, Calif., 1981. Good collection of documents, with excellent introductory essays.

Hobsbawm, Eric J. *The Age of Capital, 1848–1875.* London, 1975. Among the best introductions.

———. *The Age of Revolution, 1789–1848.* London, 1962.

———, and George Rudé. *Captain Swing: A Social History of the Great English Agricultural Uprising of 1830.* New York, 1975. Analyzes rural protest and politics.

Horn, Jeff. *The Path Not Taken: French Industrialization in the Age of Revolution, 1750–1830.* Cambridge, 2006. Argues that industrialization in France succeeded in ways that other historians have not appreciated, and was much more than a failed attempt to imitate the British model.

Jones, Eric. *The European Miracle: Environments, Economies and Geopolitics in the History of Europe and Asia.* Cambridge, 2003. Argues that the Industrial Revolution is best understood as a European phenomenon.

Kemp, Tom. *Industrialization in Nineteenth-Century Europe.* London, 1985. Good general study.

Kindelberger, Charles. *A Financial History of Western Europe.* London, 1984. Emphasis on finance.

Landes, David S. *The Unbound Prometheus: Technological Change and Industrial Development in Western Europe from 1750 to the Present.* London, 1969. Excellent and thorough on technological change and its social and economic context.

Langer, William L. *Political and Social Upheaval, 1832–1852.* New York, 1969. Comprehensive and detailed survey.

McNeill, J. R. *Something New under the Sun: An Environmental History of the Twentieth-Century World.* New York and London, 2000. Short section on the nineteenth century.

Mokyr, Joel. *The Lever of Riches: Technological Creativity and Economic Progress.* New York, 1992. A world history, from antiquity through the nineteenth century

O'Gráda, Cormac. *Black '47 and Beyond: The Great Irish Famine.* Princeton, N.J., 1999.

———. *The Great Irish Famine.* Cambridge, 1989. A fascinating and recent assessment of scholarship on the famine.

Kenneth Pomeranz. *The Great Divergence: China, Europe, and the Making of the Modern World Economy.* Princeton, N.J., 2000. Path-breaking global history of the Industrial Revolution that argues that Europe was not as different from other parts of the world as scholars have previously thought.

Rendall, Jane. *The Origins of Modern Feminism: Women in Britain, France and the United States, 1780–1860.* New York, 1984. Helpful overview.

Rose, Sonya O. *Limited Livelihoods: Gender and Class in Nineteenth-Century England.* Berkeley, Calif., 1992. On the intersection of culture and economics.

Sabean, David Warren. *Property, Production, and Family Neckarhausen, 1700–1870.* New York, 1990. Brilliant and very detailed study of gender roles and family.

Sabel, Charles, and Jonathan Zeitlin. "Historical Alternatives to Mass Production." *Past and Present* 108 (August 1985): 133–176. On the many forms of modern industry.

Schivelbusch, Wolfgang. *Disenchanted Night: The Instrialization of Light in the Nineteenth Century.* Berkeley, Calif., 1988.

———. *The Railway Journey.* Berkeley, 1986. Schivelbusch's imaginative studies are among the best ways to understand how the transformations of the nineteenth century changed daily experiences.

Thompson, E. P. *The Making of the English Working Class*. London, 1963. Shows how the French and Industrial Revolutions fostered the growth of working-class consciousness. A brilliant and important work.

Tilly, Louise, and Joan Scott. *Women, Work and the Family*. New York, 1978. Now the classic study.

Valenze, Deborah. *The First Industrial Woman*. New York, 1995. Excellent and readable on industrialization and economic change in general.

Williams, Raymond. *Keywords: A Vocabulary of Culture and Society*. New York, 1976. Brilliant and indispensable for students of culture, and now updated as *New Keywords: A Revised Vocabulary of Culture and Society* (2005), by Lawrence Grossberg and Meaghan Morris.

Zeldin, Theodore. France, 1848–1945, 2 vols. Oxford, 1973–1977. Eclectic and wide-ranging social history.

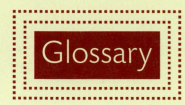

Glossary

1973 OPEC oil embargo Some leaders in the Arab-dominated Organization of the Petroleum Exporting Countries (OPEC) wanted to use oil as a weapon against the West in the Arab-Israeli conflict. After the 1972 Arab-Israeli war, OPEC instituted an oil embargo against Western powers. The embargo increased the price of oil and sparked spiraling inflation and economic troubles in Western nations, triggering in turn a cycle of dangerous recession that lasted nearly a decade. In response, Western governments began viewing the Middle Eastern oil regions as areas of strategic importance.

Abbasid Caliphate (750–930) The Abbasid family claimed to be descendants of Muhammad, and in 750 they successfully led a rebellion against the Umayyads, seizing control of Muslim territories in Arabia, Persia, North Africa, and the Near East. The Abbasids modeled their behavior and administration on that of the Persian princes and their rule on that of the Persian Empire, establishing a new capital at Baghdad.

Peter Abelard (1079–1142) Highly influential philosopher, theologian, and teacher, often considered the founder of the University of Paris.

absolutism Form of government in which one body, usually the monarch, controls the right to make war, tax, judge, and coin money. The term was often used to refer to the state monarchies in seventeenth- and eighteenth-century Europe. In other countries the end of feudalism is often associated with the legal abolition of serfdom, as in Russia in 1861.

abstract expressionism The mid-twentieth-century school of art based in New York that included Jackson Pollock, Willem de Kooning, and Franz Kline. It emphasized form, color, gesture, and feeling instead of figurative subjects.

Academy of Sciences This French institute of scientific inquiry was founded in 1666 by Louis XIV. France's statesmen exerted control over the academy and sought to share in the rewards of any discoveries its members made.

Aeneas Mythical founder of Rome, Aeneas was a refugee from the city of Troy whose adventures were described by the poet Virgil in the *Aeneid,* which mimicked the oral epics of Homer.

Aetolian and Achaean Leagues These two alliances among Greek poleis formed during the Hellenistic period in opposition to the Antigonids of Macedonia. Unlike the earlier defensive alliances of the classic period, each league represented a real attempt to form a political federation.

African National Congress (ANC) Multiracial organization founded in 1912 whose goal was to end racial discrimination in South Africa.

Afrikaners Descendants of the original Dutch settlers of South Africa; formerly referred to as Boers.

agricultural revolution Numerous agricultural revolutions have occurred in the history of western civilizations. One of the most significant began in the tenth century C.E., and increased the amount of land under cultivation as well as the productivity of the land. This revolution was made possible through the use of new technology, an increase in global temperatures, and more efficient methods of cultivation.

AIDS Acquired Immunodeficiency Syndrome. AIDS first appeared in the 1970s and has developed into a global health catastrophe; it is spreading most quickly in developing nations in Africa and Asia.

Akhenaten (r. 1352–1336) Pharaoh whose attempt to promote the worship of the sun god, Aten, ultimately weakened his dynasty's position in Egypt.

Alexander the Great (356–323 B.C.E.) The Macedonian king whose conquests of the Persian Empire and Egypt created a new Hellenistic world.

Tsar Alexander II (1818–1881) After the Crimean War, Tsar Alexander embarked on a program of reform and modernization, which included the emancipation of the serfs. A radical assassin killed him in 1881.

Alexius Comnenus (1057–1118) This Byzantine emperor requested Pope Urban II's help in raising an army to recapture Anatolia from the Seljuq Turks. Instead, Pope Urban II called for knights to go to the Holy Land and liberate it from its Muslim captors, which launched the First Crusade.

Algerian War (1954–1962) The war between France and Algerians seeking independence. Led by the National Liberation Front (FLN), guerrillas fought the French army in the mountains and desert of Algeria. The FLN also initiated a campaign of bombing and terrorism in Algerian cities that led French soldiers to torture many Algerians, attracting world attention and international scandal.

Allied Powers The First World War coalition of Great Britain, Ireland, Belgium, France, Italy, Russia, Portugal, Greece, Serbia, Montenegro, Albania, and Romania.

al Qaeda The radical Islamic organization founded in the late 1980s by former *mujahidin* who had fought against the Soviet Union in Afghanistan. Al Qaeda carried out the 9/11 terrorist attacks and is responsible as well for attacks in Africa, southeast Asia, Europe, and the Middle East.

Americanization The fear of many Europeans, since the 1920s, that U.S. cultural products, such as film, television, and music, exerted too much influence. Many of the criticisms centered on America's emphasis on mass production and organization. The fears about Americanization were not limited to culture. They extended to corporations, business techniques, global trade, and marketing.

Americas The name given to the two great land masses of the New World, derived from the name of the Italian geographer Amerigo Vespucci. In 1492, Christopher Columbus reached the Bahamas and the island of Hispaniola, which began an era of Spanish conquest in North and South America. Originally, the Spanish sought a route to Asia. Instead they discovered two continents whose wealth they decided to exploit. They were especially interested in gold and silver, which they either stole from indigenous peoples or mined using indigenous peoples as labor. Silver became Spain's most lucrative export from the New World.

Ambrose (c. 340–397) One of the early "fathers" of the Church, he helped to define the relationship between the sacred authority of bishops and other Church leaders and the secular authority of worldly rulers. He believed that secular rulers were a part of the Church, and therefore subject to it.

Amnesty International Nongovernmental organization formed in 1961 to defend "prisoners of conscience"—those detained for their beliefs, color, sex, ethnic origin, language, or religion.

Anabaptists Protestant movement that emerged in Switzerland in 1521; its adherents insisted that only adults could be baptized Christians.

anarchists In the nineteenth century, they were a political movement with the aim of establishing small-scale, localized, and self-sufficient democratic communities that could guarantee a maximum of individual sovereignty. Renouncing parties, unions and any form of modern mass organization, the anarchists fell back on the tradition of conspiratorial violence.

Anti–Corn Law League This organization successfully lobbied Parliament to repeal Britain's Corn Laws in 1846. The Corn Laws of 1815 had protected British landowners and farmers from foreign competition by establishing high tariffs, which kept bread prices artificially high for British consumers. The League saw these laws as unfair protection of the aristocracy and pushed for their repeal in the name of free trade.

anti-Semitism Anti-Semitism refers to hostility toward Jewish people. Religious forms of anti-Semitism have a long history in Europe, but in the nineteenth century anti-Semitism emerged as a potent ideology for mobilizing new constituencies in the era of mass politics. Playing on popular conspiracy theories about alleged Jewish influence in society, anti-Semites effectively rallied large bodies of supporters in France during the Dreyfus Affair, and then again during the rise of National Socialism in Germany after the First World War. The Holocaust would not have been possible without the acquiescence or cooperation of many thousands of people who shared anti-Semitic views.

apartheid The racial segregation policy of the Afrikaner-dominated South African government. Legislated in 1948 by the Afrikaner National Party, it existed in South Africa for many years.

appeasement The policy pursued by Western governments in the face of German, Italian, and Japanese aggression leading up to the Second World War. The policy, which attempted to accommodate and negotiate peace with the aggressive nations, was based on the belief that another global war like the First World War was unimaginable, a belief that Germany and its allies had been mistreated by the terms of the Treaty of Versailles, and a fear that fascist Germany and its allies protected the West from the spread of Soviet communism.

Thomas Aquinas (1225–1274) Dominican friar and theologian whose systematic approach to Christian doctrine was influenced by Aristotle.

Arab-Israeli conflict Between the founding of the state of Israel in 1948 and the present, a series of wars has been fought between Israel and neighboring Arab nations: the war of 1948 when Israel defeated attempts by Egypt, Jordon, Iraq, Syria, and Lebanon to prevent the creation of the new state; the 1956 war between Israel and Egypt over the Sinai peninsula; the 1967 war, when Israel gained control of additional land in the Golan Heights, the West Bank, the Gaza strip, and in the Sinai; and the Yom Kippur War of 1973, when Israel once again fought with forces from Egypt and Syria. A particularly difficult issue in all of these conflicts has been the situation of the 950,000 Palestinian refugees made homeless by the first war in 1948, and the movement of Israeli settlers into the occupied territories (outside of Israel's original borders). In the late 1970s, peace talks between Israel and Egypt inspired some hope of peace, but an on-going cycle of violence between Palestinians and the Israeli military have made a final settlement elusive.

Arab nationalism During the period of decolonization, secular forms of Arab nationalism, or pan-Arabism, found a wide following in many countries of the Middle East, especially in Egypt, Syria, and Iraq.

Arianism A variety of Christianity condemned as a heresy by the Roman Church, it derives from the teaching of a fourth-century priest called Arius, who rejected the idea that Jesus could be the divine equal of God.

aristocracy From the Greek word meaning "rule of the best." By 1000 B.C.E., the accumulated wealth of successful traders in Greece had created a new type of social class, which was based on wealth rather than warfare or birth. These men saw their wealth as a reflection of their superior qualities and aspired to emulate the heroes of old.

Aristotle (384–322 B.C.E.) A student of Plato, his philosophy was based on the rational analysis of the material world. In contrast to his teacher, he stressed the rigorous investigation of real phenomena, rather than the development of universal ethics. He was, in turn, the teacher of Alexander the Great.

Asiatic Society A cultural organization founded in 1784 by British Orientalists who lauded native culture but believed in colonial rule.

Assyrians A Semitic-speaking people that moved into northern Mesopotamia around 2400 B.C.E.

Athens Athens emerged as the Greek polis with the most markedly democratic form of government through a series of political struggles during the sixth century B.C.E. After its key role in the defeat of two invading Persian forces, Athens became the preeminent naval power of ancient Greece and the exemplar of Greek culture. But it antagonized many other poleis, and became embroiled in a war with Sparta and her allies in 431 B.C.E. Called the Peloponnesian War, this bloody conflict lasted until Athens was defeated in 404 B.C.E.

atomic bomb In 1945, the United States dropped atomic bombs on Hiroshima and Nagasaki in Japan, ending the Second World War. In 1949, the Soviet Union tested their first atomic bomb, and in 1953 both superpowers demonstrated their new hydrogen bombs. Strategically, the nuclearization of warfare polarized the world. Countries without nuclear weapons found it difficult to avoid joining either the Soviet or American military pacts. Over time countries split into two groups: the superpowers with enormous military budgets and those countries that relied on agreements and international law. The nuclearization of warfare also encouraged "proxy wars" between clients of superpowers. Culturally, the hydrogen bomb came to symbolize the age and both humanity's power and vulnerability.

Augustine of Hippo (c. 354–397) One of the most influential theologians of all time, Augustine described his conversion to Christianity in his autobiographical *Confessions* and articulated a new Christian worldview in *The City of God*, among other works.

Augustus (63 B.C.E.–14 C.E.) Born Gaius Octavius, this grandnephew and adopted son of Julius Caesar came to power in 27 B.C.E. His reign signals the end of the Roman Republic and the beginning of the Principate, the period when Rome was dominated by autocratic emperors.

Auschwitz-Birkenau The Nazi concentration camp in Poland that was designed to systematically murder Jews and gypsies. Between 1942 and 1944 over one million people were killed in Auschwitz-Birkenau.

Austro-Hungarian Empire The dual monarchy established by the Habsburg family in 1867; it collapsed at the end of the First World War.

authoritarianism A centralized and dictatorial form of government, proclaimed by its adherents to be superior to parliamentary democracy. Authoritarian governments claim to be above the law, do not respect individual rights, and do not tolerate political opposition. Authoritarian regimes that have developed a central ideology such as fascism or communism are sometimes termed "totalitarian."

Avignon A city in southeastern France that became the seat of the papacy between 1305 and 1377, a period known as the "Babylonian Captivity" of the Roman Church.

Aztecs An indigenous people of central Mexico; their empire was conquered by Spanish conquistadors in the sixteenth century.

baby boom (1950s) The post–Second World War upswing in U.S. birth rates; it reversed a century of decline.

Babylon An ancient city between the Tigris and Euphrates rivers, which became the capital of Hammurabi's empire in the eighteenth century B.C.E. and continued to be an important administrative and commercial capital under many subsequent imperial powers, including the Neo-Assyrians, Chaldeans, Persians, and Romans. It was here that Alexander the Great died in 323 B.C.E.

Francis Bacon (1561–1626) British philosopher and scientist who pioneered the scientific method and inductive reasoning. In other words, he argued that thinkers should amass many observations and then draw general conclusions or propose theories on the basis of this data.

Balfour Declaration A letter dated November 2, 1917, by Lord Arthur J. Balfour, British Foreign Secretary, that promised a homeland for the Jews in Palestine.

Laura Bassi (1711–1778) She was accepted into the Academy of Science in Bologna for her work in mathematics, which made her one of the few women to be accepted into a scientific academy in the seventeenth century.

Bastille The Bastille was a royal fortress and prison in Paris. In June of 1789, a revolutionary crowd attacked the Bastille to show support for the newly created National Assembly. The fall of the Bastille was the first instance of the people's role in revolutionary change in France.

Bay of Pigs (1961) The unsuccessful invasion of Cuba by Cuban exiles, supported by the U.S. government. The rebels intended to incite an insurrection in Cuba and overthrow the communist regime of Fidel Castro.

Cesare Beccaria (1738–1794) An influential writer during the Enlightenment who advocated for legal reforms. He believed that the only legitimate rationale for punishments was to maintain social order and to prevent other crimes. He argued for the greatest possible leniency compatible with deterrence and opposed torture and the death penalty.

Beer Hall Putsch (1923) An early attempt by the Nazi party to seize power in Munich; Adolf Hitler was imprisoned for a year after the incident.

Benedict of Nursia (c. 480–c. 547) Benedict's rule for monks formed the basis of western monasticism and is still observed in monasteries all over the world.

Benedictine Monasticism This form of monasticism was developed by Benedict of Nursia. Its followers adhere to a defined cycle of daily prayers, lessons, communal worship, and manual labor.

Berlin airlift (1948) The transport of vital supplies to West Berlin by air, primarily under U.S. auspices, in response to a blockade of the city that had been instituted by the Soviet Union to force the Allies to abandon West Berlin.

Berlin Conference (1884) At this conference, the leading colonial powers met and established ground rules for the partition of Africa by European nations. By 1914, 90 percent of African territory was under European control. The Berlin Conference ceded control of the Congo region to a private company run by King Leopold II of Belgium. They agreed to make the Congo valleys open to free trade and commerce, to end the slave trade in the region, and to establish a Congo Free State. In reality, King Leopold II's company established a regime that was so brutal in its treatment of local populations that an international scandal forced the Belgian state to take over the colony in 1908.

Berlin wall The wall built in 1961 by East German Communists to prevent citizens of East Germany from fleeing to West Germany; it was torn down in 1989.

birth control pill This oral contraceptive became widely available in the mid-1960s. For the first time, women had a simple method of birth control that they could take themselves.

Otto von Bismarck (1815–1898) The prime minister of Prussia and later the first chancellor of a unified Germany, Bismarck was the architect of German unification and helped to consolidate the new nation's economic and military power.

Black Death The epidemic of bubonic plague that ravaged Europe, Asia, and North Africa in the fourteenth century, killing one third to one half of the population.

Black Jacobins A nickname for the rebels in Saint Domingue, including Toussaint L'Ouverture, a former slave who in 1791 led the slaves of this French colony in the largest and most successful slave insurrection.

Black Panthers A radical African American group that came together in the 1960s; the Black Panthers advocated black separatism and pan-Africanism.

Blackshirts The troops of Mussolini's fascist regime; the squads received money from Italian landowners to attack socialist leaders.

Black Tuesday (October 29, 1929) The day on which the U.S. stock market crashed, plunging U.S. and international trading systems into crisis and leading the world into the "Great Depression."

William Blake (1757–1827) Romantic writer who criticized industrial society and factories. He championed the imagination and poetic vision, seeing both as transcending the limits of the material world.

Blitzkrieg The German "lightning war" strategy used during the Second World War; the Germans invaded Poland, France, Russia, and other countries with fast-moving and well-coordinated attacks using aircraft, tanks and other armored vehicles, followed by infantry.

Bloody Sunday On January 22, 1905, the Russian tsar's guards killed 130 demonstrators who were protesting the tsar's mistreatment of workers and the middle class.

Jean Bodin (1530–1596) A French political philosopher whose *Six Books of the Commonwealth* advanced a theory of absolute sovereignty, on the grounds that the state's paramount duty is to maintain order and that monarchs should therefore exercise unlimited power.

Boer War (1898–1902) Conflict between British and ethnically European Afrikaners in South Africa, with terrible casualties on both sides.

Boethius (c. 480–524) Member of a prominent Roman family, he sought to preserve aspects of ancient learning by compiling a series of handbooks and anthologies appropriate for Christian readers. His translations of Greek philosophy provided a crucial link between classical Greek thought and the early intellectual culture of Christianity.

Simon de Bolivar (1783–1830) Venezuelan-born general called "The Liberator" for his assistance in helping Bolivia, Panama, Colombia, Ecuador, Peru, and Venezuela win independence from Spain.

Bolsheviks Former members of the Russian Social Democratic Party who advocated the destruction of capitalist political and economic institutions and started the Russian Revolution. In 1918 the Bolsheviks changed their name to the Russian Communist Party. Prominent Bolsheviks included Vladimir Lenin and Josef Stalin. Leon Trotsky joined the Bolsheviks late but became a prominent leader in the early years of the Russian Revolution.

Napoleon Bonaparte (1769–1821) Corsican-born French general who seized power and ruled as dictator from 1799 to 1814. After the successful conquest of much of Europe, he was defeated by Russian and Prussian forces and died in exile.

Sandro Botticelli (1445–1510) An Italian painter devoted to the blending of classical and Christian motifs by using ideas associated with the pagan past to illuminate sacred stories.

bourgeoisie Term for the middle class, derived from the French word for a town-dweller, *bourgeois*.

Boxer Rebellion (1899–1900) Chinese peasant movement that opposed foreign influence, especially that of Christian missionaries; it was finally put down after the Boxers were defeated by a foreign army composed mostly of Japanese, Russian, British, French, and American soldiers.

Tycho Brahe (1546–1601) Danish astronomer who believed that the careful study of the heavens would unlock the secrets of the universe. For over twenty years, he charted the movements of significant objects in the night sky, compiling the finest set of astronomical data in Europe.

British Commonwealth of Nations Formed in 1926, the Commonwealth conferred "dominion status" on Britain's white settler colonies in Canada, Australia, and New Zealand.

Bronze Age (3200–1200 B.C.E.) The name given to the era characterized by the discovery of techniques for smelting bronze (an alloy of copper and tin), which was then the strongest known metal.

Brownshirts Troops of young German men who dedicated themselves to the Nazi cause in the early 1930s by holding street marches, mass rallies, and confrontations. They engaged in beatings of Jews and anyone who opposed the Nazis.

Lord Byron (1788–1824) Writer and poet whose life helped give the Romantics their reputation as rebels against conformity. He was known for his love affairs, his defense of working-class movements, and his passionate engagement in politics, which led to his death in the war for Greek independence.

Byzantium The name of a small settlement located at the mouth of the Black Sea and at the crossroads between Europe and Asia, it was chosen by Constantine as the site for his new imperial capital of Constantinople in 324 C.E. Modern historians use this name to refer to the eastern Roman Empire that persisted in this region until 1453, but the inhabitants of that empire referred to themselves as Romans.

Julius Caesar (100–44 B.C.E.) The Roman general who conquered the Gauls, invaded Britain, and expanded Rome's territory in Asia Minor. He became the dictator of Rome in 46 B.C.E. His assassination led to the rise of his grandnephew and adopted son, Gaius Octavius Caesar, who ruled the Roman Empire as Caesar Augustus.

caliphs Islamic rulers who claim descent from the prophet Muhammad.

John Calvin (1509–1564) French-born theologian and reformer whose radical form of Protestantism was adopted in many Swiss cities, notably Geneva.

Canary Islands Islands off the western coast of Africa that were colonized by Portugal and Spain in the mid-fifteenth century, after which they became bases for further expeditions around the African coast and across the Atlantic.

Carbonari An underground organization that opposed the Concert of Europe's restoration of monarchies. They held influence in southern Europe during the 1820s, especially in Italy.

Carolingian Derived from the Latin name Carolus (Charles), this term refers to the Frankish dynasty that began with the rise to power of Charlemagne's grandfather, Charles Martel (688–741). At its height under Charlemagne (Charles the Great), the dynasty controlled what is now France, Germany, northern Italy, Catalonia and portions of central Europe. The Carolingian Empire collapsed under the combined weight of Viking raids, economic disintegration, and the growing power of local lords.

Carolingian Renaissance A cultural and intellectual flowering that took place around the court of Charlemagne in the late eighth and early ninth centuries.

Carthage The great maritime empire that grew out of Phoenician trading colonies in North Africa and rivaled the power of Rome. Its wars with Rome, collectively known as the Punic Wars, ended in its destruction in 146 B.C.E.

Cassidorus (c. 490–c. 583) Member of an old senatorial family, he was largely responsible for introducing classical learning into the monastic curriculum and for turning monasteries into centers for the collection, preservation, and transmission of knowledge. His *Institutes*, an influential handbook of classical literature for Christian readers, was intended as a preface to more intensive study of theology and the Bible.

Catholic Church The "universal" (catholic) church based in Rome, which was redefined in the sixteenth century, when the Counter-Reformation resulted in the rebirth of the Catholic faith at the Council of Trent.

Margaret Cavendish (1623–1673) English natural philosopher who developed her own speculative natural philosophy. She used this philosophy to critique those who excluded her from scientific debate.

Camillo Benso di Cavour (1810–1861) Prime minister of Piedmont-Sardinia and founder of the Italian Liberal Party; he played a key role in the movement for Italian unification under the Piedmontese king, Victor Emmanuel II.

Central Powers The First World War alliance between Germany, Austria-Hungary, Bulgaria, and Turkey.

Charlemagne (742–814) As king of the Franks (767–813), Charles "the Great" consolidated much of western Europe under his rule. In 800 he was crowned emperor by the pope in Rome, establishing a problematic precedent that would have wide-ranging consequences for western Europe's relationship with the eastern Roman Empire in Byzantium and for the relationship between the papacy and secular rulers.

Charles I (1625–1649) The second Stuart king of England, Charles attempted to rule without the support of Parliament, sparking a controversy that erupted into civil war in 1642. The king's forces were ultimately defeated and Charles himself was executed by act of Parliament, the first time in history that a reigning king was legally deposed and executed by his own government.

Chartists A working-class movement in Britain which called for reform of the political system in Britain during the 1840s. They were supporters of the "People's Charter," which had six demands: universal white male suffrage, secret ballots, an end to property qualifications as a condition of public office, annual parliamentary elections, salaries for members of the House of Commons, and equal electoral districts.

Chernobyl (1986) Site of the world's worst nuclear power accident; in Ukraine, formerly part of the Soviet Union.

Christine de Pisan (c. 1364–c. 1431) Born in Italy, Christine spent her adult life attached to the French court and, after her husband's death, became the first lay woman to earn her living by writing. She is the author of treatises in warfare and chivalry, as well as of books and pamphlets that challenge longstanding misogynistic claims.

Church of England Founded by Henry VIII in the 1530s, as a consequence of his break with the authority of the Roman pope.

Winston Churchill (1874–1965) British prime minister who led the country during the Second World War. He also coined the phrase "Iron Curtain" in a speech at Westminster College in 1946.

Cicero (106–43 B.C.E.) Influential Roman senator, orator, Stoic philosopher, and prose stylist. His published writings still form the basis of the instruction in classical Latin grammar and usage.

Cincinnatus (519–c. 430 B.C.E.) A legendary citizen-farmer of Rome who reluctantly accepted an appointment as dictator. After defeating Rome's enemies, he allegedly left his political office and returned to his farm.

Civil Constitution of the Clergy Issued by the French National Assembly in 1790, the Civil Constitution of the Clergy decreed that all bishops and priests should be subject to the authority of the state. Their salaries were to be paid out of the public treasury, and they were required to swear allegiance to the new state, making it clear they served France rather than Rome. The Assembly's aim was to make the Catholic Church of France a truly national and civil institution.

civilizing mission An argument made by Europeans to justify colonial expansion in the nineteenth century. Supporters of this idea believed that Europeans had a duty to impose western ideas of economic and political progress on the indigenous peoples they ruled over in their colonies. In practice, the colonial powers often found that ambitious plans to impose European practices on colonial subjects led to unrest that threatened the stability of colonial rule, and by the early twentieth century most colonial powers were more cautious in their plans for political or cultural transformation.

Civil Rights Movement The Second World War increased African American migration from the American South to northern cities, intensifying a drive for rights, dignity, and independence. By 1960, civil rights groups had started organizing boycotts and demonstrations directed at discrimination against blacks in the South. During the 1960s, civil rights laws passed under President Lyndon B. Johnson did bring African Americans some equality with regard to voting rights and, to a much lesser degree, school desegregation. However, racism continued in areas such as housing, job opportunities, and the economic development of African American communities.

Civil War (1861–1865) Conflict between the northern and southern states of America that cost over 600,000 lives; this struggle led to the abolition of slavery in the United States.

Classical learning The study of ancient Greek and Latin texts. After Christianity became the only legal religion of the Roman Empire, scholars needed to find a way to make classical learning applicable to a Christian way of life. Christian monks played a significant role in resolving this problem by reinterpreting the classics for a Christian audience.

Cluny A powerful Benedictine monastery founded in 910 whose enormous wealth and prestige would derive from its independence from secular authorities, as well as from its wide network of daughter houses (priories).

Cold War (1945–1991) Ideological, political, and economic conflict in which the USSR and Eastern Europe opposed the United States and Western Europe in the decades after the Second World War. The Cold War's origins lay in the breakup of the wartime alliance between the United States and the Soviet Union in 1945, and resulted in a division of Europe into two spheres: the West, commited to market capitalism, and the East, which sought to build Socialist republics in areas under Soviet Control. The Cold War ended with the collapse of the Soviet Union in 1991.

collectivization Stalin's plan for nationalizing agricultural production, begun in 1929. 25 million peasants were forced to give up their land and join 250,000 large collective farms. Many who resisted were deported to labor camps in the Far East, and Stalin's government cut off food rations to those areas most marked by resistance to collectivization. In the ensuing man-made famines, millions of people starved to death.

Christopher Columbus (1451–1506) A Genoese sailor who persuaded King Ferdinand and Queen Isabella of Spain to fund his expedition across the Atlantic, with the purpose of discovering a new trade route to Asia. His miscalculations landed him in the Bahamas and the island of Hispaniola in 1492.

Committee of Public Safety Political body during the French Revolution that was controlled by the Jacobins, who defended the revolution by executing thousands during the Reign of Terror (September 1793–July 1794).

commune A community of individuals who have banded together in a sworn association, with the aim of establishing their independence and setting up their own form of representative government. Many medieval towns originally founded by lords or monasteries gained their independence through such methods.

The Communist Manifesto Radical pamphlet by Karl Marx (1818–1883) that predicted the downfall of the capitalist system and its replacement by a classless egalitarian society. Marx believed that this revolution would be accomplished by workers (the proletariat).

Compromise of 1867 Agreement between the Habsburgs and the peoples living in Hungarian parts of the empire that the Habsburg state would be officially known as the Austro-Hungarian Empire.

Concert of Europe (1814–1815) The body of diplomatic agreements designed primarily by Austrian minister Klemens von Metternich between 1814 and 1848, and supported by other European powers until 1914. Its goal was to maintain a balance of power on the Continent and to prevent destabilizing social and political change in Europe.

Congress of Vienna (1814–1815) **and Restoration** International conference to reorganize Europe after the downfall of Napoleon and the French Revolution. European monarchies restored the Bourbon family to the French throne, agreed to respect each other's borders and to cooperate in guarding against future revolutions and war.

conquistador Spanish term for "conqueror," applied to the mercenaries and adventurers who campaigned against indigenous peoples in central and southern America.

Conservatism In the nineteenth century, conservatives aimed to legitimize and solidify the monarchy's authority and the hierarchical social order. They believed that change had to be slow, incremental, and managed so that the structures of authority were strengthened and not weakened.

Constantine (275–337) The first emperor of Rome to convert to Christianity, Constantine came to power in 312. In 324, he founded a new imperial capital, Constantinople, on the site of a maritime settlement known as Byzantium.

Constantinople Founded by the emperor Constantine on the site of a village called Byzantium, Constantinople became the new capital of the Roman Empire in 324 and continued to be the seat of imperial power after its capture by the Ottoman Turks in 1453. It is now known as Istanbul.

Nicholas Copernicus (1473–1543) Polish astronomer who advanced the idea that the earth moved around the sun.

cosmopolitanism Stemming from the Greek word meaning "universal city," the culture characteristic of the Hellenistic world challenged and transformed the more narrow worldview of the Greek polis.

cotton gin Invented by Eli Whitney in 1793, this device mechanized the process of separating cotton seeds from the cotton fiber, which sped up the production of cotton and reduced its price. This change made slavery profitable in the United States.

Council of Constance (1417–1420) A meeting of clergy and theologians in an effort to resolve the Great Schism within the Roman Church. The council deposed all rival papal candidates and elected a new pope, Martin V, but it also adopted the doctrine of conciliarism, which holds that the supreme authority within the Church rests with a representative general council and not with the pope. However, Martin V himself was an opponent of this doctrine, and refused to be bound by it.

Council of Trent The name given to a series of meetings held in the Italian city of Trent (Trento) between 1545 and 1563, when leaders of the Roman Church reaffirmed Catholic doctrine and instituted internal reforms.

Counter-Reformation The movement to counter the Protestant Reformation, initiated by the Catholic Church at the Council of Trent in 1545.

coup d'état French term for the overthrow of an established government by a group of conspirators, usually with military support.

Crimean War (1854–1856) War waged by Russia against Great Britain and France. Spurred by Russia's encroachment on Ottoman territories, the conflict revealed Russia's military weakness when Russian forces fell to British and French troops.

Cuban missile crisis (1962) Diplomatic standoff between the United States and the Soviet Union that was provoked by the Soviet Union's attempt to base nuclear missiles in Cuba; it brought the world closer to nuclear war than ever before or since.

Cuius regio, eius religio A Latin phrase meaning "as the ruler, so the religion." Adopted as a part of the settlement of the Peace of Augsburg in 1555, it meant that those principalities ruled by Lutherans would have Lutheranism as their official religion and those ruled by Catholics must practice Catholicism.

cult of domesticity Concept associated with Victorian England that idealized women as nurturing wives and mothers.

cult of the Virgin The beliefs and practices associated with the veneration of Mary the mother of Jesus, which became increasingly popular in the twelfth century.

cuneiform An early writing system that began to develop in Mesopotamia in the fourth millennium B.C.E. By 3100 B.C.E., its distinctive markings were impressed on clay tablets using a wedge-shaped stylus.

Cyrus the Great (c. 585–529 B.C.E.) As architect of the Persian Empire, Cyrus extended his dominion over a vast territory stretching from the Persian Gulf to the Mediterranean and incorporating the ancient civilizations of Mesopotamia. His successors ruled this Persian Empire as "Great Kings."

Darius (521–486 B.C.E.) The Persian emperor whose conflict with Aristagoras, the Greek ruler of Miletus, ignited the Persian Wars. In 490 B.C.E., Darius sent a large army to punish the Athenians for their intervention in Persian imperial affairs, but this force was defeated by Athenian hoplites on the plain of Marathon.

Charles Darwin (1809–1882) British naturalist who wrote *On the Origin of Species* and developed the theory of natural selection to explain the evolution of organisms.

D-Day (June 6, 1944) Date of the Allied invasion of Normandy, under General Dwight Eisenhower, to liberate Western Europe from German occupation.

Decembrists Russian army officers who were influenced by events in France and formed secret societies that espoused liberal governance. They were put down by Nicholas I in December 1825.

Declaration of Independence (1776) Historic document stating the principles of government on which the United States was founded.

Declaration of the Rights of Man and of the Citizen (1789) French charter of liberties formulated by the National Assembly during the French Revolution. The seventeen articles later became the preamble to the new constitution, which the Assembly finished in 1791.

democracy In ancient Greece, this form of government allowed a class of propertied male citizens to participate in the governance of their polis; but excluded women, slaves, and citizens without property from the political process. As a result, the ruling class amounted to only a small percentage of the entire population.

René Descartes (1596–1650) French philosopher and mathematician who emphasized the use of deductive reasoning.

Denis Diderot (1713–1784) French *philosophe* and author who was the guiding force behind the publication of the first encyclopedia. The encyclopedia showed how reason could be applied to nearly all realms of thought, and aimed to be a compendium of all human knowledge.

Dien Bien Phu (1954) Defining battle in the war between French colonialists and the Viet Minh that secured North Vietnam for Ho Chi Minh and his army and left the south to form its own government, to be supported by France and the United States.

Diet of Worms The select council of the Church that convened in the German city of Worms and condemned Martin Luther on a charge of heresy in 1521.

Diocletian (245–316) As emperor of Rome from 284 to 305, Diocletian recognized that the empire could not be governed by one man in one place. His solution was to divide the empire into four parts, each with its own imperial ruler, but he himself remained the dominant ruler of the resulting tetrarchy (rule of four). He also initiated the Great Persecution, a time when many Christians became martyrs to their faith.

Directory (1795–1799) Executive committee that governed after the fall of Robespierre and held control until the coup of Napoleon Bonaparte.

Discourse on Method Philosophical treatise by René Descartes (1596–1650) proposing that the path to knowledge was through logical deduction, beginning with one's own self: "I think, therefore I am."

Dominican Order Also called the Order of Preachers, it was founded by Dominic of Osma (1170–1221), a Castilian preacher and theologian, and approved by Innocent III in 1216. The order was dedicated to the rooting out of heresy and the conversion of Jews and Muslims. Many of its members held teaching positions in European universities and contributed to the development of medieval philosophy and theology. Others became the leading administrators of the Inquisition.

Dominion in the British Commonwealth Canadian promise to maintain their fealty to the British crown, even after their independence in 1867. Later applied to Australia and New Zealand.

Dreyfus Affair The 1894 French scandal surrounding accusations that a Jewish captain, Alfred Dreyfus, sold military secrets to the Germans. Convicted, Dreyfus was sentenced to solitary confinement for life. However, after public outcry, it was revealed that the trial documents were forgeries, and Dreyfus was pardoned after a second trial in 1899. In 1906 he was fully exonerated and reinstated in the army. The affair revealed the depths of popular anti-Semitism in France.

Alexander Dubček (1921–1992) Communist leader of the Czechoslovakian government who advocated for "socialism with a human face." He encouraged debate within the party, academic and artistic freedom, and less censorship, which led to the "Prague spring" of 1968. People in other parts of Eastern Europe began to demonstrate in support of Dubček and demand their own reforms. When Dubček tried to democratize the Communist party and did not attend a meeting of the

Warsaw Pact, the Soviets sent tanks and troops into Prague and ousted Dubček and his allies.

Duma The Russian parliament, created in response to the revolution of 1905.

Dunkirk The French port on the English Channel where the British and French forces retreated after sustaining heavy losses against the German military. Between May 27 and June 4, 1940, the Royal Navy evacuated over three hundred thousand troops using commercial and pleasure boats.

Earth Summit (1992) Meeting in Rio de Janeiro between many of the world's governments in an effort to address international environmental problems.

Eastern Front Battlefront between Berlin and Moscow during the First and Second World Wars..

East India Company (1600–1858) British charter company created to outperform Portuguese and Spanish traders in the Far East; in the eighteenth century the company became, in effect, the ruler of a large part of India. There was also a Dutch East India Company.

Edict of Nantes (1598) Issued by Henry IV of France in an effort to end religious violence. The edict declared France to be a Catholic country, but tolerated some forms of Protestant worship.

Eleanor of Aquitaine (1122–1204) Ruler of the wealthy province of Aquitaine and wife of Louis VII of France, Eleanor had her marriage annulled in order to marry the young count of Anjou, Henry Plantagenet, who became King Henry of England a year later. Mother of two future kings of England, she was an important patron of the arts.

Elizabeth I (1533–1603) Protestant daughter of Henry VIII and his second wife, Anne Boleyn, Elizabeth succeeded her sister Mary as the second queen regnant of England (1558–1603).

emancipation of the serfs (1861) The abolition of serfdom was central to Tsar Alexander II's program of modernization and reform, but it produced a limited amount of change. Former serfs now had legal rights. However, farm land was granted to the village communes instead of to individuals. The land was of poor quality and the former serfs had to pay for it in installments to the village commune.

emperor Originally the term for any conquering commander of the Roman army whose victories merited celebration in an official triumph. After Augustus seized power in 27 B.C.E., it was the title born by the sole ruler of the Roman Empire.

empire A centralized political entity consolidated through the conquest and colonization of other nations or peoples in order to benefit the ruler and/or his homeland.

Enabling Act (1933) Emergency act passed by the Reichstag (German parliament) that helped transform Hitler from Germany's chancellor, or prime minister, into a dictator, following the suspicious burning of the Reichstag building and a suspension of civil liberties.

enclosure Long process of privatizing what had been public agricultural land in eighteenth-century Britain; it helped to stimulate the development of commercial agriculture and forced many people in rural areas to seek work in cities during the early stages of industrialization.

The Encyclopedia Joint venture of French *philosophe* writers, led by Denis Diderot (1713–1784), which proposed to summarize all modern knowledge in a multivolume illustrated work with over 70,000 articles.

Friedrich Engels (1820–1895) German social and political philosopher who collaborated with Karl Marx on many publications.

English Civil War (1642–1649) Conflicts between the English Parliament and King Charles I erupted into civil war, which ended in the defeat of the royalists and the execution of Charles on charges of treason against the crown. A short time later, Parliament's hereditary House of Lords was abolished and England was declared a Commonwealth.

English Navigation Act of 1651 Act stipulating that only English ships could carry goods between the mother country and its colonies.

Enlightenment Intellectual movement in eighteenth-century Europe, that believed in human betterment through the application of reason to solve social, economic, and political problems.

Epicureanism A philosophical position articulated by Epicurus of Athens (c. 342–270 B.C.E.), who rejected the idea of an ordered universe governed by divine forces; instead, he emphasized individual agency and proposed that the highest good is the pursuit of pleasure.

Desiderius Erasmus (c. 1469–1536) Dutch-born scholar, social commentator, and Catholic humanist whose new translation of the Bible influenced the theology of Martin Luther.

Estates-General The representative body of the three estates in France. In 1789, King Louis XVI summoned the Estates-General to meet for the first time since 1614 because it seemed to be the only solution to France's worsening economic crisis and financial chaos.

Etruscans Settlers of the Italian peninsula who dominated the region from the late Bronze Age until the rise of the Roman Republic in the sixth century B.C.E.

Euclid Hellenistic mathematician whose *Elements of Geometry* forms the basis of modern geometry.

eugenics A Greek term, meaning "good birth," referring to the project of "breeding" a superior human race. It was popularly championed by scientists, politicians, and social critics in the late nineteenth and early twentieth centuries.

European Common Market (1957) The Treaty of Rome created the European Economic Community (EEC) or Common Market. The original members were France, West Germany, Italy, Belgium, Holland, and Luxembourg. The EEC sought to abolish trade barriers between its members and it pledged itself to common external tariffs, the free movement of labor and capital among the member nations, and uniform wage structures and social security systems to create similar working conditions in all member countries.

European Union (EU) Successor organization to the European Economic Community or European Common Market, formed by the Maastricht Treaty, which took effect in 1993. Currently 27 member states compose the EU, which has a governing council, an international court, and a parliament. Over time, member states of the EU have relinquished some of their sovereignty, and cooperation has evolved into a community with a single currency, the euro.

Exclusion Act of 1882 U.S. congressional act prohibiting nearly all immigration from China to the United States; fueled by animosity toward Chinese workers in the American West.

existentialism Philosophical movement that arose out of the Second World War and emphasized the absurdity of human condition. Led by Jean-Paul Sartre and Albert Camus, existentialists encouraged humans to take responsibility for their own decisions and dilemmas.

fascism The doctrine founded by Benito Mussolini, which emphasized three main ideas: statism ("nothing above the state, nothing outside the state, nothing against the state"), nationalism, and militarism. Its name derives from the Latin *fasces*, a symbol of Roman imperial power adopted by Mussolini.

Fashoda Incident (1898) Disagreements between the French and the British over land claims in North Africa led to a standoff between armies of the two nations at the Sudanese town of Fashoda. The crisis was solved diplomatically. France ceded southern Sudan to Britain in exchange for a stop to further expansion by the British.

The Feminine Mystique Groundbreaking book by feminist Betty Friedan (b. 1921), which tried to define "femininity" and explored how women internalized those definitions.

Franz Ferdinand (1863–1914) Archduke of Austria and heir to the Austro-Hungarian Empire; his assassination led to the beginning of the First World War.

Ferdinand (1452–1516) **and Isabella** (1451–1504) In 1469, Ferdinand of Aragon married the heiress to Castile, Isabella. Their union allowed them to pursue several ambitious policies, including the conquest of Granada, the last Muslim principality in Spain, and the expulsion of Spain's large Jewish community. In 1492, Isabella granted three ships to Christopher Columbus of Genoa (Italy), who went on to claim portions of the New World for Spain.

Fertile Crescent An area of fertile land in what is now Syria, Israel, Turkey, eastern Iraq, and western Iran that was able to sustain settlements due to its wetter climate and abundant natural food resources. Some of the earliest known civilizations emerged there between 9000 and 4500 B.C.E.

feudalism A problematic modern term that attempts to explain the diffusion of power in medieval Europe, and the many different kinds of political, social, and economic relationships that were forged through the giving and receiving of fiefs (*feoda*). But because it is anachronistic and inadequate, this term has been rejected by most historians of the medieval period.

First Crusade (1095–1099) Launched by Pope Urban II in response to a request from the Byzantine emperor Alexius Comnenus, who had asked for a small contingent of knights to assist him in fighting Turkish forces in Anatolia; Urban instead directed the crusaders' energies toward the Holy Land and the recapture of Jerusalem, promising those who took the cross (*crux*) that they would merit eternal salvation if they died in the attempt. This crusade prompted attacks against Jews throughout Europe and resulted in six subsequent—and unsuccessful—military campaigns.

First World War A total war from August 1914 to November 1918, involving the armies of Britain, France, and Russia (the Allies) against Germany, Austria-Hungary, and the Ottoman Empire (the Central Powers). Italy joined the Allies in 1915, and the United States joined them in 1917, helping to tip the balance in favor of the Allies, who also drew upon the populations and raw materials of their colonial possessions. Also known as the Great War.

Five Pillars of Islam The Muslim teaching that salvation is only assured through observance of five basic precepts: submission to God's will as described in the teachings of Muhammad, frequent prayer, ritual fasting, the giving of alms, and an annual pilgrimage to Mecca (the Hajj).

Five-Year Plan Soviet effort launched under Stalin in 1928 to replace the market with a state-owned and state-managed economy in order to promote rapid economic development over a five-year period and thereby "catch and overtake" the leading capitalist countries. The First Five-Year Plan was followed by the Second Five-Year Plan (1933–1937) and so on, until the collapse of the Soviet Union in 1991.

fly shuttle Invented by John Kay in 1733, this device sped up the process of weaving.

Fourteen Points President Woodrow Wilson proposed these points as the foundation on which to build peace in the world after the First World War. They called for an end to secret treaties, "open covenants, openly arrived at," freedom of the seas, the removal of international tariffs, the reduction of arms, the "self-determination of peoples," and the establishment of a League of Nations to settle international conflicts.

Franciscan Order Also known as the Order of the Friars Minor. The earliest Franciscans were followers of Francis of Assisi (1182–1226) and strove, like him, to imitate the life and example of Jesus. The order was formally established by Pope Innocent III in 1209. Its special mission was the care and instruction of the urban poor.

Frankfurt Parliament (1848–1849) Failed attempt to create a unified Germany under constitutional principles. In 1849, the assembly offered the crown of the new German nation to Frederick William IV of Prussia, but he refused the offer and suppressed a brief protest. The delegates went home disillusioned.

Frederick the Great (1712–1786) Prussian ruler (1740–1786) who engaged the nobility in maintaining a strong military and bureaucracy, and led Prussian armies to notable military victories. He also encouraged Enlightenment rationalism and artistic endeavors.

French Revolution of 1789 In 1788, a severe financial crisis forced the French monarchy to convene an assembly known as the Estates General, representing the three estates of the realm: the clergy, the nobility, and the commons (known as the Third Estate). When the Estates General met in 1789, representatives of the Third Estate demanded major constitutional changes, and when the King and his government proved uncooperative, the Third Estate broke with the other two estates and renamed themselves the National Assembly, demanding a written constitution. The position of the National Assembly was confirmed by a popular uprising in Paris and the King was forced to accept the transformation of France into a constitutional monarchy. This constitutional phase of the revolution lasted until 1972, when the pressures of foreign invasion and the emergence of a more radical revolutionary movement caused the collapse of the monarchy and the establishment of a Republic in France.

French Revolution of 1830 The French popular revolt against Charles X's July Ordinances of 1830, which dissolved the French Chamber of Deputies and restricted suffrage to exclude almost everyone except the nobility. After several days of violence, Charles abdicated the throne and was replaced by a constitutional monarch, Louis Philippe.

French Revolution of 1848 Revolution overthrowing Louis Philippe in February, 1848, leading to the formation of the Second Republic (1848–1852). Initially enjoying broad support from both the middle classes and laborers in Paris, the new government became more conservative after elections in which the French peasantry participated for the first time. A workers' revolt was violently repressed in June, 1848, and in December 1848, Napoleon Bonaparte's nephew, Louis-Napoleon Bonaparte, was elected president. In 1852, Louis-Napoleon declared himself emperor and abolished the republic.

Sigmund Freud (1856–1939) The Austrian physician who founded the discipline of psychoanalysis and suggested that human behavior was largely motivated by unconscious and irrational forces.

Galileo Galilei (1564–1642) Italian physicist and inventor; the implications of his ideas raised the ire of the Catholic Church, and he was forced to retract most of his findings.

Gallipoli (1915) In the First World War, a combined force of French, British, Australian and New Zealand troops tried to invade the Gallipoli peninsula, in the first large-scale amphibious attack in history, and seize it from the Turks. After seven months of fighting, the Allies had lost 200,000 soldiers. Defeated, they withdrew.

Mohandas K. (Mahatma) Gandhi (1869–1948) The Indian leader who advocated nonviolent noncooperation to protest colonial rule and helped win home rule for India in 1947.

Giuseppe Garibaldi (1807–1882) Italian revolutionary leader who led the fight to free Sicily and Naples from the Habsburg Empire; the lands were then peaceably annexed by Sardinia to produce a unified Italy.

Gaul The region of the Roman Empire that was home to the Celtic people of that name, comprising modern France, Belgium, and western Germany.

Geneva Peace Conference (1954) International conference to restore peace in Korea and Indochina. The chief participants were the United States, the Soviet Union, Great Britain, France, the People's Republic of China, North Korea, South Korea, Vietnam, the Viet Minh party, Laos, and Cambodia. The conference resulted in the division of North and South Vietnam.

Genoese Inhabitants of the maritime city on Italy's northwestern coast, the Genoese were active in trading ventures along the Silk Road and in the establishment of trading colonies in the Mediterranean. They were also involved in the world of finance and backed the commercial ventures of other powers, especially Spain's.

German Democratic Republic Nation founded from the Soviet zone of occupation of Germany after the Second World War; also known as East Germany.

German Social Democratic Party Founded in 1875, it was the most powerful socialist party in Europe before 1917.

Gilgamesh Sumerian ruler of the city of Uruk around 2700 B.C.E., Gilgamesh became the hero of one of the world's oldest epics, which circulated orally for nearly a millennium before being written down.

globalization The term used to describe political, social, and economic networks that span the globe. These global exchanges are not limited by nation-states and in recent decades are associated with new technologies, such as the Internet. Globalization is not new, however, as human cultures and economies have been in contact with one another for centuries.

Gold Coast Name that European mariners and merchants gave to that part of West Equatorial Africa from which gold and slaves were exported. Originally controlled by the Portuguese, this area later became the British colony of the Gold Coast.

Mikhail Gorbachev (1931–) Soviet leader who attempted to reform the Soviet Union through his programs of *glasnost* and *perestroika* in the late 1980s. He encouraged open discussions in other countries in the Soviet bloc, which helped inspire the velvet revolutions throughout Eastern Europe. Eventually the political, social, and economic upheaval he had unleashed would lead to the breakup of the Soviet Union.

Gothic style A type of graceful architecture emerging in twelfth- and thirteenth-century England and France. The style is characterized by pointed arches, delicate decoration, and large windows.

Olympe de Gouges (1748–1793) French political radical and feminist whose *Declaration of the Rights of Woman* demanded an equal place for women in France.

Great Depression Global economic crisis following the U.S. stock market crash on October 29, 1929, and ending with the onset of the Second World War.

Great Fear (1789) Following the outbreak of revolution in Paris, fear spread throughout the French countryside, as rumors circulated that armies of brigands or royal troops were coming. The peasants and villagers organized into militias, while others attacked and burned the manor houses in order to destroy the records of manorial dues.

Great Schism (1378–1417) Also known as the Great Western Schism, to distinguish it from the longstanding rupture between the Greek East and Latin West. During the schism, the Roman Church was divided between two (and, ultimately, three) competing popes. Each pope claimed to be legitimate and each denounced the heresy of the others.

Great Terror (1936–1938) The systematic murder of nearly a million people and the deportation of another million and a half to labor camps by Stalin's regime in an attempt to consolidate power and remove perceived enemies.

Greek East After the founding of Constantinople, the eastern Greek-speaking half of the Roman Empire grew more populous, prosperous and central to imperial policy. Its inhabitants considered themselves to be the true heirs of Rome, and their own Orthodox Church to be the true manifestation of Jesus' ministry.

Greek Independence Nationalists in Greece revolted against the Ottoman Empire and fought a war that ended in Greek independence in 1827. They received crucial help from British, French, and Russian troops as well as widespread sympathy throughout Europe.

Pope Gregory I (r. 590–604) Also known as Gregory the Great, he was the first bishop of Rome to successfully negotiate a more universal role for the papacy. His political and theological agenda widened the rift between the western Latin (Catholic) Church and the eastern Greek (Orthodox) Church in Byzantium. He also articulated the Church's official position on the status of Jews, promoted affective approaches to religious worship, encouraged the Benedictine monastic movement, and sponsored missionary expeditions.

Guernica The Basque town bombed by German planes in April 1937 during the Spanish Civil War. It is also the subject of Pablo Picasso's famous painting from the same year.

guilds Professional organizations in commercial towns that regulated business and safeguarded the privileges of those practicing a particular craft. Often identical to confraternities ("brotherhoods").

Gulag The vast system of forced labor camps under the Soviet regime; it originated in 1919 in a small monastery near the Arctic Circle and spread throughout the Soviet Union. Penal labor was required of both ordinary criminals and those accused of political crimes. Tens of millions of people were sent to the camps between 1928 and 1953; the exact figure is unknown.

Gulf War (1991) Armed conflict between Iraq and a coalition of thirty-two nations, including the United States, Britain, Egypt, France, and Saudi Arabia. The seeds of the war were planted with Iraq's invasion of Kuwait on August 2, 1990.

Habsburg Empire Ruling house of Austria, which once ruled the Netherlands, Spain, and central Europe but came to settle in lands along the Danube River. It played a prominent role in European affairs for many centuries. In 1867, the Habsburg Empire was reorganized into the Austro-Hungarian Dual Monarchy, and in 1918 it collapsed.

Hagia Sophia The enormous church dedicated to "Holy Wisdom," built in Constantinople at the behest of the emperor Justinian in the sixth century C.E. When Constantinople fell to Ottoman forces in 1453, it became an important mosque.

Haitian Revolution (1802–1804) In 1802, Napoleon sought to reassert French control of Saint-Domingue, but stiff resistance and yellow fever crushed the French army. In 1804, Jean-Jacques Dessalines, a general in the army of former slaves, declared the independent state of Haiti. (See **slave revolt in Saint-Domingue**)

Hajj The annual pilgrimage to Mecca; an obligation for Muslims.

Hammurabi Ruler of Babylon from 1792 to 1750 B.C.E., Hammurabi issued a collection of laws that were greatly influential in the Near East and which constitute the world's oldest surviving law code.

Harlem Renaissance Cultural movement in the 1920s that was based in Harlem, a part of New York City with a large African American population. The movement gave voice to black novelists, poets, painters, and musicians, many of whom used their art to protest racial subordination.

Hatshepsut (1479–1458 C.E.) As a pharaoh during the New Kingdom, she launched several successful military campaigns and extended trade and diplomacy. She was an ambitious builder who probably constructed the first tomb in the Valley of the Kings. Though she never pretended to be a man, she was routinely portrayed with a masculine figure and a ceremonial beard.

Hebrews Originally a pastoral people divided among several tribes, they were briefly united under the rule of David and his son, Solomon, who promoted the worship of a single god, Yahweh, and constructed the first temple at the new capital city of Jerusalem. After Solomon's death, the Hebrew tribes were divided between the two kingdoms of Israel and Judah, which were eventually conquered by the Neo-Assyrian and Chaldean empires. It was in captivity that the Hebrews came to define themselves through worship of Yahweh, and to develop a religion, Judaism, that could exist outside of Judea. They were liberated by the Persian king Cyrus the Great in 539 B.C.E.

Hellenistic art The art of the Hellenistic period bridged the tastes, ideals, and customs of classical Greece and those that would be more characteristic of Rome. The Romans strove to emulate Hellenistic city planning and civic culture, and thereby exported Hellenistic culture to their own far-flung colonies in western Europe.

Hellenistic culture The "Greek-like" culture that dominated the ancient world in the wake of Alexander's conquests.

Hellenistic kingdoms Following the death of Alexander the Great, his vast empire was divided into three separate states: Ptolemaic Egypt (under the rule of the general Ptolemy and his successors), Seleucid Asia (ruled by the general Seleucus and his heirs) and Antigonid Greece (governed by Antigonus of Macedonia). Each state maintained its independence, but the shared characteristics of Greco-Macedonian rule and a shared Greek culture and heritage bound them together in a united cosmopolitan world.

Hellenistic world The various western civilizations of antiquity that were loosely united by shared Greek language and culture, especially around the eastern Mediterranean.

Heloise (c. 1090–1164) One of the foremost scholars of her time, she became the pupil and the wife of the philosopher and teacher Peter Abelard. In later life, she was the founder of a new religious order for women.

Henry VIII (1491–1547) King of England from 1509 until his death, Henry rejected the authority of the Roman Church in 1534 when the pope refused to annul his marriage to his queen, Catherine of Aragon; he became the founder of the Church of England.

Henry of Navarre (1553–1610) Crowned King Henry IV of France, he renounced his Protestantism but granted limited toleration for Huguenots (French Protestants) by the Edict of Nantes in 1598.

Prince Henry the Navigator (1394–1460) A member of the Portuguese royal family, Henry encouraged the exploration and conquest of western Africa and the trade in gold and slaves.

hieroglyphs The writing system of ancient Egypt, based on a complicated series of pictorial symbols. It fell out of use when Egypt was absorbed into the Roman Empire, and was only deciphered after the discovery of the Rosetta Stone in the early nineteenth century.

Hildegard of Bingen (1098–1179) A powerful abbess, theologian, scientist, musician, and visionary who claimed to receive regular revelations from God. Although highly influential in her own day, she was never officially canonized by the Church, in part because her strong personality no longer matched the changing ideal of female piety.

Hiroshima Japanese port devastated by an atomic bomb on August 6, 1945.

Adolf Hitler (1889–1945) The author of *Mein Kampf* and leader of the Nazis who became chancellor of Germany in 1933. Hitler and his Nazi regime started the Second World War and orchestrated the systematic murder of over five million Jews.

Hitler-Stalin Pact (1939) Treaty between Stalin and Hitler, which promised Stalin a share of Poland, Finland, the Baltic States, and Bessarabia in the event of a German invasion of Poland, which began shortly thereafter, on September 1, 1939.

HIV epidemic The first cases of HIV-AIDS appeared in the late 1970s. As HIV-AIDS became a global crisis, international organizations recognized the need for an early, swift, and comprehensive response to future outbreaks of disease.

Thomas Hobbes (1588–1679) English political philosopher whose *Leviathan* argued that any form of government capable of protecting its subjects' lives and property might act as an all-powerful sovereign. This government should be allowed to trample over both liberty and property for the sake of its own survival and that of his subjects. For in his natural state, Hobbes argued, man was like "a wolf" toward other men.

Holy Roman Empire The loosely allied collection of lands in central and western Europe ruled by the kings of Germany (and later Austria) from the twelfth century until 1806. Its origins are usually identified with the empire of Charlemagne, the Frankish king who was crowned emperor of Rome by the pope in 800.

homage A ceremony in which an individual becomes the "man" (French: *homme*) of a lord.

Homer (fl. 8th c. B.C.E.) A Greek rhapsode ("weaver" of stories) credited with merging centuries of poetic tradition in the epics known as the *Iliad* and the *Odyssey*.

hoplite A Greek foot-soldier armed with a spear or short sword and protected by a large round shield (*hoplon*). In battle, hoplites stood shoulder to shoulder in a close formation called a phalanx.

Huguenots French Protestants who endured severe persecution in the sixteenth and seventeenth centuries.

humanism A program of study associated with the movement known as the Renaissance, humanism aimed to replace the scholastic emphasis on logic and philosophy with the study of ancient languages, literature, history, and ethics.

human rights The belief that all people have the right to legal equality, freedom of religion and speech, and the right to participate in government. Human rights laws prohibit torture, cruel punishment, and slavery.

David Hume (1711–1776) Scottish writer who applied Newton's method of scientific inquiry and skepticism to the study of morality, the mind, and government.

Hundred Years' War (1337–1453) A series of wars between England and France, fought mostly on French soil and prompted by the territorial and political claims of English monarchs.

Jan Hus (c. 1373–1415) A Czech reformer who adopted many of the teachings of the English theolojan John Wyclif, and who also demanded that the laity be allowed to receive both the consecrated bread and wine of the Eucharist. The Council of Constance burned him at the stake for heresy. In response, his supporters, the Hussites, revolted against the Church.

Saddam Hussein (1937–2006) The former dictator of Iraq who invaded Iran in 1980 and started the eight-year-long Iran-Iraq War; invaded Kuwait in 1990, which led to the Gulf War of 1991; and was overthrown when the United States invaded Iraq in 2003. Involved in Iraqi politics since the mid-1960s, Hussein became the official head of state in 1979.

Iconoclast Controversy (717–787) A serious and often violent theological debate that raged in Byzantium after Emperor Leo III ordered the destruction of religious art on the grounds that any image representing a divine or holy personage is prone to promote idol worship and blasphemy. Iconoclast means "breaker of icons." Those who supported the veneration of icons were called "iconodules," "adherents of icons."

Il-khanate Mongol-founded dynasty in thirteenth-century Persia.

Indian National Congress Formed in 1885, this Indian political party worked to achieve Indian independence from British colonial control. The Congress was led by Ghandi in the 1920s and 1930s.

Indian Rebellion of 1857 The uprising began near Delhi, when the military disciplined a regiment of Indian soldiers employed by the British for refusing to use rifle cartridges greased with pork fat—unacceptable to either Hindus or Muslims. Rebels attacked law courts and burned tax rolls, protesting debt and corruption. The mutiny spread through large areas of northwest India before being violently suppressed by British troops.

Indo-Europeans A group of people speaking variations of the same language who moved into the Near East and Mediterranean region shortly after 2000 B.C.E.

indulgences Grants exempting Catholic Christians from the performance of penance, either in life or after death. The abusive trade in indulgences was a major catalyst of the Protestant Reformation.

Inkas The highly centralized South American empire that was toppled by the Spanish conquistador Francisco Pizarro in 1533.

Innocent III (1160/61–1216) As pope, he wanted to unify all of Christendom under papal hegemony. He furthered this goal at the Fourth Lateran Council of 1215, which defined one of the Church's dogmas as the acknowledgement of papal supremacy. The council also took an unprecedented interest in the religious education and habits of every Christian.

Inquisition Tribunal of the Roman Church that aims to enforce religious orthodoxy and conformity.

International Monetary Fund (IMF) Established in 1945 to ensure international cooperation regarding currency exchange and monetary policy, the IMF is a specialized agency of the United Nations.

Investiture Conflict The name given to a series of debates over the limitations of spiritual and secular power in Europe during the eleventh and early twelfth century, it came to a head when Pope Gregory VII and Emperor Henry IV of Germany both claimed the right to appoint and invest bishops with the regalia of office. After years of diplomatic and military hostility, it was partially settled by the Concordat of Worms in 1122.

Irish potato famine Period of agricultural blight from 1845 to 1849 whose devastating results produced widespread starvation and led to mass emigration to America.

Iron Curtain Term coined by Winston Churchill in 1946 to refer to the borders of Eastern European nations that lay within the zone of Soviet control.

Italian invasion of Ethiopia (1896) Italy invaded Ethiopia, which was the last major independent African kingdom. Menelik II, the Ethiopian emperor, soundly defeated them.

Ivan the Great (1440–1505) Russian ruler who annexed neighboring territories and consolidated his empire's position as a European power.

Jacobins Radical French political group during the French Revolution that took power after 1792, executed the French king, and sought to remake French culture.

Jacquerie Violent 1358 peasant uprising in northern France, incited by disease, war, and taxes.

James I (1566–1625) Monarch who ruled Scotland as James VI, and who succeeded Elizabeth I as king of England in 1603. He oversaw the English vernacular translation of the Bible known by his name.

Janissaries Corps of enslaved soldiers recruited as children from the Christian provinces of the Ottoman Empire and brought up to display intense personal loyalty to the Ottoman sultan, who used these forces to curb local autonomy and as his personal bodyguards.

Jerome (c. 340–420) One of the early "fathers" of the Church, he translated the Bible from Hebrew and Greek into a popular form of Latin—hence the name by which this translation is known: the Vulgate, or "vulgar" (popular), Bible.

Jesuits The religious order formally known as the Society of Jesus, founded in 1540 by Ignatius Loyola to combat the spread of Protestantism. The Jesuits would become active in politics, education, and missionary work.

Jesus (c. 4 B.C.E.–c. 30 C.E.) A Jewish preacher and teacher in the rural areas of Galilee and Judea who was arrested for seditious political activity, tried, and crucified by the Romans. After his execution, his followers claimed that he had been resurrected from the dead and taken up into heaven. They began to teach that Jesus had been the divine representative of God, the Messiah foretold by ancient Hebrew prophets, and that he had suffered for the sins of humanity and would return to judge all the world's inhabitants at the end of time.

Joan of Arc (c. 1412–1431) A peasant girl from the province of Lorraine who claimed to have been commanded by God to lead French forces against the English occupying army during the Hundred Years' War. Successful in her efforts, she was betrayed by the French king and handed over to the English, who condemned her to death for heresy. Her reputation underwent a process of rehabilitation, but she was not officially canonized as a saint until 1920.

Judaism The religion of the Hebrews as it developed in the centuries after the establishment of the Hebrew kingdoms under David and Solomon, especially during the period of Babylonian Captivity.

Justinian (527–565) Emperor of Rome who unsuccessfully attempted to reunite the eastern and western portions of the empire. Also known for his important codification of Roman law, in the *Corpus Juris Civilis*.

Justinian's Code of Roman Law Formally known as the *Corpus Juris Civilis* or "body of civil law," this compendium consisted of a systematic compilation of imperial statutes, the writings of Rome's great legal authorities, a textbook of legal principles, and the legislation of Justinian and his immediate successors. As the most authoritative collection of Roman law, it formed the basis of canon law (the legal system of the Roman Church) and became essential to the developing legal traditions of every European state, as well as of many countries around the world.

Das Kapital (Capital) The 1867 book by Karl Marx that outlined the theory behind historical materialism and attacked the socioeconomic inequities of capitalism.

Johannes Kepler (1571–1630) Mathematician and astronomer who elaborated on and corrected Copernicus's theory and is chiefly remembered for his discovery of the three laws of planetary motion that bear his name.

Keynesian Revolution Post-depression economic ideas developed by the British economist John Maynard Keynes, wherein the state took a greater role in managing the economy, stimulating it by increasing the money supply and creating jobs.

KGB Soviet political police and spy agency, first formed as the Cheka not long after the Bolshevik coup in October 1917. It grew to more than 750,000 operatives with military rank by the 1980s.

Chingiz Khan (c. 1167–1227) "Oceanic Ruler," the title adopted by the Mongol chieftain Temujin, founder of a dynasty that conquered much of southern Asia.

Khanate The major political unit of the vast Mongol Empire. There were four Khanates, including the Yuan Empire in China, forged by Chingiz Khan's grandson Kubilai in the thirteenth century.

Ruhollah Khomeini (1902–1989) Iranian Shi'ite religious leader who led the revolution in Iran after the abdication of the Shah in 1979. His government allowed some limited economic and political populism combined with strict constructions of Islamic law, restrictions on women's public life, and the prohibition of ideas or activities linked to Western influence.

Nikita Khrushchev (1894–1971) Leader of the Soviet Union during the Cuban missile crisis, Khrushchev came to power after Stalin's death in 1953. His reforms and criticisms of the excesses of the Stalin regime led to his fall from power in 1964.

Kremlin Once synonymous with the Soviet government, it refers to Moscow's walled city center and the palace originally built by Ivan the Great.

Kristallnacht Organized attack by Nazis and their supporters on the Jews of Germany following the assassination of a German embassy official by a Jewish man in Paris. Throughout Germany, thousands of stores, schools, cemeteries and synagogues were attacked on November 9, 1938. Dozens of people were killed, and tens of thousands of Jews were arrested and held in camps, where many were tortured and killed in the ensuing months.

Labour party Founded in Britain in 1900, this party represented workers and was based on socialist principles.

Latin West After the founding of Constantinople, the western Latin-speaking half of the Roman Empire became poorer and more peripheral, but it also fostered the emergence of new barbarian kingdoms. At the same time, the Roman pope claimed to have inherited both the authority of Jesus and the essential elements of Roman imperial authority.

League of Nations International organization founded after the First World War to solve international disputes through arbitration; it was dissolved in 1946 and its assets were transferred to the United Nations.

Vladimir Lenin (1870–1924) Leader of the Bolshevik Revolution in Russia (1917) and the first leader of the Soviet Union.

Leviathan A book by Thomas Hobbes (1588–1679) that recommended a ruler have unrestricted power.

liberalism Political and social theory that judges the effectiveness of a government in terms of its ability to protect individual rights. Liberals support representative forms of government, free trade, and freedom of speech and religion. In the economic realm, liberals believe that individuals should be free to engage in commercial or business activities without interference from the state or their community.

lithograph Art form that involves putting writing or design on stone and producing printed impressions.

John Locke (1632–1704) English philosopher and political theorist known for his contributions to liberalism. Locke had great faith in human reason, and believed that just societies were those which infringed the least on the natural rights and freedoms of individuals. This led him to assert that a government's legitimacy depended on the consent of the governed, a view that had a profound effect on the authors of the United States' Declaration of Independence.

Louis XIV (1638–1715) Called the "Sun King," he was known for his success at strengthening the institutions of the French absolutist state.

Louis XVI (1754–1793) Well-meaning but ineffectual king of France, finally deposed and executed during the French Revolution.

Ignatius Loyola (1491–1556) Founder of the Society of Jesus (commonly known as the Jesuits), whose members vowed to serve God through poverty, chastity, and missionary work. He abandoned his first career as a mercenary after reading an account of Christ's life written in his native Spanish.

Lucretia According to Roman legend, Lucretia was a virtuous Roman wife who was raped by the son of Rome's last king and who virtuously committed suicide in order to avoid bringing shame on her family.

Luftwaffe Literally "air weapon," this is the name of the German air force, which was founded during the First World War, disbanded in 1945, and reestablished when West Germany joined NATO in 1950.

Lusitania The British passenger liner that was sunk by a German U-boat (submarine) on May 7, 1915. Public outrage over the sinking contibuted to the U.S. decision to enter the First World War.

Martin Luther (1483–1546) A German monk and professor of theology whose critique of the papacy launched the Protestant Reformation.

ma'at The Egyptian term for the serene order of the universe, with which the individual soul (*ka*) must remain in harmony. The power of the pharaoh was linked to ma'at, insofar as it ensured the prosperity of the kingdom. After the upheavals of the First Intermediate Period, the perception of the pharaoh's relationship with ma'at was revealed to be conditional, something that had to be earned.

Niccolo Machiavelli (1469–1527) As the author of *The Prince* and the *Discourses on Livy*, he looked to the Roman past for paradigms of greatness, while at the same time hoping to win the patronage of contemporary rulers who would restore Italy's political independence.

Magna Carta The "Great Charter" of 1215, enacted during the reign of King John of England and designed to limit his powers. Regarded now as a landmark in the development of constitutional government. In its own time, its purpose was to restore the power of great lords.

Magyar nationalism Lajos Kossuth led this national movement in the Hungarian region of the Habsburg Empire, calling for national independence for Hungary in 1848. With the support of Russia, the Habsburg army crushed the movement and all other revolutionary activities in the empire. Kossuth fled into exile.

Moses Maimonides (c. 1137–1204) Jewish scholar, physician, and scriptural commentator whose *Mishneh Torah* is a fundamental exposition of Jewish law.

Thomas Malthus (1766–1834) British political economist who believed that populations inevitably grew faster than the available food supply. Societies that could not control their population growth would be checked only by famine, disease, poverty, and infant malnutrition. He argued that governments could not alleviate poverty. Instead, the poor had to exercise "moral restraint," postpone marriage, and have fewer children.

Nelson Mandela (b. 1918) The South African opponent of apartheid who led the African National Congress and was imprisoned from 1962 until 1990. After his release from prison, he worked with Prime Minister Frederik Willem De Klerk to establish majority rule. Mandela became the first black president of South Africa in 1994.

Manhattan Project The secret U.S. government research project to develop the first nuclear bomb. The vast project involved dozens of sites across the United States, including New Mexico, Tennessee, Illinois, California, Utah, and Washington. The first test of a nuclear bomb was near Alamogordo, New Mexico on July 16, 1945.

manors Common farmland worked collectively by the inhabitants of entire villages, sometimes on their own initiative, sometimes at the behest of a lord.

Mao Zedong (1893–1976) The leader of the Chinese Revolution who defeated the Nationalists in 1949 and established the Communist regime in China.

Marne A major battle of the First World War in September 1914, which halted the German invasion of France and led to protracted trench warfare on the Western Front.

Marshall Plan Economic aid package given to Europe by the United States after the Second World War to promote reconstruction and economic development and to secure the countries from a feared communist takeover.

Karl Marx (1818–1883) German philosopher and economist who believed that a revolution of the working classes would overthrow the capitalist order and create a classless society. Author of *Das Kapital* and *The Communist Manifesto*.

Marxists Followers of the socialist political economist Karl Marx who called for workers everywhere to unite and create an independent political force. Marxists believed that industrialization produced an inevitable struggle between laborers and the class of capitalist property owners, and that this struggle would culminate in a revolution that would abolish private property and establish a society committed to social equality.

Mary; see **cult of the Virgin**.

Mary I (1516–1558) Catholic daughter of Henry VIII and his first wife, Catherine of Aragon, Mary Tudor was the first queen regnant of England. Her attempts to reinstitute Catholicism in England met with limited success, and after her early death she was labeled "Bloody Mary" by the Protestant supporters of her half sister and successor, Elizabeth I.

mass culture The spread of literacy and public education in the nineteenth century created a new audience for print entertainment and a new class of entrepreneurs in the media to cater to this audience. The invention of radio, film, and television in the twentieth century carried this development to another level, as millions of consumers were now accessible to the producers of news, information, and entertainment. The rise of this "mass culture" has been celebrated as an expression of popular tastes but also criticized as a vehicle for the manipulation of populations through clever and seductive propaganda.

Mayans Native American peoples whose culturally and politically sophisticated empire encompassed lands in present-day Mexico and Guatemala.

Giuseppe Mazzini (1805–1872) Founder of Young Italy and an ideological leader of the Italian nationalist movement.

Mecca Center of an important commercial network of the Arabian Peninsula and birthplace of the prophet Muhammad. It is now considered the holiest site in the Islamic world.

Medici A powerful dynasty of Florentine bankers and politicians whose ancestors were originally apothecaries ("medics").

Meiji Empire Empire created under the leadership of Mutsuhito, emperor of Japan from 1868 until 1912. During the Meiji period Japan became a world industrial and naval power.

Mensheviks Within the Russian Social Democratic Party, the Mensheviks advocated slow changes and a gradual move toward socialism, in contrast with the Bolsheviks, who wanted to push for a proletarian revolution. Mensheviks believed that a proletarian revolution in Russia was premature and that the country needed to complete its capitalist development first.

mercantilism A theory and policy for directing the economy of monarchical states between 1600 and 1800 based on the assumption that wealth and power depended on a favorable balance of trade (more exports and fewer imports) and the accumulation of precious metals. Mercantilists advocated forms of economic protectionism to promote domestic production.

Maria Sybilla Merian (1647–1717) A scientific illustrator and an important early entomologist. She conducted research on two continents and published the well-received *Metamorphosis of the Insects of Surinam*.

Merovingian A Frankish dynasty that claimed descent from a legendary ancestor called Merovic, the Merovingians were the only powerful family to establish a lasting kingdom in western Europe during the fifth and sixth centuries.

Mesopotamia The "land between the Tigris and the Euphrates rivers," Tigris and Euphrates where the civilization of Sumer, the first urban society, flourished.

Klemens von Metternich (1773–1859) Austrian foreign minister whose primary goals were to bolster the legitimacy of monarchies and, after the defeat of Napoleon, to prevent another large-scale war in Europe. At the Congress of Vienna, he opposed social and political change and wanted to check Russian and French expansion.

Michelangelo Buonarroti (1475–1564) A virtuoso Florentine sculptor, painter, and poet who spent much of his career in the service of the papacy. He is best known for the decoration of the Sistine Chapel and for his monumental sculptures.

Middle Kingdom of Egypt (2055–1650 B.C.E.) The period following the First Intermediate Period of dynastic warfare, which ended with the reassertion of pharonic rule under Mentuhotep II.

Miletus A Greek polis and Persian colony on the Ionian coast of Asia Minor. Influenced by the cultures of Mesopotamia, Egypt, and Lydia, it produced several of the ancient world's first scientists and sophists. Thereafter, a political conflict between the ruler of Miletus, Aristagoras, and the Persian Emperor, Darius, sparked the Persian Wars with Greece.

John Stuart Mill (1806–1873) English liberal philosopher whose faith in human reason led him to support a broad variety of civic and political freedoms for men and women, including the right to vote and the right to free speech.

Slobodan Milosevic (1941–2006) The Serbian nationalist politician who became president of Serbia and whose policies during the Balkan wars of the early 1990s led to the deaths of thousands of Croatians, Bosnian Muslims, Albanians, and Kosovars. After leaving office in 2000 he was arrested and tried for war crimes at the International Court in The Hague. The trial ended before a verdict with his death in 2006.

Minoan Crete A sea empire based at Knossos on the Greek island of Crete and named for the legendary King Minos. The Minoans dominated the Aegean for much of the second millennium B.C.E.

Modernism There were several different modernist movements in art and literature, but they shared three key characteristics. First, they had a sense that the world had radically changed and that this change should be embraced. Second, they believed that traditional aesthetic values and assumptions about creativity were ill-suited to the present. Third, they developed a new conception of what art could do that emphasized expression over representation and insisted on the value of novelty, experimentation, and creative freedom.

Mongols A nomadic people from the steppes of Central Asia who were united under the ruler Chingiz Khan. His conquest of China was continued by his grandson Kubilai and his great-grandson son Ogedei, whose army also seized southern Russia and then moved through Hungary and through Poland toward eastern Germany. The Mongol armies withdrew from Eastern Europe after the death of Ogedei, but his descendents continued to rule his vast empire for another half century.

Michel de Montaigne (1533–1592) French philosopher and social commentator, best known for his *Essays*.

Montesquieu (1689–1755) An Enlightenment *philosophe* whose most influential work was *The Spirit of Laws*. In this work he analyzed the structures that shaped law and categorized governments into three types: republics, monarchies, and despotisms. His ideas about the separation of powers between the executive, the legislative, and the judicial branches of government influenced the authors of the United States Constitution.

Thomas More (1478–1535) Christian humanist, English statesman, and author of *Utopia*. In 1529, he was appointed Lord Chancellor of England but resigned because he opposed King Henry VIII's plans to establish a national church under royal control. He was eventually executed for refusing to take an oath acknowledging Henry to be the head of the Church of England, and has since been canonized by the Catholic Church.

mos maiorum Literally translated as "the code of the elders" or "the custom of ancestors." This unwritten code governed the lives of Romans under the Republic and stressed the importance of showing reverence to ancestral tradition. It was sacrosanct and essential to Roman identity, and an important influence on Roman culture, law, and religion.

Wolfgang Amadeus Mozart (1756–1791) Austrian composer, famous at a young age as a concert musician and later celebrated as a prolific composer of instrumental music and operas that are seen as the apogee of the Classical style in music.

Muhammad (570–632 C.E.) The founder of Islam, regarded as God's last and greatest prophet by his followers.

Munich Conference (1938) Hitler met with the leaders of Britain, France, and Italy and negotiated an agreement that gave Germany a major slice of Czechoslovakia. British prime minister Chamberlain believed that the agreement would bring peace to Europe. Instead, Germany invaded and seized the rest of Czechoslovakia.

Muscovy The duchy centered on Moscow whose dukes saw themselves as heirs to the Roman Empire. In the early fourteenth century, Moscow was under the control of the Mongol Khanate. After the collapse of the Khanate, the Muscovite grand duke, Ivan III, conquered all the Russian principalities between Moscow and the border of Poland-Lithuania, and then Lithuania itself. By the time of his death, Ivan had established Muscovy as a dominant power.

Muslim learning and culture The Crusades brought the Latin West in contact with the Islamic world, which impacted European culture in myriad ways. Europeans adapted Arabic numerals and mathematical concepts as well as Arabic and Persian words. Through Arabic translations, western scholars gained access to Greek learning, which had a profound influence on Christian theology. European scholars also learned from the Islamic world's accomplishments in medicine and science.

Benito Mussolini (1883–1945) The Italian founder of the Fascist party who came to power in Italy in 1922 and allied himself with Hitler and the Nazis during the Second World War.

Mycenaean Greece (1600–1200 B.C.E.) The term used to describe the civilization of Greece in the late Bronze Age, when territorial kingdoms like Mycenae formed around a king, a warrior caste, and a palace bureaucracy.

Nagasaki Second Japanese city on which the United States dropped an atomic bomb. The attack took place on August 9, 1945; the Japanese surrendered shortly thereafter, ending the Second World War.

Napoleon III (1808–1873) Nephew of Napoleon Bonaparte, Napoleon III was elected president of the French Second Republic in 1848 and made himself emperor of France in 1852. During his reign (1852–70), he rebuilt the French capital of Paris. Defeated in the France-Prussian War of 1870, he went into exile.

Napoleonic Code Legal code drafted by Napoleon in 1804 and based on Justinian's *Corpus Iuris Civilis*. It distilled different legal traditions to create one uniform law. The code confirmed the abolition of feudal privileges of all kinds and set the conditions for exercising property rights.

Napoleon's military campaigns In 1805, the Russians, Prussians, Austrians, Swedes, and British attempted to contain Napoleon, but he defeated them. Out of his victories, Napoleon created a new empire and affiliated states. In 1808, he invaded Spain, but fierce resistance prevented Napoleon from achieving a complete victory. In 1812, Napoleon invaded Russia, and his army was decimated as it retreated from Moscow during the winter. After the Russian campaign, the united European powers defeated Napoleon and forced him into exile. He escaped and reassumed command of his army, but the European powers defeated him for the final time at the Battle of Waterloo.

Gamal Abdel Nasser (1918–1970) Former president of Egypt and the most prominent spokesman for secular pan-Arabism. He became a target for Islamist critics, such as Sayyid Qutb and the Muslim Brotherhood, angered by the Western-influenced policies of his regime.

National Assembly of France Governing body of France that succeeded the Estates-General in 1789 during the French Revolution. It was composed of, and defined by, the delegates of the Third Estate.

National Association for the Advancement of Colored People (NAACP) Founded in 1910, this U.S. civil rights organization was dedicated to ending inequality and segregation for black Americans.

National Convention The governing body of France from September 1792 to October 1795. It declared France a republic and then tried and executed the French king. The Convention also confiscated the property of the enemies of the revolution, instituted a policy of de-Christianization, changed marriage and inheritance laws, abolished slavery in its colonies, placed a cap on the price of necessities, and ended the compensation of nobles for their lost privileges.

nationalism Movement to unify a country under one government based on perceptions of the population's common history, customs, and social traditions.

nationalism in Yugoslavia In the 1990s, Slobodan Milosevic and his allies reignited Serbian nationalism in the former Yugoslavia, which led non-Serb republics in Croatia and Slovenia to seek independence. The country erupted into war, with the worst violence taking place in Bosnia, a multi-ethnic region with Serb, Croatian and Bosnian Muslim populations. European diplomats proved powerless to stop attempts by Croatian and Serbian military and paramilitary forces to claim territory through ethnic cleansing and violent intimidation. Atrocities were committed on all sides, but pro-Serb forces were responsible for the most deaths.

NATO The North Atlantic Treaty Organization, a 1949 military agreement between the United States, Canada, Great Britain, and eight Western European nations, which declared that an armed attack against any one of the members would be regarded as an attack against all. Created during the Cold War in the face of the Soviet Union's control of Eastern Europe, NATO continues to exist today and the membership of twenty-eight states includes former members of the Warsaw Pact as well as Albania and Turkey.

Nazi party Founded in the early 1920s, the National Socialist German Workers' Party (NSDAP) gained control over Germany under the leadership of Adolf Hitler in 1933 and continued in power until Germany was defeated in 1945.

Nazism The political movement in Germany led by Adolf Hitler, which advocated a violent anti-Semitic, anti-Marxist, pan-German ideology.

Neo-Assyrian Empire (883–859 B.C.E.–612–605 B.C.E.) Assurnasirpal II laid the foundations of the Neo-Assyrian Empire through military campaigns against neighboring peoples. Eventually, the empire stretched from the Mediterranean Sea to Western Iran. A military dictatorship governed the empire through its army, which it used to frighten and oppress both its subjects and its enemies. The empire's ideology was based on waging holy war in the name of its principal god, Assur, and the exaction of tribute through terror.

Neoliberalism Neoliberals believe that free markets, profit incentives, and restraints on both budget deficits and social welfare programs are the best guarantee of individual liberties. Beginning in the 1980s, neoliberal theory was used to structure the policy of financial institutions like the International Monetary Fund and the World Bank, which turned away from interventionist policies in favor of market-driven models of economic development.

Neolithic Revolution The "New" Stone Age, which began around 11,000 B.C.E., saw new technological and social developments, including managed food production, the beginnings of permanent settlements, and the rapid intensification of trade.

Neoplatonism A school of thought based on the teachings of Plato and prevalent in the Roman Empire, which had a profound effect on the formation of Christian theology. Neoplatonists argued that nature is a book written by its creator to reveal the ways of God to humanity. Convinced that God's perfection must be reflected in nature, neoplatonists searched for the ideal and perfect structures that they believed must lie behind the "shadows" of the everyday world.

New Deal President Franklin Delano Roosevelt's package of government reforms that were enacted during the depression of the 1930s to provide jobs for the unemployed, social welfare programs for the poor, and security to the financial markets.

New Economic Policy In 1921, the Bolsheviks abandoned war communism in favor of the New Economic Policy (NEP). Under NEP, the state still controlled all major industry and financial concerns, while individuals could own private property, trade freely within limits, and farm their own land for their own benefit. Fixed taxes replaced grain requisition. The policy successfully helped Soviet agriculture recover from the civil war, but was later abandoned in favor of collectivization.

Isaac Newton (1642–1727) One of the foremost scientists of all time, Newton was an English mathematician and physicist; he is noted for his development of calculus, work on the properties of light, and theory of gravitation.

Tsar Nicholas II (1868–1918) The last Russian tsar, who abdicated the throne in 1917. He and his family were executed by the Bolsheviks on July 17, 1918.

Friedrich Nietzsche (1844–1900) The German philosopher who denied the possibility of knowing absolute "truth" or "reality," since all knowledge comes filtered through linguistic, scientific, or artistic systems of representation. He also criticized Judeo-Christian morality for instilling a repressive conformity that drained civilization of its vitality.

nongovernmental organizations (NGOs) Private organizations like the Red Cross that play a large role in international affairs.

North American Free Trade Agreement (NAFTA) Treaty negotiated in the early 1990s to promote free trade among Canada, the United States, and Mexico.

Novum Organum Work by English statesman and scientist Francis Bacon (1561–1626) that advanced a philosophy of study through observation.

October Days (1789) The high price of bread and the rumor that the king was unwilling to cooperate with the assembly caused the women who worked in Paris's large central market to march to Versailles along with their supporters to address the king. Not satisfied with their initial reception, they broke through the palace gates and called for the king to return to Paris from Versailles, which he did the following day.

Old Kingdom of Egypt (c. 2686–2160 B.C.E.) During this time, the pharaohs controlled a powerful and centralized bureaucratic state whose vast human and material resources are exemplified by the pyramids of Giza. This period came to an end as the pharaoh's authority collapsed, leading to a period of dynastic warfare and localized rule.

OPEC (Organization of the Petroleum Exporting Countries) Organization created in 1960 by oil-producing countries in the Middle East, South America, and Africa to regulate the production and pricing of crude oil.

Operation Barbarossa The codename for Hitler's invasion of the Soviet Union in 1941.

Opium Wars (1839–1842) War fought between the British and Qing China to protect British trade in opium; resulted in the ceding of Hong Kong to the British.

Oracle at Delphi The most important shrine in ancient Greece. The priestess of Apollo who attended the shrine was believed to have the power to predict the future.

Ottoman Empire (c.1300–1923) During the thirteenth century, the Ottoman dynasty established itself as leader of the Turks. From the fourteenth to sixteenth centuries, they conquered Anatolia, Armenia, Syria, and North Africa as well as parts of southeastern Europe, the Crimea, and areas along the Red Sea. Portions of the Ottoman Empire persisted up to the time of the First World War, but it was dismantled in the years following it.

Reza Pahlavi (1919–1980) The Western-friendly Shah of Iran who was installed during a 1953 coup supported by Britain and the United States. After a lengthy economic downturn, public unrest, and personal illness, he retired from public life under popular pressure in 1979.

Pan-African Conference 1900 assembly in London that sought to draw attention to the sovereignty of African people and their mistreatment by colonial powers.

Panhellenism The "all Greek" culture that allowed ancient Greek colonies to maintain a connection to their homeland and to each other through their shared language and heritage. These colonies also exported their culture into new areas and created new Greek-speaking enclaves, which permanently changed the cultural geography of the Mediterranean world.

pan-Slavism Cultural movement that sought to unite native Slavic peoples within the Russian and Habsburg empires under Russian leadership.

Partition of India (1947) At independence, British India was partitioned into the nations of India and Pakistan. The majority of the population in India was Hindu and the majority of the population in Pakistan was Muslim. The process of partition brought brutal religious and ethnic warfare. More than one million Hindus and Muslims died and twelve million became refugees.

Blaise Pascal (1623–1662) A Catholic philosopher who wanted to establish the truth of Christianity by appealing simultaneously to intellect and emotion. In his *Pensées*, he argued that faith alone can resolve the world's contradictions and that his own awe in the face of evil and uncertainty must be evidence of God's existence.

Paul of Tarsus Originally known as Saul, Paul was a Greek-speaking Jew and Roman citizen who underwent a miraculous conversion experience and became the most important proponent of Christianity in the 50s and 60s C.E.

Pax Romana (27 B.C.E.–180 C.E.) Literally translated as "the Roman Peace." During this time, the Roman world enjoyed an unprecedented period of peace and political stability.

Peace of Augsburg A settlement negotiated in 1555 among factions within the Holy Roman Empire, it formulated the principle *cuius regio, eius religio*, "he who rules, his religion": meaning that the inhabitants of any given territory should follow the religion of its ruler, whether Catholic or Protestant.

Peace of Paris The 1919 Paris Peace Conference established the terms to end the First World War. Great Britain, France, Italy, and the United States signed five treaties with each of the defeated nations: Germany, Austria, Hungary, Turkey, and Bulgaria. The settlement is notable for the territory that Germany had to give up, including large parts of Prussia to the new state of Poland, and Alsace and Lorraine to France; the disarming of Germany; and the "war guilt" provision, which required Germany and its allies to pay massive reparations to the victors.

Peace of Westphalia (1648) An agreement reached at the end of the Thirty Years' War that altered the political map of Europe. France emerged as the predominant power on the Continent, while the Austrian Habsburgs had to surrender all the territories they had gained and could no longer use the office of the Holy Roman Emperor to dominate central Europe. Spain was marginalized and Germany became a volatile combination of Protestant and Catholic principalities.

Pearl Harbor The American naval base in Hawaii that was bombed by the Japanese on December 7, 1941, bringing the United States into the Second World War.

peasantry Term used in continental Europe to refer to rural populations that lived from agriculture. Some peasants were free, and could own land. Serfs were peasants who were legally bound to the land, and subject to the authority of the local lord.

Peloponnesian War The name given to the series of wars fought between Sparta (on the Greek Peloponnesus) and Athens from 431 B.C.E. to 404 B.C.E., and which ended in the defeat of Athens and the loss of her imperial power.

perestroika Introduced by Soviet leader Mikhail Gorbachev in June 1987, perestroika was the name given to economic and political reforms begun earlier in his tenure. It restructured the state bureaucracy, reduced the privileges of the political elite, and instituted a shift from the centrally planned economy to a mixed economy, combining planning with the operation of market forces.

Periclean Athens Following his election as *strategos* in 461 B.C.E., Pericles pushed through political reforms in Athens, which gave poorer citizens greater influence in politics. He promoted Athenians' sense of superiority through ambitious public works projects and lavish festivals to honor the gods, thus ensuring his continual reelection. But eventually, Athens' growing arrogance and aggression alienated it from the rest of the Greek world.

Pericles (c. 495–429) Athenian politician who occupied the office of strategos for thirty years and who presided over a series of civic reforms, building campaigns, and imperialist initiatives.

Persian Empire Consolidated by Cyrus the Great in 559, this empire eventually stretched from the Persian Gulf to the Mediterranean, and also encompassed Egypt. Persian rulers were able to hold this empire together through a policy of tolerance and a mixture of local and centralized governance. This imperial model of government would be adopted by many future empires.

Persian Wars (490–479 B.C.E.) In 501 B.C.E., a political conflict between the Greek ruler of Miletus, Aristagoras, and the Persian Emperor, Darius, sparked the first of the Persian Wars when Darius sent an army to punish Athens for its intervention on the side of the Greeks. Despite being heavily outnumbered, Athenian hoplites defeated the Persian army at the plain of Marathon. In 480 B.C.E., Darius' son Xerxes invaded Greece but was defeated at sea and on land by combined Greek forces under the leadership of Athens and Sparta.

Peter the Great (1672–1725) Energetic tsar who transformed Russia into a leading European country by centralizing government, modernizing the army, creating a navy, and reforming education and the economy.

Francesco Petrarca (Petrarch) (1304–1374) Italian scholar who revived interest in classical writing styles and was famed for his vernacular love sonnets.

pharaoh A term meaning "household" which became the title borne by the rulers of ancient Egypt. The pharaoh was regarded as the divine representative of the gods and the embodiment of Egypt itself. The powerful and centralized bureaucratic state ruled by the pharaohs was more stable and long-lived than any another civilization in world history, lasting (with few interruptions) for approximately three thousand years.

Pharisees A group of Jewish teachers and preachers that emerged in the third century B.C.E. They insisted that all of Yahweh's (God's) commandments were binding on all Jews.

Philip II (382–336 B.C.E.) King of Macedonia and father of Alexander, he consolidated the southern Balkans and the Greek city-states under Macedonian domination.

Philip II Augustus (1165–1223) The first French ruler to use the title "king of France" rather than "king of the French." After he captured Normandy and its adjacent territories from the English, he built an effective system of local administration, which recognized regional diversity while promoting centralized royal control. This administrative pattern would characterize French government until the French Revolution.

Philistines Descendants of the Sea Peoples who fled to the region that now bears their name, Palestine, after their defeat at the hands of the pharaoh Ramses III. They dominated their neighbors, the Hebrews, who used writing as an effective means of discrediting them (the Philistines themselves did not leave a written record to contest the Hebrews' views).

philosophe During the Enlightenment, this word referred to a person whose reflections were unhampered by the constraints of religion or dogma.

Phoenicians A Semitic people known for their trade in exotic purple dyes and other luxury goods, they originally settled in present-day Lebanon around 1200 B.C.E. and from there established commercial colonies throughout the Mediterranean, notably Carthage.

Plato (429–349 B.C.E.) A student of Socrates, Plato dedicated his life to transmitting his teacher's legacy through the writing of dialogues on philosophical subjects, in which Socrates himself plays the major role. The longest and most famous of these, known as the *Republic*, describes an idealized polis governed by a superior group of individuals chosen for their natural attributes of intelligence and character, who rule as "philosopher-kings."

Plotinus (204–270 C.E.) A Neoplatonist philosopher who taught that everything in existence has its ultimate source in the divine, and that the highest goal of life should be the mystic reunion of the soul with this divine source, something that can be achieved through contemplation and asceticism. This outlook blended with that of early Christianity and was instrumental in the spread of that religion within the Roman Empire.

poleis One of the major political innovations of the ancient Greeks was the *polis*, or city-state (plural *poleis*). These independent social and political entities began to emerge in the ninth century B.C.E., organized around an urban center and fostering markets, meeting places, and religious worship; frequently, poleis also controlled some surrounding territory.

Marco Polo (1254–1324) Venetian merchant who traveled through Asia for twenty years and published his observations in a widely read memoir.

population growth In the nineteenth century, Europe experienced a dramatic population growth. During this period, the spread of rural manufacturing allowed men and women to begin marrying younger and raising families earlier, which increased the size of the average family. As the population grew, the portion of young and fertile people also increased, which reinforced the population growth. By 1900, population growth was strongest in Britain and Germany, and slower in France.

Potsdam (1945) At this conference, Truman, Churchill and Stalin met to discuss their options at the conclusion of the Second World War, including making territorial changes to Germany and its allies and the question of war reparations.

Prague spring A period of political liberalization in Czechoslovakia between January and August 1968 that was initiated by Alexander Dubček, the Czech leader. This period of expanding freedom and openness in this Eastern bloc nation ended on August 20, when the USSR and Warsaw Pact countries invaded with 200,000 troops and 5,000 tanks.

pre-Socratics A group of philosophers in the Greek city of Miletus, who raised questions about humans' relationship with the natural world and the gods, and who formulated rational theories to explain the physical universe they observed. Their name reflects the fact that they flourished prior to the lifetime of Socrates.

Price Revolution An unprecedented inflation in prices in the latter half of the sixteenth century, resulting in part from the enormous influx of silver bullion from Spanish America.

Principate Modern term for the centuries of autocratic rule by the successors of Augustus, who seized power in 27 B.C.E. and styled himself *princeps* or Rome's "first man." See **Roman Republic**.

Protestantism The name given to the many dissenting varieties of Christianity that emerged during the Reformation in sixteenth-century western Europe. While Protestant beliefs and practices differed widely, all were united in their rejection of papal authority and the dogmas of the Roman Catholic Church.

Provisional Government After the collapse of the Russian monarchy, leaders in the Duma organized this government and hoped to establish a democratic system under constitutional rule. They also refused to concede military defeat, and it was impossible to institute domestic reforms and fight a war at the same time. As conditions worsened, the Bolsheviks gained support. In October 1917, they attacked the provisional government and seized control.

Claudius Ptolomeus, called Ptolemy (c. 85–165 C.E.) A Greek-speaking geographer and astronomer active in Roman Alexandria, he rejected the findings of previous Hellenistic scientists in favor of the erroneous theories of Aristotle, publishing highly influential treatises that promulgated these errors and suppressed (for example) the accurate findings of Aristarchus (who had discovered the Heliocentric universe) and Erathosthenes (who had calculated the circumference of the earth).

Ptolemaic system Ptolemy of Alexandria promoted Aristotle's understanding of cosmology. In this system, the heavens orbit the earth in an organized hierarchy of spheres, and the earth and the heavens are made of different matter and subject to different laws of motion. A prime mover produces the motion of the celestial bodies.

Ptolemy (c. 367–c. 284 B.C.E.) One of Alexander the Great's trusted generals (and possibly his half brother), he became pharaoh of Egypt and founded a new dynasty that lasted until that kingdom's absorption into the Roman Empire in 30 B.C.E.

Punic Wars (264–146 B.C.E.) Three periods of warfare between Rome and Carthage, two maritime empires who struggled for dominance of the Mediterranean. Rome emerged as the victor, destroyed the city of Carthage and took control of Sicily, North Africa and Hispania (Spain).

pyramid Constructed during the third millennium B.C.E., these structures were monuments to the power and divinity of the pharaohs entombed inside them.

Qu'ran (often Koran) Islam's holy scriptures, comprised of the prophecies revealed to Muhammad and redacted during and after his death.

Raphael (Raffaelo Sarazio) (1483–1520) Italian painter active in Rome, his works include *The School of Athens*.

realism Artistic and literary style which sought to portray common situations as they would appear in reality.

Realpolitik Political strategy based on advancing power for its own sake.

reason The human capacity to solve problems and discover truth in ways that can be verified intellectually. Philosophers distinguish the knowledge gained from reason from the teachings of instinct, imagination, and faith, which are verified according to different criteria.

Reformation Religious and political movement in sixteenth-century Europe that led to a break between dissenting forms of Christianity and the Roman Catholic Church; notable figures include Martin Luther and John Calvin.

Reich A term for the German state. The First Reich corresponded to the Holy Roman Empire (9th c.–1806), the Second Reich was from 1871 to 1919, and the Third Reich lasted from 1933 through May 1945.

Renaissance From the French word "rebirth," this term came to be used in the nineteenth century to describe the artistic, intellectual, and cultural movement that emerged in Italy after 1300, and which sought to recover and emulate the heritage of the classical past.

Restoration period (1815–1848) European movement after the defeat of Napoleon to restore Europe to its pre–French Revolution status and to prevent the spread of revolutionary or liberal political movements.

Cardinal Richelieu (1585–1642) First minister to King Louis XIII, he is considered by many to have ruled France in all but name, centralizing political power and suppressing dissent.

Roman army Under the Republic, the Roman army was made up of citizen-soldiers who were required to serve in wartime. As Rome's empire grew, the need for more fighting men led to the extension of citizenship rights and, eventually, to the development of a vast, professional, standing army that numbered as many as 300,000 by the middle of the third century B.C.E. By that time, however, citizens were not themselves required to serve, and many legions were made up of paid conscripts and foreign mercenaries.

Roman citizenship The rights and responsibilities of Rome's citizens were gradually extended to the free (male) inhabitants of other Italian provinces and later to most provinces in the Roman world. In contrast to slaves and non-Romans, Romans had the right to be tried in an imperial court and could not be legally subjected to torture.

Roman Republic The Romans traced the founding of their republic to the overthrow of their last king and the establishment of a unique form of constitutional government, in which the power of the aristocracy (embodied by the Senate) was checked by the executive rule of two elected consuls and the collective will of the people. For hundreds of years, this balance of power provided the Republic with a measure of political stability and prevented any single individual or clique from gaining too much power.

Romanticism Beginning in Germany and England in the late eighteenth century and continuing up to the end of the nineteenth century, Romanticism was a movement in art, music, and literature that countered the rationalism of the Enlightenment by placing greater value on human emotions and the power of nature to stimulate creativity.

Jean-Jacques Rousseau (1712–1778) Philosopher and radical political theorist whose *Social Contract* attacked privilege and inequality. One of the primary principles of Rousseau's political philosophy is that politics and morality should not be separated.

Royal Society This British society's goal was to pursue collective research. Members would conduct experiments, record the results, and share them with their peers, who would study the methods, reproduce the experiment, and assess the results.

The arrangement gave English scientists a sense of common purpose as well as a system to reach a consensus on facts.

Russian Revolution of 1905 After Russia's defeat in the Russo-Japanese War, Russians began clamoring for political reforms. Protests grew over the course of 1905, and the autocracy lost control of entire towns and regions as workers went on strike, soldiers mutinied, and peasants revolted. Forced to yield, Tsar Nicholas II issued the October Manifesto, which pledged individual liberties and provided for the election of a parliament (called the Duma). The most radical of the revolutionary groups were put down with force, and the pace of political change remained very slow in the aftermath of the revolution.

Russo-Japanese War (1904–1905) Japanese and Russian expansion collided in Mongolia and Manchuria. Russia was humiliated after the Japanese navy sunk its fleet, which helped provoke a revolt in Russia and led to an American-brokered peace treaty.

Saint Bartholomew's Day Massacre The mass murder of French Protestants (Huguenots) instigated by Queen Catherine de' Medici of France and carried out by Catholics. It began in Paris on 24 August 1572 and spread to other parts of France, continuing into October of that year. More than 70,000 people were killed.

salons Informal gatherings of intellectuals and aristocrats that allowed discourse about Enlightenment ideas.

Sappho (c. 620–c. 550 B.C.E.) One of the most celebrated Greek poets, she was revered as "the Tenth Muse" and emulated by many male poets. Ironically, though, only two of her poems survive intact, and the rest must be pieced together from fragments quoted by later poets.

Sargon the Great (r. 2334–2279 B.C.E.) The Akkadian ruler who consolidated power in Mesopotamia.

SARS epidemic (2003) The successful containment of severe acute respiratory syndrome (SARS) is an example of how international health organizations can effectively work together to recognize and respond to a disease outbreak. The disease itself, however, is a reminder of the dangers that exist in a globalized economy with a high degree of mobility in both populations and goods.

Schlieffen Plan Devised by German general Alfred von Schlieffen in 1905 to avoid the dilemma of a two-front war against France and Russia. The Schlieffen Plan required that Germany attack France first through Belgium and secure a quick victory before wheeling to the east to meet the slower armies of the Russians on the Eastern Front. The Schlieffen Plan was put into operation on August 2, 1914, at the outset of the First World War.

Scientific Revolution of Antiquity The Hellenistic period was the most brilliant age in the history of science before the seventeenth century C.E. Aristarchus of Samos posited the existence of a heliocentric universe. Eratosthenes of Alexandria accurately calculated the circumference of the earth. Archimedes turned physics into its own branch of experimental science. Hellenistic anatomists became the first to practice human dissection, which improved their understanding of human physiology. Ironically, most of these discoveries were suppressed by pseudo-scientists who flourished under the Roman Empire during the second century C.E., notably Claudus Ptolomeus Ptolemy) and Aelius Galenus (Galen).

second industrial revolution The technological developments in the last third of the nineteenth century, which included new techniques for refining and producing steel; increased availability of electricity for industrial, commercial, and domestic use; advances in chemical manufacturing; and the creation of the internal combustion engine.

Second World War Worldwide war that began in September 1939 in Europe, and even earlier in Asia (the Japanese invasion of Manchuria began in 1931), pitting Britain, the United States, and the Soviet Union (the Allies) against Nazi Germany, Italy, and Japan (the Axis). The war ended in 1945 with Germany and Japan's defeat.

Seleucus (d. 280 B.C.E.) The Macedonian general who ruled the Persian heartland of Alexander the Great's empire.

Semitic The Semitic language family has the longest recorded history of any linguistic group and is the root for most languages of the Middle and Near East. Ancient Semitic languages include those of the ancient Babylonians and Assyrians, Phoenician, the classical form of Hebrew, early dialects of Aramaic, and the classical Arabic of the Qu'ran.

Sepoy Mutiny of 1857 See **Indian Rebellion of 1857**.

serf An unfree peasant laborer. Unlike slaves, serfs are "attached" to the land they work, and are not supposed to be sold apart from that land.

William Shakespeare (1564–1616) An English playwright who flourished during the reigns of Elizabeth I and James I, Shakespeare received a basic education in his hometown of Stratford-upon-Avon and worked in London as an actor before achieving success as a dramatist and poet.

Shi'ites An often-persecuted minority within Islam, Shi'ites believe that only descendants of Muhammad's successor Ali and his wife Fatimah (Muhammad's daughter) can have any authority over the Muslim community. Today, Shi'ites constitute the ruling party in Iran and are numerous in Iraq, but otherwise comprise only 10 percent of Muslims worldwide.

Abbé Sieyès (1748–1836) In 1789, he wrote the pamphlet "What is the Third Estate?" in which he posed fundamental questions about the rights of the Third Estate and helped provoke its secession from the Estates-General. He was a leader at the Tennis Court Oath, but he later helped Napoleon seize power.

Sinn Féin The Irish revolutionary organization that formed in 1900 to fight for Irish independence.

Sino-Japanese War (1894–1895) Conflict over the control of Korea in which China was forced to cede the province of Taiwan to Japan.

slave revolt in Saint-Domingue (1791–1804) In September of 1791, the largest slave rebellion in history broke out in Saint-Domingue, an important French colony in the Caribbean. In 1794, the revolutionary government in France abolished slavery in the colonies, though this act was essentially only recognizing the liberty that the slaves had seized by their own actions. Napoleon reestablished slavery in the French Caribbean in 1802, but failed in his attempt to reconquer Saint-Domingue. Armies commanded by former slaves succeeded in winning independence for a new nation, Haiti, in 1804, making the revolt in Saint-Domingue the first successful slave revolt in history.

slavery The practice of subjugating people to a life of bondage, and of selling or trading these unfree people. For most of human history, slavery had no racial or ethnic basis, and was widely practiced by all cultures and civilizations. Anyone could become a slave, for example, by being captured in war or by being sold for the payment of a debt. It was only in the fifteenth century, with the growth of the African slave trade, that slavery came to be associated with particular races and peoples.

Adam Smith (1723–1790) Scottish economist and liberal philosopher who proposed that competition between self-interested individuals led naturally to a healthy economy. He became famous for his influential book, *The Wealth of Nations* (1776).

Social Darwinism Belief that Charles Darwin's theory of natural selection (evolution) was applicable to human societies and justified the right of the ruling classes or countries to dominate the weak.

social democracy The belief that democracy and social welfare go hand in hand, and that diminishing the sharp inequalities of class society is crucial to fortifying democratic culture.

socialism Political ideology that calls for a classless society with collective ownership of all property.

Society of Jesus; see **Jesuits**.

Socrates (469–399 B.C.E.) The Athenian philosopher and teacher who promoted the careful examination of all inherited opinions and assumptions on the grounds that "the unexamined life is not worth living." A veteran of the Peloponnesian War, he was tried and condemned by his fellow citizens for engaging in allegedly seditious activities, and was executed in 399 B.C.E. His most influential pupils were the philosopher Plato and the historian and social commentator Xenophon.

Solon (d. 559 B.C.E.) Elected archon in 594 B.C.E., this Athenian aristocrat enacted a series of political and economic reforms that formed the basis of Athenian democracy.

Somme (1916) During this battle of the First World War, Allied forces attempted to take entrenched German positions from July to mid-November of 1916. Neither side was able to make any real gains despite massive casualties: 500,000 Germans, 400,000 British, and 200,000 French.

Soviet bloc International alliance that included the East European countries of the Warsaw Pact as well as the Soviet Union; it also came to include Cuba.

soviets Local councils elected by workers and soldiers in Russia. Socialists started organizing these councils in 1905, and the Petrograd soviet in the capital emerged as one of the centers of power after the Russian monarchy collapsed in 1917 in the midst of World War I. The soviets became increasingly powerful and pressed for social reform, the redistribution of land, and called for Russian withdrawal from the war effort.

Spanish-American War (1898) War between the United States and Spain in Cuba, Puerto Rico, and the Philippines. It ended with a treaty in which the United States took over the Philippines, Guam, and Puerto Rico; Cuba won partial independence.

Spanish Armada Supposedly invincible fleet of warships sent against England by Philip II of Spain in 1588 but vanquished by the English fleet and bad weather in the English Channel.

Sparta Around 650 B.C.E., after the suppression of a slave revolt, Spartan rulers militarized their society in order to prevent future rebellions and to protect Sparta's superior position in Greece, orienting their society toward the maintenance of their army. Sparta briefly joined forces with Athens and other poleis in the second war with Persia in 480–479 B.C.E., but these two rivals ultimately fell out again in 431 B.C.E., when Sparta and her Peloponnesian allies went to war against Athens and her allies. This bloody conflict lasted until Athens was defeated in 404 B.C.E., after Sparta received military aid from the Persians.

Spartiate A full citizen of Sparta, hence a professional soldier of the hoplite phalanx.

spinning jenny Invention of James Hargreaves (c. 1720–1774) that revolutionized the British textile industry by allowing a worker to spin much more thread than was possible on a hand spinner.

SS (Schutzstaffel) Formed in 1925 to serve as Hitler's personal security force and to guard Nazi party (NSDAP) meetings, the SS grew into a large militarized organization that became notorious for their participation in carrying out Nazi policies.

Joseph Stalin (1879–1953) The Bolshevik leader who succeeded Lenin as the leader of the Soviet Union and ruled until his death in 1953.

Stalingrad (1942–1943) The turning point on the Eastern Front during the Second World War came when the German army tried to take the city of Stalingrad in an effort to break the back of Soviet industry. The German and Soviet armies fought a bitter battle, in which more than half a million German, Italian, and Romanian soldiers were killed and the Soviets suffered over a million casualties. The German army surrendered after over five months of fighting. After Stalingrad, the Soviet army launched a series of attacks that pushed the Germans back.

Stoicism An ancient philosophy derived from the teachings of Zeno of Athens (fl. c. 300) and widely influential within the Roman Empire; it also impacted the development of Christianity. Stoics believe in the essential orderliness of the cosmos, and that everything that occurs happens for the best. Since everything is determined in accordance with rational purpose, no individual is master of his or her fate, and the only agency that human beings have consists in their responses to good fortune or adversity.

Sumerians The ancient inhabitants of southern Mesopotamia (modern Iraq and Kuwait) whose sophisticated civilization emerged around 4000 B.C.E.

Sunnis Proponents of Islam's customary religious practices (*sunna*) as they developed under the first two caliphs to succeed Muhammad, his father-in-law Abu-Bakr and his disciple Umar. Sunni orthodoxy is dominant within Islam, but is opposed by the Shi'ites (from the Arabic word *shi'a*, "faction").

Syndicalists A nineteenth century political movement that embraced a strategy of strikes and sabotage by workers. Their hope was that a general strike of all workers would bring down the capitalist state and replace it with workers' syndicates or trade associations. Their refusal to participate in politics limited their ability to command a wide influence.

tabula rasa Term used by John Locke (1632–1704) to describe man's mind before he acquired ideas as a result of experience; Latin for "clean slate."

Tennis Court Oath (1789) Oath taken by representatives of the Third Estate in June, 1789, in which they pledged to form a National Assembly and write a constitution limiting the powers of the king.

Reign of Terror (1793–1794) Campaign at the height of the French Revolution in which violence, including systematic executions of opponents of the revolution, was used to purge France of its "enemies" and to extend the revolution beyond its borders; radicals executed as many as 40,000 persons who were judged enemies of the state.

Tetrarchy The result of Diocletian's political reforms of the late third century C.E., which divided the Roman Empire into four quadrants.

Theban Hegemony The term describing the period when the polis of Thebes dominated the Greek mainland, which reached its height after 371 B.C.E., under leadership of the Theban general Epaminondas. It was in Thebes that the future King Philip II of Macedon spent his youth, and it was the defeat of Thebes and Athens at the hands of Philip and Alexander—at the Battle of Chaeronea in 338—that Macedonian hegemony was forcefully asserted.

theory of evolution Darwin's theory that linked biology to history. Darwin believed that competition between different organisms and struggle with the environment were fundamental and unavoidable facts of life. In this struggle, those individuals who were better adapted to their environment survived, while the weak perished. This produced a "natural selection," or favoring of certain adaptive traits over time, leading to a gradual evolution of different species.

Third Estate The population of France under the Old Regime was divided into three estates, corporate bodies that determined an individual's rights or obligations under royal law. The nobility constituted the First Estate, the clergy the Second, and the commoners (the vast bulk of the population) made up the Third Estate.

Third Reich The German state from 1933 to 1945 under Adolf Hitler and the Nazi party.

Third World Nations—mostly in Asia, Latin America, and Africa—that are not highly industrialized.

Thirty Years' War (1618–1648) Beginning as a conflict between Protestants and Catholics in Germany, this series of skirmishes escalated into a general European war fought on German soil by armies from Sweden, France, and the Holy Roman Empire.

Timur the Lame (1336–1405) Also known as Tamerlane, he was the last ruler of the Mongol Khans' Asian empire.

Marshal Tito (1892–1980) The Yugoslavian communist and resistance leader who became the leader of Yugoslavia and fought to keep his government independent of the Soviet Union. In response, the Soviet Union expelled Yugoslavia from the communist countries' economic and military pacts.

towns Centers for markets and administration. Towns existed in a symbiotic relationship with the countryside. They provided markets for surplus food from outlying farms as well as producing manufactured goods. In the Middle Ages, towns tended to grow up around a castle or monastery which afforded protection.

Treaty of Brest-Litovsk (1918) Separate peace between imperial Germany and the new Bolshevik regime in Russia. The treaty acknowledged the German victory on the Eastern Front and withdrew Russia from the war.

Treaty of Utrecht (1713) Resolution to the War of Spanish Succession that reestablished a balance of power in Europe, to the benefit of Britain and in ways that disadvantaged Spain, Holland, and France.

Treaty of Versailles Signed on June 28, 1919, this peace settlement ended the First World War and required Germany to surrender a large part of its most valuable territories and to pay huge reparations to the Allies.

trench warfare Weapons such as barbed wire and the machine gun gave tremendous advantage to defensive positions in World War I, leading to prolonged battles between entrenched armies in fixed positions. The trenches eventually consisted of twenty-five thousand miles of holes and ditches that stretched across the Western Front in northern France, from the Atlantic cost to the Swiss border during the First World War, On the eastern front, the large expanse of territories made trench warfare less significant.

triangular trade The eighteenth-century commercial Atlantic shipping pattern that took rum from New England to Africa, traded it for slaves taken to the West Indies, and brought sugar back to New England to be processed into rum.

Triple Entente Alliance developed before the First World War that eventually included Britain, France, and Russia.

Truman Doctrine (1947) Declaration promising U.S. economic and military intervention to counter any attempt by the Soviet Union to expand its influence. Often cited as a key moment in the origins of the Cold War.

tsar Russian word for "emperor," derived from the Latin *caesar* and similar to the German *kaiser,* it was the title claimed by the rulers of medieval Muscovy and of the later Russian Empire.

Ubaid culture An early civilization that flourished in Mesopotamia between 5500 and 4000 B.C.E., it was characterized by large village settlements and temple complexes: a precursor to the more urban civilization of the Sumerians.

Umayyad Caliphate (661–930) The Umayyad family resisted the authority of the first two caliphs who succeeded Muhammad, but eventually placed a member of their own family in that position of power. The Umayyad Caliphate ruled the Islamic world from 661 to 750, modeling their administration on that of the Roman Empire. But after a rebellion led by the rival Abbasid family, the power of the Umayyad Caliphate was confined to their territories in al-Andalus (Spain).

Universal Declaration of Human Rights (1948) United Nations declaration that laid out the rights to which all human beings were entitled.

University of Paris The reputation of Peter Abelard and his students attracted many intellectuals to Paris in the twelfth century, some of whom began offering instruction to aspiring scholars. By 1200, this loose association of teachers had formed themselves into a UNIVERSITAS, or corporation. They began collaborating in the higher academic study of the liberal arts with a special emphasis on theology.

Pope Urban II (1042?–1099) Instigator of the First Crusade (1096–1099), who promised that anyone who fought or died in the service of the Church would receive absolution from sin.

urban populations During the nineteenth century, urban populations in Europe increased six fold. For the most part, urban areas had medieval infrastructures, which new populations and industries overwhelmed. As a result, many European cities became overcrowded and unhealthy.

Utopia Title of a semi-satirical social critique by the English statesman Sir Thomas More (1478–1535); the word derives from the Greek "best place" or "no place."

Lorenzo Valla (1407–1457) One of the first practitioners of scientific philology (the historical study of language), Valla's analysis of the so-called Donation of Constantine showed that the document could not possibly have been written in the fourth century C.E., but must have been forged centuries later.

vassal A person who pledges to be loyal and subservient to a lord in exchange for land, income, or protection.

velvet revolutions The peaceful political revolutions throughout Eastern Europe in 1989.

Verdun (1916) This battle between German and French forces lasted for ten months during the First World War. The Germans saw the battle as a chance to break French morale through a war of attrition, and the French believed the battle to be a symbol of France's strength. In the end, over 400,000 lives were lost and the German offensive failed.

Versailles Conference (1919) Peace conference between the victors of the First World War; resulted in the Treaty of Versailles, which forced Germany to pay reparations and to give up its colonies to the victors.

Queen Victoria (1819–1901) Influential monarch who reigned from 1837 until her death; she presided over the expansion of the British Empire as well as the evolution of English politics and social and economic reforms.

Viet Cong Vietnamese communist group formed in 1954; committed to overthrowing the government of South Vietnam and reunifying North and South Vietnam.

Vikings (800–1000) The collapse of the Abbasid Caliphate disrupted Scandinavian commercial networks and turned traders into raiders (the word "viking" describes the activity of raiding). These raids often escalated into invasions that contributed to the collapse of the Carolingian Empire, resulted in the devastation of settled territories, and ended with the establishment of Viking colonies. By the tenth century, Vikings controlled areas of eastern England, Scotland, the islands of Ireland, Iceland, Greenland, and parts of northern France. They had also established the beginnings of the kingdom that became Russia and made exploratory voyages to North America, founding a settlement at Newfoundland (Canada).

Leonardo da Vinci (1452–1519) Florentine inventor, sculptor, architect, and painter whose breadth of interests typifies the ideal of "the Renaissance man."

A **Vindication of the Rights of Woman** Noted work of Mary Wollstonecraft (1759–1797), English republican who applied Enlightenment political ideas to issues of gender.

Virgil (70–19 B.C.E.) An influential Roman poet who wrote under the patronage of the emperor Augustus. His *Aeneid* mimicked the ancient Greek epics of Homer, and told the mythical tale of Rome's founding by the Trojan refugee Aeneas.

Visigoths The tribes of "west" Goths who sacked Rome in 410 C.E. and later established a kingdom in the Roman province of Hispania (Spain).

Voltaire Pseudonym of French philosopher and satirist Francois Marie Arouet (1694–1778), who championed the cause of human dignity against state and church oppression. Noted deist and author of *Candide*.

Lech Walsea (1943–) Leader of the Polish labor movement Solidarity, which organized a series of strikes across Poland in 1980. They protested working conditions, shortages, and high prices. Above all, they demanded an independent labor union. Solidarity's leaders were imprisoned and the union banned, but they launched a new series of strikes in 1988, which led to the legalization of Solidarity and open elections.

war communism The Russian civil war forced the Bolsheviks to take a more radical economic stance. They requisitioned grain from the peasantry and outlawed private trade in consumer goods as "speculation." They also militarized production facilities and abolished money.

Wars of the Roses Fifteenth-century civil conflict between the English dynastic houses of Lancaster and York, each of which was symbolized by the heraldic device of a rose (red and white, respectively). It was ultimately resolved by the accession of the Lancastrian king Henry VII, who married Elizabeth of York.

Warsaw Pact (1955–1991) Military alliance between the USSR and other communist states that was established as a response to the creation of the NATO alliance.

The **Wealth of Nations** 1776 treatise by Adam Smith, whose laissez-faire ideas predicted the economic boom of the Industrial Revolution.

Weimar Republic The government of Germany between 1919 and the rise of Hitler and the Nazi party.

Western Front Military front that stretched from the English Channel through Belgium and France to the Alps during the First World War.

Whites Refers to the "counterrevolutionaries" of the Bolshevik Revolution (1918–1921) who fought the Bolsheviks (the "Reds"); included former supporters of the tsar, Social Democrats, and large independent peasant armies.

William the Conqueror (1027–1087) Duke of Normandy who laid claim to the throne of England in 1066, defeating the Anglo-Saxon King Harold at the Battle of Hastings. He and his Norman followers imposed imperial rule in England through a brutal campaign of military conquest, surveillance, and the suppression of the indigenous Anglo-Saxon language.

William of Ockham (d. 1349) An English philosopher and Franciscan friar, he denied that human reason could prove fundamental theological truths, such as the existence of God: he argued that there is no necessary connection between the observable laws of nature and the unknowable essence of divinity. His theories, derived from the work of earlier scholastics, form the basis of the scientific method.

Woodrow Wilson (1856–1924) U.S. president who requested and received a declaration of war from Congress so that America could enter the First World War. After the war, his prominent role in the Paris Peace Conference signaled the rise of the United States as a world power. He also proposed the Fourteen Points, which influenced the peace negotiations.

Maria Winkelmann (1670–1720) German astronomer who worked with her husband in his observatory. Despite discovering a comet and preparing calendars for the Berlin Academy of Sciences, the academy would not let her take her husband's place within the body after he died.

Witch craze The rash of persecutions that took place in both Catholic and Protestant countries of early modern Europe and her colonies, facilitated by secular governments and religious authorities.

women's associations Because European women were excluded from the workings of parliamentary and mass politics, some women formed organizations to press for political and civil rights. Some groups focused on establishing educational opportunities for women, while others campaigned energetically for the vote.

William Wordsworth (1770–1850) Romantic writer whose central themes were nature, simplicity, and feeling. He considered nature to be man's most trustworthy teacher and source of sublime power that nourished the human soul.

World Bank International agency established in 1944 to provide economic assistance to war-torn nations and countries in need of economic development.

John Wyclif (c. 1330–1384) A professor of theology at the University of Oxford, Wyclif urged the English king to confiscate ecclesiastical wealth and to replace corrupt priests and bishops with men who would live according to the apostolic standards of poverty and piety. He advocated direct access to the Scriptures and promoted an English translation of the Bible. His teachings played an important role in the Peasants' Revolt of 1381 and inspired the still more radical initiatives of a group known as Lollards.

Xerxes (519?–465 B.C.E.) Xerxes succeeded his father, Darius, as Great King of Persia. Seeking to avenge his father's shame and eradicate any future threats to Persian hegemony, he launched his own invasion of Greece in 480 B.C.E. An allied Greek army defeated his forces in 479 B.C.E.

Yalta Accords Meeting between President Franklin D. Roosevelt, Prime Minister Winston Churchill, and Premier Joseph Stalin that occurred in the Crimea in 1945 shortly before the end of the Second World War to plan for the postwar order.

Young Turks The 1908 Turkish reformist movement that aimed to modernize the Ottoman Empire, restore parliamentary rule, and depose Sultan Abdul Hamid II.

ziggurats Temples constructed under the Dynasty of Ur in what is now Iraq, beginning around 2100 B.C.E.

Zionism A political movement dating to the end of the nineteenth century holding that the Jewish people constitute a nation and are entitled to a national homeland. Zionists rejected a policy of Jewish assimilation, and advocated the reestablishment of a Jewish homeland in Palestine.

Zollverein In 1834, Prussia started a customs union, which established free trade among the German states and a uniform tariff against the rest of the world. By the 1840s, the union included almost all of the German states except German Austria. It is considered an important precedent for the political unification of Germany, which was completed in 1870 under Prussian leadership.

Zoroastrianism One of the three major universal faiths of the ancient world, alongside Judaism and Christianity, it was derived from the teachings of the Persian Zoroaster around 600 B.C.E. Zoroaster redefined religion as an ethical practice common to all, rather than as a set of rituals and superstitions that cause divisions among people. Zoroastrianism teaches that there is one supreme god in the universe, Ahura-Mazda (Wise Lord), but that his goodness will be constantly assailed by the forces of evil until the arrival of a final "judgment day." Proponents of this faith should therefore help good to triumph over evil by leading a good life, and by performing acts of compassion and charity. Zoroastrianism exercised a profound influence over many early Christians, including Augustine.

Ulrich Zwingli (1484–1531) A former priest from the Swiss city of Zurich, Zwingli joined Luther and Calvin in attacking the authority of the Roman Catholic Church.

Text Credits

Leon B. Alberti: "On the Importance of Literature" from *University of Chicago Readings in Western Civilization, Vol. 5*, eds. Cochrane & Krishner. Copyright © 1986 by The University of Chicago. Reprinted by permission of The University of Chicago Press. "On the Family" from *The Family in Renaissance Florence*, trans./ed. by Renée Neu Watkins (University of South Carolina Press, 1969), pp. 208–213. Reprinted by permission of the translator.

Armand Bellee (ed.): *Cahiers de plaintes & doleances des paroisses de la province du Maine pour les Etats-generaux de 1789*, 4 vols. (Le Mans: Monnoyer, 1881–92), 2: 578–82. Translated by the American Social History Project, "Liberty, Equality, Fraternity: Exploring the French Revolution" by Jack R. Censer and Lynn Hunt. Reprinted by permission.

Henry Bettenson (ed.): "Obedience as a Jesuit Hallmark" from *Documents of the Christian Church*, 2nd Edition. Copyright © 1967, Oxford University Press. Reprinted by permission of Oxford University Press.

Gabriel Biel: "Execrabilis." Reprinted by permission of the publisher from *Defensorium Obedientiae Apostolicae Et Alia Documenta* by Gabriel Biel, edited and translated by Heiko A. Oberman, Daniel E. Zerfoss and William J. Courtenay, pp. 224–227, Cambridge, Mass.: The Belknap Press of Harvard University Press, Copyright © 1968 by the President and Fellows of Harvard College.

Boyer, Baker & Kirshner (eds): "Declaration of the Rights of Man and of the Citizen", "Napoleon's Letter to Prince Eugene" and "Circular Letter to Sovereigns" from *University of Chicago Readings in Western Civilization, Vol. 7*, pp. 238–239; 419–420; 426–427, Copyright © 1987 by The University of Chicago. Reprinted by permission of The University of Chicago Press.

David Brion Davis: From *Encyclopédie*, Vol. 16, Neuchâtel, 1765, p. 532 as cited in David Brion Davis, *The Problem of Slavery in Western Culture*. (Ithaca, N.Y.: Cornell University Press, 1966), p. 416. Copyright © 1966 by David Brion Davis. Reprinted by permission.

Michel de Montaigne: From *Montaigne: Selections from the Essays*, translated and edited by Donald M. Frame (Harlan Davidson, Inc., 1973), pp. 34–38. Reprinted by permission of Harlan Davidson, Inc.

Rene Descartes: From *A Discourse on the Method of Correctly Conducting One's Reason*, trans. Ian Maclean. Copyright © Ian Maclean 2006. Reprinted by permission of Oxford University Press.

Armand J. du Plessis: "Cardinal Richelieu on the Common People of France," pp. 31–32 from Hill, Henry Bertram, *The Political Testament of Cardinal Richelieu.* © 1961 by the Board of Regents of the University of Wisconsin System. Reprinted by permission of The University of Wisconsin Press.

Galileo Galilei: From *Discoveries and Opinions of Galileo* by Galileo Galilei, translated by Stillman Drake, copyright © 1957 by Stillman Drake. Used by permission of Doubleday, a division of Random House, Inc.

Rosemary Horrox (ed.): From *The Black Death*, by Horrox (Trans., Ed.), 1994, Manchester University Press, Manchester, UK. Reprinted with permission.

Carolyne Larrington: "The Condemnation of Joan of Arc by the University of Paris" from *Women and Writing in Medieval Europe*, Carolyne Larrington, Copyright © 1995 Routledge. Reproduced by permission of Taylor & Francis Books UK.

L.R. Loomis (ed. and trans.): "Haec Sancta Synodus" and "Frequens" from *The Council of Constance* (New York: Columbia University Press, 1961), pp. 229, 246–247. Copyright © 1962, Columbia University Press. Reprinted by permission of the publisher. We have made diligent efforts to contact the copyright holder to obtain electronic permission to reprint this selection. If you have information that would help us, please write to Permissions Department, W.W. Norton & Company, Inc., 500 Fifth Avenue, New York, NY 10110.

Konstantin Mihailovic: *Memoirs of a Janissary*, trans. Benjamin Stolz. Michigan Slavic Translations no. 3 (Ann Arbor: Michigan Slavic Publications, 1975), pp. 157–159. Copyright © 1975, Michigan Slavic Publications. Reprinted by courtesy of Michigan Slavic Publications, Ann Arbor, Mich.

E.M. Plass: From *What Luther Says, Vol. II*, (pgs. 888–889) © 1959, 1987 Concordia Publishing House. Used with permission of CPH. All rights reserved.

Jean Rousseau: From *Rousseau's Political Writings: A Norton Critical Edition*, edited by Alan Ritter and Julia Conaway Bondanella, translated by Julia Conaway Bondanella. Copyright © 1988 by W.W. Norton & Company, Inc. Used by permission of W.W. Norton & Company, Inc. This selection may not be reproduced, stored in a retrieval system, or transmitted in any form or by any means without the prior written permission of the publisher.

M.C. Seymour (ed.): "The Legend of Prester John" from *Mandeville's Travels*, pp. 195–199. Copyright © 1967, Clarendon Press. Reprinted by permission of Oxford University Press.

Professor of Russian Studies, Rollins College; **p. 476**: Giraudon/Art Resource, NY; **p. 477**: Giraudon/Art Resource, NY; **p. 480**: Ali Meyer/Corbis; **p. 482**: Corbis; **p. 484**: John R. Freeman & Co.; **p. 485**: Gianni Dagli Orti/Corbis; **p. 486**: Warder Collection, NY.

Chapter 16: p. 492: Cellarius, Andreas/The Bridgeman Art Library; **p. 495**: Jeffrey Coolidge/Getty Images; **p. 497**: Erich Lessing/Art Resource, NY; **p. 498 (left)**: The Granger Collection, New York; **p. 498 (right)**: Wikimedia Commons; **p. 499 (left)**: Image Select/Art Resource, NY; **p. 499 (right)**: Royal Astronomical Society/Photo Researchers, Inc.; **p. 500**: Stapleton Collection/Corbis; **p. 501**: Erich Lessing/Art Resource, NY; **p. 503**: John P. McCaskey cropped by Smartse/Wikimedia Commons; **p. 506**: Rene Descartes, L'homme de René Descartes, et la formation du foetus....Paris: Compagnie des Libraires, 1729/Courtesy of Historical Collections & Services, Claude Moore Health Sciences Library, University of Virginia.; **p. 508**: Bodleian Library; **p. 509**: Thysania agrippina, white witch—Caterpillar, cocoon and adults of a white witch moth (Thysania agrippina). Plate 20 from Metamorphosis Insectorum (1705) by Maria Sybilla Merian (1647–1717). © The Natural History Museum, London/The Image Works; **p. 510**: Bettmann/Corbis; **p. 511**: Bodleian Library; **p. 512**: Bettmann/Corbis; **p. 513**: Giraudon/Art Resource, NY.

CHAPTER 17: p. 516: Bridgeman Art Library; **p. 518**: Elizabeth Nesbitt Room Chapbook Collection/Information Sciences Library/University of Pittsburgh; **p. 519**: Bibliotheque Nationale, Paris, France/Lauros/Giraudon/The Bridgeman Art Library; **p. 522**: Giraudon/Art Resource, NY; **p. 523**: Bettmann/Corbis; **p. 524 (left)**: Historisches Museum der Stadt Wien; **524 (right)**: Historisches Museum der Stadt Wien; **p. 529**: Stapletib Collection/Corbis; **p. 530 (left)**: Sir Joshua Reynolds/Omai of the Friendly Isles/nla.pic-an5600097/National Library of Australia; **p. 530 (right)**: William Hodges/King of Otaheite/nla.pic-an2720588/National Library of Australia; **p. 531**: Francesco Bartolozzi/A view of the inside of a house in the island of Ulietea, with the representation of a dance to the music of the country/nla.pic-an9184905/National Library of Australia; **p. 532**: Bibliotheque Nationale, Paris, France/Bridgeman Art Library, Flammarion; **p. 534**: © Tate Gallery, London/Art Resource, NY; **p. 538**: A Literary Salon in the 18th Century (pen and sepia wash on paper), Dandre-Bardon, Michel Francois (1700–83)/Louvre (Cabinet de dessins), Paris, France, (Archives Charmet/www.bridgeman.co.uk); **p. 540**: Bettmann/Corbis; **p. 541**: Erich Lessing/Art Resource, NY; **p. 542**: Erich Lessing/Art Resource, NY.

Chapter 18: p. 544: Erich Lessing/Art Resource, NY; **p. 548 (left)**: akg-images; **p. 548 (right)**: The Art Archive/Musée Carnavalet Paris/Marc Charmet; **p. 549**: Giraudon/The Bridgeman Art Library; **p. 551**: Chateau de Versailles, France/The Bridgeman Art Library; **p. 553**: Musee de la Ville de Paris, Musee Carnavalet, Paris, France/Giraudon/The Bridgeman Art Library; **p. 554**: Musee de la Revolution Francaise, Vizille, France/The Bridgeman Art Library; **p. 560**: Bibliotheque Nationale, Paris, France/The Bridgeman Art Library; **p. 561**: The Death of Marat, by Jacques Louis David (Giraudon/Art Resource); **p. 562**: Bettmann/Corbis; **p. 563**: Giraudon/Art Resource, NY: Musée de la Ville de Paris, Musée Carnavalet, Paris, France; **p. 566 (left)**: Risma Archivo/Alamy; **p. 566 (right)**: The Art Archive; **p. 567 (left)**: Musee de la Ville de Paris, Musee Carnavalet, Paris, France/Lauros/Giraudon/The Bridgeman Art Library; **p. 567 (right)**: Courtesy of the Warden and Scholars of New College, Oxford/The Bridgeman Art Library; **p. 570**: The Gallery Collection/Corbis; **p. 571**: Erich Lessing/Art Resource, NY; **p. 572**: Museo del Prado, Madrid; **p. 576**: Gianni Dagli Orti/Corbis.

Chapter 19: p. 578: National Gallery, London/Art Resource, NY; **p. 580**: Peak District National Park; **p. 582**: Stefano Bianchetti/Corbis; **p. 584 (left)**: The National Archives of the UK; **p. 584 (right)**: The Granger Collection, New York; **p. 585 (bottom)**: Hulton-Deutsch Collection/Corbis; **p. 585 (right)**: The Hulton Deutsch Collection; **p. 586**: Hulton-Deutsch Collection/Corbis; **p. 587**: Bibliotheque des Arts Decoratifs, Paris, France/Archives Charmet/The Bridgeman Art Library; **p. 592**: HIP-Archive/Topham/The Image Works; **p. 593**: HIP-Archive/Topham/The Image Works; **p. 594**: Hulton Deutsch Collection/Corbis; **p. 595 (left)**: Fotomas/Topham/The Image Works; **p. 595 (right)**: Mary Evans/The Image Works; **p. 597**: Hulton Archive/Getty Images; **p. 600**: Geoffrey Clements/Corbis; **p. 602**: Giraudon/Art Resource, NY; **p. 603**: North Wind/Nancy Carter/North Wind Picture Archives; **p. 607**: The Granger Collection, NY; **p. 609**: The Granger Collection, NY.

Index

art (continued)
  one-point perspective in, 383, *383*
  of portraiture, 339, 383, 387
  realism in, 338, 341
  Renaissance, 340, 378, 379, 383–84,
    391, 394–96, 397
  Venetian School of, 386–87
  Virgin Mary in, *325,* 340, 341, *341*
artillery, 362–63
Assembly of Notables (France), 551
astrolabes, 361
astrology, 494, 495
Astronomia Nova (Kepler), 500
astronomy, *495,* 498–99
  Copernican Revolution in,
    496–98, *498*
  emergence of, 494–96
  Kepler's laws and, 498–99, 511
  Tychonic system of, *497*
As You Like It (Shakespeare), 450
Augsburg, 414
  League of, 469
  Peace of (1555), 430–31,
    430, 432, 434
Augustine, Saint (354–430), 381–82,
  393, 401, 413
Austen, Jane, 539
Austerlitz, battle of (1805), 568
Australia, 480, 585
Austria, 325, 437, 469–73, 487
  absolutism in, 458, 459
  French Revolution and, 556, 561
  in Industrial Revolution, 587,
    589, 590
  Napoleon vs., 564, 568, 572–76
  partition of Poland and, 477–78, *477*
Austrian empire, 470–71
authority, search for, 447–49
autocracy, absolutism and, 474–78
Auvergne, 457–58
Avignon, "Babylonian Captivity" in,
  312, 325, 329–30, *330,* 378, 399
Azores, 359, 362, 363, 364, 365
Azov, 476
Aztecs, *364,* 368, *368*

Babylonian Captivity (papal;
  1309–1378), 312, 325,
  329–30, *330,* 378, 399
Bach, Johann Sebastian (1685–1750),
  541
Bacon, Francis (1561–1626), 494,
  503–7, *503,* 519, 520
Baconians, 507
Bahamas, 366
balance of power, 469–70, 477–78
Balboa, Vasco Nuñez de (1475–1519),
  367

Balkans, 354, 356
Balzac, Honoré de (1799–1850), 601
Bamberg, witch hunts in, 447
Banker and His Wife, The (Massys), *317*
Bank of England, 487
banks, banking:
  commerce and, 317, 487
  in Industrial Revolution, 587–88
  in Italy, 317
  Medici family and, 317, 325, 378
Baptism, sacraments of, 410–11
Barbados, 486
Barberini, Cardinal Maffeo, *see* Urban
  VIII, Pope
Baronius, Cardinal, 501
Basel, 392, 411
  Council of, 331
Bassi, Laura, 508
Bastille, 545, 552
Battle of the Nations (1813), 573
Bavaria, 325, 470
Beaumarchais, Pierre Augustin de, 543
Beccaria, Cesare Bonesana de
  (1738–1794), 518, 523
Becket, Thomas (c. 1118–1170), 338
Beirut, 351, 353, 354, 355, 362
Belarus, 327, 328
Belgium, 432
  in Industrial Revolution, 586,
    587, 588
Benz, Carl, 590
Bergundy, 439
Berlin, 464, 472, 478
Berlin Academy of Science, 509
Berlin Royal Academy, 536
Bernini, Gianlorenzo (1598–1680),
  450, 451–52
Berry, duke of, *319*
Bible, 311, 401, 421, *421,* 425
  Luther's translation of, *401*
  printing of, 344
  Vulgate, 380, *421*
Bill of Rights, British, 467
birth control, 604–5
Birth of Venus (Botticelli), 384, *384*
Black Death (plague), 311–17, *312,* 320,
  334, 336, 337, 345, 353
  causes of, 316
  demographics, 312–15, *313*
  Jews blamed for, 314–15
  recurrences of, 429, 478
  rural areas and, 316, 320
Black Gazette, The, 535
Black Sea, 351, 353
Blake, William (1757–1827), 583
Blenheim, battle of (1704), 470
Boccaccio, Giovanni (1313–1375),
  337–38

Bodin, Jean (1530–1596), 449, 468
Bohemia, 330, 434, 471–72
  heretical movements in, 336–37
Boilly, Louis Léopold, 567
Boleyn, Anne (c. 1507–1536), queen of
  England, 416, 418, 419
Bolivia, 370
Bologna, University of, 391
Bonaparte, Napoleon, *see* Napoleon I,
  emperor of France
Boniface VIII, Pope (1294–1303), 329
Book of Marvels (Mandeville), 347, *351,*
  352–53, 365
Book of the City of Ladies, The (Christine
  de Pisan), 338
Book of the Courtier, The (Castiglione),
  382–83
Book of the Deeds of Arms and of Chivalry,
  The (Christine de Pisan), 339
books:
  censorship of, 421, 501–3, 535
  Enlightenment and, 535–36,
    538–41
  nationalism and, 344–45
  on navigation, 362
  printing of, 342, *343,* 344–45
Bora, Katharina von, 403
Bordeaux, 342, 609
  siege of (1453), 363
Borgia, Cesare (c. 1475–1507),
  380–81, 382
Borgia, Lucrezia (1480–1519), 406
Borneo, 485
Borodino, battle of (1812), 572
Bossuet, Jacques-Benigne (1627–1704),
  460, 468
Boston, 488
Botticelli, Sandro (1445–1510), *380,*
  384–85, *384, 385*
Bougainville, Louis-Anne de
  (1729–1811), 527–28, 529
Boulton, Matthew (1728–1809), 584
Bourbon, Antoine de, 431
Bourbon dynasty, 431
bourgeoisie, 602
Boyle, Robert (1627–1691), 507,
  508, 511
Boyne, battle of the (1690), 468
Brahe, Tycho (1546–1601), 497–500,
  499, 500
Bramante, Donato (c. 1444–1514), 389
Brandenburg, 325
Brandenburg-Prussia, 325, 472–73, *472*
Brassey, Thomas, 585
Brazil, 364, 485, 486
Britain, *see* Great Britain
British East India Company, 487, 488
Brontë, Charlotte (1816–1855), 604

commercial revolution and, 478, *479*
in Industrial Revolution, 580, 587, 594, 597, 599
portolan charts, *361, 362*
Portrait of Omai (Reynolds), *528*
Portugal, 326, 484, 485
expansion and exploration by, 354–55, 359, 361, 362, 363–64, 367, 371, 458
independence of, 437
slave trade and, 363–64, 485, 486
potato cultivation, 478, 480
Potosí, Bolivia, 369, 370
Poullain de la Barre, François, 508
Prague, 336, 391
Praise of Folly, The (Erasmus), 393, 406
predestination, doctrine of, 401
Presbyterians, 413
Prester John, legend of, 352–53, 363
Price Revolution, 428–29
Pride and Prejudice (Austen), 539
Prince, The (Machiavelli), 381, 382
Principia Mathematica (Newton), 494, 508–11
printing, 479, 494
invention of, 342, *343,* 344–45
Luther's use of, 344, 403
Private Lives of Louis XIV, The, 535
prostitution, 601, 606, 608
Protestantism:
discipline and, 413–14
in England, 425, 433, 434, 466
family and, 413–16
French Revolution and, 553
marriage and, 413–16
national identity and, 425
in post-Reformation Europe, 428
rise of, 394
spread of, 408, *409,* 410–14, 416–20
state power and, 425
women and, 413–16, 422
see also specific denominations
Protestant Reformation, 331, 333, 393, 394, 397, 400–425
Calvinism and, 411–13
Catholic Reformation and, 420–24
Christian humanism and, 420, 425
domestication of, 413–16
in England, 416–20
German princes and, 408
in Germany, 400–410
Hussite Revolution and, 337
Lollardy and, 337
Lutheran Reformation and, 400–410
onset of, 402–3
Renaissance and, 425
in Switzerland, 410–13
Prussia, 325, 469–70, 476, 478, 487

absolutism in, 459
French Revolution and, 556
in Industrial Revolution, 587
Junker class of, 472, 473
militarism of, 472–73
Napoleon vs., 568, 571–72, 573
partition of Poland and, 477–78, *477*
in Seven Years' War, 487, *488*
Silesia seized by, 473
Ptolemy I, king of Egypt (323–285 B.C.E.), 494, 495, *495,* 496, *498*
Ptolemy of Alexandria, 365
public opinion, 539
Pugachev, Emelyan (1726–1775), 477
Puritans, 413, 442–43, 451
English Civil War and, 442–43

quadrants, 361
Quakers, 484
Qubilai (Kublai) Kahn, 347, 350, 351, *351,* 352
Quebec, battle of (1759), 487
Quietists, 464

Rabelais, François (c. 1494–1553), 394
Radcliffe, Ann (1764–1823), 539
railways:
in Industrial Revolution, 584–86, *585, 586*
Raphael (Raffaello Sanzio; 1483–1520), 387–88, *388,* 403
rationalism, 424
Raynal, Guillaume Thomas François, 526, 527, 535
Razin, Stenka, 474
reading glasses, 494
Reflections on the Revolution in France (Burke), 556, 558–59
Reformation, *see* Protestant Reformation
Regiomontanus, Johannes, 495
regionalism, 430
in France, 431, 460–61, 464
Reims, France, 323
religion:
colonization and, 481, 482
Encyclopedia and, 522
Enlightenment and, 524
French Revolution and, 553–56, 560
in Late Middle Ages, 329–37
in Ottoman Empire, 357
philosophy and, 446
power of state and, 446–47
scientific revolution and, 494–96, 500–503
tolerance and, 428, 473
wars of, 428–37, 455
see also mysticism; papacy; *specific religions*

Rembrandt van Rijn (1606–1669), *452,* 454–55
Renaissance, 373–97
architecture of, 389–90
art of, 340, 378, 379, 383–89, 394–96, 397
classical learning and, 373–77, 378, 391, 397
commerce in, 374–75, 391
decline of, 390–91
definition of, 374
education in, 375–77, 378, 391–92, 397
English, 392, 396, 450–51
in Florence, 379, 380–82, 383–86, 387, 388, 391
humanism of, 375–77, 379, 392–94, 397
ideal of courtier in, 382–83
Italian, 340, 374, 397
Italian political and military disasters and, 381, 382, 390–91
Latin in, 375–77, 379
literature of, 373, 375, 378, 379, 382–83, 392–94, 397
Middle Ages and, 373–74, 391, 397
music of, 396
Neoplatonism in, 380, 384, 387, 389
northern, 391–97
origins of, 374
papacy and, 375, 378–79
patronage in, 391, 392
philosophy in, 380, 391–94
scientific revolution and, 495
textual scholarship in, 379–80
women in, 375, 377, 379, 383, 397
Rend, W. P., *600*
Reni, Guido (1575–1642), *421*
revolutions, Atlantic, *546*
Reynolds, Joshua (1723–1792), 528, *530,* 531
Rhineland, 469
Richard II, king of England (1377–1399), 321
Richardson, Samuel (1689–1761), 539
Richelieu, Cardinal (1585–1642), 434, 439
Rigaud, Hyacinthe, 462, *462*
Rights of Man, The (Paine), 558–59
Robespierre, Maximilien (1758–1794), 561–62, *562,* 563, 573
Robinson Crusoe (Defoe), 539
Rocroi, battle of (1643), 437, *438*
Roman calendar, 496
Roman Empire, slavery in, 356
Romanov dynasty, 474
Romanticism, 533

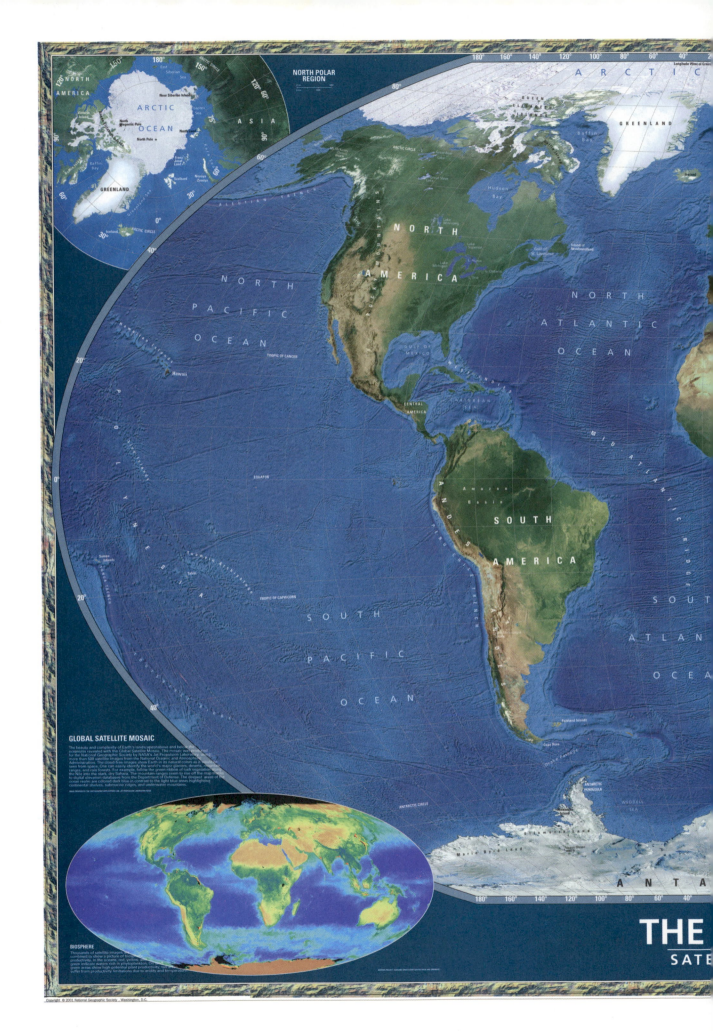

NORTH POLAR REGION

ARCTIC OCEAN

GREENLAND

ASIA

NORTH AMERICA

North Pole
North Magnetic Pole

ARCTIC

GREENLAND

NORTH AMERICA

Queen Elizabeth Islands

Arctic Circle

Hudson Bay

Lake Winnipeg
Lake Superior
Lake Michigan
Lake Huron
L. Erie

Gulf of Mexico

CENTRAL AMERICA

Gulf of St. Lawrence

NORTH ATLANTIC OCEAN

WEST INDIES
CARIBBEAN SEA

NORTH PACIFIC OCEAN

ROCKY MOUNTAINS

Hawaii

TROPIC OF CANCER

EQUATOR

SOUTH AMERICA

Amazon Basin

ANDES

SOUTH ATLANTIC OCEAN

MID ATLANTIC RIDGE

SOUTH PACIFIC OCEAN

TROPIC OF CAPRICORN

POLYNESIA
MELANESIA
Samoa Islands
Tahiti
Tuamotu Archipelago

PERU CHILE TRENCH

Falkland Islands
Cape Horn
Drake Passage

ALEUTIAN TRENCH

ANTARCTIC PENINSULA

WEDDELL SEA

ANTARCTIC CIRCLE

Marie Byrd Land

ANTA

GLOBAL SATELLITE MOSAIC

The beauty and complexity of Earth's landscapes—above and below the oceans—is revealed with the Global Satellite Mosaic. The mosaic was produced for the National Geographic Society by NASA's Jet Propulsion Laboratory, using more than 500 satellite images from the National Oceanic and Atmospheric Administration. The cloud-free images show Earth in its natural colors as it would be seen from space. One can easily identify the world's major glaciers, deserts, mountain ranges, and rain forests. For example, follow the green ribbon of lush vegetation along the Nile into the dark, dry Sahara. The mountain ranges seem to rise off the map thanks to digital elevation databases from the Department of Defense. The deepest areas of the ocean realm are colored dark blue in contrast to the light blue areas highlighting continental shelves, submarine ridges, and underwater mountains.

BIOSPHERE

Thousands of satellite images were combined to show a picture of biosphere productivity. In the oceans, red, yellow, and green indicate waters rich in phytoplankton. On land, green areas show high-potential plant productivity. Tan and brown areas suffer from productivity limitations due to aridity and temperature.

THE
SATE

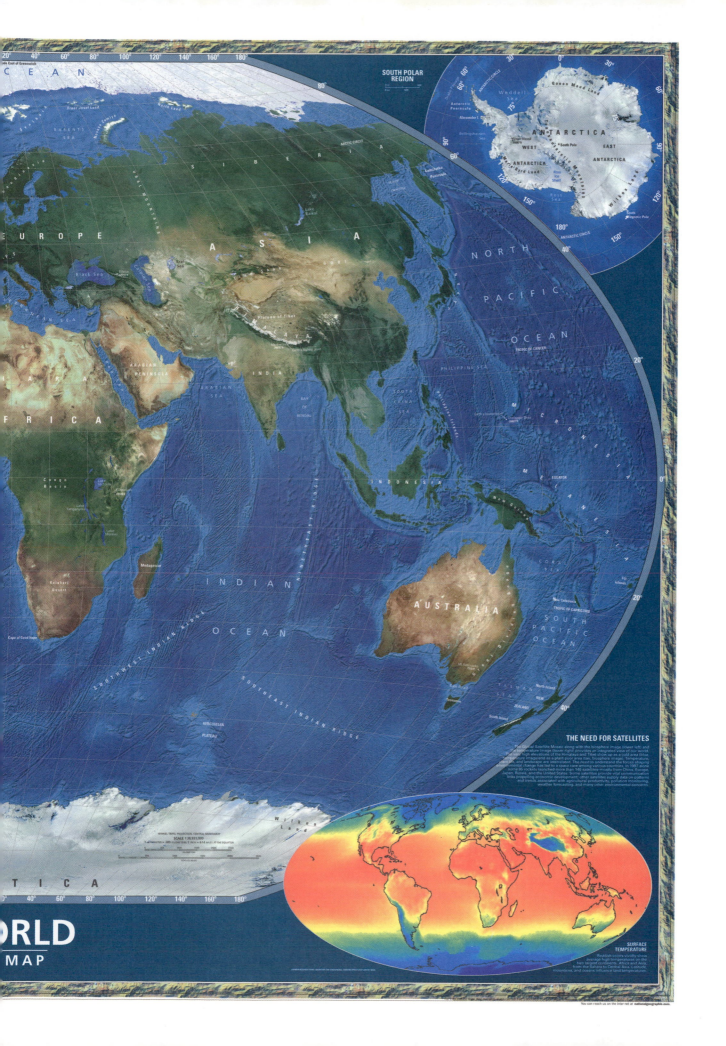

SOUTH POLAR REGION

ANTARCTICA

NORTH

PACIFIC

OCEAN

SIBERIA

ASIA

EUROPE

AFRICA

ARABIAN
PENINSULA

INDIA

INDONESIA

AUSTRALIA

INDIAN

OCEAN

NEW
ZEALAND

TROPIC OF CAPRICORN

SOUTH
PACIFIC
OCEAN

THE NEED FOR SATELLITES

The Global Satellite Mosaic along with the biosphere image (lower left) and the temperature image (lower right) provides an integrated view of our world. The sea-high elevations of the Himalaya and Tibet show up as a cold area (blue temperature image) and as a plant-poor area (tan, biosphere image). Temperature, plants and landscape are interrelated. The need to understand the forces shaping environmental change has led to a space race among various countries. In 1997 alone, some 85 rockets launched more than 140 satellites—mostly from China, Europe, Japan, Russia, and the United States. Some satellites provide vital communication links propelling economic development; other satellites supply data on patterns and trends associated with agricultural productivity, pollution monitoring, weather forecasting, and many other environmental concerns.

WORLD
MAP

SURFACE TEMPERATURE

Reddish colors vividly show average high temperatures on the two largest continents, Africa and Asia, from the Sahara to Central Asia. Latitude, mountains, and oceans influence land temperatures.

You can reach us on the Internet at nationalgeographic.com